The Practice of Judicial Interaction in the Field of Fundamental Rights

JUDICIAL REVIEW AND COOPERATION

Under the general editorship of Fabrizio Cafaggi, Hans Wolfgang Micklitz, Dominique Hascher, and Torben Melchior, this Judicial Review and Cooperation series is a forum for monographs and collaborative volumes on the role of the judiciary in present day Europe. Each of the books in the series will appeal not only to an academic audience but will also engage policy makers and practitioners concerned with judicial practice in Europe.

Titles in the series include:

Regulating Judicial Activity in Europe
A Guidebook to Working Practices of the Supreme Courts
Edited by Network of the Presidents of the Supreme Judicial Courts of the European Union

National Courts and EU Law
New Issues, Theories and Methods
Edited by Bruno de Witte, Juan A. Mayoral, Urszula Jaremba, Marlene Wind and Karolina Podstawa

Judicial Cooperation in European Private Law
Edited by Fabrizio Cafaggi and Stephanie Law

The Practice of Judicial Interaction in the Field of Fundamental Rights
The Added Value of the Charter of Fundamental Rights of the EU
Edited by Federica Casarosa and Madalina Moraru

The Practice of Judicial Interaction in the Field of Fundamental Rights

The Added Value of the Charter of Fundamental Rights of the EU

Edited by

Federica Casarosa

Centre for Judicial Cooperation, European University Institute, Italy and Visiting Fellow, Masaryk University, Czech Republic

Madalina Moraru

Centre for Judicial Cooperation, European University Institute, Italy and Senior Research Fellow, Law Faculty, Masaryk University, Czech Republic

JUDICIAL REVIEW AND COOPERATION

EE Edward Elgar PUBLISHING

Cheltenham, UK • Northampton, MA, USA

Published by
Edward Elgar Publishing Limited
The Lypiatts
15 Lansdown Road
Cheltenham
Glos GL50 2JA
UK

Edward Elgar Publishing, Inc.
William Pratt House
9 Dewey Court
Northampton
Massachusetts 01060
USA

A catalogue record for this book
is available from the British Library

This book is available electronically in the **Elgar**online
Law subject collection
http://dx.doi.org/10.4337/9781800371224

ISBN 978 1 80037 121 7 (cased)
ISBN 978 1 80037 122 4 (eBook)

Ad Alba e Bianca
(Federica Casarosa)
Tatălui meu, Vasile Moraru
(Madalina Moraru)

Contents

Contributors

Prof. Matej Accetto
Judge of the Constitutional Court of the Republic of Slovenia and University of Ljubljana

Prof. Raluca Bercea
University of West Timişoara and trainer at the National Association of the Romanian Bars (UNBR)

Prof. Maria Bergström
University of Uppsala

Fabrizio Cafaggi
Judge of the Italian Council of State

Raffaella Calò
Italian Ministry of Justice

Prof. Federica Casarosa
Centre for Judicial Cooperation at European University Institute and Visiting Fellow at Masaryk University

Marc Clement
Judge of the Court of Appeal of Lyon

Stephen Coutts
Lecturer at University College Cork

Prof. Deirdre Curtin
Director of Centre for Judicial Cooperation at European University Institute

Lilla Farkas
Senior legal policy analyst for the Migration Policy Group at European University Institute

Martina Flamini
Judge of the Tribunal of Milan

Rita Gião Hanek
University of Lisbon

Mateusz Grochowski
Senior Researcher at Max Planck Institute for Comparative and International Private Law (Hamburg)

Jarosław Gwizdak
Institute of Law and Society and former judge at District Court of Katowice

Prof. Gábor Halmai
European University Institute

Prof. Paola Iamiceli
University of Trento

Alexandros-Ioannis Kargopoulos
Judge of the Court of First-Instance in Athens

Dr. Marjan Kos
University of Ljubljana

Ass. Prof. Nicole Lazzerini
University of Florence

Magdalena Ličková
Référendaire at the Court of Justice of the European Union

Bernard McCloskey
Lord Justice of Appeal, N. Ireland Court of Appeal

Ass. Prof. Madalina Moraru
Centre for Judicial Cooperation, European University Institute and Senior Research Fellow, Law Faculty, Masaryk University

Dr. Karolina Podstawa
University of Maastricht, European Centre on Privacy and Cybersecurity

Prof. Nina Półtorak
Judge at the General Court of the European Union and Jagiellonian University

Florentino-Gregorio Ruiz Yamuza
Senior Appeal Court Judge of Huelva

Raffaele Sabato
Judge at the European Court of Human Rights

Prof. Joan Solanes Mullor
Pompeu Fabra University

Hans Sundberg
Legal secretary at General Court of the European Union

Maciej Taborowski
Deputy Commissioner for Human Rights, Poland

Markus Thoma
Judge at Austrian Supreme Administrative Court

Gabriel Toggenburg
EU Fundamental Rights Agency

Dr. Lavinia Vizzoni
University of Siena

Prof. Saša Zagorc
University of Ljubljana

Edith Zeller
Judge at the Administrative Court of Vienna

Foreword

This book reveals a living epistemic community – one that came into being during the lifespan of the EC funded training project Active Charter Training Through Interaction of National Experiences (ACTIONES) and has been actively nourished ever since. This legal epistemic community engages intensely across the boundaries of practice and of academia, and has at its core the representatives of the original 17 partners to the project but it reaches much wider in terms of scope and relevance. The editors of this volume are to be congratulated for their systematic efforts to keep this community alive and kicking. Two years after the project ended, they organised a meeting in November 2019 with the contributors to this book, agreeing the overall approach of the book, the terminology to be followed and the research questions to be answered. The book has been constructed in an insightful manner in order to stimulate debate and dialogue across the boundaries of practice (lawyers, judges, officials) at European and national level and academia with every chapter written by an academic having a 'comment' chapter by a practitioner (and occasionally vice versa).

The idea has been from the very beginning to stimulate exchanges but also learning as to what the provisions of the EU Charter can and should mean in the real world of courts and litigants. The papers underlying the chapters in this book (some 25 in all including the comments) were nascent only 18 months ago. How much has changed in the wider context in this still short space of time. The COVID-19 public health crisis still now in its second wave at the beginning of May 2021 with no certainty as to its definitive or likely end. The crisis not only caused almost inevitable delays in the production process of the book but more fundamentally revealed and intensified already existing trends on a number of themes hugely central to this book. Events – crises in particular – can gloss over legal and technical problems when the need is great or perceived to be so. As we now hopefully emerge from this crisis, this book is very timely in identifying a number of gaps and issues for the future that the serious underlying work reflected in this book can underpin in a context where the centrality of the importance of the EU Charter cannot be underplayed. The editors are to be warmly congratulated for the long path they have trodden together on this theme of judicial interactions in and around the Charter of Fundamental Rights from conception to adolescence to what is now most likely a vigorous young adulthood in terms of the salience and centrality of this topic in European law and in legal practice.

The editors' introduction to the book positions the topic in a much broader field of enquiry. They deliberately and convincingly choose the umbrella term of 'judicial interactions' rather than the narrower judicial dialogue to include vertical and horizontal exchanges of various types. This inclusive approach enables specifically the analysis, in their words, of 'the multi-dimensional impact of a wide array of judicial interaction techniques such as the preliminary reference procedure, consistent interpretation, comparative reasoning, mutual recognition and disapplication, between courts from various jurisdictions, with various specialisations, at various levels in the judicial hierarchy'. The specific issue to explore across the rich content of the many chapters is whether such interactions have in fact, in a coherent and coordinated manner, contributed to the safeguarding of human rights through the medium of the EU Charter in the various legal orders.

While progress is evident and positive points noted, it seems more in the line of the EU Charter having an incremental and indirect effect on national constitutional case law rather than a revolutionary one. Where Member States do not comply with the values enshrined in Article 2 Treaty on European Union in general, and the fundamental rights protection standards of the Charter in particular, there are gaps in the protection of fundamental rights, especially in Member States (Halmai). Sensitive political aspects of judicial interactions in particular at the horizontal levels are never far from the mind with topics such as judicial independence under the spotlight, as in the contributions of Podstawa and Gwizdak. Even with Brexit there is some optimism from both the judiciary (McCloskey) and commentator (Coutts) that one way or another the provisions of the EU Charter will continue to resonate and be applied, albeit perhaps indirectly, to ensure effective legal protection across a host of roles, including as a source of legislative and judicial inspiration as well as in the context of transnational forms of judicial cooperation that are retained in some form and with new ways of participating.

In terms of substance, Part II of the book focuses on a selection of legal areas where the EU Charter is particularly prominent or salient, in particular in the areas of migration and asylum, non-discrimination and consumer protection. Time has not stood still since the academic meeting in 2019 and the drafting of these chapters and if anything the relevance of the topic is ever more acute and urgent given developments in the meantime, in particular relating to the pandemic. The topic of the book as a whole and the importance of having a living and active epistemic community have got a considerable boost in COVID times in a manner that is likely to impact the specifics of the judicial cooperation and further interactions that are the thrust of this book.

Digitalisation is partly through relying on private actors and pushing out the boundaries of the public-private divide and this leads to possible de-politicisation/de-legalisation in a context of Europeanisation. It was already there but COVID-19 makes it crystal clear in a manner that was less structurally visible before. The broader topic of judicial interaction lends itself quite naturally to expanded frontiers, especially in the context of digitalisation, and topics such as the digitalisation of evidence in the context of criminal law proceedings, European Production Orders and European Preservation Orders indicate new boundaries for judicial interactions in Europe where the need to ensure fundamental rights protection is essential. It is fascinating moreover to discover in this specialised area of criminal law the extent to which direct public-private avenues of law enforcement cooperation including the judiciary are being envisaged in European regulations. This reflects a more fundamental paradigm shift away from the more traditional international law instruments enabling law enforcement cooperation, in particular the treaty based Mutual Legal Assistance (MLA) mechanisms and the general principle of non-interference in another State's affairs.

The main idea behind the proposal by the Commission to facilitate cross-border access to electronic evidence is that certificates of judicial orders will be transmitted directly to the legal representatives of online service providers. The intention is to reduce response times in comparison to the more traditional state to state instruments; service providers will be obliged to respond within ten days or, in urgent cases, within six hours. The proposal comes in reaction to the perceived acute need to provide law enforcement and judicial authorities with modern instruments tailored to the new digital realities for obtaining cross-border access to data.

The proposal for a European Production Order and the European Preservation Order both allow the judicial authority of a Member State, the issuing State, to directly 'order' (note the recalibration from 'assistance') a provider offering the service in the EU to hand over or store the electronic evidence. They imply an extraordinary simplification of the procedure, with a significant reduction in deadlines for delivery of the evidence. But the most interesting general point is the obligation placed on the service provider irrespective of where they are and independent of the authority of another State and its legal system. Such extraterritorial or even de-territorialised criminal enforcement challenges long-established notions of international law and of the protection of individual rights and certainly leads to the risk of de-legalisation and the inability to ensure the effective protection of fundamental rights.

It is in my view not exaggerated to speak of a potentially tectonic shift in the way that judicial cooperation is being envisaged in these new European draft instruments for legislation given that the Commission conceives of mutual recognition as taking place not by any second judicial authority, but by the private service provider. Article 82(1) ensures mutual recognition of judicial decisions by which a judicial authority in the issuing State addresses a legal person in another Member State and even imposes obligations on it, without prior intervention of a judicial authority in that other Member State. Critically, legal representatives must comply with orders regardless of where the crime took place, where the provider is established, or where the evidence is stored, and irrespective of the nationality or residence of the target. The European Production or Preservation Order can lead to the intervention of a judicial authority of the executing State when necessary to enforce the decision. It is too early to say how exactly this will work in practice but it does seem like a very radical change to the existing system of judicial interactions, even as broadly framed in this book.

As this latter example shows the stage is set for interesting years ahead in terms of the manner in which judicial cooperation will take place, how and with whom. The frontiers are shifting through not only the new technological realities but also the envisaged actors including not only non-judicial public actors but also, more radically, completely private actors who are assigned tasks and functions within the emerging system of governance. This throws up a host of potential risks from the perspective of the effective protection of fundamental rights for the affected individuals and calls for sustained vigilance by joined-up epistemic communities as to how this may and should pan out in practice. This book represents the end of the beginning and reveals in a timely and salient fashion the need to carry this topic actively forward in new and creative ways.

Deirdre Curtin, Director of the Centre for Judicial Cooperation

Acknowledgements

We wish to express our gratitude to the scholars and the legal practitioners who took part in the Active Charter Training Through Interaction of National Experiences (ACTIONES) training project during 2015–17. The representatives of the 17 partners to this European Commission DG Justice supported project were the load-bearing engine that allowed the achievement of the project objectives and of this book.

The collaboration and willingness of lawyers and judges across the EU countries to share their practices and experiences on the application of the EU Charter of Fundamental Rights has allowed the creation of an epistemic community able to identify and address the most topical questions that national and European courts face in their ongoing efforts to enhance the level of protection of fundamental rights.

Last but not least, the editors would like to thank the contributors to this volume for their wonderful collaboration and their patience in addressing all the editors' comments.

Table of cases

Court of Justice of the European Union

Joined Cases C-148/13 to C-150/13 *A, B and C v Staatssecretaris van Veiligheid en Justitie* ECLI:EU:C:2014:2406
Case C-112/13 *A v B* ECLI:EU:C:2014:2195
Case C-243/19 *A v Veselības ministrija* ECLI:EU:C:2020:872
Case C-824/18 *A.B. and Others (Nomination des juges à la Cour suprême – Recours)* ECLI:EU:C:2021:153
Joined Cases C-585/18, C-624/19 and C-625/19 *A.K. (Independence of the Disciplinary Chamber of the Supreme Court)* ECLI:EU:C:2018:910
Case C-157/15 *Achbita and Centrum voor gelijkheid van kansen en voor racismebestrijding v G4S Secure Solutions NV* ECLI:EU:C:2017:203
Case C-517/17 *Addis* ECLI:EU:C:2020:579
Case C-652/16 *Ahmedbekova* ECLI:EU:C:2018:801
cases C-201/15 *AGET Iraklis* ECLI:EU:C:2016:972
Case C-617/10 *Åklagaren v Åkerberg Fransson*, EU:C:2013:105
joined cases C-317/08 *Alassini v Telecom Italia SpA*, C-318/08 *Califano v Wind SpA*, C-319/08 *Iacono v Telecom Italia SpA* and C-320/08 *Multiservice Srl v Telecom Italia SpA* EU:C:2010:146
Case C-585/16 *Alheto* ECLI:EU:C:2018:584
Case C-106/77 *Amministrazione delle Finanze dello Stato v Simmenthal SpA* EU:C:1978:49
Joined Cases C-404/15 and C-659/15 *Aranyosi and Căldăraru v Generalstaatsanwaltschaft Bremen* ECLI:EU:C:2016:198
Case C-488/11 *Asbeek Brusse and de Man Garabito v Jahani BV* EU:C:2013:341
Case C-176/12 *Association de médiation sociale* ECLI:EU:C:2014:2
Case C-64/16 *Associação Sindical dos Juízes Portugueses v Tribunal de Contas* ECLI:EU:C:2017:395
Case C-413/12 *Asociación de Consumidores Independientes de Castilla y León* ECLI:EU:C:2013:800
Case C-81/12 *Asociaţia Accept v. Consiliul Naţional pentru Combaterea Discriminării* ECLI:EU:C:2013:275
Case C-235/09 *Association Belge des Consommateurs Test-Achats ASBL and Others v Conseil des ministres* ECLI:EU:C:2011:100
Case C-268/17 *AY* ECLI:U:C:2018:602
Case C-415/11 *Aziz v Caixa d'Estalvis de Catalunya, Tarragona i Manresa (Catalunyacaixa)* EU:C:2013:164
Case C-618/10 *Banco Español de Crédito, SA v Joaquín Calderón Camino* EU:C:2012:349
Case C-128/12 *Banco Português de Negócios SA* ECLI:EU:C:2013:149

case C-421/14 *Banco Primus* EU:C:2017:60
Joined cases C-96/16 and C-94/17 *Banco Santander SA* ECLI:EU:C:2018:643
Case C-274/14 *Banco de Santander SA* ECLI:EU:C:2020:17
Case C-472/11 *Banif Plus Bank Zrt v Csaba Csipai and Viktória Csipai* ECLI:U:C:2013:88
Case C-109/17 *Bankia SA v Juan Carlos Mari Merino and Others* EU:C:2018:735
Case C-427/06 *Bartsch* ECLI:EU:C:2008:517
Case C-682/15 *Berlioz Investment Fund* ECLI:EU:C:2017:373
Case C-5/12 *Betriu Montull* ECLI:EU:C:2013:571
Case C-119/15 *Biuro podróży 'Partner' Sp. z o.o, Sp. komandytowa w Dąbrowie Górniczej v Prezes Urzędu Ochrony Konkurencji i Konsumentów* EU:C:2016:987
Case C-438/14 *Bogendorff von Wolffersdorff* ECLI:EU:C:2016:401
Case C-2/92 *Bostock* ECLI:EU:C:1994:116
Case C-249/13 *Boudjlida v Préfet des Pyrénées-Atlantiques* ECLI:EU:C:2014:2431
Case C-188/15 *Bougnaoui and Association de défense des droits de l'homme (ADDH) v. Micropole S* ECLI:EU:C:2017:204
Case C-122/15 *C* ECLI:EU:C:2016:391
Case C-210/06 *Cartesio* ECLI:EU:C:2008:723
Case T-452/10 *ClientEarth v Council* ECLI:EU:T:2011:420
Case C-380/05 *Centro Europa 7 Srl v Ministero delle Cominicazioni et al.* ECLI:EU:C:2008:59
Case C-54/17 *Centrum voor gelijkheid van kansen en voor racismebestrijding v. Firma Feryn NV* ECLI:EU:C:2008:397
Case C-83/14, *CHEZ Razpredelenie Bulgaria AD v. Komisia za zashtita ot diskriminatsia* ECLI:EU:C:2015:480
Case C-482/10 *Cicala*, ECLI:EU:C:2011:868
Case C-578/16 *CK and Others v Republika Slovenija* EU:C:2017:127
Case 45/76 *Comet BV v Produktschap voor Siergewassen* EU:C:1976:191
Case C-673/16 *Coman* ECLI:EU:C:2018:385
Case C-416/17 *Commission v France* ECLI:EU:C:2018:811
Joined Cases C-715/17, C-718/17 and C-719/17 *Commission v Republic of Poland, Commission v Hungary, Commission v Czech Republic* ECLI:EU:C:2020:257
Case C-192/18 *Commission v Poland* ECLI:EU:C:2019:924
Case C-619/18 *Commission v Poland (Independence of the Supreme Court)* ECLI:EU:C:2019:531
Case C-791/19 *Commission v Poland (Independence of the Disciplinary Chamber of the Supreme Court)* ECLI:EU:C:2020:277
Case C-286/12 *Commission v Hungary (Retirement age of judges)* ECLI:EU:C:2012:687
Case C-235/17 *Commission v Hungary* ECLI:EU:C:2019:432
Case C-78/18 *Commission v Hungary* ECLI:EU:C:2020:476
Case C-203/14 *Consorci Sanitari del Maresme* ECLI:EU:C:2015:664
Case C-152/17 *Consorzio Italian Management and Catania Multiservizi* ECLI:EU:C:2018:264
Case C-561/19 *Consorzio italiano management* ECLI:EU:C:2021:799
Case C-466/11 *Gennaro Currà* ECLI:EU:C:2012:465
joined cases C-224/19 and C-259/19 *CY and Others v Caixabank SA and Banco Bilbao Vizcaya Argentaria SA* ECLI:EU:C:2020:578
Case C-333/13 *Dano* ECLI:EU:C:2014:2358 par 88–92

Case C-441/14 *Dansk Industri (DI) acting on behalf of Ajos A/S v. Estate of Karsten Eigil Rasmussen* ECLI:EU:C:2016:278
Case C-395/15 *Daouidi* ECLI:EU:C:2016:917
Case C-279/09 *DEB* ECLI:EU:C:2010:811
Case C-201/13 *Deckmyn, Vrijheidsfonds VZW v. Helena Vandersteen, Christiane Vandersteen, Liliana Vandersteen, Isabelle Vandersteen, Rita Dupont, Amoras II CVOH, WPG Uitgevers België* ECLI:EU:C:2014:2132
Case C-650/13 *Delvigne* ECLI:EU:C:2015:648
Joined Cases C-177/17 and C-178/17 *Demarchi Gino Sas* ECLI:EU:C:2017:65
Joined Cases C-596/16 and C-597/16 *di Puma and Zecca* ECLI:EU:C:2018:192
Case C-118/17 *Dunai* ECLI:EU:C:2019:207
Case C-260/18 *Dziubak* ECLI:EU:C:2019:819
Case C-310/16 *Dzivev* ECLI:EU:C:2018:623
Case C-71/14 *East Sussex County Court* ECLI:EU:C:2015:656
Case C-414/16 *Egenberger v. Evangelisches Werk für Diakonie und Entwicklung eV* ECLI:EU:C:2018:257
Case C-403/16 *El Hassani* ECLI:EU:C:2017:960
Case C-448/17 *EOS KSI Slovensko s.r.o. v Ján Danko and Margita Danková* EU:C:2018:745
Case T-94/07 *EREF v Commission* ECLI:EU:T:2009:451
Case C-56/13 *Érsekcsanádi Mezőgazdasági* ECLI:EU:C:2014:352 par 54–57
Case C-260/89 *ERT* ECLI:EU:C:1991:254
Case C-244/13 *Ewaen Fred Ogieriakhi* ECLI:EU:C:2014:323
Case C-645/19 *Facebook Ireland and Others* ECLI:EU:C:2021:483
Case C-354/13 *Fag og Arbejde (FOA), acting on behalf of Karsten Kaltoft, v Kommunernes Landsforening (KL), acting on behalf of the Municipality of Billund* ECLI:EU:C:2014:2463
Case C-368/95 *Familiapress* ECLI:EU:C:1997:325
Case C-160/14 *Ferreira da Silva and Brito* ECLI:EU:C:2015:565
Case C-497/13 *Froukje Faber v Autobedrijf Hazet Ochten BV* ECLI:U:C:2015:357
Case C-314/08 *Filipiak* ECLI:EU:C:2009:719
Case C-49/14 *Finanmadrid EFC SA v Jesús Vicente Albán Zambrano and Others* EU:C:2016:98
Case C-258/14 *Florescu et al. v Sibiu et al.* ECLI:EU:C:2017:448
Case C-924/19 *FMS and others* ECLI:EU:C:2020:367
Case C-422/18 *FR* ECLI:EU:C:2018:784
Case C-614/10 *Football Dataco Ltd* ECLI:EU:C:2012:115
Case T-247/16 *Fursin and Others v ECB* ECLI:EU:T:2017:623
Case C-383/13 *G & R* ECLI:EU:C:2013:533
Case C-537/16 *Garlsson Real Estate and Others* ECLI:EU:C:2018:193
Case C-467/04 *Gasparini and others* ECLI:EU:C:2006:610
Case C-18/18 *Glawischnig-Piesczek v Facebook Ireland Limited* ECLI:EU:C:2019:821
Case C-189/18 *Glencore Agriculture Hungary* ECLI:EU:C:2019:861
Case C-507/17 *Google* ECLI:EU:C:2019:772
Case C-528/11 *Halaf v Darzhavna agentsia za bezhantsite pri Ministerskia savet* ECLI:EU:C:2013:342
Case C-198/13 *Hernández* ECLI:EU:C:2014:2055
Case C-40/11 *Iida* ECLI:EU:C:2012:691
Case C-11/70 *Internationale Handelsgesellschaft mbH v Einfuhr- und Vorratsstelle für Getreide und Futtermittel* ECLI:EU:C:1970:114

Joined Cases C-411/10 and C-493/10 *NS v Secretary of State for the Home Department and ME and Others v Refugee Applications Commissioner and Minister for Justice, Equality and Law Reform* ECLI:EU:C:2011:865

Joined cases C-154/15 and C-307/15 *Francisco Gutiérrez Naranjo v Cajasur Banco SAU, Ana María Palacios Martínez v Banco Bilbao Vizcaya Argentaria SA (BBVA), Banco Popular Español SA v Emilio Irles López and Teresa Torres Andreu* EU:C:2016:980

Joined cases C-349/18 to C 351/18 *Nationale Maatschappij der Belgische Spoorwegen (NMBS) v Mbutuku Kanyeba and Others* ECLI:EU:C:2019:936

Case C-246/06 *Navarro* ECLI:EU:C:2008:19

Case C-472/10 *Nemzeti Fogyasztóvédelmi Hatóság v. Invitel Távközlési Zrt* ECLI:EU:C:2012:242

Case C-507/18 *NH v. Associazione Avvocatura per i diritti LGBTI – Rete Lenford* ECLI:EU:C:2020:289

Case C-4/73 *Nold KG v Commission* ECLI:EU:C:1974:5

Case C-305/05 *Ordre des barreaux francophones and germanophones and Others* ECLI:EU:C:2007:383

Case C-543/14 *Ordre des barreaux francophones et germanophone and Others* ECLI:EU:C:2016:157

Case C-199/11 *Otis* ECLI:EU:C:2012:684

Case C-392/18 *P Bettani v Commission* ECLI:EU:C:2019:186

Case C-573/11 *P ClientEarth v Council* ECLI:EU:C:2013:564

Joined Cases C-663/17 P, C-665/17 *P* and C-669/17 *P European Central Bank (ECB) v Trasta Komercbanka AS and Others* ECLI:EU:C:2019:923

Joined cases C-402/05 P and C-415/05 *P Kadi and Al Barakaat* ECLI:EU:C:2008:461

Case C-422/11 *P* and C-423/11 *P Prezes Urzędu Komunikacji Elektronicznej v Commission* EU:C:2012:553

Joined cases C-515/17 P and C-561/17 P Uniwersytet Wrocławski and Poland v REA EU:C:2020:73

Case C-653/19 *PPU DK* ECLI:EU:C:2019:1024

Case C-168/13 *PPU Jeremy* F ECLI:EU:C:2013:358

Joined Cases C-354/20 *PPU L* and C-412/20 *PPU P (Openbaar ministerie)* ECLI:EU:C:2020:1033

Case C-216/18 *PPU LM (Celmer)* ECLI:EU:C:2018:117

Case C-237/15 *PPU Lanigan* ECLI:EU:C:2015:474

Case C-220/18 *PPU ML* ECLI:EU:C:2018:589

Case C-129/14 *PPU Spasic* ECLI:EU:C:2014:586

Case C-638/16 *PPU X and X v État belge* ECLI:EU:C:2017:173

Case C-503/15 *Panicello* ECLI:EU:C:2017:126

Case C-243/08 *Pannon GSM Zrt. v Erzsébet Sustikné Győrfi* EU:C:2009:350

Case C-28/14 *Pańczyk* ECLI:EU:C:2014:2003

Case C-443/15 *Parris v Trinity College Dublin and Others* ECLI:EU:C:2016:897

Case C-34/02 *Pasquini v Istituto nazionale della previdenza sociale (INPS)* EU:C:2003:366

Case C-483/12 *Pelckmans Turnhout NV* ECLI:EU:C:2014:304

Case C-453/10 *Pereničová and Perenič v SOS financ spol. s r. o.* ECLI:EU:C:2012:144.

Case C-390/12 *Pfleger* ECLI:EU:C:2014:281

Case C-470/12 *Pohotovosť* ECLI:EU:C:2014:101

Case C-63/08 *Pontin v T-Comalux SA* EU:C:2009:666 [2009] ECR I-10467

Case C-632/17 *Powszechna Kasa Oszczędności (PKO) Bank Polski S.A. w Warszawie v Jacek Michalski* EU:C:2018:963
Case C-176/17 *Profi Credit Polska S.A. w Bielsku Białej v Mariusz Wawrzosek* EU:C:2018:711
Case T-226/10 *Prezes Urzędu Komunikacji Elektronicznej v Commission* ECLI:EU:T:2011:234
Case C-73/16 *Puškár v Finančné riaditeľstvo Slovenskej republiky and Kriminálny úrad finančnej správy* ECLI:EU:C:2017:725
Joined cases C-225 and C-226/19 *R.N.N.S. and K.A.* ECLI:EU:C:2020:951
Case C-377/14 *Radlinger and Radlingerová v Finway a.s.* EU:C:2016:283
Joined cases C-698/18 and C-699/18 *SC Raiffeisen Bank SA and BRD Groupe Societé Générale SA v JB und KC* ECLI:EU:C:2020:537
Case C-467/18 *Rayonna prokuratura Lom and Others* ECLI:EU:C:2019:765
Case C-896/19 *Repubblika v Il-Prim Ministru* ECLI:EU:C:2020:1055
Case C-33/76 *Rewe-Zentralfinanz eG and Rewe-Zentral AG v Landwirtschaftskammer für das Saarland* EU:C:1976:188
Case C-147/08 *Römer* ECLI:EU:C:2011:286
Case C-34/09 *Ruiz Zambrano* ECLI:EU:C:2011:124
Joined cases C-141/12 and C-372/12 *S and Others* ECLI:EU:C:2014:2081
Case C-256/19 *S.A.D. Maler und Anstreicher OG v Magistrat der Stadt Wien and Bauarbeiter Urlaubs- und Abfertigungskasse* ECLI:EU:C:2020:523
Case C-276/12 *Sabou* ECLI:EU:C:2013:678
Case C-348/16 *Sacko Moussa* ECLI:EU:C:2017:591
Joined cases C-381/14 and C-385/14 *Sales Sinués and Youssouf Drame Ba v Caixabank SA and Catalunya Caixa SA (Catalunya Banc S.A.)* EU:C:2016:909
Case C-208/09 *Sayn-Wittgenstein* ECLI:EU:C:2010:806
Case C-278/16 *Sleutjes* ECLI:EU:C:2017:757
Case C-206/13 *Siragusa* ECLI:EU:C:2014:126
Case C-258/13 *Sociedade Agrícola e Imobiliária da Quinta de S. Paio Lda* ECLI:EU:C:2013:810
Case C-349/07 *Sopropé* ECLI:EU:C:2008:746
Case C-180/17 *Staatssecretaris van Veiligheid en Justitie* (Suspensory effect of the appeal) EU:C:2018:775
Joined cases C-569/16 and C-570/16 *Stadt Wuppertal and Volker Willmeroth als Inhaber der TWI Technische Wartung und Instandsetzung Volker Willmeroth e.K. v. Maria Elisabeth Bauer and Martina Broßonn* ECLI:EU:C:2018:871
Case C-29/69 *Stauder v City of Ulm* EU:C:1969:57
Case C-329/13 *Stefan* ECLI:EU:C:2014:815
Case C-367/15 *Stowarzyszenie* ECLI:EU:C:2017:36
Case C-93/12 *Stoyanov* ECLI:EU:C:2013:432
Case C-53/03 *Syfait and Others* ECLI:EU:C:2005:333 para 21
Case C-222/13 *TDC* ECLI:EU:C:2014:2265
Case C-105/14 *Taricco and Others (Taricco I)* ECLI:EU:C:2015:555
Case C-418/11 *Texdata Software GmbH* ECLI:EU:C:2013:588
Case C-213/89 *The Queen v Secretary of State for Transport, ex parte: Factortame Ltd and others* EU:C:1990:257
Case C-32/20 *TJ* ECLI:EU:C:2020:441
Case C-17/74 *Transocean Marine Paint Association v Commission* ECLI:EU:C:1974:106
Case C-168/15 *Tomášová* ECLI:EU:C:2016:602

Case C-265/13 *Torralbo Marcos* ECLI:EU:C:2014:187
Case C-556/17 *Torubarov v Bevándorlási és Menekültügyi Hivatal* EU:C:2019:626
Joined cases C-609/17 and C-610/17 *TSN* ECLI:EU:C:2019:981
Case C-491/07 *Turanský* ECLI:EU:C:2008:768
Case C-205/08 *Umweltanwalt von Kårnten* ECLI:EU:C:2009:767
Case C-432/05 *Unibet (London) Ltd and Unibet (International) Ltd v Justitiekanslern* EU:C:2007:163
Case C-222/86 *Union nationale des entraîneurs et cadres techniques professionnels du football (Unectef) v Heylens and Others* ELCI:EU:C:1987:442
Case C-437/13 *Unitrading* ECLI:EU:C:2014:2318
Cases T-137/16 *Uniwersytet Wrocławski v REA* ECLI:EU:T:2017:407
Case C-26/62 *Van Gend en Loos v. Netherlands Inland Revenue Administration* ECLI: EU:C:1963:1
Case C-61/65 *Vaassen-Gőbbels* ECLI:EU:C:1966:39
Case C-191/15 *Verein für Konsumenteninformation v. Amazon EU Sàrl* ECLI:EU:C: 2016:612
Case C-680/17 *Vethanayagam and Others* ECLI:EU:C:2019:627
Case C-659/18 *VW (Right of access to a lawyer in the event of non-appearance)* ECLI: EU:C:2020:201
Case C-5/88 *Wachauf* ECLI:EU:C:1989:321
joined cases C-65/09 *Gebr. Weber GmbH v Jürgen Wittmer* and C-87/09 *Ingrid Putz v Medianess Electronics GmbH* EU:C:2011:396 [2011] ECR I-05257
Case C-419/14 *WebMindLicenses Kft*. ECLI:EU:C:2015:832
Case C-452/18 *XZ v Ibercaja Banco SA* EU:C:2020:536
Case C-363/12 *Z. v A Government department* ECLI:EU:C:2014:159
Case C-491/10 *Zarraga* ECLI:EU:C:2010:82.
Case C-300/11 *ZZ* ECLI:EU:C:2013:363
Opinion 2/2013 ECLI:EU:C:2014:2454
Opinion 1/2009 ECLI:EU:C:2009:739

European Court of Human Rights

A and B v Norway App. nos. 24130/11 and 29758/11
A.S. v Poland , App. nos.37042/20 and 37691/20
Abdulaziz, Cabales and Balkandali v The United Kingdom, App. nos. 9214/80; 9473/81 and 9474/81
Airey v. Ireland, App. no. 6289/73
Almaši v Serbia, App. no. 21388/15
Artico v Italy, App. no. 6694/74
Baka v. Hungary, App. n. 20261/12
Beizaras and Levickas v. Lithuania App. no. 41288/15
Beuze v Belgium, App. no. 71409/10
Bochan v Ukraine (no. 2), App. no. 22251/08
Bosphorus Hava Yollar, App. no. 45036/98
Correia de Matos v Portugal, App. no. 56402/12
Croissant v Germany, App. no. 13611/88
Czekalla v Portugal, App. no. 38830/97
Dayanan v Turkey, App. no. 7377/03
Doyle v Ireland, App. No. 51979/17

Dvorski v Croatia, App. no. 25703/11
Edizioni Del Roma Societa Cooperativa A.R.L. and Edizioni del Roma S.R.L. v Italy App. no. 68954/13
Engel and others v the Netherlands, App. nos. 5100/71; 5101/71; 5102/71; 5354/72; 5370/72
Eremia v. the Republic of Moldova, App. no 3564/11
Fazia Ali v the United Kingdom, App. no. 40378/10
G.I.E.M. S.R.L. and Others v Italy, App. nos. 1828/06, 34163/07 and 19029/11
Galstyan v Armenia, App. no. 26986/03
Gestur Jónsson and Ragnar Halldór Hall v Iceland, App. nos. 68273/14 and 68271/14
Grande Stevens and others v Italy, App. nos. 18640/10, 18647/10, 18663/10, 18668/10 and 18698/10
Guðmundur Andri Ástráðsson v. Iceland, App. n.26374/18
Güveç v Turkey, App. no. 70337/01
Halime Kilic v. Turkey, App. no. 22492/93
Harabin v. Slovakia, App. no. 58688/11
Ibrahim and Others v the United Kingdom, App. nos. 50541/08, 50571/08, 50573/08
Identoba and Others v Georgia, App. no. 73235/12
Janosevic v Sweden App. no 34619/97
Jussila v. Finland, App. no. 73053/01
Kamasinski v Austria, App. no. 9783/82
Kremzow v Austria, App. no. 12350/86
Lagerblom v Sweden, App. no. 26891/95
Lala v The Netherlands, App. no. 14861/89
Lucky Dev v Sweden, App no 7356/10
Lykourezos v Greece, App. no. 33554/03
M.C. and A.C. v. Romania, App no 12060/12
M.G. v. Turkey, App. no. 646/10
Maširević v Serbia, App. no. 30671/08
Mehmet Zeki Çelebi v Turkey, App. no. 27582/07
Menarini Diagnostics v Italy, App. no. 43509/08
Michaud v France, App. no. 12323/11
Morice v. France, App. n.29369/10
Moustaquim v Belgium, App. No. 12313/86
MSS v Belgium and Greece, App. no. 30696/09
Nilsson v Sweden, App. no. 73661/01
Oberschlick v. Austria, App. n. 11662/85
Oliary v Italy, App. nos. 18766/11 and 36030/11
Pajič v Croatia, App. no. 68453/13
Paluda v. Slovakia, App. no. 33392/12
Panovits v Cyprus, App. no. 4268/04
Pelladoah v The Netherlands, App. no. 16737/90
Poitrimol v France, App. no. 14032/88
Ramos Nunes de Carvalho e Sá v Portugal, App. nos. 55391/13, 57728/13 and 74041/13
Rosenquist v Sweden, App. no. 60619/00
Ruotsalainen, App. no. 13079/03
Ruşen Bayar v Turkey, App. no. 25253/08
Salduz v Turkey, App. no. 36391/02
Schmautzer v. Austria, App. no. 15523/89

Sejdovic v Italy, App. no. 56581/00
Sen v. the Netherlands, App. no. 31465/96
Senchishak v Finland, App. no. 5049/12
Simeonovi v Bulgaria, App. no. 21980/04
Sitnevskiy and Chaykovskiy v Ukraine, App. nos. 48016/06 and 7817/07
Sramek v. Austria, App. n. 8790/79
Stanev v Bulgaria, App. no. 36760/06
Taddeucci and McCall v Italy App. no. 51362/09
Tarakhel v Switzerland, App. No. 29217/12
Tolmachev v Estonia, App. no. 73748/13
Twalib v. Greece, App. no. 24294/94
Valeriy Lopata v Russia, App. no. 19936/04
Vallianatos v Greece, App. nos 29381/09 and 32684/09
Van Geyseghem v Belgium, App. no. 26103/95
Vasenin v Russia, App. no. 48023/06
Västberga Taxi and Vulk v Sweden, App. no. 36985/97
Vaudelle v France, App. no. 35683/97
Welch v UK, App. no. 17440/90

Member States caselaw

Belgian Council of Alien Law Litigation, case No. 126.219, judgment of 25 June 2014
Belgian Council of Alien Law Litigation, case No. 230.293, judgment of 24 February 2015
Belgian Council of Alien Law Litigation, case No. 230.293, judgment of 24 February 2015
Belgian Council of Alien Law Litigation, case No. 233.257 judgment of 15 December 2015
Bulgarian Burgas Administrative Court, decision No. 564, case No. 1786/2017
Dutch Council of State, decision 201208550/1/V2
Dutch Council of State, decision 201110141/1/V2
Dutch Council of State, decision 201210441/1/V2
Dutch Council of State, decision 201407197/1/V3
Dutch Court of first instance of The Hague, branch Zwolle, n. 14/4276, 27 January 2015
French Administrative Court of Lyon, *M. Halifa*, no 12LY02704, 14 March 2013
French Administrative Court of Lyon, *Préfet de l'Ain c/ M. Bepede Guehoada*, no 12LY02737–12LY02739, 14 March 2013
French Administrative Court of Marseille, no 12MA04450, 8 June 2013
French Administrative Court of Nancy, no 12NC01805, 16 May 2013
French Council of State, *Barjamaj*, no 307999, 28 November 2007
French Council of State, *Hammou* no 306821–30682, 19 October 2007
French Council of State, *Préfet de Police v Demir*, no 120435, 19 April 1991
French Council of State, *Silidor*, no 315441, 26 November 2008
German Federal Constitutional Court, decision 24 April 2013, 1 BvR 1215/07
German Federal Constitutional Court, decision 5 May 2020, 2 BvR 859/15
Italian Appeal Court of Milan, 3 May 2011
Italian Appeal Court of Turin, Decision 23 September 2011
Italian Constitutional Court Decision n. 24/2017, 26 January 2017
Italian Court of Cassation, decision n. 27527, 30 December 2014

Italian Court of Cassation, decision n. 9116, 23 April 2014
Italian Tribunal of Naples, 9 December 2011
Italian Tribunal of Rome, 25 March 2011
Italian Tribunal of Rome, 27 April 2012
Lithuanian Supreme Administrative Court, *M.S. v Migration Department under the Ministry of Interior*, case No. A-69/2013, 20 June 2013
Lithuanian Supreme Administrative Court, *Z.K. v Kaunas County Police Headquarters*, case No. A-2681/2012, 3 September 2013
Polish Constitutional Court, K 1/12 (12 December 2012) PL CR OTK-A 2012/11/134
Polish Constitutional Court, K 27/12 (27 March 2013) OTK ZU 3A/2013
Polish Supreme Administrative Court, (7 December 2017) I OSK 857/17
Polish Supreme Administrative Court, (5 April 2019) II OSK 3210/18
Polish Supreme Administrative Court, (30 May 2019) II OSK 3559/18
Polish Supreme Court, Decision (13 May 2010) III SK 29/09
Polish Supreme Court, Decision (5 June 2007) I CSK 117/07
Polish Supreme Court, Decision (October 2008) III CZP 80/08
Polish Supreme Court, Resolution (13 July 2006) III SZP 3/06
Polish Supreme Court, Resolution (28 January 2014) BSA I-4110-4/13
Spanish Supreme Court, 8 June 2017, RJ 2017/2509
Slovenian Administrative Court, Judgment No. 2016 I U 645/2016 of 4 May 2016
Spanish Commercial Court of Barcelona No. 9, No. 413/14-D3, 11 July 2016
Swedish Court of Appeal for Western Sweden, Case B 2432-09 *MO v Ekobrottsmyndigheten*, 23 June 2010
Swedish Supreme Administrative Court, RÅ 2009 ref 94
Swedish Supreme Court, NJA 2010 p 168
Swedish Supreme Court, NJA 2013 s 502.
Swedish Supreme Court, NJA 2013 s 746
UK Court of Appeal, Benkharbouche v Embassy of Sudan [*2015*] *EWCA Civ 33*
UK High Court (*United Kingdom, High Court of England and Wales, R (AZ) v Secretary of State for the Home Department* [2015] EWHC 3695, 18 December 2015, [2016] 4 WLR 12
UK Supreme Court, [2014] UKSC 3 of 22 January 2014
UK Supreme Court, R (Kiairie and Byndloss) v SSHD [2018] UKSC 67
UK Supreme Court, R (on the application of Miller) v The Prime Minister [2019] UKSC 41
UK Upper Tribunal, Immigration and Asylum Chamber, Abdul [2016] UKUT 106 (IAC)
UK Upper Tribunal, Immigration and Asylum Chamber, R (AM) v Secretary of State for the Home Department [2017] UKUT 262 (IAC)
UK Upper Tribunal, Immigration and Asylum Chamber, R (Mohibullah) v SSHD [2016] UKUT (IAC) 561
UK Upper Tribunal, Immigration and Asylum Chamber, R (on the application of Hagos) v Secretary of State for the Home Department [2015] UKUT 0271 (IAC)
UK Upper Tribunal, Immigration and Asylum Chamber, R (on the application of ZAT and Others) v Secretary of State for the Home Department, IJR [2016] UKUT 61 (IAC)
UK Upper Tribunal, Immigration and Asylum Chamber, R (Saha) v Secretary of State for the Home Department (IJR) [2017] UKUT 17 (IAC)

1. Judicial interactions in action – a tool for a more powerful and influential EU Charter of Fundamental Rights

Federica Casarosa and Madalina Moraru

1. THE MULTI-FACETED DIMENSIONS OF THE EU SYSTEM OF PROTECTION OF FUNDAMENTAL RIGHTS

The multilevel system of fundamental rights protection that applies in Europe may be interpreted as the result of national, regional and international legislators' shared concerns about the protection of rights and principles essential in democratic societies.[1] However, the normative hierarchy, the overlap and the cross-referencing between national and European bills of rights creates a complex fundamental rights web that is difficult for those willing to put these principles into practice to untangle.[2]

---

[1] A. Barbera, 'Le tre Corti e la tutela multilivello dei diritti' in P. Bilancia and E. De Marco (eds), *La tutela multilivello dei diritti: Punti di crisi, problemi aperti momenti di stabilizzazione* (Giuffrè, Milano, 2004), 81 ff.; A. Cardone, *La tutela multilivello dei diritti fondamentali* (Giuffrè, Milano, 2012); M. Cartabia, '"Taking Dialogue Seriously": The Renewed Need for a Judicial Dialogue at the Time of Constitutional Activism in the European Union', Jean Monnet Working Papers 12 (2004); F. Sorrentino, 'La tutela multilivello dei diritti', 2004, available at www.archivio.rivistaaic.it (last visited 20 October 2021).

[2] I.E.A. Pernice, 'Multilevel Constitutionalism and the Treaty of Amsterdam: European Constitution-Making Revisited?', *Common Market Law Review*, 36 (1999), 703 ff.; I. Pernice, 'Multi-Level Constitutionalism and the Treaty of Amsterdam: European Constitution-Making Revisited?', *Common Market Law Review*, 36(4) (1999), 703. Note that the concept of multilevel structure has been criticised and reformulated by S. Cassese, 'Fine della solitudine delle corti, ovvero il dilemma del porcospino', Accademia delle Scienze di Torino, *Ars interpretandi*, 1 (2015), 21.

The coexistence of multiple levels and decision-making centres,[3] generating a sort of multilevel governance, has on the one hand undermined classic institutions such as sovereignty and the protection of rights as an absolute State prerogative; on the other hand, it has pushed forward the process of European integration. Safeguarding and guaranteeing fundamental rights therefore take place between the different layers of this system without, however, completely coinciding with them.[4] In Europe, this integrated system of protection of fundamental rights includes the supranational level (represented by the European Convention on Human Rights (ECHR), the case law of the European Court of Human Rights (ECtHR) and the EU Charter of Fundamental Rights as well as the case law on fundamental rights of the Court of Justice of the European Union (CJEU)) and the national level.[5] The integration of these levels results in a multilevel protection of rights comprising constitutionally recognised rights, those protected by the Convention and those provided for in the EU Charter.

This 'inter-constitutional order' finds its main legitimisation in the national constitutions, which become 'inter-constitutions': charters that are open to international declarations which can also offer effective contributions to the full safeguarding of the fundamental values of freedom and equality.[6] Consequently, constitutional provisions addressing fundamental rights cannot be disentangled from the interpretation of these rights provided by the Strasbourg and Luxembourg courts.[7]

Within this system, the EU Charter stands as a recent addition. The Charter's entry into force a little more than a decade ago allowed legal practitioners to explore – although still timidly – the potential of this bill of rights to resolve cases involving a violation of fundamental rights.[8] However, this did not happen smoothly as several doubts emerged during this period, in particular

---

[3] M. Luciani, 'Costituzionalismo irenico e costituzionalismo polemico', *Giurisprudenza costituzionale*, IV (2006), 1660.

[4] A. Ruggeri, 'La tutela "multilivello" dei diritti fondamentali, tra esperienze di normazione e teorie costituzionali', *Politica del diritto*, 3 (2007), 317.

[5] D. Tega, 'La Cedu e l'ordinamento italiano' in M. Cartabia (ed.), *I diritti in azione: Universalità e pluralismo dei diritti fondamentali nelle Corti europee* (il Mulino, Bologna, 2007), 68.

[6] A. Ruggeri, 'Sovranità dello Stato e sovranità nazionale, attraverso i diritti umani, e le prospettive di un diritto europeo "intercostituzionale"', *Rivista di diritto pubblico comparato ed europeo*, fasc. 2 (2001), 544.

[7] A. Ruggeri, 'La tutela "multilivello" dei diritti fondamentali, tra esperienze di normazione e teorie costituzionali', cit., 129.

[8] According to FRA, 'references to the Charter in national courts' decisions are growing more frequent and less superficial'. In 2019, over 11 per cent of the requests for preliminary rulings contained questions related to the Charter (see FRA, *Ten Years On: Unlocking the Charter's Full Potential* (Publications Office of the European Union, Luxembourg, 2020), 7).

regarding: what is the precise scope of application of the Charter compared to the scope of application of EU law?[9] What is the relationship between the rights in the Charter and the general principles of EU law,[10] the ECHR[11] and national constitutions?[12] What are the different forms of justiciability of its provisions?[13]

On many occasions, national courts were unable to disentangle this knot so they sought guidance, directly from the CJEU through the preliminary reference procedure or indirectly through comparative analysis of foreign decisions on similar issues. These vertical and transnational judicial interactions had an immediate impact on the resolution of specific conflicts of interpretation of the EU Charter and at the same time they have influenced the subsequent application of the Charter by other courts in new legal fields.[14]

The number of judicial interactions on the clarification of the Charter has been constantly growing over the last decade,[15] due to the decentralised and non-hierarchical nature of EU law. National courts as well as EU law courts have sought guidance on how to interpret the new bill of rights, and vertical and transnational judicial interactions have proved to avert inconsistent application of international legal norms and inter-court conflicts.[16] Also, judicial interactions have covered more and more rights from the EU Charter[17] and legal areas, including those perceived as pertaining to the core of national procedural autonomy, such as national organisation of courts.[18] The EU Charter has been at the forefront of judicial interactions addressing the chal-

---

[9] C-617/10 *Åkerberg Fransson* ECLI:EU:C:2013:105. For an in-depth analysis, see Chapters 2, 3 and 20 in this book.

[10] See more in Chapter 18 in this book.

[11] See Article 53(2) EU Charter.

[12] C-399/11 *Melloni* ECLI:EU:C:2013:107; see more in Chapters 5, 6 and 7 in this book.

[13] See Article 52(5) and Case C-176/12 *AMS* ECLI:EU:C:2014:2; see more in Chapter 2 in this book.

[14] For cross-sectoral and transnational ripple effects of judicial interactions, see Chapter 18 in this book.

[15] FRA, *Ten Years On: Unlocking the Charter's Full Potential*, cit., 9.

[16] On judicial interactions averting conflicts between Constitutional Courts and the CJEU, see the *Taricco* saga commented on in Chapter 5 in this book; while on judicial interaction averting conflicts between the CJEU, ECtHR and national constitutional courts, see Chapter 15 in this book, discussing the rights of same-sex couples from the perspective of the Romanian Constitutional Court.

[17] Such as Article 16, see more in Chapters 3 and 4 in this book.

[18] On judicial independence and domestic systems and organisation of judiciary, see Case C-64/16 *Associação Sindical dos Juízes Portugueses v Tribunal de Contas* ECLI:EU:C:2017:395 and the growing list of cases on judicial independence commented on in Chapters 8 and 9 in this book.

lenges raised by the various crises affecting the EU – economic,[19] so-called refugee,[20] rule of law.[21] In spite of the prolific judicial interactions identified in this book, new challenges to effective judicial interaction are developing, risking to diminish both the quantity and quality of judicial interactions. The rule of law backsliding is endangering effective judicial interactions in multiple ways. First of all, the threat of disciplinary actions[22] and criminal liability[23] for addressing preliminary questions to the CJEU has a chilling effect on direct vertical judicial interaction between domestic judges and the CJEU. The long-established right of ordinary courts to interact with the CJEU under Article 267 Treaty on the Functioning of the European Union (TFEU), unrestricted by substantial or procedural limitations set out in national laws, constitutions[24] or judicial hierarchy,[25] is under threat, leading the European Commission to lodge infringement procedures to protect the EU right of domestic courts to vertical judicial interaction.[26] Furthermore, the undermined judicial independence of some domestic courts diminishes the mutual trust which is the stepping stone for efficient transnational judicial interaction under the Area of Freedom, Security and Justice.[27] In addition to the variable flux

---

[19] Joined Cases C-8/15 P to C-10/15 P *Ledra Advertising* ECLI:EU:C:2016:701; Case C-258/14 *Florescu et al. v Sibiu et al.* ECLI:EU:C:2017:448.

[20] C-924/19 *FMS and others* ECLI:EU:C:2020:367.

[21] C-585/18 *A.K.* ECLI:EU:C:2019:982.

[22] K. Gajda-Roszczynialska and K. Markiewicz, 'Disciplinary Proceedings as an Instrument for Breaking the Rule of Law in Poland', *Hague Journal on the Rule of Law*, 12 (2020), 451; P. Bárd, 'Luxemburg as the Last Resort: The Kúria's Judgment on the Illegality of a Preliminary Reference to the ECJ', *VerfBlog*, 23 September 2019, available at https://verfassungsblog.de/luxemburg-as-the-last-resort/ (last visited 20 October 2021), DOI: 10.17176/20190923-232735-0.

[23] See M. Jałoszewski, 'Will Judge Igor Tulea be Apprehended by Force?', (2021), available at https://ruleoflaw.pl/will-judge-igor-tulea-be-apprehended-by-force/#:~:text=Judge%20Igor%20Tuleya%20is%20a,harshly%20reviewed%20the%20PiS%20MPs (last visited 20 October 2021).

[24] C-188/10 *Melki and Abdeli* ECLI:EU:C:2010:363; C-112/13 *A v B* ECLI:EU:C:2014:2195; C-416/10 *Križan* ECLI:EU:C:2013:8.

[25] C-210/06 *Cartesio* ECLI:EU:C:2008:723; C-314/08 *Filipiak* ECLI:EU:C:2009:719. For more details see *ACTIONES Handbook on the Techniques of Judicial Interactions in the Application of the EU Charter* (EUI, 2017), available at https://cjc.eui.eu/wp-content/uploads/2019/03/D1.1.b-Module-2.pdf (last visited 20 October 2021).

[26] European Commission, 'European Commission refers Poland to the European Court of Justice to protect independence of Polish judges and asks for interim measures', 31 March 2021, Press release, available at https://ec.europa.eu/commission/presscorner/detail/en/IP_21_1524 (last visited 20 October 2021).

[27] C-216/18 *LM* ECLI:EU:C:2018:586; Joined Cases C-354/20 PPU and C-412/20 PPU *L and P* ECLI:EU:C:2020:1033; P. Bárd and J. Morijn, 'Domestic Courts Pushing

and patterns of judicial interactions, changes are occurring also in the modes of judicial interaction. A new form of judicial interaction emerges – 'abusive comparativism' – whereby captured constitutional courts indirectly interact with the CJEU and ECtHR, by way of a smoke-screened consistent interpretation, to legitimise the constitutionality of 'unconstitutional legislation'.[28]

The various facets, process and outcomes of judicial interaction on the Charter have, so far, not been fully investigated in academic research. Unlike the existing literature, which mostly focuses solely on direct vertical means of dialogue, namely the preliminary reference,[29] or is limited to particular legal fields,[30] the contributions in this book analyse the multi-dimensional impact of a wide array of judicial interaction techniques, such as the preliminary reference procedure, consistent interpretation, comparative reasoning, mutual recognition and disapplication, between courts from various jurisdictions, with various specialisations, at various levels in the judicial hierarchy, and over a decade.

The book aims to fill the abovementioned gap regarding the role of judicial interactions in the application of the EU Charter across various fields and jurisdictions. It aims to provide a comparative assessment of selected horizontal and sector-specific legal issues regarding the interpretation and application of

---

for a Workable Test to Protect the Rule of Law in the EU: Decoding the Amsterdam and Karlsruhe Courts' Post-LM Rulings (Part II)', VerfBlog, 19 April 2020.

28 M. Ziółkowski and B. Grabowska-Moroz, 'Enforcement of EU Values and the Tyranny of National Identity: Polish Examples and Excuses', VerfBlog, 26 November 2019; G. Halmai, 'National(ist) Constitutional Identity? Hungary's Road to Abuse Constitutional Pluralism', EUI Working Paper LAW 2017/08.

29 J. Krommendijk, 'It Takes Two to Tango: An Introduction', *European Papers*, 5(2) (2020), 745; A. Pahladsingh and R. Grimbergen, *The Charter and the Court of Justice of the European Union: Notable Cases from 2016–2018* (Wolf Legal Publishers, Tillburg, 2019); Stacy A. Nyikos, 'The Preliminary Reference Process: National Court Implementation, Changing Opportunity Structures and Litigant Desistment', *European Union Politics*, 4 (2003), 399–401; Michal Bobek, 'Of Feasibility and Silent Elephants: The Legitimacy of the Court of Justice through the Eyes of National Courts' in Maurice Adams, Henri de Waele, Johan Meeusen and Gert Straetmans (eds), *Judging Europe's Judges: The Legitimacy of the European Court of Justice Examined* (Hart, Oxford, 2013), 197; Thomas de la Mare and Catherine Donnelly, 'Preliminary Rulings and EU Legal Integration: Evolution and Stasis' in Paul Craig and Grainne de Búrca (eds), *The Evolution of EU Law* (OUP, Oxford, 2011), 363.

30 Such as M. Moraru, G. Cornelisse and P. de Bruycker, *Law and Judicial Dialogue on the Return of Irregular Migrants from the European Union* (Hart, Oxford, 2020); D. Baldinger, *Vertical Judicial Dialogues in Asylum Cases: Standards on Judicial Scrutiny and Evidence in International and European Asylum Law* (Brill-Nijhoff, Leiden, 2015); J. Krommendijk, 'The Preliminary Reference Dance between the CJEU and Dutch Courts in the Field of Migration', *European Journal of Legal Studies*, 4 (2018), 101.

the Charter with a profound impact on jurisprudence, legislation and administrative practices at both the EU and domestic levels. In order to provide an overall methodological framework, it is crucial to identify the boundaries of the concept of judicial interactions (section 2) and introduce the book's main research question, namely whether and how judicial interaction techniques employed by courts and judges have solved issues of normative or judicial interpretation incompatibility in a way that has ensured coherence and coordination among different legal and judicial systems in safeguarding human rights in various legal orders (section 3).

2. JUDICIAL INTERACTIONS: A DEFINITION

The phenomenon of judicial dialogue between courts at the European and national levels is one of the most interesting topics in contemporary law and it has been widely discussed in the doctrine to the point that, prima facie, it would seem to constitute a subject now widely studied, already exhaustively examined in all its many facets and consequently lacking in food for thought. Numerous pages of literature have been devoted to the topic, and various conceptualisations and applications have developed to the point that it is difficult to find a clear and generally accepted definition, which has further contributed to the development of a diversity of theoretical approaches to judicial dialogue.

At the beginning of the 1990s, the 'dialogue' metaphor was used to describe the use of the so-called comparative jurisprudence method: when a judge examined the case law of other courts, in particular in the field of fundamental rights, it was claimed that the choice of the best solution was the result of dialogue with other courts.[31] This was referred to as dialogue between different

[31] Cfr. C. L'Heureux-Dubè, 'The Importance of Dialogue: Globalization and the International Impact of the Rehnquist Court', *Tulsa Law Journal*, 34 (1998), 15 ff.; J. Polakiewicz and V. Jacob-Foltzer, 'The European Human Rights Convention in Domestic Law: The Impact of the Strasbourg Case Law in States where Direct Effect is Given to the Convention', *Human Rights Law Journal*, 12 (1991), 125 ff.; for later literature, see A. Tzanakopoulos, 'Judicial Dialogue as a Means of Interpretation' in H.P. Aust and G. Nolte (eds), *The Interpretation of International Law by Domestic Courts: Uniformity, Diversity, Convergence* (OUP, Oxford, 2016), 3.

jurisdictions,[32] judicial dialogue, horizontal and vertical communication,[33] transjudicial communication,[34] interjudicial dialogue[35] and reception.[36]

As a result of the increasing relations among legal systems – and consequently the increased opportunities for judges in different countries to interact – dialogue between courts was strengthened: references to statements and principles on fundamental rights formulated in foreign jurisprudence flourished.[37] Moreover, the idea of a 'global legal space' based on common values in which different jurisdictions can interact to solve questions concerning the protection of rights supported this trend.[38] The idea that 'in fundamental rights there is an aspiration towards universality, which justifies the need to go beyond the boundaries of the individual legal system'[39] is not entirely abstract. The safeguarding of fundamental rights is, in fact, an area of constitutional law common to all legal systems, especially those inspired by the principles of liberal democratic constitutionalism,[40] and the universal nature of these rights means that they can be interpreted both in the light of national experiences and through comparison with foreign experiences. This in itself fosters dialogue between judges from different countries and the creation of a virtual legal space in which an increasing number of legal systems identify themselves around a common core of principles and discuss the solutions to be adopted in the field of rights.

---

32 J. Polakiewicz and V. Jacob-Foltzer, 'The European Human Rights Convention in Domestic Law', cit., 125.

33 M. Slaughter, 'A Global Community of Courts', *Harvard International Law Journal* 44 [2003], 191.

34 M. Slaughter, 'A Typology of Transjudicial Communication', *University of Richmond Law Review*, 29 (1994), 99 ff.

35 P.W. Almeida, 'The Asymmetric Judicial Dialogue between the ICJ and the IACtHR: An Empirical Analysis', *Journal of International Dispute Settlement*, 11 (2020), 1.

36 C. L'Heureux-Dubè, 'The Importance of Dialogue', cit., 17.

37 B. Markesinis and J. Fedtke (eds), *Giudici e diritto straniero: La pratica del diritto comparato* (Il Mulino, Bologna, 2009), 17.

38 S. Cassese, 'La funzione costituzionale dei giudici non statali: Dallo spazio giuridico globale all'ordine giuridico globale', *Rivista trimestrale di diritto pubblico*, fasc. 3 (2007), 609 ff. and id., *I tribunali di Babele: I giudici alla ricerca di un nuovo ordine globale* (Donzelli, Roma, 2009).

39 M. Cartabia, 'La Costituzione italiana e l'universalità dei diritti umani', *Rassegna*, 27 (2008), available at www.astrid-online.it (last visited 20 October 2021).

40 A. Barbera, 'Le basi filosofiche del costituzionalismo', in id. (ed.), *Le basi filosofiche del costituzionalismo* (Roma, Laterza, 1997), 3; S. Bartole, 'Costituzione e costituzionalismo nella prospettiva sovranazionale', *Quaderni costituzionali*, fasc. 3 (2009), 569 ff.

There are a large number of articles documenting how judicial interactions take place between the CJEU and the ECtHR,[41] between national courts from different jurisdictions and the CJEU,[42] between national courts and the ECtHR,[43] between European and international courts[44] and between national supreme or constitutional courts across Europe and around the world.[45] However, there is no general agreement among academics and legal practitioners on how to name these types of interaction, and neither a uniform theory nor a definition.[46] More recently terms such as 'transnational judicial dialogue'[47] and 'conver-

---

41 See, e.g., L. Scheeck, 'Competition, Conflict and Cooperation between European Courts and the Diplomacy of Supranational Judicial Networks', GARNET Working Paper 23/07; S. Douglas Scott, 'A Tale of Two Courts: Luxembourg, Strasbourg and the Growing European Human Rights Acquis', CMLRev, 43 (2006), 3; K. Dzehtsiarou, T. Konstadinides, T. Lock and N. O'Meara, *Human Rights in Europe: The Influence, Overlaps and Contradictions of the EU and the ECHR* (Routledge, Oxon, 2014).

42 On interaction between constitutional courts and the CJEU, see G. Martinico, 'Judging in the Multilevel Legal Order: Exploring the Techniques of "Hidden Dialogue"', *King's Law Journal*, 21(2) (2010), 257.

43 A. Føllesdal, B. Peters and G. Ulfstein, *Constituting Europe: The Court of Human Rights in a National, European, and Global Context* (Cambridge University Press, Cambridge, 2013).

44 Consider, e.g., N. Lavranos, 'The CJEU's Relationship with Other International Courts and Tribunals', 6 September 2010, available at <http://papers.ssrn.com/sol3/papers.cfm?abstract_id=1672727> (last visited 8 March 2012); Y. Shany, *Regulating Jurisdictional Relations between National and International Courts* (OUP, Oxford, 2007).

45 M. Bobek, S. Muller and S. Richards, 'Highest Courts and Globalisation'; T. Groppi and M. Ponthoreau, 'The Use of Foreign Precedents by Constitutional Judges'; J. Mendez, 'Constitutionalism and Transitional Justice', in Michel Rosenfeld and András Sajó (eds), *The Oxford Handbook of Comparative Constitutional Law* (OUP, Oxford, 2012), 1272.

46 For a legal perspective, see among others A.M. Slaughter, 'A Global Community of Courts', *Harvard International Law Journal*, 44 (2003), 191; A.T. Pérez, *Conflicts of Rights in the European Union: A Theory of Supranational Adjudication* (Oxford University Press, Oxford, 2009); A. Arnull, 'Judicial Dialogue in the European Union' in J. Dickson and P. Eleftheriadis (eds), *Philosophical Foundations of European Union Law* (Oxford University Press, Oxford, 2012), 109; for a political science perspective, see U. Sadl and Y. Panagis, 'The Force of EU Case Law: An Empirical Study of Precedential Constraint' (JURIX proceedings, The Foundation for Legal Knowledge Based Systems, 2015); U. Sadl and H. Palmer, 'Can Quantitative Methods Complement Doctrinal Legal Studies? Using Citation Network and Corpus Linguistic Analysis to Understand International Courts', *Leiden Journal of International Law*, 30 (2017), 327.

47 See M. Bobek, *Comparative Reasoning in European Supreme Courts* (OUP, Oxford, 2013); A. Slaughter, *A New World Order* (Princeton University Press, Princeton, 2009).

sation'[48] have also been employed.The term judicial *dialogue*, which so far seems to be the commonest term,[49] seems restrictive and unable to grasp the whole range of contacts (either intentional or casual) between courts within the same Member State, between ones in different Member States, between national and the European supranational courts and between the two European supranational courts – the CJEU and the ECtHR – in the most comprehensive manner. Judicial dialogue entails an ongoing exchange of arguments in order to reach common understandings.[50] Therefore, dialogue requires some sort of reciprocity among the judicial actors involved and it develops on a case by case basis over time.[51] However, scholars noted that reciprocity and continuity over time occur rarely in practice. Other scholars criticise the idea of a judicial dialogue in itself, contending that dialogue is a common practice in political institutions but it is almost impossible among courts and judges,[52] that it is difficult to identify as it can often happen implicitly and not explicitly,[53] and it requires an ongoing exchange of ideas, whereas in judicial practice there is more often a monologue rather than dialogue.[54]

---

48 M. Claes, M. de Visser, P. Popelier and C. van de Heyning (eds), *Constitutional Conversations in Europe: Actors, Topics and Procedures* (Intersentia, Antwerp, 2013), 1.

49 A. Rosas, 'The European Court of Justice in Context: Forms and Patterns of Judicial Dialogue', EJLS, 1/2 (2007), 1; L.B. Tremblay, 'The Legitimacy of Judicial Review: The Limits of Dialogue between Courts and Legislatures', *International Journal of Constitutional Law*, 3 (2005), 617; F. Jacobs, 'Judicial Dialogue and the Cross-Fertilization of Legal Systems: The European Court of Justice', *Texas International Law Journal*, 38 (2003), 54.

50 Opinion of AG Bot delivered on 14 May 2014 in Case C-244/13 *Ewaen Fred Ogieriakhi* ECLI:EU:C:2014:323.

51 A. Torres Pérez, 'Judicial Dialogue and Fundamental Rights in the European Union: A Quest for Legitimacy', in G. Jacobsohn and M. Schor (eds), *Comparative Constitutional Theory* (Edward Elgar Publishing, Cheltenham, UK and Northampton, MA, USA, 2018), 104. As a consequence 'conversation' is also a wider category than 'dialogue' as it also includes instances where more than two actors are involved and interactions that have a more informal character or are not geared towards achieving a particular aim. For more details on 'conversations' as a form of judicial interaction, see M. Claes, M. de Visser, P. Popelier and C. van de Heyning, 'Introduction: On Constitutional Conversations', in id. (eds), *Constitutional Conversations in Europe, Actors, Topics and Procedures* (Intersentia, Antwerp, 2012), 1.

52 See B. De Witte, 'The Closest Thing to a Constitutional Conversation in Europe: The Semi-Permanent Treaty Revision Process' in P. Beaumont, C. Lyons and N. Walker (eds), *Convergence and Divergence in European Public Law* (Hart, Oxford, 2002), 137.

53 David S. Law and Wen-Chen Chang, 'The Limits of Global Judicial Dialogue', *Washington Law Review*, 86 (2011), 523.

54 A. Torres Pérez, 'Judicial Dialogue and Fundamental Rights in the European Union', cit., 104–5.

This book instead endorses the term 'judicial interaction' in order to propose a category that reflects instances of interaction that may differ in intensity, outcome and typology, and that aims to construct a better interpretation of a legal norm without necessarily involving reciprocity or continuity over time. At the basic level, judicial interaction can be qualified as a sequence of judgments that refer to each other involving at least two courts and which are not necessarily in a hierarchical relation, with a shared intention of improving the practice of interpreting or reviewing a supranational norm. Therefore, judicial interactions embed a set of techniques used by courts and judges to promote coherence and coordination (or at least minimise the risk of conflicts) among different legal and judicial systems in safeguarding constitutional goods that are protected by various levels of governance. As a result, the cooperative contraposition[55] with foreign experiences is not interpreted as a transplant of law through case-law decisions, but instead as a form of dynamic flow of knowledge aimed at ensuring respect for the principles of the constitutional state of law.[56]

In addition to judicial interactions which take place through courts cross-referencing or comparative reasoning, whether explicit or implicit, over recent decades judges and courts around the world, and especially in the European Union, have increased their interaction,[57] also directly through meetings, exchanges in workshops and conferences, delegations from one court to another, in institutional forms of cooperation[58] or indirectly via online platforms, such as e-platforms and blogs.[59] The judicial networks existing within the EU have contributed immensely to the increase in judicial interactions.

---

55 G. Zagrebelsky, *La legge e la sua giustizia* (Il Mulino, Bologna, 2008), 400.

56 E.F. MacGregor, 'What Do We Mean When We Talk about Judicial Dialogue? Reflections of a Judge of the Inter-American Court of Human Rights', *Harvard Human Rights Journal*, 30 (2017), 89.

57 Different types of classifications of the ways courts interact with each other are used in the literature: Frishman refers to three categories: face to face interactions, IT-based communication and cross-citations; see, O. Frishman, 'Transnational Judicial Dialogue as an Organisation Field', *European Law Journal*, 19 (2013), 739, 747; different types of classification have been used by A. Slaughter, 'Judicial Globalization', *Virginia Journal of International Law*, 40 (1999–2000), 1103, 1104; E. Lazega, 'Mapping Judicial Dialogue across National Borders: An Exploratory Network Study of Learning from Lobbying among European Intellectual Property Judges', *Utrecht Law Review*, 8 (2012), 115, 118.

58 For instance, European Judicial Training Network, Association of European Administrative Judges, Consultative Councils of European Judges, European Network of Councils for the Judiciary, Network of the Presidents of the Supreme Courts, European Network of Councils for the Judiciary.

59 This method of judicial cooperation is better developed in EU countries that recognise precedent as legally binding, e.g. the UK and Ireland, while civil law systems

The great value of these informal meetings is that they offer national judges an opportunity to discuss and exchange views on the development of jurisprudence, tackling problems of interpretation and application in diverse areas of law, including European fundamental rights. Although these judicial interactions which take place between judges often materialise in cross-referencing (formal judicial interactions), this book does not consistently include in its analysis this type of judicial interactions, but will limit itself to providing anecdotal evidence, where relevant, to the main claims in the chapters.

3. A TENTATIVE TAXONOMY OF JUDICIAL INTERACTIONS

As mentioned above, judicial interactions may differ from each other in intensity, outcome and typology. This volume analyses judicial interactions in the EU and looks at three dimensions. First, it considers judicial interactions that habitually occur between national judges and the CJEU, most notably in the form of preliminary reference procedures, but also when national judges engage with the case law of the CJEU in other ways. We call this *vertical judicial interaction*. We also use this term for engagement by national judiciaries with ECtHR case law. Second, there will often be interactions between judges within the same Member State, which we call *horizontal judicial interaction.* Third, national judges may engage with the case law of other Member States' courts, which we call *transnational judicial interaction*. The term transnational judicial interaction can also describe interactions between the CJEU and the ECtHR. As we employ a broad understanding of the concept, judicial interaction can take various forms, of which the most important are: (1) the duty of consistent interpretation of national law with EU legal obligations as interpreted by the CJEU; (2) the preliminary reference procedure; (3) disapplication; (4) comparative reasoning with national legislation and jurisprudence from other Member States; and (5) mutual recognition of foreign judgments.[60]

This volume moves well beyond simply reflecting on vertical judicial interaction between national courts and the CJEU in the context of preliminary reference procedures. The main novelty of the book lies in the plentiful examples and case studies it offers regarding how courts in a Member State, through a transnational judicial interaction, work out how specific issues in the

(e.g. France and Romania) do not recognise legal precedent as *stare decisis* and so the use of national foreign judgments is less common.

[60] For a more in-depth analysis of 'Judicial Interaction Techniques', see M. Moraru, 'ACTIONES Module of Judicial Interaction Techniques' (2017), available at https://cjc.eui.eu/wp-content/uploads/2019/03/D1.1.b-Module-2.pdf (last visited 20 October 2021).

horizontal or sectoral application of the EU Charter can be best accommodated in their national judicial practices through the application of the EU's bill of rights.

The third dimension of judicial interaction discussed in the volume is *transnational judicial interactions*, which capture how national courts from different jurisdictions, and also supranational courts, chief among them the CJEU and the ECtHR, engage with each other's case law. The authors of this volume have engaged in more than just a jurisdiction by jurisdiction description of how the EU Charter is received by the national courts. The cross references, the contextualised discussion of the themes, the rich representation of case law selected in each chapter and commentaries will give the reader a compelling account of the three dimensional judicial interaction taking place in relation to the EU Charter. The volume reveals both positive outcomes, whereby national courts have made the EU Charter a real living instrument, but also a still limited impact of the Charter due to persistent lack of clarity regarding its scope of application (see Chapter 20) or the concrete added value of the Charter when there is already extensive EU secondary legislation in a particular sector (see Chapter 14), and a growing gap between the reach of the EU Charter and the needs of society in certain sectors (such as migration).

The premise of this book is that judicial interaction can answer complex legal questions relating to the implementation of the EU Charter. Several questions accordingly guide the assessment of judicial interaction in this volume.

- Have judicial interactions among courts contributed to making the multilevel system of fundamental rights one of mutual agreement or understanding?
- Have they contributed to an enhancement of fundamental rights or has this only been an incidental repercussion spinning off the enhancement of effective enforcement of EU law?
- How have policies and governance regimes been challenged and reconciled in courts, as spaces/forums of contestation?
- How have judicial interactions benefited national courts? Or have only some courts been benefiting from interactions?
- How have judicial interactions benefited the individual?
- Have judicial interactions contributed to transplanting fundamental rights standards across legal fields (e.g. right to be heard standards developed first in competition law, moved to smart sanctions and then to asylum and immigration)? Should there be a limit to these spillover effects? (Are remedies for the violation of the right to be heard in competition just for violation of the right to be heard in asylum and immigration?)

To comprehensively address these questions, the book brings together leading authors from various backgrounds, including scholars, lawyers, judges and policy officers. The true hallmark of the entire volume is the extensive underlying research carried out in the framework of two European Commission-funded projects dedicated to judicial training, namely European Judicial Cooperation and Fundamental Rights Practice of National Courts – Unexplored Potential of Judicial Dialogue Methodology (JUDCOOP)[61] and Active Charter Training Through Interaction of National Experiences (ACTIONES),[62] which had the opportunity to train and involve a total of 600 national judges. The book includes several contributions addressing either horizontal or sectoral issues that will provide scholars and professionals with practical guidelines regarding the current and forthcoming challenges related to the application of fundamental rights.

Mirroring the experimentalist approach adopted in the abovementioned training projects, which triggered the creation of an epistemic community composed of academics and professionals, each contribution is written as a collaboration between one academic and a legal practitioner (i.e. a judge or a lawyer). The purpose is to provide the occasion for an exchange of expertise and knowledge, able not only to stimulate a deeper connection between theoretical analysis of rules and principles, but also their practical implementation in real life cases. The result is the provision of guidelines able to provide readers with reference to landmark cases and decisions at both the European and national levels. Along with each chapter, a comment by an academic or practitioner follows, highlighting the underlying principles of judicial interaction and their contribution to the application of the EU Charter.

---

[61] European Judicial Cooperation and Fundamental Rights Practice of National Courts – Unexplored Potential of Judicial Dialogue Methodology (JUDCOOP) financed by the European Commission and coordinated by the Centre for Judicial Cooperation. The results of the project are available at https://cjc.eui.eu/projects/european-judicial-cooperation-in-fr/ (last visited 20 October 2021).

[62] Active Charter Training Through Interaction of National Experiences (ACTIONES) funded by the European Commission and coordinated by the Centre for Judicial Cooperation, see more at https://cjc.eui.eu/projects/actiones/ (last visited 20 October 2021).

4. OVERVIEW OF THE CONTRIBUTIONS – EXPLORING THE OUTCOMES OF JUDICIAL INTERACTIONS ON THE APPLICATION OF THE EU CHARTER

The Charter not only provides a written catalogue of fundamental rights but it also contains a set of rules known as 'general provisions' or 'horizontal clauses' concerning: the scope of application of the Charter (Article 51); the interpretation of the Charter's fundamental rights that 'correspond' to rights granted in the ECHR or 'result from the constitutional traditions common to the Member States' (respectively, Article 52, para. 3 and Article 52, para. 4); the different effects of the Charter's provisions that contain 'rights' or 'principles' (Article 52, para. 5); and its relationship with sources external to the EU legal order, notably domestic constitutions (Article 53).

Part I of the book provides an overview of the most relevant – and complex – issues emerging from the interpretation and application of horizontal provisions,[63] taking into account the case law of the Court of Justice providing interpretation of them.

Judge Półtorak explores the limitations of the application of the rights and principles enshrined in the EU Charter by the Member States in order to highlight how the EU Charter may benefit, if not trigger, judicial interactions. She points out that the first step (although not necessarily the last one) for national courts is a clear qualification of the field of application, as enshrined in Article 51(1) of the Charter, which as a consequence sheds light on the scope of the obligation on the Member States to respect and apply the Charter but also to analyse the consequences of this obligation for national courts. Półtorak suggests that the question of the scope of application of the Charter should be distinguished from the question of its actual application in place of national constitutional rights and freedoms, and concludes that the Charter may operate in parallel with national fundamental rights – it may be put on standby and only step in when a national law does not guarantee an adequate level of protection or when the implementation of EU law is put in jeopardy.

Toggenburg's commentary starts from Półtorak's analysis and addresses three main questions. (1) How far does the 'field of application of Union law'

[63] 'General provisions' or 'horizontal clauses' concerning: the scope of application of the EU Charter (Article 51); the interpretation of the Charter's fundamental rights that 'correspond' to rights granted in the ECHR or 'result from the constitutional traditions common to the Member States' (respectively, Article 52, para. 3 and Article 52, para. 4); the different effects of the Charter's provisions that contain 'rights' or 'principles' (Article 52, para. 5); and its relationship with sources external to the EU legal order, notably domestic constitutions (Article 53).

reach? (2) How many rights in the Charter provisions are rights in the strict sense, and of these how many are directly applicable between individuals? (3) What entails from the EU and the Member States being obliged to 'promote the application' of the Charter?

Zagorc and Kos address the interplay between constitutional values and the EU Charter. They describe how European values form and what their relationship with national constitutions is today, arguing that a decoupling has occurred forming a relatively independent EU value system which can now be employed against non-compliant Member States. As a result, their contribution suggests that the EU Charter should feature more prominently in legal conflicts between the EU and Member States which are essentially value-underpinned. The contribution then explores the use of the EU Charter which would be in line with the current constitutional setup of the EU, both within and outside its scope of application.

The comment by Lazzerini highlights the crucial role of the Charter as a bridge to national (constitutional) standards rather than as a pair of scissors. Lazzerini supports this argument by providing several examples emerging from the jurisprudence of the CJEU determining the standard of fundamental rights protection. Moreover, she shows that the Court's approach may become more open to contributions from Member States' constitutional standards thanks to the contribution of national courts.

The contribution by Judge Accetto assesses the impact of the EU Charter on the jurisprudence of national courts already vested with the duty of safeguarding fundamental rights – constitutional courts. He evaluates the import of the Charter as a recent addition to a relatively saturated field of laws and mechanisms of human rights protection, comprising not only the national constitutional orders but also the system under the ECHR and the development of human rights as general principles of EU law prior to the adoption of the Charter. His analysis takes into account a brief retrospective look at the 'constitutionalisation' of the EU legal order and the development of EU human rights law prior to the adoption of the Charter. Accetto then concludes that in the relatively short span of the first ten years the effects of the Charter are limited and indirect rather than dramatic and direct. Nevertheless, its formal and symbolic significance has contributed to the recently bolstered judicial interaction between the national apex courts and their European counterpart in reconciling overlapping fundamental rights regimes. Perhaps this indirect effect of the Charter may be the true catalyst of its long-term significance.

Halmai's comment investigates the original and the changed aims of the Charter's Article 51 to make sure that Member States respect fundamental rights, which is followed by a closer look at the right to effective remedy and fair trial guaranteed in Article 47 of the Charter. The conclusion of the commentary is that the Charter's effect on national constitutional jurisprudence is more incremental and indirect than revolutionary, and it seems to be insufficient to protect fundamental rights, especially in Member States which do not comply with the values enshrined in Article 2 Treaty on European Union (TEU) in general, and the fundamental rights protection standards of the Charter in particular.

Podstawa and Gwizdak's contribution addresses one of the most sensitive issues emerging from the interplay between Articles 2 and 19(1) TEU, and Article 47 EU Charter, and the principle of effectiveness of EU law. It addresses judicial independence, showing that its meaning is far from clear and uniform and its application far from straightforward. In particular, the contribution highlights that judicial independence in the CJEU case law involves three essential elements, namely the brewing conflict in the 'new' states of the European Union against the background of the judiciary reforms, the willingness of the CJEU to accept jurisdiction according to Article 19 TEU and finally the crucial role played by judicial interactions among national and European courts. Although the case law so far seems to align towards an increasing jurisdictional power in the EU legal order, according to the authors, the ongoing evolution does not conceal the fact that judges continue to seek support from the case law of the CJEU to make the standard of judicial independence more specific and less prone to manipulation.

Judge Zeller's commentary highlights that the standards adopted by the CJEU and other European bodies in addressing the weakness of EU legal systems vis-à-vis judicial independence are not always uniformly applied and interpreted. Zeller compares the Hungarian and Austrian legal systems, showing that elements pointed out as proofs of the erosion of rule of law in the Hungarian legal system are not so different from features that characterise the Austrian one, which, however, have never been criticised or contested at the EU level.

Ličková and Solanes Mullor focus their contribution on the right to be advised, defended and represented enshrined in Article 52(3) EU Charter. They assess whether the EU-specific articulation of fundamental-right standards remains coherent with their development before the ECtHR and concludes that cross-fertilisation between the two systems can work to some extent in both directions, as is shown by the ECtHR case law on Article 6(1)(c) ECHR and the regime of permissible restrictions on the right to legal advice under the Access to Lawyer Directive. The role of the EU Charter so far can only be acknowledged as a tool to interpret notions of EU law and to test the EU-law compatibility of Member States' actions when they implement EU law within the meaning of Article 51(1) of the Charter, although the number of cases decided by the CJEU on the meaning and specific implications of the provisions of the Access to Lawyer Directive so far remains rather limited, and many aspects therefore still remain to be explored.

In the commentary by Judge Kargopoulos, the CJEU jurisprudence is analysed through the lens of the limits on approximation of criminal procedure laws set out in the Treaties (Article 5 TEU, Articles 67 and 82(2) TFEU). It is argued that often the CJEU does not properly reflect the limitations of the Treaties in its analysis, which risks overextending the application of secondary instruments in criminal proceedings, with the indirect effect of impairing national criminal justice systems and their formulations of defence rights, resulting in distrust of EU law rather than promoting mutual trust among Member States.

Judge McCloskey's contribution addresses the aetiology of the Charter and, in particular, its future influence in the post-Brexit United Kingdom. McCloskey affirms that the EU Charter, if deployed to its full potential, should emerge as one of the most powerful instruments of human rights protection in the globe and will progressively expose the folly of Brexit. The contribution concludes that the exile of the Charter after Exit Day will not be final and absolute. McCloskey supports this conclusion with several arguments, underlining in particular the fact that fundamental rights or principles of EU law, which exist irrespective of the Charter, will be retained in domestic UK law. Although there will be no right of action in domestic UK law after Exit Day based on a failure to comply with EU general principles, and courts will not be empowered to disapply domestic laws post-Exit Day on the basis that they are incompatible with EU general principles, McCloskey trusts the innovation and creativity of UK lawyers and judges: effective human rights protection, particularly in a country which has no constitution, will be heavily dependent on a strong rule of law culture.

Coutts's comment focuses on the roles the Charter will play in the UK legal system: a side-constraint on the exercise of state power; a source of legislative and judicial inspiration; and a means of underpinning transnational systems of cooperation. The analysis concludes that the exclusion of the Charter from retained EU law will remove the first but not the second, while making achievement of the third more difficult in any future relationship.

Part II of the book is dedicated to a selection of legal areas where the EU Charter has a relevant impact, namely migration and asylum, non-discrimination and consumer protection. The selection of these areas is based on the case law of the CJEU interpreting the EU Charter. Its impact is particularly evident in areas where EU rules touch on vulnerable categories of individuals, such as in the non-discrimination, migration and asylum fields. However, the 'presence' of the Charter is also more and more visible in fields in which, until now and for different reasons, the fundamental rights dimension has remained underdeveloped, such as consumer law.

Gião Hanek and Farkas's analysis starts from the limits emerging from the approach adopted by the EU non-discrimination acquis, which tends to be limited to the gender equality and non-discrimination directives, therefore showing a gaping difference between the level of protection accorded to certain groups and others. Therefore, the contribution broadens the perspective to secondary legislation, procedural and soft law measures pertaining to criminal forms of discrimination, yielding more nuanced insights. The contribution documents the emergence of a 'continuum of equality' between the civil and the criminal branches in EU anti-discrimination law, particularly through the Victims' Rights Directive. It shows that the EU Charter can play an important role in approximating EU norms to international human rights standards and offers strategies for addressing legislative deadlock to equalise protection across discriminated groups.

The comment presented by Attorney Bercea focuses on the CJEU's decision in *Coman*. It points out that despite the framing of the Romanian Constitutional Court's questions and the Advocate General's Opinion, the CJEU disregarded Article 21 of the Charter. This deliberate absence of reference is interpreted not as a form of deference to the national legal systems and judges but to the ECtHR. Accordingly, the CJEU's decision appears not only as a 'free movement' but also a 'human rights' case, as Article 21 of the Charter is discretely very much present in the decision as Article 14 ECHR is.

Grochowski and Taborowski's contribution addresses EU consumer law through the lens of its most important principle, namely the principle of effectiveness. This concept has recently been significantly reframed and reinvigorated in the CJEU case law on EU consumer law by two interconnected dynamics: the introduction of Article 47 EU Charter and the current debate over the axiological foundations of EU private law. Effectiveness has thus been elevated to a more prominent position, being situated at the intersection of policy and fundamental rights. The contribution then delves into the role of effectiveness in the protection offered by EU law to the consumer as a domain of dialogue between the CJEU and domestic courts, and adopts in this respect two focal points. It pays particular attention to the ways of proliferating the standard of effectiveness through instruments of judicial dialogue. In this regard the text adopts a two-pronged perspective. On the one hand, it seeks to identify the ways for domestic courts to bring the problem of effectiveness before the CJEU in the preliminary procedure. On the other hand, it attempts to understand the extent to which (and under what premises) the notion of effectiveness construed by the CJEU can be reflexively translated into domestic legal systems.

Iamiceli's comment highlights the multiple dimensions of effectiveness: the effectiveness of EU law and *effet utile* are boosted by effective judicial protection. The comment moves from these multiple dimensions and presents the different ways that other principles of EU law, such as proportionality and dissuasiveness, interact with them. Whereas proportionality enables a fair balancing when the right to an effective remedy needs to be limited against other fundamental rights or freedoms, dissuasiveness tends to serve *effet utile*, sometimes beyond the boundaries of effective judicial protection.

Moraru and Judge Clement's contribution delves into the role played by the EU Charter in asylum-, return- and visa-related hearing procedures through the lens of judicial interactions. Through an analysis of European and domestic cases spanning over a decade, the authors provide evidence of the crucial role played by judicial interaction in identifying which of the various EU legal sources of the right to be heard are applicable to asylum seekers, returnees and visa applicants at the domestic level. They continue by investigating how judicial interactions have contributed to the development of concrete standards for the conduct of administrative hearings. The chapter proceeds with an analysis of how judicial interactions have empowered domestic courts to shape new remedies for violation of the right to be heard outside the confines of EU secondary legislation and domestic procedural law directly on the basis of the EU law general principle of the right to defence and Article 47(2) EU Charter. Notwithstanding the positive impact of the EU Charter, the authors also identify shortcomings of judicial interaction for the uniform application of the EU fundamental right to be heard of asylum seekers and immigrants across the Member States.

Judge Flamini comments on a concrete case of judicial interaction, offering the perspective of a national judge who has to address the challenges of implementing a preliminary ruling from the CJEU in a context of divergent domestic jurisprudence and overlapping legal sources of fundamental rights. Although procedural law is a flexible means able to ensure respect for the fundamental right to international protection, it would remain a mere declaration of principle to affirm the fundamental nature of this right if effective procedural guarantees were not available to safeguard the substantive legal condition.

Part III of the book is dedicated to the role of judicial interactions in shaping remedies for fundamental rights violations on the basis of the EU Charter. The selection of these areas is based on the CJEU case law interpreting the EU Charter and extending its application in ever wider fields making it instrumental not only in settling individual violations of fundamental rights but also in shaping national legal systems to ensure respect of the EU Charter.

Bergström and Judge Sundberg investigate the principle of *ne bis in idem*, taking into account its explicitation in numerous international, regional and bilateral instruments. The interrelationship and parallel application of these legal instruments by a variety of courts may entail a number of legal challenges but also opportunities. In particular, Bergstrom and Sundberg start from the well-known *Åkerberg Fransson* saga, showing its enormous impact on fundamental rights protection. At the same time, judicial interaction between national and European courts played a significant role during this saga. Then, the contribution aims to analyse the judicial interaction involved in the light of more recent developments before the CJEU and the ECtHR. As a result, the authors conclude that courts are instrumental not only in the settlement of individual disputes but also in changing the legal system.

Judge Ruiz Yamuza's commentary addresses the CJEU's *AY* decision, where the Court made some remarkable contributions concerning the construction of the *ne bis in idem* principle in Council Framework Decision 2002/584/JHA. The analysis allows a comparison with the approach adopted by the CJEU in the *Åkerberg Fransson* case. In this case the axis on which the CJEU's analysis revolved was the relationship between administrative penalties and criminal law, whereas in *AY* it was criminal cooperation within the Area of Freedom, Security and Justice. Nevertheless, both cases are exponents of the CJEU's doctrine on the *ne bis in idem* principle and they present different areas of intersection.

Casarosa and Judge Sabato take stock of the increasing role of administrative enforcement in EU law through the allocation of regulatory and sanctioning powers to independent administrative authorities at the national level. The consequence is an institutional setting that relies on the interplay between administrative and judicial enforcement, which exerts an impact on the exercise of the right to an effective remedy. The contribution analyses the jurisprudence of the CJEU, showing that the time and methods of coordination between administrative and judicial enforcement are crucial from different perspectives. A first perspective is that of achieving effective judicial protection without undue delay and excessive cost of the proceedings. A second and equally important perspective is the role of judicial review in safeguarding fair trial guarantees. Administrative decisions are not outside the domain of effective judicial protection. Instead, they provide an added level of protection that should follow and comply with the same principles applicable to judicial ones. Only through interventions by national courts through preliminary rulings has the CJEU had the opportunity to identify the limits and conditions for specific institutional settings.

The comment by Judge Thoma analyses the branches of administration and the (administrative) judiciary, showing that in principle the relation between them seems clear at first sight: in a context of checks and balances it is up to the third power, the judiciary, to control the second one (the executive branch). But on a closer look this clear distinction is blurred: the directions of control may seem uneven and the range of control limited. The question posed by Thoma is what the essentials of a (administrative) judiciary are for it to be able to fulfil its function of control vis-à-vis the executive branch.

Casarosa and Judge Calò's contribution evaluates the recent legislative intervention on collective action, taking stock of the long and ongoing process that characterised the development of a European framework for this remedy. The contribution then compares the approach adopted by national and European courts both in terms of preventive remedies (e.g. injunctions) and in terms of reparatory remedies (e.g. class actions). In particular, the authors highlight the clear hierarchy between individual and collective action acknowledged in the CJEU's jurisprudence, which leaves collective actions playing only a complementary role. The authors affirm that this approach conflicts with the underlying objectives of collective remedy, namely the possibility of enhancing access to justice through the collective management of disputes addressing the same claim against the same plaintiff.

Vizzoni's comment starts its argument with the assumption that the mechanisms of collective redress ought to be applied with a clear view of the fundamental rights sphere from the perspective of maintaining a proper balance between effectiveness of protection and the requirements arising from the overall fundamental standards and guarantees existing in national legal systems. In order to evaluate the newly adopted European (and Italian) legal framework for collective redress, Vizzoni compares it with that available in antitrust law. The analysis allows a specific 'antitrust light' to be shed on collective mechanisms, disclosing some potentialities still in the direction of effective protection of the parties involved, but also some fallacies which deserve distinct consideration.

The vertical, horizontal or transnational judicial interactions analysed in this volume have produced concrete changes in the national legislation, on the relation between the domestic judiciaries, on the competences of the courts vis-à-vis the executive, and on domestic judicial doctrines, for the purpose of securing the supremacy and direct effect of EU law and the EU Charter. Ultimately, it is clear that judicial interaction has contributed first to a more coherent application of the EU Charter and, secondly, to an enhanced fundamental rights protection for individuals. They may have also offered national judges a cost-effective inspirational legal source for solving the difficult questions concerning the application of the EU Charter raised before them.[64]

64 The chapters in this volume were submitted around November 2020.

PART I

Horizontal issues

2. The application of the rights and principles of the Charter of Fundamental Rights

Nina Półtorak[1]

PREAMBLE

This chapter explores the limitations of the application of the rights and principles enshrined in the Charter of Fundamental Rights of the EU (hereafter CFR or Charter). It is impossible to discuss here all the issues related to the application of the Charter. Given that, viewed from the perspective of judicial interactions, the most problematic questions are those regarding the application of the Charter by the Member States, the chapter will focus on these questions and will point out, when necessary, some other problems such as the distinction between rights and principles and their application in horizontal relations. Application of the Charter by courts of the Member States requires interpretation of the field of application of the Charter to the Member States (Article 51(1) CFR). This is a necessary first step but, of course, not the last one. Therefore, this study tries to define the scope of the obligation on the Member States to respect and apply the Charter but also to analyse the consequences of this obligation for national courts. Hence, it presents, first, the problems in the binding force of the Charter for the Member States (points II–III) and, next, the problems of its application by national courts in relation to their constitutional powers (point IV). Finally, it suggests that the question of the scope of application of the Charter (regulated by Article 51(1)) should be distinguished from the question of its actual application in place of national constitutional rights and freedoms (point V). It argues that the latter question

[1] All the views and opinions of the author are strictly personal. The extended version of this article was published under the title 'The application of the rights and principles of the Charter of Fundamental Rights', in *European University Institute Working Papers*, 2021/34, Robert Schuman Centre for Advanced Studies Centre for Judicial Cooperation, European University Institute.

should be answered on the basis of Article 53 CFR and its interpretation by the Court of Justice of the European Union (CJEU). Article 51(1) CFR allows a broad scope of applicability of the Charter which should not depend on the special needs of EU law to apply the Charter. Such needs may be, however, used as criteria justifying intervention by the Charter in lieu of national fundamental rights. In other cases, the Charter may operate in parallel with national fundamental rights – it may be put on standby and only step in when a national law does not guarantee an adequate level of protection or when the implementation of EU law is put in jeopardy.

I. PRELIMINARY REMARKS

The Charter is about people and their rights. As is stated in its preamble, the EU places the individual at the heart of its activities and contributes to the preservation and development of common values. By strengthening the protection of fundamental rights, the Charter serves these aims. Therefore, the ultimate objective of the Charter is to put people and their rights at the centre of the integration process.[2] This aim should determine the rules of interpretation and application of the Charter in EU law and that of the Member States. However, while the Charter was adopted to strengthen the protection of fundamental rights of individuals in the EU, it just codifies and reaffirms the rights and principles already recognised in European Union law and makes them more visible. Moreover, the Charter does not change any EU power or extend the scope of application of European law (Article 6(1) Treaty on European Union (TEU), Article 51(2) CFR).[3] Thus, the legal and practical constraints on the Charter might have provoked questions as to its practical effectiveness. Nevertheless, more than 10 years after its entry into force as a binding legal Act the Charter has proved to be a milestone in the development of the legal systems of the EU and its Member States. It has become an important part of EU and national jurisprudence – not only does the CJEU invoke its provisions and use them as a legal basis for its decisions but the same is true of national courts. This process has not been easy and hassle-free from the point of view

[2] This correlates with the policies of the EU as expressed by the European Parliament: 'It is only by placing the well-being of the people and the respect of their rights at the centre of the EU's policies and decisions, that we will manage to counteract Euroscepticism'. Explanatory statement to the Report on the situation of fundamental rights in the European Union in 2017 of 13 December 2018 (2018/2103(INI).

[3] For more, see, e.g., Koen Lenaerts, 'Respect for fundamental rights as a constitutional principle of EU' *Columbia Journal of European Law* 6 (2000), 1; Piet Eeckhout, 'The EU Charter of Fundamental Rights and the federal question' CMLRev 39 (2002), 945.

of the constitutional identity of the Member States. It has not been possible to avoid interactions between the national constitutional orders and the Charter.

As part of EU law with the same legal value as the Treaties, the Charter acquires the same quality, meaning that the fundamental rights enshrined in it can have direct effect and primacy over national law. In consequence, national courts not only examine the compliance of national law with EU law but also its compliance with the fundamental rights recognised in the EU system. Applying the Charter, the national judge not only adjudicates a concrete case but also faces the problems of the complicated relations between the Charter and constitutional fundamental rights; the problem of the competences of the ordinary judge versus the competences of the constitutional judge; and the issue of the division of competences between constitutional courts and the CJEU in the field of fundamental rights. These are all valid and complex problems underlining the challenging aspect of the Charter for national legal systems and national judges. However, they should not overshadow the importance and usefulness of the Charter in helping national courts to protect European and national constitutional values. The Charter, which was initially seen as a legal instrument serving the EU and making the EU fundamental rights more visible, now more than ever can protect and support the constitutional values of the Member States.

II. RIGHTS AND PRINCIPLES IN THE CHARTER

It will be useful to first explain the character of the provisions in the Charter and particularly the distinction between rights and principles. As will be clarified later, this distinction is not relevant to the problem of the applicability of the Charter to the Member States as defined in Article 51(1) CFR but it introduces the main modality for judicial authorities to apply the provisions of the Charter and must always be taken into account when analysing the problem of application of the Charter.

The terminology used in the Charter to describe its content is not quite coherent. First, the preamble states that the European Union recognises the rights, freedoms and principles set out in the Charter. Then Article 51(1) provides that the EU and the Member States should respect the rights and observe the principles. Finally, Article 52(5) provides for the distinction between the rights and principles of the Charter. This distinction is introduced to find a compromise as to the justiciability of economic and social rights and is well known in national constitutional systems (yet under different names and not always as exactly the same legal concept – e.g. subjective rights, programmatic norms, constitutional principles).[4] The principles referred to in Article 52(5) CFR should not be confused with general principles of EU law. This last concept is developed in the case law of the CJEU and is not limited to fundamental rights (or principles) and does not impose any constraints as to the justiciability of these general principles. Therefore, the terminology used in the case law of the CJEU, particularly from the time before the entry into force of the Charter should not be relevant to interpretation of Article 52(5) CFR. Also in the present work, the terminology used in its further parts does not refer to the distinction made in Article 52(5) CFR.

From the point of view of entities applying the Charter, whether they are EU or national institutions and courts, the distinction between rights and principles directly provided in Article 52(5) will influence the way the Charter is applied. As they are part of the primary law of the EU, both rights and principles in the Charter have the qualities of direct effect and primacy over national law. However, their functioning in national and EU law is different. As is provided for in Article 52(5) CFR, the provisions of the Charter which contain principles may be implemented by legislative and executive acts taken by institutions, bodies, offices and agencies of the Union and by acts of Member States when they are implementing Union law in the exercise of their powers. They are only judicially cognisable in the interpretation of such acts and in the ruling on their legality. The effects of the principles are therefore limited in comparison to the rights. The rights contained in the Charter may be fully judicially operational – they can be invoked and enforced before courts and be a direct legal basis for judicial decisions, while the principles should be implemented by legislative or executive acts and their judicial operationality is limited to the interpretation and legality of such acts. Therefore, the principles may not be a direct and autonomous basis for judicial decisions but need to be implemented by further acts and are used for the purpose of deciding on the interpretation or validity of these acts.

It is not always easy to classify a given provision in the Charter as a right or a principle. Of course, the title of a given provision in the Charter is not decisive in this respect. Moreover, the same provision may contain both rights and principles.[5] There are still not many directions in the case law of the CJEU

---

[4] See, e.g., Steven Peers, Sacha Prechal, 'Article 52: scope and interpretation of rights and principles' in Steven Peers, Tamara Hervey, Jeff Kenner, Angela Ward (eds), *The EU Charter of Fundamental Rights: A Commentary* (Hart, Oxford 2014), p 1505.

[5] As the explanations of the Charter state, examples of principles include Articles 25 (rights of the elderly), 26 (rights of persons with disabilities) and 37 (environmental protection) and provisions which contain both elements of a right and of a principle, e.g. Articles 23 (equality between women and men), 33 (right to family and professional life) and 34 (social security and social assistance).

about the distinction between rights and principles. The CJEU has already confirmed that Article 21 CFR prohibiting discrimination on the basis of the grounds established therein, Article 47 CFR establishing the right to effective judicial protection and Article 31(2) granting the right to paid annual leave are sufficient in themselves and do not need to be made more specific by provisions in EU or national law to confer on individuals these rights.[6] Therefore, we may state that these provisions contain rights and not principles in the meaning of Article 52(5) CFR.

The application of both rights and principles of the Charter often requires courts to balance the interests which they represent and to find the right equilibrium between them using the proportionality rule and taking into account indications that may be derived from legal acts of the EU where such balancing might have already been done. The CJEU has confirmed that such balancing of rights has no effect on the possibility of relying on the rights in question before a court.[7]

III. THE FIELD OF APPLICATION OF THE CHARTER TO THE MEMBER STATES (AN ATTEMPT AT SYSTEMATISATION)

Article 51(1) CFR stating that the provisions of the Charter are addressed to the Member States 'only when they are implementing Union law' stirred controversies and disputes from the very beginning. Various suggestions as to the interpretation of this provision attempting to dispel doubts have been formulated in opinions of Advocates General as well as in the doctrine.[8] The

---

[6] Cases C-414/16 *Vera Egenberger* ECLI:EU:C:2018:257, par 78; C-243/19 *A v Veselības ministrija* ECLI:EU:C:2020:872, par 36; C-569/16 and C-570/16 *Stadt Wuppertal v Maria Elisabeth Bauer* ECLI:EU:C:2018:871, par 87.

[7] C-414/16 *Vera Egenberger* ECLI:EU:C:2018:257, par 80.

[8] See, e.g., Allard Knook, 'The Court, the Charter, and the vertical division of powers in the European Union' CMLRev 42 (2005), 367; Koen Lenaerts, 'The Court of Justice of the European Union and the protection of fundamental rights' *Polish Yearbook of International Law* 31 (2011), 79; Koen Lenaerts, 'Exploring the limits of the EU Charter of Fundamental Rights' *European Constitutional Law Review* 3 (2012), 375; Marek Safjan, 'Areas of application of the Charter of Fundamental Rights of the European Union: fields of conflict?' EUI Working Papers LAW 22 (2012); Alan Rosas, 'When is the EU Charter of Fundamental Rights applicable at national level?' *Jurisprudence* 19 (2012), 1269; Armin von Bogdandy, Matthias Kottmann, Carlino Antpöhler, Johanna Dickschen, Simon Hentrei, Maja Smrkolj, 'Reverse Solange: protecting the essence of fundamental rights against EU Member States' CMLRev 49 (2012), 489; Bas van Bockel, Peter Wattel, 'New wine into old wineskins: the scope of the Charter of Fundamental Rights of the EU after Åkerberg Fransson' *European Law Review* 6 (2013), 866; Koen Lenaerts, 'Trybunał Sprawiedliwości Unii Europejskiej

Court formulated the first systematic interpretation of Article 51(1) CFR in its 2013 judgment in the *Åkerberg Fransson* case.[9] This judgment has been widely commented on in legal works[10] and national case law.[11] It explains the interpretation of Article 51(1) CFR but it does not give a ready-to-use pattern suitable for every case. After the *Åkerberg Fransson* judgment it is clear that 'the Charter does not grant "free-standing" fundamental rights – that is, rights that have no point of attachment to what lies within the competence of the Union'.[12] What comes from *Åkerberg Fransson* and has been confirmed by further case law is that citizenship of the EU may not be regarded in itself as justifying application of the Charter towards individuals. In other words, there must be some EU provision concretising the rights stemming from citizenship for a case to be considered to fall within the scope of the Charter.[13] Neither is EU citizenship in itself a link sufficient to justify application of the Charter and nor does the Charter extend the rights granted to EU citizens. The question remains, however, of what this point of attachment (link) enabling a national court to conclude that a given case falls within the scope of application of the Charter could be.

---

a ochrona praw podstawowych' *Europejski Przegląd Sądowy* 1 (2013), 4; see also Nina Półtorak, 'Zakres związania państw członkowskich Kartą Praw Podstawowych UE' *Europejski Przegląd Sądowy* 9 (2014), 17, where several theses developed in this chapter have been formulated. As for the opinions of the AG, see the opinion of Advocate General Sharpston in case C-34/09 *Gerardo Ruiz Zambrano* ECLI:EU: C:2010:560, par 163; Opinion of Advocate General Cruz Villalon in case C-617/10 *Åkerberg Fransson* ECLI:EU:C:2012:340, par 27.

[9] Case C-617/10 *Åkerberg Fransson* ECLI:EU:C:2013:105. For the full background to this case, see Chapter 20 in this book.

[10] See, e.g., Daniel Sarmiento, 'Who's afraid of the Charter? The Court of Justice, national courts and the new framework of fundamental rights protection in Europe' CMLRev 50 (2013), 1267; Michael Dougan, 'Judicial review of Member State action under the general principles and the Charter: defining the "scope of Union law"' CMLRev 52 (2015), 1201.

[11] In its judgment of 24 April 2013 the German Bundesverfassungsgericht held that the *Åkerberg Fransson* judgment must be interpreted as referring to the specific case of VAT regulations, since if it were to have a larger scope it would have to be regarded as issued *ultra vires* and thus infringing the constitutional identity of the Member States, Decision of 24 April 2013, 1 BvR 1215/07, accessed 20 October 2021 at http://www.bundesverfassungsgericht.de/pressemitteilungen/bvg13-031en.html. This decision was also invoked by the UK Supreme Court, [2014] UKSC 3 of 22 January 2014.

[12] As Advocate General Sharpston has put it in her opinion in case C-456/12 *O. v Minister voor Immigratie* ECLI:EU:C:2013:837, par 60.

[13] Contrary to what was proposed in *Reverse Solange*, Von Bogdandy and others *supra* note 8.

On the basis of the case law of the CJEU it is possible to list a few groups of situations which fall under the terms of implementation of EU law as provided for in Article 51(1) CFR.[14]

1. Direct Implementation of EU Law

First is the situation when Member States directly implement EU law, which may be called acting 'as agents' or as the executive power of the EU.[15] It is reflected in the first criterion usually checked by the CJEU when deciding on the applicability of the Charter, which is whether the national legislation in question aims to implement provisions of EU law.[16] This happens in cases such as those governed by directly effective EU legislation (most of all by the Treaties or regulations[17]) or governed by national provisions directly implementing EU law (mainly directives).[18] In most of these cases, the principles of primacy and direct effect of EU law come into play, which might be a simple indication for the national court that the Charter is also applicable.

The question of the applicability of the Charter does not depend on whether a Member State uses its discretionary power when implementing EU law (however, this criterion may be of importance when the CFR overlaps with a constitutional standard, which will be analysed further on). Such a conclusion may already be drawn from the *ERT* case and has been confirmed in later case law.[19]

---

[14] There might be many possible systematisations, e.g. Advocate General Bobek lists three groups: direct application, indirect application and derogations, opinion in C-298/16 *Ispas* ECLI:EU:C:2017:650, par 32. See also e.g. N. Lazzerini, *ACTIONES Handbook on the Techniques of Judicial Interactions in the Application of the EU Charter, Module 1: The EU Charter of Fundamental Rights – Scope of Application, Relationship with the ECHR and National Standards, Effects*, accessed 20 October 2021 at https://cjc.eui.eu/wp-content/uploads/2019/03/D1.1.a-Module-1.pdf.

[15] Cases C-5/88 *Wachauf* ECLI:EU:C:1989:321; C-2/92 *Bostock* ECLI:EU:C:1994:116. For more, see Joseph H.H. Weiler, Nicolas J.S. Lockhart, '"Taking rights seriously" seriously: the European Court and its fundamental rights jurisprudence – part I' CMLRev 32 (1995), 51.

[16] E.g. case C-265/13 *Emiliano Torralbo Marcos* ECLI:EU:C:2014:18, par 30.

[17] E.g. case C-559/14 *Meroni* ECLI:EU:C:2016:349, par 44.

[18] E.g. cases C-528/13 *Geoffrey Léger* ECLI:EU:C:2015:288, par 46–47; C-418/11 *Texdata Software GmbH* ECLI:EU:C:2013:588.

[19] Cases C-260/89 *ERT* ECLI:EU:C:1991:254; C-411/10 and C-493/10 *N.S.* ECLI:EU:C:2011:865, par 68; C-276/12 *Jiří Sabou* ECLI:EU:C:2013:678, par 25–26; C-329/13 *Ferdinand Stefan* ECLI:EU:C:2014:815, par 34; C-258/14 *Eugenia Florescu and others* ECLI:EU:C:2017:448, par 48. See also the opinion of Advocate General Mengozzi in C-638/16 PPU *X and X v État belge* ECLI:EU:C:2017:93, par 81–83.

2. Indirect Implementation of EU Law

A second group covers situations when the case is governed by national provisions which are not aimed at the implementation of EU law but which affect EU law (we may call this situation an indirect implementation of EU law).[20] This was the case in the *Åkerberg Fransson* judgment. It was also the case in the *Berlioz* judgment, in which a national provision regulating sanctions for refusing information and not aimed to transpose a directive was treated as implementation of EU law since the application of that national provision 'was intended to ensure that of the directive'.[21] In the *Delvigne* case, the CJEU decided that the Member State must be considered to have been implementing EU law when adopting general provisions on the right to vote if it influenced the right to vote in elections to the European Parliament.[22] In these cases the general obligations of the Member States stemming from EU law could be affected by the application of the national provisions in question.

However, the mere fact that a national measure comes within an area of the competences of the EU is not enough to bring the case within the scope of EU law.[23] EU competence should be executed, so there should be EU rules (not necessarily a legislative Act, but a rule coming from EU legal acts or from the case law of the CJEU) which imply an obligation on the Member State and within which the national measure falls. Moreover, indirect interference between national and EU law is not always sufficient as the concept of implementation of EU law requires 'a certain degree of connection above and beyond the matters covered being closely related or one of those matters having an indirect impact on the other'.[24] This degree of connection should be determined on a case by case basis using the criteria formulated by the CJEU such as: whether the given national legislation is intended to implement a provision of EU law; the nature of that legislation and whether it pursues objectives other than those covered by EU law, even if it is capable of indirectly affecting EU law; and whether there are specific rules in EU law on the matter

---

[20] Case C-40/11 *Y. Iida* ECLI:EU:C:2012:691, par 79. See also C-206/13 *Cruciano Siragusa* ECLI:EU:C:2014:126, par 25.

[21] Case C-682/15 *Berlioz Investment Fund* ECLI:EU:C:2017:373, par 40.

[22] Case C-650/13 *Delvigne* ECLI:EU:C:2015:648, par 24–34. According to EU law, the electoral procedure is to be governed in each Member State by its national provisions. However, when exercising that competence the Member States are bound by EU law in order to ensure that the members of the European Parliament are elected by direct universal suffrage in a free and secret ballot.

[23] E.g. case C-198/13 *Víctor Manuel Julian Hernández* ECLI:EU:C:2014:2055, par 36.

[24] Case C-206/13 *Cruciano Siragusa*, par 24.

or capable of affecting it.[25] It seems, therefore, that if the national law is not intended to implement EU law and it serves objectives other than that of EU law, in order to qualify that national law as being in the scope of the Charter there must be a particular EU rule imposing an obligation on the Member State and in consequence concerning or affecting the issue regulated by the national law (such as the VAT directive and Article 325 Treaty on the Functioning of the European Union (TFEU) in the *Åkerberg Fransson* case).

This indirect implementation group also comprises procedural measures adopted by the Member States within their procedural autonomy but which may affect the effective enforcement of EU law. In the *DEB* case, Article 47 CFR was applied to verify national provisions concerning legal aid in compensation claims, although EU law does not regulate the question of legal aid in such claims.[26] Similarly, in the *Stoyanov* case the CJEU held that the question of jurisdiction of courts which adjudicate on agricultural subsidy issues falls under the Charter.[27]

The indirect implementation of EU law category also includes cases where EU legislation exists but cannot be directly applicable at the national level because of the constraints of the doctrine of the direct effect of EU law especially in relation to the directives. It can be inferred from the case law of the CJEU that fundamental rights (at least non-discrimination) can be relied on in cases in which a directive itself might not be applied. It is because the sheer existence of a directive regulating the same matters as the relevant national legislation is a link with EU law, which triggers the application of the fundamental rights.[28] However, the subsequent case law explains that what should be actually taken into account in such situations is the existence of national provisions regulating the same issues as the directive and which might undermine the effectiveness of the directive after the transposition deadline.[29]

That leads us to the problem of the applicability of the Charter in horizontal situations. The CJEU has stated that the Charter may be applicable in relations

---

25 *Ibidem*, par 25.

26 Case C-279/09 *DEB* ECLI:EU:C:2010:811; see also C-199/11 *Otis* ECLI:EU:C:2012:684, par 45.

27 Case C-93/12 *Velko Stoyanov* ECLI:EU:C:2013:432.

28 Cases C-555/07 *Seda Kücükdeveci* ECLI:EU:C:2010:21; C-144/04 *Werner Mangold* ECLI:EU:C:2005:709, par 78; C-246/06 *Josefa Velasco Navarro* ECLI:EU:C:2008:19, par 32.

29 Case C-427/06 *Birgit Bartsch* ECLI:EU:C:2008:517, par 24. See also case C-147/08 *Jürgen Römer* ECLI:EU:C:2011:286, par 61–64. See the opinion of Advocate General E. Sharpston of 22 May 2008 in case C-427/06 *Birgit Bartsch*, par 69. See also Xavier Groussot, Laurent Pech, Gunnar T. Petursson, 'The scope of application of EU fundamental rights on Member States' action: in search of certainty in EU adjudication' Eric Stein Working Paper 1 (2011).

between private parties.[30] This does not mean, however, that the Charter may be always invoked in a horizontal relation in order to disapply a national provision. Here, the CJEU has indicated that it depends on the character of the provision of the Charter. If the provision in the Charter is sufficient in itself to confer on individuals a right which they may rely on as such, it may be invoked in horizontal relations in order to disapply national provisions.[31] If the Charter provision does not suffice to confer on individuals a right and it needs more specific expression in an EU directive, it cannot be invoked in a dispute between individuals in order to disapply the national provision. These statements are probably based on the premise that, in the case of the Charter provisions which need to be implemented with a directive, it is in fact the directive which would be applied in horizontal relations, and this is not permitted by EU law. In the case of a Charter provision being a directly applicable general principle of EU law (e.g. the non-discrimination principle), it is this provision that is applied in a horizontal relation, so there is no back door for the horizontal effect of directives.

As to the problem of the relation between Article 51(1) CFR and the horizontal direct effect of the Charter, it should be stated that the provision in question does not address the question of whether individuals might be directly bound by the Charter and it cannot be interpreted as systematically precluding such a possibility. If the Charter provision is sufficient in itself to confer rights on individuals, meaning that it is both mandatory and unconditional in nature, it may be relied on in disputes between individuals in a field covered by EU law and therefore falling within the scope of the Charter.[32] This means that Article

---

[30] Case C-414/16 *Vera Egenberger* ECLI:EU:C:2018:257, par 82. On the horizontal effect of the Charter, see, e.g., Marek Safjan, 'The horizontal effect of fundamental rights in private law: on actors, vectors, and factors of influence' in Kai Purnhagen, Peter Rott (eds), *Varieties of European Economic Law and Regulation: Studies in European Economic Law and Regulation*, vol 3. (Springer, Cham 2014) p 123; Eleni Frantziou, 'Mangold recast? The CJEU's flirtation with Drittwirkung in Egenberger' *European Law Blog*, 24 April 2018; Eleni Frantziou, 'Joined cases C-569/16 and C-570/16 Bauer et al: (most of) the Charter of Fundamental Rights is horizontally applicable' *European Law Blog*, 19 November 2018, accessed 20 October 2021 at www.europeanlawblog.eu; Aurelia Colombi Ciacchi, 'The direct horizontal effect of EU fundamental rights, CJEU 17 April 2018, case C-414/16, *Vera Egenberger v Evangelisches Werk für Diakonie und Entwicklung* e.V and CJEU 11 September 2018, case C-68/17, *IR v JQ*' *European Constitutional Law Review* 15 (2019), 294.

[31] Cases C-414/16 *Vera Egenberger*, par 76–78; C-176/12 *Association de médiation sociale* ECLI:EU:C:2014:2, par 47.

[32] Such arguments have been used by the CJEU in order to declare the right to paid annual leave as expressed in Article 31(2) CFR to be horizontally effective, case C-569/16 and C-570/16 *Stadt Wuppertal v Maria Elisabeth Bauer* ECLI:EU:C:2018:871, par 87, 79–92.

51(1) CFR does not govern the question of the application of the Charter in disputes between individuals and that this question should instead be answered on the basis of the established case law of the CJEU on the horizontal effect of primary EU law.[33] Thus, the Charter's provisions may be horizontally applicable in the fields covered by EU law and therefore falling within the scope of the Charter, which is a criterion different from implementation of EU law used in Article 51(1) CFR.

From this reasoning, it also results that the distinction between rights and principles introduced in Article 52(5) of the Charter, which may be of relevance to the question of the horizontal application of the Charter, should not be relevant for the analysis of the scope of application of the Charter as defined in Article 51(1). Not only is the question of the horizontal application of the Charter distinct from the question of its scope of application towards Member States but also the character of the Charter's provisions (a right or a principle) should not be a factor taken into account when analysing the problem of the applicability of the Charter to the Member States. However, even when the case before a national judge falls under the implementation of EU law and therefore the Charter is applicable, Article 52(5) CFR may still limit the actual application of the Charter's principle. This shows the complexity of the process of application of the Charter by a national judge, as well as how many different but overlapping questions it provokes.

The next subcategory in this indirect implementation of EU law group concerns national measures which limit the freedoms of the internal market (situations of derogation).[34] In its judgment in the *Pfleger* case, the CJEU answered the question of whether the Charter should apply when a Member State introduces regulations providing criminal penalties for organising games of chance without a licence.[35] It applied the *ERT* line of case law and concluded that where a Member State relies on public interest requirements in order to justify national restrictions on the freedoms of the internal market it must be subject to examination in the light of the rights guaranteed by the Charter. In consequence, '(t)he use by a Member State of exceptions provided for by EU law in order to justify an obstruction of a fundamental freedom guaranteed by the Treaty must, therefore, be regarded (…) as "implementing Union law"

[33] See *ibidem*, par 88.

[34] Cases C-260/89 *ERT* ECLI:EU:C:1991:254; C-368/95 *Familiapress* ECLI:EU:C:1997:325.

[35] Case C-390/12 *Robert Pfleger* ECLI:EU:C:2014:281. See also cases C-201/15 *AGET Iraklis* ECLI:EU:C:2016:972, par 63–64; C-235/17 *Commission v Hungary* ECLI:EU:C:2019:432, par 64–65; C-78/18 *European Commission v Hungary* ECLI:EU:C:2020:476, par 101–104.

within the meaning of Article 51(1) of the Charter'.[36] It should be added, that in situations of derogation, the question is often whether a given national law falls within the category of rules limiting the freedoms of the internal market.[37] Therefore, the question of the applicability of the Charter in situations of derogation has been answered by the CJEU on the basis of the *ERT* case law but the underlying analysis concerned the scope of EU law itself (i.e. whether the EU law covers the national derogating regulations).

Concluding this part of the analysis, it might be said that any obligation to enforce EU law by a Member State could be a link enabling applicability of the Charter. This comprises situations where national legislation affects enforcement of an obligation coming from EU law (it either serves or jeopardises the enforcement of EU law), even if it is not aimed at its implementation. This may include: national procedural provisions established within the procedural autonomy of Member States but falling under the requirement of the effectiveness of EU law; national law falling within the scope of EU provisions lacking direct effect but enforcement of which might be put into question by this national law; and national provisions limiting the basic freedoms of the internal market. It follows then that the Charter may cover not only situations where a Member State acts under the principles of primacy and direct effect but also under the principle of effectiveness of EU law.[38]

3. The Given Case Falls under EU Law

For the Charter to be applicable it is not enough for a national provision to fall within the scope of EU law but this provision must also be applicable in the given case before the national judge.[39] This approach was confirmed by the judgment in the *Iida* case, which although it concerned national provisions directly implementing EU regulations it was treated as not falling under the Charter because the facts of this particular case remained outside the scope of EU law.[40] In the *Mohamed Daouidi* case the CJEU stated that since the question of the application of EU law in this case had to be established by the

36 C-390/12 *Robert Pfleger* ECLI:EU:C:2014:281, par 36.

37 See, e.g., cases C-483/12 *Pelckmans Turnhout NV* ECLI:EU:C:2014:304, par 25; C-122/15 *C* ECLI:EU:C:2016:391, par 29 and the opinion of Advocate General Kokkot ECLI:EU:C:2016:65, par 66–67; C-235/17 *European Commission v Hungary* ECLI:EU:C:2019:432, par 65.

38 See van Bockel, Wattel, *supra* note 8, p 878.

39 E.g. cases C-258/13 *Sociedade Agrícola e Imobiliária da Quinta de S. Paio Lda* ECLI:EU:C:2013:810, par 23; C-56/13 *Érsekcsanádi Mezőgazdasági* ECLI:EU:C:2014:352, par 54–57.

40 Case C-40/11 *Y. Iida*, par 80.

referring court following a previous judgment of the CJEU, at that stage in the proceedings it was not determined that the situation of the applicant in the national proceedings came within the scope of EU law.[41] The CJEU did not find the Charter applicable in a case concerning court fees when, contrary to the *DEB* case mentioned above, the litigation before the national court did not concern a matter regulated by EU law.[42] Also when a case before a national court concerned the execution of a judgment ordering compensation by the State for the excessive length of legal proceedings referring to a bankruptcy, the CJEU decided that there was nothing indicating that the dispute before the national court related to the interpretation or application of a rule of EU law other than the Charter itself.[43] The Charter will not be applicable even if the domestic provisions applied by the national court form part of a regulation transposing an EU directive but these provisions do not implement a specific obligation with regard to the situation at issue in the proceeding before the national court.[44]

The above does not mean, however, that the Charter cannot apply in the cases of an 'abstract review' of national provisions which implement the EU law if this abstract verification is necessary for the national court in order to issue a decision in a given case.[45]

4. The Scope of EU Law

As has already been pointed out with respect to situations of derogation, interpretation of the concept of implementation of EU law may also be problematic because of difficulties in defining the scope of EU law as such. This can be illustrated by different views of the scope of regulation of the EU Visa Code presented by the Advocate General and the CJEU acting in the Grand Chamber. According to the Advocate General, when applying the Visa Code, a Member State acts within the scope of EU law, but for the CJEU the national authorities were wrong to qualify the factual situation as being within the scope of the Visa Code and to decide on the request for a visa. In consequence, such a situation is outside of the scope of EU law and so it is not subject to the Charter.[46]

---

41 Case C-395/15 *Mohamed Daouidi* ECLI:EU:C:2016:917, par 60–68.

42 Case C-265/13 *Emiliano Torralbo Marcos* ECLI:EU:C:2014:187.

43 Case C-177/17 and C-178/17 *Demarchi Gino Sas* ECLI:EU:C:2017:656, par 28.

44 Case C-32/20 *TJ* ECLI:EU:C:2020:441, par 27.

45 See also opinion of Advocate General Bobek in cases C-83/19, C-127/19 and C-195/19 *Asociația 'Forumul Judecătorilor din România'* ECLI:EU:C:2020:746, par 200–202.

46 Case C-638/16 PPU *X and X v État belge* ECLI:EU:C:2017:173.

This was also the problem in many cases decided after *Åkerberg Fransson.* The CJEU has rejected application of the Charter in cases remaining clearly outside the scope of EU law, such as concerning immunity from a suit enjoyed by Germany in Italian courts in cases concerning compensation for its actions during WWII[47] and the pensions of former functionaries of Polish *ancien régime* security services.[48] However, there have also been less obvious cases, such as *Banco Português de Negócios*, in which the CJEU decided that national measures on salary reductions in a nationalised bank introduced in order to fulfil the obligations under the Stability and Growth Pact did not fall under EU law,[49] and in the *Montull* case, in which the CJEU held that since no provision of EU law precludes discrimination between adoptive and biological fathers when it comes to parental leave, the case remained outside the scope of EU law.[50] In the *Dano* case, the CJEU analysed first whether the Member State acted in compliance with an EU directive by excluding entitlement to certain social benefits and then declared that the Member States had competence to determine the conditions for granting these benefits. Therefore, when exercising this competence, they were not implementing EU law.[51] Similarly in the *DK* case, the CJEU stated that the situation to which the question of the national court referred was not covered by a directive, therefore the Charter could not be applied in this situation.[52]

A new chapter in the problem of defining the scope of EU law concerns the question of whether and to what extent the independence and organisation of a national judiciary is subject to EU law. This new chapter was opened by the judgment of the CJEU in the *Associação Sindical dos Juízes Portugueses* case concerning the interpretation of Article 19(1) TEU in the context of the principle of judicial independence. The basic question coming out from the preliminary reference by the Portuguese Supremo Tribunal Administrativo was whether EU law (Article 19 TEU and Article 47 CFR) might apply to the principle of judicial independence of a national court, the Tribunal de Contas.[53] Answering that question, first, the CJEU indicated that Article 19(1) TEU related to 'the fields covered by Union law', irrespective of whether the Member State was implementing EU law within the meaning of Article 51(1) CFR. Second, the CJEU stated that to the extent that the Tribunal de Contas

47 Case C-466/11 *Gennaro Currà* ECLI:EU:C:2012:465.

48 Case C-28/14 *Ryszard Pańczyk* ECLI:EU:C:2014:2003.

49 Case C-128/12 *BPN – Banco Português de Negócios SA* ECLI:EU:C:2013:149.

50 Case C-5/12 *Marc Betriu Montull* ECLI:EU:C:2013:571, par 67, 73.

51 Case C-333/13 *Dano* ECLI:EU:C:2014:2358, par 88–92.

52 Case C-653/19PPU *DK* ECLI:EU:C:2019:1024, par 40–42.

53 Case C-64/16 *Associação Sindical dos Juízes Portugueses* ECLI:EU:C:2018:117, par 29–30, 40–41.

might have ruled on questions concerning the application or interpretation of EU law, the Member State had to ensure that that court met the requirements necessary for effective judicial protection in accordance with Article 19(1) TEU. In this respect, it was essential to guarantee independence of the national court as required in Article 47 CFR. Finally, the CJEU did not base its decision on the Charter but on interpretation of Article 19 TEU. Therefore, it treated Article 19 TEU as justification for the application of the Charter to establish the standard of judicial protection as required by this provision, but not as an argument that when Article 19 TEU can be applicable to national law, it constitutes the implementation of EU law in the meaning of Article 51(1) CFR.

Deciding a case concerning an infringement procedure against Poland due to violations of the principle of judicial independence regarding the judges of the Supreme Court, the CJEU confirmed the reasoning applied in the *Associação Sindical dos Juízes Portugueses* case and explained that this judgment was based on Article 19(1) TEU because the national court in question could rule on questions concerning the application or interpretation of EU law.[54] This logic was also applied to several preliminary references addressed by Polish courts to the CJEU concerning reform of the national judiciary. The courts asked whether Article 19(1) TEU in connection with Article 47 CFR allowed changes to the retirement age of the judges of the Supreme Court and to the nomination process of the judges, together with new rules on disciplinary proceedings. The underlying argument in these references was that the courts of the Member State deciding cases with elements of EU law are European courts bound by Article 19(1) TEU.[55] Deciding on a few of these referrals, the CJEU confirmed once more that Article 19(1) TEU applied if the national court could rule on questions concerning the application or interpretation of EU law and therefore falling within the fields covered by EU law. Hence, application of Article 19(1) TEU requires verification of whether Member States provide remedies that are sufficient to ensure effective legal protection within the meaning of Article 47 CFR.[56]

Some conclusions may be drawn from this CJEU case law. First, national court cases applying EU law fall under the implementation of EU law in the

---

[54] See Case C-619/18 *European Commission v Poland* ECLI:EU:C:2019:531, par 50–54.

[55] And as stated by Advocate General Bobek, any transversal structural changes to the national judiciary will by definition be applicable to any and all functions exercised by national judges, case C-556/17 *Alekszij Torubarov v Bevándorlási és Menekültügyi Hivatal* ECLI:EU:C:2019:339, par 54.

[56] Cases C-585/18, C-624/18 and C-625/18 *AK and others* ECLI:EU:C:2019:982, par 82–86; C-558/18 and C-563/18 *Miasto Łowicz and Prokurator Generalny* ECLI:EU:C:2020:234, par 34.

meaning of Article 51(1) CFR and consequently Article 47 CFR regulates the standard of these court proceedings (e.g. in the *DEB*, *Stoyanov* and *AK* cases).[57] In such cases, analysis of national remedies on the basis of Article 47 CFR makes an analysis of Article 19(1) TEU redundant because it can only reinforce the conclusion already set out on the basis of the Charter.[58] Second, when national court cases do not concern EU law, a possible but unlikely impact of these cases on the effectiveness of EU law is not sufficient to fulfil the conditions of Article 51(1) CFR (as, e.g., in the *Demarchi Gino* case[59]). Nevertheless, Article 47 CFR may still be applicable in those cases which do not qualify as implementation of EU law but which fall within fields covered by EU law within the meaning of Article 19(1) TEU. Then, this provision is applied as a rule being a part of Article 19 TEU and serving its interpretation, as it defines the standard of effective legal protection which has to be ensured by the Member States in the fields covered by EU law.[60]

IV. APPLICATION OF THE CHARTER AND APPLICATION OF THE CONSTITUTIONAL STANDARDS OF THE MEMBER STATES

1. Competences of National Judges Deriving from the Charter

Defining the scope of application of the Charter is the first problem, and of course it is followed by others such as: how the Charter interacts with constitutional basic rights and the constitutional identity of the Member States; whether the Charter precludes application of the national standard of fundamental rights protection; which standard prevails in the case of conflict and who decides this; and finally whether the Charter is useful or needed by the courts of the Member States if they already have their established fundamental constitutional rights.

By making the fundamental rights recognised by the EU more visible and more convenient to use in practice, the Charter encouraged national judges to rely on EU fundamental rights. It can be stated with some simplification

---

57 Cases C-279/09 *DEB* ECLI:EU:C:2010:811; C-93/12 *Velko Stoyanov* ECLI:EU:C:2013:432; C-585/18, C-624/18 and C-625/18 *AK and others*, par 78–81.

58 Case C-585/18, C-624/18 and C-625/18 *AK and others*, par 168–169.

59 Case C-177/17 and C-178/17 *Demarchi Gino Sas* ECLI:EU:C:2017:656. See also case C-256/19 *S.A.D. Maler und Anstreicher OG* ECLI:EU:C:2020:523, par 33–34.

60 Case C-585/18, C-624/18 and C-625/18 *AK and others*, par 168. See also opinion of Advocate General Hogan in case C-896/19 *Repubblika v Il-Prim Ministru* ECLI:EU:C:2020:1055, par 42–47.

that just as the *van Gend en Loos* judgment gave national courts the power to review the compliance of national legislation with EU law, the Charter gave them the power to review the compliance of national legislation with fundamental rights.[61] Of course, it was not the Charter itself but rather the doctrine of direct effect and primacy of EU law. The Charter, as part of EU law with the same legal value as the Treaties, acquires the same quality, meaning that the provisions in the Charter can have direct effect and supremacy over national law. In consequence, national courts examine the compliance of national law with the fundamental rights recognised in the EU system.

This competence was confirmed in the *Åkerberg Fransson* judgment, in which the CJEU precluded application of national procedural rules on reviewing the compliance of domestic law with fundamental rights. It held that Swedish law could not make application of the Charter conditional on whether incompatibility with fundamental rights was manifest, 'since it withholds from the national court the power to assess fully, with, as the case may be, the cooperation of the Court of Justice of the European Union, whether that provision is compatible with the Charter'.[62] That was also directly confirmed in the *A v B* judgment concerning the Austrian legal system, in which the CJEU stated that the ordinary courts might not be under a duty to apply to the constitutional court for statutes to be annulled with *erga omnes* effect if that obligation prevented the courts from exercising their right to make a reference to the CJEU. It was, however, allowed if the court remained free to refer questions for preliminary rulings and to fulfil its obligations arising from the principles of primacy and direct effect of EU law.[63] This means that applying the Charter is the autonomous competence and duty of national courts, which are supported in this task by the CJEU through the preliminary rulings procedure.

This leads to the question of division of competence. As long as the EU had no single legal Act regulating fundamental rights, national constitutional or supreme courts remained the courts of last instance in matters of fundamental rights (of course without prejudice to the role of the European Court of Human Rights (ECtHR)[64]). Once such an Act came into force, the problems with

---

[61] Case C-26/62 *Van Gend en Loos* ECLI:EU:C:1963:1.

[62] Case C-617/10 *Åkerberg Fransson*, par 48.

[63] Case C-112/13 *A v B* ECLI:EU:C:2014:2195.

[64] Judicial dialogue between national courts and the ECtHR is significantly enhanced by Protocol 16 to the Convention, which gives the highest courts and tribunals of the Member States of the Convention the possibility to ask the ECtHR for advisory opinions on questions of principle relating to the interpretation or application of the rights and freedoms defined in the Convention, which entered into force on 1 August 2018. The ECtHR has already delivered its first opinions.

delimiting the jurisdictions of constitutional courts and the CJEU reappeared.[65] National courts examine the compliance of domestic law with the fundamental rights recognised in the EU system, even if under national law they do not have the competence to review the compliance of national provisions with constitutional rights (which is often reserved to the constitutional or highest courts). Nevertheless, EU law gives national courts the competence, right and obligation to apply the Charter autonomously and independently of national procedures. It may be said that application of the Charter bestows on national courts the role of constitutional courts – not only examining the compliance of national law with EU law, but also its compliance with the fundamental rights recognised in the EU system. In some cases, reference to the Charter and the preliminary ruling procedure may also be seen as allowing the established national interpretation of the fundamental rights to be changed when it is considered by the domestic courts to be unjustified, outdated or not complying fully with international standards.[66]

2. Diverging EU and National Standards of Protection of Fundamental Rights

The most problematic situation arises when the Charter is applicable and the standard of protection of fundamental rights it provides is different to that provided for in national law. If this standard is higher than that offered by national law, there is no doubt that it prevails. If the standard is seen by a national court as lower than that offered by the national law, on the basis of Article 53 CFR, Member States can apply the national standard. As we already know from the case law, there might, however, be situations where application of national standards leads to infringement of EU law. Would it then be allowed?

In the *Åkerberg Fransson* judgment, the CJEU, finding the Charter applicable, held at the same time that national courts were free to apply constitutional standards in a situation where action by the Member State was not entirely determined by EU law as long as the level of protection provided for by the

---

65 As reflected, e.g., in verdicts of constitutional courts using the concept of *ultra vires* jurisdiction of the CJEU in the scope of the fundamental rights – e.g. the decisions of the Bundesverfassungsgericht of 6 July 2010, 2 BvR 2661/06; *Honeywell* of 5 May 2020, 2 BvR 859/15, 2 BvR 1651/15, 2 BvR 2006/15, 2 BvR 980/16; the judgment of the Czech Constitutional Court of 15 February 2012 (TZ 8/12), *Slovak pensions.*

66 It seems that the Charter was viewed as such by the Social Court of Barcelona in case C-395/15 *Daouidi*, where the court underlined that it is clear from the case law of the Supreme Court of Spain that dismissal on grounds of illness or of temporary disability resulting from an accident at work is not considered to be discriminatory, with the result that that dismissal cannot be considered 'void', but asked the CJEU whether such a dismissal is contrary to Articles 21(1), 30, 31, 34(1) and 35 of the Charter, par 32–33.

Charter and the primacy, unity and effectiveness of EU law were not thereby compromised.[67] Moreover, the CJEU authorised the national court to assess the compliance of the regulations in question with the constitutional standards.[68] In the *Melloni* judgment, the CJEU interpreting Article 53 CFR held that 'where an EU legal act calls for national implementing measures' national courts remained free to apply national standards of protection of fundamental rights, provided that the level of protection guaranteed by the Charter as interpreted by the CJEU and the primacy, unity and effectiveness of EU law were not thereby compromised.[69] Finally, it held that a national constitutional order could not be allowed to undermine the effectiveness of EU law and to disapply EU harmonised legal rules which were in compliance with the Charter.

The CJEU in both the *Åkerberg Fransson* and *Melloni* judgments used the same formula but for different reasons. In *Åkerberg Fransson* it was used to justify the application of the national standard (possibly higher than the EU); in *Melloni* it was used to exclude such application as interfering with the primacy of EU law. This distinction is justified in view of the differences between these two cases: the first one concerned the indirect implementation of EU law which did not provide a common standard of protection of the fundamental right in question (*ne bis in idem* in the case of tax infractions[70]); the second one concerned direct implementation of EU law which concretised and defined the level of protection of the fundamental right (right to defence as one of the conditions of execution of a European arrest warrant, defined in Framework Decision 2002/584[71]).

The foregoing considerations lead to the conclusion that two situations should be distinguished: where action by the Member State is entirely determined by EU law; and where national action is not fully regulated by EU law. Actions by Member States which are straightforward implementations of obligations under EU law (they are entirely determined by EU law) are primarily subject to evaluation in the light of the Charter and Member States may not invoke their national standards of protection of fundamental rights to avoid fulfilment of obligations arising from EU law. In cases where action by

---

[67] Case C-617/10 *Åkerberg Fransson*, par 29.

[68] *Ibidem*, par 36.

[69] Case C-399/11 *Stefano Melloni* ECLI:EU:C:2013:107, par 60, 58. See also Nik de Boer, 'Case C-399/11, Stefano Melloni v Ministerio Fiscal, Judgment of the Court (Grand Chamber) of 26 February 2013' CMLRev 50 (2013), 1083; Marek Safjan, Dominik Düsterhaus, Antione Guérin, 'La Charte des droits fondamentaux de l'Union européenne et les ordres juridiques nationaux, de la mise en œuvre à la mise en balance' RTD Eur (2016), 219.

[70] Case C-617/10 *Åkerberg Fransson*, par 36.

[71] Case C-399/11 *Stefano Melloni*, par 63.

the Member State is not entirely determined by EU law, national courts may in principle apply their national standard of protection of fundamental rights. The Charter is to intervene in situations where the primacy, unity or effectiveness of EU law may be jeopardised.[72] In other words, courts may primarily apply the constitutional standard and national procedures for its protection but if it compromises the principles of primacy or effectiveness of EU law they should turn to the EU standards and the protection it offers.[73]

Advocate General Bobek explained this problem with reference to the distinction between situations where national rules fall under EU harmonised rules and where national rules do not interact directly with such harmonised EU rules but still fall within the scope of EU law. In the first situation, it may be assumed that the EU legislature has already struck a balance between, on the one hand, the protection of fundamental rights and, on the other hand, the overall efficacy of the measure at issue with regard to its objectives, so in such a case only the EU standard of protection of fundamental rights should apply. In the second situation, Member States exercising their discretion can apply their own concept of fundamental rights as long as they do not provide less protection than that guaranteed in the Charter.[74] It may be added that in the first situation (a national rule coming directly within the scope of harmonised or unified EU rules) it should be assumed that the EU legislator not only struck a balance between the fundamental rights and the effectiveness principle but also defined the standard of protection of fundamental rights by striking a proper balance between overlapping or conflicting EU fundamental rights.[75] Therefore, it can be assumed that EU legislation is compliant with the Charter and Member States cannot invoke their fundamental rights in order to justify noncompliance with this legislation. Otherwise, they put into question the primacy, unity and effectiveness of EU law. However, in the case of doubt they can challenge such EU legislation by contesting the relevant EU Act before the CJEU as infringing the Charter.[76] This possibility, although limited, is

---

72 See Sarmiento, *supra* note 10, p 1290.

73 Case C-168/13 PPU *Jeremy F* ECLI:EU:C:2013:358, par 53.

74 Opinion of Advocate General Bobek in case C-310/16 *Petar Dzivev* ECLI:EU:C:2018:623, par 84–88. Similarly, Advocate General Bot in the *Melloni* case distinguished between situations where the level of protection of fundamental rights is defined by the EU and cases where it is not. In the first case, the EU definition 'reflects a balance between the need to ensure the effectiveness of European Union action and the need to provide adequate protection for fundamental rights', par 124–125.

75 As explained in relation to the specific circumstances in case C-399/11 *Melloni*, par 62.

76 It seems that this was the aim of the preliminary reference of the Irish court in case C-363/12 *Z. v A Government department* ECLI:EU:C:2014:159, where the court asked if Directive 2006/54 is compatible with the Charter if it is interpreted as allowing

also granted to individuals who may contest an EU legal Act before a national court, which may in consequence refer the case to the CJEU. Conversely, if the level of protection of a given right or freedom in the Charter is not defined by EU legislation, Member States may use their constitutional standards of protection but they have to keep the minimal standard as provided by the Charter. Referring to the concepts used by K. Lenaerts, it may be said that in the first situation (existing harmonised or unified EU rules) there exists an EU legislative consensus which must be in compliance with the EU constitutional consensus; in the second case (no EU legislation or rules), there is no legislative consensus but the constitutional consensus might still apply.[77]

Coming back to the relation between fundamental rights protection and the effectiveness principle, it should be added that tensions between these two rules may occur not only when national and EU standards of protection of fundamental rights are different but it may also occur within the EU system itself – when the EU effectiveness principle interferes with the fundamental rights recognised by the EU. In the *M.A.S.* (*Taricco II*) judgment, the CJEU was confronted with a question from the Italian Corte Costituzionale on whether it was possible to disapply national rules on the prescription periods for tax frauds preventing the imposition of effective and dissuasive penalties affecting the financial interests of the EU and required by the CJEU's *Taricco I* judgment.[78] The problem was that this disapplication might constitute a breach of a national principle that the applicable law on criminal sanctions had to be precise. Before giving the answer, the CJEU referred to and explained the same principle concerning criminal sanctions enshrined in Article 49 CFR, which must have been observed by the Member States when they implemented the EU law. It seems, therefore, that the CJEU treated the national principle invoked by the Italian court as an EU law principle enshrined in the Charter which must also be respected by the national court when the effectiveness of EU law is at stake. Finally, the CJEU stated that the national court should have complied with the rule that offences and penalties must be defined by law, even if it would not guarantee the whole effectiveness of the implementation of the EU law.[79] What could be derived from these statements is confirmation that the effectiveness of EU law is not an absolute principle and may not require

to refuse maternity leave to a mother whose genetic child has been born through a surrogacy arrangement.

[77] Koen Lenaerts, 'EU values and constitutional pluralism: the EU system of fundamental rights protection' *Polish Yearbook of International Law* 34 (2014), 135.

[78] Case C-105/14 *Taricco and others* ECLI:EU:C:2015:555.

[79] Case C-42/17 *M.A.S.* ECLI:EU:C:2017:936, par 51–61.

Member States to omit or diminish the level of protection of fundamental rights as provided for in both the Charter and national constitutional law.[80]

A preliminary conclusion may be that in cases of direct implementation of EU law by Member States, the Charter should be the main fundamental rights Act applied by national courts. In cases of indirect implementation of EU law, the Charter is applicable but not necessarily applied – if the national standard of protection of fundamental rights is sufficient, it is enough to rely on this standard and the Charter applies if it provides a higher level of protection or if the unity, primacy or effectiveness of EU law may be compromised. This approach seems compatible with the principle of subsidiarity of protection adopted in the European Convention on Human Rights (ECHR) system. The ECtHR recognises both national constitutional courts and the CJEU as guarantors of human rights observance in national and the EU systems. It also establishes a rebuttable presumption that the EU legal system offers an equivalent level of protection of human rights. In cases where Member States act in compliance with their obligations stemming from EU law, it can be presumed that they also act in compliance with fundamental rights and the responsibility for human rights observance rests on the CJEU and EU law. In cases where Member States exercise their discretionary power, the responsibility for fundamental rights observance rests primarily on national courts.[81] However, as has been clarified by the CJEU, even in such cases Member States cannot ignore the Charter if it can pose a threat to EU law or principles of primacy, unity and effectiveness.

3. Consistent EU and National Standards

The next question is whether the Charter is applicable in cases where the EU and national standards of protection of fundamental rights are consistent.[82] This question, even if not in an obvious way, is relevant to the problem of protection of the constitutional identity of the Member States. When discussing challenges that the Charter brought to national legal orders, it might be wrongly assumed that constitutional identity is a concept that serves to emphasise the differences in understanding or application of common values and fundamental rights in the Member States. Indeed, this concept is usually used to justify possible derogations or exceptions from EU common rules, as it is obvious that there is no need to rely on or invoke national identity just to

[80] See also Nina Półtorak, *European Union Rights in National Courts* (Wolters Kluwer, Alphen aan den Rijn 2015), p 339.

[81] Judgment of the ECtHR of 30 June 2005, no. 45036/98 *Bosphorus Hava Yollar*; judgment of 6 December 2012, no. 12323/11, *Michaud v France*.

[82] For more, see Chapter 6 in this book.

justify compliance with common rules. However, we should not forget that the constitutional identity of a given Member State does not consist only of deviating rules but also comprises rules which are common to all Member States and are codified in the Charter. In the majority of cases, constitutional identity is equal to or corresponds directly to European values. These cases are just not as noticeable as deviating standards cases are. Consequently, the EU and national standards of fundamental rights protection are very often the same. Nevertheless, even in the case of such convergence, the principles of direct effect and primacy allow national courts to rely on the Charter in order to examine whether the standard of fundamental rights protection has been guaranteed without a need to refer any questions on this matter to the supreme or constitutional court. Therefore, even in such cases, the national judge acquires the competences of the constitutional judge verifying whether national law complies with EU fundamental rights.

V. APPLICABILITY AND APPLICATION OF THE CHARTER

1. Arguments against a Functional Interpretation of Article 51(1)

The above analysis shows the tensions between the need to apply the Charter as a legal instrument serving effective implementation of EU law by the Member States and the problems it may create for the fragile equilibrium of EU law and national constitutional fundamental rights. For effective implementation of EU law, the intervention of the Charter should be possible in all situations that fall – even indirectly – within the scope of EU law. However, every decision on the applicability of the Charter to the Member States provokes complex problems related to the constitutional laws of Member States and the division of competences between the CJEU and national constitutional courts. Should this affect the interpretation of Article 51(1) CFR? Should we advocate for a functional interpretation of Article 51(1) CFR[83] which could lead to limitation of the applicability of the Charter to cases where the intervention of the Charter is

---

[83] The concept of functional interpretation of Article 51(1) is not the same as the functional approach proposed by Marek Safjan. The functional approach – in the concept of Judge Safjan, located halfway between the restrictive and abstract approaches – allows applicability of the Charter in cases of national law implementing EU law only indirectly, but at the same time requires that there must be a specific rule of EU law applicable to this national law. See Marek Safjan, 'Fields of application of the Charter of Fundamental Rights and constitutional dialogues in the European Union' in Fabrizio Cafaggi, Stephanie Law (eds), *Judicial Cooperation in European Private Law* (Edward Elgar Publishing, Cheltenham, UK and Northampton, MA 2017), p 51.

needed to eliminate the risk to the unity, primacy and effectiveness of EU law, so in practice to the effective enforcement of EU law by the Member States?[84] In the opinion of the author of this chapter, it is doubtful. There are a few reasons for this. First, there is the formal argument grounded in the wording of Article 51(1). It does not provide that the Charter binds Member States only if it is required for effective implementation of EU law, and neither does it make any other referral to the function of the Charter. It defines the scope of applicability of the Charter as being based just on the notion of implementing EU law. Second, a functional interpretation of Article 51(1) might influence interpretation of another concept – the scope of EU law. In other words, the scope of EU law should not be interpreted in the context of a need to apply the Charter in a given case. Defining the scope of EU law affects not only the applicability of the Charter but also the applicability of EU primary and secondary law, of the preliminary ruling procedure and the infringement procedure instituted by the European Commission. Therefore, linking the interpretation of the scope of EU law with the need to apply the Charter might lead to a restrictive interpretation of the range of EU law itself. This would be particularly alarming in cases concerning rights resulting from citizenship of the EU. As we know, the Charter does not grant any further rights not comprised already in the concept of EU citizenship, but the scope of rights originating from this citizenship should not depend on the necessity to apply the Charter in a given case.[85] The next, third, reason is based on the consequence of a functional interpretation of Article 51(1) CFR. Linking the decision on the scope of application of the Charter with the need of effectiveness of the EU law may result in restrictive interpretation of the former in the cases where there is no risk for the latter. This risk may, however, appear in other cases, but it would be difficult to take it into account if it was already decided that similar situations did not constitute implementation of EU law. And, finally, the fourth reason is the function of the Charter, which is, as its preamble states, 'to strengthen the protection of fundamental rights in the light of changes in society, social progress and scientific and technological developments by making those rights more visible'. The

[84] The absence of risk to the unity, primacy and effectiveness of EU law was treated in C-206/13 *Cruciano Siragusa*, par 32 and C-198/13 *Víctor Manuel Julian Hernández*, par 47 as an additional justification for declaring the Charter not applicable in these cases. See also the opinion of Advocate General Saugmandsgaard Øe in case C-235/17 *European Commission v Hungary* ECLI:EU:C:2018:971, par 95–112.

[85] For example, the CJEU has established that EU law also embraces situations which are outside the scope of application of secondary EU law but which have the effect of depriving EU citizens of the genuine enjoyment of the substance of the rights conferred by EU citizenship, case C-165/14 *Rendón Marín* ECLI:EU:C:2016:675, par 74 and the case law quoted therein.

main aim of the Charter is not to guarantee effective enforcement of EU law by the Member States. The Charter is there to reaffirm and protect the rights of individuals. Of course, this is possible only within the limits established in Article 51(1) CFR, thus within the boundaries of EU law, but it does not mean that these limits may be further restricted by a functional interpretation of Article 51(1). Such interpretation would not only be against the aims and objectives of the Charter but also contrary to the expectations of the addressees of the fundamental rights and principles – the people of Europe. The fact that the Charter only applies to Member States when they implement EU law is already perceived as insufficient and unsatisfactory for many citizens and this situation can create more alienation from the Union – as has been stated by the European Parliament.[86] This can only be worsened by a restrictive interpretation of Article 51(1) CFR.

2. A Functional Interpretation of Article 53 of the Charter or What Triggers the Application of the Charter

Rejection of a functional interpretation of Article 51(1) CFR does not mean that the need to apply the Charter cannot be taken into account when the CJEU or a national court decides on the actual application of the Charter in a given case. For this aim, it is important to differentiate between the scope of application of the Charter to the Member States and putting it into operation, i.e. to separate the question of applicability of the Charter from its actual application in a given case in lieu of a national standard. Finding that a given case before a national court falls within the scope of application of the Charter opens the possibility of its application, but it does not create an obligation to replace national constitutional fundamental rights with those in the Charter. While applicability of the Charter is regulated by Article 51(1) CFR, its actual application may be limited by Article 53 CFR. Unlike Article 51, Article 53 may be subject to a functional interpretation which takes into account the need to apply the Charter. The objective interpretation of the applicability of the Charter as regulated in Article 51(1) allows keeping under potential scrutiny all national actions which are covered by EU law (in the words of the CJEU: 'situations cannot exist which are covered (…) by European Union law without (…) fundamental rights being applicable'[87]). A different question is deciding whether intervention of the Charter is needed and to what extent it should be applied

[86] The European Parliament called on the EU institutions to consider an enhancement of the scope of application of the Charter, Explanatory statement to the Report on the situation of fundamental rights in the European Union in 2017 of 13 December 2018 (2018/2103(INI).

[87] Case C-617/10 *Åkerberg Fransson*, par 21.

in the place of a national standard of protection of fundamental rights.[88] This question should be answered on the basis of Article 53 CFR and the meaning given it by the CJEU in the *Melloni* and *Åkerberg Fransson* cases.

What can be derived from *Melloni* and *Åkerberg Fransson* is that when a Member State directly implements EU law which harmonises the standard of legal protection of fundamental rights, it has to apply the Charter instead of national standards. However, when a Member State only indirectly applies EU law and does not establish the common standard of protection of fundamental rights, applicability of the Charter would not necessarily lead to its actual application in place of the national standards. In such a case and under the condition that the national standards are adequate (they do not pose a threat to the standards of the Charter or obligations of the Member States), the role of the Charter may be secondary – it supports national standards and may be applied together with or as a subsidiary to national fundamental rights but does not have to be the legal basis of national court decisions. This may, however, change over time, and in the same kind of cases a Member State may not be able to provide the adequate level of protection of fundamental rights. If this happens, application of the Charter should be activated. The factor triggering its application in the cases of indirect implementation of the EU law should be the existence of a threat to the Union standard of fundamental rights protection or to the principles of primacy, unity and effectiveness of EU law.

Such a threat may arise not only in situations where the EU and national standards are at variance but also where they are generally convergent but there are deficiencies in the national legal and institutional system guaranteeing this convergent standard. Then, not only is the national law at risk but so is the EU level of fundamental rights protection. If the national law or institutions are not effective in guaranteeing the domestic basic rights, protection of the EU fundamental rights is also put in jeopardy, which justifies intervention of the Charter and the EU fundamental rights enforcement mechanisms. As a result, when individuals and national courts are able to invoke and apply the Charter to reinforce their constitutional values, the Charter helps to protect and support the national constitutional identity.[89]

A reference could be made at this point to the central thesis formulated by the Bundesverfassungsgericht in its so-called *Solange* rulings, in which the

---

[88] A different approach seems to be taken by Mark Dawson, who argues for a sliding scale rather than a binary approach to the operation of Article 51 CFR, *The Governance of EU Fundamental Rights* (Cambridge University Press, Cambridge 2017), p 77.

[89] Which is confirmed by the considerable increase in the number of references to the Charter in referrals for preliminary rulings in general and particularly to Article 47 in cases concerning the rule of law.

German constitutional court held that as long as European law observes the fundamental rights guaranteed in the national system there is no need for the national standard or the constitutional court to intervene.[90] We could formulate a mirror image of the *Solange* ruling – let us call it *Union Solange* – which says that as long as the national law of a given Member State observes the EU standard of fundamental rights and does not pose a risk of compromising the primacy, unity or effectiveness of EU law, the Charter is applicable but it does not have to be put into operation (there is such a possibility but there is no need to turn to the Charter). The above paraphrase is different from the *reverse Solange* proposal because in the latter the need for an intervention by the Charter was to define its scope of application to Member States even outside EU law.[91] In *Union Solange* as proposed above, the scope of application of the Charter is an objective and not functional notion while the need for the Charter's intervention justifies its actual operation in lieu of national standards.

3. Applicability and Application of the Charter – Consequences for Judicial Interactions

The above approach has certain procedural consequences. First, it gives the courts of the Member States the possibility to treat the Charter as applicable in all cases which directly or indirectly fall within the scope of EU law. Second, in a situation of indirect implementation, it gives them the possibility to actually apply the Charter in lieu of national standards if they conclude that the national law fails to guarantee the adequate protection of fundamental rights or that the unity, primacy or effectiveness of EU law is at risk. In such cases, national courts must also have the possibility (and obligation, in the case of courts of last instance) to use the procedure of dialogue with the CJEU in which the CJEU exercises its competences and obligations to ensure that the law is observed in the interpretation and application of the Treaties. This approach also allows national courts and the CJEU to treat the changing situation of implementation of EU law in a Member State as a relevant factor since it keeps open the actual application of the Charter by not locking it in the stage of applicability of the Charter based on a restrictive interpretation of Article 51 CFR. In grey area cases of indirect implementation of the Charter, the national judge may decide that the Charter is applicable and, taking into account the circumstances indicated by the CJEU based on Article 53 CFR, that it should or should not be applied instead of the national law.

---

[90] E.g. in judgment of 22 October 1986, FCT, 2 BvR 97/83; of 7 June 2000, 2 BvL 1/97210; of 9 January 2002, 1 BvR 1036/99211.

[91] Von Bogdandy and others, *supra* note 8.

It is finally interesting to analyse the milestone decisions of the Bundesverfassungsgericht, which seem to implement the rules coming from the case law of the CJEU as interpreted in this chapter from the perspective of national law.[92] The Bundesverfassungsgericht has stated that the Charter might be a standard for the constitutional review of national law or practice falling within the scope of EU law. First, it relied on the distinction between legislation fully and not fully harmonised under EU law. In the first case, EU fundamental rights should be applied instead of the national standard. In the second case, the national fundamental rights should be applied. This follows from the finding that where EU law does not fully harmonise the given question it seeks to accommodate the diversity of fundamental rights regimes; and it rests on the rebuttable presumption that the application of national fundamental rights ensures the level of protection required by the EU fundamental rights. Second, the constitutional court may and should review compliance with the Charter of the application of EU law by the national authorities because the Charter takes precedence over German fundamental rights in cases of fully harmonised legislation. The Bundesverfassungsgericht added that an additional review on the basis of EU fundamental rights is only necessary if there are specific and sufficient indications showing that the constitution does not afford adequate fundamental rights protection.[93]

From the point of view of the subject matter of this chapter, it should be first underlined that in the cases described above the Charter was applicable and that the decisions of the Bundesverfassungsgericht did not concern the applicability of the Charter in the meaning of Article 51 CFR. Second, the Bundesverfassungsgericht made the distinction between cases of fully harmonised legislation – where the Charter must be applied for the constitutional review exercised by the constitutional court – and legislation not fully harmonised – where the national standard of fundamental rights protection should be the basis for such a review. This distinction and its consequences for the national system were based on Article 53 CFR as interpreted by the CJEU in the *Melloni* judgment. It most probably means that the Bundesverfassungsgericht agreed with the CJEU that in cases of fully harmonised EU law, the Member States are obliged to apply the Charter and might not rely on their own standards of fundamental rights protection. Then, like all other national courts, the constitutional court should ensure the protection of the EU fundamental rights and it should do so by incorporating these fundamental rights into its standard of constitutional review. By doing so, it ensures effective legal protection

---

[92] Orders of 6 November 2019, 1 BvR 16/13 and 1 BvR 276/17.

[93] As stated in Bundesverfassungsgericht Press release no 83/2019 of 27 November 2019.

giving the individuals additional constitutional guarantees of their EU fundamental rights. In this review, the Bundesverfassungsgericht is expected to seek close cooperation with the CJEU and refer questions for preliminary ruling where they have not already been clarified by the CJEU case law. In the situation of not fully harmonised cases, even though the Charter is applicable in the meaning of Article 51(1) CFR, the national constitutional law and not the Charter should be the benchmark for the constitutional review. This is because in such cases it is the national law that guarantees the effective fundamental rights protection required by the Charter. Nevertheless, this guarantee might not be sufficient and then the constitutional court might be obliged to verify compliance of the national law with the Charter.

VI. CONCLUSIONS

With the Charter as a legal Act with a constitutional character, the judicial and legal interactions in the EU's multi-layered legal and judicial system were taken to another level, which is both challenging and full of opportunities. National courts can indirectly derive from the Charter certain extended or even new competences of constitutional review, which can be enforced without the intervention of constitutional or higher courts and which may lead to substantial changes in the interpretation and application of national standards of fundamental rights protection. The dialogue between national courts, including constitutional courts, and the CJEU shows that the main problems and questions of division of competences originating from this new deal have been solved. Now, when interpreting and applying the solutions developed through judicial interactions both EU and national judges should remember the promise of the Charter, which is to place the individual at the heart of the activities of the EU and in consequence to guarantee the effective fundamental rights protection of individuals at both EU and national levels. One of the main prerequisites of this promise is to assure applicability of the Charter in all cases covered by EU law and to reassure national judges in their interpretation of the scope and modes of application of the Charter that, while respecting the restrictions of the scope of the Charter, guarantee the genuine protection of fundamental rights. This chapter has therefore postulated that the question of applicability of the Charter should be separated from the question of its application in specific cases in lieu of national standards. The former should be decided on the basis of Article 51(1) CFR and the latter on the basis of Article 53 CFR and the functional interpretation of it given by the CJEU. Where the Member States directly implement EU law, the Charter should be the primary fundamental rights protection Act for national courts. In the case of indirect implementation of EU law, the Charter should step in where a given fundamental right may be at risk of being insufficiently protected or where effective implementation of European Union law is under threat. The option to apply the Charter should be available in the largest possible range of situations – as large as the scope of EU law – yet a need for its application may occur when national standards and measures for fundamental rights protection are insufficient or inadequate for the implementation of EU law.

The Charter's entry into force was an occurrence of both legal and symbolic significance. It emphasises the fact that the European Union is an organisation uniting European countries through a set of shared values and it constitutes another declaration by the Member States that they are committed to observing these values, which are and must remain the foundation of integration. It also gives individuals and national courts a powerful tool to protect the fundamental values common to the Member States and the EU. The Charter offers national courts supranational fundamental rights guarantees, which are crucial in the case of serious deficiencies of domestic legal systems. If fundamental rights in the Member States are compromised, the Charter and the CJEU can provide a guarantee of protection which might be more effective than domestic measures or an intervention by the ECtHR. Finally, it is extremely important in cases where national fundamental rights protection proves to be dysfunctional. This means that in certain situations the EU becomes an organisation protecting human rights and the CJEU a court of fundamental rights. It also means that in such situations national judges may rely on the Charter to protect the constitutional values of a Member State which might be jeopardised. Such situations are still exceptional even if they tend to happen more often. The Charter does not replace national constitutional standards of fundamental rights protection and does not take over the responsibility for fundamental rights protection in national systems. This responsibility still rests primarily with national courts, yet the rights and principles of the Charter can help them discharge this duty.

3. Comment: the Charter and its triple challenge: unclear applicability, a foggy distinction between rights and principles and a lack of engagement at the national level

Gabriel Toggenburg[1]

By introducing the Charter 20 years ago, the three EU institutions erected a big billboard stressing that the EU 'is founded on the indivisible, universal values of human dignity, freedom, equality and solidarity', placing 'the individual at the heart of its activities' and committing 'to strengthen the protection of fundamental rights in the light of changes in society, social progress and scientific and technological developments'.[2] These are big words.

At the same time, the Charter came along with a series of caveats as if the Union had grown fearful of its own courage. Most prominently, in its notorious Article 51 (hardly any other provision has received so much attention) the Charter stresses that it 'does not extend the field of application of Union law beyond the powers of the Union or establish any new power or task for the Union, or modify powers and tasks as defined in the Treaties'.[3] A constitutional document without constituting anything new? In addition, Article 52 explains that not all the Charter's provisions are rights and therefore many of them will be of limited practical value before a court.[4] Read in combination, these two provisions might give the impression of a sort of inverted tobacco package warning message: 'This Charter has no effect'. Indeed, in a way the Charter builds a list of fundamental rights while leaving the fundaments unchanged. Is the hopeful idea of a Charter that makes a difference on the ground therefore built on sand?

[1] This contribution is written in a private capacity and cannot be attributed to the European Union Fundamental Rights Agency (FRA).

[2] Preamble of the Charter.

[3] Art. 51 (2) of the Charter.

[4] Art. 52 (5) of the Charter.

What is the reply to such a provocative question? Exploring the potential reach and impact of the Charter requires answers to at least three foundational questions:

- How far does the 'field of application of Union law' reach?
- How many rights in the Charter provisions are rights in the strict sense, and of these how many are directly applicable between individuals?
- What does it entail for the EU and the Member States to be obliged to 'promote the application' of the Charter?[5]

Let us have a brief look at these three questions. While the first has received overwhelming interest in academia[6] and the second is being increasingly discussed,[7] the third one has remained ignored to a surprising degree.[8]

THE CHARTER'S FOGGY APPLICABILITY

Among the stumbling blocks on the way towards a more frequent application of the Charter and a more prominent promotion of its application is the lack of clarity about its scope and the distinction between rights and principles. Both questions – the Charter's scope of application and the distinction between rights and principles – are like floodgates determining the impact of the Charter. And both are left in the hands of the EU Court in Luxembourg.

Being part of supranational rather than international law, the Charter efficiently enters national legal systems. How and to what degree this happens depends first on its field of application and second on how it interacts with the constitutional reality of the Member States. It bestows on national courts the role of constitutional courts – they examine not only the compliance of national law with EU law but also its compliance with the fundamental rights recognised in the EU system. Indeed, the Charter has also led some constitutional courts to re-assert their role as EU courts. Against the background of the new prominence of EU fundamental rights, both the Austrian (in 2012) and the German (in 2019) constitutional courts have stressed that in the future they will

---

5 Art. 51 (1) of the Charter.

6 A huge number of articles have been written on this topic. See, for instance, recently Benedikt Pirker, Mapping the Scope of Application of EU Fundamental Rights: A Typology, (2018) 3 *European Papers* 133–56.

7 See, e.g., Jasper Krommendijk, Principled Silence or Mere Silence on Principles? The Role of the EU Charter's Principles in the Case Law of the Court of Justice, (2015) 11 *European Constitutional Law Review* 321–356.

8 See, however, recently, Bruno de Witte, The Strange Absence of a Doctrine of Positive Obligations under the EU Charter of Rights, [2020] (4) *Quaderni costituzionali* 854–7.

also check national law against EU law and – where areas are fully harmonised by the EU legislator – the Charter forms the only relevant standard against which the relevant national legislation has to be checked.[9] The distinction between fully harmonised fields and other fields of EU law reflects the *Melloni* case law allowing national constitutional law to provide more protection than the Charter in all areas where the EU legislator has not harmonised the relevant level of protection, including the eventual need to define the appropriate balance between conflicting rights.

The *Melloni* doctrine affirms that 'national authorities and courts remain free to apply national standards of protection of fundamental rights, provided that the level of protection laid down in the Charter, as interpreted by the Court, and the primacy, unity and effectiveness of EU law are not thereby compromised'.[10] However, Nina Półtorak disagrees – and rightly so – with what she calls a 'functional interpretation' of Article 51 (1) of the Charter limiting its applicability to cases in which the intervention of the Charter is needed to eliminate the risk to the unity, primacy and effectiveness of EU law.[11] She stresses the important distinction between applicability and the application of the Charter. When it comes to the application dimension, it indeed makes sense to bring in the element of functionality, which is why she states that:

> as long as the national law of a given Member State observes the EU standard of fundamental rights and does not pose a risk of compromising the primacy, unity or effectiveness of EU law, the Charter is applicable but it does not have to be put into operation (there is such a possibility, but there is no need to turn to the Charter).

Where the application of national standards would compromise the primacy, unity or effectiveness of EU law, it is the Charter that needs to be applied – this is what Nina Półtorak calls '*Union Solange*'. However, this mechanism is far from providing a Charter solution to all rule of law problems given that it only triggers the application, not the applicability, of the Charter. Therefore '*Union Solange*' will not trigger the application of the Charter where the Charter is not applicable, i.e. in areas falling outside the scope of Union law. At the same time, recent judgments of the Court of Justice of the European Union might signal that the Charter may also play a role beyond the strict limits set by Article 51, especially when interplaying with Article 19 Treaty on European

---

9 Austria, Verfassungsgerichtshof, case U466/11, 14 March 2012; Germany, Bundesverfassungsgericht, case 1 BvR 276/17, 6 November 2019.

10 Case C-399/11, *Melloni* ECLI:EU:C:2013:107, para 60.

11 See Chapter 2 in this volume.

Union, i.e. in the context of judicial independence and fair trial.[12] In this sense, the Charter also reminds us that the process of European integration is just this – a process without any predefined end.

THE UNCLEAR DISTINCTION BETWEEN RIGHTS AND PRINCIPLES

Just like the question of the Charter's field of application, also the distinction between rights and principles is of considerable practical relevance and impact. The more the mix of rights vs. principles leans towards rights, the more individuals will be able to profit from the Charter. Moreover, a Charter that is composed of rights rather than principles is more likely to provide the basis for claims that have financial implications and may indirectly lead to an extension of the EU's role in the fields of social and economic policies.[13]

As is well known, the distinction between rights and principles was already introduced by the Convention drafting the Charter in order to find a compromise between those who wanted to introduce social provisions in the Charter and those who wanted to avoid the Charter establishing enforceable social rights.[14] The rather cryptic wording in Article 51 that the EU and its States have to 'respect rights' and 'observe principles' was only to a certain degree clarified in the 2001/2002 second Convention by introducing the fifth paragraph in Article 52.[15] Whereas it is up to the Court to provide final guidance, three criteria are often referred to when distinguishing rights from principles:[16]

- Does the provision oblige the EU and the States to respect a specific value or good rather than aim to protect the rights of individuals?
- Does execution of the provision depend on further concretisation in legislation?

[12] On this indirect effect, see Aurora Rasi, Effetti indiretti della carta dei diritti fondamentali?, (2019) 4 *European Papers* 615–28.

[13] This at least was the fear of those who were against the introduction of social *rights* in the Charter.

[14] The introduction of social rights then also triggered the strengthening of economic rights such as Art. 16 (the right to conduct a business) as one of the fathers of the Charter explains in Gabriel N. Toggenburg, Die Geburtsstunde der EU-Grundrechtecharta: ein Gespräch mit dem Konventsmitglied Heinrich Neisser, in Peter Hilpold, Andreas Raffeiner, Walter Steinmair (eds), *Rechtsstaatlichkeit, Grundrechte und Solidarität in Österreich und in Europa* (facultas.wuv Universitäts, Vienna 2021), 98–106.

[15] See CONV 3454/02, explaining that the provision was meant to add legal clarity.

[16] See Jasper Krommendijk, op. cit., 332–4.

- Does the Charter provision provide a large margin of discretion, for instance by referring to conditions provided in EU and/or national law?

If these three questions are answered in the affirmative, the provision is more likely to be a principle than a right. However, whereas the case law of the Court on the Charter's field of applicability already allows sufficient guidance to legal practitioners,[17] the identification of Charter provisions as either rights or principles requires additional clarification.

THE NEED TO PROMOTE THE APPLICATION OF THE CHARTER PROVISIONS

Looking at the modest level of engagement in promoting the application of Charter rights at the national level,[18] one might conclude that many governments do not see a need to take active steps to conform with the duty to promote the application of the Charter. Admittedly, Article 51 states that the Charter does not modify 'powers' or 'tasks' as defined in the Treaties. However, this can hardly mean that the Charter's call on the EU and its Member States to 'promote' the application of Charter rights is a meaningless statement meant to be ignored. Instead, this formulation is a reminder of an obligation under existing EU law: EU fundamental rights enshrine, just like human rights law in general, positive obligations. The European Court of Human Rights has developed a rich doctrine of positive State obligations and according to Article 52 whenever Charter rights correspond to European Convention on Human Rights provisions their 'meaning and scope' should be the same.[19] Just as the FRA has repeatedly reminded governments, it is timely and important to invest considerably more energy in the promotion of the actual application of Charter rights, and the revised strategy of the European Commission on the application of the Charter provides a new push in this regard.[20] Efforts in this sense include all three branches of government and range from the establishment of

---

[17] FRA, *Applying the Charter of Fundamental Rights of the European Union in Law and Policymaking at National Level: Guidance* (2018).

[18] A fact often described by the FRA, see most recently, FRA, *Ten Years on: Unlocking the Charter's Full Potential* (2020).

[19] De Witte, op. cit.

[20] Ten years ago, the European Commission adopted the first Charter strategy (see Communication COM(2010)573 final, Strategy for the effective implementation of the Charter of Fundamental Rights by the European Union). At the end of 2020 a revised 'strategy to strengthen the application of the Charter within the EU' was adopted, see COM(2020) 711 final, 2 December 2020. It clearly moved the focus from EU-level implementation to implementation at the national level.

'Charter focal points' in public administration to the revision of procedures in parliaments and a more regular exchange of Charter practices between courts.

It is in this regard worthwhile to draw attention to the history of the Canadian Charter of fundamental rights and freedoms. Adopted back in 1982, over the years it became a widely recognised success with impacts across the legal and political systems. However, it was recognised that the Charter was not – as no human rights bill is – a self-activating instrument. What triggered the potential of the Canadian Charter was a major investment in the support structure for legal mobilisation. This included, for instance, setting up a Court Challenges Programme – a set of funds created specifically to finance test cases.[21] There is no reason to believe that the European Charter of Fundamental Rights would not equally depend on political investment to fully unfold its potential. And, in fact, there is no lack of ideas and guidance on how to guarantee that the Charter rights do not remain just an ambition 'up in the air', but translate into a situation where fundamental rights are upheld in daily practice 'on the ground'.[22]

---

[21] See Charles R. Epp, Do Bills of Rights Matter? The Canadian Charter of Rights and Freedoms, (1996) 90 *American Political Science Review* 764–78.

[22] Gabriel N. Toggenburg, The Implementation of the Charter of Fundamental Rights by the EU Member States, in Steve Peers et al. (eds), *The EU Charter of Fundamental Rights* (Hart 2021).

4. European values and national constitutions: bringing the EU Charter in from uncharted waters

Saša Zagorc and Marjan Kos

1. INTRODUCTION[1]

Any law is value-dependent. In legal business-as-usual mode, values remain a silent force and only come into effect if 'ordinary' tools of interpretation[2] lead to unsatisfactory conclusions. While they also inform the quality of law, they primarily act as an essential fabric in any society. If this is negated, i.e. with genuine dissent about common values in society, such an unbalanced situation implies that values have not been or are not fully internalised. This leads us to two simple conclusions. First, a proclamation of values does not necessarily guarantee living them (the *Sein und Sollen* dichotomy).[3] Second, heavyweight conflict-solving techniques with value judgements come in handy only in times of crisis when other lightweight avenues falter (the cascade method of subsidiarity). In our view, both these conclusions are informative for an assessment of the current state of the European Union (EU) crisis related to ongoing clashes with some Member States (MSs) about the specific substance of fundamental values and principles in the EU.

This chapter is divided in two parts. First, we explore how the relationship between European values and national constitutions has gradually changed with the development of the case law of the Court of Justice of the European

1 We would like to thank Dimitry Kochenov, Madalina Moraru, Gábor Halmai, Samo Bardutzky, Matej Accetto and Jaka Kukavica for helpful comments on early versions of the chapter.

2 See, for example, Koen Lenaerts and José A. Gutiérrez-Fons, 'To Say What the Law of the EU Is: Methods of Interpretation and the European Court of Justice' (2013) EUI Working Paper AEL 2013/9 <https://cadmus.eui.eu/handle/1814/28339> accessed 21 June 2020.

3 Hans Kelsen, *General Theory of Norms* (Michael Hartney, tr, OUP, Oxford 1991) 58–60.

Union (CJEU) and modifications to the texts of the Treaties. We focus on judicial interaction and pertinent case law and explore what this relationship can tell us about value conflicts in the EU. We argue that a 'decoupling' has occurred, meaning that EU values have gained relative independence from national values and constitutions over time. Second, we look at the possible ways in which the Charter of Fundamental Rights of the European Union (EU Charter), as an important source of European values also tied with national constitutions, can inform the resolution of value conflicts in the EU. We argue for a more decisive reliance on the Charter, which we consider to be in line with the existing institutional framework.

2. NATIONAL AND EUROPEAN VALUES

Common values are the fundamental pillars which *constitute* a society. They are the connecting tissue and in diverse societies the existence and robustness of this bond is essential for their continued existence. From a constitutional perspective, it is constitutional texts and their interpretation which will most commonly expose the common values of a certain community,[4] and in this chapter we take a constitutional approach to EU law.[5] We consider primary law to be the constitutional basis for the functioning of the EU[6] and the case law of the CJEU pertaining to the application of primary law to be a source of constitutional law. In this part of the chapter, we try to determine the interplay between European values and national constitutions and values and we explore the possibility of a conflict and possible solutions.

2.1 What are the European Values?

Looking at the texts of the Treaties, we can recognise a number of references to values which are fundamental to the structure and the functioning of the

---

[4] Values may be referenced explicitly in the text or implicitly follow from the phrasing of constitutional rights or principles.

[5] On the constitutional approach to EU primary law specially focussing on the founding principles, see Armin von Bogdandy, 'Founding Principles of EU Law: A Theoretical Sketch' [2010] 12 *Revus* 35, 36–8.

[6] Following the CJEU in C-294/83 *Les Verts* EU:C:1986:166 para 23.

EU.[7] Among these, the pedestal is of course reserved for Art. 2 TEU,[8] which explicitly states that '[t]he Union *is founded on the values* of respect for human dignity, freedom, democracy, equality, the rule of law and respect for human rights', and that '[t]hese values *are common to the Member States* [...]'.[9] The fundamental nature of these values is also reflected in the case law of the CJEU.[10] As von Bogdandy expresses it, Art. 2 TEU positivises the EU's self-understanding as a community of values.[11]

Since Art. 2 TEU speaks of *values*, this mention begs the question of whether these values, usually understood as a moral category, can produce legal effects. Without delving into theoretical factors more than is necessary here, we accept the shared conviction among theorists that the values in Art. 2 TEU function as legal principles, indeed fundamental principles of EU law, and can therefore produce legal effects[12] making Art. 2 TEU enforceable.[13] The legal nature of these values, in particular the rule of law, has been recognised by the CJEU too.[14] It is noteworthy that when speaking of democracy and rule of law, the

---

7 For example, Arts 2, 3, 4, 6, 7, 13, 21 and 49 of the Consolidated version of the Treaty on European Union [2016] OJ C 202/13 (TEU) and the Preamble to the Charter of Fundamental Rights of the European Union [2016] OJ C 202/391 (EU Charter), which speaks both of values (human dignity, freedom, equality and solidarity) and principles (democracy and the rule of law).

8 This article in a different form was inserted with the Treaty of Amsterdam [1997] OJ C 340/1.

9 Emphasis added.

10 C-216/18 *LM* EU:C:2018:586 para 35.

11 Armin von Bogdandy, 'Principles and Challenges of a European Doctrine of Systemic Deficiencies' (2019) MPIL Research paper 2019-14, 8 <https://ssrn.com/abstract=3431303> accessed 17 June 2020.

12 von Bogdandy (n 5) 50.

On this discussion, see also Dimitry Kochenov, 'The Acquis and Its Principles: The Enforcement of the "Law" versus the Enforcement of "Values" in the EU' in András Jakab and Dimitry Kochenov (eds), *The Enforcement of EU Law and Values: Ensuring Member States' Compliance* (OUP, Oxford 2017) 9–10; Laurent Pech, 'The Rule of Law as a Constitutional Principle of the European Union' (2009) Jean Monnet Working Paper 04/09, 20–21 <https://ssrn.com/abstract=1463242> accessed 17 June 2020. On individual values, see Marcus Klamert and Dimitry Kochenov, 'Article 2 TEU' in Manuel Kellerbauer, Marcus Klamert and Jonathan Tomkin (eds), *The EU Treaties and the Charter of Fundamental Rights: A Commentary* (OUP, Oxford 2019) 27–30.

13 Kochenov (n 12) 11; Cristophe Hillion, 'Overseeing the Rule of Law in the EU: Legal Mandate and Means' in Carlos Closa and Dimitry Kochenov (eds), *Reinforcing the Rule of Law Oversight in the European Union* (CUP, Cambridge 2016) 62–4.

14 For example, in C-64/16 *ASJP* EU:C:2016:62 paras 30, 32, C-216/18 *LM* paras 35, 48–50, C-619/18 *Commission v Poland* EU:C:2019:531 paras 42, 47, 50, C-192/18 *Commission v Poland* EU:C:2019:924 paras 98, 106, C-791/19 *Commission v Poland* (order) EU:C:2020:277 paras 32, 92, C-585/18 *A.K.* EU:C:2019:982 paras 120–124, 167.

EU Charter characterises them as 'principles'.[15] The values mentioned in Art. 2 TEU were in fact called 'principles' until the Treaty of Lisbon.[16]

Among the fundamental values listed, respect for human rights is the most prominent example of how what today are labelled the common EU values were historically formed.[17] There was no mention of fundamental rights, let alone fundamental values of the EU, in the Treaty of Rome.[18] The development of the EU's constitutional structure, especially human rights, leaned extensively on national constitutions.[19] These values only found their way into the text of primary EU law over time after having been 'discovered' by the CJEU when interpreting the nature of the new European legal order.[20] EU human rights protection was born from the vertical contestation between the European and the national legal orders in *Stauder*[21] and *Internationale Handelsgesellschaft*,[22] where the CJEU incorporated fundamental rights into EU law as general principles of Community law, which was later reaffirmed in

---

[15] See Preamble to the EU Charter.

[16] Klamert and Kochenov (n 12) 24–5.

[17] The narrative is well known and has been studied extensively, which is why we only focus on the key points in this development. See Damian Chalmers, Gareth Davies and Giorgio Monti, *European Union Law: Cases and Materials* (2nd edn, CUP, Cambridge 2010) 232–6; Paul Craig and Gráinne de Búrca, *EU Law: Text, Cases, and Materials* (5th edn, OUP, Oxford 2011) 366–71; Jürgen Kühling, 'Fundamental Rights' in Armin von Bogdandy and Jürgen Bast, *Principles of European Constitutional Law* (Hart, Oxford 2009) 482–9. It should be noted that not all Art. 2 TEU values formed via general principles of EU law, but were construed more as programmatic values. See Klamert and Kochenov (n 12) 25.

[18] Although democracy and the rule of law were important unwritten principles. See Kochenov (n 12) 12–13.

[19] Jaka Kukavica, '"Constitutional Traditions Common to the Member States" in Fundamental Rights Litigation before the CJEU: A Catchphrase or a Genuine Interpretative Technique?' (LLM thesis, University of Cambridge 2018, manuscript available on request) 18.

[20] For an overview of the development, see Oreste Pollicino and Massimo Fichera, 'The Dialectics between Constitutional Identity and Common Constitutional Traditions: Which Language for Cooperative Constitutionalism in Europe?' [2019] 20 *German Law Journal* 1097, 1102–5.

[21] C-29/69 *Stauder v City of Ulm* EU:C:1969:57 esp. para 7.

[22] C-11/70 *Internationale Handelsgesellschaft mbH v Einfuhr- und Vorratsstelle für Getreide und Futtermittel* EU:C:1970:114 esp. para 4.

Nold.[23] It follows that fundamental rights were derived directly from national[24] constitutional law.[25]

Although recognition by other EU institutions already came in 1977,[26] this method of comparative reasoning as a source of the EU's constitutional substance was only reflected in the texts of the Treaties in the Treaty of Maastricht with the insertion of Art. F(2)[27] and it took its current form in the Treaty of Lisbon with the formal recognition[28] of the EU Charter as primary law. This concluded the evolution and, in a way, changed the role of national constitutions in the field of human rights protection in the EU.[29]

A somewhat similar yet distinct development occurred concerning the rule of law.[30] In its proclamation of the European Economic Community as a 'Community, based on the rule of law [...]' regarding review of the legality of its acts with the Treaties in *Les Verts*,[31] there is no explicit reference to the source of this constitutional principle.[32] The reason is probably that although there is consensus on the importance of the rule of law, there is dissent on its exact substance.[33] Nevertheless, it is safe to assume that, as with other principles, it is sourced from national constitutional law.[34]

---

23 C-4/73 *Nold KG v Commission* EU:C:1974:5 para 13.

24 The European value dimension relating to the ECHR is here intentionally omitted, although it is obvious that the CJEU drew from that source as well, which was itself sourced from national constitutional traditions. See C-4/73 *Nold* para 13.

25 C-4/73 *Nold* para 4. Also see Koen Lenaerts, 'The Role of National Constitutions in the EU Law: From Shared Values to Mutual Trust and Constructive Dialogue (Editorial)' [2019] 73 *Pravnik* 5, 12–14.

26 Joint Declaration by the European Parliament, the Council and the Commission [1977] OJ C 103/1.

27 As Kukavica notes, the introduction of common constitutional traditions as a source of EU fundamental rights in the TEU did not have an effect on the understanding of the role of national constitutions in EU fundamental rights protection. This is in line with our understanding, that the 'decoupling' ensued with the insertion of Art. 6(1) TEU in the Treaty of Amsterdam and advanced with the Treaty of Lisbon [2007] OJ C 306/1, also formally recognising the binding nature of the EU Charter.

28 On a substantive level, the framing of the Charter was already an important step, as the Charter drew from national constitutional traditions.

29 On the changed role of national constitutional traditions in EU law, which goes beyond the scope of our argument, see Pollicino and Fichera (n 20).

30 For an in-depth analysis, see Pech (n 12) 10–21.

31 C-294/83 *Les Verts* para. 23. Reaffirmed in C-402/05 P and C-415/05 P *Kadi and Al Barakaat* EU:C:2008:461 para 281.

32 For a list of CJEU cases referring to the rule of law up to 2002, see Pech (n 12) 58, n 190.

33 Pech (n 12) 4.

34 See Preamble to the TEU: '[Drawing inspiration] from the cultural, religious and humanist inheritance of Europe, from which have developed the universal values of the

After the insertion of vague references to the rule of law in the Treaties in 1992,[35] it was finally recognised as a founding principle of the EU in the Treaty of Amsterdam in Art. 6(1) TEU and reformulated into a value in what is now Art. 2 TEU in the Treaty of Lisbon. This latter provision does not require consideration of national constitutions when interpreting the principle, but it can be asserted that the principle originated from the common European legal heritage while at the same time retaining autonomous substance within the EU's constitutional structure.[36] This origin follows from the final wording of the provision, stating that '[t]hese values are common to the Member States [...]'.[37]

Fundamental values featured prominently in what is known as the Copenhagen criteria,[38] framed in 1993, which laid out the preconditions for central and eastern Europe candidate countries. These included 'stability of institutions guaranteeing democracy, the rule of law, human rights and respect for and protection of minorities'[39] and through the practice of EU institutions contributed to demystifying the concrete substance of the Art. 2 TEU values.[40]

The above-described examples show how national constitutions were formative in relation to EU values. Nevertheless, the substance of fundamental values remains somewhat vague[41] leaving a wide margin for interpretation. Relying on this, non-compliant MSs claim to respect these values while understanding their substance in a different way.[42] It should suffice to say that the substance of the fundamental EU values, although not explained in more detail in the text, should be understood in line with the liberal-democratic constitutional tradition.[43] The European value system is built on the constitu-

---

inviolable and inalienable rights of the human person, freedom, democracy, equality and the rule of law [...]'.

35 Included by the Treaty of Maastricht [1992] OJ C 191/1. See TEU Preamble, Art. 11 TEU and Art. 177(2) Treaty establishing the European Community (TEC, consolidated version) [1992] OJ C 224/6.

36 Similarly, see Pech (n 12) 5–7, 21.

37 Lenaerts argues that this is actually a reference to common constitutional traditions. See Lenaerts (n 25) 5–6.

38 Conclusions of the Presidency – Copenhagen, 21–2 June [1993] SN 180/1/93 REV 1. For a critical analysis, see Dimitry Kochenov, 'Behind the Copenhagen Façade: The Meaning and Structure of the Copenhagen Criterion of Democracy and the Rule of Law' [2004] 8 *European Integration Online Papers* 1.

39 Klamert and Kochenov (n 12) 23–4.

40 Hillion (n 13) 67–9.

41 On the issue of vagueness, see Hillion (n 13) 67–70.

42 The example being how Poland argues for a different understanding of the rule of law under which its judicial reforms would be compliant. See von Bogdandy (n 11) 23, n 150.

43 von Bogdandy (n 5) 49.

tional traditions of the MSs, which sublimated them into the new independent constitutional order.

2.2 The Decoupling of European Values: Independent Value Systems?

Although national values were a crucial source of inspiration for EU values, the latter have become more and more independent, gaining autonomy through their implementation in the constitutional structure of the EU. A qualitative leap, which saw the formation of an autonomous EU value system which cannot be equated with any single MS's value system, occurred.[44]

Apart from the above-mentioned Copenhagen criteria, this leap began with the proclamation of the fundamental *principles* in the Treaty of Amsterdam in Art. 6(1) TEU. As noted elsewhere, this provision by far exceeds the constitutional dimension of the Maastricht Treaty, moving from restrictive to constructive constitutionalism[45] since it proclaims that the EU itself is founded on these principles.[46] The provision was reformulated[47] in the Treaty of Lisbon into what is now Art. 2 TEU. It is unclear whether the change in terminology has particular relevance, but it would seem that it was for symbolic reasons.[48] Even more importantly, the EU Charter was incorporated into primary law.

The Treaties are instruments of international law which all the MSs agreed.[49] This includes the proclamation of fundamental values and the decision to state those values as foundational to the EU. The MSs therefore agreed to establish a union with its own set of fundamental values, which are no longer exclusively and directly tied to national values. The European values express the nature of the Union itself rather than only being descriptive of the situation in the MSs.

---

[44] We follow this proposition without delving into (but bearing in mind) theoretical inquiries into whether it is even possible for the EU to properly have its own set of values or identity.

[45] von Bogdandy (n 5) 49, 54.

[46] Note that this was before the Treaty Establishing a Constitution for Europe [2004] OJ C 310/1 (CT).

[47] The listed values were also expanded, replacing liberty with freedom and adding equality and human dignity. Compare Art. 2 TEU with Art. 6 Consolidated Version of the TEU [1997] OJ C 340/145.

[48] The change from 'principles' to 'values' happened with the CT, which also included the flag, anthem and motto of the EU. We thank Samo Bardutzky for this observation.

[49] Art. 54 TEU, Art. 357 Consolidated Version of the Treaty on the Functioning of the European Union [2016] OJ C 202/47 (TFEU). Regarding Treaty amendments, see Art. 48 TEU.

This qualitative leap is also represented by the EU Charter being given primary law status. The EU Charter partially functions as legalisation of the status quo (the CJEU's case law) and follows the minimum level of protection by the European Convention on Human Rights (ECHR) and national constitutional traditions but, importantly, goes further by establishing a wider array of rights.[50] The adoption of the Charter was therefore an important constitutional moment for the EU since it brought about a notable widening of the field of fundamental rights protection.[51] This leap was not founded exclusively on national constitutions, as was already expressed in the Preamble to the EU Charter. By doing this, it could be argued, the EU also importantly expanded its value base. This is also reflected in the CJEU case law, briefly discussed below, which shows a diminishing role of common constitutional traditions corresponding to an increasing role of the EU Charter. Paradoxically, the formal adoption of the Charter actually meant, on the one hand, legalisation of national constitutional law as a source of inspiration for EU constitutional law, but at the same time a break between the two in the sense that it went a step further by establishing the Union's own value base in the field of human rights, separating it from the national constitutions.

It is important to note here that we are not arguing that a complete schism occurred or that this process has been finalised. The distancing between national constitutions and values on the one hand and European values on the other remains a dynamic process.

2.3 The Current Nexus between the Two Value Systems

The remaining nexus between European values and national constitutions is mainly reflected in the reference to the common constitutional traditions of MSs in Art. 6(3) TEU and the Preamble and Art. 52(4) of the EU Charter, both in relation to fundamental rights.[52] Outside these concrete references, national values still remain informative of European values, but even their interpretative potential remains limited. In the area of fundamental rights, the common constitutional traditions, in line with Art. 52(4) EU Charter, now serve as an interpretative guide to the proclaimed existing EU values only when a right in the EU Charter is based on national constitutional traditions.[53] They only sup-

---

50 Pollicino and Fichera (n 20) 1107.

51 With the important limitation incorporated in Art. 51(2) EU Charter, which is discussed in more detail below.

52 Also see Art. 340 TFEU.

53 Kukavica (n 19) 39.

plement EU values in a limited number of concrete cases.[54] This is reflected in the case law of the CJEU after the 'decoupling' too. Already after the adoption of the Charter, but especially after its formal recognition as a source of primary law, the role of national constitutions in the interpretation of EU fundamental rights diminished, or at least changed.[55] With the Treaty of Lisbon, the EU Charter became the main source of fundamental rights in the EU.[56]

Regarding other values in Art. 2 TEU, the current text of the TEU does not create such a link to national constitutions, recognising only that they are common to the MSs. Nevertheless, as was explained above, at least the rule of law was inspired by national constitutional traditions, and national understandings will probably continue to inform its substance at the EU level.

The 'decoupling' left behind other ways in which national constitutions can have a direct impact, such as through Art. 4(2) TEU. This highlights a serious problem which has been unveiled by recent attempts to circumvent the enforcement of European values by invoking national values.[57] The relative autonomy of European values is manifested here by the premise that even when arguing for a departure from EU law based on national constitutional arguments, the latter need to remain within the contours of European law, including especially Art. 2 TEU.[58] Hence, no national arguments for deviations contravening fundamental EU values can be considered valid.[59]

The 'decoupling' thesis first means that a change in an MS's value system does not have a direct impact on the EU value system as it is determined in the texts of the Treaties. A change in national value systems, even if it is reflected at the level of constitutional law, would not per se cause a change in EU values.[60] For such a change, an incentive would have to come from

---

[54] For a differing view and a possible new role of common constitutional traditions in the post-EU Charter, see Pollicino and Fichera (n 20) 1107–8.

[55] Pollicino and Fichera (n 20) 1107ff.

[56] Kukavica (n 19) 39.

[57] Examples are Hungary, which actually changed the Fundamental Law, and Poland, which argued for a different understanding of the rule of law. See Marjan Kos, 'The Relevance of National Identity in European Union Law and Its Potential for Instrumentalisation' [2019] 79 *Zbornik znanstvenih razprav* 41, 56–61.

[58] Editorial Comments, 'Safeguarding EU Values in the Member States: Is Something Finally Happening?' [2015] 52 CMLR 619, 628; Hillion (n 13) 63.

[59] For example: AG Sharpston in C-715/17 *Commission v Poland, Slovakia and the Czech Republic* paras 212, 216. Also see C-438/14 Bogendorff von Wolffersdorff EU:C:2016:401 para 71; C-208/09 Sayn-Wittgenstein EU:C:2010:806 para 91.

[60] This argument does not go against the ideas expressed in Piotr Bogdanowicz, Iris Canor, Matthias Schmidt, Maciej Taborowski and Armin von Bogdandy, 'Guest Editorial: A Potential Constitutional Moment for the European Rule of Law – The Importance of Red Lines' [2018] 55 *Common Market Law Review* 983 (similarly, von Bogdandy (n 11) 3), where it is claimed that if the EU failed to act against authoritarian

within, meaning that either the institutions would begin interpreting the core values differently or a change in the Treaties would occur. Second, changes in national constitutional frameworks and the corresponding values may not go against the fundamental EU values in Art. 2 TEU, which prevents illegitimate national autonomy claims.

2.4 Value Conflicts in the EU

Not every conflict between national and European law may be considered a value clash. Such a clash only occurs when there is an elementary difference in the understanding of one of the fundamental values nominally common to the two systems. As the illiberal turn in some MSs in the past decade illustrates, value clashes may take different procedural and operational forms, from an MS simply disapplying or violating secondary law[61] to a more systemic change resulting from a changed understanding of the principle of division of powers as a cornerstone of the rule of law.[62]

What is the cause of these clashes? The EU proclaims that the Art. 2 TEU values are fundamental to the EU and the MSs. The latter additionally agreed to respect these values, most recently when they ratified the Treaty of Lisbon. The EU also required, as it still does, respect for these values by acceding countries in the Copenhagen criteria[63] and in Art. 49 TEU, which was, formally, satisfied by acceding MSs. The fundamental values should therefore not only be viewed as a prerequisite for accession but also for continued membership.[64] It would appear that this convergence only occurred on paper (*Sein*) and was not really internalised, although it ought to be (*Sollen*). It can be argued that the discrepancy unmasked the real underlying values, which lay dormant

---

practices it could be argued that these would become part of the EU's understanding of the rule of law. This could, in our view, be confirmed, since such a decision by the EU institutions could perhaps be seen as a change in the understanding of the rule of law that came from within the EU. However, a failure to act on behalf of the EU would be in contravention of the EU constitutional structure. This is corroborated by Arts 3(5), 32 and more specifically Art. 21 TEU. See also Carlos Closa, Dimitry Kochenov and JHH Weiler, 'Reinforcing Rule of Law Oversight in the European Union' (2014) EUI Working Paper 2014/25, 6 <http://hdl.handle.net/1814/30117> accessed 17 June 2020. Even UN SC Resolutions may not justify a derogation from these fundamental principles. See C-402/05P and C-415/05P *Kadi and Al Barakaat* para 285. On this question, see Koen Lenaerts, 'The Kadi Saga and the Rule of Law within the EU' [2014] 67 SMU L. Rev. 707.

61 With regard to asylum and migration, see C-715/17 *Commission v Poland, Hungary and Czech Republic.*

62 C-585/18 *A.K.*

63 See above, n 38.

64 Closa, Kochenov and Weiler (n 60) 7.

until the position of those MSs consolidated within the EU. If this is the case, it of course begs the question of whether it is possible, in legal venues, to achieve the internalisation of these values.[65] Bearing this in mind, we nevertheless need to consider what legal options are at the disposal of the relevant institutions.

We argue that the European values have come full circle: from the point where the EU sourced its fundamental principles from national constitutional orders to the decoupling of the EU values from the national systems, and finally to the point where EU values act as a force for change of national values. This can either be achieved organically, when EU MSs have already incorporated and adopted EU values in their own legal systems, or coercively, when the EU attempts to force the MSs to adapt.

In line with the cascade method of subsidiarity, recourse to heavyweight conflict-solving techniques loaded with value judgements is only viable in times of serious crisis. Deep cuts in the vertical division of powers are only legitimate if they follow the most serious encroachments on common values. The same approach is valid for a proper argumentation by the CJEU. In the current situation in which the most fundamental constitutional premises of the EU legal order are being questioned, a more or less coercive approach is warranted.[66]

Since the two value systems are interconnected but separate, a clash can only be solved by a change on one of the two sides. As the promotion and cultivation of its own set of fundamental principles is a major reason for its existence, the EU cannot withdraw from them without losing its purpose. *Ceteris paribus*, there are therefore only two legally coherent long-term solutions, and they both focus on the MSs: either the reluctant MS conforms to the fundamental values of the Union or, alternatively, it leaves the Union.

Following this line of thought, the next step is to consider the possible venues for European value enforcement. There is an ongoing surge in the literature on this topic,[67] to which we wish to add by exploring possible exploitation of the EU Charter.

---

[65] For the sake of consistency, it needs to be highlighted that it is not only the new MSs which suffer from these discrepancies, since there are traits of authoritarian practices in the 'old democracies' (usually referred to as such *a contrario* by the MSs from the eastern side of the Iron curtain, which only democratised after 1990) too.

[66] The sharpest possible approach is promoted by Laurent Pech and Kim Lane Scheppele in 'Illiberalism Within: Rule of Law Backsliding in the EU' [2017] 19 *Cambridge Yearbook of European Legal Studies* 1, 5: 'If this problem of rogue Member States within the EU is to be solved, we believe that all EU institutions must use all of the tools at their disposal.'

[67] For an overview, see Closa, Kochenov and Weiler (n 60) 12ff; von Bogdandy (n 11) 17.

3. THE ROLE OF THE CHARTER IN VALUE CONFLICTS

Values present themselves in different ways in the EU legal order. For example, the right to effective judicial protection is one of the Charter rights and a general principle of EU law inspired by common constitutional traditions, the ECHR and international law and, as a subset of the rule of law,[68] it impacts as a value that is concretised in the primary law of the EU. While multiple sources do not change the core of its substance as recognised in the European judicial system,[69] its jurisdictional, material and operative scope varies profoundly. For example, the *ASJP* judgment of the CJEU instructs that 'fields covered by Union law' in Art. 19(1) TFEU do not match 'implementing EU law' in Art. 51(1) of the Charter.[70]

We proceed from the understanding, which by now seems to have also been internalised by the EU institutions,[71] that the EU should act in the face of ongoing value clashes which have resulted mainly in serious rule of law concerns in some MSs.[72] If an MS acts in violation of fundamental values, it is (among other things) up to the EU institutions to take appropriate action to protect them.[73] This is especially so when it is clear that national institutions are unable to ensure an effective response.[74] Ideally, in order to succeed EU

---

[68] We are aware of an important distinction between rule of law and the Rule of law highlighted by Kochenov in Dimitry Kochenov, 'The Missing EU Rule of Law?' in Carlos Closa and Dimitry Kochenov (eds), *Reinforcing Rule of Law Oversight in the European Union* (CUP, Cambridge 2016) 290–91 and Gianluigi Palombella, 'Beyond Legality: Before Democracy – Rule of Law Caveats in the EU Two-Level System: Reinforcing Rule of Law Oversight in the European Union' in Carlos Closa and Dimitry Kochenov (eds), *Reinforcing Rule of Law Oversight in the European Union* (CUP, Cambridge 2016) 38–40. In our contribution, we refer to the rule of law as *gubernaculum*.

[69] Cf. AG Tanchev observed in the *LM* case, para 38, that, while there is a clear overlap between the values contained in Art. 2 TEU and the specific rights guaranteed by the Charter, they are nevertheless distinct concepts. It is unclear if he refers to a substantive or other scope of these values and provisions.

[70] C-64/15 *ASJP* para 29. Also see Luke Dimitrios Spieker, 'Commission v. Poland: A Stepping Stone towards a Strong "Union of Values"?' (Verfassungsblog, 30 May 2019) <https://verfassungsblog.de/commission-v-poland-a-stepping-stone-towards-a-strong-union-of-values/> accessed 17 June 2020.

[71] Not least by the Commission, which has initiated several proceedings, but also by the CJEU, which has issued two judgments referring to the situation in Poland (C-192/18, C-619/18, C-715/17 and a number of preliminary rulings).

[72] For reasons supporting EU action in enforcing values, see von Bogdandy (n 11) 7–9; Closa, Kochenov and Weiler (n 60) 3–7.

[73] See in this sense Closa, Kochenov and Weiler (n 60) 5–7.

[74] Closa, Kochenov and Weiler (n 60) 15.

institutions would need to have a counterpart in at least one national institution rooting for the rule of law in the MS. Normally, this would be ordinary courts.[75] In specific cases, problems may also arise if only the compromised courts have – due to the national distribution of competences – the possibility of requesting a preliminary ruling and they do not avail themselves of it to act. Without 'un-captured' institutions, the effectiveness of EU action is questionable.[76]

It is self-evident that the role and impact of the Charter cannot be regarded as an omnipresent[77] one-size-fits-all[78] final[79] solution to these problems. What we argue here is that it has nevertheless not been utilised to the fullest potential. It is our understanding that the main reason for this is the established division of competences between the EU and the MSs as is elaborated in the Treaties,[80] on which Art. 51 of the EU Charter as the key limitation on the use of the EU Charter in ongoing conflicts is based.[81] Although we fully share Jakab's (pre-*ASJP*) conviction that 'if we aim for a fully-fledged values community which benefits all its citizens equally, then the Charter should gain as

---

[75] Examples of how this may be obstructed are the disciplinary proceedings against judges in Hungary and Poland. For example, see Dániel G. Szabó, 'A Hungarian Judge Seeks Protection from the CJEU: Part I' (Verfassungsblog, 28 July 2019) <https://verfassungsblog.de/a-hungarian-judge-seeks-protection-from-the-cjeu-part-i/> accessed 17 June 2020; Laurent Pech and Patryk Wachowiec, '1095 Days Later: From Bad to Worse Regarding the Rule of Law in Poland (Part II)' (Verfassungsblog, 17 January 2019) <https://verfassungsblog.de/1095-days-later-from-bad-to-worse-regarding-the-rule-of-law-in-poland-part-ii/> accessed 17 June 2020.

[76] Despite this being one of the main criticisms by Kochenov concerning why reliance on preliminary rulings is doubtful, it is clear that even in non-independent judiciaries defiant judges are willing to ask tough questions and put themselves to the fore. See, e.g. C-558/18 *Miasto Łowicz v Skarb Państwa – Wojewoda Łódzki* EU:C:2020:234 (which was finally decided as inadmissible).

[77] See below on limitations of the material scope of application of the Charter.

[78] The role of the Charter is twofold at least. It may act, first, as a tool that removes unwanted divergences in the interpretation of EU secondary law and, second, as a tool which the EU legal system applies to address systemic and/or intentional violations of fundamental rights.

[79] Due to limitations in the scope of application of the Charter, other legal bases and avenues, such as Arts 2, 4(3) and 19(1) TEU seem more appropriate to provide the ultimate protection ground.

[80] See Chapter 2 in this volume.

[81] Torres Pérez argues that it might have been for prudential and strategic reasons, in order to strengthen Art. 19(1) TEU and avoid contestation of the use of the EU Charter. See Aida Torres Pérez, 'From Portugal to Poland: The Court of Justice of the European Union as Watchdog of Judicial Independence' [2020] 27 *Maastricht Journal of European and Comparative Law* 105, 117.

such full applicability in every case',[82] there are still normative restrictions[83] in place preventing such an overarching approach.[84] Even reading Art. 19(1) along the lines of the United States' due process clause, thereby including the rights in the EU Charter, while theoretically possible, seems improbable.[85] Nevertheless, a use of the Charter more in line with its place in the EU's constitutional constellation while respecting the normative framework and the general balance of powers is possible.

3.1 The Use of the EU Charter in 'Undisputed Waters' – within the Field of Application of EU Law

Value conflicts are often masked behind more tenable violations of concrete provisions of secondary law. Here, the issue of EU competence is beyond doubt and the EU institutions could base infringement procedures more directly on the Charter. For example, the Commission could initiate infringement proceedings if an MS treats asylum seekers in violation of ECHR or CJEU standards, causing a violation of Art. 4 EU Charter.

We understand that this may be a provocative proposal and it could be construed as the CJEU (and the Commission) putting themselves in the role of the ECHR as the human rights arbiter in Europe.[86] In addition, putting less reliance on more concrete provisions of secondary law than the Charter rights obfuscates the subsidiary nature of values and principles in comparison to rules. However, if the EU wishes to retain the moral high ground, a decisive step in defending its values is necessary, in particular if responses by MSs are grossly inadequate. This is also why we argue that only the most serious or systemic violations would justify such a Charter-focussed infringement procedure.[87]

---

[82] András Jakab, 'The EU Charter of Fundamental Rights as the Most Promising Way of Enforcing the Rule of Law against EU Member States' in Carlos Closa and Dimitry Kochenov (eds), *Reinforcing Rule of Law Oversight in the European Union* (CUP, Cambridge 2016) 194.

[83] Namely, Art. 6(1)(2) TEU and Art. 51(1) and (2) EU Charter. Even following Torres Pérez's argument that Art. 19(1) TEU functions as a trigger for the application of the EU Charter, it does not necessarily mean the application of the EU Charter in all cases. See Torres Pérez (n 81) 112–18.

[84] See, e.g., Kühling (n 17) 500–501; Closa, Kochenov and Weiler (n 60) 12.

[85] Torres Pérez (n 81) 118–19.

[86] Cf. Jakab (n 82) 199–202.

[87] Von Bogdandy, in the context of Art. 2 TEU, speaks of 'red lines'. See von Bogdandy (n 11) 27–9. This proposal, if aimed at systemic or most serious human rights violations, resonates somewhat with Scheppele's systemic infringement procedure proposal. See Kim Lane Scheppele, 'Enforcing the Basic Principles of EU Law through Systemic Infringement Actions' in Carlos Closa and Dimitry Kochenov (eds),

Besides the standard issues tied to infringement proceedings,[88] the setback of this approach is that such measures may not be able to reach across the whole spectrum of issues emanating from illiberal tendencies in MSs.[89] Approaching a systemic deficiency with narrowly aimed kicks is less likely to, by itself, put the system back in its place. A human rights-centred approach is predestined to focus on specific cases, making it hard to grasp the problem of authoritarian practices in institutional development completely.[90] However, this approach has an important advantage, which is that it is usually much easier to establish a violation of a human right than a systemic deficiency in an institutional setup. Another possibility is to combine the two approaches.

Second, the EU institutions could refer to the EU Charter even if a fundamental rights violation has not yet been established but there exists a serious risk of such a violation. The EU Charter would here be used as a value-filled principle base guiding the interpretation in the given case. One such example is the C-715/17 *Commission v Poland et al.* case,[91] where MSs were brought before the CJEU for refusing to participate in the refugee allocation schemes. We believe that a reference to a potential violation of Charter rights which carry strong value credit would importantly benefit the legitimacy of the legal argument in the case. Unfortunately, AG Sharpston stopped just short of this[92] and the CJEU, in that sense, followed suit.[93]

This approach would also send a signal to national courts, which could then interpret national law in line with the EU Charter and invoke it as a reference to a common value system, reinforcing the protection of European values.

Reinforcing Rule of Law Oversight in the European Union (CUP, Cambridge 2016) 105.

[88] E.g. Dimitry Kochenov, 'On Policing Article 2 TEU Compliance: Reverse Solange and Systemic Infringements Analysed' [2013] 33 *Polish Yearbook of International Law* 145, 167–8.

[89] The fundamental rights issue is only part of the existing value clash problem. See Closa, Kochenov and Weiler (n 60) 12.

[90] Similarly, see von Bogdandy and others (n 60) 988, 990.

[91] C-715/17, C-718/17 and C-719/17 *Commission v Poland, Hungary and the Czech Republic* ECLI:EU:C:2020:257.

[92] See AG Sharpston in C-715/17, C-718/17 and C-719/17 EU:C:2019:917 paras 211 *et seq.*, where it is established that even when MSs are arguing for an exception to an EU rule they must act in line with 'the overarching principles' that they accepted when they joined the Union. See also a critique of an early meek stance by EU institutions in Hungary's illiberal democracy turn, in, e.g., Bojan Bugarič, 'Protecting Democracy inside the EU: On Article 7 TEU and the Hungarian Turn to Authoritarianism' in Carlos Closa and Dimitry Kochenov (eds), *Reinforcing Rule of Law Oversight in the European Union* (CUP, Cambridge 2016) 82–101.

[93] CJEU judgment in C-715/17, C-718/17 and C-719/17 *Commission v Poland, Hungary and the Czech Republic*.

Considering Art. 4(3) TEU, the national courts would interpret national law in line with EU values.[94] This would be especially valuable, since if national courts invoke such arguments against their governments the situation with regard to perceived legitimacy is very different to when appeals for change come from the EU.[95]

In such cases, bringing the Charter into the equation reinforces the position of the EU, particularly with a view to the fundamental nature of the values it underpins. When a human rights violation can be established, the strength of the argument is reinforced, since compared to other fundamental values the room for manoeuvre is narrow. The authority of the European Court of Human Rights (ECtHR) will benefit the EU's position too. However, even in cases where there only exists a risk of human rights violations, referring to the EU Charter will benefit the legitimacy of the case.

3.2 The Use of the EU Charter in 'Disputed Waters' – outside the Field of Application of EU Law

The second group includes cases where the EU Charter would generally not be applicable under Art. 51 EU Charter.[96] This is also the main problem with referring to it in cases of fundamental value clashes, which are currently in the fore in the EU, since these deal mainly with institutional developments which generally[97] fall outside the scope of EU competences and the field of application of the EU Charter. The question here is whether Charter rights may, at least to a limited extent,[98] be operationalised outside the scope of EU law in what would otherwise be, described in simplified form, 'purely internal situa-

---

[94] Armin von Bogdandy and Luke Dimitrios Spieker, 'Countering the Judicial Silencing of Critics: Art. 2 TEU Values, Criminal Liability and Reverse Solange' [2019] MPIL Research Paper 2019-08, 4 <https://ssrn.com/abstract=3365013> accessed 17 June 2020.

[95] Jakab (n 82) 198.

[96] For a discussion on the scope of application of the EU Charter following Art. 51, see Koen Lenaerts, 'EU Values and Constitutional Pluralism: The EU System of Fundamental Rights Protection' [2014] 34 *Polish Yearbook of International Law* 135, 137–42.

[97] For a convincing account of how Art. 19(1) TEU should be seen as a trigger for the EU Charter, see Torres Pérez (n 81).

[98] This could be argued at least in connection with some Charter rights, such as the freedom of speech and the prohibition of torture and inhuman or degrading treatment or punishment. See below.

tions'[99] by way of including these rights in Art. 2 TEU, which is considered to be generally applicable.[100]

The above-mentioned different emanations of the same values result in differences in the material and operational scope of these provisions. Following this realisation, we propose a four-part cascaded approach to establishing the justiciability of the values in Art. 2 TEU.

A first reflection of this is a 'mutual amplification' approach[101] achieved through a systematic reading of the Treaties, which to some degree is already accepted by the CJEU when it comes to Arts 2 and 19 TEU and 47 EU Charter.[102] The CJEU accepted this in *LM*[103] and *ASJP*[104] dealing with the independence of the judiciary. There, justiciability of Art. 2 TEU is achieved via a nexus with Art. 19(1)(2) TEU, which, indirectly by establishing a link to EU law, expands the scope of the right to a fair trial before an independent tribunal in Art. 47 EU Charter[105] beyond the confines of Art. 51 EU Charter.[106] As is shown in the literature, Treaty provisions can mutually reinforce one another leading to a qualitative leap in the protection of common values.[107] As Torres Pérez notes, such a reading of Art. 19(2) TEU could become the trigger for the application of the Charter even more generally.[108] In any case, the CJEU is (for now) indirectly applying Art. 47 EU Charter outside the scope of EU law by relying on the authority of Art. 2 TEU, which contains values to be observed regardless of whether an MS is applying EU law or not.[109] This is the first and strongest possible position an Art. 2 TEU value can have since it gains justiciability via Art. 19(2)(1) TEU and clear substance via Art. 47 EU Charter.

Based on these arguments and following von Bogdandy and Spieker,[110] we argue that this approach could also be possible for fundamental rights in the

---

99 The evolution of EU law in general and of free movement law in particular has rendered the concept somewhat obsolete, turning it into a rather rough and inaccurate approximation of the scope of EU law in the majority of cases. See Sara Iglesias Sánchez, 'Purely Internal Situations and the Limits of EU Law: A Consolidated Case Law or a Notion to be Abandoned?' [2018] 14 *European Constitutional Law Review* 7.

100 von Bogdandy (n 11) 8; von Bogdandy and Spieker (n 94) 10.

101 The term is borrowed from von Bogdandy and Spieker (n 94) 14.

102 AG Tanchev defines this link in C-192/18 *Commission v Poland* EU:C:2019:529 as a 'constitutional passerelle'.

103 C-216/18 *LM* paras 49–51.

104 C-64/16 *ASJP* paras 29–32.

105 C-64/16 *ASJP* para 51; C-216/18 *LM* para 53.

106 von Bogdandy and Spieker (n 94) 12; Spieker (n 70).

107 von Bogdandy and Spieker (n 94) 14.

108 Torres Pérez (n 81) 115–18.

109 von Bogdandy and Spieker (n 94) 12.

110 von Bogdandy and Spieker (n 94) 14ff.

EU Charter. Following the line of the *reverse-Solange* idea,[111] the protection of fundamental values in Art. 2 TEU by way of including the core of fundamental rights in the Charter[112] can be adopted. In this sense, the essence of a particular right is understood to be protected under the values in Art. 2 TEU.[113] This would not only confirm the general applicability of parts of the EU Charter but also make them justiciable. Compared to the previous case, the legal position of this second argument is weaker since reference to Art. 19(1)(2) as the anchor for justiciability is generally[114] off the table.[115]

Operationalisation of human rights through Art. 2 TEU was indirectly accepted by the CJEU in C-216/18 *LM* with regard to judicial independence.[116] We believe that other fundamental rights could be operationalised in this way. As with effective judicial protection, Art. 2 TEU would grant general applicability while specific EU Charter provisions would guarantee substance and justiciability.[117]

There are two additional options which are, however, not directly tied to the EU Charter. One is to construe the values in Art. 2 TEU as legal obligations by

---

[111] On the Reverse-Solange idea, see Armin von Bogdandy, Matthias Kottmann, Carlino Antpöhler, Johanna Dickschen, Simon Hentrei and Maja Smrkolj, 'Reverse Solange: Protecting the Essence of Fundamental Rights against EU Member States' [2012] 49 CMLR 489. For the application of Reverse Solange to Art. 2 TEU, see von Bogdandy and Spieker (n 94) 8ff. For a critical analysis of this theory, see Kochenov (n 88) 153–62.

[112] The CJEU uses the term 'the essence' of a fundamental right. See C-216/18 *LM* para 59. Also see Art. 52(1) EU Charter. On the notion of the essence of fundamental rights, see von Bogdandy and others (n 111) 510ff. Also see von Bogdandy and Spieker (n 94) 17–18.

[113] von Bogdandy and Spieker (n 94) 3, on the example of the freedom of expression.

[114] Another, less persuasive, argument could be based on a wide reading of Art. 19(1)(2), under which 'effective legal protection' would entail the protection of an individual under the law, understood broadly, covering more rights than just Art. 47 EU Charter.

[115] Cf. AG Tanchev warns in C-192/18 against a direct use of Art. 47 of the Charter in situations outside the notion of implementation of EU law under Art. 51(1) of the Charter (paras 99–100). See also Martina Coli, 'The Judgment of the CJEU in Commission v. Poland II (C-192/18): The Resurgence of Infringement Procedures as a Tool to Enforce the Rule of Law?' (Diritti Comparati, 21 November 2019) <http://www.diritticomparati.it/judgment-cjeu-commission-v-poland-ii-c-192-18-resurgence-infringement-procedures-tool-enforce-rule-law/> accessed 21 November 2019.

[116] C-216/18 *LM* paras 48, 49 and C-64/16 *ASJP* para 31.

[117] The effectiveness of this approach is reinforced by a recent judgment of the CJEU which takes another step forward by requiring national authorities to disapply if need be for the sake of judicial independence any contrary provision of national law to a Charter right. See C-585/18 *A.K.* paras 155–156. This opinion is also expressed in von Bogdandy and Spieker (n 94) 4.

connecting them to the principle of sincere cooperation. This would imply that MSs are obliged to ensure the full application of the Art. 2 TEU values within their national legal systems. However, relying solely on the general obligations of the MSs' clashes with the existing CJEU case law requires a specific obligation.[118] The other is sole reliance on Art. 2 TEU as a self-standing legal basis for EU action. However tempting it may be, it would enable jurisprudence based solely on value judgements without any further concretisation in the primary and secondary law of the EU. Not only would this head for adjudging on matters of morality but also it would lead to a threat of secular papacy[119] in the hands of the CJEU, which stands for the third possibility too. Rightly, the Court remains reserved.

Most fundamental rights included in the Charter undoubtedly pertain to the fundamental values enshrined in Art. 2. This indirect extension of the use of a part of the EU Charter therefore does not strain the scope of the Charter so as to negatively affect the federal balance within the EU or unduly encroach on national sovereignty and autonomy.[120] Only the parts of fundamental rights entailed in the Charter which are so fundamental ('core rights') that they belong within Art. 2 TEU obtain general application and justiciability. Charter rights in their entirety only apply where an MS is implementing EU law, therefore complying with Art. 51(1) of the Charter.[121]

Splitting values between core and non-core values is of course a doubled-edged sword. Any substantive breach of the core values of the Union reveals a denial of elementary commonality and implies that the unbearable situation will be resolved through agents and processes different from these values. Despite this and referring to already proposed methods, we suggest that several groups of rights in the EU Charter could be identified as belonging to the 'core' of human rights, thus falling within the material scope of Art. 2 TEU.[122]

This understanding of Charter rights as fundamental values on which the EU is based is made less problematic by the fact that all the EU MSs are (1) members of the Council of Europe, and (2) protect these fundamental rights in

---

[118] E.g. C-609/17 and C-610/17 *TSN* EU:C:2019:981 para 53.

[119] Ronald Dworkin, 'Secular Papacy' in Robert Badinter and Stephen Breyer (eds), *Judges in Contemporary Democracy: An International Conversation Preface* (NYU Press, New York 2004) 67.

[120] See Art. 4(2) TEU.

[121] von Bogdandy and Spieker (n 94) 17. On the broad interpretation of this notion by the CJEU, see Chapter 2 in this volume.

[122] See n 98. On the notion of the essence of fundamental rights, see von Bogdandy and others (n 111) 510ff; Maja Brkan, 'The Concept of Essence of Fundamental Rights in the EU Legal Order: Peeling the Onion to Its Core' [2018] 14 *European Constitutional Law Review* 332.

their own constitutions.[123] As has been explained, the latter were a source for the formulation of the EU's values themselves and in a sense the protection of these (decoupled) values is now, in cases of deviations by MSs, vested in the EU. Applying the EU Charter beyond a narrow reading of Art. 51(1) EU Charter in only extreme cases therefore does not create new or unexpected obligations for MSs but instead only reprimands them for violations of their already existing obligations under international, national and EU law.

Additionally, looking at Art. 2 TEU values, one might ask oneself why only the value of the rule of law would find its legal justiciability and all the other fundamental values in the same provision would not. Why would anyone a priori treat the rule of law as a value more favourably than democracy? This seems coincidental, perhaps strengthening the expounded systemic argument.

4. CONCLUSION

Two processes of decoupling, namely of EU from national constitutional values and of 'fields covered by EU law' from the 'implementing EU law' notion together produce a synergy that sways rigid limits of the EU institutional design into a more coherent protection of the common values. Putting strong, yet still relative, decoupling of the EU and national values into a historical context reveals that, first, EU institutions use an autonomous understanding of values as a shield against national interpretation of them and, second, they apply it now as a spear against deviating national conceptions of common values in the EU. While the Chinese idiom of attacking one's shield with one's own spear appears to have a completely different meaning, we should still be wary of the literal understanding of it in the current context of solving crises in the EU. While trying to prevent national deviations from the common values, it is of utmost importance to remain unreservedly loyal to them. Only in this way can the full circle of the autonomous nature of EU values, as discussed in this chapter, remain stable.

The EU has gradually developed an immune system against intrusions into the values it cherishes the most. As an overt expression of values common to the union of European states, the EU Charter should be brought from uncharted waters into the common vocabulary of value protection. As has been shown, there are several paths for using the Charter which would enable this without disturbing the balance between state sovereignty and the EU's autonomy. The force applied by the EU to deflect national attempts at fundamental value distortion, and the proposed paths taken, should correspond to the seriousness of the attempts.

---

123 Similarly, see C-216/18 *LM* para 57.

Putting all the eggs into the basket of legal remedies would, however, be a symptom of misdiagnosis. Reliance on specific values, including the rule of law, has its limits. In other words, and figuratively speaking, a modified Peter Principle for values informs us that the tendency in most organisational hierarchies, such as that of the EU, is for every value to gain prominence in the resolution of conflicts until it reaches the level of its non-utility. Warnings that law has a limited capacity to resolve hard cases of populist encroachment on democracy, separation of powers and the rule of law are not new but they are becoming more ominous.[124] Jakab put it bluntly: 'thinking that the rule of law is an Archimedean point in modern constitutionalist states is lawyerly hubris'.[125] Nevertheless, shying away from the exploration of new legal pathways in the noble endeavour to protect common values would deny their central importance in the fabric of any non-homogeneous society. We consider, optimistically, that the current institutional design of the EU still offers some room for further strengthening of the legal impact of values and principles without compromising it. In our view, bringing the EU Charter, the mutually agreed codification and concretisation of the core values of the EU, in from unchartered waters while maintaining the institutional design intact is the right path.

---

[124] Bojan Bugarič, 'Can Law Protect Democracy? Legal Institutions as "Speed Bumps"' [2019] 11 *Hague Journal on the Rule of Law* 447.

[125] András Jakab, 'Stakeholder Contribution on Rule of Law' (European Commission, 18 July 2019) <https://ec.europa.eu/info/sites/info/files/stakeholder_contribution_on_rule_of_law_-_prof._dr._andras_jakab_0.pdf> accessed 22 November 2019.

5. Comment: the standard of fundamental rights protection according to the EU Charter: what is the role of national standards (and courts)?

Nicole Lazzerini

INTRODUCTION

The reflection that follows is prompted by an interesting point made by Saša Zagorc and Marjan Kos in Chapter 4. They observe that the drafting of the EU Charter and the subsequent recognition of its primary law status contributed to a 'decoupling' of the fundamental rights systems[1] of the Member States from that of the EU.

The phenomenon described by Zagorc and Kos has distant roots. Since the judgment in *Internationale Handelsgesellschaft*,[2] the Court of Justice of the European Union (CJEU), has been emphasising that '[the] protection of [fundamental] rights, whilst inspired by the constitutional traditions common to the Member States, must be ensured within the framework of the structure and objectives of the [Union]'.[3] This approach reflects the Union's *existential* need to ensure the uniformity and effectiveness of its law, which would be compromised if the Member States could systematically rely on their domestic catalogues of fundamental rights to override contrasting EU law provisions.[4]

---

1 More precisely, Zagorc and Kos refer to the EU's and the Member States' value systems. The focus in this commentary will be limited to fundamental rights (Article 6 Treaty on European Union (TEU)) rather than to values (Article 2 TEU).

2 Case 11/70 *Internationale Handelsgesellschaft mbH v Einfuhr- und Vorratsstelle für Getreide und Futtermittel* [1970] EU:C:1970:114.

3 Ibid., para. 4.

4 Ibid., para. 3.

Moreover, the justification for a (partly) autonomous system of fundamental rights protection in the EU is also substantive. As Advocate General Bot observed in his opinion in *Melloni*,

> fundamental rights reflect the choices of a [community] as regards the proper balance to be achieved between the interests of individuals and those of the community to which they belong [, which] is closely linked to assessments which are specific to the legal order concerned, relating particularly to the social, cultural and historical context of that order, and cannot therefore be transposed automatically to other contexts.[5]

In this respect, I agree with Zagorc and Kos that the Charter, being tailored to the specific features and needs of the Union, has enhanced the degree of autonomy of the EU system of fundamental rights from those of the Member States.

At the same time, however, I believe that the Charter – and more generally the legal and judicial environment that has been taking shape since the recognition of its primary law status – has an interesting potential to act as a bridge to national (constitutional) standards, rather than as a pair of scissors. To substantiate this claim, I will first discuss the current approach of the Court of Justice to the determination of the standard of fundamental rights protection. I will argue that it is imbued – rightly, in my view – with a subsidiarity rationale. As a second step, I will reflect on how, thanks to the role of national courts, the Court's approach may become more open to the contribution of the Member States' constitutional standards.

THE COURT, THE CHARTER AND CONSTITUTIONAL STANDARDS: AN APPROACH INSPIRED BY SUBSIDIARITY

The Charter contains two references to the 'constitutional traditions common to the Member States'. According to the fifth recital in the Preamble, the Charter reaffirms the rights as they result, *inter alia*, from those traditions. Article 52(4) then lays down an *ad hoc* interpretative rule for this set of rights, which 'shall be interpreted in harmony with those traditions'. In addition, Article 53 states that '[n]othing in [the] Charter shall be interpreted as restricting or adversely affecting human rights and fundamental freedoms as recognised, in their respective fields of application, by (…) the Member States' constitutions'.

---

5 Case C-399/11 *Melloni* [2013] Opinion of AG Bot, ECLI:EU:C:2012:600, para. 109.

So far, the Court of Justice has never referred to Article 52(4). By contrast, it engaged with the meaning and implications of Article 53 in the well-known *Melloni* preliminary ruling.[6]

The Court stressed that primacy 'is an essential feature of the EU legal order' and rejected the interpretation whereby Article 53 would grant precedence to higher constitutional standards of fundamental rights protection. At the same time, however, the Court did not read Article 53 as a safeguard against the possibility that Member States rely on the Charter as a justification to lower domestic standards of protection *outside* the field of Union law. Had the Court endorsed this interpretation, Article 53 would have been deprived of any autonomous meaning, given that Article 51 already establishes that the Charter is legally binding on the Member States only *within* the field of Union law.[7]

In fact, taking some distance from the wording of Article 53, the Court read this clause as granting the application of constitutional standards only where the EU act or provision at issue does not itself establish a common standard of protection, leaving it to national implementing measures *as long as* 'the level of protection provided for by the Charter, as interpreted by the Court, and the primacy, unity and effectiveness of EU law are not thereby compromised'.[8] By contrast, when the standard is determined by the EU act or provision, there is no space for constitutional protection. Instead, one could challenge the compatibility with the Charter of the EU harmonised standard.

In my view, this interpretation of Article 53 is an expression of – and gives substance to – the concept of subsidiarity endorsed by the Charter. Notably, Article 51(1) states '[t]he provisions of [the] Charter are addressed to the institutions, bodies, offices and agencies of the Union with due regard for the principle of subsidiarity'.[9] I read this as an invitation to carefully consider *whether* the effective achievement of the objectives pursued by the act at issue requires the harmonisation of the standard of protection or, by contrast, it is

---

6 Case C-399/11 *Melloni* [2013] ECLI:EU:C:2013:107, para. 26.

7 See Case C-617/10 *Åkerberg Fransson* [2013] ECLI:EU:C:2013:105, paras 17 to 22.

8 *Melloni* [judgment], cit., 60.

9 See also the fifth recital in the Preamble to the Charter ('This Charter reaffirms, with due regard for the powers and tasks of the Union and for the principle of subsidiarity, ...'). Arguably, the references to subsidiarity in the Preamble and Article 51(1) of the Charter should not be read through the lens of Article 5(3) TFEU, concerning subsidiarity as a limit to the exercise of EU non-exclusive competences: on the one hand, the Charter does not confer competences or powers on the Union (Articles 6(1) TEU and 51(2) Charter); on the other hand, the duty of the EU institutions to respect the Charter cuts across any competences attributed by the Treaties, regardless of their nature.

more appropriate to defer to national standards. The primary addressees of this invitation are the institutional actors involved in the EU law-making process, whereas national courts are not *directly* involved at this stage. However, the Member States' representatives within the Council and national parliaments should approach the question(s) of *which* common standard of fundamental rights protection is desirable, *if any*, in the light of the respective domestic standards and the relevant case law.

The interpretation of Article 53 provided by the Court in *Melloni* adds teeth to this subsidiarity rationale by delineating the consequences of each alternative (common European standard vs national standards). Moreover, it sets the framework for the contribution of national courts, in cooperation with the Court of Justice, to the determination of the standard of protection. Concerning this, it is convenient to address the two scenarios identified in *Melloni* one by one.

A NOVEL FRAMEWORK FOR JUDICIAL COOPERATION: THE ROLE OF NATIONAL COURTS IN SITUATIONS WHERE THE STANDARD OF PROTECTION IS NOT HARMONISED …

When the level of fundamental rights protection is not harmonised by EU legislation, the conditions identified by the Court of Justice in *Melloni* may suggest that in practice the space for national standards is very limited. Notably, the requirement that the primacy, unity and effectiveness of EU law cannot be compromised by the application of those standards secures a significant margin of appreciation for the Court of Justice.[10] However, the Court may use this to accommodate national choices concerning the protection of fundamental rights. The '*Taricco/M.A.S.* saga' is a case in point.

In the *Taricco* judgment,[11] on a request for preliminary ruling by a first instance court, the Court of Justice held that a provision contained in the Italian Criminal Code was incompatible with Article 325 of the Treaty on the Functioning of the European Union (TFEU) on the protection of the financial interests of the Union and should be disapplied. The Court also added that such a disapplication did not infringe the rights of the accused, notably the rule of the non-retroactivity of criminal law as guaranteed by Article 49(1) of the Charter.

10 Cf N. De Boer, 'Addressing rights divergence under the Charter: *Melloni*' [2013] 50 *Common Market Law Review* 1083, p. 1096.

11 Case C-105/14 *Taricco and Others* (*Taricco I*) [2015] ECLI:EU:C:2015:555.

This conclusion, which endorsed the case law of the European Court of Human Rights on the *procedural* nature of the regime of limitation periods,[12] was highly problematic for the Italian legal order, where that regime belongs, by contrast, to *substantive* criminal law; the *constitutional* principle that offences and penalties must be defined by law therefore applies. Thus, in the following *M.A.S.* case (also known as *Taricco II*)[13] the problem was brought before the Italian Constitutional Court, which decided to raise a reference for preliminary ruling to the Court of Justice on the scope of the duty of disapplication established in *Taricco*.[14]

Relying on its *controlimiti* doctrine, the Constitutional Court made clear that the principle of legality is an overriding constitutional principle, which the primacy of EU law cannot discard. The Court of Justice, after recalling that the *controlimiti* issue '[was] not drawn to its attention in the case in which the *Taricco* judgment was given'[15] concluded that, in the absence of harmonisation of the rules on limitation periods, '[t]he Italian Republic was thus, at that time, free to provide that in its legal system those rules (…) form part of substantive criminal law, and are thereby, like those rules, subject to the principle that offences and penalties must be defined by law'.[16] The underlying premise to this conclusion was the distinction introduced in *Melloni* between situations 'entirely determined' by Union law or not.[17]

From the perspective of judicial interaction, the *Taricco/M.A.S.* saga triggers (at least) two considerations.

On the one hand, the rather opaque reasoning in the *M.A.S* preliminary ruling (which is, in principle, criticisable)[18] and the outcome achieved (notably, the 'permission' not to disapply a national provision that was previously held incompatible with EU – secondary – law)[19] suggest that the Court of Justice was willing to use its leeway under the *Melloni* test in order to accommodate

---

12 This classification implies that the regime of limitation periods does not fall within the scope of the legality principle under Article 7 European Convention on Human Rights.

13 Case C-42/17 *M.A.S. and M.B.* (*Taricco II*) [2018] ECLI:EU:C:2017:936.

14 Corte costituzionale, ordinanza n. 24/2017 (26 January 2017), ECLI:IT:COST:2017:24.

15 *M.A.S. and M.B.*, cit., para. 28.

16 Ibid., para. 45.

17 The reference to the *Melloni* test in *Taricco II* is indirect via a quotation of para. 29 of *Åkerberg Fransson*, which in turn refers to *Melloni*.

18 See N. Lazzerini, 'Il rapporto tra primato del diritto dell'Unione e tutela costituzionale dei diritti fondamentali nella sentenza *Taricco-bis*: buona la seconda?' [2018] *Rivista di diritto internazionale* 234.

19 Cf C. Rauchegger, 'National constitutional rights and the primacy of EU law: *M.A.S.*' [2018] 55 *Common Market Law Review* 1521.

fundamental national value choices (not compromising the Charter standard) and to avoid a hard conflict with a Member State's Constitutional Court.

On the other hand, this judicial saga highlights that the attempt to reconcile the Member States' choices concerning the protection of fundamental rights with the effective achievement of common European goals should not be the consequence (and last resort solution) of a collision between the Court of Justice and the constitutional courts. The need for improved cooperation by both the national and the European sides is quite evident: domestic courts should provide all relevant information concerning their constitutional frameworks which may be touched (or even upset) by the findings of the Court of Justice; in turn, the latter should devote closer attention to these frameworks and to the case law of constitutional courts before concluding that the more protective national standard cannot be maintained, as it did in the *Taricco I* judgment.[20]

... AND IN SITUATIONS WHERE THE STANDARD OF PROTECTION IS HARMONISED AT THE EU LEVEL

In the alternative scenario identified in *Melloni*, namely the situation where the standard of fundamental rights protection is harmonised at the Union level, the institutional actors involved in the EU law-making process should bear the primary responsibility, under Article 52(4) of the Charter, to take into account the constitutional frameworks and practices of the Member States on the issues dealt with, or touched by, draft legislation.

In line with the approach followed by the Court of Justice in its case law on the general principles of Union law, Article 52(4) must not be read as endorsing either a 'lowest common denominator' approach or a 'maximum standard' approach. As the Explanations to the Charter[21] point out, 'the Charter rights concerned should be interpreted in a way offering a high standard of protection which is adequate for the law of the Union and in harmony with the common constitutional traditions'. In other words, against the backdrop of these traditions, and taking into account the goals pursued by the measure at issue, the EU

---

[20] In its recent judgment on the European Central Bank's decisions on the Public Sector Purchase Programme, the German Federal Constitutional Court observed that the Court of Justice would exceed the mandate conferred on it by Article 19(1) TEU if 'the general legal principles that are common to the laws of Member States [were] manifestly disregarded'. See BVerfG, Judgment of the Second Senate of 5 May 2020 – 2 BvR 859/15, notably para. 112.

[21] Explanations relating to the Charter of Fundamental Rights, OJ C 303, 14 December 2007, pp. 17–35.

harmonised standard must be appreciated as offering a high level of protection (though not necessarily *the highest*).

Does this mean that an *uncommon* constitutional tradition cannot contribute to the interpretation of the Charter? I would argue that the rationale behind Article 52(4) suggests that it can when the relevant standard stands out because it offers *uncommonly high* protection. The definition of an EU harmonised standard, in conformity with the Charter, implies that more protective national standards cannot supersede the common one. Accordingly, it would be wise to consider the negative consequences that the harmonised level of protection may have in some Member States: whilst the maximum standard approach cannot be generalised, one cannot exclude *a priori* the possibility of reconciling the objectives pursued by the legislation at issue and the *uncommonly high* protection afforded to the fundamental rights involved by one Member State. By endorsing the latter standard, EU harmonisation would contribute to enhancing the protection of fundamental rights in the European legal space. The definition of a harmonised standard would otherwise inevitably entail a sacrifice of existing more protective national standards and an impediment to the development of broader protection in the other Member States.

Now, the main obstacle to this approach is of a political nature: as practice shows, the Member State governments may indeed be willing to level down the protection of the fundamental rights involved in order to find a compromise on the proposed legislation.[22] Here comes the role of national courts, in cooperation with the Court of Justice. Rather than challenging the EU harmonised standard (simply) because it does not align with (or leave space for) the allegedly broader domestic standard, national courts should act as guardians of the methodology endorsed by Article 52(4). In other words, they should trigger a review by the Court of Justice when, having regard to the relevant constitutional frameworks and practices of the Member States, and to the objective(s) pursued by the EU act at issue, the harmonised standard cannot be regarded as offering a 'high protection'.

CONCLUSION

The Charter has the potential to fuel a process of 'decoupling' between the fundamental rights systems of the Member States, on the one hand, and the EU's, on the other. At the same time, however, it offers an occasion (and

---

22 The case of asylum legislation is illustrative: see C. Favilli, 'The standard of fundamental rights protection in the field of asylum: The case of the right to an effective remedy between EU law and the Italian Constitution' [2019] 12 *Review of European Administrative Law* 167.

a framework) for reconceptualising the relationship between the EU's and constitutional standards of fundamental rights protection in a logic of mutual enrichment. The Court of Justice, being the ultimate interpreter of the Charter, is a crucial player in this respect. Interestingly, its current approach to the determination of the standard of fundamental rights protection also assigns – in principle, at least – a significant role to national courts. Thus, the formal premises for the abovementioned logic of mutual enrichment have been set. The following essential step should be a stable attitude of direct and indirect dialogue between the Court of Justice and national courts, inspired, on both sides, by the common objective of ensuring a high standard of fundamental rights protection.

6. The potential and the limits of the impact of the Charter on constitutional jurisprudence

Matej Accetto

1. INTRODUCTION

On 23 December 2009, three weeks after the entry into force of the Treaty of Lisbon and with it the Charter of Fundamental Rights of the European Union (the Charter, or CFR), in the *Detiček* case the Court of Justice (CJEU) issued the first judgment based on a reference for a preliminary ruling from a Slovenian court.[1] In substantive terms, the CJEU judgment was one of the first decisions (if not the very first one) of the Court of Justice after the formal entry into force of the Charter which meaningfully relied on it. In a delicate matter concerning parental responsibility and the rights of the child, the Court invoked Article 24 CFR, which helped guide it to a decision.[2] Apart from resolving a sensitive case necessitating an urgent procedure, however, the decision – and the preliminary reference itself, lodged with the Court only some two months earlier – also signified a symbolic end to the reference drought of Slovenian courts, which had finally made use of the preliminary rulings procedure some five and a half years after Slovenia acceded to the EU. This drought was a point of some concern. During a visit to Slovenia in spring 2009, the then vice president of the European Parliament Diane Wallis and the Slovenian Justice Minister Aleš Zalar met with Slovenian judges to try to identify the reason. A lack of familiarity with EU law on the part of the judges was still the preferred candidate five years after the accession. Once the first reference was finally made, there was therefore a collective sigh of relief. While the case was still pending, the judge who drafted it was even awarded a special commendation 'for the greatest

1 Case C-403/09 PPU *Detiček*, ECLI:EU:C:2009:810.
2 See *Detiček*, n. 1 above, paras 53–61.

accomplishments in recognition and establishment of Slovenia in the EU' by the organisers of a conference on EU law.[3]

Ten years later, contemplating on the success of the CFR in guiding national jurisprudence and judicial interactions between the CJEU and its national counterparts, a similar type of hopeful optimism may be in order. With notable exceptions, the Charter largely seems to be absent from the daily practice of national courts. In Slovenia, for instance, in the first nine years until the end of 2018 there were a little fewer than 400 cases decided by the higher-level ordinary courts in which the Charter was referenced, with almost 77 per cent of these cases comprising decisions by the specialised Administrative Court,[4] and with over 83 per cent of all the cases pertaining to one exceptional area, that of asylum and immigration. For its part, the Slovenian Constitutional Court has referred to the Charter in some three dozen cases, and many of these did not include a substantive reference in the Court's own assessment of the case. All over Europe, national reports paint a similarly reticent picture.[5]

This highlights the important question of the nature and the extent of the necessity or utility of the Charter, something that was already raised at its original inception and that has not (yet) lost its currency almost two decades later. Has the Charter filled an important lacuna or entered an already saturated field of laws and mechanisms of human rights protection? The question can be posed in the context of the EU law framework and perhaps even more in the context of national constitutional orders, and it invites us to contemplate the possible 'added value' of the Charter for the EU constitutional framework, for national constitutional jurisprudence and, finally, for judicial interactions between the European and national judicial actors, which is a common theme of the contributions to this volume.

In endeavouring to provide (a small part of) the answer, we now also have the benefit of the first ten years of its use by courts, reticent though this may be. After all, it is precisely and only through the use of the Charter by courts (the Court of Justice and its national counterparts) that the full extent of the Charter's force can be revealed. In saying this, we merely echo Cardozo, who

---

[3] On this see Matej Accetto, '(Ustavno)sodna presoja in predhodno odločanje v pravu EU' [2011] (11) *Pravna praksa* 24, 24.

[4] A more thorough overview of the use of the CFR by Slovenian courts is provided in Matej Accetto, 'Trials, Tributes and Tribulations: EU Charter before Slovenian Courts' in Michal Bobek and Jeremias Adams-Prassl (eds), *The EU Charter of Fundamental Rights in the Member States* (Hart, Oxford 2020). In this report, reference is also made to Cardozo to frame the discussion of the Charter's possible added value, which is repeated below.

[5] For an overview, see the contributions to the edited volume cited in the preceding footnote.

stated that once it is judicially recognised a principle will tend to expand to the limits of its logic, even if it is not always consistently followed by courts[6] and even when it needs to be balanced against the limits of its history.[7] Ten years is most certainly too short a period to reach the limits of the Charter's logic, but perhaps we may at least identify the direction in which these limits are sought. Then, we are left with the final and perhaps the most difficult question: which of the (judicial) developments identified would not have occurred *but for* the Charter, i.e. in what ways would the landscape of human rights jurisprudence – and judicial interactions – be different if the Charter had never been adopted?

To provide some thoughts and tentative conclusions on these issues, this chapter proceeds as follows. First, it provides a brief retrospective look at the 'constitutionalisation' of the EU legal order and the development of EU human rights law prior to the adoption of the Charter. Then it assesses the role of the Charter in the development of EU law, and how the Charter may have substantively affected national constitutional jurisprudence. Finally, it attempts to identify the impact of the Charter on judicial interactions between European courts, in particular between national (constitutional) courts and the Court of Justice.

2. EUROPE'S CONSTITUTIONAL PROJECT AND HUMAN RIGHTS: A LOOK AT THE PAST

The story of the important and sometimes pivotal role of law in the process of European integration is a familiar one. We can remind ourselves of Hallstein's characterisation of the European Community as a Rechtsgemeinschaft, meant not only as a 'community of law' based on respect for the rule of law but even, lacking the usual substrate of people and territory, as a 'creation of law';[8] of Stein famously lauding the seminal role of the European Court of Justice in fashioning the new polity's constitutional order;[9] and of the way in which the

---

6 Benjamin N. Cardozo, *The Growth of the Law* (Yale University Press, New Haven 1927) 57.

7 Benjamin N. Cardozo, *The Nature of the Judicial Process* (Yale University Press, New Haven 1921) 51. For more on his views on the four methods in the judicial process, see Edwin W. Patterson, 'Cardozo's Philosophy of Law: Part II' [1939] 88 *University of Pennsylvania Law Review and American Law Register* 156, 160.

8 Walter Hallstein, *Die Europäische Gemeinschaft* (Econ Verlag, Düsseldorf 1974) 33.

9 Eric Stein, 'Lawyers, Judges and the Making of a Transnational Constitution' [1981] 75 *American Journal of International Law* 1, 1.

integration process was perceived to be, and at times surely was, driven by law and the members of the legal (interpretative) community.[10]

Even this familiar tale, however, needs to be understood in its context. The success of the European integration project is also owed to accommodating both idealist and realist visions of European integration, fashioning not only its particular brand of a supranational legal order caught between international and constitutional law but also a supranational political order caught between a classic international organisation and a federal polity. The viability of this construction depended not only on the initiative of those advocating for an emerging European polity but also on its acceptance by those who might have objected to it. It was by understanding and accommodating these particular interests that a common polity could be construed.

In a provocative essay on European constitutionalism, Allott describes the European Union as a 'mass of contradictions', among them 'a treaty [which] is not a constitution', 'the "masters of the Treaty" heresy', 'a final court which does not have the final word', and so on.[11] Allott considers these contradictions to be evidence of Europe's failure in the process of social self-constitution,[12] with the Member States still standing apart as solitary points in need of a Euclidean *ecthesis* to become a true community.[13] However, it may have been precisely by appreciating the many contradictions defining its integration process that the Union could develop as a supranational polity as well as a legal community.

The same can be said of its supranational legal order. In substantive terms, it was helped by the fact that the doctrines of direct effect and supremacy as developed by the Court were not without respect for the national legal orders.[14] In structural terms, the requirement for unanimity for 'constitutional' decisions which had been in practice for several decades for all decision-making could also be used to advance the supranational character of the established order.

---

10 See, e.g., Harm Schepel and Rein Wesseling, 'The Legal Community: Judges, Lawyers, Officials and Clerks in the Writing of Europe' [1997] 3 *European Law Journal* 165.

11 Philip Allott, 'Epilogue: Europe and the Dream of Reason' in Joseph H.H. Weiler and Marlene Wind (eds), *European Constitutionalism beyond the State* (Cambridge University Press, Cambridge 2003) 215.

12 Ibid. at 223–4.

13 Ibid. at 203.

14 See the critical account of EU concepts when compared to classical international law in Ole Spiermann, 'The Other Side of the Story: An Unpopular Essay on the Making of the European Community Legal Order' [1999] 10 *European Journal of International Law* 763.

If any state could veto a measure from even being adopted, why would it later deny its supranational effect?[15]

It was in this context that the Court of Justice first developed the doctrine of fundamental rights in EU law with little to no constitutional foothold in the Treaties. In the early years, being confined to a more textual interpretation of the Treaties, the Court's original stance was that fundamental rights were simply not a feature of (the then) Community law.[16] That stance might not have raised particular problems at the beginning of the 1960s in the context of a law-making process that was still dependent on the requirement for unanimity and at a time when the fundamental doctrines of a new supranational legal order were yet to be developed. By the late 1960s, however, the established doctrines of direct effect and supremacy, coupled with the planned – even if practically limited by virtue of the Luxembourg Compromise – shift to majority voting in the Council, rendered it constitutionally fraught and politically untenable. Barring a treaty revision, the Court of Justice had little choice but to resort to its own version of transnational judicial interaction: drawing inspiration from the constitutional traditions common to the Member States (and international documents, notably the European Convention on Human Rights (ECHR)), it recognised fundamental rights as enshrined in the general unwritten principles of EU law.[17]

This approach, call it functionalism or judicial activism, posed a few difficult questions of its own. First, while it underscored the significant contribution of the Member States' legal orders and their (constitutional) courts to identifying and shaping the rights that should receive judicial recognition by the Court of Justice as general principles of EU law, it also brought into focus the difficulties in determining the precise scope and content of these rights at the European level, in particular when – or rather insofar as – national standards differed.[18] The content of a given general principle of EU law could

---

[15] See, e.g., Joseph H.H. Weiler, 'Journey to an Unknown Destination: A Retrospective and Prospective of the European Court of Justice in the Arena of Political Integration' [1993] 31 *Journal of Common Market Studies* 417, 436.

[16] See a stark expression of this position, albeit in the ambit of the Treaty establishing the European Coal and Steel Community, in Joined Cases 36, 37, 38 and 40/59 *Geitling v. High Authority*, ECLI:EU:C:1960:36, [1960] ECR 423, at 439: 'Moreover Community law, as it arises under the ECSC Treaty, does not contain any general principle, express or otherwise, guaranteeing the maintenance of vested rights.'

[17] Case 29/69 *Stauder*, ECLI:EU:C:1969:57, [1969] ECR 419, para. 7; Case 11/70 *Internationale Handelsgesellschaft*, ECLI:EU:C:1970:114, [1970] ECR 1125, paras 3–4.

[18] On such challenges, see Joseph H.H. Weiler, *The Constitution of Europe: 'Do the New Clothes Have an Emperor?' and Other Essays on European Integration* (Cambridge University Press, Cambridge 1999) 102–16.

therefore not be easily determined either by reference to any single national order or through a comparative analysis of all national legal orders, since it was both a mix of various legal influences[19] and developed in the shadow of EU law as an autonomous legal order with an accentuated role for the Court of Justice to reshape it as required in the European context.[20]

Consequently, and just as importantly, this development highlighted the difficult challenge of reconciling possible tensions between EU law and the national legal orders that were likely to arise, especially since in practical terms EU fundamental rights operated as work migrants of sorts,[21] departing from the national legal orders as sources of inspiration for the Court of Justice but then returning back home enshrined – and sometimes substantively transformed – as general principles of EU law. It also put into question the proper role of the Court of Justice, having to navigate the jurisprudential minefield while trying to avoid charges of unbridled judicial discretion and 'legislative' activism as an engine of integration.[22]

Finally, while the national constitutional frameworks certainly preceded the elaboration of an EU fundamental rights regime, was this really a case of the European level trailing – or even being forced to catch up with – the well-established national regimes, or were they but two parts of the same transformative development?[23]

In any event, the resulting regime of rights protection in EU law was therefore neither clearly (pre-)defined nor particularly well-suited to resolving pos-

---

[19] Notably, in the early days, French administrative law and jurisprudence (which was the first to incorporate general legal principles) and German constitutional law with the bolstered interpretative role of the constitutional court – see Tim Koopmans, 'General Principles of Law in European and National Systems of Law: A Comparative View' in Ulf Bernitz and Joakim Nergelius (eds), *General Principles of European Community Law* (Kluwer Law International, The Hague 2000) 26.

[20] Takis Tridimas, *The General Principles of EC Law* (Oxford University Press, Oxford 1999) 4.

[21] According to Koopmans, n. 19 above, at 25.

[22] For some, like the early critic of the Court's alleged activism Rasmussen, the Court was too likely to draw inspiration for its decisions from political considerations – see Hjalte Rasmussen, *On Law and Policy in the European Court of Justice: A Comparative Study in Judicial Policy-Making* (Martinus Nijhoff Publishers, Dordrecht/Boston 1986) 62. For others, the Court managed to avoid the appeal of 'legislating' – see Harm Schepel and Erhard Blankenburg, 'Mobilizing the European Court of Justice' in Graínne de Búrca and Joseph H.H. Weiler (eds), *The European Court of Justice* (Oxford University Press, Oxford 2001) 41.

[23] For the proponents of the latter view, see, e.g., Giacomo Delledone and Federico Fabbrini, 'The Founding Myth of European Human Rights Law: Revisiting the Role of National Courts in the Rise of EU Human Rights Jurisprudence' [2019] 44 *European Law Review* 178, 194.

sible tensions between EU and national law, which was evidenced by varied constitutional challenges to the unfettered reign of the supranational doctrines of EU law by national courts.[24] Fundamental rights also feature in two of Allott's 19 contradictions in the European project mentioned above:[25] he criticises them for not being *fundamental*, because they were developed as general principles of law rather than hierarchically elevated criteria for the validity of EU law, and for being *disintegrated*, because EU law lacks a mechanism to resolve discrepancies between two or three human rights regimes in individual Member States (EU, ECHR and national).

This criticism, again, can be tempered by understanding the limits of the Court-centred development of human rights as general principles of EU law. After all, what other choice did the Court of Justice have given the lack of a more surefooted constitutional foothold in the Treaties? If what the EU fundamental rights regime needed was a transformative or self-constitutive moment of *ecthesis*, surely it was not for the Court of Justice but for the European constitution-makers to provide it? Was this challenge addressed by the Charter? And if so, was it met?

3. THE CHARTER AND NATIONAL (CONSTITUTIONAL) JURISPRUDENCE

The point that the Charter was finally filling a crucial lacuna in the EU constitutional order was certainly often made in many public debates on the Union in the run-up to the referenda on the Constitutional Treaty. Finally, or so the claim would go, EU primary law would contain a bill of rights, which is indispensable in any constitutional order, remedying a regrettable omission of the original European construction and providing citizens with a clear expression of a catalogue of their inalienable rights that the Union was there to promote and protect. On the face of it, this claim was so indisputable as to make it almost redundant. Indeed, who could object to the idea of adding a bill of rights to a constitutional document that had previously lacked one?

However, reservations have been expressed about the implied corollary of such appeals to the Charter's ostensible added value – that this formal lacuna also signified a substantive drought, i.e. that before the Charter EU

---

24 There is no need to rehash this story here. I provide a more thorough account, including the *Solange* cases of the German Federal Constitutional Court, in Matej Accetto, 'Constitutional Courts and EU Law' in Maria Lúcia Amaral and Selma Pedroso Bettencourt (eds), *Estudos em Homenagem ao Conselheiro Presidente, Volume I: Direito Constitucional, Direito Constitucional Europeu, Direito Europeu* (Almedina, Coimbra 2016) 778.

25 Allott, n. 11 above, at 217.

law provided no (adequate) protection of individuals' fundamental rights.[26] What of the respect given to constitutional doctrines and to the ECHR? What of the well-established doctrine of fundamental rights being enshrined in the unwritten general principles of EU law, as elaborated by the Court of Justice and demanding universal recognition in the implementation and application of EU law? Seen through such a critical lens, the public endorsements of the Charter's added value might perhaps be more closely connected to the positioning of the European Union vis-à-vis its Member States than to the position of individual citizens vis-à-vis Union law. Put differently, one could wonder whether a comprehensive bill of rights incorporated in EU primary law might be needed more to substantiate the Union's claim to be a fully functional constitutional order or to address any shortcomings in the various fundamental rights regimes applicable in its Member States.[27]

It may well be that the Charter achieves both of these aspirations to some extent and neither of them fully. As for the assumption that the Charter might be an indispensable cog in the process of constitutionalising the EU, we need only remind ourselves that such a narrative, namely that the operation of EU law and in particular the jurisprudence of the Court of Justice has constitutionalised EU primary law, has been around for several decades and long predated even the drafting, let alone the entry into force of the Charter.[28] Rasmussen and Martinsen have recently been critical of this traditional narrative, claiming that this process was often opposed or checked by the Member States and that the EU has not (yet) been successfully constitutionalised.[29] However, it is also telling that in revisiting the constitutionalisation process, devoting a larger part of their analysis to the earlier years and only a four-page section to developments after the Treaty of Maastricht,[30] they make no reference to the Charter,

---

26 See, e.g., Weiler, n. 18 above, at 334–5, noting that notwithstanding possible gaps in rights protection many European states are defined by a culture of rights saturation rather than rights deprivation and that a point of diminishing returns has been reached as far as adding new lists of rights to the existing catalogues is concerned.

27 The provocative tone of this query notwithstanding, I do not wish to imply that significant lacunae or practical difficulties in protecting fundamental rights would not exist, or that the Union and its citizens would not benefit from a bolstered commitment to human rights, or indeed that human rights might not obtain a(n ever) more central role in the EU framework. See, e.g., the discussion (and further sources listed in fn. 4 on p. 324) in Samantha Besson, 'The European Union and Human Rights: Towards A Post-National Human Rights Institution?' [2006] 6 *Human Rights Law Review* 323, 324–7.

28 See, e.g., the discussion mentioned in Stein, n. 9 above.

29 Morten Rasmussen and Dorte S. Martinsen, 'EU Constitutionalisation Revisited: Redressing a Central Assumption in European Studies' [2019] 25 *European Law Journal* 251, 270–72.

30 Ibid. at 267–70.

let alone discuss its significance in advancing (the acceptance of) constitutional practice in EU law. While the Charter certainly forms part of EU primary law, and can be said to at least enshrine if not establish fundamental rights as one of the pillars of the EU constitutional order,[31] it will not necessarily be seen as a definitive or inevitable element in the constitutionalisation process.

As for the aspiration to provide Union citizens with fundamental rights, on the other hand, while it is true that the Charter was hardly revolutionary in this sense, entering a saturated field of various rights regimes including the doctrine of human rights enshrined in the general principles of EU law, we can remind ourselves that these are exactly the reasons Allott gives when criticising EU fundamental rights as disintegrated and not at all fundamental. On the face of it, it seems that the Charter could provide an answer to his critique: rather than developing them as general principles, the Charter also symbolically enshrines fundamental rights as hierarchically superior criteria for the validity of EU law, and should perhaps also serve as a tool to be used when resolving potential conflicts between the various fundamental rights regimes.

It is hard to see the Charter as bringing about the transformative *ecthesis* of social self-constituting desired by Allott. However, to the extent that it does achieve its potential, it may nevertheless help in both the areas discussed above: help create a clear constitutional foothold for the Union aspiring to achieve a full constitutionalisation of its legal order; and consequently provide a mechanism that integrates and marshals common standards of fundamental rights within the ambit of EU law.

In this regard, the somewhat underwhelming conclusion is that, given the nature of the issue and the context in which the Charter is to operate, ten years may not have been long enough for true transformative change. Its tendency to expand to the limits of its logic may well need more time to come to fruition, all the more so when its impact on national legal orders and national courts is concerned. After all, it is already true that within EU law the development of the Charter's role was incremental rather than monumental, molecular rather than molar, a nice and informative example being offered in the area of free movement law, where the Charter was originally not mentioned much but where a shift from the ECHR to the Charter did slowly occur.[32] Could the same not occur, albeit even more slowly, when it comes to national courts?

---

[31] See, e.g., Koen Lenaerts, 'Exploring the Limits of the EU Charter of Fundamental Rights' [2012] 8 *European Constitutional Law Review* 375, outlining the important ways in which the Charter has informed the jurisprudence of the Court of Justice and focusing on the significance of Article 53 CFR as an expression of constitutional pluralism (at 398) while underscoring the constitutional autonomy of the Union (at 402).

[32] See the account in Hester Kroeze, 'The Substance of Rights: New Pieces of the *Ruiz Zambrano* Puzzle' [2019] 44 *European Law Review* 238, 250–53.

Snapshots of the national court practice in Slovenia, to take the example I am most familiar with, seem to temper this optimism even further.[33] As stated above, while by the end of 2018 there were almost 400 cases (counting only the decisions of higher-level courts) in which a reference to the Charter was made, not only did the vast majority pertain to the area of asylum and immigration but very rarely did a court engage with the Charter in detail, and more rarely still did the Charter form the definitive basis for the court's decision in the case. Instead, the Charter provisions were most often referred to as additional support or rather simply as reaffirmation of standards derived from the relatively extensive bill of rights contained in the Slovenian Constitution.

One notable exception was Article 1 CFR, since the Slovenian Constitution does not contain a similar explicit reference to human dignity as a fundamental right: although it is usually still invoked by courts alongside a constitutional provision such as Article 34 (safeguarding personal dignity and security)[34] or Article 18 (prohibiting torture, inhumane and degrading treatment),[35] in these cases the Charter was brought to the fore precisely because the courts felt that the constitutional foothold of these rights was uncertain.[36] For its part, the Constitutional Court adopted a decision in 2011 in which it also invoked the preamble and Article 1 CFR alongside many other sources in order to substantiate the interpretation of human dignity as a fundamental right forming part of the Slovenian Constitution, which is expressed in a number of constitutional provisions and grounded as a particular constitutional principle in Article 1 of the Constitution (which states that Slovenia is a democratic republic).[37] In the other rare cases where the standards of protection under the Charter and the Constitution were compared, the courts typically found that the Charter provided a standard no higher than the corresponding national provisions.[38]

---

[33] In the following four paragraphs I summarise some of the points elaborated in Accetto, n. 4 above, which contains a more thorough analysis of the Slovenian judicial practice by both ordinary courts and the Constitutional Court.

[34] See, e.g., I U 2750/2017 of 21 December 2017, ECLI:SI:UPRS:2017:I.U.2750.2017.8, paras 40–44.

[35] I U 1921/2012 of 17 January 2013, ECLI:SI:UPRS:2013:I.U.1921.2012.

[36] See, e.g., IV Cp 3279/2013 of 29 January 2014, ECLI:SI:VSLJ:2014:IV.CP.3279.2013, where the Higher Court of Ljubljana explicitly stated that while human dignity was undoubtedly recognised as a constitutional value, it was not clear which part of the Constitution enshrined the principle.

[37] Decision U-I-109/10 of 26 September 2011, ECLI:SI:USRS:2011:U.I.109.10, paras 6–10.

[38] E.g., the decision of the Higher Court of Ljubljana II Cp 4904/2010 of 13 April 2011, ECLI:SI:VSLJ:2011:II.CP.4904.2010, dealing with references to Articles 16(4) and 17(5) CFR.

The same could be said to apply to the jurisprudence of the Slovenian Constitutional Court: while it undoubtedly treats the fundamental rights and general principles in EU law as domestic constitutional principles which are binding with the force of the national constitution,[39] the relatively extensive catalogue of constitutional provisions coupled with the court's broad interpretative approach imbuing constitutionally recognised rights with the scope awarded to corresponding rights in international human rights documents effective in Slovenian law means that the Charter has not featured in a free-standing fashion. Instead, it has typically been used to underscore or at most further bolster particular constitutional rights, such as the right to collective bargaining,[40] children's rights[41] and religious freedom.[42]

Finally, in a case concerning a constitutional complaint filed by the European Central Bank (ECB) against an ordinary court decision which allegedly violated its rights under Articles 22 and 23 of the Constitution, Article 6 ECHR and Article 47 CFR, the Constitutional Court held that in the circumstances of the case the ECB did not have standing to lodge a constitutional complaint alleging a violation of its fundamental rights.[43] The Constitutional Court reached its decision notwithstanding the application of the general principle of effective judicial protection, noting the limits to demands imposed by EU law on national procedural autonomy and concluding that the issue of standing before the Constitutional Court was to be determined by the standards of national law without needing to answer whether, as a matter of EU law, the ECB as an EU institution could invoke the protection of Article 47 of the Charter.[44]

---

39 See, e.g., Decision U-I-155/11 of 18 December 2013, ECLI:SI:USRS:2013:U.I .155.11, para. 14.

40 See Decision U-I-249/10 of 15 March 2012, ECLI:SI:USRS:2012:U.I.249.10, paras 18–24, with Article 28 CFR being used alongside other sources to strengthen interpretation of Article 76 of the Constitution.

41 See Decision Up-748/16 of 25 April 2018, ECLI:SI:USRS:2018:Up.748.16, with Article 24(2) CFR being used alongside other sources and the jurisprudence of the two European courts to recognise the importance of the principle of the child's best interests in interpreting the children's rights provision in Article 56 of the Slovenian Constitution.

42 Decision U-I-92/07 of 15 April 2010, ECLI:SI:USRS:2010:U.I.92.07, paras 77–78 and 84, in which Article 10(1) CFR was again referred to alongside Article 41 of the Constitution and several other international sources, but in which the Court went on to state that the other cited provisions expressed the positive aspect of religious freedom more precisely than the Constitution.

43 Decision U-I-157/16, Up-729/16, Up-55/17 of 19 April 2018, ECLI:SI:USRS: 2018:U.I.157.16.

44 Ibid. para 31. The Court here also made reference to the judgment of the Court of Justice in Case C-521/15 *Spain v. Council*, ECLI:EU:C:2017:982, paras 87 and 89,

Had the Constitutional Court determined otherwise, namely that in the circumstances of the case the question of the ECB's eventual standing depended on interpretation of EU law, not one but two preliminary references to the Court of Justice might have been likely to follow. The first one would have sought to determine whether, as a matter of EU law, the ECB could invoke the Charter in such a manner, and had the answer been yes, in deciding on the merits of the complaint the Constitutional Court might have agreed that the ordinary court erred in disposing of the substantive issue on its own, in which case the usual approach would dictate sending the case back to the ordinary court to remedy its error. As it happened, the preliminary reference was not made. It was, however, made in the earlier *Kotnik* case,[45] in part concerning Article 17(1) of the Charter, where in its follow-up decision the Constitutional Court again reiterated that Articles 33 and 67 of the Constitution ensured the same level of protection of private property and that it would therefore review the alleged violation in the light of the two constitutional provisions but also take into account the preliminary ruling of the Court of Justice in the *Kotnik* case.[46]

These examples also lead us to address the last question: what impact has the Charter had on the frequency or nature of judicial interactions between national courts and their European counterpart?

4. THE CHARTER AND JUDICIAL INTERACTIONS

Elsewhere,[47] I have discussed the different guises of transnational judicial dialogue as conducted from the bench, all of which are also relevant in the present discussion in the context of EU law: *judicial dialogue as inspiration*, courts looking beyond their national borders for inspiration or comparative experiences of other jurisdictions in solving the challenges they face; *judicial*

---

in which the Court of Justice was faced with the issue of Spain invoking Article 41(1) CFR and held that in any event that right reflected a general principle of EU law which Member States could also rely on.

[45] The reference in Case U-I-295/13 of 6 November 2014, decided by the Court of Justice in C-526/14 *Kotnik and Others*, ECLI:EU:C:2016:570. Two further preliminary references were since made by the Constitutional Court in cases C-486/20 and C-45/21, lodged in late 2020 and early 2021, respectively.

[46] Decision U-I-295/13 of 19 October 2016, ECLI:SI:USRS:2016:U.I.295.13, para. 107.

[47] Matej Accetto, 'Pride and Precedent: On Judicial Interpretation and Dialogue in European Law' in *Europeanization of Constitutional Law and Constitutionalization of European Law: Challenges for the Future*, a compendium of papers prepared in celebration of the 25th anniversary of the Constitutional Court of Albania (Tirana, 2017) 133.

dialogue as instruction, courts engaging in direct conversation with transnational courts (one need not be reminded of the preliminary references to the Court of Justice or the fresh possibility of requesting advisory opinions from the European Court of Human Rights) so as to obtain authoritative guidance on interpretation of the law to employ in a given case; and *judicial dialogue as disagreement*, courts addressing not only their domestic audience but also their European (national or transnational) counterparts, with their judicial opinions serving also to advance the arguments of their own interpretation of the law in the face of divergent positions of their counterparts.

Without time or a need to revisit the argument in detail, one could claim that, beyond the already stated increased attention to comparative 'precedents' which is present both within and outside Europe, although not without its discontents,[48] the different modalities of judicial dialogue may actually reinforce one another. For instance, it can be argued that in EU law the preliminary rulings procedure not only introduced a mechanism for providing an authoritative interpretation of EU law but it also introduced a new dynamic between the Court of Justice and national (apex) courts, one in which the former could at least sometimes appear to be concerned with application and compliance rather than (merely) interpretation[49] and the latter with testing the limits of their duty to refer under Article 267(3) Treaty on the Functioning of the European Union and the *CILFIT* doctrine.[50] On the other hand, however, the practical implications of notable disagreements, while certainly occasioned by strong discontent with a particular decision or position, may also be to reinforce the possibility of engaging in an earnest judicial dialogue and the willingness to do so. Put bluntly, the invitation to learn may also be seen as an invitation to disagree, and disagreement as engagement, both reaffirming the important role of transnational judicial dialogue in charting the uncertain waters of an ever more interdependent or globalised law. In this regard, the manner in which national

---

48 Consider the so-called 'culture wars' regarding US constitutional identity following modest comparative references in six Supreme Court cases at the turn of the millennium (see Mark Tushnet, 'Referring to Foreign Law in Constitutional Interpretation: An Episode in the Culture Wars' [2006] 35 *University of Baltimore Law Review* 299) or the selectivity in identifying pertinent comparative examples (on the Israeli experience, see Ran Hirschl, *Comparative Matters: The Renaissance of Comparative Constitutional Law* (Oxford University Press, Oxford 2014) 23).

49 See, e.g., Hjalte Rasmussen, 'The European Court's Acte Clair Strategy in CILFIT – Or: Acte Clair, of Course! But What Does it Mean?' [2015] 40 *European Law Review* 475, 477–82 (first published in (1984) 9 E.L. Rev. 242).

50 Case 283/81 *CILFIT*, ECLI:EU:C:1982:335. After all, the national courts already took a similar approach following the earlier decision in Joined Cases 28–30/62 *Da Costa*, ECLI:EU:C:1963:6, as already noted by AG Capotorti in his opinion in the *CILFIT* case, para. 4.

(constitutional) adjudication is undertaken has also been changing. National courts are becoming inextricably tied to a transnational – or at least, for the time being, European – judicial community, with international/European courts and their national counterparts mutually shaping and being guided by the new constitutional pluralism, finding their way across a common sea populated by the many overlapping jurisdictions and multiple legal sources.[51]

In other words, both their legal environment and the role that (constitutional) courts are to perform have already been changing for other reasons not attributable to the Charter. The processes of globalisation have not only occasioned an increasing economic interdependence of states but also invite us, and soon may require us, to abandon the cosy living rooms of our established national legal systems constructed on the foundations of traditional nation-state paradigms and consider that law is (again becoming) a global phenomenon that can be neither developed nor taught or practised as a self-contained 'monist' discipline within the geographical and regulatory confines of a single sovereign state.[52] Accordingly, one can also talk of a multifaceted international constitutionalism which in part increasingly relies on the role of the courts and judicial review,[53] and – as is also evidenced in the brief snapshot of Slovenian practice – it is certainly true that courts have increasingly also referred to international legal norms when scrutinising domestic legal regimes and institutions.[54] Whether this so-called second wave of judicial review has then been followed by a committed effort to reverse the scrutiny, i.e. for national courts to also start scrutinising international institutions and legal regimes, is perhaps still open to debate.[55] One can certainly agree that national (constitutional)

---

[51] Cf. Miguel Poiares Maduro, 'Interpreting European Law: Judicial Adjudication in a Context of Constitutional Pluralism' [2007] 1 *European Journal of Legal Studies* 1, 137.

[52] See, e.g., Randal Lesaffer, 'The Lighthouse of Law' [2012] 17 *Tilburg Law Review* 153.

[53] For an elaboration of the main elements of international constitutionalism, i.e. its normative, institutional, judicial, coordinative and self-referential functions, see Andraž Zidar, *The World Community between Hegemony and Constitutionalism* (Eleven International Publishing, The Hague 2019) 165–216.

[54] Cf. Doreen Lustig and Joseph H.H. Weiler, 'Judicial Review in the Contemporary World: Retrospective and Prospective' [2018] 16 *International Journal of Constitutional Law* 315, 327.

[55] See ibid. at 345–54 and several responses to Lustig and Weiler's foreword in the subsequent volume of the *International Journal of Constitutional Law*. This general point does not seek to neglect or deny that, in the context of EU law, courts of most Member States have at one time or another critically addressed the supremacy or effect of (specific instances of) EU law and the pronouncements of the Court of Justice, and that several continue to do so.

identity has been increasingly invoked in judicial interactions,[56] even if its indeterminacy and nationalist tinge render it a dangerous tool.[57]

For all these reasons – in brief, the relative frugality of national courts in their use of Charter provisions and the more general changes in the (trans) national scenery of judicial review – it is difficult to ascertain the precise effect that the Charter has had on judicial interactions in Europe. In other words, what is the Charter's *but-for* effect, i.e. which of the developments concerning the protection of fundamental rights and judicial review would not have occurred in the absence of the Charter's provisions? After all, even at the Court of Justice some of the most significant developments in the interaction between EU law and national legal orders have occurred outside the Charter. It was acknowledged as a sort of eureka moment when the Court of Justice in the *Associação Sindical dos Juízes Portugueses*[58] case found EU law to apply not by virtue of Article 47 CFR – which would first necessitate overcoming the hurdle of Article 51 CFR – but instead with reference to Article 19(1) Treaty on European Union it opened the way for the Commission to successfully bring an action against Poland for infringing judicial independence through measures which on their own had nothing to do with the implementation of EU law.[59]

One thing that has changed, and in which the Charter has a potential to change the scenery even more, is the way national courts – and *which* national courts – interact with the Court of Justice through the preliminary ruling procedure. This interaction has already changed in two ways, one quantitative and the other qualitative. Early on, the Court of Justice did not have many national interlocutors and often depended on the idea that lower national courts would be empowered by having a direct route to an authoritative European interlocutor.[60] In practice, this sometimes meant a smaller group of motivated judges who took on disproportionately active roles. For example, while mentions have been made of the enthusiasm with which lower Italian courts made use

---

56 Doreen Lustig and Joseph H.H. Weiler, 'Judicial Review in the Contemporary World: Retrospective and Prospective – A Rejoinder' [2019] 17 *International Journal of Constitutional Law* 40, 41.

57 See Federico Fabbrini and András Sajó, 'The Dangers of Constitutional Identity' [2019] 25 *European Law Journal* 457, 472–3.

58 Case C-64/16 *Associação Sindical dos Juízes Portugueses*, ECLI:EU:C:2018:117, paras 19–37.

59 Case C-619/18 *Commission v. Poland*, ECLI:EU:C:2019:531, paras 42–59.

60 See, e.g., Tommaso Pavone and R. Daniel Kelemen, 'The Evolving Judicial Politics of European Integration: The European Court of Justice and National Courts Revisited' [2019] 25 *European Law Journal* 352, 353–7.

of the procedure after 1970,[61] it is telling that the numbers were still relatively small and mostly produced by repeat actors: of the 89 preliminary references made by Italian courts between 1964 and 1980, 60 were made by the same four judges.[62] Since the mid-1980s, this has been changing with the docket growing to such an extent that in the past several decades the Court's operation and growing workload have been followed with consistent calls for reform.[63]

In qualitative terms, after many years of reluctance on their part to engage with the Court of Justice, national apex courts have recently started to engage more in interactions with the Court of Justice, a phenomenon some explain as a maturing of the EU legal order in which judicial interactions have started to resemble more those that take place in the traditional judicial hierarchy.[64] While this may jeopardise the established understanding of the significant role of the lower national courts in ensuring the effectiveness of EU law,[65] it is perhaps also the inevitable and welcome solution to the increased workload at the Court of Justice in a system that was always more welcoming of preliminary references from national courts in principle than it was able, if the national courts were to wholeheartedly subscribe to the thesis and start sending references across the board, to sustain in practice.

This increased role of national courts is at least in harmony with, if not occasioned by, the elevated status of the Charter. After all, the Charter provisions may be the closest that EU law comes to overlapping with the traditional purview of national constitutional jurisprudence based on national bills of rights.[66] As the Italian Constitutional Court said in its decision in 2017 when discussing the interplay between the preliminary reference procedure and constitutionality review,

> it bears considering that the aforementioned Charter of Rights is a part of Union law that is endowed with particular characteristics due to the typically constitutional stamp of its contents. The principles and rights laid out in the Charter largely

---

[61] Francesco P. Ruggeri, 'Report on Italy' in Anne-Marie Slaughter, Alec Stone Sweet and Joseph Weiler (eds), *The European Court and National Courts: Doctrine and Jurisprudence* (Hart, Oxford 2000) 149.

[62] Rasmussen and Martinsen, n. 29 above, at 260.

[63] I provide more detail on this in Matej Accetto, 'The Past and Possible Futures of European Union Judicature' [2011] *Czech (& Central European) Yearbook of Arbitration* 3, 7–17.

[64] Pavone and Kelemen, n. 60 above, at 355.

[65] Pavone and Kelemen call this the 'darker side' of the apex courts' increased role, potentially also limiting the possibility for private actors to effectively safeguard their EU rights – ibid. at 355 and 372.

[66] Cf. Danielle Gallo, 'Challenging EU Constitutional Law: The Italian Constitutional Court's New Stance on Direct Effect and the Preliminary Reference Procedure' [2019] 25 *European Law Journal* 434, 445.

> intersect with the principles and rights guaranteed by the Italian Constitution (and by other Member States' constitutions). It may therefore occur that the violation of an individual right infringes, at once, upon the guarantees enshrined in the Italian Constitution and those codified by the European Charter, as recently occurred in reference to the principle of the legality of crimes and punishments.[67]

The increased role of national apex and constitutional courts may therefore also be seen as an attempt to be actively engaged in accommodating a potential clash between the two fundamental rights regimes,[68] which has been made apparent all the more by the formal and symbolic significance of the Charter.

This, in turn, has potential consequences both for the nature of judicial interactions and for the substantive import of the Charter's provisions. As for the first, unlike lower national courts, whose empowerment lay in obtaining direct access to the authoritative European interlocutor, apex courts may be motivated more by a desire and the possibility to see the preliminary reference procedure as a reciprocal dialogue, one in which they are able to shape the European understanding of particular rights as much as take on board the authoritative pronouncements of the Court of Justice.[69] A part of the reason may well lie in the intermingling of the two rights regimes and the approach of constitutional courts, such as that outlined with regard to the Slovenian Constitutional Court above, which are averse to treating sources of law on fundamental rights applicable in national legal orders as separate regimes whose varied substantive standards would be applicable in an isolated manner within their distinct jurisdictional spheres. Therefore, while the Charter, which on its own terms is limited to the scope of implementation (or application) of EU law, may not directly play the role of the key transformative 'actor' in occasioning legal transplants across legal fields, it may nevertheless indirectly exert a broader influence on the development of national legal orders. Notably, it may serve as an inspiration for an extension of the same standards to other comparable situations governed by domestic law, as constitutional courts may feel hard-pressed to engage in a sort of reverse discrimination, recognising certain higher standards of human rights protection when the EU Charter is to apply but not extending the same level of human rights protection to situations falling outside its scope of application.

---

67 Decision of the Italian Constitutional Court No. 269/2017 of 14 December 2017, §5.2.

68 Gallo, n. 66 above, at 445, refers to the concern that the counter-limits might be violated.

69 Cf. Pavone and Kelemen, n. 60 above, at 367.

5. CONCLUSION

The formal significance of the Charter as one of the pillars of the Union constitutional order has clearly been recognised by both the Court of Justice and national courts. Accordingly, in the last ten years it has also served as the legal basis for important decisions of the Court of Justice, further buttressing the constitutional role of fundamental rights in EU law. What has been less clear so far is the substantive added value of the Charter, i.e. whether and to what extent development in the light of the Charter has gone further or in a different direction than it would in a legal order that still had to rely on the pre-established doctrine of fundamental rights enshrined in the general unwritten principles of EU law, drawing inspiration from constitutional traditions common to the Member States and international human rights documents.

This question can be posed both with regard to the jurisprudence of the Court of Justice and as far as the constitutional jurisprudence of national courts is concerned. As for the former, one can assume that most of the important decisions of the Court of Justice relying on the Charter would not come out differently now – at least not significantly so – if the frame of reference were the general principles of EU law. After all, even now the Court may sometimes rely on general principles to affirm a particular fundamental right, especially if the application of the Charter is doubtful. In this regard, the effect of the Charter may well be incremental rather than revolutionary, its text leading the Court ever more towards the limit of its logic.

As for national constitutional jurisprudence, the substantive effect of the Charter may be even more indirect, in particular where a particular right recognised by the Charter is already firmly enshrined in a national constitution. It seems unlikely that the Charter provisions on their own would directly affect the reasoning of national constitutional courts to such an extent that they would significantly advance or amend the substantive standards of fundamental rights arising under domestic constitutional rules.[70] After all, with the provisions and application of the Charter firmly confined within the limits of EU law, national courts, even constitutional courts, may be reluctant to break entirely new interpretative ground on their own initiative. Instead, the more likely route for the 'domestication' of the Charter may well still lie in the national courts taking on board the implications of authoritative pronouncements by the Luxembourg

[70] This point also applies with regard to those fundamental rights that do not yet have a clear constitutional foothold in a particular national legal order: while national courts will be bound to acknowledge the Charter provisions within its sphere of application, it is far less certain that the Charter could serve as a formal point of intrusion (*Einbruchsstelle*) through which new fundamental rights would automatically be introduced as fully fledged items in domestic constitutional bills of rights.

Court. However, by drawing the legal regimes even closer in the significant role their bills of rights assume in their constitutional orders, the Charter may well bolster the understanding that the judicial enterprise of discovering its limits is a joint one. In this regard, the increasing judicial interactions may well play a crucial role, with the apex national courts encouraging and following, but possibly also evaluating and checking the pronouncements of their Luxembourg interlocutor.

Is the individual still – always – at the centre of this enterprise? I would certainly hope so.

7. Comment: can the Charter help to protect rights in the Member States?

Gábor Halmai

Matej Accetto in Chapter 6 deals with the impact of the EU Charter of Fundamental Rights (Charter, CFR) on fundamental rights protection through the jurisprudence of well-functioning courts, particularly that of the Slovenian Constitutional Court. The chapter also discusses the role of judicial dialogue in this as inspiration, instruction or disagreement. My short contribution raises the question, whether the Charter can help to protect fundamental rights in Member States, where ordinary and constitutional courts fail to do so, and are unwilling to engage in dialogue with European courts. First I investigate the original and the changed aim of the Charter's Article 51 to make sure that Member States respect fundamental rights, followed by a closer look at the right to effective remedy and fair trial guaranteed in Article 47 of the Charter.

THE INTERPRETATION OF ARTICLE 51 OF THE CHARTER IN DOMESTIC MATTERS

According to the literal, rather restrictive interpretation of Article 51(1) CFR, the Charter does not apply to cases where Member States do not implement EU law but act in a purely domestic matter: '[t]he provisions of this Charter are addressed to the institutions and bodies of the Union with due regard for the principle of subsidiarity and to the Member States only when they are implementing Union law'. Article 51(2) further stresses that the 'Charter does not establish any new power or task for the Community or the Union, or modify powers and tasks defined by the Treaties'. This means that the Charter is predominantly applicable to EU institutions, and does not want to protect fundamental rights provided by the Member States' constitutions. This interpretation has been confirmed by the current President of the European Court of Justice (CJEU), Koen Lenaerts, as well: '[f]rom the fact that the Charter is now legally binding it does not follow that the EU has become a "human rights organisation" or that the CJEU has become "a second European Court on Human Rights" (ECtHR)'.[1]

This narrow interpretation has firstly been challenged by Advocate General Miguel Maduro in his 2008 opinion in the case *Centro Europa*. Maduro indicated that a citizen of a Member State, in response to a substantial breach of the rights, laid down in the Charter of Fundamental Rights, may invoke against his/her state the protection of the Charter on the basis of European citizenship.[2] After the newly elected government of Viktor Orbán enacted a new media law dismantling freedom of the media in Hungary in 2010, Armin von Bogdandy and his colleagues published the so-called 'reverse Solange' academic proposal.[3] The line of thought advanced in the proposal argues that the commitment to protect fundamental rights expressed in Article 2 of the Treaty on European Union may be invoked by any citizen in the court of a Member State in opposition to such measures by the given Member State that substantially violate fundamental rights. This right, which stems from Union citizenship, is derived by the authors from the practice of the CJEU, especially the *Ruiz Zambrano* judgment, which stated that any measures by a Member State '[w]hich have the effect of depriving citizens of the Union of the genuine enjoyment of the substance of the rights conferred by virtue of their status as citizens of the Union violate Article 20 of the Treaty on the Functioning of the European Union (TFEU), which creates Union citizenship and its component rights'.[4] The *Åkerberg Fransson* judgment[5] from 2013 also made it clear that the CJEU has moved away from the former literal interpretation by arguing that any material link and potential law-making are sufficient for the application of the Charter, provided that the case comes under the scope of EU law underpinned by certain EU regulation.[6]

---

[1] Cf. Koen Lenaerts, 'Exploring the Limits of the EU Charter of Fundamental Rights' (2012) 8(3) *European Constitutional Law Review*, 375, 377.

[2] See: Opinion of Advocate General Poiares Maduro, delivered on 12 September 2007, Case C-380/05 *Centro Europa 7 Srl v Ministero delle Comunicazioni e Autorità per le Garanzie nelle Comunicazioniand Direzione Generale Autorizzazioni e Concessioni Ministero delle Comunicazioni*.

[3] Armin von Bogdandy, Mattias Kottmann, Carlino Antpöhler, Johanna Dickschen, Simon Hentrei and Maja Smrkolj, 'Reverse Solange: Protecting European Media Freedom against EU Member States' (2012) 49 *Common Market Law Review*, 489.

[4] C-34/09 *Ruiz Zambrano*, para. 42.

[5] Case C-617/10 *Åkerberg Fransson*, ECLI:EU:C:2013:105, judgment of 26 February 2013.

[6] In the case *Sándor Nagy and others*, decided in the same year, the ECJ found the case to be inadmissible. The case concerned the Hungarian law, which permitted the dismissal of civil servants without justification. Despite the fact that this was clearly irreconcilable with Article 30 of the Charter, which provides that '[e]very worker has the right to protection against unjustified dismissal, in accordance with Union law and

Those arguing against the literal interpretation of Article 51 of the Charter, taking into account that a Treaty change is not a viable solution, favour the creative reinterpretation of Article 51(1), which can make the Charter also applicable in purely domestic cases.[7]

THE USE OF ARTICLE 47 CFR TO DETERMINE THE INDEPENDENCE OF NATIONAL COURTS

Domestic courts are not only part of the national judiciary but also part of the EU justice system playing an important role in the enforcement of EU law, for instance deciding on extradition based on the Framework decision on the European Arrest Warrant (EAW). The principle of mutual recognition in surrender proceedings prescribes that 'the Member States are in principle obliged to give effect to a European Arrest Warrant'.[8] Recital 10 of the 2002 Framework decision on EAW states that '[t]he implementation may be suspended only in the event of a serious and persistent breach of Article 6(1) TEU (currently Article 2) determined by the Council pursuant to Article 7 TEU'. Even though until triggering Article 7 in December 2017 against Poland no such procedure had occurred, the CJEU allowed deviations from the mutual trust principle in 'exceptional circumstances' already in 2016. The *Aranyosi and Căldăraru*[9] case concerned the surrender of individuals to countries with detention conditions that amounted to violations of Article 4 CFR prohibiting torture, inhuman, degrading treatment or punishment. The CJEU established a two-prong test for checking the fundamental rights situation in the issuing Member State. If the risk of fundamental rights violation is established, in the second step, it must be determined whether the person concerned by the EAW will be exposed, because of the conditions of his or her detention in the issuing Member State within the meaning of Article 4 EU Charter.

---

national laws and practices', the ECJ found that the impugned legislation was not part of Hungary's implementing EU law, and thus, Article 51 precluded the application of the Charter.

7 A. Jakab, 'The EU Charter of Fundamental Rights as the Most Promising Way of Enforcing the Rule of Law against EU Member States' in C. Closa and D. Kochenov (eds), *Reinforcing Rule of Law Oversight in the European Union* (Cambridge University Press, Cambridge 2016).

8 Case C-237/15 PPU *Lanigan*, [2015] ECR 474, para. 36.

9 Judgment of the Court (Grand Chamber) of 5 April 2016, *Pál Aranyosi and Robert Căldăraru v Generalstaatsanwaltschaft Bremen*, Requests for a preliminary ruling from the Hanseatisches Oberlandesgericht in Bremen, Joined Cases C-404/15 and C-659/15 PPU. See W. van Ballegoooij and P. Bárd, 'Mutual Recognition and Individual Rights: Did the Court Get it Right?' (2016) 7(4) *New Journal of European Criminal Law*, 439.

Two years later the CJEU further clarified the requirements of the exceptions in the *LM* case.[10] Here the question has been whether Artur Celmer, a crime suspect, should be surrendered from Ireland to Poland when the Irish judge has serious doubts as to whether the suspect would receive a fair trial in Poland, due to the lack of independence of the judiciary resulting from the 'reform' of the Polish judicial system. The CJEU ruled that the two-step test in *Aranyosi* needs to be followed by the Irish judge when making a decision on surrender. Regarding the first prong of the test on judicial independence, the CJEU relied on the Portuguese judges' case,[11] and emphasised that both judicial independence and impartiality are crucial for the right to fair trial guaranteed in Article 47 CFR to be respected. By treating Articles 4 and 47 of the Charter as analogous in the second step of the investigation, the CJEU disregarded the fact that while prison conditions can vary within the country, the lack of judicial independence either exists or not and cannot be remedied. This makes the second prong superfluous and warrants the CJEU as the ultimate decision-making body in the cases targeting judicial independence. Also, with the two-step test the CJEU entered into a judicial dialogue with a national court unwilling to negotiate, and made an unjustified distinction between surrender proceedings and infringement procedures.[12]

One of those infringement proceedings concluded in the judgment in *Commission v Poland*, where the CJEU, with reference to the independence of the judiciary, called Poland to forthwith suspend the application of the national law lowering the retirement age for Supreme Court judges.[13] Here the CJEU stated the lack of independence of the national judiciary, as opposed to the similar case in *Commission v Hungary*[14] six years earlier, when the justices reasoned with the prohibition of discrimination based on age. On 18 November

---

[10] Judgment of the Court (Grand Chamber) of 25 July 2018, *Minister for Justice and Equality v LM*, Requests for a preliminary ruling from the High Court (Ireland), Case C-216/18 PPU, ECLI:EU:C:2018:586.

[11] Judgment of the Court (Grand Chamber) of 27 February 2018, *Associação Sindical dos Juízes Portugueses v Tribunal de Contas*, Request for a preliminary ruling from the Supremo Tribunal Administrativo, Case C-64/16, ECLI:EU:C:2018:117.

[12] 'The competence of the Court under Article 19(1) TEU and 47 of the Charter and the competence of the European Council under Article 2 and 7 TEU are parallel'. Cf. Michal Krajewski, 'Who is Afraid of the European Council? The Court of Justice's Cautious Approach to the Independence of Domestic Judges, ECJ 25 July 2018, Case C-216/18 PPU, The Minister for Justice and Equality v LM' (2018) 14(4) *European Constitutional Law Review*, 792.

[13] Order of 15 November 2018, *Commission v Poland*, C-619/18, ECLI:EU:C:2018:910.

[14] Judgment of 6 November 2012, *Commission v Hungary*, C-286/12, ECLI:EU:C:2012:687. See the detailed discussion of the case by Gábor Halmai, 'The Early Retirement Age of the Hungarian Judges' in Fernanda Nicola and Bill Davies (eds), *EU*

the CJEU ruled in the *A.K. and others v Sąd Najwyższy* case,[15] which combined three referrals from the Polish Supreme Court regarding the Disciplinary Chamber of the Polish Supreme Court and, indirectly, the National Council of Judiciary. The referrals expressed concerns about a new system of disciplinary proceedings against judges, as well as about the election of the members of the National Council of Judiciary by the parliamentary majority instead of by judges themselves. Contrary to its judgment a year earlier the CJEU did not assess the independence of the Disciplinary Chamber on its own, instead, it elaborated a test of the 'appearance' of judicial independence, avoiding a direct reference to Article 19(1) Treaty on European Union on judicial independence arguing that the 'standard solution' of applying a specific substantive EU legal norm coupled with Article 47 CFR was available.

*

In his chapter, Matej Accetto concluded that the Charter's effect on national constitutional jurisprudence is rather incremental and indirect than revolutionary. After investigating the possible impact of the Charter in the Member States I also came to the conclusion that it seems to be insufficient to protect fundamental rights.

Law Stories: Contextual and Critical Histories of European Jurisprudence (Cambridge University Press, Cambridge 2017) 471.

15 Case C-585/18 *A.K. and others v Sąd Najwyższy*.

8. Judicial independence – the EU's prescription in the making to the Polish (and other) maladies

Karolina Podstawa and Jarosław Gwizdak[1]

I. INTRODUCTION

Whilst it is up to the European Union's Member States to 'provide remedies sufficient to ensure effective legal protection in the fields covered by Union law' (Art. 19(1) Treaty on European Union (TEU)), the determination and enforcement of the European (Union) standard of 'effective legal protection', encompassing judicial independence, has become the challenge for the rule of law (in the light of Art. 2 TEU), the right to a fair trial (Art. 47 Charter of Fundamental Rights of the European Union (CFR)), for the effectiveness of Union law[2] and, as a result, for the entirety of the European Union legal system. In particular, judicial independence has become a subject for many discussions: in political plenums, during the unprecedented marches gathering judges in their official gowns and ordinary citizens,[3] and in courts. The phrase

1 The authors would like to express their gratitude to Madalina Moraru and Federica Casarosa for excellent comments on earlier versions of this text and the team of ACTIONES and TRIIAL projects for their continuous support and intellectual stimulation.

2 European Commission, 'Rule of law report – communication and country chapters' (*European Commission*, 13 September 2020) <https://ec.europa.eu/info/publications/2020-rule-law-report-communication-and-country-chapters_en> accessed 25 January 2021.

3 To mention just the most impressive ones: massive protests in front of the Supreme Court in Warsaw 'Chain of lights' starting on Sunday, 16 July 2017 when the first draft of the justice system reform was introduced: See: Themis, Stowarzyszenie Sędziów, 'Spotkajmy się 16 lipca aby wyrazić swój sprzeciw wobec ustaw o Sądach powszechnych, Krajowej Radzie Sądownictwa i Sądzie Najwyższym' (*Themis*, 14 July 2017) <spotkajmy-sie-16-lipca-aby-wyrazic-swoj-sprzeciw-wobec-ustaw-o-sadach-powszechnych-krajowej-radzie-sadownictwa-i-sadzie-najwyzszym> accessed 2 February 2021; and the March of 1000 Robes with members of European Judiciary and bar associa-

'judicial independence' on the lips of so many would imply that globally its meaning is clear and uniform and its application straightforward.

In this chapter we examine this assumption offering the account of the evolution of the understanding of the judicial independence in the case law of the Court of Justice of the European Union (CJEU) as involving three essential elements. The underlying claim of this analysis is of no little consequence. Specifically, judging on the example of the Art. 19 TEU and Art. 47 CFR-rooted standard of judicial independence, it seems that, even in the contexts where the European Union misses an implied competence, the Court is capable of developing a legal construct allowing it to incorporate essential elements of the functioning of Member States under its jurisdiction in order to safeguard the unity of the European Union legal order. However, to be able to do so, the CJEU needed favourable circumstances.

The first essential ingredient of the recipe involved the emergence on the part of the judges of a will to take a stance and root their domestic position in the European Union law. The favourable circumstance consisted in a brewing conflict focused on reform of the justice system in some Central and Eastern European (CEE) states of the European Union and, in particular, in Poland. It was the conflict that pushed the CJEU to develop a narrative on its Art. 19 TEU jurisdiction – the second ingredient. And thirdly, the courts at both European and national level needed to be ready to engage in many judicial interactions, which, as we will see below, was the case. In fact, this readiness of judges to engage in various forms of a dialogue allows us to hope that instead of a crisis of judicial culture or rule of law we should be speaking of the growth of the juridical power and impact in the European Union legal order.

Each of these elements will be examined in turn in the subsequent parts of this chapter. Due to the limitation of the writing and publishing process, the discussion will be limited to the period of the 2010s and finalizing with 2 March 2021. What needs to be emphasized is that the evolution will surely continue, for, as we speak, judges continue to seek support in the case law of the CJEU to make the standard of judicial independence more specific and less prone to manipulation.[4]

---

tions, to show solidarity with Polish colleagues, see more Gwizdak, Jarosław, 'Neither Portraits Nor Pictures' (*Visegrad Insight*, 9 June 2020) <Neither Portraits Nor Pictures – Supreme Court in Poland – On Central Europe, from Central Europe> accessed 27 January 2021 and Gwizdak, Jarosław, 'Twist in the Legal Universe Finding a Real European Foundation for the Rule of Law in Poland' (*Visegrad Insight*, 11 February 2020) <Twist in the Legal Universe – The Rule of Law in Poland> accessed 27 January 2021.

[4] Ziółkowski, M, 'Two Faces of the Polish Supreme Court after "Reforms" of the Judiciary System in Poland: The Question of Judicial Independence and Appointments'

II. INGREDIENT NO 1 – THE CIRCUMSTANCES – THE POLISH BACKGROUND STORY

The discussion will start with the first of the ingredients: the circumstances that forced the hand of the CJEU. In particular, the focus shall be placed on Poland, arguably the most problematic of CEE states.

The current conflict among the Polish judiciary and lawyers and between the Polish government and the European Union institutions has been repeatedly described in academic literature[5] and in policy papers[6] together with the instances of judicial and societal activism emerging in response to it. Whereas what the academic public has grown to know as the Polish democratic backsliding[7] dates to the period between 2015 and today, the origins of the internal feud reach to the period directly after the Polish democratic transition and to the period of the gradual building of the democracy. We will not repeat the story of the former here. Instead, we would like to draw attention to the latter.[8]

(2020) 5 *European Papers (European Forum Insight)* 352. The change of the paradigm is pointed to indirectly by Lenaerts, K, 'On Judicial Independence and the Quest for National, Supranational and Transnational Justice' in Selvik, G, Clifton, M-J, Haas, T, Lourenço, L and Schwiesow, K (eds), *The Art of Judicial Reasoning* (Springer Nature Switzerland AG, Cham, Switzerland 2019) 158.

5 See, for instance: Kochenov, D and Pech, L, 'Better Late than Never? On the European Commission's Rule of Law Framework and its First Activation' (2016) 54 *Journal of Common Market Studies* 1062, Sadurski, W, *Poland's Constitutional Breakdown* (Oxford University Press, Oxford 2019), Kochenov, D and Bárd, P, 'The Last Soldier Standing? Courts versus Politicians and the Rule of Law Crisis in the New Member States of the EU' in Ballin, EH, van der Schyff, G and Stremler, M (eds), *European Yearbook of Constitutional Law 2019* (Springer, Cham, Switzerland 2020) 243.

6 The civil society organizations were aware of the context and meaning of changes since 2017. See, for instance: Civil Development Forum, 'Analysis 8/2017: The draft amendments to the National Council of the Judiciary – another attempt to limit the rule of law' <https://for.org.pl/en/a/5322,analysis-8/2017-the-draft-amendments-to-the-national-court-register-another-attempt-to-limit-the-rule-of-law> accessed 2 February 2021. See, also the dedicated organization established on 4 June 2018: Komitet Obrony Sprawiedliwości (Justice Defense Committee): Justice Defense Committee Homepage <https://ruleoflaw.pl/tag/kos/> accessed 2 February 2021.

7 Bermeo, Nancy, 'On Democratic Backsliding' (2016) 27 *Journal of Democracy* 1, 5. In the Polish context, the concept was introduced by Wojciech Sadurski: Sadurski, W, 'How Democracy Dies (in Poland): A Case Study of Anti-Constitutional Populist Backsliding' Sydney Law School Research Paper 72 (2018).

8 The main narrative aiming to support the first attempt to reform the system of justice focuses on the elitism of the professional group: Goryczka-Jezierska, Justyna, 'Min. Gowin: środowisko sędziów jest elitarne, podzielone i oddzielone od społeczeństwa' (*Prawo.pl*, 22 August 2014) <https://www.prawo.pl/prawnicy-sady/min

Since 1989 judges have generally refrained from speaking out in the public debate, using the notions of judicial independence and impartiality as reasons for their seclusion from the public sphere.[9] In line with this approach, the core of their work entailed literal interpretation of the letter of law and did not reflect the spirit of the law, nor the context of its application. Perhaps this is the reason why the conflicts within the justice system have not been known to the broader public.

The persistent squabbles entailed on one hand the differences in interpretation among different courts,[10] including the highest courts (the Supreme Court and the Constitutional Court),[11] between judges of different instances,[12] and

-gowin-srodowisko-sedziow-jest-elitarne-podzielone-i-oddzielone-od-spoleczenstwa,179305.html> accessed 2 February 2021.

[9] See also the statements made by various judges in the previously cited report by Amnesty International: '"We have never spoken out before. Now we do [...] Yes, we feel the pressure, but I don't believe we will be silenced," commented Judge Dorota Zabłudowska from the District Court in Gdańsk' Amnesty International, 'Poland: Free Courts, Free People, Judges Standing for Their Independence' (2019), available at https://www.amnesty.org/en/documents/eur37/0418/2019/en/ accessed 25 October 2021. As to the requirements defining ethics for judges, see: 'Code of Professional Ethics for Judges': 'Judges are obliged to exercise restraint in use of social media' National Council of the Judiciary, 'Code of Professional Ethics for Judges' (*Krajowa Rada Sądownictwa*, 13 January 2017) <https://krs.pl/pl/o-radzie/zbior-zasad-etyki-zawodowej-sedziow/591-uchwala-nr-25-2017-krajowej-rady-sadownictwa-z-dnia-13-stycznia-2017-r.html> accessed 2 February 2021, para 23. See also the communication of the disciplinary commissioner for the ordinary court judges on proceedings focused on Twitter activity of a judge, Rzecznik Dyscyplinarny Sędziów Sądów Powszechnych (*Rzecznik Dyscyplinarny Sędziów Sądów Powszechnych*, 18 January 2020, Saturday, evening) <http://rzecznik.gov.pl/wp-content/uploads/2020/01/komunikat-Jaroslaw-O.pdf> accessed 2 February 2021.

[10] The need for unifying interpretation of legal provisions was expressed, for instance, during the conference in the Supreme Court. See: 'Studia i analizy Sądu Najwyższego: Grochowski, Mateusz, Raczkowski, Michał and Żółtek, Sławomir (eds), '"Jednolitość orzecznictwa. Standard – instrumenty – praktyka. Materiały z konferencji naukowej", 21 November 2013' (2015) *Studia i analizy Sądu Najwyższego* 5, 11.

[11] For the discussion of the competence of the Supreme Court to examine the constitutionality of provisions: Grochowski, Mateusz, Raczkowski, Michał and Żółtek, Sławomir (eds), *Jednolitość orzecznictwa. Standard – instrumenty – praktyka. Materiały z konferencji naukowej, 21 November 2013* (Biuro Studiów i Analiz Sądu Najwyższego, Warsaw 2015) 50.

[12] 'For while the previous "dual power" legislature and executive tended to violate the rights of lower-level judges and collaborate with judicial elites, the current reforms reach to the top of the feudal judicial pyramid.' Królikowski, Mariusz, 'Z pamiętnika prostego sędziego' (*Rp.pl*, 24 December 2016) <https://www.rp.pl/Rzecz-o-prawie/312249997-Mariusz-Krolikowski-Z-pamietnika-prostego-sedziego.html> accessed 2 February 2021.

between ordinary and administrative courts.[13] Arguably, these early stages of the brewing conflict were characterized by a high level of a formalized judicial dialogue among the Polish judiciary (in particular, through the question of law procedure under Art. 193 of the Constitution of the Republic of Poland).[14]

It is against this backdrop that the first reforms of the justice system were introduced in September 2008 and resulted in weeks long protests (the 'no docket days'). The conflict concerned judges' remuneration[15] and culminated with the 'betrayal' of the Constitutional Court that approved the possibility not to adapt judicial salaries to the altered economic circumstances.[16] Of similarly contentious nature was the selection of judges to the Polish National Council of the Judiciary. Only judges of regional and appellate courts would be appointed on the basis of informal networks. In such a way judges of district courts had neither representation nor influence.[17]

Another reform follows in 2013 known by the name of the minister sponsoring it: the 'Gowin's reform'.[18] Officially, in order to render the work of the courts more effective and, informally, to abolish the local camaraderie net-

---

[13] See a controversial judgment of the Supreme Administrative Court which was reluctant to assess the validity of appointments to judicial office: Naczelny Sąd Administracyjny, I OSK 857/17 (7 December 2017). Subsequently, however, the Supreme Administrative Court felt compelled to seek assistance from the CJEU. See: Case C-824/18 *A.B. and Others (Nomination des juges à la Cour suprême – Recours)*, ECLI:EU:C:2021:153.

[14] For the English version, see: Constitution of the Republic of Poland (the official translation available on the website of the Polish Sejm) <https://www.sejm.gov.pl/prawo/konst/angielski/kon1.htm> accessed 26 January 2021.

[15] See, for instance: Iustitia, 'Komunikat Zarządu na temat "dni bez wokandy"' (*Iustitia Stowarzyszenie Sędziów Polskich*, 10 September 2008) <https://www.iustitia.pl/83-komunikaty-i-oswiadczenia/199-komunikat-zarzadu-na-temat-dni-bez-wokandy> accessed 2 February 2021.

[16] Polish Constitutional Court, K 1/12 (12 December 2012) PL CR OTK-A 2012/11/134, Królikowski, Mariusz, 'Z pamiętnika prostego sędziego', op. cit. n (12).

[17] Consider that during the term 2014–18, of 17 judges appointed to the National Council of the Judiciary, none sat on a district court. In the term starting with 2018, 13 of 15 judges originated from district courts. Krajowa Rada Sądownictwa, 'Historia Krajowej Rady Sądownictwa' (*Krajowa Rada Sądownictwa*, 2020) <https://krs.pl/pl/o-radzie/historia/527-historia.html> accessed 3 February 2021.

[18] For a brief critical account see: Pośpiech, Paweł, 'Po reformie Gowina, czyli mała sądowa apokalipsa' (*Kwartalnik IUSTITIA* 2(16)/2014) <https://www.kwartalnikiustitia.pl/po-reformie-gowina-czyli-mala-sadowa-apokalipsa,6637> accessed 26 January 2021. For important *votum separatum* of Judge Wojciech Hermeliński to the approving verdict of the Constitutional Tribunal in K 27/12 (27 March 2013) PL CR OTK ZU 3A/2013, poz. 29 <https://ipo.trybunal.gov.pl/ipo/Sprawa?cid=2&dokument=9020&sprawa=9572> accessed 3 February 2021, paras 164–210.

works,[19] as of 1 January 2013, 79 smallest district courts were transformed into branch offices of bigger courts. Basing their protest on the formal shortcoming alone[20] the transferred judges refused to sit on benches in their 'new' courts. Whereas it is not within the jurisdiction of the Supreme Court to adjudicate on the validity of Polish laws and whilst continuing to endorse the literal interpretation of provisions of the law on the organization of common courts,[21] the Supreme Court offered a historical account of attribution of competence in exercising the power of transfer pointing to the fact that ministerial prerogative in this context has been a relic of the Second Polish Republic (1918–39) subsequently abused under the Polish People's Republic (1947–89) and brought back to life through Gowin's reform.[22] Manifesting the conflicted nature of the relationship between the two top courts, the Constitutional Court evaluated the reform as constitutional.[23] The strong opposition to the reform, however, forced the Minister of Justice to withdraw it and to reinstate the abolished courts (all but ultimately three).

In this context Law and Justice yet again aspired to reshuffle privileged positions within courts and to finally ensure the 'just' system of appointments to the judicial bodies and the long awaited system of judicial accountability.[24]

---

[19] Królikowski, Rafał, 'Krajobraz sądów po reformie Gowina' (*Rp.pl*, 2 January 2016) <Królikowski: Krajobraz sądów po reformie Gowina – Sędziowie i sądy – rp.pl> accessed 26 January 2021.

[20] The decision to transfer the judges was signed by the deputy minister, and not the Minister of Justice.

[21] Prawo o organizacji sądów powszechnych, Dz.U. 2016 poz. 2062 (OJ PL 2016(2062)).

[22] Polish Supreme Court, Resolution (full composition) BSA I-4110-4/13 (28 January 2014) <http://www.sn.pl/sites/orzecznictwo/Orzeczenia2/BSA-I-4110-4-13.pdf> accessed 26 January 2021 at 5–12.

[23] Constitutional Tribunal, K 27/12 (27 March 2013) OTK ZU 3A/2013, poz. 29 <https://ipo.trybunal.gov.pl/ipo/Sprawa?cid=2&dokument=9020&sprawa=9572> accessed 26 January 2021.

[24] Importantly, there is a general consensus among the members of the judiciary and the broader public that the reform of the organization of the system of justice has been essential. See, for example: Ochremiak, Anna, Szymaniak, Piotr and Kryszkiewicz, Małgorzata, 'Reforma sądownictwa: potrzeba ustrojowa czy polityczna', *Dziennik Gazeta Prawna: prawo, biznes, polityka* (2017/220) B8–B9, Kryszkiewicz, Małgorzata, 'Reforma sądownictwa: potrzebne są zmiany, a nie rewolucja/Bartosz Pilitowski, Sławomir Pałka, Michał Laskowski, Stanisław Trociuk, Marek Celej, Zbigniew Krüger: debatę prowadziła Małgorzata Kryszkiewicz', *Dziennik Gazeta Prawna: prawo, biznes, polityka* (2017/166) B8–B9, Gwizdak, Jarosław, '100 idei dla Polski: Reforma wymiaru sprawiedliwości' (*Wszystko co najważniejsze*, 18 grudnia 2016), Agenda Polska Związku Pracodawców Polskich, 'Wymierna sprawiedliwość: Projekt reformy sądownictwa' (*Agenda Polska Związku Pracodawców Polskich*, 2018) <https://zpp.net.pl/wp-content/uploads/2018/03/Agenda-Polska-Wymierna-sprawiedliwość.-Projekt

The background story sheds a bit of light on how, once through the reform of the Polish judicial system, the renewed redistribution of privilege distorted a relative (albeit conflict-based) balance.

III. INGREDIENT NO 2 – JURISDICTION – THE TRIAD OF ART. 47 CFR, ART. 2 TEU AND ART. 19 TEU

The discussion of judicial independence in the European Union context necessitates anchoring of the concept in the law of the European Union. In fact, as outlined by Torres Pérez,[25] the permissibility of the CJEU to pronounce itself on the topic and the subsequent related legislative activity of the Council of the European Union and the European Parliament would have not progressed far, had it not been for the decision taken by the judges of the CJEU to explore the position of Art. 19 TEU and its relationship to fundamental rights architecture including the CFR, in particular, its Art. 47.

As early as in *Associação Sindical dos Juízes Portugueses v Tribunal de Contas (ASJP)*, the Court takes a step in differentiating between the material scope of Art. 19 TEU and triggering the applicability of the CFR. The Court emphasized above all that the concept of 'the fields covered by Union law' is broader than that of Art. 51(1) CFR, for Art. 19 TEU will apply irrespective of whether the Member States are implementing Union law (and so irrespective whether there was a clear competence conferred on the EU to act in a given area by adopting legislation or triggering Member States' duty of sincere cooperation[26]).

-reformy-sądownictwa.pdf> accessed 3 February 2021, Sokołowski, Jacek, 'Spór o sądy w 16 punktach' (*Klub Jagielloński*, 11 July 2018) <https://klubjagiellonski.pl/2018/07/11/spor-o-sady-w-16-punktach/> accessed 3 February 2021.

[25] Torres Pérez, A, 'From Portugal to Poland: The Court of Justice of the European Union as Watchdog of Judicial Independence' (2020) 27(1) *Maastricht Journal of European and Comparative Law* 115–18.

[26] For more see: Spaventa, Eleonor, 'The Interpretation of Article 51 of the EU Charter of Fundamental Rights: The Dilemma of Stricter or Broader Application of the Charter to National Measures' (Study for the PETI Committee of the European Parliament, 2016) <https://www.europarl.europa.eu/RegData/etudes/STUD/2016/556930/IPOL_STU(2016)556930_EN.pdf> accessed 30 January 2021 or Pirker, Benedikt, 'Mapping the Scope of Application of EU Fundamental Rights: A Typology' (2018) 3 *European Papers* 133 or Lazzerini, N, 'The Scope and Effects of the Charter of Fundamental Rights in the Case Law of the European Court of Justice' in Palmisano, G (ed.), *Making the Charter of Fundamental Rights a Living Instrument* (Brill/Nijhoff, The Hague 2014), 30.

Later on, in *Commission v Poland*[27] the CJEU clarifies that, even when exercising their own competence, Member States are still required to comply with their obligations derived from EU law and specifically from Art. 19(2) in this specific case.[28] As Torres Pérez rightly observes, in both cases a clear EU law element was ultimately discerned by the Court, unlike in two parallel in time preliminary reference procedures initiated by two Polish judges without a clear link to EU law, ultimately declared inadmissible by the CJEU on grounds of their hypothetical character.[29]

Thus, with the elaboration of the interpretation of Art. 19 TEU and with the determination of its jurisdiction, the CJEU has forged an additional strong instrument capable of defending Art. 2 TEU. What remained was the determination of the content of obligations of Member States under Art. 19 TEU and, in other words, the meaning of the notion of 'effective judicial protection of rights of individuals'. There, the Court builds on the foundations of its justice system: the concept of 'a court or a tribunal' within the meaning of Art. 267 Treaty on the Functioning of the European Union (TFEU) and the concept of an 'effective remedy' and 'fair trial' resulting from the common constitutional traditions of Member States of the EU and subsequently reaffirmed by Art. 47 CFR.[30] This 'hermeneutical' approach to Art. 47 CFR has been reaffirmed by the CJEU also in *Commission v Poland*[31] which has been considered as a missed opportunity to further explore Art. 51(1) CFR.[32] Torres Pérez points to a clear path through which the trigger effect can be activated: through bringing a given situation in the field of EU law as in the *Åkerberg Fransson*[33] scenario and an analogous one in *Ruiz Zambrano*[34] in relation to Art. 20 TEU. From the perspective of judicial independence, however, the hermeneutical approach is sufficient to determine the standard of judicial independence applicable in a systematic manner by Member States who are to fulfil their obligations under Art. 19 TEU.

To sum up, even though the trigger effect has not been fully discerned from the combination of rules, the Court has endorsed the hermeneutic construction

---

27 Case C-619/18 *Commission v Republic of Poland (Independence of the Supreme Court)*, ECLI:EU:C:2019:531, para 52.

28 Ibid.

29 Joined Cases C-558/18 and C-563/18 *Miasto Łowicz* and *Prokuratura Okręgowa w Płocku (Miasto Łowicz)*, ECLI:EU:C:2020:234.

30 Case C-64/16 *Associação Sindical dos Juízes Portugueses (ASJP)*, ECLI:EU:C:2018:117, para 35.

31 Case C-619/18 *Commission v Republic of Poland (Independence of the Supreme Court)* op. cit. n (27), para 52.

32 Torres Pérez, A, 'From Portugal to Poland …' op. cit. n (25), 115–18.

33 Case C-617/10 *Åkerberg Fransson*, ECLI:EU:C:2013:105.

34 Case C-34/09 *Ruiz Zambrano*, ECLI:EU:C:2011:124.

and seems to be simplifying it with time. In fact, in the more recent *A. K. (Independence of the Disciplinary Chamber of the Supreme Court)*, it stated:

> The principle of the *effective judicial protection* of individuals' rights under EU law, referred to in the second subparagraph of Article 19(1) TEU, is a *general principle of EU law* which is *now enshrined in Article 47 of the Charter*, so that the former provision *requires Member States to provide remedies that are sufficient to ensure effective legal protection, within the meaning in particular of the latter provision*, in the *fields covered by EU law*[35] (emphasis added).

The most clearly observable shortcut is that a general principle of EU law of effective judicial protection is enshrined now in Art. 47 CFR hence arguably does not require a trigger as it would be in any case directly effective vis-à-vis individuals.[36]

Admittedly, the construct developed by the Court is not a perfect one, however, it addresses a number of problems the European Union has been facing in the past years.

Firstly, establishing a reliable link between Art. 2 TEU, Art. 19 TEU and Art. 47 CFR allows the EU justice systems to be subject to scrutiny regardless whether a state in question has been a part of the EU since its conception, or joined the 'gentlemen's club' relatively recently. It offers an opportunity to abolish the double standards applied by the European Union to states within and outside its borders. Thus making the judicial systems of the Member States subject to scrutiny on the basis of Art. 2, Art. 19 TEU and Art. 47 CFR means that the gentleman's club must not only let some fresh air in but also leave the view through the windows unobstructed.

Finally, pairing Art. 19 and Art. 2 TEU implies that following up on the framing of the standard of judicial independence linked to the rule of law may, in the long term, bring about further clarification of standards that pertain to such democratic guarantees as freedom of association or freedom of the press.

IV. INGREDIENT NO 3 – JUDICIAL DIALOGUE

The recipe for European Union judicial independence culminates with the final ingredient: judicial dialogue. In this section we will trace the evolution from the CJEU's 'hands-off' approach to the position of the national judges within national legal systems[37] to the development of a more elaborate standard.

---

35 Joined Cases C-585/18, C-624/19 and C-625/19 *A. K. (Independence of the Disciplinary Chamber of the Supreme Court)*, ECLI:EU:C:2018:910, para 168.

36 As per original C-144/04 *Mangold*, ECLI:EU:C:2005:709, paras 74–77.

37 Case C-286/12 *Commission v Hungary (Retirement age of judges)*, ECLI:EU:C: 2012:687.

Importantly, the standard's evolution is the result of an extensive interaction of both formal and informal types among courts and judges.

1. Judicial Independence under Art. 267 TFEU as a Constitutive Feature of 'Courts and Tribunals'

Whereas this contribution is primarily concerned with the most recent developments with respect to the standard of judicial independence in the European Union, the origins of the current approach, as substantiated by the Court when developing a link between Art. 2 TEU, Art. 19 TEU and Art. 47 CFR, can be found in the case law relating to the EU law's autonomous concept of 'courts or tribunals' under Art. 267 TFEU. This concept has been developed as a guarantee for the effective implementation of EU law by national courts acting in their capacity as European Union courts. The importance of how the notion of 'courts or tribunals' is interpreted lies in the fact, as emphasized by Lenaerts,[38] that it is not the Member States' law that will ultimately decide as to whether a given body will be considered as 'a court or a tribunal' under Art. 267 TFEU, but, in fact the CJEU. The 'decision' will lie with the EU law determined factors such as 'whether the body is established by law, whether it is permanent, whether its jurisdiction is compulsory, whether its procedure is *inter partes*, whether it applies rules of law and whether it is independent'[39] that have been long accepted as a standing interpretation of the concept through the case law of the CJEU.[40]

The concept of judicial independence, as an attribute of 'a court or a tribunal' under Art. 267 TFEU, found first its clear expression in the *Wilson* judgment[41] whereby the CJEU distinguished between the external and internal independence of judges required for a body to be permitted to refer a question to the CJEU to be granted a standing.[42] Internally, national law must guarantee

---

[38] Lenaerts, K, 'On Judicial Independence and the Quest for National, Supranational and Transnational Justice' op. cit. n (4) 158.

[39] Case C-296/14 *MT Højgaard and Zűblin*, ECLI:EU:C:2016:347, para 23.

[40] See, for example: Case 61-65 *Vaassen-Gőbbels*, ECLI:EU:C:1966:39, Case C-205/08 *Umweltanwalt von Kårnten*, ECLI:EU:C:2009:767, para 35, Case C-203/14 *Consorci Sanitari del Maresme*, ECLI:EU:C:2015:664, para 17. For extensive discussion of the concept of a court or tribunal, see: Rodriguez-Medal, J, 'Concept of a Court or Tribunal under the Reference for a Preliminary Ruling: Who Can Refer Questions to the Court of Justice of the EU?' (2015) 8 *European Journal of Legal Studies* 104; see also Casarosa, Federica, 'ACTIONES Handbook – Module 3 Fair Trial' <https://cjc.eui.eu/wp-content/uploads/2019/03/D1.1.c-Module-3.pdf> accessed 2 February 2021.

[41] Case C-506/04 *Wilson*, ECLI:EU:C:2006:587, paras 49–52.

[42] A similar notion is also present in Case C-175/11 *H. I. D.*, ECLI:EU:C:2013:45. See also the commentary in Moraru, Madalina, Penasa, Simone, and Strazzari, Davide,

a 'level playing field' and so impartiality. Externally, members of the judiciary must be shielded from external pressures or influences that may affect their independent judgement. In practical terms, the EU law demands that the Member States' law provides for guarantees from removal from office and protection of constraints imposed by hierarchy or subordination.[43]

The two elements of judicial independence have been used by the Court as a basis for the establishment of the admissibility criterion specifically in the context of ensuring the incoming of preliminary references to the CJEU, as it seems to delineate between administrative bodies of the state and the judiciary. In fact, most frequently, the CJEU would deny the attribute of independence to bodies in reference to which the removal from office would not be guaranteed by national rules. This was the case in the context of *Syfait*,[44] where the Greek competition authority was a referring body, or in the more recent *Banco de Santander SA*,[45] where the position of the Spanish Central Tax Tribunal was evaluated.

In addition, in the view of the CJEU, external independence requires that a referring body is not subject to the constraints stemming from hierarchy or subordination that may lead to the duty to follow orders or instructions.[46]

Whereas the independence of a court or a tribunal is protected by EU law as a means of warranting that the stream of questions arriving at the CJEU's threshold indeed originates with bodies whose decision making processes focus on the material content of EU law, the protection of judges whose independence is at risk seems to be a logical and necessary evolution of the case law of the CJEU.[47] And thus both aspects of judicial independence find their further reflection in a more recent case law, however, with an altered optics focused, on the one hand, on the obligations of Member States under Art. 19 TEU and, on the other, on protection of judges as individuals whose position guarantees fulfilment of conditions of the right to a fair trial under Art. 47 CFR.

We have explored the utilitarian origins of the notion of judicial independence, such that was to enable the functioning of national courts as European courts capable of freely evaluating concrete problems of European Union law. The CJEU's reliance on the concept was the essential element for the courts to

---

'RE-JUS Casebook on Effective Justice in Asylum and Immigration' (2018) <https://www.rejus.eu/sites/default/files/content/materials/rejus_casebook_effective_justice_in_asylum_and_immigration.pdf> accessed 29 January 2021, at 104.

43 Case C-222/13 *TDC*, ECLI:EU:C:2014:2265, paras 32 and 35.

44 Case C-53/03 *Syfait and Others*, ECLI:EU:C:2005:333, para 21.

45 Case C-274/14 *Banco de Santander SA*, ECLI:EU:C:2020:17, paras 54–60.

46 Case C-503/15 *Margarit Panicello*, ECLI:EU:C:2017:126, paras 41–42.

47 Lenaerts, K, 'On Judicial Independence and the Quest for National, Supranational and Transnational Justice' op. cit. n (4) 160–61.

take on the subsequent task of clarifying the meaning of the concept of judicial independence.

2. The Judiciary of the Member States of the European Union Unite!

Indeed, it is in the European Union setting that judicial interactions increase in their intensity and range. For one part, they are of formal and informal nature. The former involves either the national internal procedures enabling courts to refer questions of law to Constitutional or Supreme Courts (such as the said procedure under Art. 193 of the Polish Constitution), the EU's preliminary reference procedure or the essential interaction between the courts in the course of procedures based on mutual trust. Formal interactions also include in their range European Union constitutional obligations binding national courts: duty of consistent interpretation, obligation to disapply national rules incompatible with the European Union law. The informal interactions refer to the cross-fertilization of the application of national law with reflection on the interpretation of a given standard of rights protection by other, domestic or international, courts.

Subsequently, interactions may be of vertical or horizontal character. In the former case involving courts within hierarchical relationships and, in the latter case, courts of the same level engaging with courts of their own or other states. This final form of judicial interaction may involve a vertical element if judgments of relevance have gone through various levels of adjudication. It may be ventured that judicial dialogue on effective judicial protection is prone to produce a particularly dense landscape of judicial dialogue – after all, who else is to contribute to the understanding of their own position if not judges themselves?

Indeed, it seems that to date we have seen an unprecedented initiative on the part of the European judiciary: from Poland who sought help in supporting their opposition to governmental 'reforms',[48] or similar ones from Hungarian courts;[49] judges from other Member States who sought to advance the interpretation of the notion of judicial independence and verify their own position

---

48 These cases will be discussed in detail below.

49 Case C-564/19 *IS* (request for a preliminary ruling, 24 July 2019). Importantly, the procedure of the referral under Hungarian law is subject to the control by the Supreme Court (Kúria) having a clearly deterring effect from referring further questions by Hungarian judges. For more, see: Bard, Petra, '"Am I Independent?": A Hungarian Judge Asks the CJEU in a Struggle against Judicial Capture' (*RECONNECT Project Blog Post*, 27 September 2019) <https://reconnect-europe.eu/blog/politics-newep-krum-2/> accessed 26 January 2021.

in this context;[50] and finally judges who followed the guidance of the CJEU in adjudicating on the rule of law in a state requesting a transfer of individual in conditions of the European Arrest Warrant (EAW).[51] It becomes clear that both the national courts and judges have gone a long way from the original misconstruction of a clear judicial independence case under the guise of non-discrimination in the Hungarian early retirement case[52] to the flurry of questions. In this section we will trace this development starting from *AFSJ*[53] to the currently accepted standard of judicial independence.

The tale of judicial dialogue on judicial independence starts with the austerity measures of the EU. By Law 75/2014, the Portuguese legislator introduced a temporary reduction, starting in October 2014, in salaries of a certain number of public sector office-holders and persons. Under the administrative acts on the 'implementation of remuneration' issued under this law, the remuneration of judges of the Tribunal de Contas (Court of Auditors) was also decreased. The judgment delivered on 27 February 2018 only brought relief to the Polish judges already suffering under the strain of Law and Justice measures. This is acknowledged in paragraph 44 of the CJEU's decision.[54] That is consistent with the *Wilson* pronouncement, and the established verification mechanism, and becomes a permanent feature of the argumentation on the independence of the courts.

Paradoxically, a judgment that was unfavourable to Portuguese judges of the Court of Auditors gave hope to Polish judges when further reforms and attempts to subordinate the judiciary to the executive were to come.

The argument that did not allow the salary demands of Portuguese judges to be recognized helped the Court to assess the changes being made to the Polish

---

50 As in cases C-272/19 *Land Hessen*, ECLI:EU:C:2020:535 or C-256/19 *S.A.D. Maler und Anstreicher OG v Magistrat der Stadt Wien and Bauarbeiter Urlaubs- und Abfertigungskasse*, ECLI:EU:C:2020:523.

51 See C-216/18 PPU *LM (Celmer)*, ECLI:EU:C:2018:117 and its origin: Case C-404/15 *Aranyosi and Câldâraru*, ECLI:EU:C:2016:198 as well as implementation: Biernat, S and Filipek, P, 'The Assessment of Judicial Independence Following the CJEU Ruling in C-216/18 LM' in von Bogdandy, A, Bogdanowicz, P, Canor, I, Grabenwarter, C, Taborowski, M and Schmidt, M (eds), *Defending Checks and Balances in EU Member States: Taking Stock of Europe's Actions* (Springer, Berlin Heidelberg 2021) 403.

52 C-286/12 *European Commission v Hungary (Early retirement of judges)* op. cit. n (37).

53 Case C-64/16 *Associação Sindical dos Juízes Portugueses* op. cit. n (30).

54 C-216/18 PPU *LM (Celmer)* op. cit. n (51), para 44; see also the critical approach in: Lane Scheppele, Kim, 'Rule of Law Retail and Rule of Law Wholesale: The ECJ's (Alarming) "Celmer" Decision' (*VerfBlog*, 28 July 2018) <https://verfassungsblog.de/rule-of-law-retail-and-rule-of-law-wholesale-the-ecjs-alarming-celmer-decision/> accessed 5 February 2021.

justice system. In *LM (Celmer)*, three EAWs addressed to Ireland resulted in the High Court of Ireland asking for a preliminary ruling.[55]

The CJEU answered the Irish court's question, ordering, in particular, a two-stage verification of the requests made by the courts. In addition, the Court drew attention to the threat to independence and sovereignty of the judiciary that disciplinary proceedings not falling within the standard of independence may pose.[56]

It has turned out that there is greater confidence in the decisions of a single judge, who is increasingly willing to use questions for a preliminary ruling, than in the whole system. This confidence was also placed in the judges of the national courts whose task was to evaluate the structural guarantees of the rule of law in the receiving Member States and that with mixed effects.[57]

Whilst the European judges decide whether the Polish legal system could be trusted enough to offer a fair trial to suspects of criminal acts, the Polish government and its loyal institutions continued with a full-frontal push directed at the Polish (disloyal) judicial environment thus inevitably offering further opportunities to European courts to scrutinize the Polish judicial system. And these opportunities were tragically taken by a variety of judges sitting on various benches with, frequently, dire consequences.[58]

For example, the Polish Disciplinary Chamber of the Supreme Court (suspended by a CJEU's preliminary ruling in C-791/19 R) issued on 23 September 2020 a judgment II DO 52/20[59] deciding as follows:

> It should be added that the judgement of the CJEU […] in Joined Cases C-585/18, C-624/18 and C-625/18, cannot be regarded as binding on the grounds of the Polish legal system, since in all proceedings before the Supreme Court Chamber of Labour and Social Security in which questions for a preliminary ruling were submitted to

---

55 C-216/18 PPU *LM (Celmer)* op. cit. n (51).

56 C-216/18 PPU *LM (Celmer)* op. cit. n (51), para 67.

57 Biernat, S and Filipek, P, 'The Assessment of Judicial Independence Following the CJEU Ruling in C-216/18 LM' in von Bogdandy, A, Bogdanowicz, P, Canor, I, Grabenwarter, C, Taborowski, M and Schmidt, M (eds), *Defending Checks and Balances in EU Member States: Taking Stock of Europe's Actions* (Springer, Berlin Heidelberg 2021) 403.

58 See, for instance, the case of Igor Tuleya and his continuous 'fall-outs' with the government. See: Jałoszewski, Mariusz, 'Ziobro's Man Censors Judge Igor Tuleya: He Banned His Columns about the Courts on the Radio' (*ruleoflaw.pl*, 26 February 2021) <https://ruleoflaw.pl/ziobros-man-censors-judge-igor-tuleya/> accessed 26 February 2021.

59 Polish Supreme Court, II DO 52/20 (official translation) <http://www.sn.pl/aktualnosci/SiteAssets/Lists/Komunikaty_o_sprawach/AllItems/Case%20II%20DO%2052-20.pdf> accessed 5 February 2021.

> the CJEU [...], activities were carried out in the compositions contrary to legal regulations.

The use of the phrase 'unlawful composition' of another court by a court appointed contrary to and unknown to the Constitution is telling. The battle continues.

In this context one should recall the Polish Muzzle Law,[60] which prevents judges from speaking out in the public debate. The Law does not comply with any European standard at the first glance. First and foremost, it requires judges to disclose their affiliation with associations, societies and political parties throughout their careers. This is not just about judicial associations, which are in regular opposition to the actions of the government. Such actions can lead to the disclosure of sensitive data of judges (e.g. association of those suffering from a terminal illness) and constitute an attack on their privacy.

The law also prohibited: threatening with a disciplinary procedure against any judge who may question it, the review of judicial appointments by the National Council of the Judiciary. In substance, the law stopped the implementation of a CJEU decision.

Polish judges, feeling the threat to their ethos of independence and impartiality, sought help from the CJEU requesting intervention in cases where their issuing of the judgment could have been subject to a subsequent 'sanction'.[61] Unfortunately, of the series of questions, two have been declared inadmissible due to the potential character of the threat to judicial independence.[62] Arguably, the judges should have waited until their fears materialized.

---

[60] That is a nickname of another amendment to the law on ordinary courts prohibiting judges from questioning the appointment of other judges, forcing judges to reveal their affiliation in social associations (judges associations, sport clubs, support groups, etc.): Ustawa z dnia 20 grudnia 2019 r. o zmianie ustawy – Prawo o ustroju sądów powszechnych, ustawy o Sądzie Najwyższym oraz niektórych innych ustaw, Dz.U. 2020 poz. 190 (PL OJ (2020) 190). For the commentary, see: Przymusiński, Bartłomiej, 'I Am a Judge, I Will Tell You why I Am Going out on the Street' (*IUSTITIA*, 29 January 2020) <https://www.iustitia.pl/en/3654-i-am-a-judge-and i-will-tell-you-why-i-am-going-out-on-the-street> accessed 5 February 2020 and Mazur, Dairusz, 'Annual Report for 2020: From Bad to Worse the Polish Judiciary in the Shadow of the "Muzzle Act"' (*Themis*, 31 December 2020) <http://themis-sedziowie.eu/wp-content/uploads/2021/01/Themis_From-bad-to-worse_ang.pdf> accessed 5 February 2021.

[61] See, for instance, the circumstances around the preliminary references giving the rise to the judgment in Joined Cases C-558/18 *Miasto Łowicz* op. cit. n (29) and more recently C-824/18 *A.B. and Others (Nomination des juges à la Cour suprême – Recours)* op. cit. n (13).

[62] Joined Cases C-558/18 *Miasto Łowicz* op. cit. n (29).

Simultaneously, the judges of states plied with afflictions similar to the Polish one decided to act (see the pending Romanian cases[63]). In the meantime, the standard has taken a discernible shape.

V. BREWING THE STANDARD OF JUDICIAL INDEPENDENCE IN THE EUROPEAN UNION LEGAL SYSTEM

The standard of judicial independence to be applied across the European Union is composed of ingredients resultant from grievances visible in a variety of jurisdictions and against the background of facts of the case. As we saw, it is a mix of a utilitarian approach reflecting the minimum threshold a referring entity must meet to be able to enquire about the meaning of the validity of EU law under Art. 267, in part reflecting constitutional traditions of Member States, or in nuanced manner, problems with them.

The recipe for judicial independence is to be discerned in the clearest manner from the judgment resulting from the infringement procedure in *Commission v Poland (Independence of the Supreme Court)*, however, by then the Court could root the standard at stake in the multitude of case law that emerged between the original *Commission v Hungary (early retirement age of judges)*[64] and the contemporary setting of judicial quasi-reforms across the European Union.

And so firstly, the court concerned must be able to exercise its functions wholly autonomously without being subject to any hierarchical constraints.[65] Secondly, the court concerned and judges must display objectivity and the absence of any interest in the outcome of the proceedings apart from the strict application of the rule of law.[66] Thirdly, 'rules, particularly as regards the composition of the body and the appointment, length of service and grounds for abstention, rejection and dismissal of its members, that are such as to dispel any reasonable doubt in the minds of individuals as to the imperviousness

---

63 See for the context of Romanian cases: Dragoș, Călin, 'The Court of Justice of the European Union is Facing a New Challenge: Compliance with the Rule of Law or Not as a Result of the Effects of Decisions Delivered by the Constitutional Court of Romania' (*UNIO Official Blog*, 25 January 2021) <https://officialblogofunio.com/2021/01/25/the-court-of-justice-of-the-european-union-is-facing-a-new-challenge-compliance-with-the-rule-of-law-or-not-as-a-result-of-the-effects-of-decisions-delivered-by-the-constitutional-court-of-romania/> accessed 18 February 2018.

64 Case C-286/12 *European Commission v Hungary (Early retirement of judges)*, ECLI:EU:C:2012:687.

65 Case C-619/18 *Commission v Republic of Poland (Independence of the Supreme Court)* op. cit. n (27), para 72 following up on Case C-64/16 *ASJP* op. cit. n (30).

66 idem, para 73.

of that body to external factors and its neutrality with respect to the interests before it'.[67] Fourthly, the CJEU in discussing freedom of judges from external and internal pressures focuses on the principle of irremovability and related guarantees.[68]

Finally, and most controversially, the standard of judicial independence discerned by the CJEU contains a subjective element. Namely, in line with *A. K. (Indépendence de la chambre disciplinaire de la Cour Supreme)*,[69] the Court will not be seen as independent 'if the objective circumstances in which that court was formed, its characteristics and the means by which its members have been appointed "*are capable of giving rise to legitimate doubts, in the minds of subjects of the law*" as to the imperviousness of that court to external factors (direct or indirect influence of the legislature and the executive) as to its neutrality with respect to the interests before it' (emphasis added).

This standard emerged against the uprising in the CEE states and the question remains: is it sufficient? Voices from the judiciary, in particular in states affected by the anti-democratic backsliding reply in unison that this is not the case. It seems that the guidance offered by the CJEU so far does not guarantee the manipulation-proof application of the standard. In fact, as argued by Ziółkowski, this strategy was probably the most compatible with the pluralistic standard of judicial independence that amounts to, regrettably, the 'appearance of independence' rather than the substantive minimum of strict guarantees to be put in place for the benefit of the judiciary.

It may be indeed the case that the words of the CJEU may be applied in a distorted manner, or even declared unlawful as in the above-mentioned judgment of the Disciplinary Chamber of the Polish Supreme Court.[70] However, arguably, such an ignorant judgment, which is blatantly contrary to European Union obligations of the Polish state, could have not been prevented even if the CJEU had offered a more detailed guidance.

At the same time after the period of relative activism, the CJEU took again a step back somewhat playing to the critique by Ziółkowski. Symbolically, in *Openbaar Ministerie (Independence of the issuing judicial authority)*[71] the CJEU again addressed the issue of the independence of the Polish court issuing the EAW. This time the preliminary question was raised by the Amsterdam Rechtbank requesting the CJEU to aid national judges in application of the two-tier test developed in *LM.* The CJEU essentially emphasized that the mere

67 idem, para 74.

68 idem, paras 75–76.

69 Joined Cases C-585/18, C-624/19 and C-625/19 *A. K.* op. cit. n (35), para 171.

70 Polish Supreme Court, Case II DO 52/20, op. cit. n (59).

71 Joined Cases C-354/20 PPU *L* and C-412/20 PPU *P (Openbaar ministerie)*, ECLI:EU:C:2020:1033.

existence of systemic or generalized deficiencies affecting the independence of the issuing Member State's judiciary is not enough for the issuing authority in a given case (court) to be by default non-independent and for the affected individual's right to a fair trial to be at risk. The Court prescribed for national courts the two-tier test and in particular the need to conduct a subjective evaluation of the case at hand and the individual's position (and so the assessment of the situation of the requested person, the nature of the offence in question and the factual context which forms the basis of the EAW, such as statements by public authorities which are liable to interfere with the way in which the individual case is handled).[72] Probably, the most clear indication the courts received in terms of how the situation of the issuing authorities should be assessed is that until the Art. 7(2) TEU procedure is brought to an end, declaring the systemic deficiencies concerning EU values, the subjective evaluation must be conducted by national courts executing EAWs.[73]

Whereas it may be alleged that in the *Openbaar Ministeri*e the CJEU approached dismissively the plight of European judges who need to apply the two-prong *LM* test in execution of the EAW, in the 2 March 2021 judicial independence judgment *A.B. and Others (Nomination des juges à la Cour suprême – Recours)*[74] it took a more demonstrative approach (albeit safeguarded by multiple reminders about the role of referring courts). The CJEU dealt here with the question of the impact of the lack of judicial review for the procedure of appointments of judges to the positions on the Supreme Court. The judicial nominations are effectuated by the President of Poland, however, the *de facto* selecting body is the National Council of the Judiciary which by means of a resolution presents the candidatures to the President. The question was referred by the Polish Supreme Administrative Court, responsible for the judicial review of all nominations but, under the amended rules, those of the judges of the Supreme Court.

This narrow question allowed the CJEU to showcase the application of the standard that has been developed in the previous case law. It is done in a concise, yet comprehensive manner, emphasizing the contextual and legal elements as well as the role of national courts in evaluation of the circumstances that may 'give rise to reasonable doubts, in the minds of individuals, as to the imperviousness of the judges concerned to external factors and as to their neutrality with respect to the interests before them'.[75] In its almost linear reasoning, the CJEU draws attention to the three ingredients that, as argued in

[72] Ibid, para 58.

[73] Ibid, para 57.

[74] C-824/18 *A.B. and Others (Nomination des juges à la Cour suprême – Recours)* op. cit. n (13).

[75] Ibid, para 123.

this chapter, were essential for the constitution of the standard of judicial independence under the European Union law. Most unusually the CJEU applied the standard and indicated to national judges the instances when national rules were to be disapplied.

The CJEU in the first place asserted its jurisdiction and the need to evaluate the position of national courts vis-à-vis requirements of Art. 267 TFEU and, therefore, obligations of the Member States under Art. 19(1) TEU read in the light of Art. 47 CFR. By now the CJEU relying on its earlier case law recalls the rule seamlessly: it starts from recalling the relationship between Art. 267 TFEU and Art. 4(3) TEU emphasizing the duty of sincere cooperation resting on the Member States to enable national courts to refer questions to the CJEU.[76]

Subsequently, the CJEU recalled the relationship between the EU values and the second subparagraph of Art. 19(1) TEU, in barely five paragraphs.[77] The Member States must guarantee to their citizens adequate remedies and procedures that will guarantee effective legal protection.[78] The latter is the general principle of European Union law, 'stemming from the constitutional traditions common to the Member States, which has been enshrined in Articles 6 and 13 [European Convention on Human Rights], and which is now reaffirmed by Article 47 of the Charter'.[79] Finally, this obligation applies to fields covered by Union law, irrespective of whether Member States are implementing it (as per Art. 51 CFR).

Finally, the CJEU draws attention to the fact that:

> to ensure that such bodies are in a position to ensure the effective judicial protection thus required under the second subparagraph of Article 19(1) TEU, maintaining their independence is essential, as confirmed by the second paragraph of Article 47 of the Charter, which refers to access to an 'independent' tribunal as one of the requirements linked to the fundamental right to an effective remedy.[80]

The elements of judicial independence have been identified in the previous case law by CJEU and imply the existence in a given jurisdiction of

> rules, particularly as regards the composition of the body and the appointment, length of service and grounds for abstention, rejection and dismissal of its members, that are such as to dispel any reasonable doubt in the minds of individuals as to the

---

76 Ibid, paras 90–107.
77 Ibid, paras 108–139.
78 Ibid, para 109.
79 Ibid, para 110.
80 Ibid, para 115.

> imperviousness of that body to external factors and its neutrality with respect to the interests before it.[81]

The protection should focus on the maintenance of the tripartite division of powers and protection from any direct or indirect influence over the work of the judiciary.[82]

Against the backdrop of this outlined standard of judicial independence, the CJEU endeavours to perform a rather acrobatic activity: on the one hand, it proceeds to analyse the context within which the referring court operates and thus the circumstances that may give rise to a reasonable doubt about the independence of a court. At the same time, the CJEU reminds all courts about their duties under the EU law both to conduct such analysis on their own, and to disapply national provisions that might impact the effectiveness of EU law.[83]

It seems that whereas the logic behind the development of the standard and its application is considered ripe by the CJEU, what courts are struggling with is the subjective elements of the test. Can any guidance be discerned from the reasoning of the Court?

There are three elements the Court considered: the *de facto* position of the appointing body vis-à-vis the legislature and the executive, the broader context of rules focusing on judicial appointments, and the resulting legislative intent. So, in the first place the Court assessed the position of the National Council of the Judiciary and the fact that changed rules of appointment may lead to a 'special' relationship between its members and the appointing parliamentarians. Secondly, the CJEU paired this conclusion with the legislative intervention in the determination of the retirement age thus opening up multiple positions on the Supreme Court. And, finally, it observed that the entirety of the judicial reform was conducted consciously with the precise intent of creating such circumstances as to allow for the appointments to be conducted in a strictly prescribed manner.[84]

It remains to be seen whether national judges will consider such guidance as sufficient in determining the EU law compliance of national rules affecting independence of the judiciary. Certainly, the three elements taken into consideration, including the subjective element of the test on the systemic level, are helpful. The real question that remains pertains to the assessment of whether

---

81 Ibid, para 117.

82 Ibid, paras 118–119.

83 See, in particular, the extensive summary of the case law on primacy and disapplication, ibid, paras 140–150, but also a clear indication to disapply national provisions precluding the possibility of lodging the appeal against the decision of the National Council of the Judiciary on putting forward a judge's candidature, ibid, paras 153, 167.

84 Ibid, paras 129–139.

a given court in a given case within the contexts of mutual recognition can be considered as independent as per the *LM* dictum.

VI. THE POLISH EPILOGUE AND THE FUTURE OF THE DIALOGUE

In the conclusion of their recent study, Gutmann and Voigt state that adoption of legislation focusing on judicial independence (*de jure* independence) is, in fact, negatively correlated with the actual independence (*de facto* independence). This is connected with the fact that judicial independence as an ideal strived for should be considered as, in fact, beyond the control of politicians and lawmakers. It is more of a function of a generalized trust in institutions in a given society and the position of individualism as a foundational element of such society.[85] The Polish case study offers a strong case in point.[86] The saga of abusive laws, chilling measures, judgments and judicial dialogues initiating in the Polish context is bound to continue through the hands of the affected judges but also the European Union judicial community. The Polish context is ripe with the judicial problems concerning judicial appointments, judicial accountability and irremovability and, finally, the organization of courts.

As far as the judicial appointments are concerned, two issues emerge: the position of the National Council of the Judiciary (already assessed by the CJEU) and of the judges appointed by this arguably unlawful body.

Shortening the term of office of the National Council of the Judiciary proved to be the 'original sin' of all subsequent attempts to change the Polish justice system. The Council, itself appointed in violation of the Constitution, took part in the judicial appointment procedure and gave its opinion on candidacies for promotion in a context of clear conflict of interests.

Aleksander Kappes and Jacek Skrzydło comment on the position of the judges appointed by the Council, pointing to the fact that the key problem lies in the assessment of the presidential appointment, in particular whether it has a capacity to validate legal errors that had been committed at the earlier stages

---

[85] Gutmann, J and Voigt, S, 'Judicial Independence in the EU: A Puzzle' (2020) 49 *European Journal of Law and Economics* 83, 84.

[86] Among many examples see: Horne, CM, *Building Trust and Democracy: Transitional Justice in Post-Communist Countries* (Oxford University Press, Oxford 2017); Horne, CM, 'Lustration, Transitional Justice, and Social Trust in Post-Communist Countries: Repairing or Wresting the Ties that Bind?' (2014) 66 *Europe-Asia Studies* 225. In the context of the EU courts, see, for instance, Mayoral, JA, 'Impact through Trust: The CJEU as a Trust-Enhancing Institution' in Wind, Marlene and Follesdal, Andreas (eds), *International Courts and Domestic Politics* (CUP, Cambridge 2018).

of the judicial appointment procedure. They emphasize that even the Supreme Court took the position that such validation did not take place.[87]

The scale of the problem is rather large as there are more than 500 judges appointed with the participation of the National Council of the Judiciary (and a further 1048 vacant positions await appointments). Circa 70 000 judgments were passed with the participation of such judges. The position of the Council and of the appointed judges will definitely be a subject of the evaluation by the CJEU in the near future as the result of pending cases initiated by prosecutors' offices in a variety of seats in Poland.

Disciplinary proceedings against judges are the second legal minefield. Despite the CJEU granting interim measures to the European Commission[88] and ordering the suspension of the functioning of the Disciplinary Chamber of the Supreme Court, the Chamber continued to function. Whereas it does not pass judgments concerning disciplinary proceedings per se, it adjudicates on immunities of judges. Such decisions, in the understanding of the Disciplinary Chamber, do not lead to the accountability of judges or prosecutors but only potentially enable further accountability related proceedings. At the end of 2020, judge activists of the judicial associations: Beata Morawiec[89] and Igor Tuleya[90] were deprived of immunities in such a manner. Proceedings concerning Judge Iwulski are still pending.[91]

It is clear that the government has been planning to silence the activist judges through the use of disciplinary proceedings on a much larger scale given the reward system put in place for disciplinary commissioners.[92] As soon as the government feels less scrutinized, the proceedings are likely to start anew.

---

87 Kappes, Aleksander and Skrzydło, Jacek, 'Czy wyroki neo-sędziów są ważne? Rozważania na tle uchwały trzech połączonych izb Sądu Najwyższego z 23 stycznia 2020 roku (BSA I-4110-1/20)' (2020) *Palestra* 5 <https://palestra.pl/pl/czasopismo/wydanie/5-2020/artykul/czy-wyroki-neo-sedziow-sa-wazne-rozwazania-na-tle-uchwaly-trzech-polaczonych-izb-sadu-najwyzszego-z-23.01.2020-r.-bsa-i-4110-1-20> accessed 10 March 2021.

88 C-791/19 *European Commission v Republic of Poland (Independence of the Disciplinary Chamber of the Supreme Court)*, ECLI:EU:C:2020:277.

89 The decision was taken on 12 October 2020, however, has not been officially published since.

90 See Jałoszewski, Mariusz, 'Ziobro's Man Censors Judge Igor Tuleya …' op. cit. n (58).

91 Żaczkiewicz-Zborska, Katarzyna, 'SN: Decyzja w sprawie uchylenia immunitetu prezesa Izby Pracy odroczona' (*Prawo.pl*, 21 January 2021) <https://www.prawo.pl/prawnicy-sady/uchylenie-immunitetu-prezesowi-iwulskiemu,505939.html> accessed 10 March 2021.

92 See <https://oko.press/wierny-zolnierz-ziobry-prezesem-najwiekszego-sadu-w-polsce/> accessed 25 October 2021.

The final minefield, so far untouched by the judicial proceedings, concerns the organization of courts, including meddling with the appointments to the positions of presidents of courts, promotions (to higher courts) and court attributions as well as attribution of cases to individual judges.[93]

All of the above-mentioned aspects of reforms of the judiciary in Poland have a potential to produce further litigation at national and international level and further clarifications to the existing standard. Hopefully, the Polish judiciary will withstand the pressure in the meantime.

VI. CONCLUSIONS

This chapter presented a contextualized enquiry into the development of the standard of judicial independence by European courts. The context within which the standard has been brewed is that of the Polish reform of the judicial system in the period of anti-democratic backsliding. The identified modus operandi was that of a (mostly formalized) judicial dialogue. In the chapter we focused on the period of the past six years: the time of the controversial rule by the Law and Justice party elected to power in two consecutive terms. As the result of the judicial preliminary references to the CJEU but also of activities of individual judges, a common baseline standard has been emerging. Its characteristic feature across jurisdictions lies in two constitutive elements of the developed tests: the objective one focused on the existence of guarantees protecting judges from internal and external influences (and providing for in particular the principle of irremovability), and the subjective one focused on the conviction that a given court in a given case may not be independent and may, in its decisions, limit the right to a fair trial of an affected individual. Given the avalanche of preliminary questions to the CJEU, it seems rather clear that the standard in its current form is not considered to be sufficiently ripe by the judges.

Whereas this may be true, and this contribution may soon require an update, what makes the standard of judicial independence so extraordinary and outstanding against the background of issues related to Art. 47 CFR is that the protection of the right to a fair trial of ordinary citizens resulted as secondary. The first and foremost subject of protection is the persona of a judge: both a judge, a professional whose job description is being rapidly adjusted; and a judge, an abstract guarantor of the tripartite division of powers whose posi-

---

93 This was extensively described, for instance, in Grabowska-Moroz, Barbara and Szuleka, Małgorzata, 'It Starts with the Personnel: Replacement of Common Court Presidents and Vice Presidents from August 2017 to February 2018' (2018) <https://www.liberties.eu/en/stories/polish-court-chiefs-sacked-via-fax/14946> accessed 25 October 2021.

tion results both from Art. 19 TEU and from the constitutional traditions of democratic Member States of the European Union.

Whereas both aspects of persona undoubtedly merit protection, it does not escape one's attention that today both Polish, but also Romanian, German, and other, judges use preliminary questions mainly to clarify their own status or that of their courts.

Such actions are, on the one hand, an easy target for the authorities, who frighten the public with the pernicious influence of the EU. These threats hit very fertile ground, and do not increase trust in the judiciary. On the other, it is clear that the judicial profession, so long associated with remaining in the shadows, applying unassumingly the letter of the law and protecting its separateness, in fact needed an occasion in reshaping the modality in which the judicial power is exercised. Finally, as it seems, the European judges found not only the venue to have their voices heard but also multiple interlocutors in the cross-jurisdictional judicial dialogue before European apex courts. The hope remains that the latter will not abuse the trust.

9. Comment: Austro-Hungarian partnership? A brief comparison between an old democracy and a new democracy

Edith Zeller

1. INTRODUCTION

The rule of law crisis in Poland has spotlighted the underlying fundamentals of EU values. Previously, it had hardly ever been seriously questioned whether all the EU Member States – once they have fulfilled the formal criteria to become members of the EU – continue to meet these requirements.

The Polish case and the erosion of the rule of law in Poland not only bring to light deficiencies in the Polish judicial system but should be a warning call for other national judicial systems. They also provide politicians or actors who would like to see the judiciary as a part of government policy or the policies of other influential interest groups with a simple example. A Polish colleague once commented that the Polish legislator wants to produce a Frankenstein-like judiciary system, a so-called 'Frankensteinisation of legislation'.[1]

Like viruses, such negative examples can easily spread. Immunisation is necessary to avoid being infected by a virus which can easily destroy a functioning justice system. Once a justice system is not strong and robust it can easily get affected. The question remains whether old democratic systems – i.e.

[1] Polish politicians argue that their reform is in line with European standards because certain aspects of it also exist in other countries. This is seen as an invalid argument and accepting such arguments would amount to a possible 'Frankensteinisation of legislation', which would be based on a combination of the 'worst practices' existing in other countries instead of on best practice and common European standards. For more detail, see Council of Europe, Parliamentary Assembly, Doc. 15025, Report of 6 January 2020 on 'The functioning of democratic institutions in Poland', draft resolution, para. 9, available at https://assembly.coe.int/nw/xml/XRef/Xref-XML2HTML-en.asp?fileid=28330&lang=en (accessed 19 February 2021).

those of old EU Member States with consolidated democracies – are more immunised against such a virus than young democratic systems and transitional democracies.

This brings me away from Poland to these old Member States with consolidated democracies. Not only since the Secretary General of the Council of Europe noted a race to the bottom[2] has it become worth taking a closer look in the mirror and at systems which are not (yet) under open attack. If politicians in new democracies take parts of other structures as role models for their judicial reform plans, the question arises of whether their arguments can easily be washed away as a 'Frankensteinisation' or whether they are poking their fingers into open wounds in the judicial systems of old democracies.

Legal cultures and historical legal developments differ from country to country. Because of this diversity it is not possible to use one template for all and on all systems. Nevertheless, certain factors exist in all our judiciaries which are similar and function as custodians of independence – be it individual or structural independence.[3]

Knowing the administrative judicial system of Austria best,[4] in this chapter I will use this old EU Member State as a model for comparison.

2. POINTS OF COMPARISON

Given that the Hungarian authorities drew on the systems established in Austria and Bavaria,[5] the question arises of how the Austrian Administrative Judiciary system differs from the – heavily criticised – Hungarian plans to reform the administrative judiciary.

First, we can briefly mention that the Austrian model does not provide a judicial council at all, whereas such a specific judicial council is foreseen in the Hungarian bill. However, let us turn to similar features.

The main structural weaknesses which were specifically criticised by the Venice Commission in the Hungarian case were a need to enhance elements

---

2 Report by Secretary General of the Council of Europe Thorbjörn Jagland, 2017, 'State of Democracy, Human Rights and the Rule of Law', available at https://edoc.coe.int/en/an-overview/7381-pdf-state-of-democracy-human-rights-and-the-rule-of-law.html (last accessed 25 October 2021).

3 See Edith Zeller, 'Access points for infringements of judicial independence: a practical tour d'horizon' (2019) 20 *ERA Forum* 129–39, page 130.

4 As the federal system and the administrative courts have separate laws for the organisation and service of judges and the courts it is hardly possible to go into details on each administrative court system. However, the basic provisions are alike in all the Austrian judicial systems for administrative courts of first instance.

5 European Commission for Democracy Through Law (Venice Commission), Opinion no. 943/2018, CDL-AD(2019)004, para. 25.

of judicial self-governance and also to identify other means to counterbalance the prerogatives of the Minister of Justice and the president of the Hungarian Supreme Administrative Court, together with recommendations to amend the appointment procedure for court presidents and new administrative judges.

Therefore, the main critics of the Hungarian reform plans concentrated on the unbalanced powers (of the minister and court presidents) in the area of judicial administration and the appointment procedures for new administrative judges. Let us compare these two main points.

2.a The Role of Court Presidents

It goes without saying that judicial administration is an 'entrance gate' to courts and it has an influence on courts. It is necessary to have self-administration within the judiciary to the greatest possible extent and to have effective gatekeepers. Court presidents play an important role in this respect.[6]

The position of court president includes power over judicial careers, administrative power, budgetary power, media power, ambassadorial power and jurisprudential power, all in different forms and with different intensity.[7] Court presidents are actors in judicial self-government. That the role of court presidents is of importance for political leaders has become visible as in the Hungarian bill they are to be selected and appointed by free decisions of the executive power. This allows direct political influence on the selection process.[8]

In Austria, in each of the nine different federal provinces and in each of the federal administrative courts the court president monocratically directs the judicial administration.[9] Court presidents are appointed for an unlimited period of time. Hence, under the present organisational laws of all Austrian admin-

---

6 Adam Blisa and David Kosar, 'Court Presidents: the missing piece in the puzzle of judicial governance' (2018) 19 *German Law Journal*, No. 7 on Judicial Self Governance in Europe, page 12 *et seq*.

7 Idem.

8 In Poland, the Minister of Justice could freely dismiss and appoint court presidents during a certain period of the so-called Polish judicial reform phase. Austria must also be mentioned as a negative example of such a relevant structural weakness in the administrative judiciary. See also European Commission, Rule of Law Report 2020 on Austria, SWD(2020) 319 final, page 3. The factual background for the decisions of the European Court of Human Rights in the cases *Baka v Hungary* and *Harabin v Slovakia* – affecting Mr Baka and Mr Harabin in their specific functions as court presidents – shows the specific importance of these positions.

9 A monocratic administration must be seen in contrast to a collective judicial administration which is executed either by the plenary assembly of judges or by two judicial committees.

istrative courts, presidents of the courts must and do exercise comprehensive powers under organisational laws because monocratic administrations regulate most areas of judicial administration.

Except in a few provinces, the court president is subordinate to the orders of the executive power of the province by law.[10]

In addition, so far all court presidents have been appointed in full discretion of the executive power.[11] There is no appointment procedure involving the court judges and neither does the appointment procedure correspond to the way that (other) court judges are appointed.[12] Therefore, the selection and appointment of the presidents of all the Austrian administrative courts remain in the full discretion of the executive power (i.e. the provincial or federal government), allowing direct political influence on the selection process – hand in hand with a high risk of a politically based decision on who will be chosen for the position of court president. At the same time, these administrative courts, led by these court presidents, have the legal competence to monitor the administrative acts/omissions of these governments.

Furthermore, no legal protection mechanisms exist for unsuccessful candidates.[13] Therefore, the (possibly politically determined) selection process cannot be legally challenged and no access to courts exists. The process is not transparent either.

One additional point to make is that the president of an administrative court need not have served as a judge ahead of his/her appointment as president.

The powers of the monocratic judicial administration which are implemented by the respective court president include: the recruitment, supervision and dismissal of all court personnel; the design, definition and modification of the internal organisation of the court (without transparency and without

---

[10] In most of the provinces where no subordination exists by law, the president is legally obliged to report to the local government on all business.

[11] A few of the organisational laws in the federal provinces provide for a kind of 'expert objectification commission' which has no decision-making powers, does not work transparently and is only involved in the selection process so that it can give scores and provide an opinion. These committees are not formally subordinated to orders but members of the judiciary are under-represented without a majority. Neither is there any legal protection mechanism nor transparency concerning the decisions (opinions) of this committee.

[12] This circumstance already contrasts with the position of opinion CCJE No 19 (2016) on the role of the Presidents of the Court, para. 38, and is also considered relevant in opinion CCJE-BU(2019)3 of 29 March 2019.

[13] Who have applied unsuccessfully for the position of court president. Legal protection only exists to claim pecuniary damages in cases in which the candidate has been discriminated against based on certain grounds and under certain restricted conditions there is state liability.

the possibility of challenging such decisions); budgetary responsibilities and executing financial power; the assignment of cases (the decision is made by a judicial senate); providing informal statements on the court judges when they apply for positions for their career development; controlling all the material resources of the court (without transparency and without the possibility of such decisions being contested – also in cases in which the court president allocates resources to the judges unequally); supervising the judges outside their judicial office[14] as well as in their judicial work – in addition to a judicial self-governing body which can evaluate the work of the judges;[15] and *ex officio* chairing all judicial self-governing bodies with the rights and responsibilities of the chair.[16] Concerning disciplinary regimes, in most of the federal provinces the president handles complaints against judges from outside and within the court and initiates disciplinary proceedings against judges in all cases where 'reasonable suspicion of disciplinary behaviour' exists (in general without any further legal concretisation of the criteria). An initiation of disciplinary proceedings by the court president may not be challenged on its own, but this does not necessarily have to be the case.[17]

When looking at the Austrian system, it emerges that neither mechanisms ensuring transparency nor participation rights, rights to information or counterbalancing mechanisms are available in these areas of judicial administration of the court which fall under the competence of the president. Hardly any legal protection mechanisms exist.[18]

Let us now turn to Hungary and the opinion issued by the Venice Commission. It focuses on the specific prerogatives of the Minister of Justice.[19] The planned new Judicial Council does not seem to be able to be an effective

---

[14] E.g. the approval of holidays.

[15] In most of the administrative courts no regular evaluation takes place, although in some courts regular evaluation by this judicial committee takes place. In many of these administrative courts two negative evaluations result in an *ex lege* (!) dismissal of the judge concerned.

[16] As noted above, in Art. 134 para. 2 and Art. 135 para. 2 the Federal Constitution provides for two judicial committees or the competence of the plenary assembly of the court to decide on the allocation of cases and to make non-binding proposals for the appointment of new administrative judges.

[17] Opinion CCJE, BU(2019)3 of 29 March 2019, paras 32, 33. However, the CCJE has seen it to be problematic if there are not sufficiently clear criteria which the President needs to follow in a disciplinary procedure.

[18] The judge's 'subjective rights' must be involved in order to have justiciable rights.

[19] It must be stressed that Hungary is not a federal state like Austria but more centralised. The judiciary is also centrally organised.

counterbalance to the Minister of Justice.[20] The Venice Commission stressed that it is hard to justify the powers of the Minister of Justice in the appointment procedures for court presidents.

In brief, in Hungary the appointment of court presidents is only possible for a (renewable) limited period of time, court presidents must have previously served as judges and administrative and organisational power is shared by the Minister of Justice, the president of the Supreme Administrative court and the respective court president – partly counterbalanced by a National Judicial Council. The deficiencies that emerge are comparable to those in the Austrian Administrative Judiciary model.

Executivist systems like the Austrian system with court presidents having broad powers with most responsibilities for the proper administration of the court have more vulnerable structures: possible subordination in decision-making activity can be manifold, with implications in terms of the amount of support for non-judicial court staff, logistic handling or restrictions on court rooms and going up to the question of which (kind of) court decisions are published and made publicly available in databases or search options.

These deficiencies were confirmed by the Consultative Council of European Judges (CCJE),[21] the Group of States against Corruption (GRECO) expressed its concern[22] and the European Commission stressed some issues in its first Rule of Law Report in 2020.[23]

An interim conclusion is that the open criticism of the planned Hungarian model is equally valid for the Austrian model, bearing in mind the benchmark that an internal judicial hierarchy must not be permitted in the exercise of judicial functions.[24] It can be tricky to distinguish between what is a judicial func-

---

20 European Commission for Democracy Through Law (Venice Commission), Opinion no. 943/2018, CDL-AD(2019)004, para. 47.

21 Opinion CCJE, BU(2019)3 of 29 March 2019 on the Viennese administrative court system.

22 The expert group of the Council of Europe, the Group of States against Corruption, heavily criticised the non-transparent appointment procedures in the 2016, Fourth Evaluation Round, Corruption Prevention in respect of members of parliament, judges and prosecutors, Evaluation Report Austria, GrecoEval4Rep(2016)1 of 13 February 2017, available at https://rm.coe.int/CoERMPublicCommonSearchServices/DisplayDCTMContent?documentId=09000016806f2b42/ (accessed 16 February 2021). Also see Fourth Evaluation Round, GrecoRC4(2018)15 of 17 July 2019, Compliance Report Austria, available at https://uvsvereinigung.wordpress.com/2019/07/17/greco-sieht-nur-sehr-geringe-fortschritte-im-oesterreichischen-justizsystem/ (accessed 16 February 2021).

23 European Commission, Rule of Law Report 2020 on Austria, SWD(2020) 319 final. One major strength of the Austrian model lies in its quite strong protection concerning the allocation of cases.

24 Rec. CM (2010)12, para. 30.

tion and what is an administrative function (like for any other civil servant). Grey areas remain in this executivist model and this is not a point of strength of the Austrian system of administrative justice.[25]

2.b Judicial Appointment Procedures

Attention has been turned to the issue of judicial appointments regarding the erosion of the rule of law in Poland. The recent landmark decision of the European Court of Human Rights[26] has contributed to these debates.

In principle, each judge who is appointed in accordance with the constitution and other applicable rules thereby obtains his or her constitutional authority and legitimacy. The Hungarian reform plans put the main prerogatives for the recruitment of new judges in the hands of the Minister of Justice. The Venice Commission – in principle – did not see a problem when recruitment is not driven by a judiciary's self-governing body but by the Minister of Justice.[27]

However, the Commission found the provisions on the power of the Minister to change the ranking of candidates prepared by the Judicial Council at his discretion without any explanation or recourse 'most problematic'[28] and it noted that it was 'most regrettable' that the draft law contained no explicit and effective means of controlling the use of the power conferred on the Minister of Justice regarding the appointment of future administrative judges. So far, so unpleasant. A – not even closer – look at the Austrian system for recruiting new administrative judges reveals a much darker picture:

The selection procedures for new judges vary among the Austrian federal provinces. No uniform procedure or criteria exist except one provision at the constitutional level.[29] The general assembly of a court's judges (or the respective judicial committee) can make non-binding proposals for three candidates for each vacant judicial post. However, the whole selection procedure – in the hands of the executive power of the province – in general lacks transparency. Furthermore, there is neither a right to have a legal review of the decision of these administrative selecting authorities nor reasoned decisions for (unsuc-

---

[25] A practical example is orders given by judges to the non-judicial court staff versus contrary orders ('recommendations') given by the court president to the court staff.

[26] Judgment of the European Court of Human Rights, Grand Chamber, of 1 December 2020, in the *Gudmundur Andri Astradsson vs Iceland* case, Appl. No. 26374/18.

[27] European Commission for Democracy Through Law (Venice Commission), Opinion no. 943/2018, CDL-AD(2019)004, paras 49 and 51.

[28] European Commission for Democracy Through Law (Venice Commission), Opinion no. 943/2018, CDL-AD(2019)004, paras 56 and 57.

[29] Article 134 Federal Constitution.

cessful) candidates. The selection practice of some of the authorities in the federal provinces (e.g. in Vienna and reportedly Lower Austria) shows that there have been cases where they have not followed the recommendations of the committee of judges[30] and not the first of the three proposed candidates has been selected but number two or three (even though the first choice would have been available), or none of the proposed candidates (but someone else not listed) has been appointed.[31] The Vienna federal province organisation laws even provide for two different selection steps in the overall procedure. The first by only the executive power itself,[32] in a non-transparent way in which a ranking of candidates is made through hearings, and then the non-binding proposals are obtained from the judicial committee of the administrative court.

Unlike the Hungarian draft, in Austria no obligation exists to give reasons for deviating from the proposals of the judicial committees.[33] Specifically noteworthy is the fact that no explicit and effective means of controlling the use of the power conferred on the governments of the federal provinces or of the federal government exist regarding the appointment of future administrative judges. This seems even more striking as in the Hungarian case the Venice Commission noted a lack of criteria for a ministerial override and of a mechanism to review the Minister's decision, although the bill foresaw some safety measures to counterbalance the Minister's power.[34]

There is no doubt that it would be mischievous to argue that having no procedure with no legal review rights of unsuccessful candidates implies that no violation of Art. 6 European Convention on Human Rights (ECHR) can take place and so the judicial system serves well all aspects of the rule of law benchmarks simply because no infringement of the nomination process takes place when there is no established nomination process. On the contrary, flagrant mistakes in an appointment procedure can lead to a lack of independence and

---

30 However, see point 47 of CM/Rec (2010)12) and the clear notes in its explanatory memorandum, paras 51 and 52, Council of Europe, European Committee on Legal Co-operation (CDCJ) – CM(2010)147-add1 of 21 October 2010, available at https://search.coe.int/cm/Pages/result_details.aspx?ObjectID=09000016805ce0df #globalcontainer (accessed 15 February 2021).

31 Three appointments have been made at the Viennese administrative court since 2015 in which none of the proposed candidates were appointed, i.e. appointments made in free discretion of the executive power (of approximately 20–25 judicial replacements since 2015).

32 I.e. the administrative body of the Viennese government.

33 Very recently such an obligation has come into force for the ordinary judiciary. This provision is also applicable for the Federal Administrative Court.

34 For more detail on these provisions, see European Commission for Democracy Through Law (Venice Commission), Opinion no. 943/2018, CDL-AD(2019)004, paras 49–59.

a lack of fundamental principles of fair review of the appointment procedure, and ignorance of clear European soft law standards lead to the same result. The GRECO[35] has repeatedly expressed its concerns – with so far no response from the Austrian legislator or the Austrian administrative court administrations.

Interestingly, unlike the Hungarian case, the Austrian case is not deemed to be problematic, although the appointment system shows blatant deficiencies compared to the Hungarian draft.

3. CONCLUSION

Each of our systems has good points and weak points. We should make efforts to increase the good points and minimise the weak ones. It is no longer legitimate to differentiate between old democracies and young democracies. Polish and other politicians love to refer to the old democracies as role models and this might end up with a poisonous mixture – taking the weak points of various systems and ignoring the strong points at the same time. However, this means that all our systems must invest in becoming more robust and in minimising the weak points.

Both systems, the Austrian and the planned Hungarian one, are equally weak. Interestingly, no relevant criticism can be heard from Austrian academia although criticism of Hungarian and Polish developments is loud.[36] The national associations of administrative judges[37] and the European Association of Administrative Judges[38] have repeatedly voiced their concerns.

---

35 The expert group of the Council of Europe, the Group of States against Corruption, heavily criticised the non-transparent appointment procedures in 2016, Fourth Evaluation Round, Corruption Prevention in respect of members of parliament, judges and prosecutors, Evaluation Report Austria, GrecoEval4Rep(2016)1 of 13 February 2017, available at https://rm.coe.int/CoERMPublicCommonSearchServices/DisplayDCTMContent?documentId=09000016806f2b42/ (accessed 16 February 2021) and Fourth Evaluation Round, GrecoRC4(2018)15 of 17 July 2019, Compliance Report Austria, available at https://uvsvereinigung.wordpress.com/2019/07/17/greco-sieht-nur-sehr-geringe-fortschritte-im-oesterreichischen-justizsystem/ (accessed 16 February 2021).

36 However, see Reinhard Heinrich (Hg.), 'Kritisches Handbuch der österreichischen Demokratie', Böhlau Verlag, 2020 and the activities of the Österreichische Forschungsgemeinschaft – Zukunft der Demokratie, available at https://www.oefg.at/arbeitsgemeinschaften/zukunft-der-demokratie/ (accessed 15 February 2021).

37 See, e.g., http://www.verwaltungsrichter.at/ (accessed 15 February 2021).

38 See https://www.aeaj.org/ (accessed 15 February 2021).

There should not be a lowering of existing standards as an outcome of judicial reforms and of experiments on the lowest possible standard that can be applied.[39]

The longer we wait, the more difficult it will become to bring weaknesses back in line with European standards. These weaknesses have a role-model effect, namely the above-mentioned race to the bottom. They have the potential to spread not linearly but exponentially like a virus. Furthermore, in the worst cases this will lead to different categories of judges with many more adverse consequences. Looking at Poland, we can imagine such consequences.

Old democracies might have better semi-skilled immune systems. However, the Covid-19 pandemic has proven that persons with a good immune system can be affected and even die. It would be hazardous to believe that such an 'anti-democratic' virus can only grow in new democracies. It is our duty to discover each of the structural weaknesses in our legal systems in order to contribute to a trustable European judiciary.

---

[39] To follow the trend of increasing speed and making it more comfortable for the legislative and executive powers to handle the judiciary in a country.

10. Limitations to access to justice and Article 47 of the Charter: the right to be advised, defended and represented

Magdalena Ličková and Joan Solanes Mullor[1]

I. INTRODUCTION

Although the right to have a counsel is one of the basic components of the concept of fair trial as understood today,[2] it has manifestly not always been an undisputed element in the procedural landscape. Indeed, there have been times and places in which defendants were prohibited from receiving advice in felony trials where they risked everything, including their very lives, because, in short, an 'honest defence' was not considered to require any special skills.[3] The general belief was that 'the very Speech, Gesture and Countenance, and Manner of Defence of those who are Guilty, when they speak for themselves, may often help to disclose the Truth, which probably would not so well be discovered from the artificial Defence of others speaking for them'.[4]

Nevertheless, concerns about the injustice that could possibly be suffered by persons unfamiliar with the foreign language of law[5] gradually reversed such

1 The authors would like to thank Sara Iglesias Sanchez for her critique of this chapter. All opinions and errors remain ours.

2 Case C-305/05 *Ordre des barreaux francophones and germanophones and Others* [2007] ECR I-5305, para 31. See, for instance, *Poitrimol v France*, App. no. 14032/88 (ECtHR, 23 November 1993), para. 34; *Salduz v Turkey*, App. no. 36391/02 (ECtHR, 27 November 2008), para. 51; and *Doyle v Ireland*, App. no. 51979/17 (ECtHR, 23 May 2019), para. 67.

3 John H. Langbein, 'The Criminal Trial before Lawyers' (1978) U. Chi. L. Rev. 45(2) 263, 282–3, 310.

4 William Hawkins, *A Treatise of the Pleas of the Crown*, vol. 2, 400, London, 2 vols, 1716, 1721, quoted in John H. Langbein, 'The Prosecutorial Origins of Defence Counsel in the Eighteenth Century: The Appearance of Solicitors' (1999) *Cambridge Law Journal* 58(2) 314, 315.

5 Which possibly could indeed be a *foreign* language in the literal sense of this term, such as when in England laws were written in French and Latin. John Felipe

thinking and transformed the defendant's adviser from a *persona non grata* to a fundamental actor appearing in courtrooms. While the specific content and implications of this may differ, it is not uncommon for the right of access to a lawyer to be recognised as a fundamental constitutional right, either specifically or as a component of the right to a fair trial or to due process.[6]

At the international level, the right to a lawyer is enshrined in the European Convention on Human Rights (ECHR),[7] in the International Covenant on Civil and Political Rights,[8] in the statutes of international criminal tribunals[9] and to some extent in the Vienna Convention on Consular Relations.[10] In European Union law, the right to be advised is specifically provided for in the second paragraph of Article 47 of the Charter of Fundamental Rights of the European Union (Charter)[11] and in Directive 2013/48/EU (Access to Lawyer Directive).[12] Moreover, Directive 2012/13 (Right to Information Directive)[13] provides that suspects or accused persons must at least be informed of certain procedural

---

Acevedo, 'The Ideological Origins of the Right to Counsel' (2016) *South Carolina Law Review* 68(1) 87, 104.

[6] An early example of the constitutionalisation of the right to a lawyer can be identified in the United States legal system. Many state constitutions guarantee this right, and the Sixth Amendment to the United States Constitution recognised it in 1789. See Laura I. Appleman, 'The Community Right to a Counsel' (2012) *Berkeley Journal of Criminal Law* 17(1) 1, 42–4. For European examples, see Ed Cape, Zaza Namoradze, Roger Smith and Taru Spronken, *Effective Criminal Defence in Europe*, Antwerp, Intersentia, 2010, pp. xxxi–657 and Ed Cape and Zaza Namoradze, *Effective Criminal Defence in Eastern Europe: Bulgaria, Georgia, Lithuania, Moldova, Ukraine*, Soros Foundation–Moldova, 2012, pp. xxvii–500.

[7] Article 6(3)(c) reads as follows: '3. Everyone charged with a criminal offence has the following minimum rights: [...] to defend himself in person or through legal assistance of his own choosing or, if he has not sufficient means to pay for legal assistance, to be given it free when the interests of justice so require.'

[8] Article 14(3)(b) and (d), adopted on 16 December 1966 by the United Nations General Assembly, *United Nations Treaty Series*, vol. 999, p. 171.

[9] See, e.g., Article 21(4)(d) of the Statute of the International Criminal Tribunal for the former Yugoslavia, adopted on 25 May 1993 by United Nations Security Council Resolution 827, S/RES/827 (1993) as amended.

[10] Article 36, 24 April 1963, *United Nations Treaty Series*, vol. 596, p. 261.

[11] The second paragraph of Article 47 of the Charter corresponds to Article 6(1) ECHR on the right to a fair trial. Explanations relating to the Charter of Fundamental Rights [2007] (OJ C303). Moreover, Article 48(2) of the Charter lays down a more general guarantee of 'the rights of the defence of anyone who has been charged'.

[12] Directive 2013/48/EU on the right of access to a lawyer in criminal proceedings and in European arrest warrant proceedings, and on the right to have a third party informed upon the deprivation of liberty, and to communicate with third persons and with consular authorities while deprived of liberty [2013] (OJ L294).

[13] Article 3 of Directive 2012/13/EU on the right to information in criminal proceedings [2012] (OJ L142).

rights, including the right of access to a lawyer and entitlement to free legal advice, and of the conditions for obtaining it. Furthermore, the right to legal advice is guaranteed (although in a less detailed manner) by other EU legislative instruments outside the criminal-law context, such as acts concerned with the common rules of asylum (Asylum Procedures Directive,[14] Reception Conditions Directive,[15] Dublin Regulation[16]) and the Returns Directive.[17] 'Less assertively',[18] the right to legal assistance can also be understood as being covered by Article 9(5) of the Aarhus Convention, requiring its contracting parties to 'consider the establishment of appropriate assistance mechanisms to remove or reduce financial and *other barriers* to access to justice'.

Given its position within the autonomous constitutional framework of the European Union, the Charter constitutes a powerful basis for enhancing the rights enshrined therein. What is relevant here, since its application vis-à-vis the Member States is limited to situations in which they implement EU law,[19] is that its interpretative relevance should in principle increase with the progressive adoption of legislative acts dealing with procedural rights. But does it? One can understandably wonder what part the Charter has to play when considering that the Access to Lawyer Directive gives flesh to the right to be advised with a level of detail that simply cannot exist in an instrument of

---

14 Article 22 of Directive 2013/32/EU on common procedures for granting and withdrawing international protection [2013] (OJ L180).

15 Article 18 (2)(b)(c) of Directive 2013/33/EU of the European Parliament and of the Council of 26 June 2013 laying down standards for the reception of applicants for international protection [2013] (OJ L180).

16 Article 27(5) of Regulation (EU) No. 604/2013 establishing the criteria and mechanisms for determining the Member State responsible for examining an application for international protection lodged in one of the Member States by a third-country national or a stateless person [2013] (OJ L180).

17 Article 13(3) of Directive 2008/115/EC on common standards and procedures in Member States for returning illegally staying third-country nationals [2008] (OJ L 348). On this provision, see Nathan Cambien, 'Effective Remedies and Defence Rights in the Field of Asylum, Migration and Borders' in Sara Iglesias Sanchez and Maribel González Pascual (eds), *EU Fundamental Rights in the Area of Freedom, Security and Justice*, Cambridge, Cambridge University Press, 2021, referring to the judgment in C-249/13 *Khaled Boudjlida v Préfet des Pyrénées-Atlantiques* EU:C:2014:2431, para. 65.

18 As noted by Advocate General Sharpston in her opinion in Case C-543/14 *Ordre des barreaux francophones et germanophone e.a.* EU:C:2016:157, para. 67.

19 See Case C-617/10 *Åkerberg Fransson* EU:C:2013:105, paras 21–23. See generally K. Lenaerts and J.A. Gutiérrez-Fons, 'The Place of the Charter in the EU Constitutional Edifice,' in S. Peers, T. Hervey, J. Kenner and A. Ward (eds), *The EU Charter of Fundamental Rights: A Commentary*, Oxford, C.H. Beck, Hart, Nomos, 2014, 1559–93, and Allan Rosas, 'When is the EU Charter of Fundamental Rights Applicable at National Level?' (2012) *Jurisprudence* 19(4) 1269–88, 1277.

a constitutional nature. In the following sections, this chapter will therefore assess the role of the Charter in shaping the content of this right by examining the case law of the Court of Justice of the European Union (CJEU) which has emerged with regard to the requisite quality of lawyers (II), the conduct of suspects or accused persons (III) and the type of proceedings at issue (IV). It then turns to the question of how violations of the right to be advised are to be remedied (V) before drawing concluding remarks (VI).

II. THE RIGHT TO BE ADVISED: REPRESENTATION BY ANY LAWYER?

The effective exercise of the right to be advised is hardly imaginable without the acting lawyer meeting the necessary professional standards. Some light as to what EU law requires in this respect has been shed by recent case law dealing with the limits set (1) at the national level and (2) before the courts of the Union.

A. The Access to Lawyer Directive and National Rules on Representation

The Access to Lawyer Directive provides minimum standards from which suspects and accused persons in criminal proceedings[20] must benefit. Like this directive, other instruments adopted in the context of the same legislative package[21] detail further rights (some of which are stated in the Charter), such as the right to interpretation and translation, information and legal aid and the presumption of innocence.[22] While the immediate objective of these instruments

---

[20] And persons affected by the European arrest warrant under Council Framework Decision 2002/584/JHA on the European arrest warrant and the surrender procedures between Member States [2002] (OJ L190) ('EAW FD').

[21] Resolution of the Council on a Roadmap for strengthening procedural rights of suspected or accused persons in criminal proceedings [2009] (OJ C295) and European Council, 'The Stockholm Programme – an open and secure Europe serving and protecting citizens', point 2.4 [2010] (OJ C115).

[22] Directive 2010/64/EU on the right to interpretation and translation in criminal proceedings [2010] (OJ L280); Directive 2012/13, fn. 13 *supra*; Directive 2016/343/EU on the strengthening of certain aspects of the presumption of innocence and of the right to be present at the trial in criminal proceedings [2016] (OJ L65); Directive 2016/1919/EU on legal aid for suspects and accused persons in criminal proceedings and for requested persons in European arrest warrant proceedings [2016] (OJ L297); Directive 2016/800/EU on procedural safeguards for children who are suspects or accused persons in criminal proceedings [2016] (OJ L132); Directive 2011/93/EU on combating the sexual abuse and sexual exploitation of children and child pornography, and replacing Council Framework Decision 2004/68/JHA [2011] (OJ L335).

is to enhance these guarantees, at a more general level they aim to promote mutual trust among the Member States in the fairness of their criminal-law systems because by laying down common standards for selected aspects of criminal procedure they enhance the operation of other EU-law instruments of judicial cooperation in criminal-law matters.[23]

The Court was offered its first opportunity to interpret the Access to Lawyer Directive in the *Kolev* case,[24] which concerned criminal proceedings against customs officials accused of bribery. What is relevant here is that this case dealt with the question of whether the Access to Lawyer Directive precluded legislation under which the national court had to exclude and replace a defendant's lawyer who represented another defendant where the defence of the two defendants was in mutual conflict.

This legal question was addressed under the general provision in Article 3(1) of the Access to Lawyer Directive requiring the Member States to ensure that suspects and accused persons have the right of access to a lawyer in such time and in such a way as to allow them to exercise their rights of defence in a practical and effective manner. Although the Access to Lawyer Directive includes the much more specific restrictions-related Article 8, there was no need for the Court to engage in an analysis of that provision as it concerns a different type of intensity of the restriction on the right at issue, namely one that affects the very possibility of consulting any lawyer, not just a lawyer of one's own choosing.

Referring to the clause in Article 52(3) of the Charter, the Court turned to the case law of the European Court of Human Rights (ECtHR) to note that 'while the right of access to a lawyer [...] laid down in Article 6(3) ECHR implies that it should be open to the person concerned to use a lawyer of his own choice, that possibility is not [...] absolute'. Such restrictions are nevertheless 'subject to the test of proportionality',[25] requiring them to be prescribed by law, to pursue a public interest objective and to be proportionate to that objective. *In casu*, this test was considered to be met, with the Court noting that the (legitimate) objective of the national legislation at issue was to safeguard the right of accused persons to an effective defence, the absence of any conflict of interest on the part of the lawyer being essential for this purpose.

---

23 Opinion of Advocate General Bobek in Case C-646/17 *Moro* EU:C:2019:489, paras 39–40. See also Proposal for a Directive of the European Parliament and of the Council on the right of access to a lawyer in criminal proceedings and on the right to communicate upon arrest, COM/2011/0326 final, point 4.

24 Case C-612/15 *Nikolay Kolev and Others* EU:C:2018:392.

25 Referring to *Croissant v Germany*, App. no. 13611/88 (ECtHR, 25 September 1992), para. 29; and *Lagerblom v Sweden*, App. no. 26891/95 (ECtHR, 14 January 2003), para. 54. See *Kolev*, fn. 24 *supra*, para. 106.

Although in the *Kolev* case the Court mentioned Articles 47 and 48(2) of the Charter while observing that the Access to Lawyer Directive seeks to promote the rights enshrined in it, the Charter principally played its well-established role as a bridge to standards developed under the ECHR, thus enhancing coherence between it and European Union law. It should be noted that, contrary to Article 47 of the Charter and to the Access to Lawyer Directive, Article 6(3)(c) ECHR refers to the right to be assisted by a lawyer 'of his own choosing'. In this normative context, the ECtHR examined a similar restriction by weighing the 'defendant's wishes' against 'the interests of justice'[26] and by considering whether a restriction on these wishes relied on 'relevant and sufficient grounds'.[27] This constitutes a rather lenient test applied in situations in which there is no denial of access to a lawyer as such but in which the wishes of the represented person as to who should represent them were not honoured.

In contrast with such situations, in (subsequent) cases in which there was an outright denial of access to legal advice, the ECtHR has applied the stricter scrutiny of 'compelling reasons',[28] only allowing for a restriction to be imposed 'in exceptional circumstances'. The restriction must moreover be 'of a temporary nature and [be] based on an individual assessment of the particular circumstances of the case'.[29] The ECtHR has further verified whether a decision to restrict access to legal advice relies on a legal basis, and whether its scope and content are 'sufficiently circumscribed by law so as to guide operational decision-making by those responsible for applying them'.[30] That being said, an absence of 'compelling reasons' does not necessarily lead to a violation of the ECHR, but it triggers 'very strict scrutiny' when it comes to the assessment of the overall fairness of the criminal proceedings under Article 6(1) ECHR.[31] In such a situation, it is for the defendant government to show that 'the overall fairness of the trial [has not been] irretrievably prejudiced'.[32]

---

[26] *Croissant*, fn. 25 *supra*, para. 29; and *Lagerblom*, fn. 25 *supra*, para. 54. See also *Almaši v Serbia*, App. no. 21388/15 (ECtHR, 8 October 2019), para. 105.

[27] See *Dvorski v Croatia*, App. no. 25703/11 (ECtHR, 20 October 2015), paras 79, 81–82.

[28] Concerning the investigation phase. See *Salduz*, fn. 2 *supra*, para. 55. See further *Ibrahim and Others v the United Kingdom*, App. nos. 50541/08, 50571/08, 50573/08, 40351/09 (ECtHR, 13 September 2016), paras 257–265; *Beuze v Belgium*, App. no. 71409/10 (ECtHR, 9 November 2018), paras 137–149; *Mehmet Zeki Çelebi v Turkey*, App. no. 27582/07 (ECtHR, 28 January 2020), paras 45–51. See also *Dvorski*, fn. 27 *supra*, para. 80.

[29] *Mehmet Zeki Çelebi*, fn. 28 *supra*, para. 46; *Beuze*, fn. 28 *supra*, para. 142.

[30] *Mehmet Zeki Çelebi*, fn. 28 *supra*, para. 46.

[31] *Ibrahim and Others*, fn. 28 *supra*, paras 265 and 274. See also *Simeonovi v Bulgaria*, App. no. 21980/04 (ECtHR, 12 May 2017), paras 112–113.

[32] *Mehmet Zeki Çelebi*, fn. 28 *supra*, para. 48.

The notion of compelling reasons, together with the three elements mentioned above (exceptional circumstances, temporary nature and individual assessment) featuring in *Salduz*[33] and in the subsequent case law appear in the introductory part of Article 3(6) of the Access to Lawyer Directive. This provision then follows up with two specific scenarios of permissible restrictions, one of which later appeared in ECtHR case law.[34]

The less stringent 'relevant and sufficient reason' test and the rigorous 'compelling reasons' test constitute the two tools that the ECtHR has used to examine situations of alleged violations of the right to be advised, depending on the intensity of the alleged breach. The facts in *Kolev* make the case comparable to situations that the ECtHR has addressed using the more lenient test of 'relevant and sufficient reasons' in that the Court briefly verified the existence of a public interest objective pursued by the legislation at issue, and its proportionality, but did not engage in a fully fledged scrutiny of these elements or in a limitations of rights assessment under Article 51(2) of the Charter as it had done on other occasions.[35] That being said, situations in which there is an outright denial of access to legal advice, which in principle should trigger more thorough scrutiny, are now exhaustively covered in specific provisions of the Access to Lawyer Directive, which provides for the EU-law analytical framework to be applied in such circumstances.

As already pointed out, the restriction at issue in *Kolev* concerned the choice to be represented by a specific lawyer and not the very possibility of obtaining legal advice. The case therefore appears to bear more relevance to assessment of the effectiveness of legal assistance than to examination of a genuine restriction on the right to legal advice. Under the ECtHR case law, the ECHR contracting parties can indeed be held liable not only for a complete lack of legal assistance but also for its ineffectiveness, and not only in the context of *ex officio* representation and legal aid schemes but also regarding privately hired lawyers.[36] Therefore, an EU Member State may violate the right to legal advice

---

33 *Salduz*, fn. 2 *supra*, paras 54 *in fine* and 55; *Beuze*, fn. 28 *supra*, para. 142.

34 See *Beuze*, fn. 28 *supra*, para. 143; *Ibrahim and Others*, fn. 28 *supra*, para. 259; *Simeonovi*, fn. 31 *supra*, para. 117.

35 For an example related to Article 50 of the Charter (*ne bis in idem*), see cases C-524/15 *Menci* EU:C:2018:197; C-537/16 *Garlsson Real Estate and Others* EU:C:2018:193; C-596/16 and C-597/16 *Di Puma and Zecca* EU:C:2018:192.

36 *Güveç v Turkey*, App. no. 70337/01 (ECtHR, 20 January 2009), para. 131. See also *Artico v Italy*, App. no. 6694/74 (ECtHR, 13 May 1980), para. 33 (noting that 'mere nomination does not ensure effective assistance since the lawyer appointed for legal aid purposes may die, fall seriously ill, be prevented for a protracted period from acting or shirk his duties') or *Kamasinski v Austria*, App. no. 9783/82 (ECtHR, 19 December 1989), para. 65. See also *Czekalla v Portugal*, App. no. 38830/97 (ECtHR, 10 October 2002), para. 60.

under the ECHR standards if, without making access to a lawyer impossible, its authorities do not prevent the representation from being flawed, which was precisely the scenario that came to the fore in *Kolev*.

B. Autonomous Rules of Representation before Union Courts

As was evidenced by the outcome in *Kolev*, there are cases in which a defendant needs to be 'protected from his own lawyer'. To find further relevant case law examples shedding light in this respect, one needs for the moment to veer away from the national arena (and by the same token the criminal-law area) and turn to the rules governing proceedings before courts of the Union. In this specific context, the issue of standards of legal representation has received yet another dimension when it comes to the requirement for mandatory representation, which has to be respected by physical and legal persons wishing to appear before Union courts.[37] While their obligation to be represented is stated in Article 19 of the Statute of the CJEU,[38] courts of the Union have further defined limits that flow from (1) the concept of 'lawyer' used in that provision and (2) from the requirement of effective judicial remedy under Article 47 of the Charter.

i. Article 19 of the Statute: the requirement of independence of lawyers

The obligation to be represented is not uncommon across the Member States when it comes to representation before the highest judicial instances, and it also applies to non-privileged applicants before both of the Union's courts.[39] Under Article 19 of the Statute, non-privileged applicants must be represented by a lawyer authorised to practise before a court of a Member State (or of a party to the European Economic Area Agreement). No further condition is stipulated, and one might therefore wonder whether the capacity to act in this context depends only on national laws and professional rules determining whether a specific lawyer may represent a specific applicant in a specific dispute. The response to this question is twofold. While Article 19 of the Statute makes it clear that only lawyers qualified under national

---

37 See esp. Articles 263, fourth paragraph; 265, third paragraph; 268; 270; and 272 Treaty on the Functioning of the European Union (TFEU).

38 Consolidated version of the Treaty on the Functioning of the European Union, Protocol (No 3) on the Statute of the Court of Justice of the European Union, OJ C 202, 7 June 2016, p. 210.

39 With the exception of the preliminary ruling proceedings where reference is made to applicable national law. See Article 97(3) of the Rules of Procedure of the Court of Justice.

laws may appear before Union courts, it is also required, in what is now well-established case law,[40] that these lawyers be 'independent'. The concept is understood as an autonomous notion of EU law and was recently confirmed in the *Uniwersytet Wrocławski* case.[41] Initially, the General Court dismissed as manifestly inadmissible an action filed by this university because its lawyer did not meet the test of independence. This was because, although the lawyer was qualified under national law, he was also giving classes at the university. On appeal, however, the Court clarified that

> the lawyer's duty of independence is to be understood not as the lack of any connection whatsoever between the lawyer and his or her client, but the lack of connections which have a manifestly detrimental effect on his or her capacity to carry out the task of defending his or her client while acting in that client's interests to the greatest possible extent.[42]

In the light of that test, the Court concluded that in the absence of a hierarchical relationship the connection between the applicant and the lawyer in the case was too tenuous.[43]

Although, strictly speaking, the *Uniwersytet Wrocławski* case does not concern a case of self-representation,[44] from a broader perspective one could compare the requirement of independence developed in EU case law to the idea of a dispassionate, technically prepared and therefore effective defence, to which the ECtHR referred in *Correia de Matos v Portugal.*[45] In this case involving a lawyer claiming the right to represent himself, despite the requirement of mandatory legal representation, the ECtHR scrutinised the legislation, case law and the overall context of mandatory legal representation in Portuguese criminal proceedings. Referring to the margin of appreciation doctrine, the ECtHR subjected the requirement, as a limitation to the right to represent oneself, to scrutiny under the 'relevant and sufficient requirement'

---

40 See, e.g., cases T-94/07 *EREF v Commission* EU:T:2009:451, para. 15; T-452/10 *ClientEarth v Council* EU:T:2011:420, para. 14; C-573/11 P *ClientEarth v Council* EU:C:2013:564, para. 11; T-226/10 *Prezes Urzędu Komunikacji Elektronicznej v Commission* EU:T:2011:234, paras 16–17 and 21; C-422/11 P and C-423/11 P *Prezes Urzędu Komunikacji Elektronicznej v Commission* EU:C:2012:553, paras 32–34.

41 Cases T-137/16 *Uniwersytet Wrocławski v REA* EU:T:2017:407, C-515/17 P and C-561/17 P *Uniwersytet Wrocławski and Poland v REA* EU:C:2020:73.

42 C-515/17 P and C-561/17 P *Uniwersytet Wrocławski and Poland v REA* EU:C:2020:73, para. 64.

43 Ibid., para. 66.

44 On the issue of self-representation of an applicant before Union courts, see, e.g., Case C-392/18 P *Bettani v Commission* EU:C:2019:186.

45 *Correia de Matos v Portugal*, App. no. 56402/12 (ECtHR, 4 April 2018), paras 153–154.

test and insisted inter alia on the importance of maintaining the possibility for the accused to intervene in person so as to influence his or her defence.[46] It considered that the need to secure a dispassionate and effective defence may indeed constitute a relevant and sufficient reason for the mandatory legal representation to be required, and even if the defendant is trained in advocacy he or she 'may be unable, as a result of being personally affected by the charges, to conduct an effective defence in his or her own case'.[47] At a broader level, these considerations represent an example of the general requirement, repeatedly referred to by the ECtHR, according to which the guarantee of rights under the ECHR must be 'effective and practical, not theoretical and illusory'.[48] A similar dictum appears in Article 3(1) of the Access to Lawyer Directive.

The *Uniwersytet Wrocławski* case also raised the issue of the procedural consequences of a failure to respect the independence-related requirement. Although the solution adopted by the Court ultimately did not make it necessary to engage in such an analysis, it was explored by the Advocate General, who suggested considering such a failure to be remediable so as to avoid sanctioning the applicant for an inadequate choice of lawyer. In his view, the opposite solution would bring about a situation incompatible with Article 47 of the Charter, with the impossibility of correcting an inadequate choice of lawyer 'simply extinguish[ing] the essence of the right to an effective judicial remedy'.[49]

ii. Article 47 of the Charter: limits to the effects of national rules on legal representation

For an action by a non-privileged applicant before Union courts to be admissible, it is inter alia necessary to show that the lawyer representing the applicant has been duly authorised to do so. To verify whether this condition is satisfied in respect of, specifically, a legal person governed by private law, Article 51(3)

---

46 Ibid., paras 144–159, esp. paras 158 and 159.

47 Ibid., para. 153. In a different case, the ECtHR concluded that there was a violation of Article 6(1) ECHR due to an overly strict interpretation of the applicant's *locus standi* in a civil claim filed by an applicant – himself a practising lawyer – was dismissed due to a lack of compliance with the mandatory rules on legal representation that were, at the time, subject to diverging judicial interpretation. *Maširević v Serbia*, App. no. 30671/08 (ECtHR, 11 February 2014), paras 47–51.

48 *Artico*, fn. 36 *supra*, para. 33; *Kamasinski*, fn. 36 *supra*, para. 65; *Czekalla*, fn. 36 *supra*, para. 60. See also in this sense *Dayanan v Turkey*, App. no. 7377/03 (ECtHR, 13 October 2009), paras 30–32.

49 Opinion of Advocate General Bobek in Joined Cases C-515/17 P and C-561/17 P *Uniwersytet Wrocławski v Research Executive Agency (REA) and Republic of Poland* EU:C:2019:774, para. 151 and fn. 65.

of the Rules of Procedure of the General Court requires lawyers to lodge their authority to act. While the question as to whether the power of attorney has been issued by a person authorised to act on behalf of a legal person is a matter governed by national law, the Court has conditioned the effects of these rules on their compliance with the right to effective judicial remedy enshrined in Article 47 of the Charter. More specifically, in the *Trasta Komercbanka* case[50] the General Court initially held that there was no need to adjudicate on the action filed by a credit institution whose authorisation had been withdrawn by the European Central Bank and which went into liquidation as a consequence of the withdrawal. The decision of the General Court was based on the fact that the power of attorney of the acting lawyer was revoked by the applicant's liquidator, who was appointed after the action was brought.[51] Nevertheless, the applicant put forward the existence of a conflict of interest on the part of the liquidator appointed (and revocable) by the national authority that had participated in the procedure which had led to the withdrawal of the authorisation (and therefore to the applicant's liquidation). While acknowledging that it is for the national law to define who can act on behalf of a legal person,[52] the Court deciding on appeal rejected an overly lenient approach consisting in accepting any and all of such rules, as 'the autonomy enjoyed by the Member States […] is restricted by their obligation, in particular, to ensure compliance with the right to an effective remedy and to a fair hearing enshrined in Article 47 of the Charter'.[53] Relying on this article and ECtHR case law, it held that Union courts shall not recognise the legal consequences of such rules where their application leads to violation of the principle of the effective judicial protection of individuals' rights under EU law.[54]

When compared, the judgments in *Uniwersytet Wrocławski* and *Trasta Komercbanka* can be seen as responding to two complementary aspects of representation before Union courts: while the first case limits what was seen as an overly strict limit imposed on legal representation where national rules arguably permit it, the second one neutralises the effects of national rules when they put effective access to 'European' justice in jeopardy. Although the *Kolev* case mentioned earlier differs from both *Uniwersytet Wrocławski* and *Trasta Komercbanka* in terms of its normative context and implications, these three

---

50 Joined Cases C-663/17 P, C-665/17 P and C-669/17 P *European Central Bank (ECB) v Trasta Komercbanka AS and Others* EU:C:2019:923 and Case T-247/16 *Fursin and Others v ECB* EU:T:2017:623.

51 Case T-247/16 *Fursin and Others v ECB* EU:T:2017:623, paras 32–50.

52 *European Central Bank (ECB v Trasta Komercbanka)*, fn. 50 *supra*, paras 57–58.

53 Ibid., para. 59 and cited case law.

54 Ibid., para. 70.

cases all address issues related to the quality and status of the lawyer, and for that reason touch on an important aspect of (if not a pre-condition for) the exercise of the right to effective judicial remedy. Interestingly, the solutions by way of which these issues have been addressed embrace different conceptual approaches, in which the role of the Charter fluctuates between absence in *Uniwersytet Wrocławski* (resolved through interpretation of Article 19 of the Statute), being the traditional bridge to the ECtHR standards in *Kolev* (decided on the basis of a proportionality test) and a limit to the Member States' autonomy (confirmed, yet circumscribed) in *Trasta Komercbanka*, in which Article 47 of the Charter played a determinative role as it constituted the very basis of the Court's response to the relevant part of the appeal.

III. THE RIGHT TO BE ADVISED: A REWARD FOR APPEARING IN THE COURTROOM?

Under Article 3(2)(d) of the Access to Lawyer Directive, the possibility of consulting a lawyer must be granted to persons who have been summoned to appear before a court with jurisdiction in criminal matters in due time before they are to appear before the court. The *VW (Right of access to a lawyer in case of non-appearance)* case offered the Court of Justice an opportunity to clarify the scope of permissible derogations to this rule and to ascertain whether, in particular, the right to be advised can be used as a 'bargaining chip'[55] to make an absconding person appear. The Court responded with a clear no.[56]

The suspect in this case failed to appear despite being summoned, which, by application of Spanish legislation, resulted in his right of access to a lawyer being delayed. In a rather straightforward analysis, the Court noted that such a restriction is not among those exhaustively listed in Article 3(5) and (6) of the Access to Lawyer Directive, read in combination with Article 8(1). It concluded that to allow it would run counter to the right to be advised laid down in the second paragraph of Article 47 of the Charter and the rights of defence guaranteed by Article 48(2) of the Charter, which are among the objectives pursued by the Access to Lawyer Directive.

Similarly, ECtHR case law is rich in examples making it clear that the right of access to a lawyer cannot be made dependent on the presence of the accused.[57] While States can discourage unjustified absences, they cannot do so

---

[55] Opinion of Advocate General Bobek in C-659/18 *VW (Right to access to a lawyer in case of non-appearance)* EU:C:2019:940, para. 60.

[56] Case C-659/18 *VW (Right of access to a lawyer in the event of non-appearance)* EU:C:2020:201.

[57] That was also pointed out by Advocate General Bobek in *VW*, fn. 55 *supra*, para. 48, referring to *Pelladoah v The Netherlands*, App. no. 16737/90 (ECtHR,

by way of denial of legal assistance.[58] Therefore, delays in this respect, especially in the pre-trial phase, require rather strict scrutiny both under the Access to Lawyer Directive and the ECHR, be it through the exhaustively defined 'exceptionality' based on enumerated compelling reasons framed by a test of proportionality (as regards the former) or through the 'compelling reasons' test already referred to above and characterised as very stringent[59] framed by assessment of the overall fairness of the criminal proceedings (as regards the latter).[60]

IV. THE RIGHT TO BE ADVISED – IN WHICH PROCEEDINGS?

The next issue that the Court was asked to clarify was whether the right of access to a lawyer extends to proceedings that do not lead to the imposition of a criminal sentence, but which nevertheless result in a deprivation of liberty. *Rayonna prokuratura Lom*[61] concerned criminal proceedings brought against EP, who was arrested on suspicion of committing a serious crime while suffering from mental illness. The criminal proceedings were later closed on account of EP's mental disorder, and EP was ordered to undergo compulsory medical measures. EP was neither questioned during the investigation nor notified of the criminal procedure, and he was not given access to a lawyer.

The question which therefore arose was whether under such circumstances EP's rights could be considered to be complied with, calling for clarification as to whether the Access to Lawyer Directive, and also the Information about Rights Directive,[62] applied to judicial proceedings authorising, on therapeutic and safety grounds, the committal to a psychiatric hospital of persons who in a state of insanity have committed acts representing a danger to society. The Court concluded that the scope of the two directives is broad enough to cover such proceedings even if they do not lead to the imposition of a 'sentence' when they nevertheless result in the deprivation of liberty, and when that deprivation is based on, among other things, safety grounds.[63]

---

22 September 1994), para. 40; and *Van Geyseghem v Belgium*, App. no. 26103/95 (ECtHR, 21 January 1999), para. 34. See further *Lala v The Netherlands*, App. no. 14861/89 (ECtHR, 22 September 1994), para. 33. Compare with *Galstyan v Armenia*, App. no. 26986/03 (ECtHR, 15 November 2007), para. 89.

58 *Tolmachev v Estonia*, App. no. 73748/13 (ECtHR, 9 July 2015), para. 48.

59 For the *Ibrahim* test, based on 'compelling reasons' and defined as particularly stringent, see *Ibrahim and Others*, fn. 28 *supra*, para. 258.

60 Ibid., para. 274.

61 C-467/18 *Rayonna prokuratura Lom and Others* EU:C:2019:765.

62 And Directive 2012/13, fn. 13 *supra*.

63 See *Rayonna prokuratura Lom*, fn. 61 *supra*, para. 41.

The Court construed the scope of the two instruments as extending to the situation at hand, not through the procedural guarantees under Articles 47 or 48(2) of the Charter but through the concept of 'criminal proceedings' and the substantive protection granted to liberty and security under its Article 6, together with the relevant case law of the ECtHR on the corresponding Article 5(1)(e) ECHR.[64] It concluded that since the measures at issue came within the scope of Article 6 of the Charter, judicial proceedings related to it fell within the scope of the directives, the objectives of which included the pursuit of the right guaranteed under that provision. This conclusion was further confirmed by several articles of the Access to Lawyer Directive which underline the need to take into account the needs of vulnerable persons, in line with ECtHR case law, integrating this consideration into the assessment of the fairness of proceedings as a whole.[65]

Indeed, beyond the intrinsic vulnerability in which suspects find themselves due to the very fact of being, for instance, in police custody,[66] considering the needs of persons who are specifically vulnerable on account of, particularly, age or mental health features prominently as the first element in the *Ibrahim* test of the overall fairness of criminal proceedings.[67]

---

[64] This provision lists 'the lawful detention [...] of persons of unsound mind' among situations allowing for limitations to the right to liberty and security. The Court referred to *Stanev v Bulgaria*, App. no. 36760/06 (ECtHR, 17 January 2012), para. 120, where the ECtHR reiterated the positive obligation on states under Article 5(1) ECHR to protect liberty and to provide effective protection of vulnerable persons. For his part, Advocate General Campos Sánchez-Bordona referred to *Vaudelle v France*, App. no. 35683/97 (ECtHR, 30 January 2001), in which the ECtHR reiterated the obligations of states to take steps so as to enable a person suffering from a mental disorder to enjoy their rights. See esp. paras 59–65.

[65] *Ibrahim*, fn. 28 *supra*, para. 274; *Sitnevskiy and Chaykovskiy v Ukraine*, App. nos. 48016/06 and 7817/07 (ECtHR, 10 November 2016), para. 79; *Beuze*, fn. 28 *supra*, para. 150. See further *Valeriy Lopata v Russia*, App. no. 19936/04 (ECtHR, 30 October 2012), para. 125 (regarding the right to be heard and appear before the court in person); *Vasenin v Russia*, App. no. 48023/06 (ECtHR, 21 June 2016), paras 135–136.

[66] *Ruşen Bayar v Turkey*, App. no. 25253/08 (ECtHR, 19 February 2019), para. 134. See also *Ibrahim*, fn. 28 *supra*, para. 255.

[67] See *Ibrahim*, fn. 28 *supra*, para. 274 stating under (a): 'Whether the applicant was particularly vulnerable, for example, by reason of his age or mental capacity.'

V. REMEDIES FOR VIOLATIONS OF THE RIGHT TO BE ADVISED

Once a violation of the right to a lawyer has been established, what remedies should apply?[68] The Access to Lawyer Directive is rather brief on this point, with its Article 12(1) simply requiring the existence of remedies that are effective. The second paragraph of the same provision adds that the Member States shall ensure that the assessment of statements made by suspects or accused persons or of evidence obtained in breach of their right to a lawyer (or in cases in which a derogation to this right is authorised) respects the right to defence and to the fairness of proceedings.[69] This obligation is nevertheless 'without prejudice to national rules and systems on the admissibility of evidence'.[70] The initially drafted provision was more demanding, requiring '[t]he remedy [to] have the effect of placing the suspect or accused person in the same position in which he would have found himself had the breach not occurred'.[71] In line with the ECtHR's judgment in *Salduz*,[72] this draft article aimed to ban 'the use of evidence obtained where access to a lawyer was denied, save in those exceptional cases where the use of such evidence will not prejudice the rights of the defence'.[73]

While the current wording of Article 12 therefore leaves the Member States with a rather broad margin as to the consequences to be drawn from situations in which the right to a lawyer has been violated, Recital 50 of the Access to Lawyer Directive recalls that 'regard should be had to the case law of the [ECtHR], which has established that the right of defence will, in principle, be irretrievably prejudiced when incriminating statements made during police interrogation without access to a lawyer are used for a conviction'. The same recital nevertheless follows up with a 'without prejudice' proviso equivalent

---

68 See generally Anneli Soo, 'Article 12 of the Directive 2013/48: A Starting Point for Discussion on a Common Understanding of the Criteria for Effective Remedies of Violation to the Right to Counsel' (2017) *European Journal of Crime, Criminal Law and Criminal Justice* 25(1) 31. On the genesis of that rule, see Ilias Anagnostopoulos, 'The Right of Access to a Lawyer in Europe: A Long Road Ahead?' (2014) *European Criminal Law Journal* 4(1) 3, 15–17.

69 See also Article 8(2) of the Right to Information Directive.

70 From a different perspective, on the limits to the requirement of effectiveness in EU law in the context of illegally obtained evidence for the purpose of criminal prosecution of VAT-related offences, see Case C-310/16 *Dzivev* EU:C:2019:30.

71 Draft Article 13(2) Proposal for a directive of the European Parliament and the Council on the right of access to a lawyer in criminal proceedings and on the right to communicate upon arrest, COM(2011)326 final.

72 *Salduz*, fn. 2 *supra*.

73 Proposal COM(2011)326 final, fn. 71 *supra*, 9, point 30.

to that featuring in Article 12(2) referred to above. In this respect, it has been suggested that genuinely effective remedies should be ones that reinstate the pre-violation situation of the suspect or accused, which would result in the exclusion of evidence obtained in violation of the right to a lawyer, the exclusion of further evidence obtained on that basis, and retrial.[74] That said, and as the wording of Article 12 of the Access to Lawyer Directive attests, the solutions existing in the Member States seem to differ greatly,[75] and each of the above-mentioned options may be subject to rules further differentiating how different remedies should apply, in which stages and with what consequences.

When it comes to interpreting the proper characteristics and legal consequences of the remedies to be applied in this context, ECtHR case law cannot, by definition, offer detailed guidance since it operates on the well-established mantra advising the reopening of the trial, this being the 'most appropriate way of readdressing' violations of Article 6 of the ECHR.[76] However, this 'ideal redress' is only referred to in Article 46 of the ECHR, with the ECtHR having made it clear that it is not for it to determine 'how any new trial is to proceed and what form it is to take'.[77] Similarly, the Committee of Ministers in charge of supervising compliance with ECtHR case law has 'recommended' reopening as an ideal form of redress for violations of Article 6,[78] with many states following this recommendation.[79]

Contrary to the situation of the ECtHR, the issue of remedies is a question that the Court of Justice will in principle have to address if asked in preliminary ruling proceedings regarding interpretation of Article 12 of the Access to

---

[74] Anneli Soo, '(Effective) Remedies for a Violation of the Right to Counsel during Criminal proceedings in the European Union: An Empirical Study' (2018) *Utrecht Law Review* 14(1) 18, 19 and 48. See also the concurring opinion of Judge Zupančič in *Dvorski*, fn. 27 *supra*.

[75] Anneli Soo, '(Effective) Remedies …', fn. 74 *supra*, at 20 and 48. See further Anneli Soo, 'How Are the Member States Progressing on Transposition of Directive 2013/48/EU on the Right of Access to a Lawyer? An Inquiry Conducted among the Member States with the Special Focus on How Article 12 is Transposed' (2017) *New Journal of European Criminal Law* 8(1) 64.

[76] See, e.g., *Panovits v Cyprus*, App. no. 4268/04 (ECtHR, 11 December 2008), para. 103; *Salduz*, fn. 2 *supra*, para. 72.

[77] *Sejdovic v Italy*, App. no. 56581/00 (ECtHR, 1 March 2006), para. 127.

[78] Recommendation No. R (2000) 2 of the Committee of Ministers to member states on the re-examination or reopening of certain cases at the domestic level following the judgments of the European Court of Human Rights.

[79] See the comparative survey of domestic mechanisms providing for the possibility to request the review of civil cases undertaken by the ECtHR in *Bochan v Ukraine (no. 2)*, App. no. 22251/08 (ECtHR, 5 February 2015, rectified 11 March 2015), paras 26–27.

Lawyer Directive.[80] The Court did this to some extent in the above-mentioned *Rayonna prokuratura Lom* case,[81] in which it confirmed the incompatibility of the national rule preventing the national court from verifying whether the relevant procedural rights had been complied with in the pre-judicial stage. Reiterating 'the importance of the right to an effective remedy, protected by Article 47 of the Charter', the Court concluded, in principle, that Article 12 of the Access to Lawyer Directive 'precludes any national measure which impedes the exercise of effective remedies in the event of a breach of the rights protected by that directive'.[82] That being said, the question raised did not bring up the issue of the procedural consequences of previous flawed conduct on the part of authorities, but a somewhat upstream question whether the national judge has the competence to even examine whether such flaws had occurred.

VI. CONCLUSION

From an inter-systemic perspective, the case law of the Court of Justice concerning the right to be advised, defended and represented attests to the well-established role of the Charter serving as a bridge, ensuring through its Article 52(3) that the EU-specific articulation of fundamental-right standards remains coherent with their development before the ECtHR. This cross-fertilisation between the two systems[83] can work to some extent in both directions, as was recently evidenced by the interplay between the ECtHR case law on Article 6(1)(c) ECHR and the regime of permissible restrictions on the right to legal advice under the Access to Lawyer Directive.[84]

From a purely intra-EU perspective, the Charter can generally feature in three main roles: as a standard for judicial review of the legality of acts of Union law,[85] as a tool to interpret notions of EU law and to test the EU-law compatibility of Member States' actions when they implement EU law within the meaning of Article 51(1) of the Charter.[86] The case law which has so far engaged with the right of access to a lawyer bears out the two latter functions.

---

80 On the differences between the situations of the ECtHR and the Court of Justice in that respect, see Case C-234/17 *XC and Others* EU:C:2018:853, paras 36–48.

81 C-467/18 *Rayonna prokuratura Lom and Others*, fn. 61 *supra*.

82 Ibid., paras 57–58. The Court reached that conclusion based on 'the clear, unconditional and precise wording of Article 8(2)' of the Information about Rights Directive, and then drew the same interpretation as regards the Access to Lawyer Directive.

83 See generally, K. Lenaerts and J.A. Gutiérrez-Fons, 'The Place of the Charter …', fn. 19 *supra*.

84 See *Kolev*, fn. 24 *supra*, para. 106; *Beuze*, fn. 28 *supra*, para. 143; *Ibrahim and Others*, fn. 28 *supra*, para. 259; *Simeonovi*, fn. 31 *supra*, para. 117.

85 See recently *XC and Others*, fn. 80 *supra*, para. 37 and the cited case law.

86 Opinion of Advocate General Bobek in *Moro*, fn. 23 *supra*, paras 83–85.

More specifically, Articles 47 and 48(2) of the Charter were referred to in the *Kolev* case so as to re-enforce the boundaries set by the EU legislature in the Access to Lawyer Directive when it comes to the permissible restrictions that the Member States can impose on the choice of lawyer, and in the *VW* case regarding the conditions that can be imposed so that suspects or accused persons can benefit from legal advice. In this context, the Court exercised its scrutiny either in the light of the test provided for in the Access to Lawyer Directive (in the *VW* case) or using a more general proportionality test (in the *Kolev* case), depending on the nature and the 'intensity' with which the right to legal advice had been affected.

In the *Rayonna prokuratura Lom* case, Article 47 of the Charter and the right to effective judicial remedy enshrined in it was further relied on by the Court to clarify the scope of the powers at the disposal of the national judge in order to ascertain failures to guarantee the exercise of procedural rights in the pre-judicial stage of the proceedings. In the same case, the Court relied on Article 6 of the Charter, related to the right to liberty and security, to construe the notion of criminal proceedings under the Access to Lawyer Directive, with the result that it also extends to proceedings that result in the deprivation of liberty, albeit without there being a 'sentence'. That noted, the number of cases that have offered the Court the opportunity to shed more light on the meaning and specific implications of the provisions of the Access to Lawyer Directive so far remains rather limited, and many aspects therefore still remain to be explored. The potential of this instrument to shape national practice is nevertheless rather broad. This is because its material scope makes it clear that the guarantees specified in it apply irrespective of any trans-border element of proceedings,[87] which makes the directive a generally applicable procedural law instrument. It also means that when called upon to apply it the national judge will be able to rely on the Charter in a fully national context where no other rule of EU law is at issue.

Last but not least, recent case law of the Court such as *Uniwersytet Wrocławski* and *Trasta Komercbanka* has brought new opportunities to explore the conditions under which non-privileged applicants can access Union courts. Despite their somewhat technical appearance, the rules defining who can represent such applicants and under which conditions their representation may end are nonetheless fundamental elements defining the effectiveness of such access. In this respect, while the concept of lawyer has recently been elucidated through interpretation of Article 19 of the Statute alone, Article 47 of the Charter has played an important role in setting out the limits to the legal

---

[87] In the context of the Right to Information Directive (fn. 69 *supra*), Case C-646/17 *Moro* EU:C:2019:489, paras 29–37.

effects of national law when that law allows for rules of representation that put the applicant's right to effective judicial remedy in jeopardy.

11. Comment: the EU law on the right to access a lawyer revisited: proportionality and subsidiarity implications

Alexandros-Ioannis Kargopoulos[1]

1. INTRODUCTION

The regulation of criminal justice lies at the core of national sovereignty. The Treaty on the Functioning of the European Union (TFEU) largely reflects this: first by explicitly referring to the intended purpose, content and considerations that EU 'minimum' rules in the field should reflect; and second by providing for a special legislative process that can revert to an intergovernmental process with the use of the 'emergency brake' procedure. Viewed through the prism of the conferral of competence and the principles of proportionality and subsidiarity, the TFEU provisions providing the legal basis for the Union to legislate on criminal procedure rules and rights form a quite solid framework. Despite this framework, it has been argued that an attempt to harmonise the rights of defendants in criminal proceedings at the EU level would be a difficult task.[2] 'Minimum' rules and common definitions drafted in Brussels 'may not reflect the balance of internal criminal justice systems'.[3] In addition, by attaining the status of 'autonomous' notions of EU law and being interpreted broadly by the Court of Justice of the European Union (CJEU), such rules could seriously challenge state sovereignty.[4] The effectiveness and primacy of EU law could be seen as a way to enforce new and further limitations on existing procedural

[1] All opinions and views expressed in this chapter are solely those of the author and its content does not necessarily represent the views or position of the European Union Agency for Fundamental Rights.

[2] Valsamis Mitsilegas, *EU Criminal Law* (Hart Publishing, Oxford 2009), p. 105.

[3] Ibid.

[4] Ibid.

rights in national legal orders.[5] Moreover, broad readings of directives may damage the structural consistency of national criminal justice systems. From an instrument meant to safeguard fundamental rights in the implementation of EU law, the Charter of Fundamental Rights could transform into a tool for directly enforcing unforeseen changes in national legal orders.

This chapter briefly discusses the limitations set by primary EU law on directives establishing minimum procedural rights rules. It then critically re-reads some of the points on the case law on the Access to a Lawyer Directive made in Chapter 10. In contrast, the argument is made here that the previous concerns appear justified as the CJEU adopts a rather broad interpretation of the Access to a Lawyer Directive that hardly appears aligned with the overarching principles and interpretive limitations flowing from the Treaties. This approach risks resulting in distrust of EU law rather than promoting trust amongst Member States.

2. THE TREATY FRAMEWORK ON EU DIRECTIVES ON PROCEDURAL RULES AND RIGHTS

The architecture of the European Union is based on the principle of conferral established in Article 5(2) Treaty on European Union (TEU), which restricts Union acts 'only within the limits of the competences conferred upon it'. The principles of proportionality and subsidiarity, which derive from the principle of conferral, act essentially as the boundaries of the scope that secondary instruments can have. Directives can be annulled for exceeding the limitations imposed by these principles, although the CJEU appears to perform limited scrutiny in this regard.[6]

The Treaty on the Functioning of the EU (TFEU) pays due attention to the impact that Union law may have on national criminal justice systems. The

---

5 Alexandros I. Kargopoulos, 'Fundamental rights, national identity and EU criminal law', pp. 134–5, in Valsamis Mitsilegas, Maria Bergström and Theodore Konstantinides (eds), *Research Handbook on EU Criminal Law* (Edward Elgar, Cheltenham, UK and Northampton, MA 2016); Valsamis Mitsilegas, 'Mutual recognition, mutual trust and fundamental rights after Lisbon', pp. 156–7, in Valsamis Mitsilegas, Maria Bergström and Theodore Konstantinides (eds), *Research Handbook on EU Criminal Law* (Edward Elgar, Cheltenham, UK and Northampton, MA 2016).

6 Revekka-Emmanouella Papadopoulou, 'Article 5', p. 31, in Vasilios Christianos (ed.), *Treaty on EU & TFEU: Commentary per Article* [Συνθήκη ΕΕ & ΣΛΕΕ] (Nomiki Vivliothiki, Athens 2012); Rosaria Sicurella, 'EU competence in criminal matters', p. 69, in Valsamis Mitsilegas, Maria Bergström and Theodore Konstantinides (eds), *Research Handbook on EU Criminal Law* (Edward Elgar, Cheltenham, UK and Northampton, MA 2016).

legal basis and the limitations on directives approximating procedural rules and the rights of individuals are found in Articles 67(1)(3) and 82(2) TFEU, which must be read together with the principles of subsidiarity and proportionality.[7] Respect for the 'different legal traditions and national systems' figures prominently in these provisions, signalling the deference that such instruments should exhibit to national criminal justice systems.[8] Undisputed evidence of this deference is the 'emergency break' procedure, whereby a disagreement may be referred to the Council, triggering a process that resembles the past intergovernmental pillar structure.[9] This procedure only applies to proposals impacting on procedural laws, further showing the additional sensitivity of the issue.

According to Article 82(2) TFEU, read together with Article 67(1)(3) TFEU, directives approximating procedural rights in criminal matters are subject to the following restraints: (a) their rules should be 'minimum', i.e. they should not include overreaching rules and requirements, but instead minimal and 'patchy' solutions; (b) they should take into account 'the different legal traditions and national systems', which implies that they should not force substantial and systemic changes to national criminal justice systems. Indeed, the legitimacy and success of the area of freedom, security and justice depends on ensuring respect for the legal orders and traditions of the Member States;[10] and (c) approximated procedural rules should also aim at 'facilitating mutual recognition and judicial cooperation in criminal cases' to the extent that this is 'necessary'. Approximation is a means to achieve mutual recognition and not an aim in itself.[11] Therefore, Union rules cannot aim at other goals, e.g. at improving defence rights beyond the minimum accepted standards. It is also argued that the 'necessity' of such rules in enhancing mutual recognition should be verifiable.[12] This further implies that directives on procedural rights should not extend to matters which are not subject to mutual recognition and judicial cooperation. Nevertheless, the prevailing view appears to be that assessment of what is necessary to facilitate mutual recognition is up to the legislator and Article 82(2) TFEU does not require proof that a particular

---

7 Sicurella, 'EU competence in criminal matters', n. 6 above, p. 71.

8 It is also argued that the reference to 'respect to fundamental rights' in Article 67(1) TFEU refers to fundamental rights found in national legal orders. See Kargopoulos, 'Fundamental rights, national identity and EU criminal law', n. 5 above, p. 143.

9 Sicurella, 'EU competence in criminal matters', n. 6 above, p. 55.

10 Kargopoulos, 'Fundamental rights, national identity and EU criminal law', n. 5 above, p. 144.

11 Mitsilegas, *EU Criminal Law*, n. 2 above, p. 109; Sicurella, 'EU competence in criminal matters', n. 6 above, p. 60.

12 Mitsilegas, *EU Criminal Law*, n. 2 above, p. 110.

measure promotes mutual recognition.[13] Nonetheless, it would be problematic if a linkage between a directive on procedural rights and facilitation of mutual recognition is disproved when it is implemented in practice. The same would be the case if such a measure adversely impacts the integrity and legal tradition of a national criminal justice system. The underlying rationale of such instruments approximating procedural rights is that ensuring common minimum standards deriving from European Convention on Human Rights (ECHR) guarantees and case law promotes mutual trust amongst judicial authorities.[14] *In concreto*, these minimum rules would result from exhausting the EU legislative process without excluding the possibility of such instruments going beyond what the Treaties permit or deviating from ECHR standards. For example, the Access to a Lawyer Directive goes further than the case law of the European Court of Human Rights (ECtHR) by requiring access to a lawyer during investigative acts such as house searches.[15] A requirement, however, which may adversely impact national criminal processes.[16]

3. REVISITING THE CASE LAW ON ACCESS TO A LAWYER

a. Scope of the Access to a Lawyer Directive

The judgment in the case of *Rayonna prokuratura Lom* is an example of the CJEU appearing to have extended the scope of the Access to a Lawyer Directive beyond what is foreseen in the Treaties and the Directive itself.[17] The CJEU reasoned that the purpose of the Access to a Lawyer and Information in Criminal Proceedings Directives is to establish minimum rules on certain rights of suspects and accused persons, seeking to promote the rights enshrined in Articles 6, 47 and 48 of the Charter.[18] However, nowhere in the Charter or the Treaties is it envisaged that directives on procedural rules are legislated with the exclusive purpose of promoting Charter rights. Secondary instruments

---

13 House of Lords, European Union Committee, *The European Union's Policy on Criminal Procedure*, 30th Report of Session 2010-1, HL Paper 288 (House of Lords, 2012), pp. 20–21.

14 Jacqueline Hodgson, 'Criminal procedure in Europe's area of freedom, security and justice: the rights of the suspect', p. 170, in Valsamis Mitsilegas, Maria Bergström and Theodore Konstantinides (eds), *Research Handbook on EU Criminal Law* (Edward Elgar, Cheltenham, UK and Northampton, MA 2016).

15 Ibid., p. 179.

16 House of Lords, *The European Union's Policy on Criminal Procedure*, n. 13 above, p. 32.

17 CJEU, Case C-467/18, *Rayonna prokuratura Lom*, 19 September 2019.

18 Ibid., paras 36–37.

should comply with the Charter; they are not meant to promote its application beyond their scope. Quite the contrary, the Charter does not provide a legal basis for Union legislation and cannot extend the competences of the Union.[19] By basing its analysis on the above assumption, the CJEU seems to frustrate and extend the scope of the Charter, transforming it into a legal basis for EU action. Moreover, this reasoning does not properly reflect the *raison d'être* of the Access to a Lawyer Directive and the approximation of procedural rights, which is to promote mutual recognition of criminal judgments and judicial cooperation in criminal matters. Articles 67(1)(3) and 82(2) TFEU were not mentioned in the Court's analysis. In particular, the CJEU did not examine whether the psychiatric measure in the case could have been the subject of judicial cooperation in criminal matters, or a criminal judgment (or judicial decision) subject to mutual recognition. Without this consideration, the application of Directive 2013/48/EU to the facts of the case appears flawed. Moreover, the CJEU proceeded by holding that psychiatric measures entailing a restriction of liberty are covered by Article 5 ECHR and therefore by Article 6 of the Charter.[20] This also appears flawed, as it implies that the Charter is directly applicable to such measures irrespective of whether they are regulated by EU legislation. In addition, the use of the argument that persons of unsound mind can be subject to criminal proceedings to justify the application of the Access to a Lawyer Directive is not convincing on its own.[21] This is because the issue was not the proceedings for the determination of the criminal charge against the person involved but the psychiatric measure imposed on him.

b. The Issue of Remedies

In Chapter 10, Ličková and Mullor accurately observe that the issue of remedies for breach of the right of access to a lawyer would be a difficult question which the CJEU may have to answer in the future. Such judgments could well prove problematic. It is awkward to draw analogies between the ECtHR case law on such matters and what the CJEU could or should rule on national remedies during the preliminary ruling procedure. The ECtHR, which has the 'privilege' to deal with a case once it has been finally disposed of after all available remedies at the national level are exhausted or when such remedies would not be effective, is far better suited to the task. It has an overall picture of what happened in practice and can rule on the actual facts of the case. It can

---

19 Article 51(2) of the Charter of Fundamental Rights; Explanations relating to the Charter of Fundamental Rights [2007] (OJ C 303), Explanation of Article 51 – Field of application.

20 *Rayonna prokuratura Lom,* n. 17 above, para. 45.

21 Ibid., paras 47–48.

therefore properly examine whether a remedy was appropriate and effective to redress a violation of defence rights. In this regard, the ECtHR has even ruled that a violation of the right of access to a lawyer can be rectified in a subsequent stage of proceedings.[22] In *Twalib v. Greece*, the Strasbourg Court held that criminal proceedings at the appellate level rectified the shortcomings of the first instance, in which the lawyer appointed by the state did not have adequate time to prepare the defence.[23] What is also striking is that in this case, there was no remedy available specifically designed to address violation of the right of access to a lawyer.

Clearly, it is hard for the CJEU to perform such a scrutiny. Instead, by deciding in the abstract whether a remedy fulfils the requirements of Article 12 of the Access to a Lawyer Directive, the CJEU risks delivering a wrongful assessment of the remedies in place precisely because it would not be able to assess their effectiveness in practice.[24] This could be an impossible task to perform without examining the outcome of the case, since different legal orders provide for a variety of legal means to challenge a violation of the right of access to a lawyer, a report by the Fundamental Rights Agency shows.[25] In this way, a judgment by the CJEU holding that a certain national remedy is not effective risks adversely impacting on structural elements of national criminal proceedings. Such an outcome could contradict Articles 67 and 82(2) TFEU and the requirement to respect the different legal traditions and national systems. In addition, it is certainly debatable whether such an outcome would also be necessary to facilitate mutual recognition and judicial cooperation in criminal cases. On the other hand, the CJEU may rule that a certain remedy, or set of remedies, complies with Article 12 of the Access to a Lawyer Directive even though its violation could occur in practice. Therefore, such a judgment would risk justifying a violation of the right of access to a lawyer that may occur in practice. In conclusion, based on the above scenarios, the argument can be made that an interpretation of Article 12 of the Access to a Lawyer Directive in a preliminary ruling may go further than what is envisaged in the Treaties. This, of course, will not increase trust amongst Member States but

---

22 ECtHR, *Twalib v. Greece*, no. 24294/94, Reports 1998-IV, paras 41–42.

23 Ibid.

24 For details on the different scope of jurisdiction of the two courts, see Alexandros I. Kargopoulos, 'ECHR and the CJEU: competing, overlapping, or supplementary competences?' (2015) 3 *EuCrim* 96, pp. 97–9.

25 See the findings on eight Member States with regard to remedies against the use of defendants' statements made without the presence of a lawyer in European Union Agency for Fundamental Rights, *Rights in Practice: Access to a Lawyer and Procedural Rights in Criminal and European Arrest Warrant Proceedings* (Publications Office of the European Union, Luxembourg 2019), p. 55.

instead will create distrust of Union law for disproportionately impacting on national criminal justice systems. Deferring the question of effectiveness of remedies to the competent national court appears to be the best solution.[26]

4. CONCLUDING REMARKS

Indeed, the issues discussed above regarding the case law of the CJEU are only a few compared to those that may rise or have risen. Nevertheless, they illustrate valid concerns about the disproportionate impact that directives on procedural rules and rights may have on national criminal justice systems when broadly read. It is not necessary for this to be the case. The respect for national legal orders and traditions required by Articles 67 and 82(2) TFEU should be a guiding principle for the CJEU when interpreting directives approximating procedural rules and rights in criminal matters.[27] Restraint on broadening the scope of such directives is implied in the Treaties. Rather than easily resorting to dubious 'autonomous' concepts with unforeseen consequences for national criminal justice systems, definitions and rules in such instruments should match existing corresponding notions and rules found in national legal orders. This approach can ensure the anticipated respect for the legal orders and traditions of Member States proclaimed in the Treaties that would further foster trust in the edifice of the European Union.

---

[26] See in this regard CJEU, Case C-220/18 PPU, *ML*, 25 July 2018, paras 72–76 on examination of the effectiveness of remedies with regard to prison conditions, holding that the existence of such remedies does not suffice in itself.

[27] Kargopoulos, 'Fundamental rights, national identity and EU criminal law', n. 5 above, p. 144.

12. The Lisbon Charter and the Brexit void

Bernard McCloskey[1]

1. INTRODUCTION

The fundamental difference between the pre-Charter and post-Charter eras is that the rights of European Union (EU) citizens are now proclaimed and codified visibly and unambiguously in a model which is transparent, unequivocal and dynamic. The rights enjoyed by citizens of the Union are more concrete, tangible and accessible than ever before. A new era in the EU legal order has dawned. The hallmarks of this new legal order include visibility, coherency, accessibility and transparency. The Charter represents both the vindication and the codification of the jurisprudence of the European Court of Justice (ECJ)/Court of Justice of the European Union (CJEU), which developed the cornerstone principles of equal treatment, non-discrimination, transparency, legitimate expectations and the legal recognition and protection of other fundamental rights and freedoms.[2]

Article 6(3) Treaty on European Union (TEU) is to be viewed against the framework outlined above. It provides that fundamental rights *shall* constitute general principles of EU law. It proclaims that 'fundamental rights' consist of those rights guaranteed by the European Convention of Human Rights and Fundamental Freedoms (ECHR), together with rights embedded in the constitutional traditions common to the Member States.

---

[1] I welcome gratefully the invitation to contribute to this worthwhile publication, providing a judicial perspective. I have been preaching for several years the gospel that the EU Charter of Fundamental Rights lacks profile and visibility in the legal systems of the United Kingdom, which comprise England and Wales, Northern Ireland and Scotland. My interaction with judicial colleagues from other EU Member States suggests that the EU-wide experience has been variable. The Actiones project is, therefore, both welcome and overdue.

[2] From the earliest days of the ECJ jurisprudence, see, for example, *Stauder* – Case 29/69 – 'Fundamental Rights (are) enshrined in the general principles of Community law and protected by the Court'.

In the abstract, the operation of the EU Charter can be examined in the following separate juridical contexts:

(a) In the CJEU.
(b) In the European Court of Human Rights (ECtHR).
(c) In one's own Member State.
(d) In other Member States.

While I shall focus particularly on (c), the adoption of a somewhat broader panorama will be necessary.

2. THE TITLE DEEDS OF THE EU CHARTER

In order to assess the impact and scope of the Charter an understanding of its roots is essential. This exercise is particularly apposite at a stage in history when the EU is increasingly burdened by unprecedented doubts and challenges.

The EU Charter represented the culmination of several decades work of the CJEU and its predecessor, the ECJ, during which active, imaginative and penetrating judicial interpretation and application of EU law had discovered and proclaimed fundamental rights. The Charter is a vindication of the tireless work of dedicated supranational judges. This reflection on its own underlines the importance of the Actiones Project.

As is well known, the EU Charter had a lengthy period of gestation. It was an instrument of (mere) soft law following its initial adoption.[3] Following a sluggish, rather than meteoric, progression from the status of mere political statement, it was ultimately incarnated in the form of an international treaty of equal value with the TEU and the Treaty on the Functioning of the European Union, a directly effective measure of EU primary law, entering into force in tandem with the Lisbon Treaty on 1 November 2009.[4] From any perspective, the Charter represents a landmark achievement for the Member States of the EU. Standing proudly as one of the three dominant instruments of governance of the EU, it is, in effect, a legally binding bill of rights, resembling the catalogues of rights to be found in the constitutions of EU Member States.

The Preamble to the Charter is illuminating and instructive. It reveals its diverse origins and sources of inspiration, as well as proclaiming its rationale and aims. It recalls the post-war resolution of the peoples of Europe 'to share

---

[3] By the European Parliament, the Council and the Commission on 7 December 2000.

[4] Per Article 6(1) TEU, the Charter 'shall have the same legal value as the Treaties'.

a peaceful future based on common values'. It draws on the 'spiritual and moral heritage of the Union', which is founded on the 'indivisible, universal values of human dignity, freedom, equality and solidarity'. Its most important statement, arguably, is the reaffirmation that the Union is 'based on the principles of democracy and the rule of law'.

The Preamble boldly proclaims that through the twin mechanisms of Union citizenship and the creation of an area of freedom, security and justice, the EU 'places the individual at the heart of its activities'. It emphasises, on the one hand, the common values of the Member States and, on the other, the respect to be accorded to 'the diversity of the cultures and traditions of the peoples of Europe', their national identities and how they are governed at national, regional and local levels. Furthermore, the Preamble explicitly recognises the principle of subsidiarity.

Through the Preamble one learns that the EU Charter is not designed to be merely declaratory in nature and effect. Rather, it is based on the recognition that 'it is necessary *to strengthen* the protection of fundamental rights'.[5] What are the origins of these rights? They derive from:

> the constitutional traditions and international obligations common to the Member States, the [ECHR], the Social Charters adopted by the Union and by the Council of Europe and the case law of the Court of Justice of the European Union and of the European Court of Human Rights.

From the judicial perspective, this lengthy list of sources is important, for at least two reasons. First, it provides an insight into the scope and potential of the Charter in practice.[6] Second, it will be permissible for judges to have resort to these sources in resolving issues concerning the interpretation and application of the Charter.

The manifest diversity, breadth and versatility of the Charter are among its hallmarks. These traits can be readily traced to the UN Declaration of Human Rights (1948), the Statute of the Council of Europe (1949), the Treaty of Rome (1950) and, to a lesser extent, the Refugee Convention (1951) followed by and in tandem with the progressive jurisprudence of the CJEU *and* the increasingly influential case law of the ECtHR.

---

[5] My emphasis.

[6] The Charter on the EU statute books and the Charter in actual operation are two quite different things.

Drawing on all of these sources, the Preamble to the TEU enunciates the following:

> Drawing inspiration from the cultural, religious and humanist inheritance of Europe, from which we have developed the universal values of the inviolable and inalienable rights of the human person, freedom, democracy, equality and the rule of law.

This is to be juxtaposed with Article 2 TEU where the same values are shared both by the Union and 'Member States in a society in which pluralism, non-discrimination, tolerance, justice, solidarity and equality between men and women prevail'.

Harmonious with this provision, one of the EU's stated aims in its relations with the wider world is the protection of human rights, in particular the rights of the child.[7] The following words from the Charter's Preamble, arguably, reflect the Charter's most novel feature:

> [The Union] places the individual at the heart of its activities, by establishing the citizenship of the Union and by creating an area of freedom, security and justice.

3. THE PANORAMA OF THE EU CHARTER

Panoramically, the Lisbon Reforms of 2009 effected a significant transformation of the EU landscape, with a greater emphasis on human rights protection than ever before. The human rights development in EU law has been the product of evolution, not revolution: a gentle, orderly and judge-led process which, viewed in retrospect, appears a natural progression. It is nonetheless remarkable given that human rights did not feature in the European Treaties in their original incarnation. There was no bill of rights and nothing equivalent thereto. The founding fathers were enlightened and ambitious, but cautiously so.

But the creation of the European Economic Community (EEC) did not occur in isolation. One cannot ignore the (more or less) simultaneous adoption of the Statute of the Council of Europe which, in common with its EEC counterpart, had as one of its aims the achievement of greater unity among European states in the midst of the devastation caused by the Second World War. Thus the Statute devised an elaborate human rights protection model, the ECHR, as its marquee mechanism. The resulting interaction and approximation between the two regimes – the EU and the Council of Europe (COE) – was, in hindsight, predictable, if not seamless. With the passage of time each would, inevitably, be influenced by the other and absorb the other to an appropriate extent.

---

7 Per Article 3(5) TEU.

Viewed retrospectively, it was inevitable that the EU Institutions, in particular the CJEU, would be alert not merely to the activities under the umbrella of the ECHR. The CJEU also found itself operating in an environment in which many of the Member States had written constitutions. It is, therefore, unsurprising that these constitutions – which are given explicit recognition in the Charter – have influenced the evolution of EU law, not least because of the composition of the CJEU, particularly in cases involving an interface between EU law and national constitutional law. It is clearly foreseeable that national constitutions will have some impact in cases involving the Charter.[8]

The Charter's broad panorama and extensive reach are reflected in the post-Lisbon activities of both the CJEU and the Union legislative, executive and administrative bodies. In all of these contexts, issues of fundamental rights have centred on the Charter. In the activities of these organs, the Charter has, progressively, become a reference point. It operates as a compass, a benchmark, for the development of EU policies. *In principle*, the benefits which this should bring for EU citizens are stronger and more effective rights in the product resulting from each policy development and legislative process. Furthermore, the Charter's prominence in the jurisprudence of the CJEU has steadily increased.

As appears from the background outlined above, the rationale for this state of affairs includes the following:

(a) The Charter has enhanced legitimacy on account of its democratic origins, being preceded by two solemn Conventions reflecting the deliberations of the governments of Member States, the European Parliament *and* the national parliaments of the Member States.
(b) There are clearly identifiable constitutional elements in the two preceding Conventions.
(c) The Charter draws heavily upon the ECHR and other human rights instruments which are binding on all EU Member States.
(d) The Charter also relies on the constitutional traditions common to the Member States.
(e) The Charter is a modern, visible, comprehensible and codifying instrument.
(f) The Charter is legally binding and, generally at least, has direct effect.
(g) Finally, and fundamentally, the Charter is one of the constitutional instruments of governance of the EU and enjoys the same status as the others.

---

8 See *Kremzow v Austria* [1997] ECR I – 2629.

4. THE EU CHARTER: ASYLUM PROTECTION

Somewhat ironically, the United Kingdom (UK) has made a notable contribution to the Charter jurisprudence of the CJEU. In the field of immigration and asylum, the most important Charter decision of the CJEU is, by some measure, *NS and ME*.[9] The central issue raised in these combined Article 267 references was whether the mechanism contained in the Dublin Regulation[10] to refrain from sending an asylum applicable to the Member State which, under the Dublin Regulation criteria, is responsible for examining the application, may become a duty precluding such transfer where the responsible Member State does not respect EU fundamental rights and/or the EU measures relating to asylum.

The Charter provision which featured most prominently is Article 4, which prohibits torture and inhuman or degrading treatment or punishment. The Court held that Article 4 precludes such a transfer in circumstances where the transferring Member State cannot be unaware that systemic deficiencies in the asylum procedures and reception conditions of the responsible Member State:

> amount to substantial grounds for believing that the asylum seeker would face a real risk of being subjected to inhuman or degrading treatment.

The test is *not* that of alleged violations of fundamental rights or the EU asylum instruments. Rather, it concerns systemic and serious deficiencies in the procedures, arrangements and conditions in the responsible Member States.

In *NS and ME*, the decision under challenge entailed a proposal to return three asylum applicants from the UK and the Republic of Ireland to Greece. There was a heavy focus on the discretionary examination provision of Article 3(2) of Dublin II. The first question for the CJEU was whether a Member State's decision under Article 3(2) falls within the scope of EU law for the purposes of Article 6 TEU and/or Article 51 of the Charter. The Court answered this question affirmatively.[11] The Court's reasoning on the substantive issues drew on the Common European Asylum System, which is based on the full and inclusive application of the Geneva Convention and the guarantee that no person will be returned to a place where they risk being persecuted. The Court also referred to Article 18 of the EU Charter.[12]

Finally, the Court highlighted the principle of mutual trust among EU Member States, concluding:

---

9 Joined cases C-411/10 and C-493/10.

10 Council Regulation (EC) No 343/2003.

11 See [69].

12 See the corresponding explanation to the Charter article.

(a) There can be no conclusive presumption that the responsible Member State observes the fundamental rights of the EU.
(b) The transfer by a Member State to the responsible Member State is unlawful where the former is aware of systemic deficiencies in the asylum procedure and reception conditions of the second State such as to amount to substantial grounds for believing that the claimant would face a real risk of inhuman or degrading treatment. This would be unlawful as *contrary to Article 4 of the EU Charter.*[13]
(c) Articles 1 (the right to human dignity), 18 and 47 (the right to an effective remedy and a fair trial) of the Charter do not require a different answer to the questions raised.

Notably, the Grand Chamber declined to construe the joint UK/Polish Protocol as conferring any exemption on either of these Member States from their fundamental obligation to comply with the Charter.[14] What had once been triumphantly paraded by the United Kingdom as an 'opt out' clause, a landmark victory in the constant battle against the tide of EU legislation, dissolved, aided by a UK concession, into a veritable damp squib.

5. THE CHARTER IN THE ECTHR

Brief consideration of this topic is essential, given that post-Brexit the status of the ECHR in the UK will be unchanged.[15] The ECHR is an international treaty providing for the effective protection of a certain number of rights. It does not constitute a legal order such as that of the EU. The ECHR came into existence as a means of binding the countries of Europe to fundamental principles with a view to deterring any recurrence of the horrors of the Second World War. This was also a major aim of the EU. However, today, more than 60 years later, its function cannot be reduced to that sole purpose. As a 'first step for the collective enforcement of certain of the rights stated in the Universal Declaration',[16] the ECHR constitutes a common 'shared view' of European human rights law, defining 'the margin within which states may opt for different fundamental balances between government and individuals'.[17]

The ECtHR has developed an *assumption* that those responsible for formulating EU law intend it to be compatible with the ECHR. See, for example,

---

13 Paragraphs [94] and [106].

14 At [120].

15 See *infra*. The UK membership of the Council of Europe continues, as does the Human Rights Act.

16 ECHR Preamble para [6].

17 Weiler, J.H.H., *The Constitution of Europe* (CUP, Cambridge 1999) 107.

Bosphorus Turzim v Ireland.[18] This assumption seems unremarkable, having regard to the history of the Charter outlined above.

One finds references to the EU Charter in a small number of cases only. There are two decisions of the ECtHR which have an important bearing on the subject of the Actiones Project. The first is *MSS v Belgium and Greece*,[19] where the complaint was that the Greek procedures for the reception of asylum claimants and the processing of their claims were so inadequate that they constituted ill treatment contrary to Article 3 ECHR.

In holding that Greece was in violation of Article 3 ECHR regarding both detention and living conditions *and* that Belgium was similarly in violation of Article 3 ECHR for transferring asylum claimants to Greece, thereby exposing them to the risk of such ill treatment, the Strasbourg Court relied more on the concept of 'fundamental rights' than the EU Charter. This is understandable, given that from 1 December 2009 the TEU had provided not only that the EU 'recognises the rights, freedoms and principles set out in the Charter of Fundamental Rights', but *also* that:

> Fundamental rights, as guaranteed by the [ECHR] and as they result from the constitutional traditions common to the Member States, shall constitute general principles of the Union's law.[20]

In an equally landmark decision, *Hirsi Jamaa v Italy*,[21] where Italian authorities had intercepted a boat carrying potential asylum applicants in the Mediterranean Ocean forcing their return to Libya, the ECtHR held that both Article 3 ECHR and Article 19 Charter (prohibition against collective expulsions) had been infringed.

The following summary seems appropriate. The ECtHR is prepared to draw on the EU Charter as a source of influence, or guidance, in its interpretation and application of the ECHR. However, the Charter has not been accorded any special status. Rather, it has been treated by the ECtHR in much the same way as other sources of international law. The Charter's influence has been most noticeable in relation to Article 6 ECHR. It has also had some influence in Article 3 cases involving asylum claimants. Clearly, the Charter cannot be a source of law which in some way usurps the ECHR itself. In principle, the CJEU may interpret provisions of the Charter comparable to/overlapping with ECHR provisions more generously than the ECtHR has done to date. Equally, in principle, the ECtHR may seek to maintain its more restrictive, conservative

18 No 45036/98 at [73] especially.
19 App No 30696/09.
20 Article 6(3).
21 No 27765/09.

interpretation of such provisions. In reality, the more likely scenario appears to be that the CJEU will take its lead from the ECtHR. This would be consonant with the differing roles and specialisms of these two transnational courts. The full potential of the Charter in the realm of the ECHR remains to be achieved.

I suggest that the following proposition is tenable: in the realm of protection of human rights involving the 27 Member States of the EU and the 47 States Parties of the Council of Europe, a two-way street is discernible – the ECtHR can have resort to the EU Charter as a source of rights, while (and to a rather greater extent) the CJEU can, similarly, invoke the ECHR. Two further sources common to each of these supranational regimes are, of course, the constitutional traditions common to the Member States and other international instruments of human rights protection. All of these instruments and sources must co-exist as harmoniously as possible. This requires vigilance, flexibility and, where necessary, imaginative approaches on the part of the CJEU, ECtHR and national judiciaries.

6. PRE-BREXIT: THE CHARTER IN THE UNITED KINGDOM

The UK, though (uniquely among EU Member States) having no written constitution, is a single constitutional entity, consisting of England, Wales, Scotland and Northern Ireland. However, for reasons of history, tradition and devolution, these countries have three different legal systems. The exercise of considering the operation and influence of the Charter in these countries is not a difficult one. Furthermore, it is instructive to consider how the Charter has fared in the Republic of Ireland.

It is no understatement to suggest that the impact of the EU Charter in the UK generally has been at most tepid. An understanding of why is not altogether easy. Some of the reasons undoubtedly include the following:

(a) The distracting and somewhat confusing UK/Poland Protocol.
(b) The relative moratorium generated by the Article 267 references in *NS and ME*.[22]
(c) The inbuilt limitations of the Charter flowing from Article 51(1).
(d) The unique and challenging architecture of the Charter: rights, freedoms, principles and 'Explanations'.
(e) Debates about direct effect.
(f) The prominence of the ECHR in the UK consequent upon the Human Rights Act 1998.

---

[22] Joined cases C-411/10 and C-493/10.

(g) And, finally, possibly insufficient exposure and inadequate education in legal circles.

In the specific field of immigration and asylum, it must also be borne in mind that there is *already* extensive prescription of rights and duties. This flows not only from the Refugee Convention and its Protocol but also the series of EU legislative measures under the umbrella of the Common European Asylum System (CEAS) and the corresponding UK domestic law implementing/transposing measures. As a result, the EU Charter is rarely pleaded in immigration/asylum cases in the UK. Being a common law jurisdiction and having regard to the duty of courts and tribunals under Article 10 TEU, the absence of any such pleading does not, of course, preclude judges from proactively raising Charter issues. However, the reality of life for immigration and asylum judges in the UK is that the Charter has featured very rarely indeed.

An exception to this is found in the decision of the UK Upper Tribunal (Immigration and Asylum Chamber) (UTIAC) in *Abdul (Section 55 – Article 24(3) Charter)*.[23] This case concerned a national of Nigeria, aged 41, who had been continuously resident in the UK for 25 years and was the father of two daughters, aged 13 and 11 respectively, both British citizens. The father acquired a residence card *qua* family member of a European Economic Area (EEA) national. However, he was also a convicted offender and, following the imposition of a sentence of four and a half years' imprisonment, the Secretary of State decided to order his deportation from the UK.

In challenging this decision the Appellant relied on, inter alia, Article 24(3) of the EU Charter which provides that every child shall have the right to maintain on a regular basis a personal relationship and direct contact with both his or her parents, unless this is contrary to his or her interests. In deciding the appeal, the Upper Tribunal held, firstly, that the gateway provisions of Article 51 were satisfied. Next, it considered the decisions of the CJEU in *Deticek v Sgueglia*[24] where the Court gave consideration to the interpretation of Council Regulation (EC) 2201/2003, which concerns jurisdiction and the recognition and enforcement of judgments in matrimonial matters. The Court, reasoning that Article 24 enshrines a 'fundamental' right, concluded that a measure which prevents the maintenance on a regular basis of a personal relationship and direct contact with both parents can be justified only by another interest of the child of such importance that it takes priority over the interest underlying that fundamental right.[25]

---

23 [2016] UKUT 106 (IAC).

24 [2009] EUECJ C-403/09.

25 See [54]–[59].

The Upper Tribunal also considered a later decision of the CJEU, *MCB v ELE*,[26] a case which had a Hague Convention context involving the disputed return of a child from the UK to the Republic of Ireland. Having regard to the reasoning of the CJEU[27] the Upper Tribunal held that the Court was suggesting that Article 24(3) adds nothing of substance to Article 24(2). The kernel of the President's judgment is contained in [30].[28]

The Upper Tribunal has also ruled in a case in which the Applicant placed direct reliance on Article 18 of the Charter. In *R (Hagos) v Secretary of State for the Home Department* (Dublin Returns – Malta) IJR,[29] the Applicant, a young male adult in good physical health, though suffering from mental health problems and asserting a risk of suicide, contended that his enforced return from the UK to Malta would violate his rights under Articles 18 and 47 of the Charter, Article 3 ECHR, Article 33 of the Refugee Convention and the Qualification Directive. The Applicant's case was based on extensive evidence pointing to significant shortcomings in the Maltese processes and procedures for the consideration and determination of asylum claims, together with deficiencies in the arrangements and facilities for the treatment of asylum claimants with psychiatric problems.

The Upper Tribunal accepted, without deciding, that Article 18 of the Charter creates an individual, enforceable right to asylum, subject of course to the claimant satisfying the qualifying conditions.[30]

The Upper Tribunal noted that this was the contention of the United Nations High Commissioner for Refugees (UNHCR) in its intervention before the CJEU in *Halaf v Bulgarian State Agency for Refugees*.[31]

7. THE CHARTER POST-BREXIT: QUO VADIS?

The withdrawal of the UK, constitutionally a single Member State, from the EU became increasingly embroiled in controversy, acrimony and uncertainty at times bordering on confusion. This process has become popularly known as 'Brexit'. Withdrawal was eventually finalised on 31 December 2020, almost five years after the historic referendum.

The Brexit mechanisms, not less than complicated, are a mixture of domestic legislation and international treaty. The main legal components are the primary legislation seeking to give effect to the 2016 referendum result, the EU

---

26 [2010] EUECJ C-400/10.
27 At [60] especially.
28 Per McCloskey LJ.
29 [2015] UKUT 0271 (IAC).
30 At [29] and [51].
31 Case C-528/11.

(Withdrawal) Act 2018 (the Withdrawal Act) and subsequent legislative measures and, on the international plane, the Withdrawal Agreement and Political Declaration[32] and, most recently, the Trade and Cooperation Agreement.

The Withdrawal Act repeals the European Communities Act 1972,[33] preserves laws which were made in the UK for the purpose of implementing EU obligations and, thirdly, converts existing EU law into domestic law, *subject to* specified exceptions. The EU Charter is one of the most striking of these exceptions. Thus, it ceased to form part of domestic UK law after 'exit day'.[34]

The abolition of the Charter in the UK is a clear implementation of those aspects of the 'leave' movement which quickly found a popular (and populist?) target in the shape of a visionary and progressive instrument of EU law which (via the narrow UK majority mindset) confers a series of legally enforceable rights and benefits on the citizens of other European countries. The unassailable juridical reality that it confers precisely the same rights and benefits on *all* citizens of the UK exercising, or wishing to exercise, free movement rights in other EU countries has been diluted and ignored to the point of virtual submergence. *Ditto* the incontrovertible factual reality of the progressive, and enduring, reliance of the UK economy on the citizens of *other* EU Member States exercising their free movement rights – and doing so *strictly in accordance with the relevant legal rules*.

It is a fact that, as the UK/Poland Protocol demonstrates, from its inception the Charter was treated with suspicion by successive UK governments. It has been variously described as excessively vague and unnecessarily intrusive. The interpretation and application of the Charter by the CJEU in its jurisprudence have not been welcomed in UK political circles. Excessive intrusion, a close relative of the 'loss of sovereignty' lament which dominated the pro-Brexit movement, has been the main complaint.

In the post-Brexit world, the repeal of the Charter, an instrument of supreme EU law, will have three ineluctable consequences in the UK. *First*, as the rights protected by the Charter are more extensive than those enshrined in the ECHR (protected in domestic law via the Human Rights Act 1998), human rights protection seems destined to diminish. Contrast, for example, Article 14 ECHR with its more expansive Charter counterpart, Article 21. Furthermore, the open-ended and non-exhaustive list of protected groups contrasts with the nine closed categories specified in domestic legislation in the Equality Act 2010. Another illustration of a more expansive Charter right is that which protects personal data (Article 8). Similarly the rights to an effective remedy and a fair

32 12 November 2019.
33 The measure of primary legislation whereby the UK acceded to the EU.
34 31 January 2020.

trial (Article 47) are of greater reach than Article 6 ECHR as the limitation of the determination of civil rights and obligations or a criminal charge does not apply. Equally the provisions of Title IV ('Solidarity') have no equivalent in the ECHR.

Second, the abolition of the Charter will give rise to a significant drought in the matter of available judicial remedies. Under the scheme of the Human Rights Act if a provision of primary legislation cannot be read and given effect in a manner compatible with the Convention rights the court is empowered to make a declaration of incompatibility. This remedial order does not affect the validity, continuing operation or enforcement of the impugned statutory provision. As regards *secondary* legislation, a judicial order of striking down or setting aside is possible. In contrast, as the Charter had the status of supreme EU law in the UK legal system, it had to prevail over any conflicting UK law. Thus a judicial decision, reflected in an appropriate remedy, that a measure of UK law was incompatible with the Charter would nullify the relevant UK law immediately. This will no longer be possible.

The decision in *Benkharbouche v Embassy of Sudan*,[35] illustrates clearly the differences between remedies under the ECHR/Human Rights Act and remedies under the Charter. In that case, members of the service staff of foreign diplomatic missions to the UK wished to assert their employment rights in proceedings against their employer. This was precluded by the State Immunity Act 1978. The court decided that the primary legislation was incompatible with the claimant's rights under both Article 6 ECHR and Article 47 of the Charter. The latter instrument was engaged because the employment claims fell within the scope of EU law. The remedy granted was an order disapplying the impugned provisions of the legislation to the extent necessary to enable employment claims falling within the scope of EU law to be brought by the claimants. This would not have been possible by the mechanism of a declaration of incompatibility under the Human Rights Act. Under the EU withdrawal legislation, the power of the court will be confined to making a declaration of incompatibility.

Third, the disappearance of the Charter is likely to have a negative impact on the culture of human rights protection in the UK. It is beyond plausible dispute that even where there is theoretically strong human rights protection in the laws of any nation the mindset of its citizens, invariably shaped to some extent by the general culture and philosophy promoted by the Government of the day, elected by a majority of voters, is an essential tool in ensuring effective rights protection in practice. It seems highly likely that the overnight removal of the

---

[35] [2015] EWCA Civ 33 and the later decision of the UK Supreme Court on 18 October 2017: [2017] UKSC 62.

Charter from UK law will have a negative impact in this respect. This could prove to be the most damaging consequence of all.

Furthermore, there are at least four reasons to be concerned about the present and future rule of law culture in the UK. *One*: the 'Brexit' decision of the UK Supreme Court published in September 2019[36] provoked a vitriolic outcry against the judiciary, of unparalleled proportions, in which senior Government figures were prominent. *Two*: the Government quickly announced that there would be a fundamental review of judicial review.[37] *Three*: the Government has recently announced a review of the Human Rights Act.[38] *Four*: the UK Internal Market Bill, published on 9 September 2020, contained a provision which, succinctly, declares a Government policy of preparedness to breach an international treaty, namely UK/EU Withdrawal Agreement, i.e. to violate international law.

I elaborate on the *first* of the rule of law concerns mooted above. Certain difficult legal issues following the Brexit referendum majority leave vote had to be resolved by the senior UK courts in judicial review proceedings. The courts resolved these issues against the Government. On 24 September 2019, the UK Supreme Court (UKSC) gave judgment in the infamous case of *Millar and Cherry*.[39] The impetus for the judicial review challenge was a legal act on the part of the Government, effected by the mechanism of an Order in Council (approved by the Sovereign) – a measure of subordinate legislation – that Parliament be prorogued for a period of approximately one month. In accordance with constitutional convention, Her Majesty's approval was given upon advice received from the Prime Minister. The central question arising was the legality of this advice.

The UKSC concluded that the decision to advise Her Majesty to prorogue Parliament was unlawful because it had the effect of frustrating, indeed preventing, the ability of Parliament to discharge its constitutional functions without reasonable justification. The UKSC decision had three identifiable strands:

(a) The lawfulness of the Prime Minister's advice to Her Majesty was justiciable, that is to say it was subject to the supervisory jurisdiction of the High Court via an application for judicial review.

---

[36] Considered further *infra*.

[37] Which has now commenced.

[38] Ministry of Justice, Independent Human Rights Act Review, 7 December 2020, available at www.gov.uk/guidance/independent-human-rights-act-review, accessed 25 October 2021.

[39] [2019] UKSC 41.

(b) The power which the Prime Minister exercised in advising Her Majesty to prorogue Parliament was subject to the fundamental principles of Parliamentary sovereignty and Parliamentary accountability, each a fundamental constitutional principle.
(c) A breach of constitutional principle had occurred because the statutory measure had mothballed Parliament without lawful justification. Indeed the whole of the Parliamentary process had been frozen. This had a profound effect on democratic fundamentals.

Finally the UKSC rejected the argument that the impugned prorogation was a 'proceeding in Parliament' which, by virtue of the Bill of Rights 1688, could not be questioned in any court. One particular consequence of this discrete conclusion was that it would be open to the court to grant a remedy. Judicial review remedies lie within the discretion of the court (see *infra*). The UKSC ruled that the impugned statutory measure was unlawful as (in terms) it had been irredeemably infected by unlawful advice given by the Prime Minister to Her Majesty. It was void and of no effect. The judicial review remedy of a quashing order was granted.

Turning to the *second* rule of law concern identified above, the Internal Market Bill published by the UK Government in the Autumn of 2020 (now an enacted statute) was predominantly concerned with regulating the free movement of goods and services and the recognition of professional qualifications in the UK in the post-Brexit world. The UK Government included in this measure a provision which contemplated that the UK would fail to honour Article 4 of the Withdrawal Agreement. The purpose and effect of Article 4 were to ensure that the provisions of the Withdrawal Agreement (including the NI Protocol) could be enforced directly, in the UK courts if necessary, *and* to empower UK courts to disapply inconsistent and incompatible provisions of domestic law. The UK undertook to enact primary legislation to confer this jurisdiction on its courts. The UK then sought to implement the Withdrawal Agreement through the 2020 Act.[40] This UK Government 'declaration of intent' is found in clauses 40–45 of the Bill. In the briefest of summaries, these provisions create conflict between the UK's proposed new internal market and the operation of the NI Protocol in two respects, namely the movement of goods between NI and GB and the application of EU state aid rules. To summarise, the UK Government declared that it would refuse to honour the Withdrawal Agreement should it find it convenient to do so. Ultimately, the Government resiled from its stance.

---

[40] Which inter alia amended the Withdrawal Act by inserting sections 7A–7C which purport to secure the direct effect of the Agreement and the availability and enforcement of its provisions without further enactment: a legislative technique previously employed in section 2(1) of the European Communities Act 1972.

All of the foregoing has been unfolding in the following context. There is a broad consensus that public perceptions (many of them misconceived) relating to immigration and asylum were one of the major forces in the Brexit 'leave' vote. Pro-Brexit politicians and others campaigned forcefully on (inter alia) a 'taking back our borders' platform. There has been progressive hostility towards, and ensuing uncertainty for, the citizens of other EU Member States in the UK. It is predicted that in its new domestic law arrangements, the UK will adopt more restrictive and less liberal immigration/asylum policies and arrangements.

Pre-referendum, the prevailing environment and culture in the UK already had a hostile disposition towards non-British nationals. One of the clearest illustrations was the harsh treatment of third country unaccompanied children. The treatment of the 'Calais children' provides one of the clearest illustrations. Successive UK governments had repeatedly expressed their intention to reduce the numbers of non-British nationals in the UK. Allied to this was the adoption of policies with acutely negative impacts on the dignity and rights of asylum claimants, predominantly in the areas of accommodation, employment and the most basic of financial support for survival.

Furthermore, immigration and asylum law in the UK has long been criticised for its sheer volume and sometimes near impenetrable complexity.[41] Linked to this is a long history of serious administrative failings in the immigration/asylum sphere in the UK: a bureaucratic system which has not been fit for purpose for a long time, dysfunctional computer systems, excessive delays, the loss of key records et al. Added to the foregoing, one of the entrenched UK government policies has been, for some time, to legislate so as to drastically reduce the scope for appeals to the courts against adverse immigration/asylum decisions, while simultaneously increasing the range of so-called 'out-of-country' appeals, strongly criticised judicially.[42] Moreover, the most senior immigration/asylum court in the UK expressed in trenchant terms its concerns regarding the conduct of cases by the Government Legal Department.[43]

Yet another sobering reflection arises out of the truism that the true potential of the EU Charter remains unfulfilled. The predictable flourishing of the

---

[41] Thankfully the Law Commission has now completed a long overdue project which, at least, has the potential to give rise to much needed improvements and reforms.

[42] See, for example, my decision in *R (Mohibullah) v SSHD* [2016] UKUT (IAC) 561, endorsed by the Supreme Court in *R (Kiairie and Byndloss) v SSHD* [2018] UKSC 67.

[43] See, for example, *R (Saha) v Secretary of State for the Home Department* (IJR) [2017] UKUT 17 (IAC) at [45]–[51] and *R (AM) v SSHD* [2017] UKUT 262 (IAC) at [91]–[92].

Charter via the jurisprudence of the CJEU will have no *direct* influence on the UK legal system. Furthermore, and independently, as the doctrine of the supremacy of EU law will disappear from the UK legal system, UK courts will no longer be subject to the obligation to disapply national legal rules conflicting with directly applicable or effective EU law.[44] As already highlighted, much of the ECHR, via the Human Rights Act, will continue to form part of domestic UK law. However, the 'disapplication' duty of the UK judge, just noted, contrasts sharply with the most intrusive of the human rights remedies available under domestic law, namely a formal order of a superior court declaring that a specified provision of parliamentary legislation is incompatible with one of the protected ECHR rights[45] with the consequence that Parliament is obliged to enact appropriate remedial legislation.

Furthermore the abolition of the Charter has been effected with little real analysis of its impact during its ten year existence. While a study was conducted in 2017,[46] this does not make a persuasive case for its abolition. It remains to be seen whether effective equivalent protection will be provided by the amalgam of general principles of EU law, retained EU law, other international human rights instruments (in particular the ECHR, via the Human Rights Act 1998) and other instruments of domestic legislation. The extinction of the Charter will occur in a context where, as indicated above, its impact in the UK has been weak. It has not had the opportunity to realise its full potential.

Also gone forever – again subject to interim and special arrangements – will be the ability of any person living in the UK to challenge acts and decisions of the executive or UK legislation said to be incompatible with fundamental EU rights, the Charter or, for that matter, any measure of EU law which is not 'retained' in domestic UK law. Such a challenge will not be possible before the UK courts. Furthermore, the invaluable mechanism whereby the UK courts could seek preliminary rulings from the CJEU will be eliminated.

This significant *lacuna* will not be remedied by the continuing existence of the Agreement on the EEA to which the UK will remain a party. By virtue of the EEA principle of homogeneity, new EU legislation is routinely transformed into the body of EEA law. The mechanism for this is the simple one of annexing such legislation to the EEA agreement.[47]

---

44 See inter alia *Costa v ENEL* [1964] CMLR 425.

45 See Section 3 of the Human Rights Act 1998.

46 UK Government, Charter of Fundamental Rights of the EU Right by Right Analysis, 5 December 2017, available at https://assets.publishing.service.gov.uk/government/uploads/system/uploads/attachment_data/file/664891/05122017_Charter_Analysis_FINAL_VERSION.pdf, accessed 25 October 2021.

47 See Article 102, EEA Agreement.

Collectively, the adoption of the EU Charter, the Citizens Directive 2004/38 and a series of detailed measures in the field of asylum are arguably the most progressive and impressive EU legislative achievements. While imperfections and shortcomings have been exposed in the CEAS, the Dublin Regulation in particular, the EU, in common with the best democratic institutions throughout the world, has demonstrated its capacity for review, revision and improvement.[48] In addition, in the context of the promotion of the Treaty values of freedom, justice and security, an elaborate European Arrest Warrant Scheme has also been painstakingly devised. Many of the foregoing measures, subject only to time limited interim arrangements and the intrinsically precarious device of 'retained EU law', will fade from the UK legal system in the post-Brexit era.

The EU Charter provides visible, accessible and comprehensive protection of a broad range of individual rights and freedoms. Its potency derives in particular from the position which it occupies at the apex of the international legal order to which it belongs. The UK no longer belongs to this legal order. Does this mean that the Charter has really disappeared overnight from the UK legal system?

The answer, perhaps at first blush surprising, is 'No'. This is due to, firstly, the complex architecture of the UK domestic Brexit legislation, in particular the Withdrawal Act.[49] The Charter applies only when a Member State is acting within the scope of EU law.[50] The UK's institutions will, of course, no longer be doing so. However, the Withdrawal Act has some notable features. In particular, certain of the existing rights codified under the Charter will be retained in UK domestic law. Furthermore, any fundamental rights or principles under EU law which exist irrespective of the Charter (surely a blurred dividing line?) will likewise be retained in UK domestic law. Under the Act there are the following concepts and categories:

- 'retained EU law'
- 'retained EU case law'
- 'retained general principles of EU law'
- preserved 'EU-derived domestic legislation'
- 'retained direct EU legislation'
- 'EU rights, powers etc'
- permissible recourse to CJEU decisions, obligatory in certain instances

---

48 The current version of the Dublin Regulation and its most recent modifications provide a clear example.

49 See especially sections 2, 3, 4, 5, 6, 7 and 20 of the Act.

50 Per Article 51, as interpreted in a series of important decisions of the CJEU.

In short, the UK's post-Brexit retreat from EU law will not be abrupt. EU law will continue to form part of domestic UK law unless and until it is repealed. Repeal will be a gradual, incremental process. Furthermore, the complete repeal of EU law is unlikely to prove either viable or desirable. The Charter will remain influential in all aspects of retained EU law which it affects. It will also exert an influence via all retained EU case law in which it features. Furthermore, there will be scope for the Charter to influence the development of the common law by judges, particularly on account of its links with the ECHR. The latter measure is unaffected by Brexit. It is incorporated in large measure in UK law by the Human Rights Act 1998 and is, hence, pure domestic law.[51] These are some of the more subtle post-Brexit legal realities.

8. THE ECHR AND THE COUNCIL OF EUROPE IN THE UK CHARTER VACUUM

Post-mortems and forecasts there will inevitably be. These will, foreseeably, entail juxtaposing the EU Charter with the ECHR. The latter (most of it) will, for a period at least, continue to be a major source of directly effective human rights protection in the UK. Previously, and unlike in many other Member States, the ECHR did not form part of domestic UK law by virtue of the 'dualist' constitutional doctrine, whereby unincorporated international Treaties and Conventions form no part of municipal law unless incorporated by domestic legislation. However, most of the ECHR rights became directly effective in UK law via a measure of primary legislation namely the Human Rights Act 1998.[52]

The ECHR belongs to the realm of the COE, which remains an organisation separate from the EU governed by its own rules, norms, systems and procedures. Continued UK membership of the COE is not at present under threat. One of the post-Brexit imponderables is whether the UK's continued membership of the COE (for so long as this continues) will stimulate a *renaissance* of this organisation and its activities in this country. It is overlooked by many that the Statute of the Council of Europe predated both the Treaty of Rome and the ECHR. It was executed on 5 April 1949.

There will, I trust, be increased public awareness of the work of the COE and its achievements to date. While public debate has, predictably, been focused on (a) the influence and implications of EU law in the UK and, to a lesser extent, external EU policy and international relations, and (b) the much maligned ECHR, it being frequently overlooked that this finds expression in

---

[51] See *infra*.

[52] Largely effective from 2 October 2000.

the UK legal system in a measure of primary legislation adopted by a democratically elected legislature, namely the Human Rights Act 1998, I would expect attention to turn to some of the other COE Conventions which, for a variety of reasons, have had limited visibility and exposure.

There may, perhaps, be a reawakening of the reality that this organisation, which was born in 1949 with ten subscribing states (including the Republic of Ireland and the UK), has sought to achieve one of its aims, namely the protection and promotion of the rule of law and the fostering of legal cooperation among States Parties, by the adoption of some 200 Conventions and Treaties addressing an impressively broad range of topics.

One of the COE organs, the European Committee for the Prevention of Torture, has been particularly and visibly active in the UK during several decades. Others with an increasing profile include the European Commission for the Efficiency of Justice (CEPEJ), the Venice Commission, the European Directorate for the Quality of Medicines, the European Pharmacopoeia and the European Commission against Racism and Intolerance. Furthermore, it is not difficult to foresee a reawakening of awareness of the institutions of the COE: the Council of Ministers, the Parliamentary Assembly, the COE Secretariat, the Secretary General and the Permanent representatives and ambassadors who are accredited by each of the 47 States Parties. To this list one adds the Congress of the Council of Europe which was established in 1994 and comprises political representatives of local and regional authorities of all States Parties.

The close association between the Statute of the Council of Europe and the admittedly more elaborate and intricate constitutional instruments establishing and governing the modern EU is striking.[53] Furthermore, acceding states must affirm their commitment to harmony, cooperation, good governance and human rights, the principle of the rule of law and the guarantee of democracy, fundamental human rights and freedoms (sound familiar?).

The Human Rights Act, being a measure of pure domestic law, will remain in force. However, the EU Charter being of demonstrably greater reach than the ECHR, UK citizens will no longer have the protection of the Charter's *additional* rights, the *soi-disant* 'added value': the specific rights of the child; the array of social protections contained in Title IV; freedom to conduct a business; the strong anti-discrimination provisions; freedom of the arts and sciences; a right of conscientious objection; freedom to choose an occupation; a right to asylum and against *refoulement*; a right to data protection; the prohibition against human trafficking; a right to marry not restricted to different-sex couples; the right to physical and mental integrity; and a guarantee of human dignity. This is an impressive list indeed.

---

[53] See Art. 1(a) of the Statute.

Some of the EU Charter's *additional* rights and protections are recognised in certain measures of UK domestic law (e.g. data protection and protection from human trafficking) or in the ECtHR jurisprudence (e.g. certain types of physical and mental integrity), others will simply evaporate overnight, a particular and worrying illustration being the more expansive rights of the child. Furthermore, ensuring 'parallel' rights in UK domestic law may not benefit from the expansion and fortification which, historically, has emerged from the progressive interpretation of the CJEU. *Ditto* as regards future EU legislative measures of expansion and fortification.

However, there has been a concerted political campaign, vociferous and at times aggressive, espousing the repeal of the Human Rights Act. If this were to eventuate the UK's separation from the democratic states of Europe would become accentuated, with correspondingly enhanced isolationism. This retrograde step would result in the ECHR being banished once again to the distant plane of international law, excised from UK domestic law. Those living and working in the UK would no longer be able to invoke its protections before the courts. This would be supremely ironic in a country where imaginative and progressive lawyers and judges relentlessly developed the status and influence of this international treaty in the UK during a period of some two decades preceding the seminal Human Rights Act. The cumbersome, slow, expensive and uncertain process of individually petitioning the ECtHR – and this only after exhausting all domestic remedies – would return. It is difficult to describe this as other than profoundly retrograde.

Some of those campaigning for the repeal of the Human Rights Act have claimed that this will be counterbalanced by the adoption of a 'purely British' bill of rights. There are, of course, many imponderables. However, at this remove, particularly given Government antipathy to the Human Rights Act, it seems far from probable that any bill of rights would mirror the protections of the ECHR. What is even more predictable is that such a measure would not replicate the EU Charter.

It follows from the above that the continuing operation of (much of) the ECHR in the UK legal system will provide but a limited counterbalance to the negative post-Brexit effects identified. The limitations of Article 8 ECHR in protecting migrants will be exposed. There will be increasing awareness of the orientation of the ECtHR jurisprudence, which has entailed much deference to state sovereignty in the sphere of migration. Successful resistance of deportation based on Article 8 ECHR has been relatively infrequent. Family life has been narrowly defined and private life is routinely disregarded.[54]

---

[54] Illustrated in *Senchishak v Finland* [5049/12], unreported 18 November 2014.

The heavy balancing of the scales in favour of the state, based on the sovereign right to control the movement of persons across international borders emerges most clearly in the landmark decision of *Abdulaziz v United Kingdom* [App No 9214/80].[55] This sovereign right to control the entry of non-nationals extends to control of their residence and expulsion.[56] This trend in the Strasbourg jurisprudence has prevailed notwithstanding that, in the context of a human rights protection instrument, it gives precedence to the principle of state control, namely a provocative that neither affirms human rights nor is contained in the text of the ECHR.

The potential of Article 8 ECHR to provide a vehicle for family reunification is equally limited. Family reunification, in this context, entails the entry of non-nationals, most frequently nationals of non-EU countries, for the purpose of family life with a family member or members already lawfully present on the territory of the state concerned. The best known of the ECtHR decisions in this respect are *Sen v Netherlands*[57] and *Mayeka v Belgium*.[58] In the UK, a series of judicial decisions giving effect to this discrete stream of Strasbourg jurisprudence began with *R (ZAT) v Secretary of State for the Home Department*.[59] As these decisions demonstrate, where Article 8 can be invoked it is capable of providing the most practical and expeditious remedial mechanism available for family reunification purposes.

In the search for factors which may provide an effective foil to the foreseeable post-Brexit human rights protection backward slide in the UK, attention turns to the increasing alignment of the CJEU and the ECtHR. This belongs to a context where the EU en bloc is to accede to the ECHR.[60] There has been a progressively discernible jurisprudential dialogue between these two national courts. This has evolved almost imperceptibly in the absence of any coercive legal obligation to this effect. The 'constitutional traditions common to the Member States', a familiar phrase, has increasing resonance in this context. This 'cross-pollination' seems merely logical given the strong association between ECHR rights and the general principles of EU law. This is readily

---

[55] [1985] ECHR 7, (1985) 7 EHRR 471, IHRL 52 (ECHR 1985), 28 May 1985, European Court of Human Rights [ECHR].

[56] See, for example, *Moustaquim v Belgium* [App No 12313/86].

[57] [2003] 36 EHRR 7.

[58] [2008] 46 EHRR 23.

[59] IJR [2016] UKUT 61 (IAC).

[60] A process that is suspended following CJEU, Opinion 2/13 (ECLI:EU:C:2014:2454) which held that accession would be incompatible with the existing Treaties.

identifiable in CJEU decisions such as *NS v SSHD*[61] and *MSS v Belgium and Greece*.[62] Examples can be readily multiplied.

Thus, post-Brexit, it is foreseeable that both the EU Charter and the general principles of EU law, particularly insofar as these have been absorbed within the ECHR and the Strasbourg jurisprudence, will have *indirect* influence in the UK legal system. This will occur in a context where it is the declared philosophy of the ECtHR to treat the ECHR as a living instrument. But the concern must be that this influence will be weak.

9. SUMMARY AND CONCLUSIONS

Will the exile of the Charter after exit day be final and absolute? The answer which I would offer is 'No'. This is based on the following provisions of the UK withdrawal legislation:

(a) While the principle of the supremacy of EU law will not apply to any enactment or rule of law made on or after exit day, the supremacy principle will nonetheless continue to apply so far as relevant to the interpretation, disapplication or quashing of any enactment or rule of law passed or made before exit day. There will undoubtedly be an argument, of some plausibility, that in giving effect to this statutory provision the Charter cannot be disregarded. Inter alia, the Charter's status at the apex of the EU constitutional arrangements cannot be ignored; the Charter codifies rights and principles already existing in EU law; and secondary EU legislation frequently invokes the Charter in its recitals.
(b) Any fundamental rights or principles of EU law which exist irrespective of the Charter will be retained in domestic UK law. This gives rise to the possibility of resort to the Charter's mechanisms, for example its 'Explanations', or to Charter jurisprudence whether of the CJEU or UK courts, provided that an identifiable nexus can be established.
(c) The Charter could conceivably make a formal or official reappearance in the event of the exercise of the statutory Ministerial power to act so as to prevent, remedy or mitigate any failure of retained EU law to operate effectively or any other deficiency.
(d) The same observation applies to the separate power to make transitional arrangements by secondary legislation.

61 [2012] 2 CMLR 9.
62 [2011] 53 EHRR 2.

(e) The Charter will continue to operate, albeit on a short-term basis, insofar as relevant to any proceedings begun, but not finally determined, before a UK court or tribunal prior to exit day.
(f) Courts and tribunals are given a discretion to have regard to judgments of the CJEU postdating exit day. These may include Charter-related decisions.
(g) Domestic courts are also given a discretion to have regard to what is done by 'another EU entity of the EU', including the CJEU, insofar as relevant to any case of which they are seized. This would embrace, for example, reports and publications of the EU Fundamental Rights Agency.
(h) Charter rights which can be identified and recognised as expressing a fundamental right or principle existing irrespective of the Charter will form part of retained EU law. While this may give rise to an untidy and uncertain dichotomy, the significance of this provision is that the Charter is a codifying instrument containing at least some provisions deriving from preceding CJEU case law. This assessment is fortified by the specific provision that 'references to the Charter in any case law are, so far as necessary for this purpose, to be read as if they were references to any corresponding retained fundamental rights or principles'. It follows that certain aspects of CJEU jurisprudence with a specific focus on the Charter may continue to exert a significant influence post-dating exit day.
(i) Courts and tribunals are specifically empowered to have regard, and give effect, to post-exit day CJEU judgments which do not depart from pre-exit day CJEU judgments.
(j) A court will be able to disapply legislation or quash a relevant act where a challenge relates to something predating exit day and is made within a three year limitation period.
(k) Any court decisions pre-exit day quashing an act or decision or disapplying a provision of pre-exit secondary legislation on the ground of incompatibility with one of the general principles of EU law will continue to have effect.

Notwithstanding the foregoing, on the other side of the scales there will be no right of action in domestic UK law after exit day based on a failure to comply with EU general principles; courts will not be empowered to disapply domestic laws post-exit day on the basis that they are incompatible with EU general principles; and the same constraint will apply in relation to particular acts.

To conclude. I apprehend that the extent of the Charter's post-Brexit influence in the UK will depend significantly on two factors in particular. The first is the innovation and creativity of UK lawyers and judges. The second is the future rule of law culture in the UK. Effective human rights protection, particularly in a country which has no constitution, will be heavily dependent on a strong rule of law culture. What the future holds for this culture in the UK is something of an *incognito* and a matter of legitimate concern.

13. Comment: Brexit and the diverse functions of the Charter of Fundamental Rights

Stephen Coutts

INTRODUCTION

As pointed out by Bernard McCloskey in Chapter 12, upon exit day[1] the Charter of Fundamental Rights (the Charter or CFR) will no longer form part of the law of the United Kingdom, unlike the vast bulk of EU law, which has been transplanted into domestic law wholesale by the Withdrawal Act 2018.[2] We therefore have the rather peculiar situation of the bulk of EU law (now termed 'retained EU law') operating within a legal system, but in the absence of the Charter, at least at first glance. It therefore provides a good opportunity to assess precisely the value of the Charter to the operation of EU law. It is in this exercise that I see the contribution of Lord Justice McCloskey's chapter.

The present comment is limited to a reflection on what Lord Justice McCloskey's chapter reveals about Brexit and the value and functions of the Charter in the Union's legal order. Space precludes a more detailed discussion of issues relating to the general added value of the Charter as a human rights instrument and pluralism in human rights protection in the European legal space more generally, topics which are well covered elsewhere (see Chapters 2 and 6 in this volume).

As pointed out by Lord Justice McCloskey, the Charter, almost uniquely of EU law, will not be 'retained' as part of domestic UK law upon exit day.

---

1 Now fixed for 31 January 2021. See the European Union (Withdrawal) Act 2018 (Exit Day) (Amendment) (No 3) Regulations 2019 (2019).

2 See generally Paul Craig, 'Constitutional Principle, the Rule of Law and Political Reality: The European Union (Withdrawal) Act 2018' (2019) 82 MLR 319. The reason is clear. A substantial chunk of UK law in fact derives from EU instruments. To withdraw from the EU without providing some form of transplant would result in significant gaps in the legal system of the UK. Hence the solution is to transfer wholesale EU law into UK domestic law, henceforth known as 'retained EU law'.

While we can assume that the motivations for this are primarily political – the Charter being a particular target of Brexiteer ire since its inception[3] – what are the precise legal consequences of this removal of the Charter? The instinctive answer is that the Charter now no longer applies, leading to a loss of a progressive and effective instrument for the protection of individual's rights. And while that is correct, it is not the whole story; for the Charter performs a number of inter-related functions in the Union's legal order and a more careful consideration is required to assess the extent to which these functions are affected by Brexit. Three can be discerned. Firstly, the classic functions of a bill of human rights in a legal order, that is to act as a limitation on the exercise of public power, ie as a side-constraint.[4] Secondly, the broader functioning of the Charter as informing human rights policymaking and interpretation in the Union either by its reference in substantive legislative provisions or as a source of inspiration or interpretation by political or judicial organs. Thirdly and finally, a more particular function of the Charter in the context of the European Union is in underpinning the operation of transnational processes and cooperation between national actors, especially in the Area of Freedom, Security and Justice. This refers to the famous pairing of mutual trust and mutual recognition.[5] A consideration of the Charter in light of Brexit permits a closer analysis of these three, separate functions.

THE LOSS OF THE CHARTER AS A GROUNDS FOR REVIEW

The impact of Brexit will be felt most immediately in relation to the first function of the Charter as acting as a classic side-constraint on public action; arguably the most important function of any human rights instrument. As pointed out by Lord Justice McCloskey, the non-inclusion of the Charter of Fundamental Rights in the concept of 'retained' EU law will remove a vital tool for the protection of individual interests and the prevention of abuses by state authorities, not least in the area of asylum. The Charter itself will cease to exist in the UK legal order and, while there are complex provisions for

---

3 See McCloskey in Chapter 12 of this book.

4 As described in Robert Nozick, *Anarchy, State and Utopia* (Basic Books, New York 1974).

5 For an assessment of the operation of mutual recognition regimes in general see Christine Janssens, *The Principle of Mutual Recognition in EU Law* (OUP, Oxford 2013). For a consideration of its development in the areas of asylum transfers and the European Arrest Warrant see Ermioni Xanthopoulou, 'Mutual Trust and Rights in EU Criminal Law and Asylum Law: Three Phases of Evolution and the Unchartered Territory beyond Blind Trust' (2018) 55 CML Rev 489.

the retention of 'general principles' of EU law and of rights contained in EU law other than the Charter,[6] it is clear from the Withdrawal Act 2018 that any such principles shall not be a cause of action or a grounds of claim for any challenge. Furthermore, the validity of retained EU law cannot be challenged unless provided for in subsequent legislation.[7]

The loss is best analysed by the comparison made by Lord Justice McCloskey with the protection that remains in the shape of the European Convention on Human Rights (ECHR) and the domestic legislation implementing that Convention, ie the Human Rights Act 1998 (HRA). The ECHR/HRA cannot compensate for the loss of the Charter for two reasons. Firstly, while the broader *scope* of the ECHR – covering as it does all state action – must be acknowledged, in terms of substance, the Charter is a more complete set of rights. This is altogether fitting in light of the nature of the ECHR as a broadly applicable but minimum set of human rights. Secondly, in terms of legal impact, the Charter, once engaged, is a provision of Union law and hence enjoys both direct effect and primacy, resulting in a relatively robust set of remedies including the ability to set aside an Act of Parliament.[8] The comparable remedy in the case of violation of a right in the Human Rights Act is a 'declaration of incompatibility', declaring that the relevant Act of Parliament is incompatible with rights contained in the HRA 1998. However, it 'does not affect the validity, continuing operation or enforcement of the provision in respect of which it is given and is not binding on the parties to the proceedings in which it is made'.[9] It remains for the UK Government, if it believes compelling reasons exist, to make amendments to remove the incompatibility.[10]

THE CHARTER AS A NORMATIVE INFLUENCE AND AID TO INTERPRETATION

However, the non-inclusion of the CFR in the body of retained law will not mean the complete absence of any normative effect of the Charter on UK law in the future. This relates to the second function of the Charter: to act as a set of rights and principles for the Union's legal order and its administrative, political and judicial actors. The Charter informs the drafting of individual

---

[6] Craig, 'Constitutional Principle, the Rule of Law and Political Reality: The European Union (Withdrawal) Act 2018' (n 2) at 330ff.

[7] See ibid at 334.

[8] See McCloskey in Chapter 12 of this book. See the classic case of Case C-239/89 *R (Factortame) v Secretary of State for Transport* EU:C:1990:257.

[9] Merris Amos, 'Problems with the Human Rights Act 1998' (2009) 72 MLR 883, 892.

[10] Ibid.

pieces of Union legislation[11] and even more clearly their interpretation by the Court of Justice of the European Union (CJEU).[12] The body of that legislation, and the rights it contains, will remain in force in the United Kingdom for the foreseeable future and any judgments of the CJEU delivered prior to Brexit day will be part of retained EU law in the UK post-exit day. Furthermore, judgments of the CJEU subsequent to Brexit day interpreting such law may be taken into account by UK courts. Finally, as noted above, general principles of EU law and rights recognised in EU law other than in the Charter will be part of retained EU law (with the important caveat that they shall not constitute a ground of action).[13] Thus, as pointed out by Lord Justice McCloskey, as part of its second function of informing the interpretation and content of *other* EU law provisions, the Charter will have a lingering effect in the UK legal system, the Withdrawal Act notwithstanding.

THE CHARTER, MUTUAL RECOGNITION AND COOPERATION IN THE FUTURE RELATIONSHIP

Finally, the Charter performs a third function, particular to the transnational structure of much EU law, in underpinning systems of mutual recognition, in particular in criminal law and asylum law, ie the Area of Freedom, Security and Justice. Mutual recognition is premised on mutual trust.[14] That mutual trust is secured in the European Union through a common institutional framework, including common standards and enforcement mechanisms. The application of the Charter, with its purported high standard of fundamental rights, in all Member States whenever they act within the scope of Union law, should, ideally, provide some measure of confidence that fundamental rights will be

---

11 With the influence of the Charter sometimes cited in the preamble. See for example Directive 2011/95/EU on standards for the qualification of third-country nationals or stateless persons as beneficiaries of international protection, for a uniform status for refugees or for persons eligible for subsidiary protection, and for the content of the protection granted [2011] OJ L 337/9, recital (16).

12 See for example the interpretation of the procedures directive by the CJEU in Joined Cases C-148/13 to C-150/13 *A, B and C v Staatssecretaris van Veiligheid en Justitie* EU:C:2014:2406, in particular human dignity (art 1, CFR) and the right to a private and family life (art 7, CFR).

13 See Craig, 'Constitutional Principle, the Rule of Law and Political Reality: The European Union (Withdrawal) Act 2018' (n 2) at 330.

14 See Xanthopoulou, 'Mutual Trust and Rights in EU Criminal Law and Aslyum Law: Three Phases of Evolution and the Unchartered Territory beyond Blind Trust' (n 5). See also Valsamis Mitsilegas, 'The Limits of Mutual Trust in Europe's Area of Freedom, Security and Justice: From Automatic Inter-State Cooperation to the Slow Emergence of the Individual' (2012) 31 YEL 319.

respected by other Member States when they are engaging – either as a sending or receiving Member State – in systems of mutual recognition. These systems, it will be recalled, rely on their quasi-automatic nature for their effectiveness. Mutual trust, underpinned by the Charter, enables the paradoxical situation where fundamental rights checks are deemed unnecessary when transferring individuals within the European Union and hence increases considerably the effectiveness of these systems. It is this logic which lies behind the CJEU's somewhat dramatic statement in *NS*.[15] As is well known (and analysed at various points in this book), contrary to the pronouncements of the CJEU, mutual trust has not flowed automatically from the mere existence of the Charter and further problems in the operation of these systems has flowed from the ongoing application of the ECHR to such transfers.[16]

It is here that the refusal of the UK to carry the CFR into its domestic legal system post Brexit may have an, as yet undefined, impact on the future relationship between the UK and the EU. While much focus has been on the trade dimension of the future relationship, the UK also wishes to establish a close relationship of cooperation in justice and home affairs, possibly including an equivalent for the European Arrest Warrant Framework Decision and the Dublin system.[17] Some form of adherence to a set of fundamental rights at least equivalent to that obtaining in the European Union would appear to be necessary.[18] Indeed, the Political Declaration makes specific reference to the Charter

---

[15] Joined Cases C-411/10 and C-493/10 *NS v Secretary of State for the Home Department and ME and Others v Refugee Applications Commissioner and Minister for Justice, Equality and Law Reform* EU:C:2011:865, [2011] ECR I-13905 at para 83. A similar sentiment in relation to the European Arrest Warrant Framework Decision can be discerned in Case C-399/11 *Stefano Melloni v Ministerio Fiscal* EU:C:2013:107.

[16] In the area of asylum transfers see *Tarakhel v Switzerland* App No 29217/12 (ECtHR) and Case C-578/16 *CK and Others v Republika Slovenija* EU:C:2017:127. In the case of the European Arrest Warrant see Joined Cases C-404/15 and C-659/15 *Pál Aranyosi and Robert Căldăraru v Generalstaatsanwaltschaft Bremen* EU:C:2016:198.

[17] Such as inclusion by Norway, Switzerland and Iceland in the Dublin system or the Agreement between the European Union and the Republic of Iceland and the Kingdom of Norway on the surrender procedure between the Member States of the European Union and Iceland and Norway [2006] OJ L 292/2. It should be noted, however, that these states' close association with the European Union either as part of the European Economic Area or, in the case of Switzerland, as part of the Schengen system is what makes their quasi-participation in systems of EU mutual recognition possible. The UK has not indicated it wishes to align itself with either of these systems, meaning such cooperation as enjoyed by these states with the European Union in all likelihood will not be replicated with the UK.

[18] See references to the commitment of fundamental rights underpinning future cooperation in the Revised text of the Political Declaration setting out the framework for the future relationship between the European Union and the United Kingdom as

indicating that future judicial cooperation in criminal matters should be underpinned by ongoing commitment to the ECHR and 'should also reflect the Union's and its Member States' commitment to the Charter of Fundamental Rights of the European Union'.[19]

Adherence to the Charter is not essential for future cooperation. As noted above the Political Declaration makes reference to the ECHR, as does the Surrender Agreement between the EU and Norway and Iceland.[20] Similarly, in *RO* the CJEU held that adherence of the UK to the ECHR – and its incorporation in national legislation – was a sufficient guarantee that the fundamental rights of an individual who was being surrendered from Ireland would continue to be guaranteed after the UK withdrew from the European Union.[21] Nonetheless, the question of fundamental rights and their role in any future cooperation between the UK and the EU in these sensitive areas is raised by the UK's treatment of the Charter in the Brexit process. The problems are certainly not insurmountable in light of the *current* human rights regime that operates in the UK. The HRA 1998 does implement the ECHR and the UK is therefore broadly human rights compliant, at least to a sufficient degree that some form of mutual recognition will be possible, although probably not at the same level of automaticity. However, *future* developments including divergence between the CFR and the ECHR, where the CFR establishes higher protections operating between EU Member States and, more seriously, a possible repeal of the HRA 1998 (a proposal which has emerged periodically in UK political discourse),[22] may cause significant problems for any future instruments of mutual recognition.

CONCLUSION

The United Kingdom was long distrustful of the Charter of Fundamental Rights, as indicated by the adoption of Protocol No 30 in the Treaty of Lisbon. It brought together two things somewhat alien to the UK legal tradition: a set of human rights restrictive of parliamentary sovereignty and their interpretation

---

agreed at negotiators' level on 17 October 2019 (European Commission 2019) at para 6.

19 Ibid, para 81.

20 Surrender Agreement between the EU and Iceland and Norway (n 17), preamble.

21 Case C-327/18 *Minister for Justice and Equality v RO* EU:C:2018:733, para 53.

22 See Conor Gearty, 'The Human Rights Act Should not be Repealed' (LSE Law – Policy Briefing Papers 16, 2016) and Anne Smith, Monica McWilliams and Yarnell Priyamvada, 'Does Every Cloud Have a Silver Lining? Brexit, Repeal of the Human Rights Act and the Northern Ireland Bill of Rights' (2016) 40 Fordham Intl Law J 79, 107 ff.

by foreign courts. It is therefore not surprising that an exception was made in the great transfer of EU law into the UK domestic legal system and that the Charter was not carried forward as 'retained EU law'. Nonetheless on closer examination the Charter will continue to have some effect in the UK's legal system. Indeed, an analysis of the impact of removal of the Charter from the UK is useful in revealing the different functions its serves in the EU's legal order more broadly. Three have been identified in this chapter: as a limitation on the exercise of public power; as a normative source for the elaboration and interpretation of other provisions of EU law; and finally as a mechanism to underpin systems of mutual recognition. It is in the first category – as a means of limiting abuses of public power – that its loss in the UK will be most felt. In relation to the second category – as a normative source – its presence will continue to be felt. This will be through the existence of general principles and other rights, Charter inspired but existing in other instruments, as well as through the reference made to judgments of the CJEU relevant to retained EU law, which will no doubt continue to be heavily influenced by the Charter. Finally, in relation to the final function of the Charter identified here – as an underpinning of the systems of mutual recognition – the loss of the Charter will not necessarily be fatal to future cooperation with the European Union, although ongoing adherence and arguably incorporation of the ECHR would appear to be so. Nonetheless, it points out the inherent link between a functioning fundamental rights system, mutual trust and mutual recognition within an Area of Freedom, Security and Justice.

PART II

Sector specific issues

14. The Charter's potential in fighting hate and discrimination: levelling up to international obligations through victims' rights

Rita Gião Hanek and Lilla Farkas

1. INTRODUCTION

In 2016 the Dutch EU Presidency chose to rent a truck and officially join the Warsaw Pride Parade. The bright orange vests read 'No hate' rather than 'equality' or 'non-discrimination' indicating that characteristics protected under the EU *acquis* appear more limited for discrimination not meeting the threshold of *hate.*[1] Could the EU Presidency rally behind a statement condemning discrimination *tout court*, rather than only condemning manifestations of discrimination that amount to 'hate' at the next Parade? If so, what should be the role of EU non-discrimination law and the Charter of Fundamental Rights of the EU? Do *judicial interaction* and/or policy processes on hate speech and hate crime have the potential to meaningfully broaden the scope of protection from discrimination? These are some of the questions this chapter seeks to answer.

The literature has investigated case law that concerns a limited number of legal measures, asking whether Article 14 of the European Convention on Human Rights (ECHR) and the Strasbourg Court (ECtHR) or Article 21 of the EU Charter and the Luxembourg Court (CJEU) provides better protection against discrimination.[2] It has queried the levels of protection dependent on the

[1] Alex Duval Smith, 'Thousands March for LGBTI Rights in Warsaw amid Rising Hostility' *The Guardian* (London, 11 June 2016) C3.

[2] Christa Tobler, 'Equality and Non-Discrimination under the ECHR and EU Law: A Comparison Focusing on Discrimination against LGBTI Persons' (2014) 74 *Zeitschrift für ausländisches öffentliches Recht und Völkerrecht* 521.

ground of discrimination,[3] proposing intersectional approaches as a panacea for legislative shortcomings.[4] The dominant supranational, top-down approach can conceal the complementarity of these instruments at the national level and the fact that intersections between different branches of law are key to making progress in addressing prejudice and discrimination.[5]

Researchers have not explored the ways in which EU and domestic law and adjudication address hate speech and hate crime, unscathed by legislative deadlock that otherwise characterizes anti-discrimination provisions. The difference stems from the two tiers of protection from discrimination, i.e. 'civil' and 'criminal' wrongs, and the disconnected analysis of the civil and criminal branches of EU anti-discrimination law.

The classic legal account distinguishes between the bodies of EU anti-discrimination and criminal law, i.e. the Gender Equality Directive (Recast),[6] the Gender Goods and Services Directive,[7] the Racial Equality Directive,[8] and the Framework Employment Equality Directive[9] (hereafter 'the gender equality and non-discrimination directives') on the one hand, and the Framework Decision on combating certain forms and expressions of racism and xenophobia by means of criminal law (hereafter 'Framework Decision')[10] and the Audiovisual Media Services, the Electronic Commerce and the

---

[3] Mark Bell and Lisa Waddington, 'More Equal than Others: Distinguishing European Union Equality Directives' (2001) 38 *Common Market Law Review* 587.

[4] See, for instance, Dagmar Schiek and Victoria Chege (eds), *European Union Non-Discrimination Law: Comparative Perspectives on Multidimensional Equality Law* (Taylor and Francis, London 2008); Dagmar Schiek and Anna Lawson (eds), *European Union Non-Discrimination Law and Intersectionality: Investigating the Triangle of Racial, Gender and Disability Discrimination* (Ashgate Publishing Ltd, Aldershot 2013).

[5] Renáta Uitz, 'Lessons from Sexual Orientation Discrimination in Central Europe' (2012) 60 *American Journal of Comparative Law* 235.

[6] Directive 2006/54/EC of the European Parliament and of the Council of 5 July 2006 on the implementation of the principle of equal opportunities and equal treatment of men and women in matters of employment and occupation (recast) [2006] OJ L 204/23.

[7] Council Directive 2004/113/EC of 13 December 2004 implementing the principle of equal treatment between men and women in the access to and supply of goods and services [2004] OJ L 373/37.

[8] Council Directive 2000/43/EC of 29 June 2000 implementing the principle of equal treatment between persons irrespective of racial or ethnic origin [2000] OJ L 180/22.

[9] Council Directive 2000/78/EC of 27 November 2000 establishing a general framework for equal treatment in employment and occupation [2000] OJ L 303/16.

[10] Council Framework Decision 2008/913/JHA of 28 November 2008 on combating certain forms and expressions of racism and xenophobia by means of criminal law [2008] OJ L 328/55.

Victims' Rights Directive (hereafter 'the Victims Directive')[11] on the other. Hate-related instruments adopted in the context of criminal law cooperation also include the Guidance Document and Note on the implementation of the Victims Directive and the Framework Decision respectively; as well the Code of conduct on countering illegal hate speech online (hereafter 'the Code').[12]

This chapter explores differences and similarities between these two branches of anti-discrimination law, attributing identical significance to both, while recognizing that their mode of implementation (transposition as compared to (judicial) cooperation) may vary. Criminal codes across the EU list offences outlawing *discriminatory crimes* or *crimes with discriminatory elements*, such as hate crimes, hate speech offences or discrimination. We contend that *discriminatory crimes* form part of *equality law* broadly understood.

As concerns the EU non-discrimination *acquis*, the ability to handle diversity and dispersed authority arises from the fact that the EU itself is an intergovernmental body that coexists, operates and legislates within the diversity of its members. It must, by definition, embrace diversity. As concerns the equal treatment of diverse population groups, there is no tangible distinction between *grounds of discrimination in the civil branch* and *protected characteristics in the criminal branch.*[13] The expansion of Member States' obligations under the criminal branch demonstrates the emergence of a *continuum* of equality that

---

[11] Recital 9, Directive 2012/29/EU of the European Parliament and of the Council of 25 October 2012 establishing minimum standards on the rights, support and protection of victims of crime, and replacing Council Framework Decision 2001/220/JHA [2012] OJ L 315/57.

[12] EC European Commission, 'Guidance Document related to the transposition and implementation of Directive 2012/29/EU of the European Parliament and of the Council of 25 October 2012 establishing minimum standards on the rights, support and protection of victims of crime, and replacing Council Framework Decision 2001/220/JHA' [2013] Ref Ares (2013)(3763804) DG Justice; EU High Level Group on combating racism, xenophobia and other forms of intolerance, Guidance Note on the Practical Application of Council Framework Decision 2008/913/JHA, November 2018 ('Guidance Note'); European Commission, Code of Conduct on Countering Illegal Hate Speech Online, June 2016; Directive (EU) 2018/1808 of the European Parliament and of the Council of 14 November 2018 amending Directive 2010/13/EU on the coordination of certain provisions laid down by law, regulation or administrative action in Member States concerning the provision of audiovisual media services (Audiovisual Media Services Directive) [2018] OJ L 303/69.

[13] 'It is important to view the EU measures aimed at addressing racism and xenophobia in the context of the broader EU legislative framework. Instruments aimed at supporting victims of crime and antidiscrimination measures are of particular relevance in this respect', Vanessa Leigh, Virginia Dalla Pozza, Katalin Adamis-Császár, Emma Psaila and Marilena Verbari, 'The European Legal Framework on Hate Speech, Blasphemy and its Interaction with Freedom of Expression', Directorate-General for Internal Policies of the Union (European Parliament), 2016, accessed 28 October 2021

partly increases the coherence of EU equality law.[14] It stands in stark contrast with the civil branch, where gaping differences remain due partly to legislative deadlock concerning the draft Horizontal Directive.

We trace these developments in three steps. First, Part 1 introduces the central organizing concept, the continuum of equality, highlighting its potential in bridging the two tiers of relevant EU law, namely anti-discrimination norms adopted under Article 19 Treaty on the Functioning of the European Union (TFEU) and *hate*-related norms under Articles 82 through 86 TFEU. The analysis focuses on the asymmetries between lists of grounds (civil branch) and protected characteristics (criminal branch) in secondary legislation.

Part 2 explores the external influence of the ECtHR on the criminal branch of EU anti-discrimination law, using the examples of *sexual orientation* and *sex/gender* specific *hate*-related instruments in the ECtHR's recent jurisprudence. We find that EU secondary legislation on criminal law codifies Strasbourg jurisprudence. It does so to both circumvent legislative deadlocks within the EU on discrimination and better implement international human rights law obligations at the national level.

Part 3 investigates whether the Charter can facilitate the emergence of a continuum of equality by bridging EU Member States' obligations under EU and international law, mindful of the higher level of protection accorded under the latter, as well as the risk that a sporadic and inconsistent use of the Charter may contribute to collision with the ECtHR and its jurisprudence as long as the EU delays accession to the European Convention. We conclude that rather than this being the case, the Charter has been used for three distinct purposes: (a) to maintain the *status quo*; (b) to reinforce the salience of EU law as a catalyst for change; but also (c) to uphold/impose a narrow reading of the anti-discrimination directives.

2. TWO-TIERED APPROACH TO EU ANTI-DISCRIMINATION LAW

In the context of equal treatment, the law – through binding as well as non-binding measures – plays a symbolic yet not necessarily key role in the EU's experimentalist, multi-level governance structure, powered by policy-makers, courts and legislators.[15] Against this backdrop, this section canvasses

---

at <https://op.europa.eu/en/publication-detail/-/publication/4271d9d1-7d3e-11e5-b8b7-01aa75ed71a1>.

[14] Anti-discrimination, non-discrimination and equality law are used interchangeably throughout the chapter.

[15] Gráinne de Búrca, 'EU Race Discrimination Law: A Hybrid Model?' in Gráinne de Búrca and Joanne Scott (eds), *Law and Governance in the EU and the US* (Hart Publishing, Oxford 2006) 98.

EU anti-discrimination law from the perspective of a continuum of equality that creates bridges between the two tiers of the relevant EU *acquis* as well as between different forms of judicial and policy cooperation and exchange.

2.1 The Continuum of Equality

In practice, there exists a *continuum* of intolerance and discrimination, ranging from less severe manifestations to more serious forms. The Allport's scale of prejudice and discrimination distinguishes interlocution from avoidance, discrimination and physical attack.[16] There is a wide spectrum of discriminatory manifestations in between these forms, in turn requiring an equally wide spectrum of state measures and legislative provisions.

The *continuum* of intolerance and discrimination necessitates a *continuum* of legal and policy responses. These responses can range from non-legal, prevention-oriented measures – such as promoting tolerance and non-discrimination in schools and publicity campaigns – through countering hate speech with speech or the adoption of codes of conduct to civil law litigation, labour law inspections and the prosecution of discrimination and hate crimes.

In all forms of discrimination that have a victim wronged by a conduct, the basic discriminatory mechanism involves: (a) the existence of a 'victim'; (b) the existence of a 'discriminator' (acting with or without discriminatory intent); (c) the choice of a victim on the basis of characteristics protected by law; and (d) harm suffered by the victim.

A victim-centric perspective characterizes criminal, civil as well as administrative law but the threshold of criminal conduct is determined by national legislators in a discretionary therefore diverse manner. Criminal law represents the most intrusive measure, thus the last resort in the protection of rights and values. Only the most egregious violations tend to be criminalized and not all grounds included in anti-discrimination legislation are protected under criminal law. Hate speech offences and hate crimes are sanctioned only on a sub-set of grounds otherwise included in domestic civil or administrative laws. Logically, all the grounds protected under criminal law should also be included in other branches of anti-discrimination legislation but there are important exceptions to this rule.

Due to the open list of grounds in Article 14 ECHR that safeguards the principle of equal treatment, Strasbourg case law has levelled out protection between discrimination as a civil wrong and discrimination as a crime as concerns the grounds/protected characteristics – an issue explored in Section

[16] Gordon Allport, *The Nature of Prejudice* (Addison-Wesley, Cambridge 1954).

2.2. Rulings not only address hate speech and hate crime, but also impose positive obligations with an emphasis on *ex officio* duties to investigate and prosecute bias regardless of whether national legislation explicitly lists a given *protected characteristic*. This broadens the scope of protection from discriminatory crimes at the national level with two important consequences for EU anti-discrimination law: first, it settles the scope of the Victims Directive, and second, it informs the interpretation of the Charter of Fundamental Rights as concerns criminal forms of discrimination.

Equality and non-discrimination at the EU level have been ensured through a so-called 'hybrid' model. Complementing judicial enforcement, policy exchange and financial incentives have not only been offered but also preferred by the European Commission. This governance approach relies on 'revisability and open-endedness' and is 'more radically bottom-up, with judicial enforcement playing a residual role to monitor the adequacy of processes'.[17] Irrespective of the conceptual or political origins of this approach, the goal has been, and still is, to broaden the scope of the normative framework.[18] 'Revisability' does not mean, however, that the way is always 'forward'.

Against this backdrop, the *continuum* of equality signifies an interdisciplinary and cross-sectoral approach to equality and non-discrimination.[19] Regardless of their nature (legal, policy, other) and repressive character (criminal, administrative or civil), state responses to different manifestations of discrimination form a continuum, mirroring discrimination in practice. The continuum of discrimination encompasses all violations of law with a discriminatory element vis-à-vis an individual or a group, including direct and indirect discrimination, harassment or instruction to discriminate, hate crime and hate speech, including gender-based violence.[20]

---

[17] de Búrca (n 15) 98.

[18] Gráinne de Búrca, 'The European Union in the Negotiation of the UN Disability Convention' (2010) 35 *European Law Review* 174, 221.

[19] See, for instance, sections on hate crime and hate speech in European Union Agency for Fundamental Rights, *Handbook on European Non-Discrimination* (European Union, Bruxelles 2018) 81 and 86. As well as Council of Europe, *Links between Freedom of Expression and Other Human Rights* (2019) 82.

[20] Hate crimes are *criminal offences committed with a bias motive* according to the OSCE definition endorsed by the European Commission in the Guidance Note on the Framework Decision 2008/913/JHA.

2.2 Civil and Criminal Branches of EU Anti-Discrimination Law: Personal Scope

EU non-discrimination norms have grown from a narrowly tailored body of law on employment and market-related discrimination to a complex regime covering a much broader range of fields and a much wider scope of *grounds*.[21] The concept of 'grounds' and 'protected characteristics' can be used interchangeably but the first more often appear in the civil branch, while the second in the criminal branch. They refer to personal characteristics, including race, colour, ethnic or social origin, religion or belief, disability, age, gender, gender expression and identity, sexual orientation, and so on that are also explicitly mentioned in the open list of Article 21 of the Charter of Fundamental Rights of the EU.

The international non-discrimination framework binding EU Member States is robust. In addition to and preceding EU law, it consists of United Nations treaties including the International Covenant on Civil and Political Rights (ICCPR), on Economic, Social and Cultural Rights (ICESCR), the Convention on the Elimination of Racial Discrimination (CERD), the Convention on the Elimination of all Forms of Discrimination Against Women (CEDAW), the Convention on the Rights of Persons with Disabilities (CRPD), Council of Europe treaties such as the ECHR and the Convention on preventing and combating violence against women and domestic violence (Istanbul Convention).[22] The EU has ratified the CRPD and is set to ratify the Istanbul Convention.

In the international legal framework, the list of protected grounds is an open one, except in ground-specific treaties. Initially, this limited the protection of victims belonging to the so-called younger generation of protected characteristics – disability, sexual orientation or gender identity – but this is not the case anymore.

The TFEU in Article 19 provides for the Council and the European Parliament to take appropriate action to combat discrimination based on sex, racial or ethnic origin, religion or belief, disability, age or sexual orientation.[23] This is the basis in EU primary law for the adoption of EU norms on non-discrimination. On the other hand, Articles 82 through 86 TFEU provide for the establishment of minimum rules applicable in the Member States to facilitate mutual recognition of judgments and judicial decisions, as well as

---

[21] Elise Muir, 'Pursuing Equality in the EU' in Damian Chalmers and Anthony Arnull (eds), *The Oxford Handbook of European Union Law* (OUP, Oxford 2015) 919.

[22] This section does not provide a comprehensive overview, which can be found in European Union Agency for Fundamental Rights, *Handbook on European Non-Discrimination Law* (European Union, Bruxelles 2018).

[23] Treaty on the Functioning of the European Union [2012] OJ C 326/47.

police and judicial cooperation in criminal matters. These provisions form the basis of EU norms and standards on criminal forms of discrimination.

EU secondary law adopted under Article 19 TFEU includes the Racial Equality Directive that prohibits discrimination on the grounds of racial or ethnic origin and applies to employment, education, social services and benefits, and goods and services. The Employment Equality Framework Directive only applies to employment and prohibits discrimination on the grounds of religion or belief, disability, age or sexual orientation. The Gender Equality Directive (Recast) and the Gender Goods and Services Directive which prohibits gender discrimination apply respectively to employment and access to goods and services. At present, sexual orientation, religious belief, disability and age are only protected in the context of employment, because a proposal to extend protection to goods and services (the so-called 'Horizontal Directive'), has been stuck in the legislative process since 2008. Having appointed the first Commissioner for Equality in 2020, the European Commission is presently reviewing the implementation of EU anti-discrimination norms, determined not only to pursue the adoption of the draft Horizontal Directive but also to enhance the enforcement of existing standards through further legislation if need be.

In the criminal branch, the Framework Decision is based on Articles 29 and 31 of the TEU.[24] It aims at approximating the criminal laws of EU Member States; mandating criminalization of hate crimes and certain forms of hate speech, on the grounds of race, colour, religion or belief, descent or national or ethnic origin.[25] ICERD and the Framework Decision take similar approaches. According to the OSCE/ODHIR database of hate crime laws, EU Member States criminalize racist hate crime (except the Netherlands, Ireland and Estonia that lack hate crime provisions, but penalize hate speech). Sexual orientation is explicitly included in the hate crime provisions of 18 EU states, gender identity in nine, sex/gender in ten and disability in 13.[26]

The broadening of the ECtHR's positive obligations doctrine concerning hate crimes has resulted in the gradual expansion of protected characteristics, which has had a direct as well as indirect effect on Member States given the

---

[24] Treaty on European Union [2012] OJ C 326/13. According to Article 29 TEU, the Council can adopt decisions to define the EU's approach to a particular matter of a geographical or thematic nature. Member States shall ensure that their national policies conform to the Union positions. According to Article 31 TEU decisions must be unanimous.

[25] This should not prevent the broadening of the scope of protection, see preambular paragraph 10 of the Framework Decision.

[26] OSCE ODIHR, *What Do We Know | OSCE – ODIHR* (Hatecrime.osce.org), 2020, accessed 17 July 2020 at <https://hatecrime.osce.org/what-do-we-know>.

EU's efforts to emulate this approach.[27] This tendency has been limited to criminal cooperation, still, it may have further reaching effects when it comes to discrimination prohibited in criminal law but (also) falling under directives in the civil branch of EU anti-discrimination law.

Criminal codes across the EU outlaw discriminatory crimes or crimes with discriminatory elements, such as hate crimes, hate speech or harassment not reaching the level of hate. Directives in the civil branch define and sanction harassment, which is often used to fight hate speech under criminal, as well as civil law, depending on domestic legislation transposing the directives.[28] National courts can thus investigate, prosecute and – in theory – provide remedy to hate speech victims.[29]

In line with international obligations, EU law on the investigation and prosecution of hate crimes and hate speech, as well as on the protected characteristics in the criminal branch, is now more detailed and broader than procedural safeguards and protected grounds provided in the civil branch. The case may be that harassment under the civil branch is sanctionable in relation to a shorter 'list' of grounds and a more limited set of fields than harassment under the criminal branch, giving rise to a wedge in and across the Member States. Conspicuously, the most comprehensive list of protected characteristics can be found in the most recent criminal law instrument, the Victims Directive.[30]

The approach in the criminal branch stands in stark contrast with the take on discrimination of directives in the civil branch, with significant implications for the personal as well as material scope of protection particularly noticeable in the list of grounds. Under the Victims Directive, specific protection stems from the protected characteristic targeted by the perpetrator. This implies a state obligation to acknowledge and tackle the underlying motivation, such

---

27 Alastair Mowbrey, *The Development of Positive Obligations under the European Convention on Human Rights* (Hart, Oxford 2004).

28 Dieter Schindlauer, 'Using the Conception of Harassment in National Anti-Discrimination Legislation as a Tool in Combating Hate Speech?' (2018) 2 *European Equality Review* 78.

29 Bulgaria, Burgas Administrative Court, decision No. 564 in case No. 1786/2017, *Valery Simeonov v. A.A.*, of 23 March 2018, accessed 28 October 2021 at <www.admcourt-bs.org/CMS_ADM/images_content/1786_2017R.htm> cited by Human European Consultancy, *A Comparative Analysis of Gender Equality in Europe*, 2019, accessed 26 August 2020 at <https://www.humanconsultancy.com/downloads/1568-a-comparative-analysis-of-gender-equality-law-in-europe-2019-pdf-1-72-mb>.

30 Victims' Rights Directive recital 9, article 1 sets forth that 'any victim should be treated without discrimination based on "race, colour, ethnic or social origin, genetic features, language, religion or belief, political or any other opinion, membership of a national minority, property, birth, disability, age, gender, gender expression, gender identity, sexual orientation, residence status or health, etc."'.

as homophobia, which in practice cannot be achieved if measures are limited to criminal law alone. Can the authorities identify bias motivation and prevent secondary victimization as required under the Directive if homophobic discrimination is not outlawed in other fields?[31] A homophobic hate crime victim ought not to be discriminated by public authorities in other areas of law, otherwise his protection as a crime victim becomes meaningless. In the criminal branch it is left to prosecutors and judges to fill the gaps of an inconsistent legal and policy framework and respond to the perpetrators' prejudiced motivation.[32] This is likely to change as the European Commission will, in 2021, propose to extend the list of *euro-crimes* to include all forms of hate crime and hate speech.[33]

Fragmentation and inconsistencies in the civil branch are challenged before the CJEU, often in the form of strategic litigation. The preliminary reference procedure has been used to broaden the scope of protection, especially when national norms explicitly leave certain identity traits unprotected.[34] The ECtHR's positive obligations doctrine can engender favourable changes in the interpretation of Article 21 of the Charter of Fundamental Rights and the subsequent sections explore how, building on the relevant Strasbourg jurisprudence, courts, legislators and policymakers (can) promote the equal treatment agenda by embracing the concept of equality as a continuum.

3. ASYMMETRIC EVOLUTION OF EU ANTI-DISCRIMINATION LAW

There are discrepancies in the evolution of the normative landscape when it comes to the criminal versus the civil branch of EU non-discrimination law. This section demonstrates how the list of protected characteristics has de facto been extended as a result of interaction between courts, legislators and poli-

---

[31] OSCE/ODHIR, *Hate Crime Victims in the Criminal Justice System: A Practical Guide* (OSCE/ODHIR, Warsaw 2020) 10.

[32] See, for example, the analysis on state primary schools protests by parents in the UK against the teaching programme 'No Outsiders' aimed at promoting equality for LGBTI people and challenging homophobia in Neville Harris, *Education, Law and Diversity* (Bloomsbury Publishing, Oxford 2020) 5.

[33] Ursula von der Leyen and Maroš Šefčovič, 'State of the Union 2021: Letter of Intent to President David Maria Sassoli and Prime Minister Janez Janša', 15 September 2021, accessed 28 October 2021 at <https://ec.europa.eu/info/sites/default/files/state_of_the_union_2021_letter_of_intent_en.pdf>; and Communication from the Commission to the European Parliament, the Council, the European Economic and Social Committee and the Committee of the Regions, Commission Work Programme 2021, A Union of vitality in a world of fragility, COM/2020/690 final.

[34] Uitz (n 5).

cymakers in the criminal branch, first in relation to the Framework Decision and later the Victims Directive. Gradual improvements in the criminal branch imply that a seemingly weaker governance technique can trigger more robust approximation of legal standards when cocooned in already existing obligations under international human rights law that bind Member States.

3.1 Strasbourg Jurisprudence and EU Standards on Hate

As mentioned above, the Framework Decision mandates action against hate speech and hate crimes based on race and religion. The narrow personal scope begs the question why only these types of hate speech and crime should be prohibited under EU law when all humans are born free and equal in dignity and in rights?[35] To answer, this section revisits the tensions between universal human rights and EU anti-discrimination law as concerns the criminal branch.

ECtHR case law extends protection from discrimination in criminal law to grounds not covered by the Framework Decision. In *M.C. and A.C. v. Romania* the ECtHR extended protection from hate crimes to sexual orientation, determining that the authorities' failure to effectively investigate a homophobic attack violated the applicants' right of effective investigation in conjunction with the prohibition of discrimination (Articles 3 and 14 of the ECHR).[36] The ECtHR clarified in *Identoba and others v. Georgia* that *gender identity* is also a protected ground.[37] In *Beizaras and Levickas v. Lithuania* the court ruled that the authorities' refusal to investigate hate speech comments about a same-sex kiss on Facebook amounts to a discriminatory attitude.[38]

National authorities also seldom investigate gender-based violence as bias motivated (failing to record misogynist or sexist slurs or to take note of underlying stereotypical power relationships) or prosecute these cases as crimes against the community. They focus instead on interpersonal aspects (the perpetrator's alcoholism or unemployment) or blaming the victim. That said, the ECtHR has considered gender-based violence as discriminatory conduct in several cases as well.[39]

---

[35] Natalie Alkiviadou, 'Hate Speech on Social Media Networks: Towards a Regulatory Framework?' (2018) 28 *Information & Communications Technology Law*, 19.

[36] *M.C. and A.C. v. Romania* App no 12060/12 (ECHR 12 April 2016).

[37] *Identoba and Others v. Georgia* App no 73235/12 (ECHR 12 May 2015).

[38] *Beizaras and Levickas v. Lithuania* App no 41288/15 (ECHR 14 January 2020).

[39] *Eremia v. the Republic of Moldova* App no 3564/11 (ECHR 28 May 2013); *M.G. v. Turkey* App no 646/10 (ECHR 22 March 2016); and *Halime Kilic v. Turkey* App no 22492/93 (ECHR 28 March 2000).

Recent EU directives include provisions on incitement to violence or hatred on grounds beyond the ones listed in the Framework Decision though. The Audiovisual Media Services Directive (AVMSD) establishes that communication shall not 'include or promote any discrimination based on sex, racial or ethnic origin, nationality, religion or belief, disability, age or sexual orientation'.[40] The Victims Directive goes beyond this list without maintaining hierarchy among the grounds. It protects, among others, lesbian, gay, bisexual, transgender, intersex (LGBTI), disabled and gender victims of hate crime establishing minimum standards on the rights, support and protection of victims of crime and ensuring that they are recognized and treated with respect, receive proper protection, support and access to justice.[41]

Generally overlooked in discussions about the EU anti-discrimination *acquis*, these directives regulate equal treatment in the criminal branch.[42] They are in conformity with international law obligations stemming from the Istanbul Convention, the CRPD and ECHR. Depending on national legislation, the Victims Directive offers protection from discrimination in criminal law to grounds and in fields not covered by the EU directives in the civil branch.

3.2 Soft Law Measures

Soft law measures perform a similar function. The European Commission has adopted Guidance Documents and Notes to facilitate the implementation of both the Framework Decision and the Victims Directive. These soft law instruments do not modify the scope of secondary legislation, yet they further clarify Member State obligations.

The Victims Directive's Guidance Document affirms that Member States should pay particular attention to the principle of non-discrimination, which

---

40 See also Article 28a in the Proposal for a Directive amending Directive 2010/13/EU on the coordination of certain provisions laid down by law, regulation or administrative action in Member States concerning the provision of audiovisual media services in view of changing market realities, COM/2016/0287 final – 2016/0151 (COD).

41 'Gender identity' was first included in EU secondary legislation through Directive 2011/29/EU of the European Parliament and of the Council (recast) on Asylum Qualification [2011] OJ L 337/9. LGBTQI-specific accommodation during asylum interviews is required by Directive 2013/32/EU of the European Parliament and of the Council on common procedures for granting and withdrawing international protection (recast) [2013] OJ L 180/60.

42 The e-Commerce Directive (Directive 2000/31/EC of the European Parliament and of the Council of 8 June 2000 on certain legal aspects of information society services, in particular electronic commerce, in the Internal Market ('Directive on electronic commerce') [2000] OJ L 178/1) refers to 'incitement to hatred on grounds of race, sex, religion or nationality' (article 3(4)).

covers all possible discrimination grounds. As underlined in Recital 17, this is particularly relevant in the context of gender-based violence and hate crimes. The Guidance Document's objective is not to criminalize certain acts or behaviours in the Member States because the protection of victims depends entirely on national law. However, under Articles 52 and 53 of the Charter of Fundamental Rights of the EU the applicability of ECtHR case law must be considered, an issue explored in Section 4 below.[43] While apparently deferential to national authorities, the Guidance Note highlights that EU Member States' obligations on the inclusion of certain grounds may stem from a normative source outside EU law. The Charter may come to play a significant part by bringing Member States' international obligations into play as concerns criminal forms of discrimination.

A similar approach characterizes the Guidance Note on the practical application of the Framework Decision released by the EU High Level Group on combating racism, xenophobia and other forms of intolerance in 2018. With reference to ECtHR case law, the Guidance Note urges Member States to include in their criminal law broader lists than the one mandated by the Framework Decision.[44] This is a reminder that sexual orientation and other grounds should be included in national hate crime and hate speech laws to comply with the ECHR.

The Guidance Note is particularly oriented at implementing positive obligations under the ECHR, which operates as an external normative source in this case. The Note provides details on implementing the duty of effective investigation and prosecution of bias motivated offences, including the identification and recording of offences, evidence gathering, qualification, charging, sentencing, restitution and compensation.

In respect of the Victims Directive, it is impossible to separate out Member State obligations stemming from EU law, and those stemming from international treaties, which essentially broaden the scope of protection from discriminatory crimes under EU law. In this context, the European Parliament's call for the Commission 'to revise the Framework Decision in order to include sexism, bias crime and incitement to hatred on grounds of sexual orientation,

---

[43] 'In all individual provisions of the transposition measures of this Directive the general principles of EU law (e.g. equality and non-discrimination) and the Charter of Fundamental Rights must be respected. Moreover, it is necessary to recall the positive obligations and existing case-law standards of the European Court of Human Rights (…).' Guidance Document (n 12) 1.

[44] See *Identoba* above (n 37) and *Vejdeland and Others v. Sweden* App no 1813/07 (ECHR 9 February 2012).

gender identity and sex' seems belated and unnecessarily limited.[45] The Victims Directive both directly and indirectly broadens the scope of protection under criminal law.

In the criminal branch, a narrow interpretation of EU law cannot hold due to the influence of the ECHR through the Charter. The announcement by European Commission President Von der Leyen in September 2020 of a new initiative *to extend the list of EU crimes to all forms of hate crime and hate speech – whether because of race, religion, gender, or sexuality* would formally broaden the scope of the Framework Decision, putting an end to legal uncertainty.[46]

Part 4 explores what contribution the EU Charter can make to normative consistency overall, particularly in light of the CJEU's so far mixed responses that may erode the continuum of equality in the civil branch.

4. THE CHARTER'S POTENTIAL IN THE EVOLUTION OF EU ANTI-DISCRIMINATION LAW

Contrary to its broadening and consistency-ensuring function in the criminal branch, the Charter's potential has not yet been fully realized in the civil branch of EU anti-discrimination law. In the latter context, the Charter has been invoked as an important legal source in political and policy documents but the way in which the broad personal scope in Article 21 could be mirrored in secondary legislation or the way in which other Charter provisions could reinforce efforts to boost the enforcement of EU anti-discrimination law have not yet been laid out. As concerns adjudication, the Charter has sporadically, albeit increasingly, been called into play for three distinct purposes, namely, to maintain the (domestic) status quo, to reinforce the salience of EU law as a catalyst of change and a source of autonomous concepts, while at times it has served to legitimate an unjustifiably narrow reading of EU anti-discrimination law.

This section explores how the principle of equal treatment enshrined in Article 21 of the Charter has been used by the CJEU. It should be noted at the outset that while Article 21 has been regularly invoked in case law relating to

45 European Parliament resolution of 14 March 2017 on equality between women and men in the European Union in 2014–2015 (2016/2249(INI)) [2018] OJ C 263/49–63.

46 European Commission, State of the Union Address by President von der Leyen at the European Parliament plenary, September 2020; European Commission, Letter of Intent: Key New Initiatives for 2021, September 2020.

the anti-discrimination directives, with one notable exception it has not been used in the criminal branch due to the lack of legal challenges before the CJEU.

4.1 The CJEU's Interpretation of Article 21 of the Charter

Article 21 of the Charter prohibits discrimination with reference to an open list of grounds that explicitly mentions characteristics protected under EU law, as well as many so-called new generation grounds. The provision itself does not create power to enact EU legislation, nor does it provide for a robust prohibition of discrimination, as it does not go beyond areas covered by existing EU anti-discrimination law, while its application is limited to the actions of the EU, its bodies and institutions and the Member States when they implement EU law.[47]

Article 21 references in CJEU judgments are quite recent because the Charter was adopted in 2000, but its applicability was not settled until 2009, when the Treaty of Lisbon entered into force. The *Fransson* judgment clarified the CJEU's interpretation of the Charter's scope.[48] It is clear from *Fransson* that the Charter can apply to situations concerning the implementation of EU secondary as well as soft law.

The recently settled issue of the Charter's applicability partly explains the delay in referencing the Charter's non-discrimination principle but it cannot explain the lack of systematic references in CJEU judgments. Important rulings were delivered after 2009, in which reference to Article 21 could have resolved issues such as intersectionality[49] or reinforced judicial protection most notably in relation to sanctions and remedies.[50]

---

[47] Claire Kilpatrick, 'Article 21: Non-Discrimination' in Steve Peers, Tamara Hervey, Jeff Kenner and Angela Ward (eds), *The EU Charter of Fundamental Rights: A Commentary* (Hart, Oxford 2014) 622.

[48] Case C-617/10 *Åklagaren v. Åkerberg Fransson* [2013] ECLI:EU:C:2013:280, paras 18 and 21.

[49] Case C-443/15 *David L. Parris v. Trinity College Dublin and Others* [2016] ECLI:EU:C:2016:897. For an analysis see, Dagmar Schiek, 'On Uses, Mis-Uses and Non-Uses of Intersectionality before the European Court of Justice (ECJ): The ECJ Rulings Parris (C-433/15), Achbita (C-157/15) and Bougnaoui (C-188/15) as a Bermuda Triangle?' (2018) 7 *International Journal of Discrimination and the Law*, CETLS Online Paper Series, accessed 28 October 2021 at SSRN: <https://ssrn.com/abstract=3196036>.

[50] Case C-81/12 *Asociaţia Accept v. Consiliul Naţional pentru Combaterea Discriminării* [2013] ECLI:EU:C:2013:275. For details, see, Katrin Wladasch, 'Making Antidiscrimination Law Effective: Burden of Proof, Remedies and Sanctions in Discrimination Cases' in T. Giegerich (ed.), *The European Union as Protector and Promoter of Equality: European Union and its Neighbours in a Globalized World*, vol. 1. (Springer, Cham 2020) 235.

It is also important to note that the preliminary reference procedure has not been used to the same extent as concerns different protected grounds, so that while for instance age discrimination has generated extensive case law, the same cannot be said about racial or ethnic origin and religion, despite the slowly growing body of cases concerning the latter two grounds.[51] Conversely, Charter references seem to dominate adjudication on the grounds of religion and disability.

Still, an extensive body of case law attests to the challenges of referring national courts dealing with the implementation of the anti-discrimination directives and Article 21 of the Charter.[52] Leading verdicts provide a glimpse into the CJEU's diverse approaches to Article 21 throughout the years.[53] They also serve as indicators on how the CJEU may address lingering inconsistencies that occur in relation to obligations under EU anti-discrimination law on the one hand and Member States' international human rights obligations on the other.

Article 21 of the Charter expresses the purpose of the CJEU's interpretation of the gender quality and non-discrimination directives.[54] The CJEU's 'expansive approach adopted in *Mangold* [as] to the horizontal effect of fundamental rights in the EU and the further rooting of this approach in the Charter' is a key contribution.[55] The Court first made a link between the Charter and the principle of equal treatment in *Kücükdeveci*.[56] In *Ajos*, the Court reaffirmed that the

---

51 Several interlocking factors may explain these differences, including the relatively resourceful applicants in cases concerning age for instance, litigation strategies that focus on certain issues such as disability discrimination in Denmark, and/or the approach of national courts to making preliminary referrals – some countries being more active than others.

52 This section relies on the ACTIONES Project that identified CJEU judgments as the main vehicle of judicial dialogue vis-à-vis Member State courts (vertical judicial dialogue) as compared to cross-national, horizontal borrowing among national courts. It must be recalled that a systematic study of national case law could not be undertaken, given the linguistic barriers and the vast number of courts. See ACTIONES Project, *Handbook on Techniques of Judicial Interactions in the Application of the EU Charter: Module 6*, accessed 28 October 2021 at <https://cjc.eui.eu/projects/actiones/actiones-platform/>.

53 These judgments are discussed in Kimberly Liu and Colm O'Cinnedie, *The Ongoing Evolution of the Case-Law of the Court of Justice of the European Union on Directives 2000/43/EC and 2000/78/EC* (European Union, Bruxelles 2019), accessed 28 October 2021 at <https://op.europa.eu/en/publication-detail/-/publication/1bcea5bc-0696-11ea-8c1f-01aa75ed71a1>.

54 Ibid, 8.

55 Ibid, 92.

56 Case C-555/07 *Kücükdeveci v. Swedex GmbH & Co KG* [2010] ECLI:EU:C:2010:21, para. 21.

general principle of equal treatment was capable of having direct horizontal effect within the scope of application of EU law.[57] More recent cases attest to the Court's readiness to provide horizontal effect to related Charter rights as well,[58] thus 'constitutionalizing' certain rights enshrined in the Charter.[59]

Given the significance of Article 21 in itself but also as the expression of a general principle of EU law and given the CJEU's function as the final interpreter of EU law, it is reasonable to expect that even when national courts making preliminary referrals fail to do so, the Court would invoke this Charter provision. Simultaneously, when national courts do invoke Article 21, the CJEU should in principle respond to such preliminary questions. In practice, however, the CJEU has not taken such a principled approach to cases implicating Article 21 of the Charter.

There are important judgments in which the CJEU did not respond to questions raised by national courts in relation to the Charter. This was the case in *Coman* that concerned the relocation of a same-sex couple from a Member State that does recognize same-sex marriage and same-sex spouses as family members to another that does neither.[60] In the preliminary reference the Romanian Constitutional Court invoked EU norms on freedom of movement 'in light of' Article 21 of the Charter, but the Luxembourg verdict did not engage with the latter provision. Conversely, the CJEU instrumentalized the Charter by underlining that refusing a residence permit to a same-sex spouse would be inconsistent with the right to respect for private and family life, guaranteed by the EU Charter. The conclusion was that the contested refusal was precluded by Article 21 TFEU within the remit of the freedom of movement for EU nationals and their family members. The Court based its reasoning on free movement, invoking fundamental human rights at the justification stage, which in some commentator's view renders the judgment partly 'catalytic', missing a proactive outcome on the ground of sexual orientation.[61]

On the other end of the scale, there are examples when the CJEU made excellent use of Article 21 of the Charter. In *CHEZ*, the CJEU invoked this

---

[57] Case C-441/14 *Dansk Industri (DI), acting on behalf of Ajos A/S v. Estate of Karsten Eigil Rasmussen* [2016] ECLI:EU:C:2016:278.

[58] For instance, joined cases C-569/16 and C-570/16, *Stadt Wuppertal and Volker Willmeroth als Inhaber der TWI Technische Wartung und Instandsetzung Volker Willmeroth e.K. v. Maria Elisabeth Bauer and Martina Broßonn* [2018] ECLI:EU:C:2018:871.

[59] Liu and O'Cinnedie (n 53).

[60] Case C-673/16 *Relu Adrian Coman and Others v. Inspectoratul General pentru Imigrări and Ministerul Afacerilor Interne* [2018] ECLI:EU:C:2018:385.

[61] See Katharine G. Young, 'A Typology of Economic and Social Rights Adjudication: Exploring the Catalytic Function of Judicial Review' (2010) 8 *International Journal of Constitutional Law* 385, 413.

Charter provision to justify a broad reading of both the personal and material scope of the Racial Equality Directive as concerns the Roma minority, emphasizing the importance of effectively protecting the rights enshrined in Article 21.[62] The verdict extended protection to a non-Roma treated unfavourably 'together with the Roma' in the context of the placement of electricity meters in 'Roma districts' on poles as high as seven metres.[63]

Among several positive examples, in which the CJEU did rely on the Charter, some stand out as general references, and few as particular references to Article 21. An example of the latter is *Deckmyn*, a case concerning copyrighted work used by a third party for purposes of imparting Islamophobic messages. In this case, Article 21 of the Charter was invoked to reinforce the protection of the original work from the defendants' 'ironic' use.[64]

In relation to an unsuccessful job application due to failure to comply with occupational requirements stemming from the (Christian) religious nature of an employer in *Egenberger*, the Court held that the prohibition of discrimination on grounds of religion or belief constitutes an aspect of the general principle of equal treatment under Article 21. This case also dealt with the specific exception available under Article 4(2) of the Employment Equality Directive to churches and other religious organizations from hiring job seekers who do not fit the so-called genuine and determining occupational requirement prevalent in the employer's religious ethos. Importantly, the CJEU found that 'a determination of compliance with this exception cannot be entrusted to the organisation itself and must be subject to effective judicial review if challenged'.[65] The significance of this finding is paramount, as it contrasts with interpretation by German courts that hitherto had given priority to a broadly defined religious autonomy of religious organizations and affiliated bodies. While Article 21 has undoubtedly embellished the legitimacy of the CJEU's verdict, *Egenberger* 'has triggered a degree of controversy, and is currently the subject of a constitutional challenge before the German Constitutional Court'.[66]

---

[62] Case C-83/14 *CHEZ Razpredelenie Bulgaria AD v. Komisia za zashtita ot diskriminatsia* [2015] ECLI:EU:C:2015:480.

[63] Sara Benedi Lahuerta, 'Ethnic Discrimination, Discrimination by Association and the Roma Community: CHEZ' (2016) 53 *Common Market Law Review* 1.

[64] Case C-201/13 *Johan Deckmyn, Vrijheidsfonds VZW v. Helena Vandersteen, Christiane Vandersteen, Liliana Vandersteen, Isabelle Vandersteen, Rita Dupont, Amoras II CVOH, WPG Uitgevers België* [2014] ECLI:EU:C:2014:2132, para. 30.

[65] Case C-414/16 *Egenberger v. Evangelisches Werk für Diakonie und Entwicklung eV* [2018] ECLI:EU:C:2018:257, paras 59 and 76–77.

[66] Liu and O'Cinnedie (n 53) 12.

Jurisprudence on minority religions, such as Islam, has so far deviated from the Court's general purposive approach when interpreting Article 21 and other Charter rights. Unlike in *Egenberger*, in cases concerning religious discrimination against stigmatized and racialized Muslim women, the Advocates General and the Court referenced the ECHR, when defining the concept of 'religion or belief' and engaged with the Charter in an uneven and inconsistent manner. Inconsistency was palpable when it came to the interpretation of EU law in light of the Member States' obligations under regional human rights standards as per Article 52 of the Charter.

On one end of the scale, Advocate General Sharpston argued in *Bougnaoui* that non-discrimination is a fundamental principle of EU law whose justification is narrowly confined, which may at times necessitate the levelling up of protection from discrimination available under the ECHR in pursuance of Article 52(3) of the Charter.[67] Conversely, in *Achbita*, Advocate General Kokott made a rather troubling reference to the Charter provision on the freedom of establishment (Article 16), invoking it as a justification for religious discrimination without meaningfully balancing it against the right to equal treatment. While this type of justification may not pass the ECHR's proportionality test, it has certainly decreased the level of protection against religious discrimination under the Employment Equality Directive (EED).[68] In the Islamic veil cases the CJEU invoked Article 21 of the Charter to underline the applicability of the EED, without, however, making robust use of the principle for the protection of Muslim women.[69] The ruling in *NH (Rete Lenford)* indicates that the CJEU may be more thorough in a less politicized context, such as an employer's homophobic speech act challenged by an LGBTI organization.[70] In this case, the Advocate General argued that the employer's freedom of expression guaranteed in Article 10 ECHR can be restricted in accordance with the ECtHR's interpretation, because the exercising of that right 'carries with it duties and responsibilities', and such restriction would be necessitated under the EED as

---

[67] Opinion of Advocate General Sharpston delivered on 13 July 2016 in Case C-188/15 *Asma Bougnaoui and Association de défense des droits de l'homme (ADDH) v. Micropole S* ECLI:EU:C:2016:553, paras 58–72.

[68] Opinion of Advocate General Kokott delivered on 31 May 2016 in Case C-157/15 *Samira Achbita and Centrum voor gelijkheid van kansen en voor racismebestrijding v. G4S Secure Solutions NV* ECLI:EU:C:2016:382.

[69] Case C-157/15 *Samira Achbita and Centrum voor gelijkheid van kansen en voor racismebestrijding v. G4S Secure Solutions NV* [2017] ECLI:EU:C:2017:203, paras 25–26 and Case C-188/15 *Asma Bougnaoui and Association de défense des droits de l'homme (ADDH) v. Micropole S* ECLI:EU:C:2017:204.

[70] Case C-507/18 *NH v. Associazione Avvocatura per i diritti LGBTI – Rete Lenford* ECLI:EU:C:2020:289, paras 48–53.

well as pursuant to Article 52(1) of the Charter.[71] Embracing this argument but omitting references to the ECHR, the CJEU found that the right to free speech guaranteed in Article 11 of the Charter is not absolute and cannot therefore be invoked to trump the principle of equal treatment as expressed in Article 21.

There are several rulings in which the Charter is invoked to reinforce a narrow reading or, alarmingly, limit the scope of protection.[72] In *Kaltoft*, the Charter was invoked to reinforce the finding that disability, as a ground, should be narrowly defined.[73] In *Test-Achats*, the CJEU relied on Article 21 to support the comparability of men and women in relation to insurance, essentially to override EU legislation seeking to favour women over men in this field.[74]

The much-criticized *Jyske Finans* case is also an example of the negative trend. In this case, the opinion of Advocate General Wahl invoked the Charter for the purposes of limiting the interpretation of the ground of racial or ethnic origin in a way that weakens but does not exclude the Racial Equality Directive's applicability to xenophobia affecting persons of foreign (non-EU) origin.[75] The CJEU omitted reference to the Charter and adopted an even narrower interpretation of the Directive than the Advocate General. The judgment came under heavy criticism, with one commentator noting that both the reasoning and the result 'begs the question of what space there is for race discrimination in the Race Directive aside from discrimination based on ethnic origin'.[76] The verdict inadvertently challenges domestic jurisprudence in Denmark where similar situations used to amount to indirect discrimination beforehand. Furthermore, it challenges the foundations of EU migrant integration policies that are incidentally based on non-EU origin and stands in

---

[71] Opinion of Advocate General Sharpston delivered on 31 October 2019(1), Case C-507/18 *NH v. Associazione Avvocatura per i diritti LGBTI – Rete Lenford* ECLI:EU:C:2019:922, para. 70.

[72] Erica Howard, 'EU Anti-Discrimination Law: Has the CJEU Stopped Moving Forward?' (2018) 18 *International Journal of Discrimination and the Law* 60.

[73] Case C-354/13 *Fag og Arbejde (FOA), acting on behalf of Karsten Kaltoft, v. Kommunernes Landsforening (KL), acting on behalf of the Municipality of Billund* [2014] ECLI:EU:C:2014:2463, para. 39. The case turned on whether obesity is disability.

[74] Case C-235/09 *Association Belge des Consommateurs Test-Achats ASBL and Others v. Conseil des ministres* [2011] ECLI:EU:C:2011:100.

[75] Opinion of Advocate General Wahl delivered on 1 December 2016 in Case C-668/15 *Jyske Finans AS v. Ligebehandlingsnævnet, acting on behalf of Ismar Huskic* ECLI:EU:C:2016:914, para. 43.

[76] Shreya Atrey, 'Race Discrimination in EU Law after Jyske Finans, Case C-668/15, Jyske Finans A/S v. Ligebehandlingsnævnet, acting on behalf of Ismar Huskic, Judgment of the Court (First Chamber) of 6 April 2017 EU:C:2017:278' (2018) 55 *Common Market Law Review* 627.

stark contrast with *CHEZ*'s broad reading of racial discrimination as extending protection to racial majority individuals associated with minority groups.[77]

All in all, the Charter has been invoked in cases relating to the ground-specific directives in a far from systemic, although generally improving manner. Still, both the CJEU and the Advocates General reference Article 21 inconsistently. When referring courts rely on the Charter as a key instrument for interpreting EU law, such as in *Egenberger* and *Coman* their approach is not necessarily reflected in CJEU rulings. The overview shows that the CJEU uses the Charter for three distinct purposes:

a) to maintain the (domestic) status quo, such as in *Kaltoft*, *Bougnaoui* and *Achbita*
b) to reinforce the salience of EU law, as a catalyst of change and a source of autonomous concepts, such as in *CHEZ*, *Egenberger* and *NH*
c) to legitimate an unjustifiably narrow reading of EU anti-discrimination law, such as in *Test-Achats* and *Jyske Finans*.[78]

The CJEU's approach to Article 21 of the Charter has enabled the simultaneous advancement of opposing stances on equality and non-discrimination in different Member States, perpetuating inconsistencies between protected characteristics. The list of protected grounds has become a central theme of contestation because of the CJEU's threefold approach that distinguishes between and within protected groups, particularly on the ground of racial or ethnic origin, religion and belief, gender, and to some extent disability. Ultimately, however, the limited material scope of protection offered by EU anti-discrimination law in the civil branch that the application of Article 21 of the Charter alone cannot resolve remains the underlying issue for most identity groups.

4.2 The Charter and Member States' International Obligations

Several (international) courts, tribunals and agencies have competence to adjudicate claims relating to the principle/right to equal treatment, which is guaranteed by distinct legal regimes and a plethora of legal norms, including the Charter of Fundamental Rights of the EU. Article 21 and other Charter rights may be invoked before national courts applying EU law or the CJEU

---

77 Lilla Farkas, 'Throwing the Babies out with the Bathwater: The CJEU, Xenophobia and Equality Bodies after Jyske Finans' (2018) 1 *European Equality Law Review* 20.

78 Subsequently in Case C-457/17 *Heiko Jonny Maniero v. Studienstiftung des deutschen Volkes eV* [2018] ECLI:EU:C:2018:912 the CJEU reiterated its overly narrow approach adopted in *Jyske Finans*.

interpreting EU law.[79] Important sites of enforcement include equality bodies, i.e. bodies established to promote racial and gender equality under the relevant directives.[80] So far, the CJEU has relied on the Charter in cases referred to it by national courts in the so-called preliminary reference procedure.[81] An important characteristic of these proceedings is that the anti-discrimination regime in EU Member States is multi-sourced and interordinal, meaning that the norms stem from a host of United Nations and Council of Europe treaties, as well as the relevant EU *acquis*. National anti-discrimination laws seek to render coherent and consistent these normative sources, of which EU anti-discrimination law constitutes but one part. Once achieved, coherence and consistency give rise to a continuum of equality, which is generally the case at the national level.

The Charter mandates the CJEU to 'correct' shortcomings and inconsistencies that may occur vis-à-vis international human rights treaties.[82] This follows, on the one hand, from Article 53, pursuant to which the Charter shall not 'be interpreted as restricting or adversely affecting human rights and fundamental freedoms as recognised, in their respective fields of application, by Union law and international law and by international agreements to which the Union, the Community or all the Member States are party'. On the other hand, pursuant to Article 52(3), insofar as a right is protected under the ECHR, the meaning and scope laid down by the Convention will govern interpretation, unless Union law provides more extensive protection.[83] As mentioned in Section 2.2, this is the case in relation to the investigation of hate crimes, both in terms of personal scope and the positive obligations of national authorities.

---

[79] On the various remedial paths, see, Mark Dawson, Elise Muir and Monica Claes, 'Enforcing the Rights Revolution in the EU: The Case of Equality' (2012) 3 *European Human Rights Law Review*, accessed 28 October 2021 at <https://papers.ssrn.com/sol3/papers.cfm?abstract_id=2177929>.

[80] Interestingly, despite direct access to the European Ombudsperson via complaints and her power to open own initiative inquiries into systemic issues, Article 21 of the Charter and discrimination-relevant EU norms have rarely been invoked before or by this institution. Considering that legislation and adjudication form but one pillar of EU governance in the field of equal treatment and non-discrimination, it seems somewhat surprising that non-legal measures and tools have so far remained largely unchallenged.

[81] Article 267 TFEU. For details, see Morten Broberg, 'Acte Clair Revisited: Adapting the Acte Clair Criteria to the Demands of the Times' (2008) 45 *Common Market Law Review* 1383.

[82] These treaties are listed in the directives' Preambles.

[83] See, for instance, Opinion of Advocate General Kokott delivered on 12 March 2015 in Case C-83/14 *CHEZ Razpredelenie Bulgaria AD v. Komisia za zashtita ot diskriminatsia* ECLI:EU:C:2015:170, p. 24: 'In so far as Article 21(1) corresponds to Article 14 of the Convention, "it applies in compliance with it."'

The coexistence of parallel normative sources may trigger legal uncertainty or inconsistent legal interpretation as described in Section 3.[84] Courts naturally seek to overcome these hurdles through judicial dialogue. By safeguarding the principle of equal treatment in general and ensuring coherent interpretation with reference to international treaty law, the Charter can play a significant role in guaranteeing that the 'continuum of equality' travels safely from the national to EU level adjudication.

Reasons that may discourage victims from pursuing a criminal discrimination case include procedural difficulties such as a higher threshold of evidence concerning 'bias motivation' and the relative ineffectiveness of remedies. In hate speech cases the perpetrator seeks to harm a group or community, therefore an individual victim may run into difficulties when seeking compensation available under criminal law. As the *Feryn* and *Accept* cases show, discriminatory speech acts – based on racial or ethnic origin and sexual orientation respectively – can effectively be sanctioned under the civil branch of EU anti-discrimination law.[85] Indeed, unlike courts in criminal cases the CJEU did not dwell on the motive of biased speech when deciding whether discrimination occurred in these cases. This is because it is not necessary to establish motive or intent behind hate speech as a civil wrong, which contrasts with criminal discrimination, in which case the level of proof is 'beyond reasonable doubt'.

Preliminary referrals concerning the criminal branch of the EU anti-discrimination *acquis* or involving the criminal prosecution of discrimination under the civil branch have not yet been made. It remains to be seen how the CJEU will address stigmatization stemming from or reinforcing asymmetric power relations between majority and protected groups in relation to discriminatory crimes. Having to face such phenomena – in terms already tackled by the Strasbourg Court – may, in the long run, positively impact on the CJEU's interpretation of Article 21 of the Charter.

A key puzzle in relation to discriminatory crimes is whether preliminary references will seek to clarify the personal and material scope of the Victims Directive in view of Strasbourg case law. Victim status stemming from the Directive should be granted under national law in full compliance with the ECHR, as already stipulated in the Guidance Document of the Directive.

The list of grounds in international human rights law under which EU Member States should investigate and prosecute hate speech and hate crime

---

[84] Dean Spielmann, 'Human Rights Case Law in the Strasbourg and Luxembourg Courts: Conflicts, Inconsistencies, and Complementarities' in Philip Alston (ed.), *The EU and Human Rights* (Oxford University Press, Oxford 1999) 757.

[85] Case C-81/12 (n 50) and Case C-54/17 *Centrum voor gelijkheid van kansen en voor racismebestrijding v. Firma Feryn NV* [2008] ECLI:EU:C:2008:397.

is being clarified by courts in the Member States and in Strasbourg, setting the terms of future dialogue with the CJEU. The European Commission's announcement that it will extend the list of euro-crimes to include all forms of hate crime and hate speech would contribute to legal certainty. In the meantime, case law trends have already exceeded what an amendment to the Framework Decision may achieve.

Simultaneously, the Victims Directive has widened the scope of protection from discriminatory crimes with reference to international human rights law. These developments suggest that rather than standard-setting on substantive law, procedural harmonization building on the obligations of Member States under international human rights law may broaden the scope of protection also in relation to the civil branch of the EU anti-discrimination *acquis*.

5. CONCLUSIONS

The chapter has traced the emergence of a 'continuum of equality' of the EU anti-discrimination *acquis*, where harmonization and cooperation on criminal safeguards broaden both the personal and material scope of protection from discrimination. This silent evolution is approximating the EU anti-discrimination *acquis* to international human rights standards, offering a strategy to unlocking legislative deadlock in the civil branch.

Insufficient attention to trends in the criminal branch of EU anti-discrimination law has sparked our analytical interest in exploring the dynamic evolution of this branch in the context of multi-level governance, indicating the opportunity of broadening through procedural standard-setting. We have shown the expansion of Member States' obligations in this context and argued that this approach can fill gaps in the continuum of equality and lead to a coherent system of EU equality law.

With increased understanding of societal marginalization and vulnerability, recent years have witnessed the gradual broadening of the traditional protected grounds as concerns cooperation in criminal matters. In relation to preventing racism and xenophobia the personal scope of EU law has widened and the most comprehensive list of protected characteristics can now be found in the most recent instrument, the Victims Directive.

This Directive has redrawn the normative landscape by extending protection from criminal forms of discrimination to grounds and fields not covered by the EU anti-discrimination directives. Not only is the Victims Directive not amenable to a hierarchy of grounds, but it also widens the scope of adjudication in respect of characteristics protected by nature of Member State obligations under international human rights law.

Soft law measures perform a similar widening function, opening EU law to the influence of international human rights law through the Charter. The ECHR already exerts considerable influence on adjudication in the criminal branch, where norms not only codify Strasbourg jurisprudence thereby promoting consistency with international human rights law, but they also strengthen the clout of EU anti-discrimination law as concerns criminal forms of discrimination.

In contrast with trends in the criminal branch, the CJEU's approach to Article 21 of the Charter in the civil branch of EU anti-discrimination law has enabled the simultaneous advancement of opposing stances on equality and non-discrimination in different Member States, and across diverse protected grounds. The Charter has an increasingly important function, not necessarily an added value but a symbolic role that could be reinforced by embracing the ECtHR's more consistent notion of discrimination across grounds and fields and consciously avoiding collision with the ECtHR and its jurisprudence.

The Charter empowers the CJEU to 'correct' shortcomings and inconsistencies that may occur vis-à-vis international human rights norms, thus being instrumental in ensuring that the EU and Member States refrain from restricting human rights and fundamental freedoms enshrined in the core human rights treaties. With the European Convention providing the bottom line of protection, the Charter can contribute to the creation of a continuum of equality, particularly if it is brought to play in both the civil and criminal branches of EU anti-discrimination law. A bolder use of the Charter in and outside the preliminary reference procedure can, in the long run, positively impact on a profound and thorough exploration of the purpose of Article 21 by the CJEU, national courts and EU institutions.

15. Comment: under Article 21 EU Charter the CJEU has, for the time being, adopted a rather deferential model of judicial review

Raluca Bercea

INTRODUCTION

One of the main questions addressed by Rita Gião Hanek and Lilla Farkas in Chapter 14 is whether judicial dialogue could be qualified as constitutive of the EU standards on non-discrimination expressed in the Charter of Fundamental Rights of the European Union. As the two authors point out, EU non-discrimination law has grown from 'a narrowly tailored body of law on employment and market related discrimination' to 'a complex regime'. Against this background, the general principle of non-discrimination enshrined in Article 21 of the Charter, which has direct horizontal effect within the scope of application of EU law, is expected to bring coherence while innervating the relevant secondary legislation field, its national implementation and judicial practice in the Member States.

In this respect, Rita Gião Hanek and Lilla Farkas come to the conclusion that the Court of Justice of the European Union (CJEU) has so far used the above provision for several distinct purposes: (a) to maintain the (domestic) status quo (in *Kaltoft*);[1] (b) to reinforce the salience of EU law as a catalyst for change and a source of autonomous concepts (in *CHEZ*,[2] *Egenberger*[3] and *Coman*[4]); and (c) to legitimate an unjustifiably narrow reading of EU

[1] CJEU, Case C-354/13 *Fag og Arbejde (FOA) v Kommunernes Landsforening (KL)*, ECLI:EU:C:2014:2463.

[2] CJEU, Case C-83/14 *CHEZ Razpredelenie Bulgaria*, ECLI:EU:C:2015:480.

[3] CJEU, Case C-414/16 *Egenberger*, ECLI:EU:C:2018:257.

[4] CJEU, Case C-673/16 *Coman et al.*, ECLI:EU:C:2018:385.

anti-discrimination law (in *Test Achats,*[5] *Achbita*[6] and *Jyske Finans*[7]). As one is forced to conclude, the added value of recourse to Article 21 of the Charter is so far symbolic: when it does not reinforce the national status quo or, worse, allow for a regretfully narrow reading of secondary legislation, it functions at best as 'a catalyst of change and a source of autonomous concepts'.

While I fully agree with this conclusion and, more specifically, with the nuance that the two authors make when they claim that trying 'to be a catalyst' is, in this context, tantamount to 'falling short of [a] rights-proactive outcome' (I), I argue that a form of judicial dialogue is nonetheless noticeable in the CJEU narrative, providing answers as to whom the European judge is deferential (II).

Given the limits of these comments, I will myself refer to one of the judgments already mentioned in this chapter.[8] As already pointed out by the two authors, the case concerns the relocation of a same-sex couple from the Netherlands to Romania, an EU Member State that does not recognise same-sex partners as family members. Before the national courts, Coman and Hamilton argued that the Romanian Civil Code was unconstitutional and infringed the provisions of the national Constitution that protected the right to personal life, family life, private life and the principle of equality. The Romanian Constitutional Court made a reference for a preliminary ruling to the European Court of Justice (ECJ) asking whether a Union citizen who had exercised free movement rights could enjoy, with his same-sex spouse, family reunification rights under EU law. The Court decided that:

> in a situation in which a Union citizen has made use of his freedom of movement by moving to another Member State and taking up genuine residence there, in accordance with the conditions laid down in Article 7(1) of Directive 2004/38/EC and, whilst there, has created and strengthened a family life with a third-country national of the same sex to whom he is joined by a marriage lawfully concluded in the host Member State, Article 21(1) TFEU [Treaty on the Functioning of the European Union] must be interpreted as precluding the competent authorities of the Member State of which the Union citizen is a national from refusing to grant that third-country national a right of residence in the territory of that Member State on the ground that the law of that Member State does not recognise marriage between persons of the same sex.

---

5 CJEU, Case C-236/09 *Association Belge des Consommateurs Test-Achats and Others*, ECLI:EU:C:2011:100.

6 CJEU, Case C-157/15 *G4S Secure Solutions*, ECLI:EU:C:2017:203.

7 CJEU, Case C-668/15 *Jyske Finans*, ECLI:EU:C:2017:278.

8 See *Coman* (fn4).

Subsequently, the Constitutional Court decided that the relevant provisions of the Romanian Civil Code were constitutional only if interpreted in accordance with the ECJ's judgment.

(I) Remaining in the Shadows

In its first referral to the ECJ, the Romanian Constitutional Court explicitly framed its questions within the ambit of the Charter. In the decision of 29 November 2016 received at the Court on 30 December 2016, it asks:

> Does the term spouse in Article 2(2)(a) of Directive 2004/38, read *in the light of Articles 7, 9, 21 and 45 of the Charter of Fundamental Rights of the European Union*, include the same-sex spouse, from a State which is not a Member State of the European Union, of a citizen of the European Union to whom that citizen is lawfully married in accordance with the law of a Member State other than the host Member State?

In consistence with the question, the *Opinion* delivered on 11 January 2018 by AG Wathelet mentions the word *Charter* 38 times, the summary of it notes among the key words *Articles 7 and 21 of the Charter of Fundamental Rights of the European Union* and the reasoning substantially includes Article 21 as well. The AG's Opinion is explicitly 'human rights based'. It focuses on Directive 2004/38, Recital 31 of which is extensively quoted, bringing in substance Article 21 of the Charter to the front of the stage:

> *This Directive* respects the fundamental rights and freedoms and *observes the principles recognised in particular by the Charter of Fundamental Rights of the European Union. In accordance with the prohibition of discrimination contained in the Charter*, Member States should implement this Directive without discrimination between the beneficiaries of this Directive on grounds such as sex, race, colour, ethnic or social origin, genetic characteristics, language, religion or beliefs, political or other opinion, membership of an ethnic minority, property, birth, disability, age or sexual orientation.

According to the AG Wathelet 'refusal to grant the application for entry and residence of a third-country national, of the same sex as the citizen of the European Union to whom he or she is married in accordance with the law of a Member State, may not be solely or decisively based on his or her sexual orientation, without infringing *Articles 7 and 21 of the Charter*' (§98).

However, the Grand Chamber judgment of 5 June 2018 omits to refer to Article 21 of the Charter and focuses on Article 21 TFEU. The human rights field as such is much diminished with only 11 references to the word *Charter* and none to Article 21 of the Charter either in the Court's reasoning or among the key words. The judgment acknowledges, however, that 'a national measure that is liable to obstruct the exercise of freedom of movement for persons may be justified only where such a measure is consistent with the fundamental rights guaranteed by the Charter, it being the task of the Court to ensure that those rights are respected' (§47). However, among the rights in the Charter, the Grand Chamber only refers to Articles 7 and 52:

> As regards the term 'spouse' in Article 2 of Directive 2004/38, the right to respect for private and family life guaranteed by the Charter is a fundamental right. In that regard, as is apparent from the Explanations relating to the Charter of Fundamental Rights [...] in accordance with Article 52(3) of the Charter, the rights guaranteed by Article 7 thereof have the same meaning and the same scope as those guaranteed by Article 8 of the European Convention for the Protection of Human Rights and Fundamental Freedoms.

In this context, according to the Grand Chamber, the contested refusal would be inconsistent with the right to respect for private and family life guaranteed by the EU Charter of Fundamental Rights (the Court did not mention the principle of non-discrimination (§47–49)).

To partly question Rita Gião Hanek and Lilla Farkas' conclusion, I wonder whether the ruling in the *Coman* case has genuinely been 'a catalyst of change and a source of autonomous concepts'. At the European Union level, *Coman* is 'practically and symbolically' important as ever since for the purposes of EU family and reunification law married same-sex couples must be considered to be in the same position as married opposite-sex couples. It is, however, doubtful that things have changed at the national level. A person's status continues to fall within Member State competence, although when exercising that competence in an EU law field Member States must comply with the latter. Can one hope at least for a voluntary harmonisation of purely internal situations subsequent to the *Coman* decision? Quite contrarily, in Romania, at least, *Coman* could not prevent the opposite effect. Only a few months later, in October 2018, a referendum was organised for the purpose of introducing a constitutional ban on same-sex marriages, which was unsuccessful only as it failed to reach the rather high required turnout threshold (of 30 per cent). Is *Coman* at least 'a source of autonomous concepts'? Again the answer is negative: while AG Wathelet favoured the adoption of an autonomous uniform EU interpretation of the term 'spouse' (§32), the Grand Chamber refused to follow that path.

(II) Being Deferential

If, despite the framing of the Romanian Constitutional Court's questions, the Grand Chamber does not make use of Article 21 of the Charter, is it because the ECJ is deferential? And, in the affirmative, to whom? The Court is not deferential to national legal systems as in any event Member States preserve their freedom to authorise or not marriage between persons of the same sex. According to my reading of *Coman*, the ECJ is instead deferential to the European Court of Human Rights. In the Opinion of AG Wathelet, reference is made to its vast jurisprudence.[9] The Grand Chamber itself finds that 'It is apparent from the case law of the European Court of Human Rights that the relationship of a homosexual couple may fall within the notion of "private life" and that of "family life" in the same way as the relationship of a heterosexual couple in the same situation' (§50). If one is prepared to concede that *Coman* is not only a 'free movement', but also a 'human rights' case, Article 21 of the Charter is as discrete as Article 14 of the Convention is very much present. As the AG argued 'based on sexual orientation, [such] a difference in treatment would be unacceptable under Directive 2004/38 and the Charter, as it must be interpreted in the light of the ECHR'. In that regard,

> although protection of the traditional family may, in some circumstances, amount to a legitimate aim under Article 14 [of the ECHR, which prohibits discrimination], the [European] Court [of Human Rights] considers that, regarding the matter in question here — *granting a residence permit for family reasons to a homosexual foreign partner* — it cannot amount to a 'particularly convincing and weighty' reason capable of justifying, in the circumstances of the present case, discrimination on grounds of sexual orientation (§98).

CODA

On 16 June 2020, the Romanian Parliament modified the National Education Law by adding to it an article according to which in all educational institutions 'activities susceptible to spread the theory of gender identity (understood as the theory that gender is a different concept from biological sex and that the two are not always the same) shall be prohibited'. Highly contested by the universities, the law amendment is now hoped not to pass the presidential filter. This news agrees with the argument put forward by Rita Gião Hanek and Lilla Farkas when they note that most of the challenges the non-discrimination principle has to face at the European Union level consist in it being a field of shared competence within which conflicting actors, values and standards will incessantly compete.

---

[9] See e.g. ECtHR, Case of *Taddeucci and McCall v Italy* (Application no. 51362/09); *Oliary v Italy* (Application nos 18766/11 and 36030/11); *Pajič v Croatia* (Application no. 68453/13); *Vallianatos v Greece* (Applications nos 29381/09 and 32684/09).

16. Effectiveness and EU consumer law: the blurriness in judicial dialogue

Mateusz Grochowski and Maciej Taborowski

1. INTRODUCTION: THE CONCEPTUAL STRUGGLE

It is not an exaggeration to state that effectiveness is the 'most important principle'[1] of European consumer law. It organizes its political agenda and institutional matrix, being present at all levels of legislative and judicial discourse.[2] It also links European private law with the entirety of the EU *acquis* and provides an inherent part of effectiveness as a foundational principle of EU law. At the same time, despite its unquestioned status, effectiveness seems to be one of the most vague and uncharted concepts of the EU legal order, which lacks systematic elucidations both in legislation, as well as in the doctrinal analysis[3] and case law. This visible void is mostly a consequence of intrinsic methodological issues.[4] The conceptual agenda of effectiveness in EU law is

---

[1] Arthur Hartkamp, *European Law and National Private Law: Effect of EU Law and European Human Rights Law on Legal Relationships between Individuals* (Intersentia, Cambridge 2016) 98.

[2] On the particular sources of the effectiveness requirement in EU consumer law see also Fabrizio Cafaggi, Paola Iamiceli, 'The Principles of Effectiveness, Proportionality and Dissuasiveness in the Enforcement of EU Consumer Law: The Impact of a Triad on the Choice of Civil Remedies and Administrative Sanctions' (2019) 25 ERPL 575, 581.

[3] On more precise reconstructions of the actual meaning of this principle and its components in European private law see especially Norbert Reich, 'The Principle of Effectiveness and EU Contract Law', in Jacobien Rutgers, Pietro Sirena (eds), *Rules and Principles in European Contract Law* (Intersentia, Cambridge 2015) 45; Norbert Reich, *General Principles of EU Civil Law* (Intersentia, Cambridge 2014); Hartkamp, above n. 1. From a more general perspective on the relevance of this principle see also Matej Accetto, Stefan Zlepnig, 'Principle of Effectiveness: Rethinking Its Role in Community Law' (2005) 11 *European Public Law* 375.

[4] On the methodological problems associated with effectiveness see also Hartkamp, above n. 1, at 98.

predominantly shaped by the Court of Justice of the European Union (CJEU), and thus emerges in a 'bottom-up' fashion – inherently nebulous and difficult to systematize. For this reason, effectiveness in EU consumer law is far from consistent, both as a theoretic concept and as an argument applied in the CJEU's reasoning.

This incoherence triggers significant consequences not only for EU law as such, but, more importantly, for interactions between the CJEU and domestic courts and authorities. The concept of effectiveness gains its highest practical relevance as a 'yardstick' for reviewing compliance of domestic law with EU principles and provisions. For this reason, it creates one of the key platforms for challenging domestic rules before the CJEU by means of the preliminary reference procedure. As a consequence, effectiveness is also the primary conceptual 'vehicle' for bringing EU values and standards back to national systems when CJEU decisions (especially those that confirm non-compliance of domestic rules with Union law) are sought to be implemented by the Member States. The concept of effectiveness is hence not merely a parameter for conformity-checking, but is rather much more – a pivotal standard for harmonizing domestic law with the EU *acquis*, carried out mostly by domestic courts. This is particularly important in the domain of private law, where EU law (and especially, consumer protection rules) often collide with or subvert long-established structures and concepts.

It is worthwhile, therefore, to seek a more systematized and coherent understanding of effectiveness in EU consumer law. Even if in the final outcome such an enquiry will divulge only approximate explanations, it can nevertheless elucidate an improved understanding of the mechanics of effectiveness as a playground for judicial dialogue. With this in mind, the following observations commence with a preliminary attempt to better recognize the three principal layers of effectiveness in EU consumer law, i.e. *effet utile*, the principle of effectiveness and effective judicial protection (section 2). In the second step, the analysis delves into various interactions between these concepts in CJEU case law, framed in response to preliminary questions of domestic courts. In so doing, the chapter attempts to untangle the conceptual framework of effectiveness, as both a criterion for reviewing conformity of domestic law, and as a point of reference for domestic courts in implementation of standards set by the CJEU (section 3). In the further part, the chapter focuses on the most important – and most problematic in practice – consequences of the CJEU's concept of effectiveness for dialogue with domestic courts (section 4). In this regard, the chapter pays particular attention to opposition between 'eliminatory' and 'creative' functions of effectiveness in domestic legal orders, and to possible collisions between various dimensions of effectiveness.

In this way the chapter attempts to draw a basic explanatory framework for effectiveness in EU consumer law. It approaches it as a 'discursive' phenomenon, framed through interaction between CJEU case law and domestic judicial practice. The text does not aspire to provide an all-embracing explanation for all the aspects of judicial dialogue established around the concept of effectiveness. It attempts, however, to identify the main parameters of this dialogue that stream from CJEU consumer case law and to better understand its possible impact on EU–domestic discourse in consumer law.

2. EFFECTIVENESS: UNPACKING THE QUANDARY

At the outset of the further analysis, it is necessary to grapple with the problem of exact content of effectiveness in the structure of EU consumer law. As will be further explained below, the conceptual framework of effectiveness is rather blurred and hard to be grasped both at the theoretic level and in the practice of judicial reasoning. Notwithstanding this, it seems possible to distinguish three principal dimensions that comprise the notion of effectiveness in EU consumer law – and which, consequently, underpin argumentative patterns of the CJEU.

2.1 *Effet utile* as a 'Meta-Principle' (Standard)

The core understanding of effectiveness in European consumer law is derived from the general concept of effectiveness of the EU legal order in its entirety, commonly referred to as the *effet utile* or 'the effectiveness principle' (which should be, however, distinguished from the effectiveness principle discussed in section 2.2). It rests on the assumption that the EU law establishes an autonomous legal order, which has to be integrated with domestic systems of the Member States, through legislation, administrative ordering and judicial practice. Each of the particular components of EU law should be able to contribute to this aim. In other words, it should maintain a particular level of effectiveness – namely, be capable of achieving regulatory aims set by EU law.[5] Every element of the EU legal order should hence participate in providing the full effectiveness (*effet utile*)[6] of the EU law, i.e. to exert the expected effect in economic or social spheres.

The existing CJEU decisions do not give a precise account of the *effet utile* principle. Quite certainly, however, it does not constitute a general principle of EU law in a strict sense, but is rather a 'meta-principle' (or: an overall stand-

---

[5] So also, with different wording ('effectiveness of ... system' of protection established by the 93/13/EEC directive on Unfair Contractual Terms – hereinafter UCTD), CJEU case C-452/18 *XZ v Ibercaja Banco, SA* EU:C:2020:536 [2020], para 76.

[6] So esp. case 106/77 *Amministrazione delle Finanze dello Stato v Simmenthal SpA* EU:C:1978:49 [1978] ECR 629, paras 18–23.

ard), which encapsulates other principles and standards. Under Article 4(3) Treaty on European Union (TEU) the obligation to provide sufficient effectiveness to EU law pertains to all domestic authorities, which includes also courts and other bodies.[7] From the perspective of judicial dialogue it remains, nonetheless, unclear to what extent *effet utile* can operate merely as a criterion for understanding EU rules and domestic law (within an EU law conforming interpretation), and to what extent it may provide a basis for a more creative approach in European and national case law. While the literal wording of the Treaties seems to advocate for the first, the more conservative attitude (Article 19 TEU vests the CJEU directly only with guardianship over the EU primary law), the actual case law of the Court, reaches visibly far beyond this premise. It quite amply establishes new principles,[8] granting individual rights and awarding domestic courts entitlements, which reach beyond the verbatim content of the EU primary and secondary rules. In doing so, the CJEU awards *effet utile* a strong legitimizing power in the creation of measures that could safeguard the actual effectiveness of EU law in domestic orders.

2.2 The Principle of Effectiveness as a Limit to Procedural Autonomy

The first of more detailed variants of effectiveness addresses the division of tasks between the European law and domestic law, encapsulated in the concept of procedural autonomy.[9] Under the general principle of cooperation (loyalty), set forth in Article 4(3) TEU, domestic courts are obliged to provide judicial protection of rights set in the EU law. In so doing they should apply domestic provisions on procedure and jurisdiction unless EU law regulates this sphere.

The equivalence principle limits this freedom by prohibiting Member States to differentiate between rules of the EU and of domestic origin. In this under-

---

[7] See also Maciej Taborowski, *Konsekwencje naruszenia prawa Unii Europejskiej przez sądy krajowe* (Wolters Kluwer, Warsaw 2012) 66ff.

[8] Such an understanding of the requirement to ensure the full effectiveness of EU law constitutes the axis around which the CJEU has built over the years the 'core' of the most important principles of the EU legal system that do not have a direct normative basis in the treaties. These principles include the principle of primacy of EU law, the principle of direct effect, the principle of interpretation of national law in accordance with EU law, and the principle of State liability for breach of EU law.

[9] On delimitation of the effectiveness principle and effective judicial protection cf. Jasper Krommendijk, 'Is there Light on the Horizon? The Distinction between "Rewe Effectiveness" and the Principle of Effective Judicial Protection in Article 47 of the Charter after Orizzonte' (2016) 53 CMLR 1395, 1404–12.

standing, established through the '*Rewe/Comet* formula',[10] EU law cannot be treated less favourably than the Member States' own rules, in particular at the level of enforcement.[11]

The effectiveness principle in turn prohibits the creation of national rules that would make the application of EU law impossible or excessively difficult. That principle is not treated as a general principle of EU law (as is the case with the principle of effective judicial protection – see section 2.3). In fact, effectiveness in that sense is a label for a kind of 'rule of reason' test which national courts are obliged to perform under Article 4(3) TEU in regard to national procedural rules serving the protection of EU law derived rights of individuals. Those national rules must not prevent or unduly impede the exercise of EU rights. If they meet this standard, they can be applied. If they do not, they should not be applied by the national court.[12]

The effectiveness principle addresses, hence, primarily the question of mutual subsidiarity of EU and domestic law. Combined with the direct effect of EU provisions and the need to provide equivalence between EU law and instruments created in domestic law,[13] it provides a common ground for implementation of the broader *effet utile* principle. All those principles thus jointly oblige Member States to treat EU-originating rules not only on an equal footing with domestic provisions but also to provide EU rules the expected

---

[10] Set in case 33/76 *Rewe-Zentralfinanz eG and Rewe-Zentral AG v Landwirtschaftskammer für das Saarland* EU:C:1976:188 [1976] ECR 01989 and case 45/76 *Comet BV v Produktschap voor Siergewassen* EU:C:1976:191 [1976] ECR 02043; see also e.g. cf. Michael Dougan, 'Primacy and the Remedy of Disapplication' (2019) 56 CMLR 1459, 1471; Anthony Arnull, 'The Principle of Effective Judicial Protection in EU Law: An Unruly Horse?' (2011) 36 *European Law Review* 51, 55ff.

[11] The CJEU treats the equivalence principle as an expression of the principle of equal treatment, see case C-34/02 *Sante Pasquini v Istituto nazionale della previdenza sociale (INPS)* EU:C:2003:366 [2003] ECR I-06515, para 70.

[12] As to the criteria used for the court's assessment, see case C-432/05 *Unibet (London) Ltd and Unibet (International) Ltd v Justitiekanslern* EU:C:2007:163 [2007] I-02271, para 54. In that regard, each case which raises the question whether a national procedural provision renders the application of Community law impossible or excessively difficult must be analysed by reference to the role of that provision in the procedure, its progress and its special features, viewed as a whole, before the various national instances.

[13] In the recent consumer case law so e.g. joined cases C-381/14 and C-385/14 *Jorge Sales Sinués and Youssouf Drame Ba v Caixabank SA and Catalunya Caixa SA (Catalunya Banc S.A.)* EU:C:2016:909 [2016] ECR I-00, para 85; joined cases C-698/18 and C-699/18 *SC Raiffeisen Bank SA and BRD Groupe Societé Générale SA v JB und KC* EU:C:2020:537 [2020], paras 59–60; and joined cases C-224/19 and C-259/19 *CY and Others v Caixabank SA and Banco Bilbao Vizcaya Argentaria SA* EU:C:2020:578 [2020], paras 83–84.

effect despite national hurdles.[14] Such a dimension of effectiveness is also expressed directly in EU secondary law. It is included in the provisions present in all consumer directives[15] that require Member States to introduce dissuasive, proportional and effective remedies.[16] In the area of consumer case law, such formulas are often treated as an independent source of the effectiveness principle (as a constraint to procedural autonomy). It can be also understood in a rather more compound way, by being intertwined with *effet utile* or (which occurs ever more frequently in recent CJEU case law) with effective judicial protection.[17]

2.3 Effective Judicial Protection

The third dimension of effectiveness rests on the premise that while enjoying procedural autonomy, Member States should observe a common and basic set of standards regarding the way in which EU law is enforced domestically. Understood in this way, effectiveness aims to guarantee that rights awarded to individuals under EU law can be effectively claimed before domestic and EU bodies and that their protection will not be subject to substantial legal or factual constraints. It intertwines with the classic right to a fair trial as well as more specific guarantees, peculiar for the EU regulatory agenda.

Currently, in EU legislation and case law the notion of effective judicial protection is becoming separated into a principle of EU law and a fundamental right. In the former sense, it is understood as a set of rules and standards that allow individuals to receive effective protection of their rights granted in EU law. In this understanding, effectiveness of judicial protection is perceived not as a set of measures ('judicial remedies'[18]) that allow for effective and equivalent enforcement of EU law. Rather, effective judicial protection is a more

---

[14] See also Anna Wallerman, 'Towards an EU Law Doctrine on the Exercise of Discretion in National Courts? The Member States' Self-Imposed Limits on National Procedural Autonomy' (2016) 53 CMLR 339, 352.

[15] See e.g. Article 7(1) UCTD which requires Member States to ensure that, in the interests of consumers and of competitors, adequate and effective means exist to prevent the continued use of unfair terms in contracts concluded with consumers by sellers or suppliers.

[16] Cf. Cafaggi, Iamiceli, above n. 2.

[17] See, amongst many others, case C-421/14 *Banco Primus* EU:C:2017:60 [2017] ECR I-00, para 48; and case C-377/14 *Ernst Georg Radlinger and Helena Radlingerová v Finway a.s.* EU:C:2016:283 [2016] ECR I-00, paras 45–46. Particularly important for development of this thread of CJEU case law was Article 7(1) UCTD, which mandated Member States to provide 'adequate and effective means' that can prevent use of unfair terms.

[18] See case *Unibet*, above n. 12, para 47.

detailed and specialized component of the effectiveness principle, discussed in section 2.2.[19] For this reason, as will be further discussed in section 3.3, the dividing line between the effectiveness principle and effective judicial protection in the CJEU decisions is often blurred and inconsequent.[20] In parallel, effective judicial protection is also framed as a fundamental right in the sense of Article 47(1) Charter of Fundamental Rights of European Union (CFREU) which, according to Article 19(1) TEU, has to be guaranteed by Member States in the fields covered by EU law.[21] In this sense effective judicial protection should be qualified as one of the foundational values of the EU legal order,[22] but at the same time is not fully equivalent either with *effet utile* nor with the effectiveness principle. It is primarily concerned with safeguarding individuals' rights to receive effective enforcement of the rights guaranteed under EU law. As opposed to the effectiveness principle and *effet utile*, it does not pay attention primarily to the regulatory aims of EU law – however (as is the case for consumer law[23]), it may protect them secondarily or as a spillover.

3. EFFECTIVENESS IN JUDICIAL DIALOGUE: CJEU ARGUMENTATIVE PATTERNS

3.1 The Dimensions of Effectiveness and Judicial Dialogue: the Framing Remarks

All three dimensions comprise the notion of effectiveness in EU consumer law.[24] Summing up the preliminary conclusions from the previous section, the

---

19 See also case *Unibet*, above n. 12, para 65.

20 On allocation of effective judicial protection in the EU legal order see also case C-389/10 P *KME Germany AG, KME France SAS and KME Italy SpA v European Commission* EU:C:2011:816 [2011] ECR I-13125, para 52.

21 The overlap of these two dimensions was directly reflected in the case C-619/18 *European Commission v Republic of Poland* EU:C:2019:615 [2019], paras 47–49. It ascertains that Member States are obliged to provide actual and full applicability of EU law, as well as 'judicial protection of rights that subject to the law derive from that right'.

22 The principle of effective judicial protection is part of the Rule of Law mentioned in Article 2 TEU; see case *European Commission v Republic of Poland*, above n. 21, para 47; cf. Piotr Bogdanowicz, Maciej Taborowski, 'How to Save a Supreme Court in a Rule of Law Crisis: The Polish Experience: ECJ (Grand Chamber) 24 June 2019, Case C-619/18, European Commission v Republic of Poland' (2020) 16 *European Constitutional Law Review* 306.

23 See cases discussed below in sections 3 and 4 where Article 47(1) CFREU was used as an instrument for guaranteeing effective application of UCTD.

24 On the complementarity of particular sub-types of effectiveness, see also case C-224/01 *Gerhard Köbler v Republik Österreich* EU:C:2003:513 [2003] I-10239, para. 47.

interrelation between the three dimensions of effectiveness can be, in some approximation, illustrated as follows:

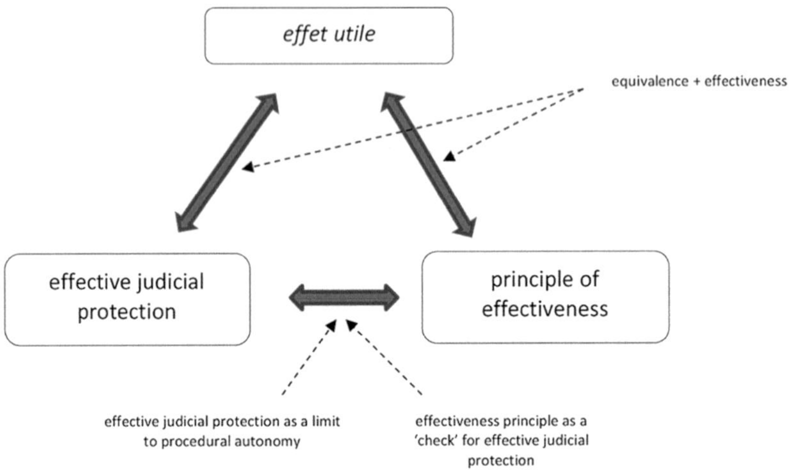

Figure 16.1 *The three dimensions of effectiveness*

Although the three dimensions are distinguishable conceptually, they are much further from being clear in the existing CJEU case law. While referring to effectiveness, the Court invokes various dimensions of this provision and puts them into divergent argumentative patterns. This incoherence can only in part be justified in terms of the development of the effectiveness doctrine over time. Indeed, in its more recent decisions, the CJEU often puts effective judicial protection and Article 47 CFREU in the foreground, as opposed to the earlier cases which perceived effectiveness rather through the prism of the principle of effectiveness and *effet utile*. This change can be attributed, in part, to the increasing proliferation of fundamental rights reasoning in EU private law, and to the growing focus on the procedural aspects of consumer protection.[25] Such explanations do not deal with all the questions triggered by the development of CJEU consumer case law over the past few decades. Clearly in many instances the Court builds on the interchangeable use of various meanings of effective-

[25] Cf. e.g. Fabrizio Cafaggi, Stephanie Law, 'Judicial Dialogue in European Private Law: Introductory Remarks', in F. Cafaggi, S. Law (eds), *Judicial Cooperation in European Private Law* (Edward Elgar, Cheltenham, UK and Northampton, MA 2017) 22–6; Anna Van Duin, 'Justice for Both: Effective Judicial Protection under Article 47 of the EU Charter of Fundamental Rights and the Unfair Contract Terms Directive' (University of Amsterdam 2020, doctoral thesis) 36–9.

ness to construe the same argument.[26] The choice between dimensions of effectiveness is not merely a question of choosing between alternative rhetorical framings, but entails also several more substantial consequences. Each of the building blocks of effectiveness are embedded in its context in EU primary and secondary law and accompanied by a number of more detailed instruments and concepts developed by the CJEU.

In consequence, reference to each of the types of effectiveness have different argumentative weight and create different legitimization for intervention into domestic legal orders. Furthermore, each of these choices are also relevant (directly) for the manner in which domestic courts should implement the CJEU decision, as well as (indirectly) for the framing of future preliminary references in the particular sub-domain of consumer law. For these reasons it is important to take a closer look at the most typical areas of incoherence between various dimensions of effectiveness, which substantially impact the mechanics of judicial dialogue: the overlap between the *effet utile* standard, the effectiveness principle and the position of the effective judicial protection vis-à-vis other types of effectiveness.

3.2 *Effet utile* vs Effectiveness Principle

In most instances, effectiveness as a principle of EU law and the *effet utile* standard are not fully separable in the CJEU case law, at both conceptual and policy-related levels. The overlap of both provisions can be further broken down to two groups.

First of all, in several decisions, the CJEU refers to *effet utile* as a 'meta' principle, which embraces other types of effectiveness. This was frequently the case for CJEU decisions that tackled the *ex officio* power of domestic courts to review terms in consumer agreements under UCTD. Along this line, in *Pannon GSM*[27] the Court referred to *effet utile* as a ground for imposing on domestic courts a duty to examine unfairness by its own motion. Similarly, in *Asbeek*[28] the Court mentioned 'the full effectiveness of the protection provided for by the directive', ascertaining that it can be satisfied only inasmuch as the domestic court can derive on its own motion all the legal consequences

---

[26] Beyond consumer law, this approach is also traceable in CJEU decisions concerning interim measures, such as case C-213/89 *The Queen v Secretary of State for Transport, ex parte: Factortame Ltd and others* EU:C:1990:257 [1990] I-02433, para. 21 and case *Unibet*, above n. 12, paras 67, 77, 79.

[27] Case C-243/08 *Pannon GSM Zrt. v Erzsébet Sustikné Győrfi* EU:C:2009:350 [2009] I-04713, para 32.

[28] Case C-488/11 *Dirk Frederik Asbeek Brusse and Katarina de Man Garabito v Jahani BV* EU:C:2013:341 [2013], para 50.

from the fact of unfairness of a clause.[29] The wording and context of both decisions makes it very clear that effectiveness is considered as an 'umbrella' formula that encompasses not merely *effet utile* as such, but also delves more deeply into the domestic procedural rules – and hence, expresses either the effectiveness principle or effective judicial protection. In turn, the more recent CJEU decisions, such as *Profi Credit I*,[30] visibly tend to replace the general effectiveness formula (*effet utile*) with more precise standards, especially the effectiveness principle (derived from Article 7(1) UCTD) and to the effective judicial protection in the sense of Article 47 CFREU. It would be rather hard to argue that both types of reasoning differ substantially. Quite the opposite, the latter group seems to merely divide the 'umbrella' standard of *effet utile* into more precise categories.[31]

Secondly, in other CJEU cases particular types of effectiveness are treated in a different manner – as principles organized in a hierarchical way. So, in *Banco Español*,[32] the principle of effectiveness seems to be considered as a prerequisite of effective judicial protection. From this vantage point, the removal of procedural hurdles in domestic law (i.e. a constraint to domestic procedural autonomy) is considered as a step necessary to guarantee a proper standard of judicial protection (Article 47 CFREU). In the same way, the CJEU linked the effectiveness principle and effective judicial protection in a series of decisions concerning order of payment and default judgment procedures in Poland and Spain.[33] They ascertained that enforcement schemes created domestically

---

[29] Joined cases C-154/15 and C-307/15 *Francisco Gutiérrez Naranjo v Cajasur Banco SAU, Ana María Palacios Martínez v Banco Bilbao Vizcaya Argentaria SA (BBVA), Banco Popular Español SA v Emilio Irles López and Teresa Torres Andreu* EU:C:2016:980 [2016] ECR I-00, para 59.

[30] Case C-176/17 *Profi Credit Polska S.A. w Bielsku Białej v Mariusz Wawrzosek* EU:C:2018:711 [2018] ECR I-00.

[31] Notably, however, in the *Alassini* case the CJEU took a different approach, and clearly separated the effectiveness principle and effective judicial protection on the grounds of the Universal Service Directive 2002/22/EC – by referring to these concepts as complementary, yet distinct grounds for review of domestic rules for compliance with EU law; joined cases C-317/08 *Rosalba Alassini v Telecom Italia SpA*, C-318/08 *Filomena Califano v Wind SpA*, C-319/08 *Lucia Anna Giorgia Iacono v Telecom Italia SpA* and C-320/08 *Multiservice Srl v Telecom Italia SpA* EU:C:2010:146 [2010] ECR I-02213, para 37.

[32] Case C-618/10 *Banco Español de Crédito, SA v Joaquín Calderón Camino* EU: C:2012:349 [2012] ECR I-00, paras 46, 49, 56 (effectiveness principle), as opposed to para 53 (*effet utile*).

[33] Case *Banco Español*, above n. 32; case *Profi Credit I*, above n. 30; case C-49/14 *Finanmadrid EFC SA v Jesús Vicente Albán Zambrano and Others* EU:C: 2016:98 [2016] ECR I-00; case C-448/17 *EOS KSI Slovensko s.r.o. v Ján Danko and Margita Danková* EU:C:2018:745 [2018] ECR I-00; case C-632/17 *Powszechna Kasa*

should meet the minimal criteria of equivalence and effective judicial protection, in the meaning of Article 47(1) CFREU. Such 'hierarchical' view of effectiveness was drawn even further in *Radlinger* where the CJEU revoked the effectiveness principle as a precondition for both effective judicial protection and *effet utile*. As was observed,

> the specific characteristics of court proceedings cannot constitute a factor which is liable to affect the legal protection from which consumers must benefit under the provisions of Directive 93/13 [...] a restriction on the power of the national court of its own motion to set aside unfair terms is liable to affect the effectiveness of the protection intended by Articles 6 and 7 of Directive 93/13.[34]

In all these cases the choice of effective judicial protection (or effective judicial protection and *effet utile*) as a superior type of effectiveness could be, at least to some extent, explained in terms of the cases' subject matter (which in all instances tackled domestic procedural rules as possible obstacles to substantive consumer rights). Nonetheless, even such an elucidation is not universal for the entirety of CJEU case law. In some situations, the CJEU puts *effet utile* in a clear foreground – even when effective judicial protection seems to provide a more direct and precise response to the issue discussed in a case. For instance, in *Aziz*[35] the CJEU concluded that the impossibility to award consumers interim protection in mortgage enforcement proceedings infringes the *effet utile* of the UCTD. The judgment mentions *effet utile* as the only kind of effectiveness, referring neither to the effectiveness principle[36] in the context of domestic procedural autonomy[37] nor to effective judicial protection and Article 47 CFREU.[38]

Aside from these two principal ways of structuring the concept of effectiveness, in numerous decisions the CJEU seems to revoke effectiveness as a general rhetoric figure, without explicating its precise understanding. For

---

Oszczędności (PKO) Bank Polski S.A. w Warszawie v Jacek Michalski EU:C:2018:963 [2018] ECR I-00; case C-495/19 *Kancelaria Medius SA v RN* EU:C:2020:431 [2020].

[34] Case *Radlinger*, above n. 17, paras 50, 57; further on *effet utile* see also paras 66 and 77 of this decision.

[35] Case C-415/11 *Mohamed Aziz v Caixa d'Estalvis de Catalunya, Tarragona i Manresa (Catalunyacaixa)* EU:C:2013:164 [2013].

[36] The same conclusion was repeated in case C-109/17 *Bankia SA v Juan Carlos Mari Merino and Others* EU:C:2018:735 [2018] ECR I-00, para 39, where the Court also referred to *effet utile* in verification whether the lack of domestic interim protection measures does not violate EU law.

[37] Case *Aziz* (above n. 35) invokes procedural autonomy only in the context of the equivalence principle (para 49), but does not link it with the effectiveness principle.

[38] Noteworthily, in *Aziz* (above n. 35) and *Bankia* (above n. 36) cases *effet utile* was invoked in order to verify the EU-conformity of omissions in domestic law.

instance, in *Bankia*[39] the Court ascertained that compensatory liability of a professional may constitute a measure that is both 'adequate' and 'effective' to combat unfair commercial practices under UCPD. The judgment does not indicate any hints on how to understand effectiveness referred to in the judgment. Although at first sight the effectiveness in question could be associated with *effet utile*, coupling this notion with adequacy suggests the CJEU might have referred to the effectiveness principle or to an unspecified combination of this principle and the *effet utile* standard. Neither of these readings seems, however, fully recognizable against the background of the decision.

3.3 Autonomy of Effective Judicial Protection?

The conceptual struggle in perceiving effectiveness in EU consumer cases is clearly observable also with regard to effective judicial protection. Apart from a very vague – almost non-existent in practice – distinction between effective judicial protection as a principle and as a fundamental right,[40] CJEU case law seems far from coherent in other aspects as well.

On the one hand, in all CJEU consumer cases, not one of the obligations imposed on Member States were derived from effective judicial protection,[41] but the Court always accompanied it with at least *effet utile* or the effectiveness principle. The Court seems to approach effective judicial protection not as a self-standing type of effectiveness, but rather as an ancillary concept, which only supplements the two other kinds of effectiveness. In this way, the *Aziz* decision ascertains that an interim relief to stay or terminate the mortgage proceedings is not available to a domestic court and does not comply with EU law as long as 'such relief is necessary to ensure the full effectiveness of its final decision'.[42] Quite clearly, by referring to effectiveness, the Court did not indicate only effectiveness of the judicial protection as such, but also mentioned thus the general notion of *effet utile* – which, in turn, is understood as effective protection against unfair terms (in the meaning of Article 7(1) UCTD), i.e. with regard to the effectiveness principle.[43]

---

[39] Case *Bankia*, above n. 36, para 46.

[40] See section 2.3.

[41] Especially, in none of the discussed decisions did the Court include one of the usual formulas used while referring to EJP; see e.g. case 222/84 *Marguerite Johnston v Chief Constable of the Royal Ulster Constabulary* EU:C:1986:206 [1986] ECR 01651.

[42] Case *Aziz*, above n. 35, para 59.

[43] Notably, the reasoning in *Aziz* (above n. 35) and the *Unibet* case (above n. 12, para. 77). Thereby, effective judicial protection was linked with effectiveness of a particular judgment – and hence, implicitly, with *effet utile*. A similar three-pronged argument, which combines all three dimensions of effectiveness, was presented also in

In some decisions, the CJEU goes even further and frames *effet utile* and the effectiveness principle as derivatives of effective judicial protection. This attitude was originally formed in public law[44] and later proliferated into the consumer contracts domain. For instance, in *Finanmadrid*[45] where the Court ascertained that 'effective protection of the rights' under the UCTD can be provided only as long as the domestic procedural rules allow for *ex officio* review of contract terms.[46] This path was further followed in *Banif*[47] and *Profi Credit I*.[48] In the latter decision, the Court referred explicitly to a procedural standard derived from both Article 47 CFREU and Article 7(1) UCTD. Understood in this way, effective judicial protection was perceived by the Court as a component and a guarantee of effectiveness in the sense of the effectiveness principle (i.e. as the possibility to obtain effective judicial protection for the substantive rights awarded to consumers under the UCTD).

On the other hand, however, in more recent CJEU case law, effective judicial protection is gaining vivid prevalence.[49] In the vast majority of consumer decisions, the Court does not revoke its classic *Rewe/Comet* formula, but refers either to the effectiveness principle or (more recently) to effective judicial protection as the independent bases for intervention into Member States' procedural autonomy.[50] It was, amongst others, the case for the CJEU decisions that tacked on the domestic order of payment procedures. While in *EOS KSI Slovensko* the EU-compliance of domestic rules was perceived through the prism of *effet utile*, in other cases the Court framed this problem as an issue of the effectiveness principle. For instance, in *Banco Español*,[51] while discussing the judicial obligation to review unfairness of clauses *ex officio*, the CJEU concluded that a rule that limits this possibility in domestic law 'appears not to

case C-75/16 *Livio Menini and Maria Antonia Rampanelli v Banco Popolare – Società Cooperativa* EU:C:2017:457 [2017] ECR I-00, para 51.

44 Case C-63/08 *Virginie Pontin v T-Comalux SA* EU:C:2009:666 [2009] ECR I-10467, paras 43–44 and C-268/06 *Impact v Minister for Agriculture and Food and Others* EU:C:2008:223 [2008] I-02483, paras 46–47.

45 Case C-49/14 *Finanmadrid EFC* EU:C:2016:98.

46 Further on the concept of effectiveness in this judgment see Krommendijk, above n. 9, at 1411–12, 1417.

47 Case C-472/11 *Banif Plus Bank Zrt v Csaba Csipai and Viktória Csipai* EU:C:2013:88 [2013] ECR I-00, paras 28, 36. Notably, in this decision the CJEU attempted to balance the principle of effectiveness with procedural guarantees (right to be heard), by mandating domestic courts to allow parties to take a stand regarding unfairness of a clause.

48 Case *Profi Credit I*, above n. 30, paras 62–63.

49 Further on the growing impact of Article 47 CFREU in EU private law see Reich, *General Principles*, above n. 3, at 90–91.

50 See e.g. case *Profi Credit I*, above n. 30.

51 Case *Banco Español*, above n. 32, para. 56.

comply with the principle of effectiveness, in so far as it makes impossible or excessively difficult, in proceedings initiated by sellers or suppliers in which consumers are defendants, the application of the protection which Directive 93/13 seeks to confer on those consumers'.

4. THE PARTICULAR OUTCOMES FOR JUDICIAL DIALOGUE

4.1 Challenges for Domestic Courts

The variety of dimensions in which the CJEU perceives the effectiveness of consumer law triggers direct and meaningful consequences for interaction between the Court and the national judiciary. Member States' courts do not only need to follow the view of effectiveness featured in a particular decision – especially when the CJEU tackled their 'own' domestic system. Within the EU-conforming interpretation they also have to respect the overall standard of effectiveness set for the particular domain of EU law, even if a particular issue has not been addressed directly through the preliminary ruling procedure. The evident incoherence in the ways of perceiving and applying this notion by the CJEU makes this task substantially complicated.

The lack of a coherent conceptual and argumentative framework for effectiveness (even in such classic instances as the *ex officio* review of contract terms[52]) poses two principal challenges. First of all, in most instances a national judge has to decode the exact meaning of effectiveness that has been adopted by the CJEU for the certain problem or sub-section of EU law. This pertains, in particular, to distinguishing between the substantive and procedural dimension of effectiveness, as well as between effectiveness as a principle and as a fundamental right (especially on the grounds of Article 47 CFREU). Secondly, domestic courts need to derive consequences from the EU notion of effectiveness on the grounds of national legal systems. This pertains not merely to interpreting domestic law in the effectiveness-conforming way, but in many instances entails also making more radical choices – such as disapplication of a domestic rule in part or in total or creation of a new solution to fill a lacuna in national system. From this vantage point, the manner in which a national judge deciphers the concept of effectiveness for the sake of a particular case may be decisive for the final resolution of the dispute – and may directly shape the actual level of consumer protection in the domestic order.

The gravity of these challenges can be clearly illustrated by three issues, in which understanding of effectiveness by domestic judges may profoundly

---

[52] See section 3.2.

impact national systems of consumer protection. At the most general level, this pertains to the choice between the 'negative' ('eliminatory') and the 'positive' ('creative') notion of effectiveness. Further, the interpretation of the effectiveness concept directly impacts also the possibility and extent of an innovative approach by domestic courts towards the creation of instruments and remedies in national legal systems. Lastly, the notion of effectiveness adopted in the particular case may also lead a court towards balancing rights – and, thereby, directly underpin a particular version of proportionality that will be adopted in the case. The subsequent remarks will delve more deeply into these three problems.

4.2 Effectiveness as a 'Negative' and a 'Creative' Factor

The classic accounts of effectiveness in EU law frequently distinguish between its 'negative' and 'positive' side.[53] Under this view, effectiveness can either lead to elimination of certain elements of domestic legal orders to provide efficacy of EU law or may ground the creation of new instruments in domestic law, wherever they are needed to provide satisfactory effects of EU rules. From a conceptual perspective, both concepts are in fact two sides of the same coin. The sufficient degree of effectiveness of EU law requires not only to remove obstacles in domestic legal orders, but also to create new instruments – wherever necessary – to 'operationalize' the proper functioning of EU law.

At the same time, both concepts are appropriate for two components of judicial dialogue in EU consumer law. The 'eliminatory' role of effectiveness is most prominent in preliminary references, which often seek to ascertain EU-conformity of particular elements of domestic law. Consumer law opens a particularly broad field for such application of effectiveness. Since the vast majority of consumer issues are regulated through directives, this domain of EU *acquis* creates frequent doubts regarding proper transposition into domestic law. This pertains both to substantive law issues (encompassed mostly by *effet utile* and the effectiveness principle) and to procedural instruments (covered, to a varying extent, by all the three dimensions of effectiveness discussed in section 2).

From the CJEU's vantage point, a preliminary question that seeks to review compliance of domestic rules with EU law triggers an obvious need to resort to effectiveness as a criterion of critical assessment of domestic provisions. In other words, while deciding on a preliminary question the CJEU has to ascer-

[53] Cf. e.g. Reich, *General Principles*, above n. 3, at 91–5, who speaks about 'eliminatory' role of effectiveness; Cafaggi, Iamiceli, above n. 2, at 581, who refer to '(affirmative) identification of available procedures, remedies and sanctions'.

tain to what extent domestic law may lack a sufficient degree of effectiveness. By referring to the concept of effectiveness (and by choosing between various dimensions of this concept), the CJEU does not aim hence to determine what is effective, but rather to identify possible areas of ineffectiveness. The situation differs from the perspective of the second party to the dialogue – i.e. domestic courts that need to subsequently implement CJEU rulings on the grounds of the domestic legal orders.

The CJEU case law has also witnessed the adoption of a different attitude, by empowering domestic courts to safeguard effectiveness by creating new instruments (or by substantially reinterpreting[54] the ones already existing in national systems). In this regard as well, the CJEU was building on various dimensions of effectiveness. The most elementary basis for a creative (innovative) attitude was provided by *effet utile*,[55] understood as a general rationale for protection of rights granted to individuals under EU law. Under this view, the inherent and unelidable part of systemic effectiveness of EU law is the sufficient level of protection rights awarded in EU substantive law.

Unsurprisingly, the bulk of problems concerning the 'creative' role of effectiveness tackles domestic procedural rules. By referring in this way to effectiveness, the CJEU usually recognizes the need to create procedural measures in domestic legal orders that would safeguard effective enforcement of individuals' rights awarded in the EU substantive law. Understood in this way, the creative dimension of effectiveness may come into play in two types of situations. First of all, it may be explicitly required by the CJEU in instances where ineffectiveness of EU law is caused by the deficit or inoperability of a particular instrument in domestic legal systems. In this way, for instance, the CJEU revoked effective judicial protection in a series of decisions regarding lack of interim measures in mortgage enforcement proceedings in Spanish law. Secondly, the 'positive' potential of effectiveness may also emerge in the outcome of a 'negative' decision, which extracts certain element from the domestic legal order.

The gap that arises in this way needs to be supplemented with direct reference to effectiveness – i.e. in a way that would respect the same degree of effectiveness that has been indicated by the CJEU. Both scenarios trigger two types of problems. First of all, they pose a plea for a clear(er) division of tasks between the CJEU and domestic legal orders in determining the content of an effective procedural toolbox for EU substantive rights. Secondly, the concept

---

[54] Similarly, on effectiveness as a 'hermeneutical' principle, Reich, *General Principles*, above n. 3, at 95–7.

[55] Cf. cases *Simmenthal* (above n. 6) and *Factortame* (above n. 26), more recently also case C-556/17 *Alekszij Torubarov v Bevándorlási és Menekültügyi Hivatal* EU:C:2019:626 [2019] ECR I-00.

of effectiveness developed by the CJEU calls domestic courts to clarify values and policy considerations that should be taken as a point of reference for effective-based innovation. The following remarks do not aspire to exhaust the constitutional and pragmatic questions triggered by pushing domestic courts to innovate *praeter* or *contra legem* with effectiveness as the sole justification.[56] It seems, however, worthwhile to delve more deeply into the precise understanding of effectiveness in the 'creation-oriented' CJEU decisions and into the dynamic between EU and domestic law that ensues upon them.

4.3 Effectiveness as a Basis for Judicial Innovation

The distinction between 'negative' and 'creative' roles of effectiveness is not always easily identifiable against the background of CJEU decisions. Most often it is an implicit outcome of an 'eliminatory' application of effectiveness, where eradication of a particular element of the domestic legal order calls upon domestic courts to identify a substitute that fills the void generated in this way. In the existing case law, most of such instances tackle procedural issues, calling domestic courts to identify or create a rule that could supplement a gap resulting from a CJEU ruling. As a consequence, most of these issues put effective judicial protection (including Article 47 CFREU)[57] in the foreground – and requires domestic courts to understand what is the exact procedural standard that can be derived from this fundamental right. Only after such interpretive effort at the domestic level (and in the context of national law) it is possible to facilitate a certain rule or remedy to fill a void.

In the recent CJEU case law, such a plea for innovation in judicial dialogue has been conspicuously created by a series of decisions concerning effectiveness of consumer protection in accelerated order of payment procedures in Spain and Poland.[58] In all these decisions the CJEU set, in a more or less pronounced way, positive obligations for domestic courts, deriving them typically from the effective judicial protection standard, coupled with Article 47 CFREU. As has been already explained in section 3.2, the notions of *effet utile*

---

[56] See Peter Van Cleynenbreugel, 'The Confusing Constitutional Status of Positive Procedural Obligations in EU Law: Observations on Effective Judicial Protection and National Procedural Autonomy in the Wake of Boxus' (2012) 5 *Review of European Administrative Law* 81, 88ff.; Maciej Taborowski, 'Case 432/05 Unibet: Some Practical Remarks on Effective Judicial Protection' (2008) 14 *Columbia Journal of European Law* 621, 629ff., along with further references.

[57] Apart from the consumer context, see also case 222/86 *Union nationale des entraîneurs et cadres techniques professionnels du football (Unectef) v Georges Heylens and Others* EU:C:1987:442 [1987] 04097, case *Johnston* (above n. 41) and case *Unibet* (above n. 12).

[58] Case *Banco Español*, above n. 32, paras 53, 56.

and the effectiveness principle are revoked in these decisions rather as a criterion for verification whether particular domestic rules meet the procedural dimension of effectiveness. In other words, while effective judicial protection is considered on these grounds as both a negative criterion (addressed to the CJEU) and a positive premise (directed towards domestic courts), the other two dimensions are considered only to play the former role.[59]

Notably, this attitude is not fully consequent across CJEU case law. For instance, in *Faber*[60] the Court referred to the principle of effectiveness in a dual role – as both a 'negative' standard (in order to repeal domestic procedural rules that limited enforcement of the 1999/44/EC directive) and as a source of 'positive' obligation of domestic courts (to allow an *ex officio* check whether a buyer was acting in a consumer capacity).

Lastly, depending on the particular case, the 'negative' and the 'positive' side of effectiveness may rest on the same or on various genres of effectiveness. This diversity can be illustrated by comparison between two cases concerning the order of payment procedure. In *EOS KSI Slovensko* the Court ascertained that 'effective protection of the rights' (*effet utile*) under UCTD requires that while issuing an order of payment a domestic court should be capable of performing an *ex officio* review of contract terms. At the same time, the CJEU mingled this approach with the effectiveness principle, by indicating that domestic law (within procedural autonomy) cannot introduce measures that could deter consumers from submitting objections to the order of payment.[61] Similarly, in the earlier *Aziz* decision, the Court – while indicating a need for interim relief in a consumer eviction procedure – referred to the concept of 'effective mean' in the sense of Article 7(1) UCTD. Interestingly, this provision – as opposed to previous CJEU decisions – was understood through the prism of effective judicial protection,[62] rather than through the more substantive law-oriented effectiveness principle. At the same time, the Court referred, indeed, to the effectiveness principle – however, only in the 'eliminatory' fashion, i.e. in order to exclude provisions of Spanish law that

[59] The same attitude is adopted also beyond consumer law, for instance in *Unibet* case, above n. 12. In this context cf. joined cases C-295/04 *Vincenzo Manfredi v Lloyd Adriatico Assicurazioni SpA*, C-296/04 *Antonio Cannito v Fondiaria Sai SpA*, C-297/04 *Nicolò Tricarico* and C-298/04 *Pasqualina Murgolo v Assitalia SpA* EU:C:2006:461 [2006] ECR I-06619, para 95, where (with regard to competition harm) the Court grounded the need to create compensatory mechanisms on a general 'principle of effectiveness' (in this context quite clearly understood as *effet utile*).

[60] Case C-497/13 *Froukje Faber v Autobedrijf Hazet Ochten BV* EU:C:2015:357 [2015] ECR I-00, paras 45–46.

[61] Case *EOS KSI Slovensko*, above n. 33, para 51.

[62] Case *Aziz*, above n. 35, para 63.

hinder effective enforcement of UCTD.[63] A divergent argument was construed in *Profi Credit I* and *PKO* decisions where the Court reached similar conclusions combining *effet utile* and the effective judicial protection (without any explicit reference to domestic procedural autonomy).

Putting several dimensions of effectiveness together renders it even more difficult for domestic judges to understand their role in filling a gap created by a CJEU decision. This pertains, first of all, to identifying whether a particular issue is of substantive or of procedural character. It requires understanding whether a dominant criterion applied by the CJEU is the effectiveness principle (in its 'substantive' role[64]) or the effective judicial protection. Secondly, it is also necessary to understand whether effectiveness – if referred to as effective judicial protection – is considered as a principle (e.g. in the sense of Article 7 UCTD) or as a fundamental right (Article 47 CFREU). These decisions may determine not only the choice between substantive and procedural instruments that can be used to supplement a void in the domestic system. They can also directly impact the admissibility of using certain gap-filling techniques (e.g. in particular domestic legal orders analogous reasoning may be available to a broader extent than in procedural law). Finally, it also can diametrically alter the type of adjustments and value balancing that a domestic court will have to make. In particular, effective judicial protection as a fundamental right can be balanced with other rights or principles, as will be illustrated in the following section.

4.4 Effectiveness and Proportionality

Under particular circumstances, various notions of effectiveness may collide with each other. This might be especially the case for the issues that involve effectiveness as a standard for substantive consumer rights and as a procedural guarantee that pertains to both parties to the proceedings at the same time. The most illustrative example for this concern has been provided in the CJEU *Partner* decision.[65] It addressed the question whether EU law permits to extend effects of contract clauses review upon professionals who did not participate

---

[63] In the conclusions (para. 64), the Court referred, however, only to Article 7(1) UCTD, without revoking effective judicial protection and the effectiveness principle. In the same way, in the case *Banco Español*, above n. 32, para 53, the CJEU approached effective judicial protection in the context of *effet utile*, referring to 'effectiveness of the protection intended by Directive 93/13'.

[64] See section 2.3.

[65] Case C-119/15 *Biuro podróży 'Partner' Sp. z o.o, Sp. komandytowa w Dąbrowie Górniczej v Prezes Urzędu Ochrony Konkurencji i Konsumentów* EU:C:2016:987 [2016] ECR I-00.

in the initial proceedings, but who use the same or a similar contract clause.[66] In so doing, the CJEU confronted effectiveness of the UCTD[67] with effective judicial protection under Article 47(1) CFREU, seeking to delimit and balance them. Upon these grounds it came to the conclusion that an extended personal scope of the consequences of unfairness can be legitimately introduced in domestic law only insofar as a professional not involved in the initial proceedings has 'an effective judicial remedy' to challenge the finding that two contract clauses express the same (unfair) content.[68]

The *Partner* decision builds on the premise that the effectiveness principle and effective judicial protection may, under particular circumstances, contradict each other[69] and, as such, they may require balancing and proportionalization.[70] From this vantage point, procedural standards derived from Article 47(1) CFREU may provide a mitigating criterion that frames enforcement of substantive consumer rights.[71] Such internal dynamic within the concept of effectiveness, which the *Partner* decision clearly evidenced, seems to be an obvious outcome of the development of EU consumer law, where Article 47(1) CFREU is visibly becoming one of the principal tools for enhancing coherence between EU protective standards and domestic legal orders. At the same time, it requires domestic courts to develop stronger constitutional sensitivity, in particular to become more aware of possible internal conflicts between various dimensions of effectiveness. This further adds up to the complexity of inter-

[66] The decision was a follow-up to an earlier case C-472/10 *Nemzeti Fogyasztóvédelmi Hatóság v Invitel Távközlési Zrt* EU:C:2012:242 [2012] I-00, which ascertained that consumers not involved in the initial proceedings can nevertheless benefit from the declaration of unfairness. Further on the concept of effectiveness in this decision Reich, 'The Principle of Effectiveness', above n. 3, at 57–9.

[67] Case *Partner*, above n. 65, para 29.

[68] Case *Partner*, above n. 65, para 40.

[69] In this sense effective judicial protection may also provide a limiting factor (or at least a yardstick) for procedural autonomy – cf. Dan Wielsch, 'Responsible Contracting: The Requirements of EU Fundamental Rights on Private Law Regimes', in H. Collins (ed.), *European Contract Law and the Charter of Fundamental Rights* (Intersentia, Cambridge 2017) 267–8.

[70] CJEU decisions based on effective judicial protection are, however, not the only ones which address the question of balancing of values within consumer law; in this sense for instance joined cases C-65/09 *Gebr. Weber GmbH v Jürgen Wittmer* and C-87/09 *Ingrid Putz v Medianess Electronics GmbH* EU:C:2011:396 [2011] ECR I-05257, paras 52, 73, where CJEU confronted 'effective protection [of] consumers' and 'effective protection of the legitimate financial interests of the seller' (in both instances understood as *effet utile*). On the concept of effectiveness in this decision cf. Reich, 'The Principle of Effectiveness', above n. 3, at 61–2.

[71] Further on the role of effective judicial protection, in particular of Article 47 CFR, in the *Partner* decision see also Cafaggi, Law, above n. 25, at 22–6 and Cafaggi, Iamiceli, above n. 2, at 582.

pretive challenge posed by the concept of effectiveness for judicial dialogue. Moreover, if Article 47(1) CFREU continues to grow in practical importance, conflicts similar to the one in *Partner* may become increasingly widespread throughout consumer law.

5. EFFECTIVENESS IN MOTION: A BLURRED MAP FOR DOMESTIC COURTS?

Quite paradoxically, although effectiveness is a core concept of EU consumer law, it remains substantially unclear and is far from conceptual stability. The understanding and internal composition of this principle depends directly on development of the CJEU case law, which remains in constant motion and – especially over the last decade – has been adopting quite incoherent approaches. This unclarity provides a substantial challenge for domestic courts, which in the EU judicial composition are the final addressees of the concepts developed by the Court of Justice. In many instances implementation of the CJEU decisions requires domestic judges not only to understand the exact conclusion of the judgment, but also its underlying values and policy framework, which in most instances is directly determined by the notion of effectiveness. Only in this way it is possible to adjust domestic law in a EU-consistent way, by curtailing the non-conforming elements and by creating new rules wherever necessary.

The lack of clarity of the notion of effectiveness renders this task somewhat arduous. Domestic courts not only need to untangle the concept of effectiveness applied by the CJEU in the particular judgment (or in the particular line of decisions, if the judgment at stake follows one). They are also confronted with a task of understanding how the deciphered 'version' of effectiveness relates with the domestic law. This entails especially a need to determine whether and to what extent the effectiveness principle calls for an active attitude of a domestic court – i.e. either for disapplication of the certain rule or for creative reasoning (either by applying analogous reasoning or by devising new instruments from scratch).

Over time, however, the lack of conceptual clarity of effectiveness in EU consumer law continues to grow, especially due to the increasing relevance of the effective judicial protection notion (understood as a principle and a fundamental right[72]). In this way, the accents within the notion of effectiveness are gradually shifted from the substantive towards procedural understanding and from the rights towards remedies and their enforcement. This poses additional questions for domestic judges, by creating a plea to distinguish whether the

---

[72] See section 2.3.

particular issue should be addressed at the level of substantive or procedural solutions, or as a combination of both. Without a doubt, the CJEU notion of effectiveness does not always reflect the same lines of division between procedure and substance that pertain to a particular domestic system. As a consequence, domestic judges not only need to understand how the CJEU relates effectiveness and the particular issue of EU consumer law – but also to figure out how this relation can be translated onto the domestic structure of substantive and procedural rules. The growing eminence of effective judicial protection calls also for more precise understanding of the extent to which the components of effectiveness may be balanced against one another. The *Partner* decision opens a discussion whether balancing of values and policy goals can be perceived as an inherent feature of effectiveness under EU law.

Finally, the apparent incoherence in approaches towards effectiveness in the CJEU's consumer case law poses an imminent question to what extent the existing edifice may allow for further coordination.[73] It seems plausible that the escalating impact of effective judicial protection may act as a harmonizing factor and provide a common denominator for various dimensions of effectiveness. Even in such case, however, the very nature of effectiveness in EU consumer law – as a notion constantly reframed by the case law – renders full and definitive coherence rather implausible. For these reasons, blurriness is likely to remain a constant trait of effectiveness, being one of the principal challenges – but also one of the main drivers – of judicial dialogue.

[73] Further on possible unification of the concept of effectiveness Krommendijk, above n. 9, at 1415–17.

17. Comment: effectiveness in EU consumer law: towards new triads

Paola Iamiceli

1. THE MULTIPLE 'SHADES' OF EFFECTIVENESS

Exploring the complexity of effectiveness in the realm of EU consumer law represents a true challenge, as shown by the intense debate flourishing among international scholars.[1] The bottom-up definition process of the principle of effectiveness, first developed within the case law of the Court of Justice, finds parallel routes in national legal traditions, where effectiveness has gained growing attention by Supreme Courts even where the principle has not been specifically codified in national constitutions and fundamental laws.[2] EU primary law itself (namely, art. 19 Treaty on European Union (TEU) and art. 47 EU Charter of Fundamental Rights (CFR)) reflects the notion of effectiveness as a judge-made principle, developed by the Court of Justice in the framework of common constitutional traditions to the Member States.[3]

Moving from this perspective, Chapter 16 by M. Grochowski and M. Taborowski explores the multiple dimensions of effectiveness in EU law and consumer law in particular. Three dimensions (three 'shades', in the authors'

[1] Takis Tridimas, *The General Principles of EU Law* (OUP, Oxford 2006) 419; Norbert Reich, *General Principles of EU Civil Law* (Intersentia, Cambridge 2014) 89 ff.; Arthur Hartkamp, *European Law and National Private Law* (Intersentia, Cambridge 2016) 100; Chantal Mak, 'Rights and Remedies: Article 47 EUCFR and Effective Judicial Protection in European Private Law Matters', in Hans-Wolfgang Micklitz (ed.), *Constitutionalization of European Private Law* (OUP, Oxford 2014) 236; Fabrizio Cafaggi, 'Towards Collaborative Governance of European Remedial and Procedural Law?' [2018] TIL 235; Emanuela Navarretta, *Costituzione, Europa e diritto privato: Effettività e Drittwirkung ripensando la complessità giuridica* (Giappichelli, Torino 2017).

[2] Examples of constitutional norms interpreted by national courts as incorporating the right to access courts and the principle of effective judicial protection are art. 24, It. Const.; art. 24, Spanish Const.; art. 19(4), German Fundamental Law.

[3] CJEU Case C-64/16 *Associação Sindical dos Juízes Portugueses*, ECLI:EU:C:2018:117 para 35.

language) are presented: (i) the one linking effectiveness and *effet utile*, which looks at the effectiveness of EU law (effectiveness of norms), as targeted through Member States' cooperation in pursuing the objectives of EU policies under art. 4(3) TEU; (ii) the one presenting effectiveness as a limitation for national procedural autonomy, therefore coupled with the principle of equivalence within the so-called *Rewe/Comet* formula[4] but also somehow connected with the triadic standard applied to (penalties and) remedies in EU secondary legislation;[5] and (iii) the one reflected in art. 47 CFR, as the legal basis for the right to an effective remedy and a fair trial. While distinguishing the three dimensions and tracing them in consumer case law, the authors themselves acknowledge that, especially in case law, boundaries are rather blurred so that shades overlap and pervade each other.

The interconnection among the multiple dimensions of effectiveness explains how, in most cases, the one approach supports the other. Then, for example, both the principle of effectiveness (intended as a ban against procedural rules making rights' protection impossible or excessively difficult, under (ii) above) and the right to effective access to justice, effective remedies and a fair trial (under (iii)) contribute to the *effet utile* of EU legislation (as a first 'shade', under (i)); indeed, the latter is often used as a reinforcing basis for the application of the former ones. Likewise, the mainly 'negative' approach, underlying the '*Rewe/Comet* formula' pertaining to the principle of effectiveness (under (ii)), is sometimes complemented by a more proactive approach by the Court, affirmatively calling for adequate remedies or procedures (e.g., interim measures and procedures thereof) in order to comply with the principle of effective judicial protection (the third 'shade').[6]

---

[4] CJEU Case C-33/76 *Rewe*, ECLI:EU:C:1976:188; CJEU Case C-45/76 *Comet*, ECLI:EU:C:1976:191.

[5] Fabrizio Cafaggi and Paola Iamiceli, 'The Principles of Effectiveness, Proportionality and Dissuasiveness in the Enforcement of EU Consumer Law: The Impact of a Triad on the Choice of Civil Remedies and Administrative Sanctions' [2017] ERPL 575; Charlotte Pavillon, 'Private Enforcement as a Deterrence Tool: A Blind Spot in the Omnibus-Directive' [2019] ERPL 1297.

[6] See Norbert Reich, *General Principles of EU Civil Law*, 97; Fabrizio Cafaggi, 'On the Transformations of European Consumer Enforcement Law: Judicial and Administrative Trialogues, Instruments and Effects', in Fabrizio Cafaggi and Stephanie Law (eds), *Judicial Cooperation in European Private Law* (Edward Elgar, Cheltenham, UK and Northampton, MA 2017) 223.

2. THE INTERPLAY BETWEEN EFFECTIVENESS AND PROPORTIONALITY

More critical is the issue on whether the multiple dimensions of effectiveness may oppose or contradict each other. Interestingly, in the authors' perspective, this seems to relate to cases in which the principle of effective judicial protection and art. 47 CFR have been applied with the latter (rather than the former) aimed at balancing the interests of counterparties. In this perspective, art. 47 CFR, rather than the principle of effectiveness, would then call for the contextual application of the principle of proportionality.

Definitively, the wider content of art. 47 CFR, expressly combining the right to access to effective remedies and the fair trial principle, more clearly links effectiveness and procedural fairness, so calling for a balancing among the different interests at stake, including those of the opponent.[7] Moreover, the Charter's recognition of the right to access to justice as a fundamental right leads to the application of the principle of proportionality under art. 52 CFR, being limitations to fundamental rights subject to such scrutiny under the Charter.[8] At the same time, however, a similar balancing has already been engaged by the Court when applying the principle of effectiveness and the *Rewe/Comet* formula, then showing additional continuity among the multiple dimensions of effectiveness more than opposition.[9]

The link between effectiveness and proportionality deserves indeed special attention. In some cases, the Court has applied the principle of proportionality to reinforce the effects of the principle of effectiveness, calling for (more) effective remedies when affected rights are particularly relevant or the consequences of infringement very severe. In other cases, proportionality is aimed at scaling down the effect of remedies or the use of procedures in order to

---

[7] The concept of procedural fairness encapsulated in art. 47 CFR may be linked, under art. 52(3) CFR, with the interpretation provided by the European Court of Human Rights as regards art. 6 European Convention on Human Rights, the latter 'intended above all to secure the interests of the parties and those of the proper administration of justice' (*Nideröst-Huber v. Switzerland*, Application no. 18990/91, 18 February 1997, § 30).

[8] Takis Tridimas, *The General Principles of EU Law*, 137; Norbert Reich, 'How Proportionate is the Proportionality Principle? Some Critical Remarks on the Use and Methodology of the Proportionality Principle in the Internal Market Case Law of the ECJ', in Hans-Wolfgang Micklitz and Bruno De Witte (eds), *The European Court of Justice and the Autonomy of the Member States* (Intersentia, Cambridge 2012) 81.

[9] CJEU Joined Cases C-317/08 to C-320/08 *Alassini*, ECLI:EU:C:2010:146 para 65.

protect counter-interests affected by such use.[10] Yet, no contradiction emerges between effectiveness and proportionality; rather, the latter complements the former. Indeed, the right to effective judicial protection does not call for the highest protection possible; being not an absolute right, proportionality is among the criteria to define contents and measure of effective remedies or procedures. Although secondary legislation tends to associate proportionality with sanctions (penalties) only, in fact the Court applies the principle of proportionality to procedures, sanctions *and* remedies. Exactly as occurs for effectiveness, the principle of proportionality plays a specific role in the area of sanctions and remedies, influencing both their choice and their grading.[11]

3. THE 'SHADES' OF EFFECTIVENESS AND THE ROLE OF DISSUASIVENESS: TOWARDS NEW TRIADS

When referred to measures adopted by Member States to address infringements of EU law, effectiveness and proportionality have been considered as part of a triad, including dissuasiveness as a third pillar. Indeed, according to EU (consumer) law, those measures shall be effective, proportionate and dissuasive. As occurs for effectiveness and proportionality, not only sanctions must be dissuasive but also remedies not having a major punitive function.[12]

The link between dissuasiveness and effectiveness can be observed having special regard to the *effet utile* dimension. Deterrence of infringements of EU law definitively improves its effectiveness and the attainment of objectives pursued by EU policy endorsed by legislation. Too lenient a measure fails to dissuade potential infringers. The same applies to incentives provided to the victims, having a remedy against the infringer: the more burdensome it is to access justice and enforce one's rights, the lower the impact on the infringer and therefore the deterring effects of enforcement measures.[13]

If dissuasiveness tends to be positively correlated with the *effet utile* dimension of effectiveness, not always does this occur with regard to effective

---

[10] Fabrizio Cafaggi (principal author), *Re-Jus Casebook on Effective Justice in Consumer Protection* (2018), accessed 28 October 2021 at https://www.rejus.eu/content/materials.

[11] Cafaggi and Iamiceli, 'The Principles of Effectiveness, Proportionality and Dissuasiveness'; F. Cafaggi, 'Rimedi e sanzioni nella tutela del consumatore: l'attuazione del New Deal', in P. Iamiceli (ed.), *Effettività delle tutele e diritto europeo* (Editoriale Scientifica, Napoli 2020) 295 ff.

[12] Cafaggi and Iamiceli, 'The Principles of Effectiveness, Proportionality and Dissuasiveness'; Pavillon, 'Private Enforcement as a Deterrence Tool'.

[13] CJEU Case C-618/10 *Banco Español de Crédito SA v Joaquín Calderón Camino* ECLI:EU:C:2012:349 paras 54 and 69.

judicial protection. Moving from this perspective, the two 'shades' of effectiveness seem indeed to expand into different directions.

The case of nullity of unfair terms provides a clear example. Though with some variations,[14] the Court of Justice is quite strict in establishing that, once the unfair term is set aside, unless the *lacuna* prevents the contract from having force and this harms the consumer, the judge may not replace or moderate the term, not even by means of application of suppletive norms, that would be applicable if parties had not adopted any term on the matter addressed by the norm.[15] The rule is intended as an application of the dissuasiveness criterion, since the infringer would not be adequately deterred from violation if he/she could rely on the subsequent judicial intervention securing at least the benefit provided by the suppletive norm. Being normally applied to cases in which the unfair term regulates the consequences of consumer's breach, the ban against judicial integration plays as a penalty for the professional, who is then substantially deprived of relief against consumer's breach, including, e.g. a fair penalty or damages.[16] If strictly applied, this approach does not only provide effective redress by placing the consumer in the position in which he/she would have been if the term was not adopted; in fact, it vests him/her with a premium corresponding to the penalty imposed on the professional. Even setting aside the question of proportionality, the ban against judicial integration could well contribute to the effectiveness of the Unfair Terms Directive, going, however, beyond what would be requested in terms of effective judicial protection. Somehow, efficiency (i.e. the aptness of effective enforcement of EU law to enable a proper and efficient functioning of the internal market) seems to prevail over an equitable balancing between the individual interests at stake. Consequently, a stronger bond between dissuasiveness and *effet utile* is established, while departing from a more balanced application of the principle of effective judicial protection.

Interestingly, in the same stream of consumer case law but in other respects, the Court seems to favour effective consumer protection over *effet utile*: when it concludes that the judge should vest the consumer with an option not only to consider the unfair term as binding, but also to oppose the 'contract rescue' enabled by default national rules in cases in which the unfair term is essential and its nullity prevents the contract to remain in existence.[17] This is concluded due to the consumer's preferences and not because total nullity rather than

[14] See a recent *revirement* in CJEU Case C-224/19 *Caixabank* ECLI:EU:C:2020:578.

[15] CJEU Case C-618/10 *Banco Español* Cases C-96/16 and C-94/17, *Banco Santander SA* ECLI:EU:C:2018:643 Case C-260/18, *Dziubak* ECLI:EU:C:2019:819.

[16] CJEU Cases C-349/18 to C 351/18 *Kanyeba et al* ECLI:EU:C:2019:936.

[17] CJEU Case C-260/18 *Dziubak*, paras 55–56.

partial would be a more effective remedy for its impact on the market and for the attainment of the directive's goals.[18] Here, effective judicial protection prevails over *effet utile*.

The research on the multiple sides of effectiveness is far from being exhausted. Future analysis could shed more light on the prism, if the interplay between effectiveness, on the one hand, and proportionality and dissuasiveness, on the other, was taken into account, the former being probably closer to the multiple facets of art. 47 CFR, the latter to those of *effet utile*.

---

[18] Indeed, in many cases the Court of Justice has concluded that the directive is not aimed at discarding from the market all contracts including unfair terms but only banning the use of the latter (CJEU Case C-453/10 *Jana Pereničová* ECLI:EU:C:2012:144).

18. Judicial interactions upholding the right to be heard of asylum seekers, returnees and immigrants: the symbiotic protection of the EU Charter and general principles of EU law

Madalina Moraru and Marc Clement

I. INTRODUCTION: TO HEAR OR NOT TO HEAR?

Asylum seekers, returnees and other third-country nationals subject to immigration procedures have faced increasing challenges in accessing effective individual hearing procedures before administrative authorities and courts across the EU, particularly after the so-called refugee crisis and the arrival in government of populist parties in several Member States.[1] In this political context, the use of fast-track procedures in both asylum and return procedures has become a key political priority aiming to tackle the high number of irregular entries into the EU and a high rate of rejected asylum applications.[2] In pursuit of this objective, governments across the EU have accelerated or reduced individual hearings in asylum and return proceedings by way of legal reforms and soft-law practices, such as: complete denials of hearings due to

[1] E. Enrione, 'Domestic Asylum Procedures between EU Law and Populist Parties' Agenda: A Growing Challenge to Asylum Seekers' Human Rights? The Cases of Italy, Sweden and the UK', Master's thesis 2019, University of Padova.

[2] The European Commission has referred to a high number of rejected asylum seekers. However, this number also includes administrative rejections that were reversed by courts on appeal. See the Commission Staff Working Document, Accompanying the Proposal for a Regulation of the European Parliament and of the Council on asylum and migration management and amending Council Directive (EC)2003/109 and the proposed Regulation SWD/2020/207 final, p 20.

an increasing use of push-backs at both sea and land borders;[3] eliminating administrative oral hearings based on loose evidence that asylum seekers are coming from safe third countries,[4] even for unaccompanied minors;[5] limiting the number of hearings by merging return-related hearings with asylum-related hearings;[6] eliminating the number of judicial hearings by cutting down the number of appeals;[7] and impairing judicial independence and impartiality by way of stripping courts of some of their judicial review and remedial powers,[8] and denying authority of judgments.[9]

The combined effect of these legal reforms and practices signals structural shortcomings in the conduct of both administrative and judicial hearings in asylum and other immigration proceedings across the Member States. In the words of Justice Nicol of the UK High Court, this trend of fast-track asylum and return proceedings showcases how governments sacrifice fairness 'on the altar of speed and convenience'.[10] Domestic judiciaries across the EU are therefore faced with complex technical questions regarding the conduct of both administrative and judicial hearings of asylum seekers and irregular migrants, such as when a third-country national should be heard regarding the administrative assessment of their right to stay in the EU (e.g. only in asylum proceedings or also separately in return proceedings); what questions the administration should address and whether the hearing should follow an adversarial model; whether, as a rule, courts should hear asylum seekers orally to remedy procedural irregularities in the conduct of administrative hearings or should they be satisfied with the evidence presented by the administration in the case file.

---

3 See EU Fundamental Rights Agency Annual Report 2020, pp 117–18.

4 In Germany, for instance, according to the facts in C-517/17 *Addis* ECLI:EU:C:2020:579. On Hungary, see C-924/19 PPU *FMS* ECLI:EU:C:2020:367.

5 See Administrative Court of the Republic of Slovenia, Judgment No. 2016 I U 645/2016 of 4 May 2016.

6 This domestic practice has increased following a 2017 recommendation by the European Commission. See Recommendation 12(a) of the European Commission of 7 March 2017 on making returns more effective when implementing Directive 2008/115/EC of the European Parliament and of the Council C(2017) 1600 final.

7 See, for instance, Italy, Law No. 46 of 13 April 2017, eliminating the one level of appeal before courts of appeal in certain circumstances.

8 For Hungary, see C-556/17 *Torubarov* ECLI:EU:C:2019:626; for Italy, see C-422/18 *FR* ECLI:EU:C:2018:784 and M. Eliantonio and C. Favilli, 'When Two Preliminary Questions Result in One and Half Answers: A "Constitutional Tragedy" in Four Acts' (2020) *European Papers*, 5(2): 911–30.

9 See *Torubarov*, cit.

10 *Detention Action v First-Tier Tribunal (Immigration and Asylum Chamber) & Ors* [2015] EWHC 1689 (Admin), para 42.

These technical questions on hearing duties also raise more general questions regarding the allocation of competences[11] and conflict resolution norms in the EU's multilayered human rights system. The complexity surrounding the right to be heard, as with several other EU fundamental rights,[12] lies in the fact that this right is protected by several different EU legal sources which are fully or partially overlapping in their scope of application and organised in a complex hierarchical relationship.[13] For instance, the right to be heard is part of three different general principles in EU law: good administration,[14] rights of defence[15] and effective judicial protection.[16] It is also part of three different fundamental rights conferred by the Charter of Fundamental Rights of the European Union (EU Charter): the right to good administration (Article 41(2)); the right to an effective remedy and fair trial (Article 47(2)); and the presumption of innocence and right of defence (Article 48(2)). In addition, specific guarantees are also conferred by EU secondary legislation regulating asylum and immigration law, such as the right to an individual administrative interview and the right to an effective remedy during asylum adjudication.[17]

Overall, the EU asylum and immigration law does not provide for a uniform right to be heard for asylum seekers and returnees across administrative and judicial proceedings. Instead the EU right to be heard is subject to a sliding regulatory scale, starting from: detailed guarantees of a mandatory, individual and oral hearing in the administrative phase of asylum adjudication;[18] no express right to an oral judicial hearing in the appeal phase of asylum adjudication, but, nevertheless, the conferral of a general right to an effective judicial remedy;[19]

---

[11] In particular, the vertical division of competences between the EU and the Member States in a field of shared competences, such as that of migration governance, according to Article 4(1) TFEU.

[12] See also the principle of non-discrimination, discussed in Chapter 14 by Rita Gião Hanek and Lilla Farkas in this edited volume.

[13] On the complexity of the general EU system of human rights, see B. de Witte, 'The European Union in the International System of Human Rights Protection: Solo Singer or Voice in the Choir?' in E. Bribosia and I. Rorive (eds), *Human Rights Tectonics: Global Perspectives on Integration and Fragmentation* (Cambridge, Intersentia 2018), pp 225–41.

[14] C-604/12 *H.N.* ECLI:EU:C:2014:302.

[15] C-17/74 *Transocean Marine Paint Association v Commission* ECLI:EU:C:1974:106; C-349/07 *Sopropé* ECLI:EU:C:2008:746.

[16] C-491/10 *Aguirre Zarraga* ECLI:EU:C:2010:828.

[17] See Article 14 and Article 46 of the Recast Asylum Procedure Directive 2013/32/EU of the European Parliament and of the Council of 26 June 2013 on common procedures for granting and withdrawing international protection OJ L 180, 29 June 2013, pp 60–95 ('Recast Asylum Procedure Directive').

[18] See Articles 14–16 of the Recast Asylum Procedure Directive.

[19] Article 46(5) of the Recast Asylum Procedure Directive.

no provision for a right to be heard in administrative return procedures, but only a right to appeal before a court or an administrative authority made up of members fulfilling the conditions of impartiality and independence;[20] no right to be heard by an administrative or judicial authority in visa application cases, but only for a general right to appeal.[21] Therefore, with the exception of the administrative phase of asylum adjudication, the EU legislation on asylum, return and visa proceedings leaves a wide margin of discretion to the Member States in the recognition and organisation of the right to be heard to asylum seekers, returnees and visa applicants. This regulatory framework signals that immigrants should have a right to be heard only once, during the administrative phase of asylum adjudication, whereas the subsequent phases in appeal and return proceedings do not require additional oral hearings. However, the practice of asylum and return adjudication has shown that additional hearings are often needed for various reasons, such as: to check the credibility of asylum seekers; fill in gaps in the administrative hearings; take into consideration new evidence related to the country of origin or the personal situation of the asylum seekers and his/her family or private life.

Faced with the challenges of normative clarification of the scope and effects of the EU fundamental right to be heard, domestic courts across the EU have resorted to transnational judicial interactions with foreign domestic courts, or to vertical judicial interaction with the Court of Justice of the European Union (CJEU) either, directly, on the basis of the preliminary reference procedure,[22] or indirectly on the basis of implementing preliminary rulings.[23] Sixteen preliminary rulings have, so far,[24] been referred from seven Member States with different migration governance systems in relation to the right to be heard in asylum and immigration cases.[25] In addition, we have collected 15 other

---

[20] Article 13 of the Return Directive (2008/115/EC).

[21] Article 32(3) of Regulation (EC) No 810/2009 of the European Parliament and of the Council of 13 July 2009 establishing a Community Code on Visas (OJ 2009 L 243, p 1), as amended by Regulation (EU) No 610/2013 of the European Parliament and of the Council of 26 June 2013 (OJ 2013 L 182, p 1).

[22] Article 267 TFEU.

[23] C-106/89 *Marleasing* ECLI:EU:C:1990:395.

[24] Up until the date of submission of the chapter, January 2021.

[25] On the right to be heard, see the CJEU cases: C-277/11 *M.M(1)* ECLI:EU:C:2012:744; C-560/14 *M.M.(2)* ECLI:EU:C:2017:101; C-249/13 *Boudjlida* ECLI:EU:C:2014:2431; C-166/13 *Mukarubega* ECLI:EU:C:2014:2336; C-383/13 *G&R* ECLI:EU:C:2013:533; C-348/16 *Sacko Moussa* ECLI:EU:C:2017:591; C-517/17 *Addis* ECLI:EU:C:2020:579 and C-670/16 *Mengesteab* ECLI:EU:C:2017:587. On remedies for violations of the right to be heard as part of wider access to justice rights, see: C-556/17 *Torubarov* ECLI:EU:C:2019:626; C-403/16 *El Hassani* ECLI:EU:C:2017:960; C-146/14 *Mahdi* ECLI:EU:C:2014:1320; C-585/16 *Alheto* ECLI:EU:C:2018:584; C-924/19 *FMS* ECLI:EU:C:2020:367; C-225/19 *R.N.N.S.* ECLI:EU:C:2020:951;

domestic judgments relying on preliminary rulings originating from foreign jurisdictions or judgments by foreign courts for the purpose of identifying the scope and effects of the right to be heard.[26] This extensive use of judicial interactions on the right to be heard in asylum and immigration proceedings can be explained by the salient role played by this right in asylum and migration cases. The right to be heard enables the competent authorities to establish the existence of a risk of refoulement. European and domestic case law has consistently shown that risks of refoulement remain unidentified, in the absence of an effective individual hearing, thus triggering the legal responsibility of states for violations of the principles of *non-refoulement* and the prohibition of ill treatment.[27]

The objective of this chapter is to analyse the role that the EU Charter has played with regard to asylum-, return- and visa-related hearing procedures and how judicial interactions have contributed to clarifying the boundaries and effects of the right to be heard as laid down in the EU Charter provisions. For this purpose, the chapter will analyse how several types of judicial interactions have helped domestic courts in, first, identifying which of the various EU legal sources of the right to be heard are applicable to asylum seekers, returnees and visa applicants at the domestic level (section II). It continues by investigating how judicial interactions have contributed to the development of concrete standards for the conduct of administrative hearings (section III). The chapter proceeds with an analysis of how judicial interactions have empowered domestic courts to shape new remedies for violation of the right to be heard outside the confines of EU secondary legislation and domestic procedural law directly on the basis of the general EU law principle of rights of defence and Article 47(2) EU Charter (section IV). The chapter concludes by finding that judicial interactions have helped national courts to achieve several objectives: to clarify the maze of multilayered EU and domestic legal norms regulating the right to be heard; to solve conflicts of interpretation between courts or

---

C-82/16 *K.A. and Others* ECLI:EU:C:2018:308; C-680/17 *Vethanayagam and Others* ECLI:EU:C:2019:627. The period selected is from the entry into force of the EU Charter until 31 January 2021. All these preliminary rulings are assessed in this chapter.

26 We have selected these judgments from approximately 30 judgments sent by 20 national judges and five national lawyers as part of the eNACT and ACTIONES projects. These 30 judgments originate from Austria, Belgium, Bulgaria, France, Greece, Ireland, Italy, Lithuania, the Netherlands, Poland and Romania. See the Centre for Judicial Cooperation database at https://cjc.eui.eu/data/data?fold=6&subfold=6.4 (last accessed January 2021).

27 For a list of this case law see M. Moraru, *e-NACT Handbook on the Application of the EU Charter in the Field of Asylum and Immigration* (Centre for Judicial Cooperation 2019), available at https://cjc.eui.eu/wp-content/uploads/2020/05/eNACT_Handbook_asylum-compresso.pdf (last accessed January 2021).

between various state powers; and to influence change of domestic policies, legislation or established judicial approaches that were not in line with EU law. Nevertheless, judicial interactions have so far not settled all the political and judicial conflicts that initially triggered the engagement of domestic courts in judicial interaction.[28]

By identifying the various judicial interactions, their objectives and outcomes on the right of asylum seekers, returnees and visa applicants to be heard, this chapter will contribute to the literature on judicial studies and fundamental rights. The case law on the right to be heard in asylum and immigration raises several politically sensitive issues regarding the separation of powers between the EU and Member States and between various branches of state power. It is therefore a fertile ground to test various theories on why domestic courts engage in judicial interactions, such as judicial empowerment,[29] inter-court competition,[30] clarification of CJEU judgments,[31] bureaucratic politics, loyalty to domestic interests (siding with domestic policies)[32] and personal and institutional reasons.[33] The chapter finds that many of these legal and non-legal explanations of judicial interactions are also present in the case law on the EU fundamental right to be heard in asylum and immigration proceedings. The chapter therefore provides a sobering analysis of how domestic courts ensure fundamental rights, be they enshrined in the EU Charter or general principles of EU law, and the political challenges courts face in promoting the rule of law in the age of migration framed as a security issue.[34]

---

28 The most salient example is the follow-up to the *Sacko Moussa* preliminary ruling in Italy. For more insights, see Chapter 19 by M. Flamini in this edited volume.

29 J.H.H. Weiler, 'The Transformation of Europe' (1991) *The Yale Law Journal*, 100: 2403–83.

30 K.J. Alter, 'Explaining National Courts' Acceptance of European Court Jurisprudence: A Critical Evaluation of Theories of Legal Integration' in A.-M. Slau ghter, A.S. Sweet and J.H.H. Weiler (eds), *The European Court and National Courts: Doctrine and Jurisprudence* (Hart, UK 1998), pp 227–52.

31 M. Eliantonio and C. Favilli (n 8).

32 G. Tridimas and T. Tridimas, 'National Courts and the European Court of Justice: A Public Choice Analysis of the Preliminary Reference Procedure' (2004) *International Review of Law and Economics*, 24(2): 125–45.

33 J. Krommendijk, 'It Takes Two to Tango: An Introduction' Special Issue of the (2020) *European Papers*, 5(2): 745–54.

34 M.J. Guia, M. van der Woude and J. van der Leun, *Social Control and Justice: Crimmigration in the Age of Fear* (Eleven International Publishing, US 2013).

II. NAVIGATING THE WEB OF EU FUNDAMENTAL RIGHTS SOURCES: THE COMPLEMENTARY PROTECTION OF THE EU CHARTER AND GENERAL PRINCIPLES OF EU LAW ON THE RIGHT TO BE HEARD

The entry into force of the EU Charter has been argued to have had a 'centralising effect' on the application of EU human rights,[35] meaning that the EU Charter has replaced the various scattered sources of EU human rights (e.g. general principles of EU law, European Convention on Human Rights (ECHR)) with one single legal source. The Charter contains some provisions specifically related to the protection of asylum seekers and irregular migrants, notably Article 18 (right to asylum) and Article 19 (protection in the event of removal, expulsion or extradition),[36] but it also contains procedural rights applicable to all individuals falling under the scope of EU law, including the right to be heard enshrined in Articles 41(2) and 47(2). Following the entry into force of the Charter, the CJEU and national courts were faced with the question of whether these provisions replaced the right to be heard safeguards scattered among three different general principles of EU law: good administration; rights of defence; and effective judicial protection.[37] Moreover, courts had to establish whether the boundaries and effects of the right to be heard of asylum seekers and irregular migrants had changed in domestic proceedings following the entry into force of the Charter.

Compared to the CJEU, national courts have an even more complicated task as they are bound by multiple legal loyalties, all of which are equally important, when implementing an EU human right.[38] Therefore, in giving priority to the EU fundamental right to be heard, domestic courts had to concomitantly ensure compliance with the right to be heard as part of the right to an effective legal remedy protected under Article 13 ECHR, which is jointly applicable with Article 3 ECHR (prohibition of ill treatment) and compliance with con-

---

[35] A. Torres Pérez, 'The Federalizing Force of the EU Charter of Fundamental Rights' (2017) *International Journal of Constitutional Law*, 15(4): 1080–97.

[36] For an exhaustive analysis of the application of Charter provisions to asylum and immigration, see M. Moraru, *eNACT Handbook*, n 27.

[37] See notes 16–18; and Herwig C.H. Hofmann and Bucura C. Mihaescu, 'The Relation between the Charter's Fundamental Rights and the Unwritten General Principles of EU Law: Good Administration as the Test Case' (2013) *European Constitutional Law Review*, 9(1): 73–101.

[38] G. Martinico, 'Multiple Loyalties and Dual Preliminarity: The Pains of Being a Judge in a Multilevel Legal Order' (2012) *International Journal of Constitutional Law*, 10(3): 871–97.

stitutional provisions.[39] Given that the right to be heard can be limited under certain circumstances,[40] domestic courts also had to balance national migration policies, some of which were democratically endorsed by the national parliaments,[41] with the protection of the EU fundamental right to be heard and the rule of law. This last issue is perhaps the most difficult, as the EU legislature left the task of establishing their procedural rules on the organisation of hearings in asylum-, return- and visa-related procedures to the Member States, setting out only a few general guarantees in EU secondary legislation.[42]

A Europe-wide judicial interaction (as shown in Figure 18.1) started in 2011 on the initiative of the Irish High Court and spread across various domestic migration governance regimes and judicial systems (e.g. France, Belgium, Italy, Lithuania and Bulgaria) with the purpose of clarifying the legal source of the EU fundamental right to be heard, its relation with EU secondary instruments and their implications in terms of fundamental rights protection at the domestic level.[43]

Horizontal judicial interaction played a key role in triggering the first request for a preliminary ruling on the right to be heard in international protection proceedings. The Irish High Court asked the CJEU to settle what appeared to be a divergent judicial interpretation of the right to be heard between Irish and Dutch courts regarding the extent to which public authorities have to disclose their intentions and evidence to asylum seekers before rejecting their asylum claims.[44]

---

39 Several constitutions provide for a right to asylum. See M. Moraru, 'A Decade of the EU Fundamental Right to Asylum: In Search of its Legal Meaning and Effects' in S. Iglesias Sanchez and M. Pascual (eds), *Fundamental Rights in the EU Area of Freedom, Security and Justice* (CUP, UK 2021) pp 139–58.

40 See Article 51(1) of the EU Charter and Articles 13 and 15 ECHR.

41 See V. Federico, M. Moraru and P. Pannia, 'Migrants and the Law: What European Courts Say on Migrants' Rights – Patterns and Variables' in Special Issue of the *European Journal of Legal Studies* (2022, forthcoming).

42 In particular, see Articles 14–18 and 46 of the Recast Asylum Procedure Directive; Article 27 of the Dublin III Regulation (Regulation (EU) No 604/2013 establishing the criteria and mechanisms for determining the Member State responsible for examining an application for international protection lodged in one of the Member States by a third-country national or a stateless person); Article 13 of the Return Directive; and Article 32 of the Visa Code.

43 This diagram offers a sample of cases involving the use of various judicial interactions among courts of different legal orders and legal hierarchy. It is based on the cases submitted by judges in the ACTIONES and eNACT projects and it is not exhaustive.

44 The Dutch Council of State had a different interpretation. It required the competent authority to inform the asylum seeker of its intention to reject the application and of the reasons for the rejection, thus giving the asylum seeker an opportunity to make

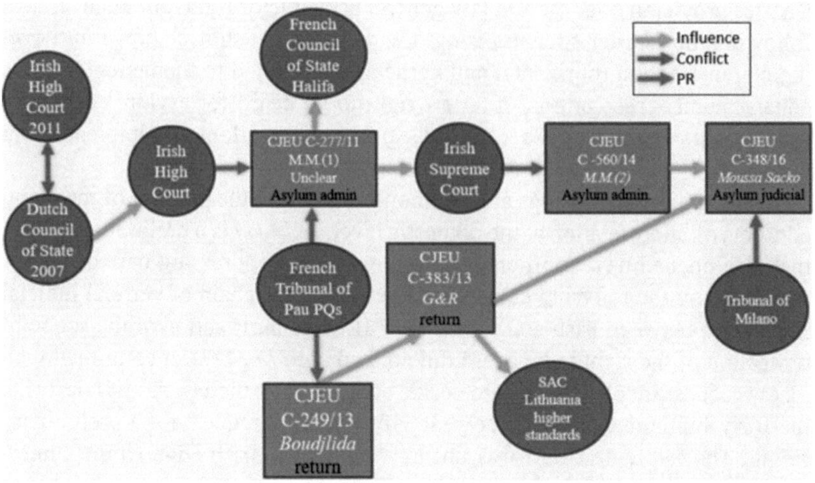

Figure 18.1 Multidimensional judicial interaction on the right to be heard

The CJEU's reply to the High Court was broader than the questions addressed by the referring court.[45] It started by considering whether in the case of a dual international protection system, such as that in Ireland,[46] asylum seekers' right to be heard must be respected both during the examination of the refugee status and subsequently before a decision on the subsidiary protection claim is adopted, although such a right was not required under the then Qualification Directive[47] and neither under the implementing Irish law. The Court held that it was necessary for the applicant to be heard both during the assessment of refugee status recognition and again for the purpose of considering his application for subsidiary protection. The Court held that the previous hearing for the purpose of refugee status determination was insufficient to fulfil the requirement of the EU fundamental right to be heard[48] as protected by Article 41(2) EU Charter. In this first preliminary ruling on the right of asylum seekers

---

his views known in writing within a prescribed period. C-277/11 *M.M. v Minister for Justice, Equality and Law Reform, Ireland* ECLI:EU:C:2012:744, para 55 ('*M.M.(1)*').

45 See J. Krommendijk (n 33).

46 Which was different from the Dutch system, which had inspired the Irish referral for preliminary questions.

47 Qualification Directive (Council Directive 2004/83/EC on minimum standards for the qualification and status of third-country nationals or stateless persons as refugees or as persons who otherwise need international protection and the content of the protection granted (OJ 2004 L 304, p 12)).

48 See *M.M.(1)*, para 90.

to be heard by public authorities, the CJEU recognised the primacy of the EU Charter provision over the EU law general principle of rights of defence, thus following the Charter's 'centralising' trend. Second, it showed how multilevel judicial interaction (horizontal and vertical) contributed to fundamental rights enhancement – recognition of a new right to be heard for asylum seekers in the absence of express EU secondary legislation[49] and domestic implementing law.

While preliminary rulings are commonly sought for the purpose of resolving conflicts of interpretation at the domestic level, *M.M.(1)* is a preliminary ruling that also opened new conflicts of interpretation by addressing new questions not raised by the referring court. For this reason, the chain of vertical judicial interaction between Irish courts and the CJEU on clarification of the scope of protection of the right to be heard did not end with *M.M.(1)*. It continued with a new request involving the same case, addressed by the last resort court (i.e. the Irish Supreme Court)[50] three years after the first request for a preliminary ruling. The Supreme Court was unsure whether the Irish High Court's interpretation of the *M.M.(1)* preliminary ruling was correct since it had deduced a new right of asylum seekers to an oral hearing before the administration adopts a decision on their claims for subsidiary protection, although the right to an oral hearing was not expressly mentioned by the CJEU but only the more general right to be heard.[51]

In *M.M.(2)*, the CJEU discarded the High Court's interpretation of the right to be heard as implying a right to an oral hearing. Nevertheless, the Court reconfirmed the obligation to ensure the right of asylum seekers to be heard in the procedure assessing the subsidiary protection claim separately from the refugee status procedure. This could take the form of written observations or an oral hearing. Although the CJEU took a step back on the protection of the right to be heard compared to *M.M.(1)* due to its limited competence over the organisation of domestic hearing procedures, the chain of judicial interaction triggered a significant domestic policy change. The Irish legislator decided to change its two-step procedure for the assessment of international protection claims into a single-step approach, which was the common practice among the Member States. Judicial interaction was perhaps only one of the factors contributing to this domestic policy change, alongside the procedural efficiency of the single-step procedure for assessing international protection claims. The single-step procedure would ease the government's procedural work as it

---

[49] Namely the Qualification Directive.

[50] C-560/14 *M v Minister for Justice and Equality* ECLI:EU:C:2017:101 ('*M.M.(2)*').

[51] This can take various forms, among others that of an oral hearing.

would no longer be required to organise two separate hearings, irrespective of the form chosen, but only one hearing to assess both refugee and subsidiary protection status.[52]

The *M.M.(1)* preliminary ruling represented a turning point for the recognition of a new right to be heard in asylum proceedings beyond the Irish frontiers. It triggered a snowball effect across jurisdictions which used different hearing models to the Irish one. For instance, some of the first-instance French courts referred to the *M.M.(1)* preliminary ruling in an attempt to influence a change in the interpretation of the right of returnees to be heard by hierarchically superior administrative courts (see Figure 18.1).[53] According to these courts, the Prefecture would as a norm be required to hear a third-country national not only regarding the refusal of a residence permit but also in terms of the return decision.[54] The courts deduced this obligation from the preliminary ruling in *M.M.(1)*, even though this ruling did not deal with return proceedings but with the unique Irish two-step international protection system. The citation of the *M.M.(1)* preliminary ruling did not convince the hierarchically superior administrative courts to endorse a broader scope of the right to be heard in French return proceedings.[55] This led the Melun Tribunal to leapfrog the domestic

---

[52] Starting from the end of 2016, the Irish International Protection Act replaced the dual system with a single procedure for assessing asylum and subsidiary protection claims in parallel. For more, see M. Moraru, 'ReJus Casebook Effective Justice in Asylum and Immigration' (2018), pp 60–70, available online at https://www.rejus.eu/sites/default/files/content/materials/rejus_casebook_effective_justice_in_asylum_and_immigration.pdf (last accessed January 2021).

[53] Such as courts of appeal and the French Council of State. Courts of appeal recognised a certain margin of discretion to national (administrative and judicial) authorities to decide on a case-by-case basis whether to hear or not third-country nationals in return-related cases (see M. Clement, 'Droit d'être entendu, droit de la défense et obligation de quitter le territoire: à propos de l'arrêt CAA Lyon du 14 mars 2013', ELSJ, 29 April 2013). From 1991, the Council of State followed a restrictive interpretation of rights of defence in immigration proceedings which excluded the application of EU general principles of law to expulsion cases and exempted the administration from a prior adversary procedure in immigration cases. See Council of State, *Préfet de Police v Demir*, no 120435, 19 April 1991; CE, *Hammou*, no 306821–30682, 19 October 2007; *Barjamaj*, no 307999, 28 November 2007; *Silidor*, no 315441, 26 November 2008.

[54] B. Jeannot, 'Le droit d'être entendu: une application décevante en droit des étrangers', La lettre du SAF, Octobre 2015.

[55] The French administrative courts of appeal had not considered it useful to submit a preliminary question following the judgment of the Lyon Administrative Court of 14 March 2013 (see CAA Lyon, 14 March 2013; *M. Halifa*, no 12LY02704, CAA Lyon, 14 March 2013; *Préfet de l'Ain c/M. Bepede Guehoada*, no 12LY02737–12LY02739, CAA Nancy, 16 May 2013, no 12NC01805, CAA Marseille, 8 June 2013, no 12MA04450).

judicial hierarchy and resort directly to the CJEU to obtain confirmation of its interpretation of the EU fundamental right to be heard. Article 267 Treaty on the Functioning of the European Union (TFEU) may thus provide domestic courts with opportunities to circumvent the hierarchy of domestic courts as *every* court in the EU may refer questions to the CJEU.

Although well argued, the reasoning provided by the referring court in *Mukarubega*[56] did not convince the CJEU to endorse its rights-oriented approach. Instead, the CJEU's interpretation of the right to be heard represents a middle ground between the opposing judicial views that had divided the French administrative judiciary. Due to its limited competence over national procedural issues, the CJEU held that, although in principle a third-country national should be heard before any individual measure is taken that adversely affects him/her,[57] where national authorities have exercised their margin of discretion allowed by the Return Directive in its Article 6(6) to simultaneously adopt a decision determining a stay to be illegal and a return decision (as was the case of France) then 'those authorities need not necessarily hear the person concerned specifically on the return decision'.[58] Nevertheless, the CJEU established clear requirements that national administrations must meet before they decide to skip a second hearing, namely that the 'person had the opportunity to effectively present his or her point of view on the question of whether the stay was illegal, and whether there were grounds which could, under national law, entitle those authorities to refrain from adopting a return decision',[59] either because of errors in assessment or because of new evidence.[60] As long as public authorities complied with the substantive content of the right to be heard, its procedural design – whether in the shape of one or multiple hearings – was left to the Member States to decide, just as the Return Directive had envisaged.

Regarding the institutional effects of the preliminary rulings, the *Mukarubega* case represents a partial success of the referring court to impose its interpretation over hierarchically superior courts. The CJEU preliminary ruling invalidated the French Council of State's restrictive interpretation.[61] Instead, the approach of the majoritarian courts of appeal in which the necessity of a second administrative hearing is to be established on a case-by-case

---

[56] Case C-166/13 *Mukarubega* ECLI:EU:C:2014:2336.

[57] Case C-349/07 *Sopropé* ECLI:EU:C:2008:746, para 49; *Mukarubega*, paras 46–48.

[58] See *Boudjlida*, para 54; *Mukarubega*, para 60.

[59] Ibid.

[60] *Boudjlida*, para 37.

[61] That is of automatic refusal of an administrative hearing before the adoption of a return decision. For more, see n 53.

basis was legitimised over the expansive interpretation of the right to be heard proposed by the referring court.

Domestic courts in Belgium,[62] Greece,[63] Lithuania[64] and the Netherlands[65] have subsequently used the French-originating preliminary rulings to require, as a rule, an administrative hearing in relation to each of the return-related decisions the administration adopts, regardless of whether the domestic return procedure is combined with or separate from asylum adjudication. The citation of preliminary rulings by domestic courts helped to increase the chances of government compliance with their interpretation of the right to be heard. For instance, in Belgium the Aliens Office began to send formal letters to invite foreign nationals to express their views before withdrawing their right to stay.[66]

Regarding the relation between the EU Charter and general principles of EU law as overlapping sources of the protection of the right to be heard, the judicial interactions analysed reveal a first phase of Charter centrism followed by a change to the general principle of rights of defence. In the 2012 *M.M.(1)* judgment, on the basis of Article 41(2) EU Charter the CJEU required the Member States to ensure that the 'right [to be heard] must apply in all proceedings which are liable to culminate in a measure adversely affecting a person'.[67] Furthermore, observance of the right to be heard is required even where the applicable EU secondary legislation does not expressly provide for such a procedural requirement, as was the case of the Qualification and Asylum Procedure Directives. It was in the next preliminary ruling delivered in 2013 following a reference sent by the Dutch Council of State that the CJEU found that Article 41(2) only applies to EU institutions, bodies and agencies.[68]

In spite of opposition by several Advocates General,[69] the CJEU has kept the general principle of rights of defence as the correct legal source for the right of

---

[62] Belgian Council of Alien Law Litigation (CALL), case No. 126.219, judgment of 25 June 2014 and later case No. 230.293, judgment of 24 February 2015; CALL, case No. 230.293, judgment of 24 February 2015; case No. 233.257, judgment of 15 December 2015. These cases are summarised in the REDIAL database, available at euredial.eu (last accessed June 2020).

[63] See, for instance, Thessaloniki Administrative Court, case No.717/2015.

[64] See I. Jarukaitis and A. Kalinauskaitė, 'The Administrative Judge as a Detention Judge: The Case of Lithuania' in M. Moraru, G. Cornelisse and P. de Bruycker (eds), *Law and Judicial Dialogue on the Return of Irregular Migrants from the EU* (Hart Publishing, UK 2020), pp 237–57.

[65] See M. Moraru and G. Renaudiere, *Redial Research Report 2016/03*, EUI (Migration Policy Centre), pp 11–13.

[66] Ibid.

[67] See *M.M.(1)*, para 85.

[68] C-383/13 *G&R* ECLI:EU:C:2013:533.

[69] In addition to the opinion of AG Wathalet, see also the opinions of AG Mengozzi in C-161/15 *Benallal* ECLI:EU:C:2016:3 and C-560/14 *M.M.(2)* ECLI:EU:C:2016:

asylum seekers, returnees and visa applicants to be heard by domestic administrative authorities before they adopt a negative decision on the legal status of these third-country nationals. Regarding the functions and level of protection conferred by the general principle of rights of defence, judicial interactions have achieved an alignment of the functions of EU Charter provisions and the general principles of right of defence and good administration.[70] The CJEU's case law shows a perfect match between the general principles of EU law and Article 41(2) in terms of content and effects. So far, the CJEU has not mentioned where the differences in content between the two sources lie, although this might be required in the future, otherwise a full application of Article 41(2) via general principles of EU law might be seen as an unlawful circumvention of the limited scope of application of Article 41(2) of the Charter.

Regarding the impact of judicial interactions on domestic jurisprudence, many domestic courts have continued to cite the two EU primary legal sources *en bloc* and used them for identical purposes, such as: filling legislative gaps in EU and domestic legislation;[71] striking down administrative decisions on third-country nationals' return to their country of origin and rejection of a form of international protection;[72] and interpretation of relevant domestic legislation.[73]

Nevertheless, the Charter plays a prominent role regarding the right to be heard during the second phase of asylum and immigration proceedings – judicial review of administrative decisions. Article 47(2) of the Charter has been confirmed to be the legal source of the right to be heard by a tribunal court during these proceedings.[74] In conclusion, the outcome of the repeated vertical judicial interaction was to create a complementary procedural protection relation, thus eliminating any conflicting or competing roles between the general principle of rights of defence and the Charter provisions (see Figure 18.2). Judicial interactions have also had a unifying force across various EU asylum and immigration procedures and across domestic migration governance systems. Notably, an individual right to be heard by administrative authorities has been recognised not only in asylum but also return adjudica-

---

320. For a different opinion, see the opinion of AG Bobek in Case C-298/16 *Ispas* ECLI:EU:C:2017:650, paras 77–79.

[70] For a similar outcome, see Chapter 22 by F. Casarosa and R. Sabato in this edited volume.

[71] Dutch Council of State, judgment of 20 November 2015, 201407197/1/V3.

[72] M. Clement (n 53).

[73] See, for instance, Lithuanian Supreme Administrative Court, *Z.K. v Kaunas County Police Headquarters*, case No. A-2681/2012, decision of 3 September 2013; *M.S. v Migration Department under the Ministry of Interior*, case No. A-69/2013, decision of 20 June 2013.

[74] See, for instance, Case C-348/16 *Sacko Moussa* ECLI:EU:C:2017:591.

tion.[75] At the domestic level, the first preliminary ruling triggered a spillover effect across jurisdictions with different migration management systems and configurations of asylum and return procedures, gradually shaping a common right to be heard.[76]

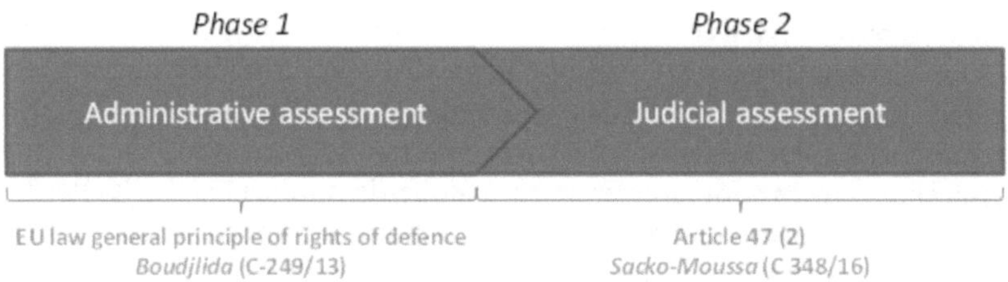

Figure 18.2 *Vertical judicial interaction clarifying the legal basis for the application of the right to be heard*

III. JUDICIAL INTERACTIONS SETTING STANDARDS FOR THE CONDUCT OF ADMINISTRATIVE HEARINGS

The previous section showed how courts and judicial interactions have used the EU law general principles of rights of defence to fill gaps in the Qualification and Return Directives. *In concreto*, new rights of asylum seekers and returnees to be heard by the administrative authorities before they adopt a decision negatively impacting individual rights have been derived at the domestic level. However, recognition of a right to be heard does not automatically secure a fair domestic administrative hearing. The case law selected for this chapter shows that there can be various shortcomings in the conduct of administrative hearings. For instance, a third-country national might come to the hearing unprepared and lacking necessary documents or information because he/she was not informed of the objective and legal consequences of the hearing, or he/she was given too little time to prepare.[77] The hearing might be too short, lacking questions related to essential individual circumstances,[78] or lack respect for other fundamental rights, such as human dignity or

---

[75] Unlike the Recast Asylum Procedure Directive, the Return Directive does not provide for a right to be heard by administrative authorities.

[76] See, for instance, Belgium and Lithuania, which are discussed in this chapter.

[77] See M. Moraru and G. Renaudiere, *REDIAL Research Report 2016/04*, EUI (Migration Policy Centre), pp 14–16.

[78] Ibid.

family and private life, by requesting or accepting too personal questions or evidentiary proof.[79] Alternatively, the hearing might be too summative either because it is only organised in a written form or because it is too short and therefore fails to raise questions that would unveil potential violations of the principle of *non-refoulement*.[80] The shortcomings in domestic administrative hearings vary among the Member States depending on the chosen model of administrative organisation. Of the various asylum- and immigration-related EU secondary instruments, only the Recast Asylum Procedure sets out more detailed safeguards, such as: a mandatory oral administrative hearing in regular asylum procedures; safeguards referring to gender and vulnerability issues; the presence of an interpreter; and the right to read and ask questions regarding the report on the interview drafted by the competent administrative authority.[81] In addition, Article 4 Qualification Directive provides circumstances that public authorities must assess as part of the credibility assessment. However, administrative hearings during subsequent asylum claims in return and visa proceedings are not subject to such detailed rules, but they are subject to a wider margin of Member State discretion.

In order to establish the requirements for the fundamental EU right to be heard in asylum-, return- and visa-related proceedings, national courts have addressed several concrete and technical questions to the CJEU. These chain judicial interactions have helped to gradually set common standards across the varied domestic procedural configurations of when and how to conduct administrative hearings.

Regarding the orality of administrative hearings during asylum proceedings, the CJEU concluded in the *M.M.(2)* case that the right to be heard did not as a general rule imply a right to a personal interview or an oral procedure in the context of an application for subsidiary protection if the person was heard orally during the refugee status determination. Contrary to the opinion of the Advocate General, which considered an oral hearing to be the rule during this administrative phase,[82] the CJEU held that the aim of respecting the right to be heard could also be achieved by means of written submissions. Nevertheless, the CJEU underlined the particular legal context of its findings: the then Irish two-step procedure. Even in such a procedure where asylum seekers were usually heard at least once, the CJEU emphasised that a second hearing might be necessary before the determination of subsidiary protection when the

---

79 Joined Cases C-148–150/13 *A.B.C.* ECLI:EU:C:2014:2406.

80 See the *M.M.* line of cases.

81 See Articles 15–17 of the Recast Asylum Procedure Directive.

82 See *M.M.(2)* ECLI:EU:C:2016:320, point 58.

applicant is 'vulnerable'.[83] As for the common one-step asylum procedure, the CJEU is stricter and requires a mandatory individual oral hearing during the administrative assessment of international protection claims, even in accelerated proceedings.[84]

Two other issues regarding the conduct of administrative hearings have divided domestic courts within both the same and different jurisdictions: the adversarial nature of administrative hearings and the extent of disclosure of evidence by the administration in national-security-related cases. Recourse to Article 267 TFEU became necessary to ensure uniform implementation of the right to be heard as part of access to justice guarantees.

In the context of two preliminary rulings originating from two different domestic migration governance regimes,[85] the CJEU rejected the full adversarial model for the conduct of administrative hearings in asylum and return proceedings. The use of the adversarial model was considered justified by the applicants' lawyers on the basis of these administrative hearings being considered under the Asylum Procedure and Return Directives as 'first-instance' decision-making resulting in enforceable decisions against third-country nationals. The CJEU continued to follow a balancing approach between the human-rights-oriented position of the referring courts and the Member States' procedural autonomy to choose the model of migration procedure.[86] The following components of the adversarial principle were rejected by the Court: the right to call and cross-examine witnesses;[87] to be warned, prior to the interview, that the administration is contemplating adopting a return decision; to have access to information on the basis of which the administration depends for justification of that decision; and to be given a period for reflection.[88] Furthermore the timing and duration of the hearing were held to be non-essential elements of the right to be heard. The CJEU therefore divested the hearing of substantive guarantees that the right to be heard has benefits

---

83 The determination of vulnerable categories was based on the following non-exhaustive criteria: age, health conditions, whether he/she is a victim of violence. In such circumstances, the CJEU held that an additional hearing could be 'necessary in order to allow him to comment in full and coherently on the elements capable of substantiating that application'.

84 *Addis* cit.

85 Ireland and France.

86 For more, see M. Moraru, 'The European Court of Justice Shaping the Right to be Heard for Asylum Seekers, Returnees and Visa Applicants: An Exercise of Judicial Diplomacy' in a Special Issue of the *European Journal of Legal Studies* (2022 forthcoming).

87 *M.M.(2)*, para 55.

88 *Boudjlida*, para 55.

in other administrative fields.[89] Nevertheless, the CJEU did recognise a more restrained adversarial principle as part of the rights of defence, taking the form of a right to be informed before the administrative hearing of the purpose(s) of the interview and the possible consequences regarding the legal status of the individual.[90] In addition, the Court also recognised the right to use legal assistance provided by a defender or legal counsel during the administrative phase of return procedures, even if only at the individual's own expense.[91] These findings are, however, specific to return procedures.

As regards the extent of disclosure of evidence held by the administration to a third-country national considered to be a threat to national security in asylum-, return- or visa-related proceedings, domestic courts have taken divergent positions. Some have extended the standards developed by the CJEU in the *ZZ* preliminary ruling[92] relating to an individual holding both EU citizenship and a third-country nationality to the above proceedings on the basis of Article 47 EU Charter,[93] while other courts have rejected this extensive application of the EU fundamental right to an effective remedy.[94] After several refusals by the Polish Supreme Administrative Court to address preliminary questions to the CJEU,[95] Dutch first-instance courts asked the CJEU to establish the requirements of Article 47 EU Charter on the duty of administrative authorities to disclose evidence in cases of Schengen short-term visa refusals on national security grounds.[96] The CJEU held that the following information has to be disclosed by the administration: the identity of the Member State which raised the objection to issuing a visa; the specific ground for refusal in the objection, accompanied, where appropriate, by the essence of the reasons for the objection; and the authority which the visa applicant may contact in order to ascertain the remedies available in the other Member

---

89 Such as competition, custom duties, taxation, smart sanctions.

90 See *Boudjlida*, para 62.

91 Ibid.

92 C-300/11 *ZZ* ECLI:EU:C:2013:363.

93 See, for instance, Court of first instance of The Hague, branch Zwolle, 14/4276, Judgment of 27 January 2015, Casesheet No. 23 in the 2019 eNACT Handbook.

94 For instance, the UK High Court (*United Kingdom, High Court of England and Wales, R (AZ) v Secretary of State for the Home Department* [2015] EWHC 3695, 18 December 2015, [2016] 4 WLR 12) and the Polish Supreme Administrative Court (e.g. Polish Supreme Administrative Court, judgments II OSK 3210/18, 5 April 2019 and II OSK 3559/18, 30 May 2019).

95 J. Bialas, 'Lawyer's Perspective on Access to Classified Evidence in Return Cases: A View from Poland' in M. Moraru and others (n 64); and pending European Court of Human Rights cases against Poland: 37042/20 and 37691/20 (*A.S. v Poland*).

96 C-225 and 226/19 *R.N.N.S. and K.A.* ECLI:EU:C:2020:951.

State.[97] Therefore, following the *ZZ*, *R.N.N.S.* and *K.A.* line of jurisprudence, a third-country national, irrespective of whether he/she also holds EU citizenship, must be informed of the essence of the grounds on which a decision refusing entry was based.[98]

Vertical judicial interactions have also helped to set a non-exhaustive list of questions that should be and should not be addressed during asylum and immigration proceedings. In *M.M. (1)* and *(2)*, the CJEU required authorities to address specific questions regarding the assessment of subsidiary protection in a two-step system of international protection, instead of relying solely on automatic use of prior credibility findings made in refugee status determination.[99] Certain questions were ruled out by the CJEU. For instance, in the *A, B and C* case, the CJEU excluded questions, and also receiving evidence (e.g. videos or photos), regarding applicants' sexual lives or practices.[100] Therefore, the permissible questioning in the context of an application for asylum should also be determined on the basis of the privacy element contained in Articles 1 and 7 of the EU Charter, which prevent applicants from performing sex acts, producing films of their sexual activity or undertaking medical testing to prove their sexual orientation.[101] Hearings regarding asylum claims based on persecution on grounds of sexual orientation are particularly sensitive. However, this should not lead to very brief or summative hearings.[102]

Regarding the content of the hearing in return proceedings, a non-exhaustive list of minimum questions was defined by the CJEU primarily in the *Mukarubega* and *Boudjlida* judgments. The CJEU has shaped in detail the content of the right to be heard. Namely, the third-country national must be able to express his/her point of view on: the legality of his/her stay; facts that could justify the authorities refraining from adopting a particular return-related decision;[103] facts that justify exception(s) to the expulsion;[104] the social circumstances of the irregular migrant, including the best interests of the child, family life and the state of health of the third-country national concerned; respect

---

97 Ibid, paras 37–48.

98 *ZZ*, para 63.

99 See in particular *M.M.(1)*.

100 Joined Cases C-148–150/13 *A.B.C.* ECLI:EU:C:2014:2406.

101 Ibid.

102 The Dutch Council of State quashed administrative decisions for these reasons: lacking the questions the administration asked; how the answers to these questions were weighted; and how the statements appraised as lacking credibility influenced the final administrative decision. See Catherine van Boven-Hartogh, 'ENACT Case note', Dutch Council of State, 201208550/1/V2, 201110141/1/V2, 201210441/1/V2, available in the CJC database.

103 *Boudjlida*, para 55.

104 Para 47.

for the *principle of non-refoulement*;[105] the detailed arrangements for his/her return, including the possibility of extending the period of voluntary departure under Article 7(2) of the Return Directive;[106] and correcting an error or submitting information relating to his/her personal circumstances.[107] The CJEU also made it clear that a return-related decision cannot be based solely on a criminal record or prior rejection of asylum illegal stay and entry, and the hearing must go beyond addressing these issues.

Overall, vertical judicial interaction has helped to shape a wider content for hearings in return proceedings compared to the practice of certain jurisdictions which used to carry out very summative hearings.[108]

IV. JUDICIAL INTERACTIONS DEVELOPING NEW REMEDIES FOR VIOLATIONS OF THE RIGHT TO BE HEARD

The previous section showed how transnational and vertical judicial interactions have contributed to the development of a common core of standards that administrative authorities have to follow under the general principle of rights of defence in the conduct of asylum- and immigration-related hearings. Nevertheless, the overall positive achievements regarding protection of the right to be heard would remain wholly theoretical in the absence of effective remedies for violations of this right. This section analyses what has been the contribution of judicial interactions to the development of effective remedies for violations of the right to be heard.

Effective remedies for violations of the right to be heard during administrative proceedings in asylum-, return- and visa-related cases and the extent of judicial review of domestic courts to establish them are only minimally harmonised at the EU level. The Recast Asylum Procedure Directive ensures only a right to an effective judicial remedy before a court,[109] but it does not prescribe harmonised standards in terms of the organisation of the appeal or the procedure to be followed. The Return Directive sets even lower standards, conferring a right to an effective *legal* remedy, which means that appeals against administrative decisions can also be legally reviewed by an administrative authority as long as it meets the requirements of impartiality

[105] Para 48.

[106] Para 51.

[107] Para 37.

[108] Such as Italy. See A. di Pascale, 'Can a Justice of Peace be a Good Detention Judge? The Case of Italy' in M. Moraru and others (n 64).

[109] See Article 46.

and independence.[110] The Visa Code is even vaguer. Article 32(2) provides a right to appeal against a short-term visa refusal without even mentioning the Return Directive's requirements of impartiality and independence if a Member State chooses an administrative appeal system. None of these EU secondary instruments set harmonised standards for the organisation of appeals against administrative decisions or a precise procedure to be followed. This silence and vagueness of EU secondary instruments has left space for the development of a rich tapestry of domestic appeal procedures among the Member States for migration-related proceedings.[111]

Regarding types of remedies, the CJEU differentiates between asylum and return proceedings. In *G&R*, the CJEU only required national courts to annul administrative decisions extending pre-removal detention made in the absence of a hearing if it is proven that the organisation of a hearing would have led to a different outcome of the procedure.[112] In *Addis*, the CJEU replaced this conditional annulment with a mandatory annulment in the case of a lack of an administrative hearing in an accelerated asylum procedure. The CJEU based this difference in types of remedies for the same violation – the absence of an administrative hearing – on the more stringent obligation to hold a hearing stipulated in the Recast Asylum Procedure, rather than the Return Directive, and not on the seriousness of the fundamental right breached. In both cases, in addition to the violation of the right to be heard, there were other rights that were affected by the lack of an administrative hearing – the right to liberty in *G&R* and the principle of non-refoulement in *Addis*.

Regarding the judicial review powers necessary for courts to establish an effective remedy, judicial interactions have empowered national courts to establish the legal accountability of the executive and establish effective remedies, either by recognising a form of international protection[113] or by deciding on the legality of a return-related decision[114] or a rejection of a short-term visa application.[115] A new era of judicial activism has developed in reaction to populist governments curbing judicial review powers. Article 267 TFEU has proved to be a protective shield for domestic courts which had lost their remedial powers in asylum and return procedures.[116]

---

110 See Article 13.

111 For a glimpse of the extent of this variety, see M. Moraru, 'ReJus Casebook' (n 52), pp 209–15.

112 See *G&R*, para 40.

113 See *Torubarov*, *Sacko Moussa* and *Alheto*.

114 *FMS* and *Mahdi*.

115 *El Hassani* and *R.N.N.S. and K.A.*

116 See *Torubarov* and *FMS*.

Article 47 EU Charter did not initially play a substantial role in the CJEU's empowerment of national court judicial reviews. In *Mahdi*, although Article 47 EU Charter was invoked by the Bulgarian referring court to obtain more extensive judicial review powers, the CJEU only relied on Article 15 of the Return Directive to prohibit a domestic rule under which courts could not assess on their own initiative new facts and legal elements outside the evidence brought by the administration for the purpose of deciding whether to prolong pre-removal detention, to establish measures alternative to pre-removal detention or release a detained returnee.[117] However, Article 47 EU Charter has slowly played a more salient role, also following invitations in Advocates General Opinions. In *El Hassani*, the CJEU required the Polish law implementing the Visa Code to introduce a new individual right to appeal before an independent court against a visa refusal by consular officials on the basis of Article 47 EU Charter. Article 47 continued to play a salient role in *FMS*, in which the CJEU required Hungarian law to ensure that the right to appeal against return decisions be secured before a court and not an independent administrative authority. In *Torubarov*, Article 47 EU Charter was used to empower Hungarian courts to recognise a form of international protection when public authorities repeatedly disregard final judgments in asylum adjudications. In *Sacko Moussa* the CJEU used Article 47(2) EU Charter together with Article 46(3) of the Recast Asylum Procedure to empower Italian first-instance courts to decide whether or not to hold an oral hearing in accelerated asylum adjudications following certain operational guidelines.[118] In *Alheto*, the CJEU established a more stringent requirement for the organisation of an oral hearing by a court on the basis of Article 47 EU Charter, namely that if in an appeal a domestic court hears for the first time a ground for inadmissibility that was not previously examined by the competent administrative authority then it must conduct a hearing of the asylum seeker.[119]

In conclusion, this section has shown that national courts have created opportunities for the CJEU to slowly but firmly enhance the legal accountability of administrations by accepting their competence to scrutinise the limits of national procedural autonomy, not only on the basis of the principles of equivalence and effectiveness but also on the higher threshold set in Article 47 EU Charter.[120] Judicial interaction has thus unravelled the potential of Article

---

[117] See the *Mahdi* case summarised in the ReJus database available at https://www.rejus.eu/db/cases/bulgaria-sofia-city-administrative-court-20-june-2014-15352014 (last accessed January 2021).

[118] For an in-depth commentary, see Chapter 19 by M. Flamini in this edited volume.

[119] *Alheto*, para 130.

[120] *Torubarov*, para 55.

47 EU Charter to: empower courts to organise judicial hearings to compensate for irregularities in administrative hearings beyond the limits of domestic procedural laws (*G&R* and *Sacko Moussa*); establish a duty for national courts to organise oral hearings as a corollary of the adversarial principle when they examine new grounds for inadmissibility in asylum adjudication for the first time (*Alheto*); extend judicial review to new facts and evidence beyond those submitted by the administration (*Mahdi* and *Ahmedbekova*[121]) and return-related administrative decisions outside the confines of domestic law (*FMS*); recognise reformatory powers to domestic courts beyond the limits of procedural law (*Torubarov*, *Mahdi*); expand access to domestic courts for the purpose of challenging the legality of consular officials refusing visas to enter a Member State (*El Hassani*); establish a duty of national courts to annul administrative decisions that were taken without organising individual oral hearings in procedures assessing the admissibility of asylum applications (*Addis*); and enhance the lower threshold of legal remedy under Article 13 of the Return Directive to a judicial remedy on the basis of Article 47 EU Charter (*FMS*).

V. CONCLUSION: THE DRIVERS AND OUTCOMES OF JUDICIAL INTERACTIONS

This chapter has shown a multitude of factors driving national courts to engage in judicial interaction with foreign domestic courts and the CJEU to clarify the boundaries and effects of the EU fundamental right to be heard in asylum-, return- and visa-related domestic proceedings, such as: changing a judicial majoritarian opinion (*Sacko Moussa*) or a hierarchically superior court's jurisprudence (*Boudjlida* and *Mukarubega*); empowering courts against an executive's lack of compliance with court judgments (*Torubarov*) or enhancing the legitimacy of judicial decisions diverging from executive practice (*Addis*, *Alheto*); enhancing the clarity and coherence of jurisprudence both in the CJEU and at the domestic level (*M.M.(1)* and *M.M (2)*); and ensuring the legitimacy of domestic migration practices (*G&R*).

The majority of judicial interactions discussed here were voluntary interactions which national courts perceived as useful to achieve normative clarity on the EU legal sources, scope, content and effects of the right to be heard in domestic asylum and return proceedings. Whether it has been the preliminary reference procedure, consistent interpretation, disapplication of national law or comparative reasoning based on foreign domestic jurisprudence, judicial interaction techniques have improved the application of the right to be heard

[121] C-652/16 *Ahmedbekova* ECLI:EU:C:2018:801.

at the domestic level. Judicial interactions have helped to clarify the relation between EU-Charter-based provisions and general principles of EU law as sources of the application of the EU fundamental right to be heard in asylum-, return- and visa-related proceedings. As was shown in Figure 18.2, the EU law general principle of rights of defence requires administrative authorities to hear a third-country national before they adopt a decision that could negatively impact his/her right to stay in the EU even if national legislation does not provide for such a right to be heard. Judicial interactions have also contributed to giving concrete shape to the content of the right to be heard by setting a non-exhaustive list of questions that should be followed or avoided during administrative hearings and the circumstances in which oral administrative hearings should be held.

Most importantly, concrete remedies have been developed for violations of the right to be heard which clarify the ambiguous legal framework set in EU secondary legislation (e.g. the Recast Asylum Procedure and Return Directive). Notably Article 47(2) EU Charter and the general principles of rights of defence ensure that administrative authorities do not evade legal accountability for their decision-making. In this sense, vertical judicial interaction has: eliminated prohibitions or restrictions on the right to access an independent court (*El Hassani*); extended judicial hearing powers beyond the limits of administrative evidence (*Mahdi*, *Abdida*, *Alheto* and *Ahmedbekova*); and guaranteed the preservation of judicial hearing powers that courts used to possess before executive or legislative reforms adopted in response to the refugee crisis (*Sacko Moussa* and *Torubarov*). The CJEU has thus given great responsibility to domestic judges, who are required to examine whether to hold an oral hearing in each asylum case regardless of whether it is an accelerated procedure. The balance tilts towards organising an oral judicial hearing once one of the circumstances of vulnerability is present in the case (*Sacko Moussa*) or new grounds of inadmissibility are considered by courts (*Alheto*). Ultimately, the powers of domestic courts further increase under the CJEU baton once procedural irregularities in the conduct of administrative hearings turn into systemic challenges to the national judicial function (*Torubarov*) or denials of the right to be heard in asylum adjudication (*Addis*, *FMS*).

In the face of growing limitations of the right to be heard, including in its essential form of accessing courts and ensuring a fair trial, domestic courts have had to ensure the rule of law by challenging asylum laws and policy before the CJEU. Cases such as *Torubarov*, *Ahmedbekova* and *FMS* show the importance of vertical judicial interaction to ensure that domestic courts can continue to play their constitutional role as rule of law gatekeepers. However, these preliminary rulings have not all achieved a unifying effect of domestic jurisprudence. For instance, domestic jurisprudence has continued to diverge in France following the *Boudjlida* and *Mukarubega* preliminary rulings, and in

Italy following *Sacko Moussa*. The inconsistent interpretation of CJEU preliminary rulings by national supreme courts and disagreements between supreme and constitutional courts have contributed to a divergent implementation of the preliminary rulings by ordinary domestic courts. Nevertheless, what the implementation of preliminary rulings clearly shows is that national courts are not mere conveyor belts for the CJEU dicta but they imprint their constructive interpretation, as was shown by the referring courts in the *Sacko Moussa* and *M.M.(1)* cases.

19. Comment: the right to be heard in international protection proceedings before an Italian judge

Martina Flamini

1. THE ROLE OF THE JUDGE IN INTERNATIONAL PROTECTION PROCEEDINGS

The judge in charge of international protection proceedings is called on to understand, interpret and verify how Union law impacts national procedural rules, despite the relatively low level of harmonisation at the European level. Procedural law is a flexible means able to ensure respect for the fundamental right to international protection. It would remain a mere declaration of principle to affirm the fundamental nature of this right if effective procedural guarantees were not available to safeguard the substantive legal condition. This premise is confirmed by the two references for a preliminary ruling made by Italian courts in the asylum field, which have as subject matter two procedural issues regarding the international protection procedure (namely, the right to be heard and the right to have the effects of a rejection order suspended after the decision by the court of first instance).

2. THE PRELIMINARY REFERENCE IN THE *SACKO MOUSSA* CASE

In Italy, international protection proceedings are examined by ordinary courts.[1] Unlike what happens in the other continental European states, where administrative jurisdiction is in charge of disputes concerning international protection,

---

[1] For a thorough analysis of the relationship between the right to an effective remedy and the right to be heard, see Davide Strazzari, 'Diritto a un ricorso effettivo e autonomia processuale degli Stati: l'audizione personale del ricorrente nelle controversie in materia di riconoscimento della protezione internazionale', Note e Commenti, DPCE on line, 2017/4.

according to the Italian legal system the judgment addresses the recognition or non-recognition of the right rather than the appeal against the administrative decision. In cases of flaws in the administrative procedure, the judge should not only nullify the administrative decision but he must also examine the merits of the right invoked in order to fully recover the guarantees violated in the administrative phase. This premise is also very important in order to understand the specificities of the rulings made by the Court of Justice of the European Union (CJEU) on preliminary rulings proposed by states where administrative judgments can only be annulled (the reference is, for example, to the recent judgment of the Second Chamber of 4 October 2018, *Nigyar Rauf Kaza Ahmedbekova, Rauf Emin Ogla Ahmedbekovc.Zamestnik-predsedatel naDarzhavna agentsia za bezhantsite*, Case C-652/16).

In the old procedure applicable to disputes involving international protection, the Court of Milan referred the matter to the CJEU (*Sacko Moussa* case, decided on 26 July 2017) for a preliminary ruling on the compatibility of Directive 2013/32/EU with the hypothesis of rejecting the *de plano* appeal, without setting a hearing in the case of manifest unfoundedness of the appeal. The Italian court affirmed that the principle provided in the 'procedures' directive, read in the light of Article 47 Charter of Fundamental Rights of the European Union (EU Charter), must be interpreted as:

> not precluding a national court, before which an appeal against a decision rejecting an application for international protection which is manifestly unfounded, from rejecting that appeal *without hearing the applicant* if the factual circumstances leave no doubt as to the merits of the decision, provided, on the one hand, that during the first instance procedure the applicant was given the opportunity to undergo a personal interview on his application for international protection in accordance with Art. 14 of the Directive, and that the transcript of that interview, if it took place, has been made available together with the file, in accordance with Article 17(2) of the Directive, and, on the other hand, that the court seised of the appeal may order such a hearing if it considers it necessary for a full and ex nunc examination of the matters of fact and law referred to in Article 46 of the Directive.

In its decision, the CJEU justified the compression of the right to be heard on the ground of the close connection between the judicial phase (referred to as a second instance with respect to the administrative phase, which is classified as the first instance procedure) and the administrative phase, using an argument never considered relevant by the European Court of Human Rights (ECtHR).[2]

---

2 For an in-depth analysis of the CJEU 's approach, see Chiara Favilli, 'The standard of fundamental rights protection in the field of asylum: The case of the right to an effective remedy between EU Law and the Italian Constitution', University of Florence, *European Administrative Law Review*, 2019, 2, 167.

After the decision by the CJEU, the Court of Milan – with a decision on 16 November 2017 – decided to order the hearing of Mr Sacko Moussa, expressly recalling the principles stated in the CJEU decision, due to the need to evaluate elements of vulnerability that did not emerge during the administrative phase and as a result of the proceedings granted him humanitarian protection.

3. THE INTERPLAY BETWEEN THE CJEU DECISION AND THE NEWLY ADOPTED NATIONAL LEGISLATION

In the aftermath of the Italian decision, Law Decree no. 13/2017, converted into Law no. 46/2017, profoundly changed the judicial procedure for the recognition of international protection. According to the new wording provided in Law 46/2017, Art. 35-bis, paras 10 and 11, Legislative Decree no. 25/2008 provides in paragraph 10 that:

> *a hearing is set for the appearance of the parties* only when the judge: a) after viewing the video recording referred to in paragraph 8, deems it necessary to order the hearing of the interested party; b) deems it essential to request clarification from the parties; c) orders technical consultancy or even ex officio, the taking of evidence.

Paragraph 11 adds that:

> *the hearing shall also be held* when at least one of the following cases occurs: a) the video recording is not available; b) the interested party has made a reasoned request in the application and the judge, on the basis of the reasons put forward by the appellant, considers the hearing to be essential for the decision to be taken; c) the appeal is based on facts not presented during the administrative procedure of first instance.

The jurisprudence of first and last instance called on to interpret the provisions of the new rules also in the light of the principles affirmed by the CJEU in the *Sacko* decision has come to hermeneutical solutions that are not always consistent. Many courts (namely Bologna, Brescia, Cagliari, Florence, Genoa, Rome, Salerno and Trieste), repeating the necessity and importance of oral hearing even in the jurisdictional phase, have decided that in the absence of a video recording a personal hearing of the plaintiff should always be arranged. Other courts (namely Naples and Milan), on the other hand, have decided to order the personal hearing (not because of unavailability of the video recording) only in cases in which the applicant's defence attorney presents new elements (not examined in the administrative phase) in the introductory appeal, or indicates circumstances which, considered previously contradictory, could otherwise be explained by the applicant.

In its judgment no. 17717/2018, the Supreme Court stated that in the absence of the video recording of the interview in the administrative phase, the judge should order the hearing of the parties, specifying, however, that in this hearing the applicant should not necessarily be heard. With reference to this hearing, the Court of Cassation briefly mentioned the CJEU judgment in the *Sacko* case without making any assessment as to the differences between the appearance hearing and the renewal of the oral hearing and the criteria for assessing whether or not to proceed with this hearing. In the subsequent ruling, no. 2817/2019, the Court of Cassation stated that, without prejudice to the obligation to fix the hearing, there is, however, 'no automatic need to hold the hearing, the obligation of which, in accordance with Directive 2013/32/EC, lies exclusively with the administrative authority responsible for examining the applicant'. It follows that 'the judge may decide solely on the basis of the elements contained in the file, including the minutes or transcript of the interview before the Commission'. In judgment no. 10786/2019, the Court of Cassation reiterated the same principle with regard to the need to fix the hearing, and pointed out that 'the fact that the applicant also failed to state the reasons why the erroneous application of the procedural rule adversely affected the decision on the merits, since the failure to videotape the interview, affecting a central element of the procedure, clearly affects his rights of defence' is not relevant.

More recently, in its 27073/2019 judgment the Supreme Court finally stated that:

> the right to effective protection, enshrined in Article 46(1) of Directive 2013/32, affects the duty of cooperation of the judge and the need to order the hearing of the applicant, which is the central moment in which this duty can be expressed, on the new issues introduced in the appeal (which are sufficiently distinct and significant), if the applicant has not been heard by the Commission.

In this ruling, therefore, the right to be heard was outlined as an expression of the duty of cooperation of the judge in the examination of the application for international protection.

With specific reference to the relationship between the administrative and the judicial phase, the Court specified that:

> if the applicant proposes in the judicial appeal new grounds, or even only new factual elements, which refer to the grounds already proposed, supplementing them significantly, and which have not been submitted to the Territorial Commission, although prior to the application for international protection, according to CJEU jurisprudence, the judge must submit them to the administrative authority and, therefore, assess them for the purposes of the decision.

This argument was supported with an express reference to the judgment by the Court of Justice in case C-652/2016 of 4 October 2018, cited above, which was made, however, with reference to a legal system in which the judge in charge of international protection procedures only has powers of annulment and not of recognition of protection, which is clearly different to the Italian system. According to the Supreme Court, if new facts not submitted to the administrative authority emerge in the proceedings before the court, the judge cannot limit himself to a hearing for the collection of such new facts (and their subsequent evaluation) but should submit them to the Territorial Commission, thus allowing the applicant to have a first oral hearing before the administrative authority regarding the new elements.

4. A COMPREHENSIVE VIEW OF THE RIGHT TO BE HEARD

This lack of uniformity of approaches reflects the different perspectives from which the interpreters address the right to be heard. First of all, a distinction should be made between the right to be heard (in the sense of stating the reasons), the right to be heard personally (the right to an oral interview) and the right to a hearing.

In international protection proceedings, the specificities of the right invoked, the specificities of the rules on evidence for the assessment of the applicant's statements (which are often the only source of evidence of the right to international protection and in which the credibility and personal experience of the applicant play a central role in the decision[3]) make it clear that the central issue revolves around the decision to order a new (oral) hearing at the judicial stage after an oral interview has taken place in the administrative stage. While there is no doubt that a new personal hearing should be held in the case of new elements being raised in the introductory appeal or in the case of the applicant wishing to clarify aspects considered to be deficient or contradictory by the Territorial Commission, the decision is much more delicate in cases in which, after a hearing before the administrative authority, the applicant generically encloses his wish to be 'heard' by the judge in order to better clarify the reasons that led him to ask for protection.

The court's decision should then be based on the principles established by the CJEU and the ECtHR, following a clear framework for the hearing

[3] According to the ECtHR, a hearing is indispensable when the decision concerns important issues, when there are facts of considerable complexity to be established or when the credibility or personal experience of the applicant plays a crucial role in the decision (ECtHR, 23 October 1995, *Schmautzer v. Austria*, 15523/89; 23 November 2006, *Jussila v. Finland*, 73053/01; 9 October 1979, *Airey v. Ireland*, 6289/73).

obligation and its aims. The right to be heard, in fact, concerns both the applicant's right to defence (and, even before that, the right to action and the fair trial principle) and the judge's duty of cooperation. With reference to the first aspect, it is important to recall that the CJEU in the *Sacko* judgment (para. 37) specified that the absence of a hearing 'constitutes a restriction of the rights of defence, which are part of the principle of effective judicial protection, enshrined in Article 47 of the Charter'. Although this right is not an absolute right, precisely because of the link between the right to an effective remedy, the right to defence and the right to a hearing, the judge must expressly state the reasons why he decides not to renew the personal hearing.

On the other hand, as far as the duty of cooperation of the judge is concerned, the correlation between the duty of cooperation of the administration and that of the court means that any deficiencies relating to the cooperation of the administration can, and must, be remedied in court. The duty of cooperation – which permeates the whole procedure – requires the judge-rapporteur to examine the previous statements made by the plaintiff (both before the police and during the hearing before the Territorial Commission) and assess whether, in view of the plaintiff's report, the presence of contradictions, the elements to be investigated or further aspects not exhaustively dealt with before the Commission (within the limits of the facts presented), it is necessary, in accordance with what has been clarified by the CJEU,[4] to order a new hearing. If the judge deems it necessary to order a new hearing of the applicant, the duty of cooperation shall be articulated by providing information on the duty to give reasons for the request[5] by asking the applicant appropriate questions during the questioning and by allowing the applicant to clarify any unsubstantiated or contradictory elements that would lead to a negative credibility assessment.

The complexity of the relationship between substantive and procedural law, the specificity of a procedure in which the decision is strongly conditioned by the applicant's statements and the particularities of the duty of cooperation require careful reflection on how the exercise of these powers implements and achieves an effective remedy for the fundamental right to international protection.

---

[4] Court of Justice, Case C-560/14 *M.M.(2)* ECLI:EU:C:2017:101; and Case C-348/16 *Moussa Sacko* ECLI:EU:C:2017:591.

[5] Court of Justice, Case C-277/11 *M.M.(1)* ECLI:EU:C:2012:744, paragraph 65.

PART III

Remedies and sanctions

20. *Ne bis in idem* – a continuing judicial dialogue

Maria Bergström and Hans Sundberg[1]

1. INTRODUCING *NE BIS IN IDEM* AND THE MULTILEVEL LEGAL LANDSCAPE

The principle of *ne bis in idem*, or the prohibition of double jeopardy, or strictly speaking the doubling of proceedings, forbids public authorities to put forth criminal charges against the same person for the same offence more than once. In domestic law, it is sometimes granted constitutional status, and it is explicitly included in numerous international, regional and bilateral instruments,[2] such as Protocol No. 7 to the European Convention on Human Rights (ECHR) (Article 4(1)), Article 50 of the Charter of Fundamental Rights of the European Union (EU Charter), and Article 54 of the Convention implementing the Schengen Agreement (Schengen Convention). The interrelationship and parallel application of these legal instruments by a variety of courts may entail a number of legal challenges, but might at the same time be beneficial for reasons of fundamental rights protection. In particular, introducing the EU Charter had an enormous impact on fundamental rights protection, *ne bis in idem* and the outcome of the well-known *Åkerberg Fransson* saga that eventually prohibited consecutive proceedings of a criminal nature with respect to

[1] This chapter partly builds on M. Bergström, 'The Impact of the Case C-617/10 – Åkerberg Fransson at National Level: The Swedish Example', in V. Mitsilegas, A. di Martino and L. Mancano (eds), *The Court of Justice and European Criminal Law: Leading Cases in a Contextual Analysis*, Modern Studies in European Law, Hart Publishing, Oxford 2019.

[2] Anne Weyembergh and Inés Armada, 'The Principle of ne bis in idem in Europe's Area of Freedom, Security and Justice', in Valsamis Mitsilegas, Maria Bergström and Theodore Konstadinides (eds), *Research Handbook on EU Criminal Law*, Edward Elgar Publishing, Cheltenham, UK and Northampton, MA 2016 with further references. See also e.g. Alexandros-Ioannis Kargopoulos, 'Ne bis in idem in Criminal Proceedings', in Maria Bergström and Anna Jonsson Cornell (eds), *European Police and Criminal Law Co-operation*, Hart Publishing, Oxford 2014.

value added tax (VAT) concerning two parallel systems of sanctions for tax fraud including administrative tax surcharges and charges for tax fraud under criminal law in Sweden.[3]

At the same time, judicial interaction between national and European courts played a significant role throughout this saga. Given the various developments on national, EU and European levels, one of the remaining questions is whether judicial interaction can provide an answer to complex legal and practical issues relating to the overlapping of fundamental rights sources in general, and *ne bis in idem* in particular, pending any further EU harmonising measures.[4] While using the *Åkerberg Fransson* saga as a reference point and illustrative example,[5] this chapter aims at analysing the judicial interaction involved in light of later developments before the Court of Justice of the European Union (CJEU) and the European Court of Human Rights (ECtHR). For the purposes of this analysis, our chosen perspective will be threefold:

First, has judicial interaction contributed to a more coherent application of the EU Charter (*sections 2 and 3*), or is the result an even more complex legal situation than without such interaction? Second, can judicial interaction provide any solutions on how to solve complex issues relating to the overlapping of fundamental rights sources (*sections 3 and 4*)? Third, and part of the concluding remarks (*section 5*), is the result an enhanced fundamental rights

---

[3] C-617/10 *Åklagaren v Hans Åkerberg Fransson*, EU:C:2013:105. See e.g. Ulf Bernitz, 'The Scope of the Charter and its Impact on the Application of the ECHR: The Åkerberg Fransson Case on *ne bis in idem* in Perspective', in Sybe de Vries, Ulf Bernitz and Stephen Weatherill (eds), *The EU Charter of Fundamental Rights as a Binding Instrument: Five Years Old and Growing*, Hart Publishing, Oxford 2015, p 155, with further references.

[4] Codified legislation on *ne bis in idem* under Article 82 TFEU, will be prioritised during the coming six year period, Comment by Peter Czonka, European Commission, at 20 Year Anniversary of the Tampere Programme: Progress and Future Priorities of the EU Area of Freedom, Security and Justice, Part of Finland's Presidency Calendar and Co-organised by CEPS, the Migration Policy Centre (MPC) and the Law Department of the European University Institute (EUI), in cooperation with the Finnish Permanent Representation to the EU, CEPS, Brussels, 3 and 4 October 2019.

[5] See Bergström (n 1), with further references e.g. to Bernitz (n 3), and (in Swedish) Ulf Bernitz, Rättighetsstadgans genomslag i svensk rätt, JT 2016-17, s 789; Katarina Fast, 'Oklart om Dubbelbestraffningsförbudets innebörd – en kommentar till generaladvokatens förslag i fallet Åkerberg Fransson', Skattenytt 2012, s 593; Katarina Fast, 'Dubbelbeskattningsförbudet i EU:s rättighetsstadga och det svenska systemet med skattetillägg och skattebrott', Svensk Skattetidning 2013, s 138ff; Magnus Gulliksson, 'Klart till halvklart – om ne bis in idem och skattetilläggen', SvJT 2013, s 658; several of the contributions in Joakim Nergelius and Eleonor Kristoffersson (eds), *Human Rights in Contemporary European Law, Swedish Studies in European Law*, Hart Publishing, Oxford 2015, vol 6; Dominique Ritleng, 'Lärdomar av EU-domstolens parallella domar i målen Åkerberg Fransson och Melloni', SvJT 2014, s 36.

protection of the individuals, and if so, in what way? The answers to these questions will be addressed in the respective section and only briefly mentioned in the concluding remarks. Yet, as a result of this analysis, we conclude that courts are instrumental not only in the settlement of individual disputes, but also in changing the legal system: in other words, pressure through law,[6] including defining the lowest level of protection for the EU legislator when proposing new harmonising legislation. Pending such harmonising EU legislation, there is still some room for national diversity, as long as the level of protection guaranteed by the ECHR and the EU Charter, including the principle of legal certainty, and the respect for the primacy, unity and effectiveness of EU law are complied with.

Whereas the application of the ECHR within the EU law context provides the lowest level of protection, the EU Charter may allow for or even require a higher level of protection. Therefore, using the ECHR as a starting point, the application of the ECtHR's jurisprudence on the *ne bis in idem* principle involves the assessment of a number of issues,[7] including: first, whether the imposition of tax surcharges is criminal in nature. Second, whether the criminal offences for which the applicant was prosecuted were the same as those for which the tax surcharges were imposed on her (*idem*). Third, whether there was a final decision, and, finally whether there was a duplication of proceedings (*bis*), including the assessment whether there is *a close connection, in substance and time*, between the criminal proceedings and the tax proceedings. Whether this last line of argument has been followed by the CJEU post *Fransson* will be briefly addressed below although the focus of this chapter is not a comparison of the legal requirements used and applied by the courts respectively per se.

Hence, as will be exemplified, the legal provisions and issues before the CJEU are not always overlapping with those emphasised by the ECtHR. The CJEU Grand Chamber rulings following *Åkerberg Fransson* have so far mainly involved Article 50 of the EU Charter, the scope of the limitation clause in Article 52(1) of the EU Charter, i.e. the justification for the limitation of the right guaranteed in Article 50 of the Charter, and the reserve in *Åkerberg Fransson* that even if the main rule is that there shall be no duplication of proceedings, it is for the national court to assess whether the remaining penalties

---

6 Referring to the concept developed by Carol Harlow and Richard Rawlings, *Pressure through Law*, Routledge, London 1992 and in Maria Bergström, 'Advocacy Groups and Multilevel Governance: The Use of EC Law as a Campaigning Tool', Doctor of Laws thesis defended at the European University Institute, Florence, March 2003.

7 *Lucky Dev v Sweden* App no 7356/10 (ECtHR, 2014), paras 50–58.

are effective, proportionate and dissuasive.[8] Irrespective of the continuous guidance by the CJEU, and the ECtHR, this is not perhaps the easiest task for national courts to embrace.

2. THE *ÅKERBERG FRANSSON* SAGA TOWARDS A CHANGE IN THE SWEDISH SYSTEM

In Sweden, the *Åkerberg Fransson* case had an enormous impact resulting in two plenary judgments where the Swedish Supreme Court, *Högsta Domstolen*,[9] and the Swedish Supreme Administrative Court, *Högsta Förvaltningsdomstolen*,[10] in June and October 2013 reversed their previous positions. This in turn gave rise to an exceptional number of petitions for a new trial.[11] In 2014, 42 individuals out of 110 serving prison sentences had been released, the remaining convicted also for other crimes than tax offences. A number of persons did not have to start their prison sentences, and 541 out of 800 individuals who had already served their sentences had filed petitions for re-opening of proceedings.[12]

Although focusing mainly on the particulars of the Swedish system, this section provides an illustrative example of the massive impact a single CJEU judgment might have not only on one national legal system, but on the relationship between national and EU law in general, and on the development of EU law and the impact of the EU Charter in particular.

2.1 Introducing the Swedish Legal System and the Initial (non-) Interaction between its Courts and the ECtHR on *ne bis in idem*

The traditional Swedish system involved two parallel systems of sanctions for tax fraud including tax surcharges, administrative law and appeal to the administrative law courts on the one hand, and charges for tax fraud under criminal law and the courts of general jurisdiction on the other. As emphasised by Appeal Court Judge Ola Zetterquist, this parallel system, introduced in 1972, had been questioned 'more or less from the outset as being incompatible with

8 *Åkerberg Fransson* (n 3), paras 34 and 36.

9 NJA (*Nytt Juridiskt Arkiv*, the Supreme Court's publication of decision) 2013, p 502.

10 RÅ 2013 ref 71 (Swedish Supreme Administrative Court).

11 Ola Zetterquist, 'Ne bis in idem and 2013 European Legal Tsunami', in Nergelius and Kristoffersson (eds) (n 5), 134.

12 Swedish Newspaper, *Dagens Nyheter*, 25 April 2014, referring to information provided by the Economic Crime Authority.

the principle of *ne bis in idem* in general, and later on, with the prohibition laid down in Article 4 of Protocol 7 to the ECHR in particular'.[13]

In relation to the first issue to assess when applying the ECtHR's jurisprudence to the facts of a case, i.e. whether the imposition of tax surcharges is criminal in nature, two rulings by the ECtHR had already in 2002 clarified that administrative tax surcharges were of a penal nature,[14] and thus fell within the scope of Article 6 ECHR. On the other hand, the Swedish system of parallel tax surcharge and tax fraud had previously been dealt with differently by the ECtHR in relation to the second issue, i.e. whether the criminal offences for which the applicant was prosecuted were the same as those for which the tax surcharges were imposed (*idem*). In the *Rosenquist* ruling from 2004,[15] the ECtHR came to the conclusion that the Swedish system of parallel tax surcharge and tax fraud constituted two different crimes.[16] In 2004, the ECtHR therefore concluded that the two offences were entirely separate and differed in their essential elements. As a result, the Swedish system did not initially infringe Article 4 of Protocol 7 to the ECHR.[17] The same assessment had been made in the relevant Swedish preparatory materials.[18]

Yet, ten years later, in *Lucky Dev v Sweden*, the ECtHR came to a different conclusion than in the *Rosenquist* case.[19] The court now held that the applicant's indictment and the imposition of tax surcharges were based on the same failure to declare business proceeds and VAT, and that the tax proceedings and the criminal proceedings concerned the same period of time and essentially the same amount of evaded taxes. As a result, the *idem* element was now fulfilled.[20]

In addition, concerning the fourth issue, i.e. whether there was a duplication of proceedings (*bis*), and whether the Swedish procedures were to be

---

[13] Zetterquist (n 11), 134.

[14] Cases *Janosevic v Sweden* App no 34619/97 and *Västberga Taxi and Vulk v Sweden* App no 36985/97. See further Bernitz (n 3), 167 and Bernitz (n 5), 802.

[15] *Rosenquist v Sweden* App no 60619/00 (ECtHR, 2004), discussed e.g. by Zetterquist (n 11), 132.

[16] For recent publications on penalty payments, see e.g. Leena Halila, Veronica Lankinen and Annika Nilsson, 'Administrativa sanktionsavgifter' (2018) *En Nordisk komparativ studie, TemaNord* 511, 289; and Vladimir Bastidas Venegas and Maria Bergström, 'Report on Sweden', in Katalin Ligeti and Stanislaw Tosza (eds), *White Collar Crime: A Comparative Perspective*, Hart Publishing, Oxford 2018.

[17] *Rosenquist v Sweden* (n 15).

[18] Government Bill 2002/03:106, pp 102ff and Committee Report 2002/03:SkU16, s 11f, referred to in Halila, Lankinen and Nilsson (n 16), 289.

[19] *Lucky Dev v Sweden* (n 7). See further Bernitz (n 3), 170; Bernitz (n 5), 810; and Halila, Lankinen and Nilsson (n 16), 289.

[20] *Lucky Dev v Sweden* (n 7), para 54.

considered as dual or as coordinated procedures which implied a combined penalty for the same act, the latter would not have infringed the *ne bis in idem* principle. In this respect, the ECtHR held that the procedures did not meet the requirements of sufficiently close connection in substance and time,[21] but were considered parallel and separate and were independent of each other. Although this duplication of proceedings did not in itself involve a breach of Article 4 of Protocol 7 of the ECHR (the Article provides no protection regarding *lis pendens*), the fact that the tax proceedings were not terminated and the tax surcharges were not quashed after the criminal proceedings had become final, meant that the applicant was tried again for an offence for which she had already been finally acquitted.[22] Hence, on 27 November 2014, the ECtHR held that there had been a violation of Article 4 of Protocol 7 to the ECHR due to the fact that the tax proceedings determining the tax surcharges continued for a further nine and a half months after the criminal proceedings had become final, to the extent that the latter involved the determination of a tax offence.

This change by the ECtHR closely followed the legal developments by the CJEU in *Åkerberg Fransson* that prohibited double proceedings of a criminal nature with regard to VAT, and the 2013 rulings by the Swedish Supreme Court that will be described and analysed briefly below. Yet, the underlying starting point was the fundamental change in the well-known ECtHR *Zolotukhin* case from 2009.[23] In other words, the above mentioned change on *ne bis in idem* was initiated by the ECtHR already in 2009.[24] Accordingly, the Swedish Supreme Court set the date for asking for a new trial based on the argument that the verdict is wrong, to the date when the ECtHR's judgment in *Zolotukhin* was delivered, i.e. 10 February 2009.[25] Nevertheless, the impact of this ECtHR case in the national Swedish order was nothing close to immediate.

What the *Zolotukhin* case changed was the second issue to be assessed, i.e. the *idem* part, 'same offence', from a legal to a factual definition: facts which constitute a set of concrete factual circumstances involving the same defendant and which are inextricably connected in substance and time.[26] This change was later confirmed, e.g. in *Ruotsalainen*, which was a case against Finland dealing explicitly with 'the relationship between a tax surcharge and a criminal charge

---

[21] Ibid, para 62.

[22] Ibid, para 63.

[23] *Zolotukhin v Russia* App no 14939/03 (ECtHR, 2009). See Magnus Gulliksson, '*Ne bis in idem* and Effective Sanctions in EU Law', in Nergelius and Kristoffersson (eds) (n 5), 156.

[24] See further Bernitz (n 3), 166 and Bernitz (n 5), 802.

[25] NJA 2013, s 746.

[26] *Zolotukhin v Russia* (n 23), discussed by Zetterquist (n 11), 132.

for the same act'.[27] In this case,[28] a person had first been sentenced to a criminal charge, and then an administrative sanction charge for the same offence.

As has been emphasised, e.g. by Appeals Court Judge Ola Zetterquist, a 2009 Supreme Administrative Court judgment and a 2010 Supreme Court judgment ignored this new approach. Whereas the Supreme Administrative Court in 2009[29] disapplied the ECHR, arguing that the Swedish system had 'distinguishing features',[30] the Swedish Supreme Court in 2010 did apply the ECHR and the new definition introduced by the ECtHR in the *Zolotukhin* case,[31] but ruled there was no *clear support* that there was an infringement of the *ne bis in idem* principle.[32]

Accordingly, up until the Supreme Court and Supreme Administrative Court reversed their positions in June and October 2013, some of the lower courts still felt obliged not to disapply provisions contrary to fundamental rights guaranteed by the ECHR, as long as the infringements were not *clear* from the text of the ECHR, or the case law relating to it. What is noteworthy, however, is that their hesitation also rhymed well with previous rulings of the ECtHR itself, such as the *Rosenquist* ruling, mentioned above.[33]

2.2 The Immediate Impact of *Åkerberg Fransson* and the EU Charter

Clearly, *Åkerberg Fransson* resulted in reversed positions by the Swedish Supreme Court, and the Swedish Supreme Administrative Court that the *Zolotukhin* case and the ECHR had not managed alone.[34] In its 2013 judgment,[35] the Supreme Court 'acknowledged simultaneous criminal and tax sanctions, for the same actions, as an illegal violation of *ne bis in idem*, as acknowledged both by the ECHR and the Charter of Fundamental Rights'.[36] This put an end to an open revolt 'unprecedented in Swedish legal history',[37]

---

27 Zetterquist (n 11), 133, discussing *Ruotsalainen* App no 13079/03 (ECtHR, 2009).

28 See also Bernitz (n 3), 164 and Bernitz (n 5), 802.

29 RÅ 2009 ref 94 (Swedish Supreme Administrative Court).

30 Zetterquist (n 11), 133.

31 *Zolotukhin v Russia* (n 23), discussed by Zetterquist (n 11), 132.

32 NJA 2010, s 168 I and II.

33 *Rosenquist v Sweden* (n 15).

34 *Zolotukhin v Russia* (n 23), discussed by Zetterquist (n 11), 132.

35 NJA 2013, s 502.

36 Joakim Nergelius, 'Human Rights in EU Law 2014: Two Key Cases of 2013', in Nergelius and Kristoffersson (eds) (n 5), 1.

37 Zetterquist (n 11), 133.

including massive academic critique,[38] and open defiance by around ten of the lower courts[39] of the two previous judgments by the Swedish Administrative Supreme Court in 2009[40] and the Swedish Supreme Court in 2010.[41]

This allegedly meant that the Supreme Court had 'previously made some severe mistakes in its handling of *ne bis in idem* matters',[42] which, in relation to EU law and the EU Charter, were specifically addressed by the CJEU in *Åkerberg Fransson*.

It was not until the origin of the *Åkerberg Fransson* case, i.e. the District Court Judge in Haparanda, that any of the so-called rebellious lower courts, still far from being the majority, argued the EU law dimension of the issue,[43] and the right of *ne bis in idem* contained in Article 50 of the EU Charter. In other words, it was not until *Åkerberg Fransson* that any Swedish or other European court argued that the tax surcharges concerning VAT, harmonised on the EU level, actually concerns EU law and the EU Charter. By requesting a preliminary ruling, the District Court 'displayed its independence and knowledge of the Charter'.[44]

Thus, adding the EU law dimension and Article 50 of the EU Charter was probably what made way for the change. It is worth repeating that EU law is clear on this point, since it precludes a judicial practice that makes the obligation for a national court to disapply any provision contrary to a fundamental right guaranteed by the Charter conditional upon that infringement being clear from the text of the Charter or the case law relating to it.[45]

---

38 See further Zetterquist (n 11), 133.

39 See e.g. Court of Appeal for Western Sweden, in Case B 2432-09 *MO v Ekobrottsmyndigheten*, judgment of 23 June 2010, in which case Ola Zetterquist was the Judge Rapporteur, Zetterquist (n 11), 133. See also Katarina Fast, 'Tusen skäl att förekomma istället för att förekommas – en kommentar till dubbelbestraffningsfallen i EU-domstolen och Högsta domstolen 2013', JT 2013–14, s 24; and Halila, Lankinen and Nilsson (n 16), 289.

40 RÅ 2009 ref 94 (Swedish Supreme Administrative Court).

41 NJA 2010, p 168 (Swedish Supreme Court) with two judges dissenting.

42 Nergelius (n 36), 6.

43 Zetterquist (n 11), 134. See, however, the Dissenting opinion by Judge Sundberg in case HfÖN B 801-09, judgment of 8 September 2010, arguing that there was no room for 'clear support' if this is a question of EU law since such a method is incompatible with EU law. Even if the case at hand did not involve application of EU law (which it, as it turned out, did), there was in the dissenting judge's opinion no room for applying a criteria of 'clear support' in any case, since it had to be applied, as a matter of EU law. Hans Sundberg, senior judge, Court of Appeals for Northern Norrland, 'The Åkerberg Fransson Saga', ACTIONES, Uppsala, 14 December 2016.

44 Bernitz (n 3), 157.

45 *Åkerberg Fransson* (n 3), para 48. See further in particular Gulliksson (n 5) and Bernitz (n 5).

As a result, the CJEU's ruling in *Åkerberg Fransson* put an end to a multi-level saga on *ne bis in idem* involving various national courts, the ECtHR and the CJEU that inspired the Swedish Supreme Court and the national lawmakers to finally change the applicable laws and practices. Since 1 January 2016, there is a joint sanction procedure in the general courts, and a barring regulation for tax surcharges and tax crimes in respect of the same mistake or invalidity regarding the same person.[46]

As stated in the beginning of this chapter, the CJEU ruling in *Åkerberg Fransson* led to tremendous repercussions in Sweden. According to a joint report by the Swedish Prosecution Authority and the Swedish Economic Crime Authority,[47] prosecutors at these authorities have reviewed more than 2,700 cases due to the changes in case law. In 580 double penalty cases, public prosecutors have applied for a new trial. To this, an unknown number of applications by convicted persons should be added.[48] Most of these cases have been heard by a court and most of these have been successful. A large part of these cases have been retried by District Courts or Courts of Appeal.[49]

Yet, whether all these steps on the national level were really necessary following *Åkerberg Fransson*, we will briefly come back to in section 3.4 below. First, some general reflections regarding the application of the EU Charter will next be provided.

2.3 Lessons from a Case Study: Towards a More Coherent Application of the EU Charter?

As emphasised by the President of the Court of Justice of the European Union, Koen Lenaerts, in his keynote speech at the 10th Anniversary of the Charter becoming legally binding,[50] the Charter is invoked in about 10 per cent of all

---

[46] Government Bill 2014/15: 131, introducing a joint sanction procedure in the general courts. A barring regulation for tax surcharges and tax crimes is introduced in respect of the same mistake or invalidity regarding the same person.

[47] Swedish Prosecution Authority and Swedish Economic Crime Authority, 'Dubbelbestraffning – åtgärder vid Åklagarmyndigheten och Ekobrottsmyndigheten med anledning av två beslut från Högsta domstolen', available at www.ekobrottsmyndigheten.se/Documents/Rapporter/Dubbelbestraffning-sammanställning-åtgärder.pdf (last accessed 11 March 2019).

[48] Hans Sundberg, senior judge, Court of Appeals for Northern Norrland, 'The Impact of Preliminary Rulings on National Case Law', ACTIONES, final conference, Brussels, 24 October 2017.

[49] Swedish Prosecution Authority and Swedish Economic Crime Authority (n 47).

[50] K. Lenaerts, Keynote Speech, Making the EU Charter of Fundamental Rights a Reality for All: 10th Anniversary of the Charter Becoming Legally Binding, High Level event jointly held by the European Commission, the Finnish Presidency of

preliminary rulings procedures, 'which indicates not only a quantitative shift in the Court of Justice's case law, but also a qualitative change, going well beyond matters that concern the regulation of the internal market'.[51]

In line with this, and in relation to the specific case of *Åkerberg Fransson*, it is clear that the preliminary reference procedure, towards the end of the *Åkerberg Fransson* saga including numerous national cases that eventually gave rise to a change in the Swedish legal system, also led towards a more coherent application of the EU Charter in all similar cases. In other words, cases when a Member State imposes tax penalties and institutes criminal proceedings against a person for breaches of the obligation to declare VAT, i.e. when the Member States are implementing EU law within the meaning of Article 51(1) of the EU Charter, and the Charter is applicable. On this general point, this clarification certainly leads towards a more coherent application of the EU Charter.

At the same time, it has been argued that the *Åkerberg Fransson* saga sends a cautious note to Luxembourg, Strasbourg and their national counterparts in considering the enormous impact an individual judgment might have not only for individuals and national legal systems, but consequently, for their respect for EU law and the ECHR.[52] Given their enormous impact, the need for clear, well-reasoned and qualitative legal precedents are crucial for the future of EU and ECHR law. In this context, the significance of the principle of legal certainty must not be taken too lightly. Hence, any development, in order not to challenge this principle, must be transparent, well reasoned and qualitative in substance, argument and clarity. The question whether this principle has been upheld in the post *Åkerberg Fransson* cases should continuously be discussed while briefly looking at the post *Åkerberg Fransson* case law from the CJEU and the ECtHR starting with five more recent Grand Chamber rulings from the CJEU.

---

the Council of the EU and the EU Agency for Fundamental Rights, Concert Noble, Rue d'Arlon 84, Brussels, 12 November 2019, available on the conference webpage: https://ec.europa.eu/info/events/2019-conference-eu-charter-fundamental-rights-2019-nov-12_en (last accessed 3 November 2021).

51 Ibid, p 2.

52 Bergström (n 1).

3. POST *ÅKERBERG FRANSSON* – AN OBSCURE EUROPEAN DIALOGUE

3.1 Five Grand Chamber Rulings by the CJEU

Between 2013, when the judgment in *Åkerberg Fransson* was delivered, and 2018, the Grand Chamber of the CJEU has given five more judgments on the application of the *ne bis in idem* principle guaranteed by Article 50 of the EU Charter,[53] all more or less explicitly dealing with the scope of the limitation clause in Article 52(1) of the EU Charter and with the reserve in *Åkerberg Fransson* that even if the main rule is that there shall be no duplication of proceedings, it is for the national court to assess whether the remaining penalties are effective, proportionate and dissuasive.[54] Given the wide discretion granted to national courts in this regard, and the continuous judicial dialogue between the CJEU and the ECtHR, these cases might shed some further light upon the specific issues concerning judicial interaction, a more coherent application of the EU Charter, and overlapping legal sources that this chapter has raised.

On 27 May 2014, in *Spasic*,[55] the CJEU found that a limitation to the *ne bis in idem* principle enshrined in Article 50 of the EU Charter may be justified on the basis of Article 52(1) thereof.[56] According to this provision, any limitation on Charter rights and freedoms must be provided for by law and respect the essence of those rights and freedoms. Further, subject to the principle of proportionality, limitations may be made only if they necessary and genuinely meet objectives of general interest recognised by the Union or the need to protect the rights and freedoms of others. In the context of a European Arrest Warrant, the CJEU concluded that Article 54 of the Schengen Convention, which makes the application of the *ne bis in idem* principle subject to the condition that, upon conviction and sentencing, the penalty imposed 'has been enforced' or is 'actually in the process of being enforced', is compatible with Article 50 of the EU Charter. Although the limitation in Article 54 of the Schengen Convention consisting of the execution requirement is not found in Article 50 of the EU Charter, the explanations relating to Article 50 of the EU Charter expressly mentions Article 54 of the Schengen Convention among the provisions covered by Article 52(1) of the EU Charter.[57] Further, although Article 52(3) of the EU Charter specifically states that if the EU Charter con-

---

[53] The principle is also referred to in the Opinion of Advocate General Bobek in Case C-574/15 *Scialdone*, EU:C:2017:553, point 125 and footnote 62.

[54] *Åkerberg Fransson* (n 3), paras 34 and 36.

[55] C-129/14 PPU *Spasic*, EU:C:2014:586.

[56] Ibid, paras 55 and 56.

[57] Ibid, paras 52–59.

tains rights that correspond to those guaranteed by the ECHR, the meaning and scope of those Charter rights shall be the same as those laid down by the ECHR, the CJEU emphasised that this provision shall not prevent Union law providing more extensive protection.[58] *Spasic* thereby provided some understanding of the interrelationship between the different provisions and instruments embracing *ne bis in idem.*

In the subsequent case *Kossowski,*[59] from 29 June 2016, the main question was whether an accused may be prosecuted in a Member State after criminal proceedings brought against him in another Member State have been terminated by the public prosecutor's office without a detailed investigation. The CJEU thereby clarified that the principle of *ne bis in idem* laid down in Article 54 of the Schengen Convention, read in the light of Article 50 of the EU Charter, must be interpreted as meaning that a decision of the public prosecutor terminating criminal proceedings and finally closing the investigation procedure against a person, albeit with the possibility of its being reopened or annulled, without any penalties having been imposed, cannot be characterised as a final decision for the purposes of those articles, when it is clear from the statement of reasons for that decision that the procedure was closed without a detailed investigation having been carried out.[60] Explicitly dealing with the Schengen Convention and the EU Charter, no reference was made to the ECHR or the jurisprudence of the ECtHR.

The case *Garlsson Real Estate,*[61] from 20 March 2018, concerned the combination of an administrative fine of a criminal nature and a final criminal conviction in a case of market manipulation and permissible limitations of the *ne bis in idem* principle guaranteed in Article 50 of the EU Charter. The case focused on justification for the limitation of Article 50 of the EU Charter. The CJEU motivated a limitation of the *ne bis in idem* principle, i.e. that it should be balanced against requirements of effective, proportional and dissuasive punishment and thus allowing for duplication of both procedures and criminal sanctions, with reference to the fact that the Member States according to the relevant directive were free to choose the penalties applicable to persons responsible for market manipulation.[62] The consequences of this opening for duplication of proceedings and criminal sanctions was in the case itself

---

58 Ibid, para 5.

59 C-486/14 *Kossowski*, EU:C:2016:483.

60 The fact that neither the victim nor a potential witness was interviewed was an indication that no detailed investigation had taken place.

61 C-537/16 *Garlsson Real Estate*, EU:C:2018:193.

62 More precisely 'Article 14(1) of Directive 2003/6, read in conjunction with Article 5 thereof', see para 49 of the judgment.

mitigated by the finding that this particular duplication appeared to go beyond what was strictly necessary in order to achieve the objective sought.

On 20 March 2018, on the same day as the ruling of *Garlsson Real Estate* and five years after *Åkerberg Fransson*, the CJEU gave judgments in the two final cases of this brief review. The first one, *di Puma*,[63] concerned the legality of administrative fines imposed in relation to insider trading, after being acquitted for the same offence in criminal proceedings. The rather odd situation in the case was that the national legislation precluded an administrative procedure after such an acquittal; a rule over which the referring court had doubts concerning its compatibility with the EU law requirement of effective, proportionate and dissuasive sanctions. The CJEU held that even if there is such a requirement in EU law that does not make the duplication of procedures mandatory, in a case where it was clear that di Puma was acquitted because there had been no offence.[64]

The second case, *Menci*,[65] like *Åkerberg Fransson*, dealt with the application of the *ne bis in idem* principle in the context of non-payment of VAT. In this case, the CJEU held that a duplication of tax and criminal proceedings and penalties constitutes a limitation on the *ne bis in idem* principle laid down in Article 50 of the Charter and consequently dealt with the justification for its limitation. For the purposes of this résumé, it is sufficient to say that the CJEU, while referring to the ECtHR case *A and B v Norway*,[66] took the opportunity to circumscribe the scope of the limitation of the *ne bis in idem* principle by providing a set of requirements for its justification. Hence, in cases where national legislation in accordance with which criminal proceedings may be brought against a person for failing to pay VAT, although that person has already been made subject in relation to the same acts, to a final administrative penalty of a criminal nature for the purposes of Article 50 of the EU Charter, i.e. a duplication of tax and criminal proceedings and penalties constituting a limitation of *ne bis in idem*, such a limitation can be justified on condition that the national legislation meets a number of conditions:[67]

First, it must pursue an objective of general interest, which is such as to justify such a duplication of proceedings and penalties, namely combating VAT offences, and those proceedings and penalties must pursue additional objectives. Second, it must contain rules ensuring coordination, limiting the additional disadvantage, which result from a duplication of proceedings to

---

63 Joined Cases C-596/16 and C-597/16 *di Puma*, EU:C:2018:192.

64 Ibid, para 44.

65 C-524/15 *Menci*, EU:C:2018:197.

66 ECtHR, 15 November 2016, *A and B v Norway*, CE:ECHR:2016:1115JUD002413011.

67 C-524/15 *Menci*, EU:C:2018:197, para 63 and operative part of the judgment.

what is strictly necessary. Third, it must provide for rules making it possible to ensure that the severity of all of the penalties imposed is limited to what is strictly necessary in relation to the seriousness of the offence concerned. The CJEU added that it is for the national court to ensure that the application of the limitation, i.e. the combined procedure and sanction, is not excessive in relation to the seriousness of the offence committed.

To summarise this short review of the CJEU's Grand Chamber case law on *ne bis in idem* after *Åkerberg Fransson,* we see that the CJEU is willing, on the basis of Article 52(1) of the EU Charter, to accept the choices made by the EU legislator as to limitations of the *ne bis in idem* principle, and that without such EU legislation, the national courts are obliged to ensure, on the one hand, that the requirements of effective, proportional and dissuasive sanctions are met and, on the other hand, that the *Menci* requirements are fulfilled, including the ensuring of a non-excessive total reaction on any given offence. In the absence of harmonised EU legislation, the CJEU guides national courts towards a more coherent application of the EU Charter. However, this line of cases is, in terms of judicial dialogue, perhaps even more interesting because of the issues they are not specifically addressing. Before going into that, we will take a quick look at the simultaneous[68] developments of the particular concept of a *sufficiently close connection in substance and time*[69] in the Strasbourg Court.

3.2 *A Sufficiently Close Connection in Substance and Time* by the ECtHR

This concept was introduced by the Strasbourg Court for the first time in *Nilsson v Sweden,*[70] a case decided long before *Zolotukhin*, concerning the combined sanctions in different proceedings of criminal punishment and withdrawal of a driving licence on the ground of a road traffic offence. It was declared inadmissible on the ground that even if there were duplication of both sanctions and procedures, this was foreseeable and the administrative (but criminal in nature) sanction of revoking the driving licence was decided on the fact that Nilsson was convicted for the offence. Thus, the administrative proceedings did not take any new facts into account, but the decision was based on the fact findings made by the criminal court.

---

[68] The case law after *Zolotukhin* is carefully summarised by the ECHR itself in *A and B v Norway* (n 66), paras 112–16.

[69] This concept was mentioned by the CJEU in the *Menci* judgment, para 61 referring to *A and B v Norway* (n 66) but not in the *di Puma* judgment.

[70] Application 73661/01, *Nilsson v Sweden*, available at http://hudoc.echr.coe.int/eng?i=001-72028 (last accessed 3 November 2021).

The above mentioned, *Lucky Dev*,[71] also involving Sweden, is illustrative of the development of this concept. It concerned, like *Åkerberg Fransson*, the administrative imposition of tax surcharges and subsequently, in criminal proceedings, the imposition of a suspended sentence and a duty to perform community service. Unlike in *Åkerberg* Fransson, the two sets of procedures were largely simultaneous. However, the ECtHR summarised[72] its finding that:

> the temporal connection on its own was evidently deemed insufficient to exclude the application of the *ne bis in idem* prohibition. It would not seem unreasonable to deduce from these judgments in cases against … Sweden that, given that the two sets of proceedings were largely contemporaneous, … it was the lack of a substantive connection that gave rise to the violation of Article 4 of Protocol No. 7.

Unlike the case of revoking a driving licence in the case of a road-traffic offence, the factual circumstances are established independently in both of these proceedings, hence the lack of 'substantive connection'.

Finally, in the case *A and B v Norway*, the ECtHR made an exercise, not unlike the CJEU made later in *Menci*, of circumscribing the applicability of the concept 'sufficiently close link in substance and time' with a series of requirements for its application.[73] According to these, the respondent State must convincingly demonstrate that the dual proceedings in question have been combined in an integrated manner so as to form a coherent whole. This implies not only that the purposes pursued and the means used to achieve them should in essence be complementary and linked in time, but also that the possible consequences of organising the legal treatment of the conduct concerned in such a manner should be proportionate and foreseeable for the persons affected. The ECtHR went on to summarise the conditions to be satisfied in order for dual criminal and administrative proceedings to be regarded as sufficiently connected in substance and in time with some material factors for determining whether there is a sufficiently close connection in substance between these proceedings, including whether they pursue complementary purposes, constitute a foreseeable consequence, avoid duplication of the collection and assessment of evidence and do not result in an excessive burden on the individual concerned.[74] The ECtHR then went on to find a sufficiently close connection in substance and time in the case at hand, by applying these conditions. Among those is the important finding that the 'establishment of facts made in one set [of proceedings] was used in the other set and, as regards

---

71 *Lucky Dev v Sweden* (n 7).

72 In *A and B v Norway* (n 66), para 114.

73 Ibid, paras 121, 125, 126 and 130.

74 Ibid, para 132.

the proportionality of the overall punishment inflicted, the sentence imposed in the criminal trial had regard to the tax penalty'.[75]

3.3 'Why Don't You Speak My Language?'

It is not an easy task to assess whether the conditions or criteria established by the CJEU are in substance the same or similar to the ones established by the ECtHR. What is clear, and equally regrettable, is that there is a substantial difference in the language deployed by the two courts. In our analysis, the perhaps most important condition for allowing duplication of proceedings is what the ECtHR identifies as the substantive link between these proceedings. In the words of the ECtHR, the state should as far as possible avoid any duplication in the collection and the assessment of the evidence. This should be done by means of adequate interaction between the various competent authorities to bring about that the establishment of facts in one set is also used in the other set. While this condition is clearly stated in the ECtHR case law, it is unspoken of in the case law of the CJEU. The closest we get to the CJEU discussing this condition is its reasoning in *di Puma*, given on the same day as *Menci*. As noted above, the latter judgment, but not the former, contained a reference to *A and B v Norway*. This lack of explicit reference is all the more noteworthy, since we learn from Advocate General Bobek's Opinion in *Scialdone*, mentioned in footnote 53 above,[76] that the very reason for attributing *Menci* to the Grand Chamber was the implications *A and B v Norway* may have had on Article 50 of the Charter. The reluctance to refer to relevant ECtHR case law is very difficult to reconcile with any ambition of transparency the CJEU may have in this field. Arguably, it was precisely the circumstance that the acquittal in the criminal proceeding was used as a bar to administrative sanctions that, in the analysis of the CJEU in *di Puma*, did not render the resulting lack of effective, proportionate and dissuasive penalties for the alleged violation of the prohibition on insider dealing incompatible with the requirement for such penalties in the relevant directive.

So, regarding the requirement of a sufficiently close substantive link, we cannot really say that there is such a condition in the CJEU case law. The mere reference to the condition of a sufficiently close link in substance and time that the CJEU gave in *Menci*[77] does not clarify whether there is such an approach in EU law as well. Given the requirement in Article 52(3) of the EU Charter that the 'meaning and scope' of Charter rights corresponding to ECHR rights 'shall

---

75 Ibid, para 146.

76 See footnote 62 of the Opinion.

77 C-18/16 *Menci* EU:C:2017:680, para 61.

be the same', it would of course be safe to say that there is such a condition also in EU law. But why then does the CJEU not say so? A possible explanation is offered by the President of the CJEU himself, Koen Lenaerts, further discussed below in section 4.1. If following Lenaerts' analysis of these cases, judicial interaction has indeed provided one possible solution on how to solve the complex issue of overlapping fundamental rights sources. First, however, a brief retrospective on the *Åkerberg Fransson* impact in Sweden.

3.4 Were the Steps Taken in Swedish Law after *Åkerberg Fransson* Really Necessary?

To recapitulate, the two Swedish Supreme Courts reversed their respective case law to rule out the separate proceedings for tax surcharge and criminal sanctions. With reference to the ECHR, and the jurisprudence of the ECtHR, this was correct, since the establishment of facts in these proceedings were separated from and independent of each other. In applying the *Menci* requirements for possible limitations of Article 50 of the EU Charter, the result would have been the same. The subsequent mass of cases in which sometimes the sanctions ended up being quite weak is of course questionable from the point of view of the – at the time seemingly innocent – reserve in *Åkerberg Fransson*, that it is for the national court to ascertain that, when not doubling the procedures, the remaining sanction is effective, proportionate and dissuasive. This is, however, rather a consequence of the way that the Supreme Court moulded the *ne bis in idem* principle into the Swedish legal system, attaching it to rules on *res judicata* and *lis pendens*. As was pointed out by the ECtHR in *Lucky Dev*,[78] *simultaneous* tax proceedings determining tax surcharges and criminal proceedings examining a corresponding tax offence would not be incompatible with Article 4 of Protocol 7 of the ECHR per se, since the Article provides no protection against *lis pendens*.

Subsequently, the legislator decided to give the general court's jurisdiction to impose both criminal law penalties and tax surcharges in cases where both were deemed necessary in order to have effective, proportionate and dissuasive sanctions. Thus, these double sanctions are decided in one set of proceedings, in which it is possible to ascertain that all of the requirements or conditions in EU law and of the ECHR are met. It would, had the legislator reacted earlier to the case law of the ECtHR, have been possible to continue with separate proceedings, as long as the fact findings of the first formed the basis for the assessment in the latter (and this was a foreseeable consequence, the proportionality of the overall sanction was guaranteed, and so on).

---

[78] *Lucky Dev v Sweden* (n 7), para 60.

4. THE OVERLAP OF FUNDAMENTAL RIGHTS SOURCES

In trying to answer the question whether judicial interaction can provide any solutions on how to solve complex issues relating to the overlapping of fundamental rights sources, legal precedent needs to be transparent, well reasoned and qualitative in substance, argument and clarity. As shown above both in relation to the *Åkerberg Fransson* saga, and the subsequent cases by the CJEU and the ECtHR, this has not always been the case, at least not without the help of convincing authoritative legal interpretation.

However, it is also argued that there is a need to take a slightly wider perspective, putting the *Åkerberg Fransson* ruling in an even wider context both in relation to other court cases as well as to legislative intervention. If doing so, there is aspiring hope that the CJEU is taking fundamental rights seriously. In this respect, fundamental rights are 'part and parcel of the rule of law within the EU, which the Court of Justice firmly upholds',[79] where it also addresses some of the complex issues relating to the overlapping of fundamental rights sources. Not only need different cases from different courts be taken into consideration, it is also important not to forget legislative initiatives on the EU level. In such a wider context, it is particularly interesting to note that the European Commission is planning to propose harmonising legislation on *ne bis in idem*.[80]

4.1 European Convention of Human Rights (ECHR) – Only Minimum Level of Protection

According to Article 52(3) of the EU Charter, the meaning and scope of the Charter rights shall be the same as those laid down by the ECHR. This means that the level of protection guaranteed by the Charter may not be lower than that guaranteed by the ECHR.[81]

---

79 Lenaerts (n 50), p 18.
80 Czonka (n 4).
81 Lenaerts (n 50).

As pointed out by Lenaerts,[82] President of the CJEU, in *Menci*,[83] the CJEU had to decide whether to align its interpretation of Article 50 of the EU Charter with the case law of the ECtHR,

> according to which the fact that the same violation of tax law is sanctioned both in tax and criminal proceedings does not infringe the *ne bis in idem* principle enshrined in Article 4 of Protocol No 7 to the ECHR, where those tax and criminal proceedings have a sufficiently close connection both in substance and in time.[84]

Lenaerts thereby observed[85] that in *Menci*, the CJEU followed a different approach, and emphasised that the ECHR 'does not constitute … a legal instrument which has been formally incorporated into EU law'.[86] In fact, after providing the conditions for limitations by national law of the *ne bis in idem* principle to be justified, the CJEU observed that its interpretation of Articles 50 and 52(1) of the EU Charter provided a level of protection of fundamental rights that was compatible with that guaranteed by the ECHR.[87] This further means that the CJEU can interpret provisions of the EU Charter with the result that the level of protection is higher than that provided by the equivalent provision in the ECHR. Important to note, therefore, is the fact that the level of protection must not be lower than that guaranteed by the ECHR, but that it may embrace a higher level of protection, as illustrated e.g. by *Menci*[88] and *Spasic*.[89]

Depending on which set of legal rules applies to a certain case, the level of protection might therefore differ. Since the ECHR has always only provided a minimum level of protection, the good news is that applying the EU Charter may rise to that level. This, however, might be difficult to foresee by individuals as well as by national courts. For the development of fundamental rights protection in Europe, the strive for clarity and consistency is therefore perhaps as important as always reaching the highest possible level of protection in

---

[82] Ibid.

[83] C-524/15 *Menci*, EU:C:2018:197. Lenaerts (n 50), p 9ff, with further references e.g. to M. Luchtman, 'The ECJ's Recent Case Law on ne bis in idem: Implications for Law Enforcement in a Shared Legal Order' (2018) 55 *Common Market Law Review* 1717, at 1730.

[84] Lenaerts (n 50), p 10, with reference to ECtHR, judgment of 15 November 2016, *A and B v Norway* (n 66), para 132.

[85] Ibid.

[86] C-18/16 *Menci*, EU:C:2017:680, para 22.

[87] Ibid, para 60, emphasised by Lenaerts (n 50).

[88] Ibid, p 9, with further references e.g. to judgments of 14 September 2017, C-18/16 *K.*, EU:C:2017:680, para 50; of 20 March 2018, C-524/15 *Menci*, EU:C: 2018:197, para 62; of 26 September 2018, C-180/17 *Staatssecretaris van Veiligheid en Justitie* (Suspensory effect of the appeal), EU:C:2018:775, para 31.

[89] C-129/14 PPU *Spasic*, EU:C:2014:586, para 5.

each individual case. The CJEU and the ECtHR must continuously guard their important roles of guiding the national courts in a transparent and foreseeable way. In this respect, the role of judicial interaction is still one of the most important tools.

4.2 Room for Diverse National Laws

In some of the most recent developments on *ne bis in idem* and Articles 50 and 52(1) of the EU Charter, the absence of harmonised EU rules has been instrumental in formulating the criteria for justification of national rules limiting *ne bis in idem* in Article 50 of the EU Charter. For instance, besides the *Menci* case in which the CJEU formulated a set of criteria for justification, *Garlsson Real Estate* emphasised the permissible choice for the Member States, according to the relevant directive, to provide either for a system in which infringements of the prohibition of market manipulation may be subject to proceedings and penalties only once, or for a system allowing a duplication, as long as the proportionality principle is complied with. According to *Menci*, such an interpretation of Articles 50 and 52(1) of the EU Charter complies with the ECHR.

Going back in time to *Åkerberg Fransson*, and regardless of the fact that *Melloni* concerned the European Arrest Warrant and not VAT or *ne bis in idem*, *Melloni* and *Åkerberg Fransson* were delivered by the CJEU on the same day and should be read together, thereby separating areas where there is a harmonised level of protection from non-harmonised.[90] In contrast to the underlying facts of *Åkerberg* Fransson, and as was stated in *Melloni*, a uniform level of protection inevitably rules out diversity as it precludes the application of higher levels of protection under national law.[91] On a more general point and in contrast to what has been argued concerning *Taricco II*,[92] this case should, according to Lenaerts, not be read as a limitation of *Melloni*.[93] This clearly separates *Melloni*, which dealt with an EU harmonised level of protection, from *Åkerberg Fransson* and *M.A.S. and M.B. (Taricco II)*,[94] at least until any harmonising EU measures on *ne bis in idem* or other fundamental rights issues have been introduced.

90 Ritleng (n 5).

91 Case C-399/11 *Melloni*, EU:C:2013:107.

92 Case C-42/17 *M.A.S. and M.B.*, EU:C:2017:936.

93 F. Vigano, 'Melloni Overruled? Considerations on the "Taricco II" Judgment of the Court of Justice' (2018) 9 *New Journal of European Criminal Law* 18, referred to by Lenaerts (n 50).

94 For an explanation of his reasoning, see Lenaerts (n 50), pp 13–15.

4.3 The Importance of Harmonisation for the Protection of Fundamental Rights

The European Commission may, as suggested above,[95] propose harmonising legislation on *ne bis in idem*, as long as the level of protection is above the levels protected by both the ECHR and the EU Charter, as laid down more in detail by the ECtHR and the CJEU. These different choices recently summarised by President Lenaerts are worth noting:[96]

> On the one hand, the EU legislator may impose a uniform level of fundamental rights protection, provided that it does not undermine the level of protection guaranteed by the Charter. Needless to say, the EU legislator is free to decide whether to impose a uniform level of protection that is higher than that guaranteed by the Charter. Any such uniform level of protection inevitably rules out diversity as it precludes the application of higher levels of protection under national law.
> On the other hand, where the EU legislator has not provided for a uniform level of protection, there is room for national diversity. However, that diversity is not absolute as it must, first, comply with the level of protection guaranteed by the Charter and, second, respect 'the primacy, unity and effectiveness of EU law'.

5. CONCLUDING REMARKS

As a result of this analysis, we conclude that courts are instrumental not only in the settlement of individual disputes, but also in changing and developing the legal system: in other words, pressure through law, including defining the lowest level of protection for the EU legislator when proposing new harmonising legislation. Pending such harmonising EU legislation, there is still some room for national diversity, as long as the level of protection guaranteed by the ECHR and the EU Charter, including the principle of legal certainty, and the respect for the primacy, unity and effectiveness of EU law are complied with.

Against the background of the particulars of the Swedish system, section 2 provided an illustrative example of multilevel judicial interaction. It further illustrated the massive impact a single CJEU judgment might have not only on one national legal system, but on the relationship between national and EU law in general, and on the development of EU law and the impact of the EU Charter in particular. The resulting clarification led towards a more coherent application of the EU Charter. Nevertheless, as illustrated by sections 3 and 4, the significance of the principles of transparency and legal certainty must not be taken too lightly even when focusing on judicial interaction and the

---

95 Czonka (n 4).
96 Lenaerts (n 50), p 12.

continuous overlap of fundamental rights sources in an increasingly important and dynamic area of European law.

Drawing from the case law of the ECtHR in *Lucky Dev v Sweden*,[97] from 27 November 2014 that followed upon *Åkerberg Fransson*, and subsequent case law of the CJEU, the application of the ECtHR's jurisprudence on the *ne bis in idem* principle involves the assessment of a number of issues. The first issue is whether the imposition of tax surcharges is criminal in nature. On the face of it, this seems to correspond to the CJEU's post *Fransson* assessment of the criminal nature of the proceedings and penalties for the purposes of Article 50 of the EU Charter.[98] The second issue is whether the criminal offences for which the applicant was prosecuted were the same as those for which the tax surcharges were imposed on her (*idem*). This in turn seems to correspond to the CJEU's post *Fransson* assessment of the existence of the same offence.[99] The third issue is whether there was a final decision, which is also discussed by the CJEU,[100] and, the fourth issue is, finally, whether there was a duplication of proceedings (*bis*), including the assessment whether there is a close connection, in substance and time, between the criminal proceedings and the tax proceedings. Whether this last line of argument has been followed by the CJEU post *Fransson* has briefly been addressed although the focus of this chapter is not a comparison of the legal requirements used and applied by the courts respectively per se.

In the post *Fransson* case law by the CJEU, the scope of the limitation clause in Article 52(1) of the EU Charter and the question of justification for the limitation of the right guaranteed in Article 50 of the EU Charter has further been discussed. At the same time, the CJEU has followed a slightly different approach compared to the ECtHR, emphasising that the ECHR 'does not constitute … a legal instrument which has been formally incorporated into EU law'.[101]

Hence, the legal provisions and issues before the CJEU are not always overlapping with those emphasised by the ECtHR. The CJEU Grand Chamber rulings following *Åkerberg Fransson* have so far mainly involved Article 50 of the EU Charter, the scope of the limitation clause in Article 52(1) of the EU Charter, i.e. the justification for the limitation of the right guaranteed in Article

---

[97] *Lucky Dev v Sweden* (n 7), paras 50–58.

[98] See e.g. C-537/16 *Garlsson Real Estate*, EU:C:2018:193, paras 34–35; and C-18/16 *Menci*, EU:C:2017:680, paras 26–33.

[99] See e.g. C-537/16 *Garlsson Real Estate*, EU:C:2018:193, paras 36–41; and C-18/16 *Menci*, EU:C:2017:680, paras 34–39.

[100] Compare e.g. the discussion by the CJEU in C-486/14 *Kossowski*, EU:C:2016:483.

[101] C-524/15 *Menci*, EU:C:2018:197, para 22, cited by Lenaerts (n 50).

50 of the Charter, and the reserve in *Åkerberg Fransson* that even if the main rule is that there shall be no duplication of proceedings, it is for the national court to assess whether the remaining penalties are effective, proportionate and dissuasive.[102] Irrespective of the continuous guidance by the CJEU, and the ECtHR, this assessment is perhaps not the easiest task for national courts to embrace.

To conclude, traditional guarantees, such as the principle of legality and *ne bis in idem* principle have been involved in the interaction between criminal liability at the national level, and rights and principles protected by EU law, and their content has been redefined. Whether the outcome of the involved judicial interaction has resulted in an enhanced fundamental rights protection of individuals is, however, not as clear-cut to answer as we would initially have thought. Fundamental rights protection is certainly developing, but the remaining inconsistencies and discrepancies between levels and different human rights instruments make it very difficult for individuals to understand and make use of these fundamental rights.[103] Clearly, given the current legal and political situation, the European courts' key role in promoting and managing that dialogue is becoming even greater.

---

[102] *Åkerberg Fransson* (n 3), paras 34 and 36.

[103] See, however, attempts to make the EU Charter accessible to all, such as the CharterClick! Project and the CharterClick tools that have recently been incorporated into the Beta version of the e-justice portal, available at https://beta.e-justice.europa.eu/581/EN/fundamental_rights (last accessed 9 June 2020).

21. Comment: objective and subjective *ne bis in idem*– the *AY* case

Florentino-Gregorio Ruiz Yamuza

The Court of Justice of the European Union (CJEU) ruling in the *AY* case on 25 July 2018 has provoked scant attention both from academics and legal practitioners.[1] Nevertheless, in this case the Court made some remarkable contributions concerning the construction of the *ne bis in idem* principle in Council Framework Decision 2002/584/JHA of 13 June 2002 on the European arrest warrant and the surrender procedures between Member States (EAW FD).[2]

The novelty of some of the topics tackled by the CJEU and the different points of view held by the Court and the Advocate General (AG) prove that there is still an ongoing debate on some *ne bis in idem* fundamentals.

In principle, the *Åkeberg Fransson* and *AY* cases may appear somewhat disconnected. In *Åkeberg Fransson* and its corresponding saga, the axis on which the analysis by the CJEU revolved was the relationship between administrative penalties and criminal law, whereas in *AY* it was criminal cooperation within the Area of Freedom, Security and Justice. Nevertheless, both cases are exponents of the doctrine of the CJEU on the *ne bis in idem* principle and they present different areas of intersection.

Among these, we must highlight the way forward concerning legislative harmonisation within the EU, the interpretation of the scope of the preliminary ruling reference, the construction of the *ne bis in idem* concept and the analysis of its nature and subjective or objective spectrum, the interrelation between the jurisprudence of the CJEU and the European Court of Human Rights (ECHR) and the need for constant dialogue between national and supranational courts, and between courts in different EU Member States.

---

1 C-268/17, *AY*, EU:C:2018:602.

2 We have to record that after the Court judgment Hungary did not surrender AY to Croatia.

1. THE SCENARIO

In 2011, the Croatian Office for Suppression of Corruption and Organised Crime (USKOK) asked the Hungarian authorities to interview AY as a suspect in the context of a corruption-related investigation carried out in Croatia. Hungary declined the cooperation request on the grounds of national interest but opened an investigation on the same facts, interviewing AY as a witness. This investigation was closed by the Hungarian National Bureau of Investigation (HNBI) in 2012. The Croatian investigation was also suspended in December 2012.

In 2013, after Croatia acceded to the EU, the USKOK issued an EAW against AY concerning the same facts. The Budapest High Court refused it, claiming that criminal proceedings had already been brought in Hungary in respect of the same acts and those proceedings had been halted. After this decision, AY moved to Germany and Austria, the authorities in which also refused to take action on the notice issued through Interpol as its execution might infringe the *ne bis in idem* principle, taking into account the Hungarian refusal of the EAW.

In 2015, after AY's indictment in Croatia, a new EAW was issued, now by the County Court of Zagreb, which was not executed by Hungary either. The EAW was re-issued in 2017, stating that the circumstances had changed and criminal proceedings against AY had been brought before the Court. Not receiving any answer from the Hungarian authorities, the Zagreb court contacted them via Eurojust to know their position: the case was already decided and therefore they were not obliged to act on the EAW.

2. THE PRELIMINARY RULING REFERENCE, THE AG'S POSITION AND THE COURT DECISION

In May 2017 the County Court of Zagreb sent a request for a preliminary ruling to the CJEU which the AG did not regard as admissible, except concerning the fifth of the questions asked, taking a stance on all of them just in case the Court did not share his view. On the contrary, the CJEU considered that the obligation to rule on the questions referred to was a general rule following its doctrine in the *Sleutjes* case.[3] Besides, it was necessary to respond so that the referring court could decide whether to withdraw or maintain the EAW, which usually impacts on the requested person's fundamental rights, the preservation of which primarily falls within the issuing authority's responsibility.

[3] C-278/16, *Sleutjes*, EU:C:2017:757.

In the fifth question, the CJEU was asked if Article 1(2) EAW FD must be interpreted as requiring the executing authority to adopt a decision on any EAW forwarded to it, even when in that Member State a ruling has already been made on a previous EAW concerning the same person and the same acts, but the second EAW has been issued by a different authority on account of the requested person's indictment. Both the AG and the CJEU agreed that Article 1(2), compels the executing authority to rule on the EAW even when in that State a previous EAW has been decided on the same person in the same criminal procedure, but the second EAW is transmitted by a different authority due to a change of circumstances in the issuing Member State. The CJEU recalled that in such circumstances the executing authority by remaining silent on the EAW fails to comply with the obligation to resolve according to Articles 1(2), 15(1), 17(1) and (6) EAW FD.

In its first to fourth questions, which were dealt with jointly by the CJEU, the referring court asked whether EAW FD Articles 3(2) and 4(3) must be interpreted as meaning that a decision by the Public Prosecutor's Office, the HNBI, terminating an investigation opened against an unknown person during which AY was interviewed merely as a witness may be relied on to refuse to execute the EAW under either of these provisions.

Concerning Article 3(2) the AG's opinion underlined that the wording 'finally judged' varied along with the linguistic versions in different Member States. Further to that, the CJEU did not give a definite answer to the question raised so far. Mr Szpunar resorted to three cases to substantiate his opinion contrary to the application of this mandatory non-execution ground.

In *Mantello*, the Court interpreted this provision widely, resorting to its case law stemming from Article 54 of the Schengen Implementation Convention.[4] According to this, a person is considered finally judged in respect of the same acts when as a result of a procedure the public action is definitively extinguished or the person definitively absolved, which has to be determined under the law of the executing State. As AY had been interviewed just as a witness, his situation did not fall into this category.

In the *Turanský* case, the Court ruled that *ne bis in idem* does not apply if before charging a person criminal proceedings are suspended where the suspension does not definitely bar further prosecution and does not preclude new criminal proceedings in respect of the same acts in that State. In that situation, public action cannot be regarded as permanently extinguished.[5]

In *Kossowski*, a prosecutor's decision terminating criminal proceedings and finally closing the investigation against a person could not be characterised

---

4 C-261/09, *Mantello*, EU:C:2010:683.
5 C-491/07, *Turanský*, EU:C:2008:768.

as a final decision when it was clear that the procedure was closed without a detailed investigation having been carried out.[6]

On its part, the CJEU determined that 'finally judged' in Article 3(2) also applies to resolutions by the public prosecutor definitely discontinuing criminal proceedings even if a court does not intervene in the decision-making process (*Kossowski*).

The 'final judgment' in Article 3(2) presupposes that criminal proceedings have been instituted against the requested person (*Mantello*, *Kossowski* and *M*), who has been finally judged in a Member State and not just interviewed as a witness (*Gasparini and others*).[7] Consequently, AY was not finally judged in Hungary. The decision by the Hungarian Prosecutor (OCI) to close the investigation, having AY deposed just as a witness, could not be invoked to refuse the surrender pursuant to Article 3(2).

As for Article 4(3) EAW FD, the AG recalled that the CJEU had not yet addressed it. Its first part and Article 3(2) have to do with *ne bis in idem*, although it has a greater scope since Article 4(3) refers to the offence instead of to the requested person. The operation of this non-mandatory ground for refusal does not require the proceedings to have been brought against the sought person but it would be excessive to interpret it as applicable when the facts were the same but the persons concerned in the proceedings were not. Additionally, a more restrictive interpretation is aligned with the national regulations that establish investigations *in rem* and then *in personam*.

According to the AG's opinion, under Article 4(3) an EAW may be refused if the executing Member State authorities have not opened or have concluded proceedings, even if the person sought has not been charged or suspected, if those authorities have examined the possibility that he committed the offence in question.

In turn, the CJEU judgment distinguished in Article 4(3) EAW FD three reasons for non-execution:

(1) The authorities of the executing State decide not to initiate criminal action, which is not the case of the Hungarian decision.
(2) The executing State authorities decide to halt proceedings in respect of the offence. The Court noted that it would be excessive to consider applicable this second ground when the EAW refers to identical facts to those that have been subject to a previous resolution adopted without considering relevant the identity of the accused or investigated person. An EAW is not issued in relation to the offence. It necessarily refers to a person

[6] C-486/14, *Kossowski*, EU:C:2016:483.

[7] C-398/12, *M*, EU:C:2014:1057 and C-467/04, *Gasparini and others*, EU:C:2006:610.

and *ne bis in idem* does not protect a person from being subjected to successive investigations for the same events in different Member States (*Kossowski*). The proceedings continued against an unknown author. AY was only a witness. The stay of the case was not decided in relation to him. Therefore, Article 4(3), second ground, could not be invoked in this case.

(3) The third ground in Article 4(3) did not apply in this case either, since it requires a final decision passed on the requested person in a third Member State preventing further proceedings.

3. COMMENTARY

Among the most relevant aspects of the case, we can distinguish three different areas:

(1) The Preliminary Ruling Reference

Without taking sides in the debate between preliminary ruling reference admissibility versus lack of jurisdiction of the CJEU, we share the AG's view that the Court's ruling may be purely advisory in this case in which the EAW had already been issued. In any case, it would not be the decision to issue but to withdraw the EAW which would justify the intervention of the CJEU.

(2) EAW

First, it is essential to affirm that in any case the executing State must give a response to the EAW issued, under Article 1(2) EAW FD. Second, the reminder made by the AG in paragraph 32 of his opinion declaring that mutual trust is one-to-one is also very interesting. Accordingly, the issuing State must also rely on the executing State when it refuses a cooperation request.

(3) *Ne bis in idem*

First, the CJEU tackled some matters for the first time and broached some others where its jurisprudence is not clear cut. Second, although the CJEU clearly stated that neither Article 3(2) nor Article 4(3) EAW FD could be relied on in the present case to justify the position of Hungary, there were areas of discrepancy between the AG and the CJEU.

They did not seem to coincide precisely regarding the subjective spectrum of *ne bis in idem*. The questions raised to the CJEU revolved around two ideas: if Article 4(3) EAW FD has an eminently objective (offence-wise) or subjective (personal) dimension and the validity of what was previously resolved in the executing State regarding the same case and person in the event of a change of circumstance in the emission status.

The AG seemed to develop a thesis that would introduce some nuances regarding the construction of Article 4(3). Even without openly abandoning the subjective conception of the whole system, he left open a divergent interpretation of Articles 3(2) and 4(3), not linking the application of *ne bis in idem* to the acquisition of the formal status as investigated or accused of the requested person, but to the production of an investigation into his possible commission of the crime.

On the other hand, the CJEU had a more restrictive vision of the application of the precept, taking the *ne bis in idem* principle onto a purely subjective terrain, requiring it to be necessary that the person has intervened in the process as accused or investigated.

Third, it is not entirely clear whether the change in circumstances mentioned in the judgment which justified a new examination of the case by the executing authority should be understood as a change in the authority dealing with the matter, formerly the Croatian prosecutor and now the Zagreb court, or the indictment of AY. We deem the latter to be the transcendent one in this case.

Fourth, although the CJEU discarded in this matter the suitability of Article 4(3), the third ground, its answer referred to both the Hungarian position and a third Member State's exam of the case.

22. The impact of judicial interactions on the interplay between administrative and judicial enforcement

Federica Casarosa and Raffaele Sabato

1. INTRODUCTION

Since the liberalisation process in the 1990s, the enforcement of EU law in many legal areas has relied on administrative enforcement mechanisms based on regulatory and sanctioning powers allocated to independent administrative authorities at the national level.[1] In order to ensure the legitimacy and accountability of these institutions, their decisions are subject to judicial review, as any party subject to a sanction has the right to appeal against the decision. The academic literature has not neglected to address this regulatory framework and analyse the interplay between national, European and global administrative law when it comes to the principles of due process regarding regulatory regimes[2] and the legitimacy of sanctioning powers allocated to administrative

[1] Independent administrative authorities acquired an increasing role in the regulation of several sectors in the European Member States. The liberalisation of network sectors at the European level triggered the creation of national regulatory authorities in utility and network-based sectors (including energy, electronic communications, and so on) and in both economic and non-economic areas (including on the one hand banking, financing and consumer protection and on the other privacy, media and non-discrimination). This institutional development was based on the assumption that independent authorities would be able to avoid the risk of capture by both the market and politics. The independence was then coupled with expertise in sector specificities allowing independent administrative authorities to regulate and supervise the behaviour of market actors according to the objectives set by the legislator. This regulatory function relies on an ability to sanction and review potential misconduct and violations. See M. Thatcher, 'Delegation to Independent Regulatory Agencies: Pressures, Functions and Contextual Mediation' (2002) 25 *West European Politics* 125; and G. Majone, 'The Rise of the Regulatory State in Europe' (1994) 17 *West European Politics* 77.

[2] S. Cassese, 'Global Standards for National Administrative Procedure' (2005) 68 *Law and Contemporary Problems* 109; C. Harlow, 'Global Administrative Law: The

authorities.[3] However, limited attention has been given to the specificities of the institutional setting in terms of compliance with EU fundamental rights and in particular to the principle of effective judicial protection. This contribution aims to shed some light on this topic and show the importance of judicial interactions between national and European courts in identifying how due process guarantees should be interpreted in the light of coordination between administrative and judicial enforcement regimes.

The institutional setting triggers an interplay between administrative and judicial enforcement: in areas where administrative authorities exercise sanctioning powers,[4] the enforcement procedure generally involves a preliminary phase before the administrative authorities and a subsequent one before judicial courts. A civil or administrative court may be asked to scrutinise a decision of a public or independent authority in order to determine whether a violation of procedural or substantial rules occurred or there is a risk of infringement. For instance, in the field of asylum and immigration, the involvement of administrative authorities consists primarily of an assessment of the facts and merits of the case for the recognition of international protection status. This process is not related to scrutiny for any kind of infringement. Subsequently, courts are responsible for providing effective remedies in cases of a procedural irregularity either by way of an administrative or judicial review or by means of parallel or sequential enforcement mechanisms.[5]

This institutional setting involving both administrative and judicial enforcement, however, has an impact on the exercise of the right to an effective remedy which is enshrined in Art. 47 of the Charter of Fundamental Rights (CFR), in particular in the definition of the content of the remedy selected and imposed as a result of the interplay between administrative and judicial proceedings.

Quest for Principles and Values' (2006) 17 *European Journal of International Law* 187.

[3] M. Bovens, D. Curtin and P. 't Hart, 'Studying the Real World of EU Accountability: Framework and Design' in M. Bovens, D. Curtin and P. 't Hart, *The Real World of EU Accountability: What Deficit?* (OUP, Oxford 2010) 31; H.C.H. Hofmann, G.C. Rowe and A.H. Türk, *Administrative Law and Policy of the European Union* (Oxford University Press, Oxford 2011).

[4] Note that these authorities did not always have sanctioning powers. In the first stage, the administrative authorities could not directly sanction a violation although they could propose a sanction to the political authority; in the second stage, the (European) legislator allocated to the administrative authority not only the sanctioning power but also the possibility of defining the sanction procedure.

[5] See the different national approaches regarding data protection enforcement regimes below in Section 3.

Since the Charter does not directly address the coordination between administrative and judicial enforcement but distinguishes between the guarantees generally applicable to any enforcement procedure and those applicable to administrative enforcement, the general features emerging from Court of Justice of the European Union (CJEU) jurisprudence are identified (Section 2) and specific examples emerging in the data protection (Section 3) and consumer protection (Section 4) areas will be discussed. Specific attention is then devoted to the case of judicial review of administrative sanctions, taking into account how the independence of administrative authorities can be guaranteed in order to enhance the collaboration between them and judicial courts (Section 5). Conclusions follow.

2. THE ROLE OF THE CHARTER IN THE INTERPLAY BETWEEN ADMINISTRATIVE AND JUDICIAL PROCEEDINGS

Art. 47 CFR provides explicit recognition of the 'right to an effective remedy and to a fair trial'. This right has two dimensions: on the one hand, the procedural right to effective access to a fair hearing and, on the other hand, the substantive right to adequate redress.[6] This article must be interpreted and exercised 'under the conditions and within the limits defined by relevant Treaty provisions which make provision for it' pursuant to Art. 52(2) CFR. The reference is to Art. 19(1) Treaty on European Union (TEU), which establishes that all national judges are judges of Union law, in that Member States 'shall provide the remedies sufficient to ensure effective legal protection in the fields covered by Union law'. Accordingly, Art. 47 CFR is applicable to all enforcement proceedings regardless of their qualification at the national level as civil, criminal or administrative.

Regarding administrative enforcement, an additional reference is Art. 41 CFR, which provides the right to good administration. There are two aspects of this right: on the one hand, the Explanations relating to the Charter and CJEU case law clarify that, as is literally indicated in the Charter, this right is to be exercised by EU institutions, bodies, offices and agencies.[7] On the other

---

[6] For a detailed analysis of Art. 47 CFR, see ACTIONES Module on The Right to an Effective Remedy, accessed 3 November 2021 at https://cjc.eui.eu/projects/actiones/actiones-platform/.

[7] See the CJEU case C-482/10 *Cicala*, EU:C:2011:868, para. 28 and later Case C-166/13 *Mukarubega*, EU:C:2014:2336, paras 43–50, with further references. Note that a different approach was taken in Case C- 277/11 *M.M.*, EU:C:2012:744, paras 81–84 in which the CJEU decided the case on the assumption that Art. 41 also binds the Member States when they act within the scope of EU law.

hand, as a general principle of EU law,[8] the right has a wider scope and the consequent obligations also bind the Member States when they act within the scope of EU law.[9]

When national authorities take measures coming within the scope of EU law, they are subject to the specific obligation to observe the rights of defence of the addressees of decisions which significantly affect their interests. However, this consequence stems from the recognition of rights of defence qualified as a general principle of EU law.[10]

A partial overlap therefore exists between the guarantees granted in Art. 47 CFR and the content of Art. 41 CFR in relation to the general EU law principle of good administration.[11] Such a partial overlap may emerge specifically, for instance, regarding the right to be heard. On the one hand, Art. 41(2)(a) provides that the right to good administration includes 'the right of every person to be heard, before any individual measure which would affect him or her adversely is taken'. On the other hand, Art. 47 includes the same right under the wider right to fair trial.[12] Similarly, the right of access to a file and the right to be given reasons by the administration laid down in Art. 41(2) may

---

[8] A general principle of EU law can be described as a fundamental principle of the legal system encompassing certain basic values and enjoying a certain amount of recognition. Given that general principles are defined on the basis of the Treaties, they are hierarchically equal to primary law and so binding on the EU and on the Member States, both in implementing Treaty obligations and when they are otherwise acting in an area falling within the scope of EU law. See T. Tridimas, 'The General Principles of EU Law and the Europeanisation of National Laws' (2020) 13 *Review of European Administrative Law* 5; C. Amalfitano, *General Principles of EU Law and the Protection of Fundamental Rights* (Edward Elgar, Cheltenham, UK and Northampton, MA 2018).

[9] In the case *S and Others*, C-141/12 and C-372/12, EU:C:2014:2081, the CJEU affirmed that Art. 41 CFR is addressed only to the institutions, bodies, offices and agencies of the European Union (para. 67). However, in the cases *Mukarubega*, C-166/13, EU:C:2014:2336 (para. 44), and *N.*, Case C-604/12, EU:C:2014:302 (para. 49), the CJEU affirmed that 'the right to good administration, enshrined in Article 41 of the Charter, reflects a general principle of EU law'.

[10] In Case C-46/16 *LS Customs Services*, EU:C:2017:839, the CJEU held that 'the right to good administration, insofar as it reflects a general principle of EU law, has requirements that must be met by the Member States when they implement EU law'.

[11] See M. Moraru, G. Cornelisse and P. De Bruycker (eds), *Law and Judicial Dialogue on the Return of Irregular Migrants from the European Union* (Hart, Oxford 2020); M. Moraru and G. Renaudiere, 'REDIAL Research Report 2016/05', accessed 3 November 2021 at http://euredial.eu/; S. Prechal, 'The Court of Justice and Effective Judicial Protection: What Has the Charter Changed?' in C. Paulussen, T. Takacs, V. Lazić and B. Van Rompuy (eds), *Fundamental Rights in International and European Law: Public and Private Law Perspectives* (Springer, The Hague 2016) 146.

[12] See Chapter 18 by Moraru and Clement.

both overlap with the protection provided under Art. 47[13] and, insofar as the latter concerns the adversarial principle, include the right to examine all the documents submitted to the court.[14]

Current developments in EU secondary legislation and case law show that guarantees similar to those provided in Art. 47 CFR should be applied to administrative enforcement. The main drivers of these developments have been the principle of good administration and the principle of effectiveness, i.e. the principle of effective protection of rights based on EU law. Clearly, the different roles played by Art. 47 CFR and the inapplicability of Art. 41 CFR to national administrative bodies make administrative enforcement not completely comparable to judicial enforcement. However, the principle of good administration and the systemic role of Art. 47 CFR as described in the CJEU decision in *Puškár*[15] may contribute to generating a common set of rules, especially if decisions of administrative enforcers are not appealed before courts.

A comparison with the standards applicable to administrative proceedings according to European Court of Human Rights (ECtHR) case law reveals a substantially different approach. The European Convention on Human Rights (ECHR) does not directly address administrative proceedings, as Art. 6 ECHR is formulated with a broad subdivision of civil and criminal proceedings so that it is up to case law to determine the guarantees applicable in proceedings which are domestically qualified as administrative. Furthermore, under the ECtHR case law, guarantees in what is viewed domestically as administrative enforcement are under different regimes when applied to 'criminal' and 'non-criminal' sanctions. As a matter of fact, the concept of 'criminal' is an autonomous concept under the Convention[16] and does not necessarily coincide with the domestic classification of sanctions. As a consequence, when the

---

13 Settled case law ever since Case 222/86 *Heylens*, EU:C:1987:442, para. 15. Cf. Case C-300/11 *ZZ*, EU:C:2013:363, para. 53 with further references. The *Heylens* case law was recently confirmed in relation to Art. 47 in, for instance, Case C-437/13 *Unitrading*, EU:C:2014:2318, para. 20.

14 Case C-300/11 *ZZ*, EU:C:2013:363, paras 55 and 56.

15 Case C-73/16 *Puškár*, EU:C:2017:725. See Section 3 below.

16 The judgments in the ECtHR cases *Engel and others v the Netherlands*, 8 June 1976 (Appl. nos 5100/71, 5101/71, 5102/71, 5354/72, 5370/72), §§ 81–83 and *Welch v UK*, 9 February 1995 (Appl. no. 17440/90) *passim*, have been the leading ones in establishing the so-called 'Engel-Welch' criteria employed by the Strasbourg Court to qualify a sanction as 'criminal' under the ECHR. For the area of administrative enforcement, see *Menarini Diagnostics v Italy*, 27 September 2011 (Appl. no. 43509/0) §§ 30 and following. See also recently the Grand Chamber judgment *Gestur Jónsson and Ragnar Halldór Hall v Iceland* (Appl. nos 68273/14 and 68271/14), 22 December 2020, although it does not concern an administrative sanction but a disciplinary sanction for 'contempt of court', the decision revises and clarifies the Engel criteria and, above all, establishes a rather high level of relevance for a pecuniary sanction to be

ECtHR establishes that sanctions in a specific case are 'criminal' a wider set of guarantees applies.

Another distinctive feature of the protection under Art. 6 ECHR is a stricter interplay between administrative and judicial enforcement than that emerging under EU law. Since administrative bodies inflicting sanctions classifiable as 'criminal' usually first investigate facts and then impose and enforce sanctions, the ECHR has not been willing to consider the so-called internal 'firewalls' established to separate investigative and quasi-judicial functions attributed to different internal bodies of the administrative authority, and has concluded that in such cases imposition and enforcement of sanctions are performed by a non-impartial body.[17] This entails, as a main consequence, that administrative enforcement is in most cases subordinate to judicial enforcement; administrative enforcement is a 'weak' system and guarantees afforded within it are almost irrelevant, as the lack of impartiality in the enforcing body, strictly construed, imposes that, on request of the transgressor, fresh judicial proceedings should be available and in practice started.[18]

It should be noted that the issue at stake is not whether a judicial remedy is available under Art. 13 ECHR. It is far more than that. A judicial remedy must in practice be started and concluded in order to remove the defect of impartiality of the enforcing authority under Art. 6. Therefore, should this development be confirmed by future case law, European systems will be obliged to restruc-

considered 'criminal' (see § 96 where, also by referring to precedents, those lower than about 50,000 euros are indicated as not criminal).

[17] 'The consecutive exercise of investigative and judicial functions within one body', i.e. including enforcement of sanctions directly issued by administrative authorities, led the ECtHR to rule that 'in criminal matters' (i.e. also for administrative sanctions that have a 'criminal' colour under case law) 'such a combination of functions is not compatible with the requirements of impartiality set out in Article 6 § 1 of the Convention' (ECtHR, *Grande Stevens and others v Italy*, 4 March 2014 (Appl. nos 18640/10, 18647/10, 18663/10, 18668/10, 18698/10), §§ 136 (on the irrelevance of firewalls) and 137 (on lack of impartiality)).

[18] If the sanction is criminal and the administrative authority has both investigative and quasi-judicial functions, the ECtHR always requires that a 'subsequent control by a judicial body that has full jurisdiction' be started to cure the original defect of impartiality, *Grande Stevens*, cit., §§ 139–140. However, the ECtHR 'does not rule out the possibility for the domestic authorities to impose "penalties" through procedures other than those classified as criminal under domestic law', *G.I.E.M. S.R.L. and Others v Italy*, Grand Chamber, 28 June 2018 (Appl. nos 1828/06, 34163/07, 19029/11), § 233. See also, *Edizioni Del Roma Societa Cooperativa A.R.L. and Edizioni del Roma S.R.L. v Italy* (Appl. no. 68954/13), 10 December 2020, where the ECtHR found that the right to a fair hearing in Art. 6(1) ECHR was not breached by the way in which the Italian communication authority imposed financial penalties on applicants because there were adequate (full jurisdiction) mechanisms of judicial review of such administrative decisions.

ture their administrative proceedings. Since the guarantees in these proceedings will become almost irrelevant under ECtHR case law, this case law may have the adverse effect of decreasing rather than increasing guarantees.

Although the two approaches may in principle run along parallel lines, the legal systems of EU Member States, and national courts in particular, are required to comply with the standards emerging from the CJEU and ECHR case law. The different approaches are likely to trigger conflicting decisions regarding compliance with the standards at the national level.

3. TYPES OF COORDINATION: AN EXAMPLE IN THE AREA OF DATA PROTECTION

Data protection is one of the areas of law where interaction between administrative and judicial enforcement has been triggered by the intervention of EU law. Since the adoption of Directive 95/46/EC, EU law has imposed the creation of independent supervisory authorities entrusted with the task of verifying the compliance of data processing provided at the national level.[19] In many countries the implementation of the Directive led to the creation of new independent bodies that were able not only to issue warnings or reprimands to the data processor/controller and order the suspension of the processing of personal data and blocking and erasure of specific data but also to impose pecuniary sanctions.[20] The General Data Protection Regulation (GDPR), then, strengthens the role of supervisory authorities allocating, pursuant to Art. 58 GDPR, also investigative, corrective and advisory powers.[21] Among the detailed list of corrective powers, Art. 58(2) GDPR also includes the possibility of imposing administrative fines, which according to Art. 83 GDPR should be proportionate, effective and dissuasive.[22]

The enforcement system adopted in the GDPR is not limited to the administrative one allocated to supervisory authorities. It is a far more complex regime calling for a dual system of supervision. Another enforcement path is entrusted

---

19 See Art. 28 Directive 95/46 on the protection of individuals with regard to the processing of personal data and on the free movement of such data, OJ L 281, 23 November 1995, p. 31.

20 Art. 28(3) Directive 95/46 provides that the supervisory authorities shall be endowed with investigative powers, effective powers of intervention and the power to engage in legal proceedings. However, no reference to sanctioning powers is included in the directive.

21 However, see Recital 151 GDPR, where it is provided that the legal systems of Denmark and Estonia do not allow for such imposition of administrative fines by the Supervisory Authorities.

22 Note that Art. 83(2) GDPR provides a list of criteria to be taken into account in order to identify whether the fine is to be imposed and the amount of it.

to the judiciary, and this can be alternative or complementary to the administrative one. Indeed, Art. 78 GDPR provides that decisions by the supervisory authority which give rise to complaints may be appealed to the courts.[23] This applies to both data subjects and controllers that have been a party to proceedings before a supervisory authority. Art. 79(1) GDPR guarantees that both enforcement procedures can be pursued by claimants, as it obliges Member States to offer data subjects whose rights have been violated a judicial channel.[24] Moreover, each Member State may establish its own judicial enforcement mechanism so as to ensure that, in the case of liability, damages may be awarded to the data subject for the data breach.[25]

As a result, the GDPR calls for a dual (administrative/judicial) system but it leaves how the two regimes may interact fully to the discretion of the Member States.[26] This is not surprising, since such issues are governed by the principle of procedural autonomy of the Member States. The lack of more detailed guidelines has led to different types of coordination between enforcement mechanisms as is shown in Table 22.1.[27]

---

[23] The GDPR, however, does not clearly identify the extent of judicial review by courts, i.e. whether it should be limited to the formal correctness of the decision of the supervisory authority (quashing the decision if appropriate, or requiring a new proceeding before the supervisory authority) or whether it may review the form and content of the decision (revising the content of the decision and the remedies provided by the supervisory authority).

[24] As highlighted by P. Voigt and A. von dem Bussche, *The EU General Data Protection Regulation (GDPR): A Practical Guide* (Springer, The Hague 2017), p. 214, Art. 79 requires specific implementation by the Member States in order to provide a judicial remedy in the case that the supervisory authority does not react in cases of violation. As a matter of fact, if a supervisory authority issues a decision, it is legally binding and can be subject to an appeal before a court, whereas when the supervisory authority remains inactive, no binding decision is issued and the party does not have any basis for a claim.

[25] For instance, in France judicial review is carried out by administrative courts and the award of damages follows the general civil law provisions that apply to civil courts.

[26] Compare the structure of the proceedings applicable in asylum law as described by Moraru and Clement in Chapter 18 of this book.

[27] In the Italian system, for instance, in cases of violation of data protection legislation two alternative enforcement systems are available: one before the supervisory authority, which has the power to adopt injunctive measures and to issue fines for breaches; and one before civil courts, where damages may also be awarded to the victim of an infringement. On the specific coordination between the two enforcement mechanisms in Italy, see Italian Supreme Court decision no. 17408/2012. For a more detailed analysis, see M. Flamini, F. Capotorti and F. Casarosa, 'Casebook italiano in materia di diritti di protezione dei dati personali' (2018), accessed 3 November 2021 at https://www.rejus.eu/sites/default/files/content/materials/italian_casebook_data_protection.pdf.

Table 22.1 Forms of coordination in data protection law

Alternative coordination	National legislation indicates that the national supervisory authority and courts are alternative means of enforcement for a violation of the data protection legislation. The claimant can either bring the claim before an administrative authority or before a court. Example: Italy
Complementary coordination	National legislation indicates that the national supervisory authority and courts afford complementary protection for a violation of the data protection legislation. The relationship between the two bodies may be one of either simultaneous or sequential remedies, with the consequent issue of the need to manage conflicting decisions. Examples: Slovakia and Ireland
Independent enforcement	In this model, national legislation is silent on the relationship between enforcement by the national supervisory authority and by the courts. As such, they operate wholly independently. Example: Estonia

The choice of a specific type of coordination between administrative and judicial enforcement can have an impact on the implementation of the right to an effective remedy. Data subjects decide whether to lodge their claim before the national supervisory authority or before a court. This is particularly relevant when the two enforcement regimes are complementary and the legal system imposes an obligation to follow a specific order regarding administrative and judicial proceedings.

In the absence of specific guidance in the GDPR on this issue, it is useful to investigate the CJEU case law in order to identify some criteria for effective coordination. Despite the lack of direct applicability of Art. 47 CFR to purely administrative enforcement procedures, judicial review of administrative decisions enforcing fundamental rights has recently been considered by the CJEU through the lens of Art. 47 CFR.

The most interesting case in the data protection area is *Peter Puškár*,[28] which addresses the coordination between administrative and judicial claims in a case of data protection breach.

Mr Puškár lodged a claim before the Supreme Court of the Slovak Republic asking for an order to remove his name from a list drawn up by the Finance Directorate. Although the list could only circulate among administrative offices, Mr Puškár held that it constituted a violation of data protection rules. The Supreme Court dismissed the claim since Mr Puškár had not exhausted the remedies before the national administrative authorities. After an appeal was presented to the Constitutional Court of the Slovak Republic, the latter affirmed that the Supreme Court had failed to take into account the factual

[28] Case C-73/16 *Peter Puškár v Finančné riaditeľstvo Slovenskej republiky and Kriminálny úrad finančnej správy*, EU:C:2017:725.

and legal arguments of the case and, most importantly, to provide a decision on the conditions that should have been met for the protection of personal data in the case of data processing by tax authorities. Therefore, the decision of the Constitutional Court completely disregarded the sequence proposed by the Supreme Court ruling regarding the preliminary administrative proceedings and the judicial proceedings, requiring the court to provide a detailed analysis of the claim and a decision on whether the processing of data by the tax authorities was lawful. The Constitutional Court affirmed that the Supreme Court had infringed the applicant's fundamental rights, namely the right to an effective remedy and a fair trial, the right to privacy and the right to protection of personal data. Therefore, the Constitutional Court referred the case back to the Supreme Court. At this point, the Supreme Court, believing that the Constitutional Court had not considered the case law of the CJEU, decided to refer to that court for a preliminary ruling.

Among the questions submitted to the CJEU, the Slovak Supreme Court included one seeking to verify whether the mandatory preliminary administrative procedure adopted by the Slovak legislature was compliant with EU law, and in particular with Art. 47 CFR.

In its decision, the CJEU pointed out that the obligation to exhaust additional administrative remedies, while not excluded by Directive 95/46, which was applicable at the time of the violation, must be scrutinised in the light of Art. 47 CFR, Art. 4(3) TEU and Art. 19(1) TEU. Since such an obligation to exhaust additional administrative remedies constitutes a limitation of the right to an effective judicial remedy, it may be justified according to the criteria set out in Art. 52(1) CFR, namely only when the restriction imposed is:

(i) provided by law;
(ii) respectful of the essence of the right;
(iii) subject to the principle of proportionality;
(iv) compliant with objectives of general interest recognised by the EU or the need to protect the rights and freedoms of others.

The Court focused on the last two criteria. Regarding the existence of objectives of general interest, the Court acknowledged that the obligation to lodge an administrative complaint before bringing a legal action has two main positive effects: first, it may relieve the courts of disputes that can be decided in a shorter time by the administrative authority concerned; and second, it may increase the efficiency of judicial proceedings in disputes in which a legal action is brought despite the fact that a complaint has already been lodged. Therefore, the general obligation pursued objectives of general interest. As for the test of proportionality, the Court relied on the AG's opinion and on its precedent in the *Alassini* case.[29] In particular, it explicitly referred to the criteria identified in the *Alassini* decision, which should guide the proportionality test vis-à-vis the additional steps imposed in the national procedure.[30]

On the basis of these criteria, the Court ruled that the obligation to exhaust the available administrative remedies appeared appropriate to achieve the aforementioned objectives of general interest, and no less onerous and efficient method was available and capable of achieving these objectives. As a result, the CJEU highlighted that the form of institutional organisation between administrative and judicial enforcement may have an impact on the achievement of effective judicial protection. However, in the specific case, the Slovak legal provisions did not infringe EU law insofar as the national provisions do not impose additional costs on the parties and lengthy proceedings. This last proportionality test is in any case allocated to the national court.

4. THE EFFECT OF ADMINISTRATIVE SANCTIONS: AN EXAMPLE IN THE AREA OF CONSUMER PROTECTION

Another area of law where the interplay between administrative and judicial enforcement may raise questions regarding the forms and manners of coordination is the consumer protection area. Consumer protection authorities were created in many Member States as a result of implementation of the Regulation on Consumer Protection Cooperation 2006/2004. In particular, the Regulation required Member States to identify enforcement authorities responsible for investigating and reacting (in a coordinated manner across Europe) in the case of cross-border infringements of EU consumer law.[31]

In almost all the EU countries the consumer authorities are responsible for enforcing the rules related to unfair commercial practices and have the powers to verify the compliance of contractual clauses with the provisions in Directive 2005/29 on unfair commercial practices. Given that in many cases administrative decisions may lead to a declaration of unfairness of the contractual terms included in consumer contracts, it is crucial to understand how this kind of decision may affect the subsequent judicial enforcement procedures, not only

---

29 Joint cases C-317/08, C-318/08, C-319/08 and C-320/08 *Rosalba Alassini v Telecom Italia SpA*, EU:C:2010:146.

30 See para. 67.

31 Note that in the most recent reform, Regulation 2017/2394 increased the scope and the powers of such authorities, which are now responsible for detecting irregularities and taking action in cases of unfair commercial practices, e-commerce, geo-blocking, package holidays, online selling and passenger rights.

in cases of judicial review but also in cases of judicial proceedings that involve parties other than those addressed by the administrative decision.

The decision of the CJEU in the Hungarian case *Pereničová*[32] provides some clues regarding the impact of an administrative decision in a separate judicial proceeding. In this case, the CJEU considered that the finding (by an administrative authority) that a commercial practice was unfair was just 'one element among others on which the competent court may, pursuant to Article 4(1) of Directive 93/13, base its assessment of the unfairness of the contractual terms (relating, in this case) to the cost of the loan granted to the consumer'.[33] Therefore, on the one hand, the CJEU affirmed the autonomy of administrative and judicial enforcement, since judicial proceedings should address the fairness of a specific contractual agreement vis-à-vis an individual consumer (who may or may not have been misled by this practice). However, on the other hand, it identified a point of contact between the two systems allowing the judge to take into account the administrative finding as an element that contributes, with others, to evaluation of the unfairness of the terms.

A more difficult situation emerges in countries where the administrative authorities may adopt injunctions that prohibit the use of particular contract clauses with an *erga omnes* effect. In this case, the use of the contractual clause is prevented not only towards the parties involved in the administrative proceedings but also to third parties. Accordingly, every business party may be obliged to refrain from using a particular clause and be subject to administrative or judicial sanctions in the case of non-compliance with the prohibition. A significant interaction on this topic emerged between the Polish court and the CJEU in the *Biuro podróży 'Partner'* case,[34] (see Figure 22.1).
Under Art. 479 of the Polish Code of Civil Procedure a judgment declaring (abstract) abusiveness of a clause is 'effective towards third persons' from the day of listing the clause in the public register administered by the President of the Office of Protection of Competition and Consumers.[35] The specialised Court for Protection of Competition and Consumers may review the fairness of standard contract terms used on the market through an *in abstracto* evaluation – i.e. regardless of whether the clause is included in any actually concluded

[32] Case C-453/10 *Jana Pereničová and Vladislav Perenič v SOS financ spol. s r. o.*, EU:C:2012:144.

[33] Ibid., para. 43.

[34] Case C-119/15, *Biuro podróży Partner*, EU:C:2016:987.

[35] For a more detailed presentation of the case see ACTIONES – Module IV – Judicial interaction on Consumer protection, accessed 3 November 2021 at https://cjc.eui.eu/projects/actiones/actiones-platform/.

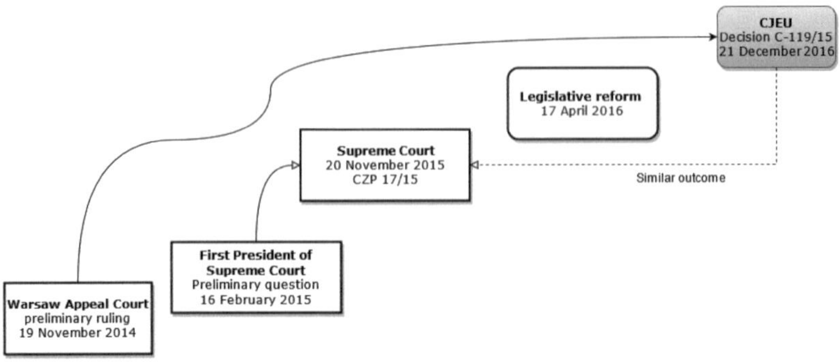

Figure 22.1 Judicial interactions in Biuro podróży 'Partner' case

contract.[36] A final judgment granting the action has an effect for third parties when a clause considered to be prohibited is included in the public register.

The case law regarding the objective limits of extended validity of an *in abstracto* judgment is not settled as in some cases the Supreme Court has interpreted the limits in a narrow way[37] whereas in other cases a broad interpretation has been adopted.[38] In a motion on 16 February 2015 (BSA I-4110-1/15) the First President of the Supreme Court used an internal procedure for the harmonisation of case law and addressed the issue of the limits of the *in abstracto* judgments vis-à-vis businesses that were not part of the initial proceedings. On 20 November 2015 (case file No. III CZP 17/18), the Supreme Court ruled. In its reasoning the Supreme Court balanced the effectiveness of consumer protection against abusive clauses and the right to fair trial in order to determine the scope of *res iudicata* of *in abstracto* review of contract clauses. Regarding consumer protection, the Court based its reasoning on Directive 93/13/EU and

[36] This specific procedure has been introduced to implement Art. 7 of Directive 93/13/EC. Standardised in Art. 47936(45) of the Code of Civil Procedure the proceedings in question are designed for the purpose of abstract control of contractual models and to protect consumers' collective interest. If an action for acknowledgement that a provision of the model agreement is prohibited is granted, the court cites the content of the provisions of the model agreement in an operative part of the judgment and prohibits their use. A copy of the final judgment, with the cause of the action granted, is sent to the President of the Office of Competition and Consumer Protection, who maintains a public register of the provisions of model agreements considered to be prohibited.

[37] Decisions of 7 October 2008 (III CZP 80/08) and of 13 May 2010 (III SK 29/09).

[38] Resolution of 13 July 2006 (III SZP 3/06) and judgment of 5 June 2007 (I CSK 117/07).

on the CJEU decision in the *Invitel* case.[39] As for the right to fair trial, the Court based its reasoning on Art. 45 of the Constitution of the Republic of Poland, Art. 6(1) ECHR and Art. 47(2) CFR. The Court determined that the:

> effectiveness of the judgment in question in favour of anyone, but with respect to the particular entrepreneur, being a defendant in the proceedings, is proportionate, as it maintains a balance between the need to guarantee the effectiveness of an abstract control [of contract clauses] and the need to respect the right to be heard, as a fundamental element of the right to fair trial, arising from the right to due process.

Therefore, the Supreme Court limited the effects of *in abstracto* review only in relation to the particular entrepreneur in the proceedings, as the decision was invokable by every consumer (including those who did not participate in the trial). Only on these conditions did the Supreme Court find this outcome proportionate and therefore compliant with the requirement of proportionality of remedies set forth in Directive 93/13/EU.

It is important to note that, before the First President referred the issue for harmonisation of case law, on 19 November 2014 the Court of Appeal in Warsaw adopted a preliminary reference to the CJEU addressing the same point in the light of EU law compliance.[40]

Before the CJEU proceedings were concluded, the legislative framework was repealed on 17 April 2016. The new legislative Act almost entirely cancelled the former provisions of the Code of Civil Procedure and introduced a new model of *in abstracto* review.[41] The amendment replaced the former judicial review with an administrative control performed by the President of the Office of Competition and Consumer Protection (the central market regulatory authority in Poland). The new regulation set forth a general prohibition of the use of unfair clauses in contracts concluded with consumers and conferred on the President of the Office the competence to issue a decision that *in abstracto* declares the unfairness of the clause. Moreover, a specific provision determined the *ratione personae* outcomes of a declaration of unfairness: it should be effective regarding the entrepreneur against whom the unfairness had been declared and all the consumers who concluded a contract with him using the standard terms indicated in the decision.

In December 2016, the CJEU decided the *Biuro* case. The judgment ascertained the limits of the *erga omnes* effect of unfairness on professionals, in

[39] Case C-472/10 *Nemzeti Fogyasztóvédelmi Hatóság v Invitel Távközlési Zrt.*, EU:C:2012:242.

[40] Request for a preliminary ruling by the Court of Appeal of Warsaw, Case C-119/15 *Biuro podróży 'Partner'*, EU:C:2016:987.

[41] See Arts 23a–23d of the Act on Competition and Consumer Protection, 16 April 2016.

particular regarding administrative remedies for violation of a judicial injunction that prohibits the use of a particular clause. The Court held that domestic law may provide the possibility of ordering injunctions that prohibit the *erga omnes* use of particular clauses in consumer contracts for being unfair. In this case, the injunction in question can be effective in favour of every consumer regardless of the date they concluded their contracts and notwithstanding whether they were involved in the initial proceedings in which the unfairness had been declared.

The Court pointed out that national administrative bodies can enforce consumer law in a way interconnected with courts. In other words, judicial and administrative enforcement may remain interdependent and there is no need to clearly separate them at the level of domestic systems. The general principles that steer the relation between these two means of enforcement are the right to effective judicial remedy (in particular the right to be heard) derived from Art. 47 CFR and the right to good administration (Art. 41 CFR).

The interaction among national and European courts, therefore, resulted in a set of factors able to steer coordination between administrative and judicial proceedings. The *erga omnes* effect of an injunction can also affect persons who have not directly participated in the administrative proceedings provided that they have an abstract right to be heard in subsequent judicial review proceedings. Therefore, the right to an effective remedy enshrined in Art. 47 CFR constitutes a boundary of the *erga omnes* effect. Although the CJEU allowed for coordination between administrative and judicial proceedings, requiring only the possibility of the exercise of the right to be heard in judicial review proceedings, the Polish legislature in its reform went further: administrative enforcement was strengthened by granting an exclusive power of review to the authority which framed the same administrative proceedings, only leaving to the courts the role of reviewing the administrative decision.

The relationship between administrative and judicial control over the unfairness of contractual clauses is still a matter for national legislation, but clearly the role of fundamental rights cannot be (any longer) ignored and will presumably be a factor in non-legislative harmonisation of the matter.

5. JUDICIAL REVIEW OF ADMINISTRATIVE SANCTIONS

As mentioned above, the decisions of administrative authorities are subject to judicial review. This is justified by the need to provide an *ex post* control mechanism enhancing the legitimacy of the overall system. As the name makes explicit, independent authorities are characterised by independence from the political system. Therefore, their impartiality vis-à-vis citizens claiming their rights before them is ensured.[42] However, the level of neutrality that characterises court proceedings, particularly regarding the rights to defence and equality of arms, cannot be found in administrative proceedings, which in almost all cases are characterised by an inquisitorial system and strong *ex officio* powers.

Judicial review is thus the means adopted by the legal system to verify the persuasiveness of an administrative decision according to a set of principles which, according to a clear classification provided by Bignami, include the following: (1) compliance with the statutory attribution provided by law to avoid cases of jurisdictional incompetence, violation or error of law, inconsistency with applicable statutes, and so on; (2) compliance with fundamental rights to avoid cases of lack of proportionality and equality of the administrative decision, unfairness and abuse of power, and so on; (3) compliance with policy rationality to avoid cases of arbitrary or capricious behaviour and evidence of a manifest error of assessment.[43]

The EU directives that impose the establishment of independent authorities[44] do not always specify in detail the features of judicial review. In particular, they lack specific guidance on the limits of the review: whether it should be limited to assessing the correctness of the decision of the supervisory authority or whether the authority may directly review the merits of the content of the decision.

According to the ECtHR case law, if administrative authorities making decisions do not themselves satisfy the requirements of Art. 6 ECHR, if they are 'criminal' in substance their decisions must be subject to subsequent control by a judicial body that has full jurisdiction. Accordingly, there will be no violation of the right to fair trial if the structural or procedural limitations emerging in an administrative procedure can be remedied in a judicial review procedure

---

[42] However, see Section 3 above concerning the opposite view of the ECtHR.

[43] F. Bignami, 'Comparative Administrative Law' in M. Bussani and U. Mattei (eds), *The Cambridge Companion to Comparative Law* (Cambridge University Press, Cambridge 2012) 145; see also S. Prechal, 'Effective Judicial Protection: Some Recent Developments – Moving to the Essence' [2020] 2 *Review of European Administrative Law* 179.

[44] Although outside the scope of this contribution, it is important to note that independent authorities have been established in several legal areas, namely the supervision of credit institutions, investment firms, insurance undertakings, electronic communication, regulated markets such as electricity and gas, and transport. For a more detailed analysis of these areas, see P. Larouche and X. Taton, 'Enforcement and Judicial Review of Decisions of National Regulatory Authorities' (2011), Centre on Regulation in Europe, accessed 3 November 2021 at https://www.cerre.eu/sites/cerre/files/110421_CERRE_Study_EnforcementAndJudicialReview_0.pdf.

able to review and quash the contested decision on questions of law and fact.[45] However, it must be acknowledged that the ECtHR also interprets the scope of review and the powers allocated to courts in a flexible manner, considering that Art. 6 ECHR does not require access to a level of jurisdiction that can substitute the opinion of the administrative authority with its own opinion.[46] Moreover, when administrative authorities make decisions in specialised areas of law requiring particular professional experience or specialist knowledge (as is the case of sector-specific legislation), states may define a different scope of the court review without any violation of the ECHR standard.[47]

As highlighted above, the CJEU's approach differs from that of the ECtHR: the CJEU does not entail that judicial review provides a remedy for a violation of fair trial guarantees in the administrative procedure. Instead, judicial proceedings add a level of protection to those already provided in the administrative proceedings.[48]

The jurisprudence of the CJEU affirms that any party affected by a decision made by a national body which violates their rights stemming from the Treaty has a right to a judicial review of this decision by a national court.[49] In accordance with the principle of procedural autonomy, in the *East Sussex Council* case,[50] the CJEU considered that where European legislation does not specify the extent of judicial review it is for the legal systems of the Member States to determine it, subject to the principles of equivalence and effectiveness.

However, more recently the CJEU has used Art. 47 CFR to justify the extent to which judicial review is to be employed by national courts. In particular, the CJEU decision relies on the principle of effective judicial protection in order to enhance not only the safeguards for the parties but also the independence

---

45 *Ramos Nunes de Carvalho e Sá v Portugal* [GC] (Appl. nos 55391/13, 57728/13, 74041/13), § 132.

46 *Fazia Ali v the United Kingdom* (Appl. no. 40378/10), §§ 75–78 and *Ramos Nunes de Carvalho e Sá v Portugal* [GC], cit., § 178.

47 For a more detailed analysis of the criteria in this case, see ECHR, *Guide to Article 6 ECHR: Right to a Fair Trial (Civil Limb)* (2019), accessed 3 November 2021 at https://echr.coe.int/Documents/Guide_Art_6_ENG.pdf.

48 Note, for instance, that the independence of administrative bodies should also be guaranteed in the case of bodies internal to the judicial institution, such as the case of court chambers responsible for addressing disciplinary sanctions. See in particular the decision in joined cases C-585/18, C-624/18 and C-625/18, *A.K.*, EU:C:2019:982.

49 This is affirmed since Case C-222/86, *Union nationale des entraîneurs et cadres techniques professionnels du football (Unectef) v Georges Heylens and others*, 1987 E.C.R. 4097, para. 14.

50 Case C-71/14 *East Sussex County Court*, EU:C:2015:656.

of the courts reviewing administrative decisions, resulting in an overall operationalisation of the rule of law.[51]

The most significant judgment in this direction is the recent *Glencore Agriculture Hungary* case.[52] The Court was asked by a Hungarian court to clarify the scope of judicial review in the specific case of the common system of value added tax in the light of Art. 47 CFR. The CJEU decision confirmed its precedent in the *WebMindLicences* case, and considered that in order to comply with Art. 47 CFR judicial review by courts should grant courts the power to verify the evidence assessed in the administrative decision, taking into account whether the evidence was obtained and used in breach of the rights guaranteed by EU law and especially by the Charter.[53] If such powers were lacking, the right to an effective remedy would be without its substantial feature of effectiveness. As a result, the findings of administrative decisions (related in this case to the application of the VAT directive) must be disregarded and the contested decision founded on that evidence must be annulled.

This is a consequence of a more general rule affirmed by the Court: the statements and findings of administrative authorities cannot bind courts. This rule is more clearly supported by the arguments of AG Szpunar's Opinion which linked judicial review to the role of courts in protecting the rule of law. Only through independence from administrative procedures and decisions in assessing the facts may national courts exercise their role in safeguarding the effective application of EU law.[54]

This reasoning went even further in the *Torubarov* case,[55] which addressed the powers of the courts vis-à-vis administrative decisions regarding eligibility for international protection. According to Hungarian law, courts can simply focus on the exercise of power by the administrative enforcer and annul an administrative decision when it is not compliant with law, and remand it to the administrative authority for fresh proceedings. However, in the specific case, such interaction was repeated as the administrative body in restarting the proceedings disregarded the indications provided by the court.

The decision of the CJEU addressing the case affirmed that, given the specificities of the case, in order to guarantee that an applicant for international protection has an effective judicial remedy within the meaning of Art. 47 CFR, not only must the national court be able to quash the decision of the adminis-

---

51 S. Prechal, 'Effective Judicial Protection: Some Recent Developments – Moving to the Essence', cit., p. 180.

52 Case C-189/18 *Glencore Agriculture Hungary*, EU:C:2019:861.

53 Case C-419/14, *WebMindLicenses Kft.*, EU:C:2015:832.

54 AG Opinion, Case C-189/18 *Glencore Agriculture Hungary*, EU:C:2019:462, para. 74.

55 Case C-556/17 *Alekszij Torubarov*, EU:C:2019:626.

trative body but also, in the case of non-compliance in the subsequent administrative proceedings, must it have the power to substitute its own decision.[56]

This approach highlights a specific allocation of powers between administrative and judicial enforcement: the courts' role is to ensure that EU law is complied with and that EU-law-based rights are protected. Although the public administration may already comply with EU law, this does not exclude the need to ensure judicial control extended to the direct issuing of measures for administrative enforcement. As AG Bobek pointed out in his Opinion in the *Torubarov* case, 'a court of law is there to review and to control the public administration, not to act as a humble "amicus administratoris" issuing suggestions as to how the law might be interpreted or what facts the administration could perhaps collect in the next round'.[57]

The CJEU's interpretation of judicial review in the cases mentioned not only adds useful elements to the dimension of the judicial independence of the judiciary[58] but also clarifies that coordination between administrative and judicial enforcement, as defined by the legislature at the national level, may not escape EU law control whenever a horizontal measure adopted by the state affects the activities and procedures of the judiciary as a whole. This is due to the fact that a horizontal measure will also impact the application of the right to an effective remedy.[59]

A number of issues have arisen concerning administrative enforcement in relation to litigation that has endeavoured to challenge (or succeeded in challenging) alleged defects in the procedure on which enforcement is based, thereby aiming to stop execution of the sanctions imposed by administrative authorities.

---

[56] Case C-556/17, cit., para. 74. It must be noted that during the proceedings – and probably as a reaction to it – the Hungarian Government provided details of a new law on administrative procedure that entered into force on 1 January 2018. This new legislation was aimed at reorganising the coordination between administrative and judicial proceedings, in particular by enabling the courts responsible for judicial review to require administrative bodies to comply with their judgments. See István Hoffman, 'Application of Administrative Law in the Time of Reforms in the Light of the Scope of Judicial Review in Hungary' (2020) 29 *Studia Iuridica Lublinensia* 101.

[57] See AG Opinion, Case C-556/19 *Alekszij Torubarov*, EU:C:2019:339, para. 102.

[58] See Chapter 6 by Accetto, Chapter 7 by Halmai and Chapter 8 by Podstawa and Gwizdak.

[59] See, in more general terms, AG Bobek's Opinion in the *Torubarov* case, para. 55. See also N. Lazzerini, '"Jurisdiction of Statutory Bodies to Disapply National Law, or Nothing": Procedural Primacy Taking over Procedural Autonomy in the CJEU's Judgment, Minister for Justice and Equality and Commissioner of the Garda Síochána' [2019] 1 *Review of European Administrative Law* 197.

A first issue concerns the fact that administrative sanctions are often deliberated on by authorities, which in a first phase investigate the transgression and, in a second phase, usually after hearing the transgressor, impose the measure. It has already been mentioned that under the ECtHR case law when sanctions may be viewed as 'criminal' the ECtHR concludes that the authority lacks impartiality because of the consecutive exercise of investigative and quasi-judicial functions, which is held to be incompatible with the requirements set out in Art. 6 § 1 ECHR regardless of the so-called internal 'firewalls', i.e. institutional separation and legal recognition of mutual autonomy of different departments within the same agency. While it is not possible to dwell here on the weakness of such indifference in the case law to 'firewalls' in administrative authorities, it is a fact that enforcement of sanctions imposed by many authorities in Europe may be easily paralysed with this argument.

A second issue, connected to the previous one, concerns the risk that investigations, and therefore enforcement based on them, may be challenged because of the exercise of administrative powers beyond the territory of the state in which the authority is based. This matter is especially relevant both because globalisation has blurred national boundaries and transactions today very frequently have a cross-country dimension and because social phenomena that are subject to administrative supervision (e.g. data, consumer contracts, financial institutions and markets, and so on) are per se trans-frontier phenomena and are components of a wider digital economy so that administrative authorities cooperate on a regular basis to ensure that territorial limits do not become functional limits.[60]

A third problematic area concerns the post-investigative stage, and in particular procedural phases in which the possible transgressor is given the possibility of submitting a written and/or oral defence to the administrative authority aiming to obtain a discontinuation of the proceedings with no sanction being inflicted. Here, again, a possible paralysis of administrative enforcement may derive from litigation based on ECtHR case law requiring – should the sanction be viewed as 'criminal' – a 'public hearing' to be held in order to comply with the requirements of Art. 6 ECHR. This line of case law leaves the only possibility of having enforcement based on a lawful background in which a full judicial review takes place in the context of proceedings that ensure the

---

[60] E.g. Art. 28(6) of Directive 95/46 – which was referred to by the European Court of Justice in the judgment cited *infra* – states, in the area of data protection, that each authority may be requested to exercise its powers by an authority of another Member State and that supervisory authorities are to cooperate with one another to the extent necessary for the performance of their duties, in particular by exchanging all useful information.

guarantee of a fair trial, including a public hearing.[61] In other words, under the ECtHR case law administrative enforcements are always defective if public hearings (and other procedural guarantees) have not been previously granted. It is self-evident that in this area no interplay is feasible since only judicial enforcement appears legitimate.

On the one hand, some of these problematic procedural issues may be addressed with adequate reforms of administrative proceedings in which public hearings and other guarantees are introduced. On the other hand, however, the attribution of both investigative and quasi-judicial powers to the same authority is a crucial feature of sanctioning authorities in Europe, hopefully completed by a convenient 'separation of powers' within the same body. In this area, only a development in the case law can ensure that administrative enforcement can fruitfully produce advantages in terms of effectiveness and promptness, these being features that are to be found to a lesser degree in judicial enforcement.

6. CONCLUSIONS

EU law enforcement relies on the capability of national systems to address and coordinate administrative and judicial enforcement in many legal areas, identifying procedures that may involve a preliminary phase before administrative authorities and a subsequent one before judicial courts.

Coordination between the two enforcement mechanisms ensures that violation of EU fundamental rights guaranteed as general principles of EU law or laid down in the EU Charter can be invoked either before an administrative authority or before a court. In both cases, the enforcement bodies should be able to provide an effective legal remedy for the violation of EU law. Moreover, if the violation occurs in the exercise of sanctioning powers by administrative authorities, the application of Art. 47 CFR in the context of fair judicial review and the principle of effectiveness of EU law allow courts to provide effective remedies, such as annulments of administrative measures or the provision of compensatory damages.

The jurisprudence of the CJEU analysed above shows that the time and methods of coordination between administrative and judicial enforcement are crucial from different perspectives. A first perspective is that of achieving effective judicial protection without undue delays and excessive costs of proceedings, as was clarified in the *Puškár* case. However, the application of Art. 47 CFR can trigger a higher level of protection which is not limited to mere

---

61 *Edizioni Del Roma Societa Cooperativa A.R.L. and Edizioni del Roma S.R.L. v Italy*, cit.

cost-effectiveness. In fact, the impacts and effects of administrative decisions on the concurrent or subsequent proceedings before courts can provide challenging issues, as the *Pereničová* and *Biuro* cases show.

In this regard, cases addressing in particular instances of judicial review highlight the equal importance that administrative and judicial enforcement have in safeguarding fair trial guarantees. Administrative decisions are not outside the domain of effective judicial protection. Instead, they provide an added level of protection that should follow and comply with the same principles applicable to judicial ones.

Only through interventions by national courts through preliminary rulings has the CJEU had the opportunity to identify the limits and conditions for specific institutional settings, although further academic work will be needed to map out the interplay between administrative and judicial enforcement.

23. Comment: checks and balances between the administration, the executive and the judiciary

Markus Thoma

1. INTRODUCTION – THE INSTITUTIONAL QUESTION

The introduction to Chapter 22 by Casarosa and Sabato opens a look at the dynamic process of integration in important fields of administration by the European (Economic) Community and the European Union and the impact on administrative enforcement. Developments in the member states set in differently, in the 'old' member states, looking back to the restoration of their democratic culture and the rule of law after World War II from the 1960s onwards and in the youngest member states in the first and second decades of the 21st century, when, after the fall of the iron curtain, they had just arrived in the western hemisphere. For some of the new and newest member states the dynamics might have been challenging, opening the experience of democracy also for national trends and spirits, being at a critical distance from European integration under a common roof of the rule of law, with the European Court of Justice (ECJ) and the European Court of Human Rights (ECtHR) at the top. The level of development in the member states was and still is different.

During these decades not only the quantity of regulations has increased but also the quality of enforcement and judicial review expected by the European Commission and the EU has improved, emphasising the rule of law, enshrining fundamental rights and requiring legal protection by independent courts in all member states at the same level in a common area of freedom, security and justice.

The relationship between administration and the administrative judiciary (or the judiciary as a whole where there is no specialised administrative one) was highly determined by the function of protecting the citizen against the state.

The process of integration in the EU changed and multiplied the function of (administrative) courts: it is still up to them to protect the citizen against the state, but now it is also up to them to guarantee the reliable application of EU law, to be the link between the member state and EU law and the last resort to force member states to fulfil their obligations to citizens and the EU.

From my point of view, in many cases administration under political control (of national politicians) is a counterpart to the (administrative) judiciary. The judiciary exercises (or should exercise) *ex post* control over the administration and the 'interplay' between them quite often reminds one more of a match (in the best sense) or of a battle (in the worst cases we face today in Europe). This leads to the crucial question of the effectiveness of judicial control, requiring independent courts to be able to resist political influence, and to the question of the institutional independence of courts. The case law of the ECJ[1] (and of the ECtHR[2]) mirrors the importance of the question of independence of judges and courts.

2. THE ROLE OF THE CFR IN THE INTERPLAY BETWEEN ADMINISTRATIVE AND JUDICIAL PROCEEDINGS – ADMINISTRATIVE COURTS AS LINKS TO EU LAW

EU law and – as part of it – the Charter of Fundamental Rights (CFR) *aim* to also change the rules on the 'interplay' between the administration and the judiciary at the institutional level: on the one hand we see guarantees in the Charter promising legal protection for citizens (in the fields of application of EU law), fitting in the traditional pattern of 'citizen vs the state'; on the other hand it aims to set up institutional guarantees for national authorities to secure the application of EU law for the match: the member state vs the EU.

A good part of this development was driven by the ECJ in recent years, giving Art. 47 CFR and Art. 19 Treaty on the Functioning of the European Union (TFEU) a broader interpretation and importance in the question of effectiveness of remedies and the independence of courts.[3] I think – and hope

---

1 CJEU C-192/18 *Commission v. Poland*; *Miasto Łowicz and Prokurator Generalny*, Joined Cases C-558/18 and C-563/18, *A.K.*, Joined Cases C-585/18, C-624/18, C-625/18, ECLI:EU:C:2019:982.

2 *Sramek v. Austria* (Appl. n. 8790/79), *Oberschlick v. Austria* (Appl. n. 11662/85), *Harabin v. Slovakia* (Appl. n. 58688/11), *Baka v. Hungary* (Appl. n. 20261/12), *Paluda v. Slovakia* (Appl. n. 33392/12), *Morice v. France* (Appl. n. 29369/10), *Ramos Nunes de Carvalho e Sà v. Portugal* (Appl. n. 55391/13), *Guðmundur Andri Ástráðsson v. Iceland* (Appl. n. 26374/18).

3 Starting with Case C-64/16 *Associação Sindical dos Juízes Portugueses v. Tribunal de Contas*, ECLI:EU:C:2018:117.

– the development is not yet finished regarding the shifting interplay between the judiciary and politics in some member states.

2.1 The Right to Good Administration

Of course, Art. 41 CFR provides the right to good administration by institutions, bodies, offices and agencies of the EU in an organisational sense. According to the prevailing opinion, national authorities applying EU law do not come within the scope of Art. 41 CFR. In its ruling of 8 May 2019 in case C-230/18 – *PI*, the ECJ interpreted Art. 49 TFEU, Arts 15(2), 16, 47 and 52 CFR *and the general principle of the right to good administration* in circumstances such as those at issue in the proceedings as precluding national legislation providing that an administrative authority may decide to close a commercial establishment with immediate effect, insofar as that legislation, first, does not require reasons, in fact and in law, to be given in writing for such a decision and to be communicated to the establishment and, second, requires that any application brought by that addressee and seeking annulment of the decision must be reasoned.

The case law of the ECJ on 'general principles' (here, in the right to good administration) in common traditions of member states stipulated fundamental rights before the CFR entered into force and fills gaps the CFR still leaves.

3. COOPERATION BETWEEN ADMINISTRATIVE AUTHORITIES AND COURTS – WHO CONTROLS WHO?

Work-sharing requires cooperation between the managing authority and (administrative) courts. However, as stated above, the task of administrative courts is to review the legality of the administration.

The limits of both cooperation and of control are reached when the administration defaults and thus shifts a substantial part of or the whole decision-making process to the administrative courts or, in particular, neglects investigative activities, thereby giving the administrative courts the role of investigative authorities. From the point of view of Union law, such as the European Convention on Human Rights (ECHR), this raises the problem of effective access to a court, a decision within a reasonable timeframe and, where the administration has control over the court's resources, the question of the court's independence. This is an issue in the ECJ's judgment in case C-685/15 – *Online Games* (see also below in section 5).

In its ruling of 10 March 2000, G 19/99, the Austrian Constitutional Court critically examined the question of institutional independence on the basis of an occasional case in the area of the Supreme Administrative Court. The

Supreme Administrative Court is also responsible for monitoring official acts of the Federal Government, including the Federal Chancellor. A constitutionally defined control system (the Supreme Administrative Court over the entire administration) does not allow any effective interference of the controlled body in the function of the controlling body. Otherwise, there would be a reversal of the control direction, which would be unconstitutional.

Cooperation between the administration and administrative courts will therefore reach its limits quickly if the Constitution, and Art. 47 CFR and Art. 6 ECHR, requires effective control by an independent court.

The contrary positions of the administration and administrative jurisdiction are also important insofar as Art. 267 TFEU only grants courts a right of referral or a requirement to refer. In particular, recent developments in some member states raise the question of whether an increasing influence of the administration on (administrative) courts could call into question the independence and therefore the right and obligation to refer under Art. 267 and thus the link between Union law and the member state.

4. DATA PROTECTION

The problem of insufficient independence described above has been judged by the ECJ precisely in the area of data protection. Already in its judgment of 9 March 2010 in the *Commission v. Germany*, C-518/07 case the ECJ held that the then Data Protection Directive 95/46/EC was violated by the fact that the German data protection authorities were subject to supervision by the state. The Court declared that by making the authorities responsible for monitoring the processing of personal data by non-public bodies and undertakings governed by public law which compete on the market (*öffentlich-rechtliche Wettbewerbsunternehmen*) in the different *Länder* subject to state scrutiny, and by thus incorrectly transposing the requirement that those authorities perform their functions 'with complete independence', the Federal Republic of Germany failed to fulfil its obligations under the second subparagraph of Art. 28(1) of Directive 95/46/EC on the protection of individuals with regard to the processing of personal data and on the free movement of such data.

In its further judgment of 16 October 2012 in C-614/10 – *Commission v Austria*, the ECJ also noted a lack of independence of the Austrian Data Protection Commission and thus a violation of the data protection directive in force at the time. Following its judgment in the *Commission v. Germany* case, the Court declared that by failing to take all the measures necessary to ensure that the legislation in force in Austria met the requirement of independence with regard to the 'Datenschutzkommission' (Data Protection Commission), more specifically by laying down a regulatory framework under which

- the managing member of the Data Protection Commission is a federal official subject to supervision,
- the office of the Data Protection Commission is integrated with the departments of the Federal Chancellery, and
- the Federal Chancellor has an unconditional right to information covering all aspects of the work of the Data Protection Commission,

Austria had failed to fulfil its obligations under the second subparagraph of Art. 28(1) of Directive 95/46/EC on the protection of individuals with regard to the processing of personal data and on the free movement of such data.

This clarifies that under Union law, independent authorities, such as in the area of data protection, must also not be subject to any supervision or interference by the state.

5. JUDICIAL REVIEW OF ADMINISTRATIVE SANCTIONS – BLIND SPOTS, LIMITS AND NEW CHALLENGES FOR THE ADMINISTRATIVE JUDICIARY

Based on the doctrine of the *marge d'appreciation* of the French *Conseil d'État*, many national legal systems confer a so-called discretionary margin or margin of appreciation on the administration.[4] The law provides a margin of discretion for an official decision-maker on the legal side, who, taking into account legally required considerations, can choose between several possible decisions in balancing.

A discretionary margin or margin of appreciation of the administrative authority does not hinder superiors (up to ministers) from giving orders to subordinates and determining the decision-making process on the merits.

Finally, the granting of discretion or a margin of appreciation to the administration may result in a restriction of administrative control by administrative courts, because the decision of the administrative authority (which may be determined by superior politicians) can remain uncontestable if and as long as it remains within the legal framework of discretion. It is for the legislator to design judicial control over the administrative authority's discretion to allow

[4] § 114 of the German Act on Administrative Court Rules (VwGO), 19 March 1991; § 28(4) of the Austrian Act on Administrative Court Proceedings (VwGVG), 13 February 2013.

the administrative court to exercise discretion instead of the administrative authority.

It should be noted that the concept of a discretionary margin or margin of appreciation has also found its way into international law and case law, in particular into the case law of the ECtHR, which gives states room for manoeuvre at the level of national legislation and also enforcement by national authorities.

Another aspect of judicial review relates to the question of cooperation between administrative authorities and courts, or control of the administrative authority by courts and the independence and impartiality of the court as discussed above.

In its judgment of 14 June 2017 in the C-685/15 – *Online Games* case, the ECJ clarified the limitations of an administrative court's investigation in an administrative criminal procedure. It held that Arts 49 and 56 TFEU read in the light of Art. 47 CFR must be interpreted as not precluding a national procedural system according to which, in administrative offence proceedings, the court called upon to rule on the compliance with EU law of legislation restricting the exercise of a fundamental EU freedom, such as the freedom of establishment or the freedom to provide services within the EU, is required to examine on its own initiative the facts of the case before it in the context of examining whether administrative offences arise, *provided that such a system does not have the consequence that that court is required to substitute itself for the competent authorities* of the member state concerned, the task of which is to provide the evidence necessary to enable that court to determine whether that restriction is justified.

Therefore, judicial control finds its limits when the court should substitute the proceeding including the investigation the administrative authority failed to do.

Last but not least, in the current context of measures against the pandemic, the question of judicial control of 'administration by regulations' arises. Whereas the criteria for an effective appeal, in particular against individual acts by administrative authorities, have been clarified, the issue of an effective remedy against regulations directly affecting the rights of a large number of citizens has not yet been the subject of the case law of the CJEU or the ECtHR, in particular whether 'administration by regulations' is in compliance with the general principle of good government (see above), for which effective remedies against this kind of administrative action must be accessible by citizens and whether it is also necessary for courts to provide interim measures.

24. The effective protection of collective interests: the interplay between jurisprudence and legislation

Federica Casarosa and Raffaella Calò[1]

1. INTRODUCTION

Collective actions are once again at the centre of political debate (and consequently of academic debate) at the European level following the intervention by the European Commission with the so-called New Deal for Consumers.[2] The intervention was initially triggered by practical difficulties encountered by citizens in obtaining an effective remedy in the case of harmful conduct by companies, banks, investment funds, producers of consumer goods, providers of electronic services and so on. In fact, the recent financial crises and the scandals involving companies such as Volkswagen, in the Dieselgate case,[3]

[1] The content of this chapter reflects merely the thoughts of the authors and does not represent the position of the Italian Ministry of Justice.

[2] Communication from the Commission to the European Parliament, the Council and the European Economic and Social Committee – A New Deal for Consumers, 11 April 2018, COM/2018/0183 final, accessed 3 November 2021 at https://eur-lex.europa.eu/legal-content/IT/TXT/?uri=CELEX:52018DC0183. See Remo Caponi, 'Ultime dall'Europa sull'azione di classe (con sguardo finale sugli Stati Uniti e il Dieselgate)' [2019] V *Foro italiano* c. 332; A. Cilento, 'New deal per i consumatori: risultati all'altezza delle ambizioni?' (2019) 3 Contratto/Impresa 1195; A. Van Duin and C. Leone, 'The Real (New) Deal: Levelling the Odds for Consumer-Litigants on the Need for a Modernisation, Part II', Amsterdam Law School Research Paper No. 2019-24, accessed 3 November 2021 at https://ssrn.com/abstract=3418275; C. Twigg-Flesner, 'Bad Hand? The "New Deal" for EU Consumers' (2018) 15 *European Union Private Law Review* 166; C. Scott, 'Consumer Law, Enforcement and the New Deal for Consumers' (2020) *European Review of Private Law*, forthcoming; A. Biard, 'Collective Redress in the EU: A Rainbow behind the Clouds?' (2018) 19 *ERA Forum* 1.

[3] The facts behind the Dieselgate scandal are well known. In 2015, the United States Environmental Protection Agency discovered that Volkswagen AG had installed a 'defeat device' on various types of its vehicles. This was a programme that could

and Facebook, in the Cambridge Analytica case,[4] have shown that the harmful effects of commercial practices can impact an extremely large number of people resident in different states, and not only in European countries.

In both the Dieselgate and Cambridge Analytica cases, consumer protection authorities and data protection authorities initiated *ex officio* administrative procedures in response to infringements suffered by consumers and data subjects,[5] while such injured parties very rarely presented claims before national courts regarding these harmful conducts. The damages suffered were

---

detect when the vehicle was tested and reduce the amount of pollutant emissions so that they appeared significantly lower (up to 40 times) than the real amount. See I. Garaci, 'Il dieselgate: Riflessioni sul private e public enforcement nella disciplina delle pratiche commerciali scorrette' (2018) 2 *Rivista di Diritto Industriale* 61.

[4] The Cambridge Analytica case affected 87 million Facebook profiles, which were profiled without the consent of the data subjects. In fact, the data collection was hidden behind a quiz application capable of accessing not only profile information but also 'friends' information. The scandal was publicly exposed in two articles published by *The Guardian* and the *New York Times* both on 17 March 2018.

[5] In the Dieselgate case, the Italian Competition and Market Authority (AGCM) closed the proceedings against the Volkswagen group in 2017, affirming that the conduct of the car manufacturer was incorrect in the light of the rules laid down in the Consumer Code relating to unfair commercial practices. For more detail, see I. Garaci and R. Montinaro, 'Public and Private Law Enforcement in Italy of EU Consumer Legislation after Dieselgate' (2019) 8 *Journal of European Consumer and Market Law* 29. In November 2017, the Dutch Consumer and Market Authority also concluded an investigation and imposed the maximum penalty that it could. Subsequently, the network of public consumer protection authorities intervened in agreement with the European Commission by adopting a common position calling for Volkswagen to improve its information practices and establish measures for consumers whose cars were defective after the so-called 'repair'. See the press release, 'Consumer Authorities and the European Commission urge Volkswagen to finalise repairs of all cars affected by emissions scandal', 7 September 2017, accessed 3 November 2021 at https://ec.europa.eu/commission/presscorner/detail/en/IP_17_3102. See also M. Frigessi Di Rattalma (ed.), *The Dieselgate: A Legal Perspective* (Springer, The Hague 2017). In the Cambridge Analytica case in the UK, the Information Commissioner's Office (ICO) extended the investigation it was already conducting into the analysis of data for political purposes also in relation to the Cambridge Analytica scandal. In October 2018, therefore, the ICO fined Facebook £500,000 for lack of transparency and security issues related to the collection of data in violation of the Data Protection Act 1998. See the measure at https://ico.org.uk/about-the-ico/news-and-events/news-and-blogs/2019/01/scl-elections-prosecuted-for-failing-to-comply-with-enforcement-notice (last accessed 3 November 2021). In Italy, in April 2018, both the Privacy Authority and the Competition and Market Authority launched an investigation into exactly what happened to the data, both in terms of individual privacy and alleged unfair business practices. In June 2019, the Privacy Authority fined Facebook €1 million. The amount of the sanction was based on several criteria, including the size of the database, the economic status of Facebook and the number of its users both in the world and in Italy. See the

so negligible for each individual that potential claimants were discouraged from engaging in long and expensive judicial procedures that could lead to extremely low levels of compensation.[6] Moreover, the injured parties were very often unaware of the remedies available to them and, even if they were, it tended to be uneconomic for individuals to pay lawyers, expert opinion costs and other costs of proceedings that could exceed the potential compensation.[7] As a result, consumers and data subjects were unable to obtain any relief for the violation they had suffered due to economic and procedural limitations affecting their right to justice.[8]

This situation may be resolved, at least partially, through collective redress mechanisms that join the efforts and the needs of all the injured parties in order to obtain compensation for the violation collectively suffered. This complies with the objective of access to justice that underlies the principle of effective remedy enshrined in Article 47 of the EU Charter (CFR). Obviously, the availability of collective redress mechanisms is not in itself sufficient to achieve an effective remedy. Instead, it requires the set of additional conditions provided by Article 47 CFR itself, namely the availability of expeditious, effective and proportionate procedural rules, and equality of arms in pursuing and defending the case collectively.[9] Unfortunately, recent analysis shows that the legal framework adopted in most EU countries is still unsatisfactory and the existing

---

measure at https://www.garanteprivacy.it/web/guest/home/docweb/-/docweb-display/docweb/9121506 (last accessed 3 November 2021).

[6] A. Giussani, 'Le azioni di classe dei consumatori dalle esperienze statunitensi agli sviluppi europei' (2019) 1 *Rivista Trimestrale di Diritto e Procedura Civile* 1572016; B. Stier and I. Tzankova, 'The Culture of Collective Litigation: A Comparative Analysis' in D.R. Hensler, C. Hodges and I. Tzankova (eds), *Class Actions in Context: How Culture, Economics and Politics Shape Collective Litigation* (Edward Elgar, Cheltenham, UK, Northampton, MA 2016), 23; Commission, Green paper on consumer collective redress, 27 November 2008, COM(2008)794 final.

[7] However, in other areas, such as competition law and environmental law, such claims require even more complex factual analysis and evidence tends to be inaccessible to individuals, which often creates a negative risk-benefit ratio and limits the effectiveness of individual claims. S. Benedi Lahuerta, 'Enforcing EU Equality Law through Collective Redress: Lagging Behind?' (2018) 55 *Common Market Law Review* 783.

[8] The above framework is not intended to deny the importance of the deterrent effect achieved through the intervention of independent authorities, which, in the case of financial penalties imposed on undertakings, may encourage undertakings to adopt virtuous behaviour under the threat of higher fines and stricter control of their conduct. Instead, it is important to highlight that complementary forms of collective redress are needed in order to extend the remedies available to injured parties, in particular in cases where public opinion has not had such a significant impact as to encourage such rapid and immediate administrative proceedings.

[9] See H. Woolf, *Access to Justice: Final Report to the Lord Chancellor on the Civil Justice System in England and Wales* (HMSO, London 1996), ch. 17.

rules are very restrictive leading to counterproductive effects on the use of collective redress mechanisms.[10]

In many countries, only intervention by courts allows the national rules to be interpreted extensively in order to enhance the use of collective remedies.[11] Therefore, this contribution will focus on the regulatory framework envisaged at the European level for collective redress and highlights the role and importance of national courts in safeguarding access to justice. Section 2 is dedicated to the definition of collective redress at the European level, with specific attention to the recent Directive on Collective redress. Section 3 analyses the most recent judicial interactions between national and European courts on this topic, highlighting the open questions left to national courts by the European legislator. Section 4 provides the example of the Italian law on collective redress adopted shortly after the presentation of the European proposal, reflecting the impact of European jurisprudence on national legislation and the importance of the principle of effectiveness in national legislation. Conclusions follow.

2. A DEFINITION OF COLLECTIVE REDRESS IN THE EU LEGAL FRAMEWORK

According to the literature, collective remedies are mechanisms that include a large number of legal instruments aimed at resolving disputes through forms

---

[10] R. Amaro, M.J. Azar-Baud, S. Corneloup, B. Fauvarque-Cosson and F. Jault-Seseke, 'Collective Redress in the Member States of the European Union', Study for JURY committee, European Parliament, 2018, accessed 3 November 2021 at https://www.europarl.europa.eu/RegData/etudes/STUD/2018/608829/IPOL_STU(2018)608829_EN.pdf, p. 43. See also BEUC, *Why We Need Collective Redress at EU Level: A Compelling Collection of Cases*, 2019, accessed 3 November 2021 at http://www.beuc.eu/publications/beuc-x-2019-062_why_we_need_collective_redress_at_eu_level.pdf.

[11] See the role of the Italian courts in interpreting the concept of 'homogeneity' among individual rights joined in class actions pursuant to Art. 140 bis of the Italian Consumer Code. Homogeneity is one of the criteria for the admissibility of collective proceedings. Accordingly, the certification of the group essentially depends on how this requirement is interpreted. In this regard, the Italian case law shows a trend towards a functional interpretation: multiple individual claims can be bundled in one single group proceeding whenever they have the same cause of action. If so, differences in the quantification of damages do not prevent the class action from being certified. See Appeal Court Turin, 23 September 2011, in Foro it., 2011, I, 3422; Tribunal of Rome, 25 March 2011, in Foro it., 2011, I, 1889; Tribunal of Naples, 9 December 2011, in www.ilcaso.it (last accessed 3 November 2021); Appeal Court Milan, 3 May 2011, ibidem; Tribunal of Rome, 27 April 2012, in Nuova giur. civ. comm. (last accessed 3 November 2021), 2012, I, 903, cited in R. Donzelli, 'Azione di classe risarcitoria', Diritto on line (2014), accessed 3 November 2021 at http://www.treccani.it/enciclopedia/azione-di-classe-risarcitoria_(Diritto-on-line)/.

of coordination among similar claims by several parties in one single action or procedure. Hodges[12] lists several mechanisms, including private collective litigation, the *partie civile* mechanism (which is linked to a criminal action), the previously mentioned proceedings before independent authorities, alternative dispute resolution (ADR) tools and ombudsmen. The so-called *actio popularis* should also be included as it allows citizens and/or certain organisations to bring a legal action in the public interest, even in the absence of an identifiable victim.[13]

From the legislative perspective, the first (yet limited) definition of collective redress is to be found in the EU Commission Recommendation on common principles for injunctive and compensatory collective redress mechanisms of 2013,[14] which selects only two types of mechanisms:

> (i) a legal mechanism that ensures a possibility to claim cessation of illegal behaviour collectively by two or more natural or legal persons or by an entity entitled to bring a representative action (injunctive collective redress); (ii) a legal mechanism that ensures a possibility to claim compensation collectively by two or more natural or legal persons claiming to have been harmed in a mass harm situation or by an entity entitled to bring a representative action (compensatory collective redress).[15]

This contribution will only focus on the first instrument, distinguishing between the two possible options through which collective actions may arise, namely (a) the mechanism in which a member of the group concerned can promote an action on behalf of the group (or class action) and (b) the mechanism in which a representative entity can promote an action on behalf of the group (or representative action). In both cases, the objective of the action may be compensation for the damage caused by a violation in favour of all the group members (such as full compensation or restitution) or aimed at

---

[12] C. Hodges, 'Collective Redress: The Need for New Technologies' (2019) 42 *Journal of Consumer Policy* 61.

[13] Cfr. L. Farkas, 'Limited Enforcement Possibilities under European Anti-Discrimination Legislation: A Case Study of Procedural Novelties – Actio popularis Action in Hungary' (2010) 3 *Erasmus Law Review* 181; S. Benedi Lahuerta, 'Enforcing EU Equality Law through Collective Redress: Lagging Behind?' (2018) 3 *Common Market Law Review* 787.

[14] Commission Recommendation of 11 June 2013 on common principles for injunctive and compensatory collective redress mechanisms in Member States concerning infringements of rights conferred by Union rules (2013/396/EU), OJEU 26 July 2013 L 201/60.

[15] Ibidem, point 3.

achieving deterrent effects, in the case of injunctive relief preventing future violations.[16]

Collective actions offer opportunities to combine several legal actions in a single legal proceeding, thus succeeding in obtaining advantages in terms of effectiveness and efficiency. At the individual level, they reduce the costs for individual claimants. Moreover, at the systemic level, they reduce the number of homogeneous cases pending before the courts, consequently limiting the risk of jurisprudential conflicts regarding assessments of potentially damaging conduct.[17]

2.1 The Directive on Representative Actions for Consumers

While historically Community law (at that time) assigned a role of particular importance to individual rightholders at the European level, as was stated in the *Van Gend en Loos* decision,[18] during the 1980s this purely individual vision attenuated and led to the introduction of collective enforcement mechanisms.[19] Indeed, in early 2010 the European Commission launched an initiative for 'A coherent European approach to collective redress', which resulted in the adoption of the previously mentioned Recommendation 2013/396/EU aimed at promoting the development of coherent principles of collective redress in all the Member States (MS) in all the areas where it could be relevant.[20] Although

---

[16] See C. Hodges, 'Collective Redress: The Need for New Technologies' (2019) 42 *Journal of Consumer Policy* 59; T. Bosters, *Collective Redress and Private International Law in the EU* (Springer, The Hague 2017); F. Cafaggi and H.-W. Micklitz (eds), *New Frontiers of Consumer Protection: The Interplay between Private and Public Enforcement* (Intersentia, Mortsel 2009). Note that damages may be either material or non-material, as happens in data protection cases, BEUC, *European Collective Redress: What is the EU Waiting For?*, BEUC initial contribution to the 2017–2018 EU initiatives on collective redress (2017), accessed 3 November 2021 at http://www.beuc.eu/publications/beuc-x-2017-086_ama_european_collective_redress.pdf.

[17] A. Giussani, 'Aggregazione di cause e aggregazione di questioni nel contenzioso di serie' (2016) 70 *Rivista Trimestrale di Diritto e Procedura Civile* 1279.

[18] See CJEU, Case C-26/62, *Van Gend en Loos v. Netherlands Inland Revenue Administration*, EU:C:1963:1. The CJEU recognised double control: institutional, by the Commission and the MS, and individual, by rightholders. This approach is also clear in the Opinion of AG Capotorti in the *Rewe* case (Case C-158/80, *Rewe v. Hauptzollamt Kiel*, EU:C:1981:71), p. 1850.

[19] European Commission, Joint information note: Towards a coherent European approach to collective redress: Next steps, SEC(2010)1192; and European Commission, Public consultation: Towards a coherent European approach to collective redress, SEC(2011)173 final.

[20] See Recommendation 2013/396/EU, recital 10.

consumer protection, competition, environment protection, protection of personal data, financial services legislation and investor protection are among the areas that are already supplemented by collective enforcement rights according to EU law.[21]

The Recommendation, based on Article 292 of the Treaty on the Functioning of the European Union (TFEU), was criticised by academics and stakeholders for being a too light intervention in the field as it was a soft law instrument unable to impose binding rules on the MS.[22] The limited impact of the Recommendation was then acknowledged in a 2018 Report on the practical implementation of the 2013 Recommendation, which showed negative results in terms of consistency and coherence of national legal frameworks for collective redress.[23] In particular, the need for a binding European instrument was highlighted in a 2018 study on 'Collective redress in the Member States of the European Union', in which the authors acknowledged the small impact of the 2013 Recommendation and pointed out that a binding instrument 'would expand the scope of collective redress, currently limited to injunctions in some countries, or would harmonise the already existing frameworks as they widely vary from one State to another'.[24]

As stated above, the results triggered a new intervention in this field.[25] In the framework of the aforementioned New Deal for Consumers, the European

---

[21] See Recommendation 2013/396/EU, recital 7.

[22] See European Consumer Association, *EU Takes Baby Step towards Collective Consumer Court Actions*, PR2013/10, June 2013, accessed 3 November 2021 at www.beuc.eu/publications/2013-00408-01-e.pdf; UEAPME, *SMEs Say No to Collective Redress, but React Positively on Antitrust Damage Proposal*, 12 June 2013, accessed 3 November 2021 at www.ueapme.com/IMG/pdf/130612_pr_Collective_redress.pdf; and Eurochambres, *Last Bad Approach on Collective Redress*, 11 June 2013, accessed 3 November 2021 at www.eurochambres.eu/objects/1/Files/EUROCHAMBRES_PR-Approach_collective_redress.pdf. All cited in A. Biard, 'Collective Redress in the EU: A Rainbow behind the Clouds?' (2018) 19 *ERA Forum* 5.

[23] The 2018 Report acknowledged that the Recommendation did not achieve its objectives and the level of fragmentation in this area was still very high. See EU Commission, Report on the implementation of the Commission Recommendation on common principles for injunctive and compensatory collective redress mechanisms in the Member State concerning violations of rights granted under Union Law, COM(2018) 40 final, 25 January 2018, accessed 3 November 2021 at www.ec.europa.eu/newsroom/just/document.cfm?action=display&doc_id=49502.

[24] R. Amaro, M.J. Azar-Baud, S. Corneloup, B. Fauvarque-Cosson and F. Jault-Seseke, 'Collective Redress in the Member States of the European Union', cit., p. 66.

[25] The New Deal for consumers also built on the findings of the Fitness Check of EU Consumer and Marketing law of May 2017 (SWD(2017)209 Final, 23 May 2017, accessed 3 November 2021 at www.ec.europa.eu/newsroom/just/item-detail.cfm?item_id=59332) and the evaluation of the 2011 Consumer Rights Directive therein.

Commission included a proposal for a directive aimed at regulating representative actions to protect the collective interests of consumers so as to reform Directive 22/2009 on injunctions for the protection of consumers' interests.[26] The proposal was then adopted on 25 November 2020, as Directive 2020/1828 on representative actions for the protection of the collective interests of consumers and repealing Directive 2009/22/EC.

As was clearly stated in the explanatory memorandum, the legal basis for such an intervention, as is the case of the current Injunctions Directive, is Article 114 TFEU, to which Article 169 TFEU refers.[27]

The European intervention is also justified by its compliance with the subsidiarity principle. In fact, as was suggested in the above-mentioned explanatory memorandum, 'action by Member States alone is likely to result in further fragmentation, which in turn would contribute to unequal treatment for consumers and traders in the internal market and create diverging levels of consumer redress in the Union'.

The Directive has a scope of application including financial services, energy, telecommunications, health, environment and so on, as it is set out in Annex I to the Directive, and also includes the protection of personal data, specifying that it only applies in the case of infringements which harm or are likely to harm the collective interests of consumers. However, the Directive does not clarify how representative actions to protect consumers and ones provided for the protection of data subjects may coordinate or even overlap, leaving many questions open.

The Directive identifies two types of collective actions:

- *a representative action for an injunction*: aimed at issuing an injunction to ascertain violation of the law and/or cessation of the practice, even if it has not yet been implemented (*ex* Art. 7);
- *a representative action for compensation*: aimed at issuing measures obliging a professional to provide 'compensation, repair, replacement, reduction

[26] Thanks to Case C-191/15, *Verein für Konsumenteninformation v. Amazon EU Sàrl*, EU:C:2016:612, in which the CJEU ruled that clauses which could lead the consumer to mistakenly believe that the law of the Member State in which a company was based governed the contract were invalid, contrary to the Rome I Regulation. Such an assessment could not, however, be influenced by the collective nature of the action, since 'the fact that such action does not relate to individual contracts concretely entered into is inherent in the very nature of such a collective and preventive action, in the context of which an abstract control is carried out'. Collective actions initiated by consumer organisations are therefore considered to contribute to the effectiveness of consumer protection legislation.

[27] See the explanatory memorandum.

of the price, termination of the contract or reimbursement of the price paid, as the case may be' (*ex* Art. 8).

Since the Directive has a minimum harmonisation objective, MS are free to provide higher levels of protection, allowing the rules to be adapted to national legal systems. This is evident from the criteria used to identify the persons entitled to bring proceedings. In this case, the Directive leaves the MS ample room for manoeuvre, allowing them to define the applicable criteria. Only in the case of representative cross-border actions are precise criteria defined pursuant to Article 4(3) of the Directive. This implies that only recognised associations have legal standing, whereas individuals are excluded.[28] The discretion given to the MS regarding the criteria for the designated bodies entitled to present a representative action could then undermine the desired harmonisation, although it might be reasonable to think that, with a view to simplification, national legislators should adopt the same criteria applicable to cross-border actions.

The Directive identifies more detailed rules on the general principles to be applied in the case of both opt-in and opt-out systems. According to the literature,[29] opt-in systems are actions where only those group members who expressly consent to it are involved in the collective litigation, whereas in opt-out systems the group members who do not want to be involved have to explicitly express their position by opting-out from the action.

In this respect, the Directive seems to leave the decision between opt-in and opt-out systems to the MS in the cases of both injunctions and actions for compensation. Only in the case of cross-border actions for compensation does the Directive provide an obligation to adopt opt-in systems. This choice represents a change compared to the past, since in Recommendation 2013/396 the European legislator instead indicated the opt-in system was preferable in order to safeguard the autonomy of individual citizens in deciding whether and how to claim against a specific violation before courts.[30] This legislative choice shows a higher level of confidence in comparisons of collective actions, which in itself does not undermine the autonomy of individuals to bring an action individually or, indeed, collectively. This also appears to be in line with the practice of most MS, since only in ten of them is an opt-in system implemented

---

28 This does not imply that class actions can be envisaged at the national level to allow individuals to present actions on behalf of groups of consumers.

29 E.F. Sherman, 'American Class Actions: Significant Features and Developing Alternatives in Foreign Legal Systems' (2003) 215 *Federal Rules Decisions* 130.

30 C. István Nagy, *Collective Actions in Europe: A Comparative, Economic and Trans-Systemic Analysis* (Springer Open, Cham 2018).

both in the framework for consumer protection and in other sectors, while in the others the opt-out system prevails.[31]

A further important factor concerns the effects of decisions in which there is interaction between administrative enforcement, operating through the intervention of the guaranteeing authorities at the national level, and judicial enforcement. Article 10 of the Directive states that final decisions by national authorities (regardless of their objective and the deciding body) are considered evidence (freely assessable by the court) that establishes the existence or non-existence of an infringement for the purpose of any other action for damages before national courts against the same professional with the same facts.

3. THE ROLE OF COLLECTIVE ACTIONS VIS-À-VIS INDIVIDUAL ACTIONS IN THE JURISPRUDENCE OF THE CJEU

Collective actions have been the subject of several pronouncements by the Court of Justice of the European Union (CJEU) aimed at resolving both procedural and substantive issues relating to the legal effects of these instruments.[32] An analysis of some of these judgments makes it possible to highlight open questions and consequently to verify whether and how the Directive can tackle these difficulties.

Among the few cases addressing collective remedies decided by the CJEU, one stands out showing how the relationship between individual and collective remedies is interpreted by the Court and how this approach affects the choices of national courts. In fact, the approach adopted by the CJEU acknowledges a hierarchy between individual and collective action, leaving the latter a complementary role.[33] This is justified by interpretation of judicial protection as a monopoly power of the individual, who is able not only to decide whether or not to lodge a claim but also whether or not to willingly participate in a collective action.

---

[31] For a more detailed analysis of several countries, see P. Leupold, 'Enforcing Consumer Rights: Collective Redress in Austria and the European Union' (2019) 8 EuCML, 121.

[32] See the analysis in R. Amaro, M.J. Azar-Baud, S. Corneloup, B. Fauvarque-Cosson and F. Jault-Seseke, 'Collective Redress in the Member States of the European Union', cit., p. 51.

[33] See Case C-470/12, *Pohotovosť*, EU:C:2014:101 and Case C-413/12, *Asociación de Consumidores Independientes de Castilla y León*, EU:C:2013:800.

The case analysed in detail here is the judicial dialogue emerging from the CJEU decision in the *Sales Sinués* case[34] (see Figure 24.1).

3.1 The Relationship between Individual and Collective Actions Addressed by Vertical Interaction between the CJEU and Spanish Courts

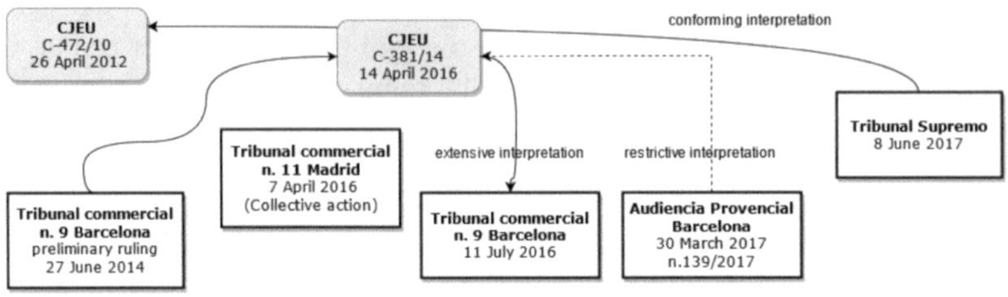

Figure 24.1 Judicial interactions in Sales Sinués case

The proceedings before the CJEU addressed three similar cases in which the fate of individual actions presented by individual consumers and the collective action brought against the same opposing party were intertwined. For the sake of simplification, only one of the three cases will be presented in the description of the facts as the CJEU decision followed the same reasoning for all three.

The case concerned a contract for the novation of a loan with a Spanish bank containing a so-called '*suelo*' clause, with which the bank imposed a stable minimum interest rate irrespective of fluctuations in market rates. In relation to this contract, Mr Sales Sinués brought an action before Barcelona Commercial Court No. 9 in order to assert the unfairness of the clause and to seek its annulment. At the same time, a consumer association brought a collective action against the same bank before the Madrid Court in order to obtain an injunction prohibiting the use of '*suelo*' clauses in loan agreements.[35] Because the

---

[34] Joined cases C-381/14 and C-385/14, *Jorge Sales Sinués and Youssouf Drame Ba v. Caixabank SA and Catalunya Caixa SA*, EU:C:2016:252. For a broader analysis of consumer protection cases in the judicial dialogue, see ACTIONES Module on consumer protection, accessed 3 November 2021 at https://cjc.eui.eu/projects/actiones/actiones-platform/; and F. Cafaggi and F. Casarosa, 'L'effettività dei rimedi nelle interazioni giudiziali fra corti nazionali e corti europee' in P. Gallo, G. Magri and M. Salvadori (eds), *Armonizzazione del diritto europeo: il ruolo delle corti* (Ledizioni, Milano 2017), 55.

[35] Case brought by Adicae (Asociación de Usuarios de Bancos Cajas y Seguros) against 72 banking institutions through a collective action.

conduct at issue was the same in the two cases, the bank asked the Barcelona Commercial Court to stay the proceedings concerning the individual action until the final judgment in the collective one.

In its assessment of the party's request, the Commercial Court of Barcelona found that the previous national jurisprudence had adopted a restrictive interpretation of the applicable national provision on *lis pendens* affirming the automatic suspension of the individual action. This interpretation, however, may have the effect of reducing the remedies available to the consumer in the case of unfair terms, contrary to Articles 6 and 7 of Directive 93/13. The Court therefore decided to stay the proceedings and to refer a number of questions to the CJEU.

In dealing with this question, the CJEU pointed out, regarding the purpose of our analysis, that the objectives for individual and collective actions may be different, since the latter may serve merely as deterrent. Following the conclusions of the Advocate General, the Court therefore underlined the differences between the two actions, implicitly adhering to the thesis of complementarity of collective action vis-à-vis individual action proposed by the Commission and adopted by the Advocate General.[36] The Court's analysis then moved on to the procedural provisions applicable to individual and collective actions.

In the light of the principle of effectiveness, the CJEU assessed the effects of the suspension of the individual action, recognising that, on the one hand, the decision in a collective action can be binding on the individual consumer even if he did not opt in to it and, on the other hand, this could prevent the national court from assessing the previous individual negotiation of the alleged unfair terms.[37] Moreover, the proportionality test applied did not change this result either, since neither the consistency between court decisions nor the need to avoid overburdening the courts could have justified such measures.[38] These elements therefore led the Court to consider the interpretation of the rule which imposes automatic suspension as an obstacle to the attainment of the objectives of Directive 93/13. The decision by the CJEU therefore stated that the Spanish national rule must be interpreted as meaning that the national court has discretionary power to assess whether it is appropriate to suspend the individual action on the basis of the functional distinction between collective and individual actions.[39]

As a result, the CJEU's approach confirmed the existing hierarchy in European case law between individual and collective actions, recognising

---

36 See also the Opinion of AG Szpunar, par. 29–30.

37 See par. 39 of the CJEU decision.

38 Cfr. par. 41–42.

39 Cfr. par. 43.

the primacy of the former and the complementary role of the latter.[40] This approach can be justified according to the interpretation of the jurisdictional protection of an individual interest as a monopolistic power of the rightholder[41] to decide whether to start and continue judicial proceedings. This approach is linked to the empowerment of jurisdictional tools in favour of consumers who are in a weaker position vis-à-vis professionals. However, this does not in any way cover the complementary aspect of the need to offer an effective remedy where the individual, precisely because of his weak position, is unable to access effective remedies.

The dialogue between the national court and the CJEU continued in the individual proceedings at the domestic level. The referring court applied the principle developed by the CJEU and continued the proceedings without imposing a suspension of the proceedings, waiting for the collective action to be decided.

In the meantime, however, the collective action ended with a declaration of the unfairness of the clauses and a prohibition against using these clauses in subsequent contracts. The proceeding before the Commercial Court of Barcelona was still open and the judge in charge questioned the effects of the judgment in the collective action on the individual action, asking whether the judgment could be used as proof of the unfairness of the clause in the individual proceeding as well. A restrictive interpretation of the CJEU's decision could totally decouple the individual action from the collective action: any result of the collective action could not affect the decision in the individual one. Instead, the Commercial Court preferred a broader interpretation of the CJEU's decision: on the one hand, the domestic court acknowledged that the autonomy of the individual to present an individual action should be safeguarded through the decoupling from collective action. On the other, the domestic court affirmed that, in order to provide 'adequate and effective means of stopping the inclusion of such [unfair] terms',[42] the individual action should benefit from the positive effects of the decision in the collective action.

---

[40] Indeed, already in Case C-413/12, *Asociación de Consumidores Independientes de Castilla y León (ACICL)*, cit., the CJEU had stated, in the light of the principles of effectiveness and equivalence, that there were no infringements in the case of a different territorial jurisdiction in the case of individual and collective actions, although the latter led to a greater difficulty for associations to pursue the objective of consumer protection. Confirming this approach also in Case C-470/12, *Pohotovost'*, cit., the CJEU had stated that, in the light of the principles of equivalence and effectiveness, the Slovak legislation on the inadmissibility of the intervention of a consumer protection association in support of a given consumer in an enforcement procedure did not infringe European law.

[41] R. Donzelli, *L'azione di classe a tutela dei consumatori* (Jovene, Napoli 2011).

[42] See the decision of the Commercial Court of Barcelona No. 9, No. 413/14-D3, 11 July 2016. Cfr Art. 7(3) Directive 93/13.

In practice, the domestic court affirmed that on the basis of the declaration of unfairness of the term in the collective action the same clause could also be declared null and void in the individual action.

In this case, the Commercial Court expressly referred to the principle of effectiveness of remedies in favour of the consumer, which led the Spanish court to an ad hoc assessment of the relationship between individual action and collective action, reviewing the model of complementarity expressed by the CJEU. More specifically, the possibility of conflicting jurisprudence on unfairness depending on whether the proceedings are brought by an individual or by an association could conflict with the objective of legal certainty, which was considered irrelevant in the CJEU's judgment, along with the issue regarding the effectiveness of the remedy. Without prejudice to the assessment of the actual circumstances under Article 4 of Directive 93/13, the difference in the assessment of unfairness depending on whether the protection is individual or collective did not appear to be logically justified.

This aspect was also addressed in a subsequent development of the Spanish jurisprudence. The decision by the Spanish Supreme Court in its judgment No. 367/2017 of 8 June 2017[43] addressed the issue of the effectiveness of decisions issued in the context of collective actions with respect to three hypotheses: (a) the effects of a decision in a collective action for a declaration of invalidity of an unfair term on a subsequent dispute brought by another consumer association concerning the same term; (b) the effects of a decision in a collective action affirming the fairness of a contractual clause on individual proceedings, where the Supreme Court concluded that such unfavourable judgments have no force of res judicata; and (c) the effects that a judgment in a collective action must have in a subsequent dispute in which an individual action for annulment is brought. The Supreme Court only addressed the hypothesis referred to in (c) and based its argument on the judgment by the CJEU in the *Invitel* case.[44] Therefore, the Supreme Court recognised that the decision stating the unfairness (and therefore the nullity) of the clause defined in the collective action may have effect in individual judgments.[45]

The issue related to the effects of collective action is only partially addressed in the Directive on representative actions as it does not offer clear indications on the coordination of actions regarding the effectiveness of remedies. In

---

[43] RJ 2017/2509. For more extensive information, see F. Cordón Moreno, 'Acción colectiva y acción individual para la defensa de los derechos de los consumidores' (2017) 31 *Derecho Privado y Constitución* 217.

[44] CJEU, Case C-472/10, *Nemzeti Fogyasztóvédelmi Hatóság v. Invitel Távközlési Zrt*, EU:C:2012:242.

[45] More problematic for the Supreme Court is precisely the definition of such effects, which cannot be those of res judicata.

fact, the aforementioned Article 10 of the Directive addresses the issue of the effects of the judgment in the case of several actions (collective or not) brought against the same party. As mentioned above, in this case decisions are considered to be evidence of the existence or non-existence of an infringement for the purposes of any other remedies, so-called follow-up actions, provided that the same damage is not compensated twice to the same consumers concerned.[46] The Directive leaves open the issue regarding the opposite situation, where a judgment has established the non-existence of an infringement. Article 10 of the Directive states that the decision in a collective action is a 'proof of the infringement' but nothing is provided in the opposite case.[47]

4. THE IMPACT OF CJEU JURISPRUDENCE ON NATIONAL LEGISLATION: THE HORIZONTAL REGULATION OF COLLECTIVE REMEDIES IN ITALY

As for the impact of CJEU jurisprudence in the matter of collective redress on national legislation, with special regard to the principle of effectiveness, an important bench test is represented by the Italian case. In fact, Law n. 31/2019 on collective redress was adopted in Italy in April 2019 and entered into force in May 2021, as provided for by Article 7.

Indeed, a year after the approval of the proposal for a Directive on representative actions, the Italian Parliament approved the national law on collective redress in order to replace the previous one adopted in 2007 and amended in 2012, which did not prove to have succeeded in legal practice.

---

[46] The practice in some European countries shows that coordination between administrative action, usually before market authorities, and collective actions before the judge is particularly useful for the selection of actions with a higher chance of winning. Paradoxical is the situation in France and Great Britain, as reported respectively in A. Biard, 'Sale temps pour l'action de groupe … la nécessaire recherche d'outils alternatifs pour résoudre les litiges de masse' (2018) 157 *Revue Lamy Droit Civil* 21; and B. Hurst, 'The "Tidal Wave" of Data Protection-Related Class Actions: Why We're Not Drowning just Yet …' (2018), accessed 3 November 2021 at https://www.twobirds.com/en/news/articles/2018/global/tidal-wave-of-data-protection-related-cases, p. 11.

[47] R. Caponi, 'Ultime dall'Europa sull'azione di classe (con sguardo finale sugli Stati Uniti e il Dieselgate)' [2019] V *Foro italiano* c. 332.

The 2019 intervention aimed to simplify the procedure applicable to collective consumer claims[48] and to improve the economic incentives to start a collective proceeding.[49]

With this in mind, the law approved in April 2019 aims to overcome the many difficulties that made class action in Italy unappealing with an intent to guarantee an effective and timely access to justice by all citizens, also in cases of small claims. The main goals of the new Italian law do not differ from the classical ones characterising the introduction of collective redress mechanisms in national legal systems: efficiency, deterrence and judicial economy. However, what is new is the very pragmatic approach adopted by the Italian legislator reflecting the idea that a new horizontal regulation of collective redress is imperative in order to achieve effective access to justice in Italy without limiting such tools to a single legal sector.

The pragmatism is expressed in a distinction between two types of collective actions, namely a compensatory procedure (so-called '*azione di classe*', or class action) and an injunctive procedure (so-called '*azione inibitoria collettiva*', or representative action).

Both actions are included in the Civil Procedure Code.[50] This choice makes it clear that Italian collective actions will be available for any sector or issue at stake, and not only by individuals but also by legal persons. At the same time, the clear distinction between the two actions reflects their different scope and emphasises their different rationales. The two actions are not only distinct but also clearly separated: even when substantial conditions exist for both compensatory and injunctive action, according to Article 840-*sexiesdecies* of the Civil Procedure Code, the two actions cannot be brought in court together.

As for compensatory collective action, the shift of the legal provisions from consumer law to the general procedural code is not only symbolic but very substantive. In fact, the new compensatory action not only operates for the protection of consumers' rights[51] but has a wide horizontal effect. While, according to the previous law, collective compensatory action was not admis-

---

48 This was confirmed by the fact that in July 2013 only one class action had ended with a favourable judicial decision awarding compensation for damages to the consumer involved.

49 The cost-benefit ratio was not very favourable for consumers and their associations as the – anticipated – legal expenses were very high and the chances of having a significant resolution were very low, partially because of the absence of punitive damages.

50 See Art. 840-*bis* ff.

51 For an accurate description of the Italian legislation on the matter before the approval of Law 31/2019, see R. Amaro, M.J. Azar-Baud, S. Corneloup, B. Fauvarque-Cosson and F. Jault-Seseke, 'Collective Redress in the Member States of the European Union', cit.

sible if brought on behalf of small stakeholders, irrespective of whether they could be regarded as weaker parties or not, the new legal instrument provided by Law 31/2019 may be used by any natural person and also by qualified legal entities. Furthermore, the collective procedure may be used for the protection of any kind of individual rights as long as they are homogeneous.

Given the broad scope of the legal provision, the new compensatory collective action is patently an alternative to the individual one, reflecting a model of complementarity more advanced than that designed by the CJEU in the above-mentioned decisions.[52] In fact, according to Article 840-*bis* Civil Procedure Code, any time individual homogeneous rights are infringed a legal action – either individual or collective – may be brought in order to obtain compensation for damages. Notably, according to the Italian law, there is not any hierarchy between individual and collective actions, but they are purely alternative. However, if the individual opts for collective action, the case will be decided by the Commercial Court instead of the ordinary one.

The new class action adopts a 'tempered' opt-in approach consisting of an 'opt-in' rule with a corrective typical of common law countries, namely the chance to join the class even after the decision accepting the class action has been pronounced by the court.[53] Pursuant to Article 840-*sexies* Code of Civil Procedure, in the 'joining' phase it is possible for the members of a class to join the action after the decision accepting the class action is pronounced by the judge. In this case, these individuals are able to take advantage of the judgment defined as *res inter alios acta* and to profit from numerous benefits: membership is possible only if the decision is favourable to the class. The individuals are not required to take part in the proceedings and they avoid the risk of losing the case. This instrument would allow those who had already introduced an individual action against the same defendant on the facts of the case to decide whether to exploit the decision in the collective action and join it or to continue with the individual action.

Although this rule goes beyond the solution provided by the Directive, partially solving the problems mentioned above regarding the effects of collective action on individuals that were not part of the initial claim, according to some commentators it may raise some doubts. While the rule provides an incentive

---

52 Note that this is in line with the previous jurisprudence of the Italian Supreme Court. The decision by the Supreme Court, Grand Chamber, 2 February 2017, no. 2610, clearly distinguished between actions for the protection of collective interests and actions for damages. In particular, it described the features of compensatory action as an alternative to individual action with the same purpose.

53 See R. Amaro, M.J. Azar-Baud, S. Corneloup, B. Fauvarque-Cosson and F. Jault-Seseke, 'Collective Redress in the Member States of the European Union', cit., p. 23.

for effective class action, the balance perhaps may seem to lead to a sacrifice of the defendant's right of defence and result in a violation of the procedural principle of contradiction,[54] which, as was also highlighted in CJEU case law in the *Biuro podróży 'Partner'* case,[55] also applies in favour of professionals.

However, this does not seem to be the case of the Italian legislation on class action. As far as the alleged sacrifice of the defendant's right of defence is concerned, the principle of equality of arms does not seem to be violated, as every person joining the class action may receive compensation only as a result of the violation effectively perpetrated by the defendant and assessed by the court. Moreover, the legislative act clearly excludes punitive damages. Therefore, the possibility for claimants to join the class action does not have any multiplying effect on compensation. Instead, it only brings more effective protection of individual rights.

Moreover, it is undoubtable that this legal solution, while it is consistent with the constitutional provisions concerning party autonomy, provides a general mechanism granting judicial protection to all weaker parties against companies and collective entities by allowing a single claimant to avail himself of a positive decision already adopted by the court in favour of the class he belongs to. In this way, the effect of the inertia of class members, which has been shown by experience, can be mitigated by the fact that joining the class after the judicial decision has been made requires much less effort than starting from scratch.

Given these premises, class action can reasonably play a fundamental role in the Italian legal system only if law firms and associations will exploit it. Therefore, the legal provisions on contingency fees for lawyers and an economic incentive for the class representatives – which can play a very propulsive effect – represent an essential part of the law reform.

The new law contains a very significant innovation as far as the injunctive procedure is concerned. In fact, while before the approval of the new law injunctive collective procedures were available only in specific sectors, the new legal instrument has a much broader scope of application.

---

[54] M. Malavasi and G. Ricciardi, 'La nuova Class action: analisi delle principali disposizioni', reperibile all'indirizzo, accessed 3 November 2021 at http://www.dirittobancario.it/approfondimenti/profili-processuali/la-nuova-class-action-analisi-delle-principali-disposizioni, p. 36; G. Ponzanelli, 'La nuova class action' (2019) 3 Danno resp 307.

[55] CGUE, C-119/15, *Biuro podróży 'Partner' Sp. z o.o*, EU:C:2016:987. See also Chapter 22 by Casarosa and Sabato in this book.

5. CONCLUSIONS

The development of a European framework for collective remedies has been a (long and) ongoing process which involves not only the European regulatory institutions but also – and most importantly – national and European courts. As the national legal systems only took into account the European recommendations in 2013 to a limited extent, interventions by courts served as triggers to adapt national provisions to the fundamental principle of access to justice, which is enshrined in the CFR and also in national constitutions.

Collective actions have been the objects of several national and European judgments, both in terms of preventive remedies (e.g. injunctions) and in terms of reparatory remedies (e.g. class actions). As mentioned above, the jurisprudence of the CJEU shows a clear hierarchy between individual and collective action, leaving the latter a complementary role.

On the one hand, the hierarchical approach between individual and collective actions can be justified by the fact that only the individual may exercise her monopoly power to seek judicial protection. This is linked to the strengthening of the procedural tools available to the individual (who is in a weaker position vis-à-vis professionals). Instead, the same weakness is missing in the case of an association presenting a collective action, or at least it has not the same intensity.[56] On the other hand, this approach conflicts with the underlying objectives of collective remedy, namely the possibility of enhancing access to justice through the collective management of disputes addressing the same claim against the same plaintiff. Therefore, the principle of effectiveness of remedies could justify a more in-depth analysis of the relationship between individual action and collective action by reviewing the complementary model developed by the court. This clearly emerges from the broad interpretation adopted by the Spanish Commercial Court vis-à-vis the CJEU decision taking into account both the need to safeguard the autonomy of the individual in seeking judicial protection through an individual action and at the same time achieving the objective of effective remedies through the coordination of the effects of individual and collective actions. An innovative example of the complementarity between the individual and collective instruments is represented by the new Italian legislation on class action, as was described above.

After the analysis of the jurisprudence, one would expect that the recent Directive on representative actions would acknowledge the problems envisaged by national courts. Unfortunately, the Directive does not solve all the problems – although it meritoriously improves the trust of European insti-

---

56 I. Benöhr, 'Collective Redress in the Field of European Consumer Law' (2014) 41 *Legal Issues of Economic Integration* 243 and ss.

tutions in opt-out mechanisms. The Directive leaves many open questions, which may have the effect of hampering the harmonisation objective. At the national level, instead, interesting developments may emerge, as is exemplified by the Italian law on collective remedies, which not only provides horizontal legislation applicable regardless of the sector but also better incentives to bring collective actions.

25. Comment: collective redress and antitrust law

Lavinia Vizzoni

INTRODUCTION

The European Union has recently approved a Directive on collective redress.[1]

At the general level, the mechanisms of collective redress ought to be applied with a clear view of the fundamental rights sphere from the perspective of maintaining a proper balance between effectiveness of protection and the requirements arising from the overall fundamental standards and guarantees existing in the national legal systems.

Based on these premises, it can be interesting to adopt the prospect of interaction between European law and national legislation in mutual directions.

The proposed comparison is particularly stimulating if applied to the Italian legal system, where the mechanisms of collective redress have so far severely struggled to find full effective implementation: art. 140 *bis* of the consumer code – now repealed[2] – was barely applied and revealed its complete inefficiency to guarantee access by consumers to an effective remedy.[3] The doctrine has actually defined the Italian class action discipline as totally disastrous and has observed that the Italian class action model has not raised the level of consumer protection and has completely disregarded the expectations of those who hoped for the achievement of the objective of collective protection.

1 Directive (EU) 2020/1828 of the European Parliament and of the Council of 25 November 2020 on representative actions for the protection of the collective interests of consumers and repealing Directive 2009/22/EC.

2 In this regard, it has been highlighted that while art. 140 *bis* has been repealed, there has been no real coordination with the so-called public class action established by the Italian d.lgs. 198/2009. See M. Franzoni, 'Azione di classe, profili sostanziali', Danno e resp., 2019, p. 309 ss.

3 A.D. De Santis, 'L'azione di classe a dieci anni dalla sua entrata in vigore', Foro it., 2019, p. 2180 ss.; R. Pardolesi, 'Inadempimento contrattuale, danno non patrimoniale, azione di classe: note minime su disvalore, disappunto, irrisorietà e altro ancora', Danno e Resp., 2020, p. 95 ss.

As will be seen, the Italian scenario of collective redress has lately undergone substantial changes, which encourages analysis of its interplay with the European level.

Additionally, a particular point of view from which it can be challenging to analyse the collective redress phenomenon is the antitrust one. Given that collective remedies are mere 'tools' whereas antitrust is a whole field of law, and it is not unusual to have tools that are used across areas, shedding a specific 'antitrust light' on collective mechanisms can disclose some potentialities still in the direction of effective protection of the parties involved but also some fallacies which deserve distinct consideration.

THE MUTUAL INTERACTION BETWEEN EUROPEAN AND ITALIAN SOLUTIONS FOR COLLECTIVE REMEDIES

The purpose of the aforementioned European Directive on collective redress has even been 'exceeded' – in a certain sense – by recent Italian legislation in the direction of overcoming the complementarity between individual and collective action.

In fact, Italian law n. 31/2019[4] seems to provide for the latter to be accessible under the same conditions as the former without establishing any hierarchical relation between the two actions – as was meaningfully anticipated by some Spanish decisions[5] – and allows the members of a class to join an action also after the decision accepting the class action is pronounced by the judge.

From a practical point of view, the goal of strengthening the application of collective redress in the European area is particularly crucial: collective action itself is a means to overcome several difficulties related to individual actions, such as the underreporting of individual claims due to the high economic costs of litigation, the complexity of the legal provisions applicable, the long duration of the judicial proceedings and the imbalance between the individual claimant and the professional counterparty. These complications and technicalities may prevent individuals from exercising their fundamental rights to access to justice.

In addition, while the scope of application of collective actions has so far been limited to consumers, the Italian law aspires to make collective action, both injunction and compensatory, a general remedy accessible by individuals

---

4 See M. Stella, 'La nuova azione inibitoria collettiva ex art. 840 sexiesdecies c.p.c. tra tradizione e promesse di deterrenza', Corriere Giur., 2019, p. 1453 ss.

5 See F. Casarosa, R. Calò, 'The effective protection of collective interests: the interplay between jurisprudence and legislation' in this same book, Chapter 24.

whose homogeneous rights are infringed.[6] This realises another step towards removing the obstacles to an effective implementation of collective redress.

This may, in turn, relaunch the debate on the effective application of collective redress to areas different to and further than the consumer one, like data protection, where the possibility of aggregated claims can be favoured in the perspective of effective protection of data subjects.[7]

Considering the centrality of collective remedies in the European area, it is meaningful that some national inputs tend to adopt relatively radical solutions in the direction of implementing the effectiveness of collective actions.

Therefore, it will be particularly interesting to understand in the near future whether there will be any chance of closer interaction between national systems and the European Union starting from the former and also due to the contribution by jurisprudence. Indeed, the Directive on representative actions for the protection of the collective interests of consumers has to be transposed into the national legislation of EU countries by 25 December 2022.

A HINT: AN 'ANTITRUST LIGHT' ON COLLECTIVE REDRESS

As anticipated, a particular point of view from which it can be interesting to analyse the collective redress phenomenon is the antitrust one. The two topics – collective action and the antitrust field – show significant overlaps and/or common points due, in the first place, to the circumstance that consumers damaged by unfair commercial practices or more generally infringements of competition law can find their effective protection (also) through a collective action.

On the one hand, although the 'consumer base' of collective redress – arising from the requirement to give consumers the protection they need in the framework of a marketplace in which they experience an asymmetrical position – has been the most highlighted recently, the non-discrimination and labour law areas also exploit collective remedies at the European and national levels.[8] Besides, the application of collective actions can per se be extended to

---

6 I. Pagni, 'L'azione inibitoria collettiva', Giur. it., 2019, p. 2329 ss., examines the extension of the collective redress remedy.

7 Exemplarily, see F. Casarosa, 'La tutela aggregata dei dati personali nel Regolamento UE 2016/679: una base per l'introduzione di rimedi collettivi?' in A. Mantelero, D. Poletti (a cura di), *Regolare la tecnologia: il Reg. UE 2016/679 e la protezione dei dati personali – Un dialogo fra Italia e Spagna*, Pisa University Press, Pisa, 2018, p. 235 ss.

8 See *Collective Redress in the Member States of the European Union*, a study commissioned by the European Parliament's Policy Department for Citizens' Rights

other areas like data protection. The new Italian class action has also expanded its scope of application, losing the consumer reference. In this way, the protection provided seems to shift more and more towards a wider notion and comes closer to the antitrust field.

In fact, on the other hand, the field of application of Directive 2014/104[9] is broader than the consumer area.[10] It is not by chance that it ensures 'anyone who has suffered harm caused by an infringement of competition law by an undertaking or by an association of undertakings' has 'the right to claim full compensation for that harm from that undertaking or association' (art. 1) and 'injured party' means 'a person that has suffered harm caused by an infringement of competition law' (art. 2). Besides, in the Italian application of the Directive – d.lgs. 3/2017 – it is specified that both natural and legal persons and also entities without legal personality fall within the notion of 'injured party' (art. 2).

Regarding the *legitimatio ad causam*, Court of Justice of the European Union (CJEU) jurisprudence has for a long time stated that the recognition of any one right to act in order to obtain full compensation for damages deriving from an infringement of antitrust rules represents the necessary prerequisite for the protection of the principles of effectiveness and equivalence of judicial protection.[11]

Likewise, looking at the Italian legislation, we notice that in law 3/2019 on collective redress *legitimatio ad causam* belongs to a vast group of actors. This particularity is well visible especially in the discipline of injunctive action, as it is provided that anyone having an interest in getting an injunction against acts and behaviours that damage a plurality of individuals or entities can start the action (art. 840-*sexiesdecies*). As has been said, the legitimation belongs then to injured individuals and entities and also to third parties having a legally appreciable interest.[12]

---

and Constitutional Affairs at the request of the Committee on Legal Affairs, aiming to assess the current state of play of collective redress at national and European levels, completed in October 2018, accessed 3 November 2021 at www.europarl.europa.eu.

[9] Directive 2014/104/EU of the European Parliament and of the Council of 26 November 2014 on certain rules governing actions for damages under national law for infringements of the competition law provisions of the Member States and of the European Union.

[10] See M. Scuffi, 'Tutela *antitrust* del consumatore e azione di classe', Dir. industriale, 2009, p. 341 ss.

[11] In the *Courage* decision, Case C-453/99, the Court of Justice stated that the principle of effectiveness of EU law requires that 'anyone' can take legal action for compensation for antitrust damage.

[12] See M. Stella, op. cit., p. 1456.

Going back specifically to the antitrust field, another of its particularities lies in the duplicity of interests protected by competition law: both the public interest in the proper functioning of the market and the private interest corresponding to that of the injured consumer in finding relief. The protection system against antitrust offences is also multilevel: in this system, 'public' protection before the competent authority does not exclude but is instead complementary to the 'private' protection understood as compensation due to the damaged party.[13]

The interaction between judicial and administrative enforcement and the subsequent need for coordination of the relative evidence and decisions certainly also characterises collective redress. The emblematic situation which could occur, linking the antitrust field and collective action, is that of a collective claim for compensation for damages arising from a conduct which has already been found anti-competitive by the national authority. In this case, art. 15 of the Directive will be particularly helpful. Regarding specifically the evidence rules, the Italian law of 2019 incorporates principles that already characterised d.lgs. 3/2017, especially in relation to access to the evidence itself. The new art. 840-*quinquies* of the Italian procedural code, in fact, lays down a special and detailed discipline for the order of exhibition of evidence, which is almost identical to that established by art. 3, d.lgs. 3/2017. Again, competition and collective action legislation seem to move together towards unity under the sign of consumer (but not only) protection.

Another relevant profile regards the issue of punitive damages. The Italian legislative act of 2019 on collective redress clearly excludes this possibility in line with Recommendation 2013/396/EU. Although there seems to be no room for punitive damages in collective actions, the new national legislation introduced (art. 840-*novies*) a special regulation on a 'rewarding' remuneration in favour of the common representative of the members of the class and of the lawyer who defended the claimant.

From the antitrust point of view, the issue relates in particular to the possibility of an effectiveness-oriented interpretation of art. 101 of the Treaty on the Functioning of the European Union (TFEU). On the one hand, it might be asked whether the national courts are to award punitive damages in excess of the advantage obtained by the offending operator, thereby deterring the use of agreements or concerted practices prohibited under that article. According

---

[13] The Italian Corte di Cassazione relates to art. 24 of the Italian Constitution (decision 23 April 2014, n. 9116). The decision does not make a direct reference to the jurisprudence of the Court of Justice or to European legislation. Nonetheless, the reference to the previous decision n. 27527 of 2013 by the Cassazione itself, which instead refers directly to the *Manfredi* decision (C-295/04) is very relevant, a real milestone in the European private antitrust enforcement system.

to the CJEU case law[14] and in the absence of EU rules governing the field, it is up to the domestic legal system of each Member State to set the criteria for determining the extent of the damages for harm caused by an agreement or practice prohibited under art. 101 of the TFEU, provided that the principles of equivalence and effectiveness are observed. In more recent decisions[15] the Court of Justice has ruled that there is no theoretical and systemic incompatibility between the EU legal system and the concept of punitive damages – provided that they do not lead to unjust enrichment – but the national judge may not award punitive damages on the sole basis of EU law in the absence of a national provision empowering the judge to award them.

On the other hand, an obstacle might certainly arise from art. 3 of Directive 2014/104, which establishes that full compensation shall not lead to overcompensation, whether by means of punitive, multiple or other types of damages.

The possibility of claiming punitive damages still remains open. A further question linking the antitrust field and the collective redress issue could be the following: what would happen if a consumer damaged by an antitrust infringement started a collective action also claiming punitive damages, maybe relying on a national discipline that allows it?[16] The underlying problem is, of course, the intersection of disciplines that may partially diverge, and the future case law may also reveal a lack of coordination.

In conclusion, a new efficient European discipline of collective redress is suitable for strengthening the principle of effective judicial protection also in favour of claimants who have suffered damages due to a violation of competition law. The combined application of the two disciplines may produce positive results in terms of access to justice and damage compensation as long as they are coherent.

14 *Manfredi*, C-295-298/04.

15 See decisions *Arjona Camacho*, C-407/14 and *Stowarzyszenie*, C-367/15.

16 On the contrary, as specifically regards the Italian legal system, it would not be simple to ask for punitive damages, as art. 1, par. 2 of d.lgs 3/2017 expressly forbids the possibility of an 'overcompensation'.

26. The impact of CJEU judgments on national legal systems: preliminary thoughts on the link with judicial dialogue[1]

Fabrizio Cafaggi

1. THE MODES OF JUDICIAL COOPERATION AND THE GEOMETRY OF DIALOGUE

This book offers a rich and diverse set of contributions to the dynamics of judicial interactions in the EU. The contributions investigate how judicial dialogue (JD) occurs and the differences emerging in various areas and countries.[2] Building on some of the analyses in the book I introduce the topic of impact evaluation of Court of Justice of the European Union (CJEU) judgments across Member States. The impact of the CJEU on national legal systems goes beyond national courts and involves both legislation and administration. CJEU judgments can modify administrative decision making and practices, and determine legislative changes.

Impact concerns the consequences and effects of judgments, both direct and indirect. The impact of CJEU judgments can refer either to the effects on the subsequent case law of the Court of Justice or to their effects on national judicial systems. The former is related to the role of precedents and the criteria to confer precedential value to a CJEU judgment within CJEU jurisprudence. The latter concerns the effects of CJEU judgments on the national courts and the

1 I would like to thank Federica Casarosa, Paola Iamiceli, Madalina Moraru and Raffaele Sabato for the numerous conversations about these issues in the course of the past years. Responsibility is exclusively mine.

2 Although the analysis provided in the book addresses judicial interactions, as the broadest terminology that could encompass the various interactions between courts, I will address in particular the occurrence of judicial dialogue intended as a case of interaction where there is continuity in time, some reciprocity among the judicial actors involved, and it develops on a case by case basis over time.

development of their case law. Whereas some relationship exists between the two forms of impact, the drivers and the metric to measure the impact differ. In this contribution the focus is on the impact of CJEU judgments on national courts and its relationship with the different forms of JD. It is contended that dialogue is one relevant factor to determine the intensity and quality of impact of CJEU judgments.

Dialogue generates the construction of common principles through repeat iterations between courts.[3] JD is not left to free choice by national courts. It is a combination of cooperation and hierarchy.[4] It is the outcome of rules that compel national supreme courts to submit preliminary references at the risk, in case of failure, of incurring liability.[5]

Dialogue may be limited to courts or may also include legislators and executives. By institutional dialogue I refer to the dialogue between the CJEU and state institutions including legislative, executive, and judicial bodies. By JD I refer more specifically to the dialogue between courts primarily driven by the preliminary reference procedure.[6] Dialogue is usually an instrument of judicial cooperation but might also be the expression of conflict.[7] In this contribution I shall focus on dialogue as an instrument of cooperation and investigate its role on the impact of CJEU judgments in national legal systems.

Judicial cooperation redefines the essence of impact, shifting from a unilateral to a dialogical approach. The impact is determined by the structure and

---

3 Repeat interaction can occur (1) with the same court (CJEU C-105/14 *Ivo Taricco and Others*, ECLI:EU:C:2015:555), (2) with different courts within the same Member State, or (3) with different national courts (see the case law concerning Kásler referred to below). In relation to the same national court it is possible that national courts refer to the CJEU within the same proceedings or different ones related to the same subject matter. For example, the Italian Council of State submitted a first preliminary reference decided by the CJEU, see Case C-152/17 *Consorzio Italian Management and Catania Multiservizi* (EU:C:2018:264) and then a second one CJEU C-561/19 *Consorzio italiano management* (ECLI:EU:C:2021:799).

4 See Takis Tridimas, 'The ECJ and the National Courts: Dialogue, Cooperation, and Instability' in Damian Chalmers and Anthony Arnull (eds), *The Oxford Handbook of European Union Law* (OUP, Oxford 2015), p. 403 ff.

5 See C-416/17 *Commission v France*, ECLI:EU:C:2018:811.

6 Court of Justice of the European Union, Recommendations to national courts and tribunals in relation to the initiation of preliminary ruling proceedings (2019/C 380/01) (hereinafter CJEU Recommendations). See CJEU C-561/19 *Consorzio italiano management*, cit.

7 See, for example, case CJEU C-399/09 *Landtová* (ECLI:EU:C:2011:415) or more recently and with a different outcome the *Taricco* saga. See R. Mastroianni, 'Sui rapporti tra Carte e Corti: nuovi sviluppi nella ricerca di un sistema rapido ed efficace di tutela dei diritti fondamentali' *European Papers*, 2020, 5, 493.

the quality of judicial interaction between national courts and the CJEU and among national courts through CJEU intervention.

JD is a form of judicial cooperation. Preliminary references under art. 267 Treaty on the Functioning of the European Union (TFEU) represent a fundamental pillar of judicial cooperation.[8] The structure of JD through preliminary references depends on (1) the identity and the number of participants, (2) the framing of the preliminary reference and (3) the framing and scope of the ruling provided by the CJEU. The analysis in this chapter is developed being aware that Advocate General Bobek has proposed a radical revision of the Court's approach to preliminary reference, more selective and directed at solving conflicting interpretations among Member States.[9] Such proposal was not adopted by the CJEU.[10]

The functions of JD are multiple. They stimulate coordination between EU and state laws, between primary and secondary EU legislation, between case law and legislation.

Trust is a pillar of the EU institutional architecture.[11] Dialogue is at the same time premised on mutual trust and generates mutual trust between the courts. The level of trust and the quality of loyal cooperation influence the intensity and breadth of the impact of CJEU judgments.[12]

The most recent developments of the case law suggest that reasons of distrust among national courts can suspend cooperation and reduce JD.[13] Judicial cooperation among national courts may be suspended when violations of fundamental rights have occurred or are likely to occur and, in particular, when systemic deficiencies may impair judicial independence.[14] When, in the context of the European arrest warrant, the court in the issuing State is likely not to be impartial and independent the court of the executing State

---

[8] See CJEU Opinion 2/2013, ECLI:EU:C:2014:2454. See CJEU Opinion 1/2009, ECLI:EU:C:2009:739, para. 84.

[9] See the proposals in A.G. Bobek Opinion, Case C-561/19 *Consorzio Italiano Management*, ECLI:EU:C:2021:291.

[10] The CJEU took a position in continuity with the *CILFIT* jurisprudence, see Case C-561/19 *Consorzio italiano management*, cit., para. 66.

[11] CJEU Opinion 2/13, cit.

[12] See Juan Mayoral, 'In the CJEU Judges Trust: A New Approach in the Judicial Construction of Europe' *Journal of Common Market Studies*, 2016, 55, 551.

[13] See the cases of 'abusive comparativism' used by Polish and Hungarian courts, B. Grabowska-Moroz, 'The Systemic Implications of the Vertical Layering of the Legal Orders in the EU for the Practice of the Rule of Law', accessed 3 November 2021 at https://reconnect-europe.eu/wp-content/uploads/2021/01/D8.3.pdf, and Casarosa and Moraru in Chapter 1 of this book.

[14] On the relationship between judicial independence and mutual trust among courts see CJEU C-216/18 *L.M.*, ECLI:EU:C:2018:586.

can suspend cooperation due to the likely violation of art. 47 Charter of Fundamental Rights (CFR).[15]

The geometry of JD follows multiple directions: vertical, horizontal and diagonal. Vertical dialogue between national and European courts, horizontal dialogue between national courts and between European courts. Diagonal dialogue between national, non-referring, courts and the CJEU.

The issue of judicial independence has offered another clear example of dialogue between the CJEU and the European Court of Human Rights (ECtHR).[16] If the divergence can be framed as a more restrictive perspective of the ECtHR from that of the CJEU then conforming interpretation can contribute to the definition of the conflict. But if the opposite situation materializes then the only possible route is represented by submitting a preliminary reference to the CJEU in order to address and possibly solve the conflict.

Horizontal and vertical dialogue are often interconnected; lack or incompleteness of horizontal dialogue between European courts can be addressed by vertical dialogue between a European and a national court. A national court may submit a preliminary reference in order to seek harmonization of its national court case law. This is particularly relevant when the European directives regulate matters that presuppose cooperation among the Member States as in the case of asylum and migration or that of the European arrest warrant. The CJEU provides the framework for mutual recognition to operate.[17]

Diagonal dialogue occurs when one national court submits a reference to clarify the application of EU law by courts of different Member States.

It is suggested that the geometry of dialogue bears consequences on both quantitative and qualitative impact. Hence *ex post* impact analysis should investigate the relationship among them (see Figure 26.1).

Often different forms of dialogue intersect. The relationship between art. 19 Treaty on European Union (TEU) and art. 47 CFR provides a good illustration of the interplay between vertical and horizontal dialogue.[18] The role of art. 19 TEU has increased tremendously in cases concerning judicial independence but it is bound to play a role well beyond independence to define Member States' responsibilities to provide their citizens with effective judicial remedies.[19] Another fertile area for JD is related to EU principles based on the

---

15 A.G. Tanchev Opinion in Case C-216/18 *L.M.*, ECLI:EU:C:2018:517, para. 133.

16 Compare ECtHR decision in *Gestur Jónsson and Ragnar Halldór Hall v. Iceland* [GC], (Appl. nos. 68271/14 and 68273/14), with CJEU decision in Case C-896/19 *Repubblika*, ECLI:EU:C:2021:331.

17 See CJEU C-216/18 *L.M.*, cit., paras 41–43; and Opinion 2/13, cit., para. 176.

18 See Case C-896/19 *Repubblika*, cit., para. 51.

19 Compare two recent judgments concerning the appointment of judges to the Supreme Court, one related to Poland and the other to Malta, respectively CJEU

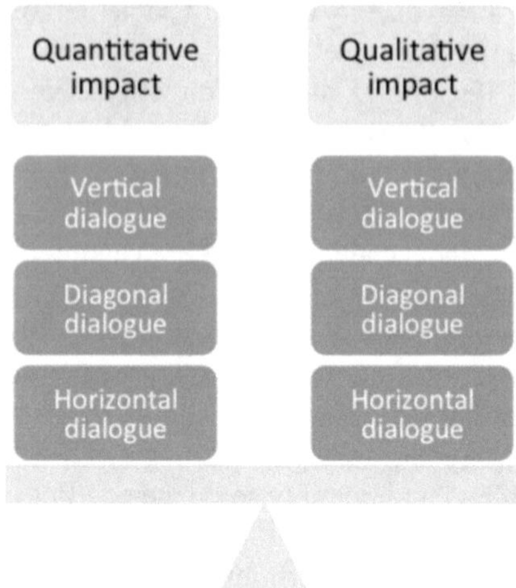

Figure 26.1 *How to evaluate impact*

existence of common constitutional traditions. Especially when there might be uncertainty over the differences between national constitutional traditions and the Charter, JD provides guides on how to harmonize the identification and interpretations of national constitutional common traditions.

National judges may face interpretative puzzles when, for example, there is a divergence between the CJEU and ECtHR and that difference cannot be solved directly by conforming interpretation according to art. 52.3 CFR. For example, art. 47 CFR on the right to an effective judicial remedy has to be interpreted consistently with the interpretation of arts 6 and 13 of the Convention provided by the ECtHR.[20] JD has created the opportunities for the creation of new remedies, and the definition of both the content and the scope of existing ones. The impact of the application of art. 47 CFR across Member States has not been even; within the same area national judges have applied differently CJEU rulings on art. 47 CFR.[21]

C-824/18 *A.B. and Others* and C-896/19 *Repubblicka*. On this issue see K. Lenaerts, 'The Role of the EU Charter in the Member States' in M. Bobek and J. Adam-Prassl (eds), *The EU Charter of Fundamental Rights in the Member States* (Hart, Oxford 2020), p.19.

20 See CJEU Case C-585/18 *A.K.*, ECLI:EU:C:2019:982, paras 116–18.

21 In the area of remedies for violation of data protection see the analysis of the *Google Spain* decision applied by national courts by F. Casarosa, 'How Judicial Interactions Steer the Application of the Right to be Forgotten by National Courts' in E. Psychogiopoulou and S. de la Sierra (eds), *Digital Media Governance and*

2. IMPACT OF CJEU JUDGMENTS: AN INTRODUCTORY FRAMEWORK

The definition of the European Court of Justice's judgments impact on national legal systems is a very complex subject. Identifying the impact and determining its intensity should be an important goal of the EU Commission and the Member States. It determines the quality of the European legal integration.

The output of the CJEU judgment coincides with the effect on the specific dispute which, in the context of preliminary reference, can only be evaluated after the final decision of the referring court.

The outcome(s) of the CJEU judgment are the direct and indirect effects on the national case laws, on the administrative practices, and on the legislation of the country of the referring court and on the other Member States. Outcomes are usually associated with the application of a CJEU judgment.[22]

Impact can be measured.

It is useful to distinguish between quantitative and qualitative impact.[23] The quantitative impact can be measured by the number of references of CJEU judgments in Member States' case law. The higher the number, the stronger the impact.

The qualitative impact may concern the relevance of EU law in national legal systems and its role in European legal integration. Clearly the impact varies depending on whether the interpretation concerns a principle or a rule.[24] The metric of qualitative impact is manyfold. For example it can be measured by evaluating the degree of uniformity of interpretation of the EU law provision within and between Member States before and after the judgment.[25] The referring court would usually focus on the conflicting interpretations within the Member State. The CJEU might expand the scope of the ruling and encompass an analysis of divergent interpretations across Member States.[26]

Supranational Courts: Selected Issues and Insights from the European Judiciary (Edward Elgar, Cheltenham, UK and Northampton, MA forthcoming).

[22] On the distinction between interpretation and application see A.G. Bobek Opinion in Case C-923/19 *Van Ameyde España SA*, EU:C:2021:125.

[23] This distinction, related to the Charter, is developed in M. Bobek and J. Adam-Prassl, 'Conclusion' in M. Bobek and J. Adam-Prassl (eds), *The EU Charter of Fundamental Rights in the Member States* (Hart, Oxford 2020), p. 559 ff.

[24] On the distinction between principles and rules see Chapter 2 by Półtorak and Chapter 3 by Toggenburg in this book.

[25] This measurement implies the definition of an indicator concerning the degree of different interpretation across MS.

[26] See CJEU Case C-160/14 *Ferreira da Silva and Brito*, ECLI:EU:C:2015:565, para. 45.

The existence of divergent interpretations of EU law at national level may depend upon wrong or right interpretations or upon multiple plausible interpretations, one of which is preferable over the others.[27] In the former case the Court's ruling should identify the 'right' interpretation. In the latter case the preferable interpretation. Qualitative impact may differ accordingly.

A more sophisticated account of measurement would require incorporating not only direct but also reverse impact. This is the case where national courts do not follow the jurisprudence of the CJEU.[28] In this case the impact is strong but it is the opposite result that the CJEU would have explicitly preferred.

Qualitative impact also concerns changes. It can be evaluated by the changes that the individual judgment or a cluster of judgments over time have produced in Member States' legislation, administration, and in judicial reasoning and interpretation.[29] Both dimensions are important. The measurement should focus on the existence and scope of the change. The wider the change, the higher the impact.

The quantitative impact may be a proxy of the authoritativeness of the judgment and its influential role.[30] The qualitative impact provides information about changes.

Within the notion of qualitative impact *it is important to further distinguish between institutional and substantive impact*. The institutional impact concerns the changes produced in Member States' legislation, administration, and judicial interpretation, and the relationship between the powers. The substantive impact may consist, for instance, in the creation of new rights and new remedies. The CJEU has 'used' art. 47 CFR and more recently art. 19.1 TEU to increase and broaden judicial protection by granting new remedies or expanding existing ones.

Very relevant is *the distinction between* ex ante *and* ex post *of judicial impact evaluation.*

The definition of the impact of the CJEU's judgments contributes to evaluate the consequences of a judgment or of a cluster of connected judgments in Member States. It ultimately contributes to the fundamental task of ensur-

---

27 There is a correlation between the nature of the interpretive divergence and the necessity to intervene according to the CILFIT principles. The Court is rethinking the prioritization of interpretive divergences to be solved by preliminary references. See the proposals in A.G. Bobek, CJEU C-561/19 *Consorzio italiano management*, cit.

28 According to A.G. Bobek Opinion, C-561/19 *Consorzio italiano management*, cit., a case in point concerns *CILFIT*, see para. 128.

29 This measurement implies the definition of an indicator concerning the change brought about by the application of the judgment.

30 There is a rich and unsettled debate on what makes a landmark case. See M. Maduro and L. Azoulai (eds), *The Past and Future of EU Law* (Hart, Oxford 2010).

ing uniform interpretation of EU law. *Ex ante* impact evaluation identifies hypothetical expected consequences of the future judgment. *Ex post* impact evaluation considers the real effects produced in national legal systems. They include both outputs and outcomes.

The binding nature of the judgment is the premise but a CJEU binding judgment may have a very different impact, depending on the context where it applies. Indicators could measure the potential expected effects.

The *ex ante* impact evaluation, based on a comparative analysis of the national case laws, could help the CJEU framing the principle in the new judgment in order to grade its consequences in all Member States.

The *ex post* impact evaluation, based on a comparative analysis of the 'effects' of the CJEU judgment among Member States, could contribute to verifying the impacts both within and between Member States. An evaluation of the *ex post* impact may reveal whether the formulation of the judgment has been differently interpreted across Member States and between institutions of the same Member State. For example, whether judgments about the right to be heard in administrative proceedings are differently interpreted by administrations and national courts.

Another important dimension of *ex post* impact evaluation concerns the consequences of the specific decision by the referring court and the courts within that national legal system. The impact differs depending on whether national judges have to set aside the domestic rule via disapplication or change their interpretation in order to conform with EU law.[31] Disapplication is usually a temporary solution, waiting for the legislators to act. Conforming interpretation produces an impact on the judicial activity without directly involving the legislators.

Institutional impact may refer to the solution/persistence of the divergence between legislators and courts or between courts within the same legal order.

Often the CJEU is asked by national courts submitting preliminary references to solve internal divergences concerning the correct interpretation of EU law within the Member State between legislators and courts or between courts.[32] The referring court asks what the correct interpretation of EU law is in order to solve that divergence.[33] Sometimes the CJEU offers the correct interpretation, abstaining from intervening in the conflict. Other times it pro-

---

31 See CJEU C-824/18 *A.B. and Others*, ECLI:EU:C:2021:153, para. 166. See more broadly joined cases C-188/10 and C-189/10 *Melki* and *Abdeli*, ECLI:EU:C:2010:363.

32 See CJEU Case C-118/17 *Dunai*, ECLI:EU:C:2019:207, para. 57 ff., part. 64.

33 Conflicts between lower courts and Tribunal Supremo in Spain. See on these issues A. Van Duin, 'Justice for Both', Phd thesis, University of Amsterdam, 2020, and ACTIONES Handbook – Module 4 – Consumer protection, 2017, accessed 3 November 2021 at https://cjc.eui.eu/projects/actiones/actiones-platform/ and ReJUS

vides guidance on how the divergence could be solved according to the interpretation given in the judgment.[34] Rarely it enters in the conflict and identifies the correct interpretation forcing the other national court (the non-referring), usually the supreme court, to change its interpretation.[35]

Currently neither an *ex ante* impact evaluation nor an *ex post* impact evaluation of CJEU judgments are formally carried out. Informally, an *ex ante* impact evaluation is sometimes performed within the Court of Justice, before issuing the judgment.[36] But an institutional methodology of impact evaluation, informing judicial decision making, is not yet available.

The introduction of both *ex ante* and *ex post* impact evaluation would certainly contribute to judicial decisions that anticipate the effects and the differences across Member States. The quality of CJEU jurisprudence would be enhanced by having a selective impact evaluation *ex ante*, and an analysis of the *ex post* impact of the judgment in different Member States. Such analysis should distinguish between output and outcomes and measure the potential quantitative and qualitative impact of the judgment through indicators. *Ex post* evaluation can offer the CJEU and the national courts accurate information that may inform both preliminary references and rulings.

Over time the *ex post* impact evaluation can contribute to better frame future judgments concerning similar issues. If the CJEU has a clear picture of the impact of previous related judgments, it can define the framing of its ruling to specify the objectives of the judgment, especially those related to the application outside the Member State of the referring court.[37]

---

casebook – Effective Justice in Consumer Protection, 2018, accessed 3 November 2021 at https://www.rejus.eu/content/materials.

34 See, for example, Case C-169/14 *Sánchez Morcillo and Abril García*, EU:C:2014:2099 as regards the obligation for the Member States to ensure the effectiveness of the rights that the parties against the use of unfair clauses, which solved a contrast between the Spanish Tribunal Supremo and Barcelona Audiencia Provincial. See more in ACTIONES Handbook – Module 4 – Consumer protection, cit..

35 See Spanish cases where the CJEU has forced the Tribunal Supremo to change its interpretation on the principle of res judicata and the limitation of retroactive effects of judicial decisions, in joined cases C-154/15 and C-307/15 *Francisco Gutiérrez Naranjo and Ana María Palacios Martínez v Cajasur Banco e Banco Bilbao Vizcaya Argentaria SA (BBVA)*, see F. Cafaggi and F. Casarosa, 'L'effettività dei rimedi nelle interazioni giudiziali fra corti nazionali e corti europee' in P. Gallo, G. Magri and M. Salvadori (eds), *L'Armonizzazione del diritto Europeo: Il ruolo delle corti* (Ledizioni, Milano 2017), p. 51.

36 Internally within the CJEU, comparative research is usually done in support of the judges' internal comparative reports circulated but they are not public. To some extent, informally, this analysis is carried out by some Advocates General.

37 To pursue the goal of uniform interpretation of EU law the CJEU must be aware of the differences across MS and how different interpretations may address them.

As we shall see JD through preliminary reference is often iterative. The impact over time should be measured not in relation to a single judgment rather in relation to a cluster of judgments that over time have defined the correct interpretation of EU law.

3. LINKING JUDICIAL DIALOGUE AND IMPACT. HOW JUDICIAL DIALOGUE INFLUENCES THE IMPACT OF THE CJEU JURISPRUDENCE IN THE MEMBER STATES

To identify which variables determine the impact of a single judgment is a challenging task. Much more modestly it is suggested that judicial cooperation and, in particular, JD plays a role in determining the impact of the CJEU case law across Member States. When defining the impact of the CJEU the dialogical structure that operates between the courts is of paramount relevance. There is not only one type of dialogue. There are different forms of dialogue between national courts and the CJEU depending on which court is referring, whether the subject matter of interpretation is a rule or a principle, how the preliminary reference is framed, how the decision in the CJEU judgment is framed. Different framings result in different dialogues with different impacts.[38]

The taxonomy of impacts of CJEU judgments is partly dependent upon the typology of dialogues.

The impact of CJEU case law on Member States is determined by many factors. Here the focus is on the relationship between impact of the CJEU and dialogue, asking whether JD may increase the impact and, in case of an affirmative answer, how that occurs.

The rules concerning the preliminary reference framing are broadly defined by the Guidelines issued by the CJEU.[39] The specific rules concerning the framing of the CJEU's rulings have been defined by the CJEU case law. Framing is relational and art. 267 TFEU provides a dialogical structure.[40]

---

[38] On framing see A. Tversky and D. Kahneman, 'The Framing of Decisions and the Psychology of Choice' *Science*, 1981, 211, 453 ff. It is beyond the scope of this contribution to explore the insights of behavioural sciences on framing the ruling. For a more detailed analysis see F. Cafaggi, 'Framing CJEU Judgments: A Behavioral Approach', on file with the author.

[39] See CJEU Recommendations on preliminary rulings, cit.

[40] The relational nature of framing implies that there is a correlation between the framing of the question and that of the answer. The correlation is not only semantic but also pragmatic. Correlation does not imply symmetry. A narrow question can turn into a broad answer and vice versa.

Impact evaluation and indicators should therefore incorporate the various framings.

The CJEU enjoys a wide discretion to define the scope of the ruling beyond the answer to the reference proposed by the national court. Depending on the objectives pursued by the judgment it may recast the questions referred or it may examine issues which have not specifically been asked by the national court.[41] Narrowing or broadening the scope of the question posed by the national court may generate different impacts of the ruling depending on whether the main focus is the solution of the dispute before the national court or an opportunity to shed light on a controversial issue addressed differently by the national courts (see Figure 26.2).

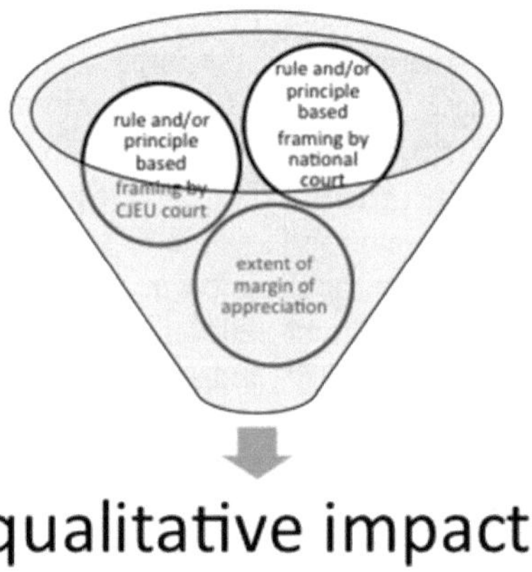

Figure 26.2 *Tentative taxonomy of qualitative impact criteria in preliminary reference procedure*

[41] Among the objectives of the CJEU case law a major task has been to define the relationship between the right to be heard, the general principles of good administration, and the right to fair administrative proceedings and to fair trial. The examination of the case law provides multiple examples of reformulation of the preliminary reference by the CJEU in order to encompass the analysis of this relationship often left out by the referring court. This example shows the objective of the CJEU to broaden the impact of their case law by using the power to reformulate the preliminary reference within the context of judicial dialogue. See Chapter 18 by Moraru and Clement in this book.

Every CJEU judgment is binding on all Member States, but the intensity of the impact depends on the framing of the question by the national referring court and its interpretation by the Court of Justice.

The binding nature of the judgment concerns the interpretation of EU law and, in theory, it applies equally across Member States. Equally binding application, however, does not result in equal impact. The context where the reference originated is not irrelevant to the framing of the answer provided by the CJEU. The courts of Member States, other than those of the referring states, have to adapt and 'translate' the principle when applied to their legal systems. Application of CJEU judgments involves a very significant process of decontextualization and recontextualization.

JD, based on preliminary references, is determined by the type and content of the referred question and by the framing of the answer provided by the CJEU.[42] In relation to framing a distinction has been proposed between outcome, guidance, and deference cases.[43] In the first instance the CJEU provides the national court with a ruling that already offers the solution to the issue standing before the court. In the second set the CJEU provides guidance but leaves the national court some space for the final decision. In the last set of cases the CJEU entirely defers the solution to the national court. The impact of the judgments differs depending on whether they are classified as outcome, guidance or deference. Subject to further research the prediction is that the impact of guidance judgment is stronger than outcome. It is likely that deference judgments might have lower impact than the other two.

Preliminary references concerning the interpretation of rules differ from preliminary references concerning the interpretation of principles. The impact of judgments concerning the former tends to be narrower and tailored to the court that has made the reference. The impact of judgments concerning princi-

---

[42] See J.H.H. Weiler, 'The Transformation of Europe' Yale L.J., 1991, 100, 2403; A.-M. Slaughter, A. Stone Sweet and J.H.H. Weiler (eds), *The European Courts and National Courts, Doctrine and Jurisprudence* (Hart, Oxford 1998); G. de Burca and J.H.H. Weiler (eds), *The European Court of Justice* (OUP, Oxford 2001); T. Tridimas, 'Knocking on Heaven's Door: Fragmentation, Efficiency and Defiance in the Preliminary Reference Procedure' *Common Market Law Review*, 2003, 40, 9; M. Bobek, 'Learning to Talk: Preliminary Rulings, the Courts of the New Member States and the Court of Justice' *Common Market Law Review*, 2008, 1611; M. Bobek, 'The Court of Justice, the National Courts, and the Spirit of Cooperation: Between Dichtung und Warheit' in A. Lazowsk and S. Blockmans (eds), *Research Handbook on EU Institutional Law* (Edward Elgar, Cheltenham, UK and Northampton, MA 2016), pp. 353–75.

[43] See T. Tridimas, 'The ECJ and the National Courts: Dialogue, Cooperation, and Instability' in Damian Chalmers and Anthony Arnull (eds), *The Oxford Handbook of European Union Law* (OUP, Oxford 2015), pp. 408–9.

ples tends to be wider and differentiated across Member States.[44] It is often the case that in the same preliminary reference a question related to a rule in a legislative instrument is followed by a question concerning the general EU principle that is needed to resolve the dispute. For example, questions concerning the unfairness of contractual terms related to interest rates are combined with questions related to the gap filling function of judges when terms are voided. The latter issue results into the definition of the scope of judicial intervention in the field of consumer contract law and the judicial gap filling powers.[45]

Rarely the CJEU explicitly contextualizes the answers provided in preliminary references because of the limits of autonomous interpretation and the necessity to ensure uniformity of the application of EU principles. However, clearly the application of the same principle and the enforcement of the same right in different contexts requires adaptation.[46] The margin of appreciation left to the Member States defines the space of discretion aimed at contextualizing the application of the judgment to the different national contexts.

In the current context the task of adaptation of the ruling is mainly on the shoulders of national courts that have to decontextualize the principle set out by the CJEU and recontextualize by applying it to their legal systems.

As a result, it is not easy for national judges to contextualize the principle and apply it to their own legal system, especially when it runs against the common interpretation given by the courts in their legal system. An *ex ante* impact evaluation could help sharing the burden of contextualization between the CJEU and national courts.

The explicit reference by CJEU judgments and by Advocates General to divergent national case law should be encouraged in order to interpret the

---

[44] The issue concerning the power of national judges to fill gaps when a term is declared unfair is illustrative. See the judicial dialogue between Hungarian courts and the CJEU and the horizontal dialogue between the Polish (C-260/18 *Dziubak*, ECLI: EU:C:2019:819) and the Hungarian (C-118/17 *Dunai*, cit.) courts developed over the interpretation of the Hungarian *Kásler* judgment (C-26/13 *Kásler and Káslerné Rábai*, ECLI:EU:C:2014:282).The vertical bilateral dialogue between the CJEU and the two national courts should be complemented by the horizontal 'implicit' dialogue between the national courts. An example is the interplay between the Hungarian courts related to judicial gap filling power.

[45] In C-118/17 *Dunai*, cit., a Hungarian court asked clarification over the interpretation of *Kásler* and more broadly what is the judicial power to fill gaps and/or avoid the entire consumer contract when a contractual term is declared unfair. In C-260/18 *Dziubak*, cit., a Polish court asked clarification over the interpretation of *Kásler* and more broadly whether the gaps in the contract may be filled by reference to equity and social rules.

[46] Adaptation results in partial differentiation which impinges on the objective of EU law uniform interpretation. See A.G. Opinion, Case C-561/19 *Consorzio italiano management*, cit.

answer given by the Court in the light of the disagreement among national courts. The objective to achieve uniform or at least compatible judicial interpretations by national courts is one of the missions of the CJEU.[47] But it cannot be the result of hierarchical command. It should be the outcome of deliberative dialogue facilitated by *ex ante* impact evaluation.

4. ART. 47 CFREU AND THE IMPACT OF THE CJEU ON NATIONAL CASE LAW

In the remaining part of this chapter, I briefly examine the impact of the CJEU on national legal systems by looking at some applications of art. 47 CFR in the context of JD between national courts and the CJEU.[48]

JD through preliminary references is based on relational framing. But the burdens are not equally shared between European and national courts. When applying the CJEU judgments national judges have to decontextualize the ruling from the legal system of the referring court and recontextualize it to their own legal system. *Ex post* impact evaluation in particular can contribute to the process of contextualization, identifying the differences in application across Member States. Objective measurement through indicators is needed to perform such an analysis.

Art. 47 is the most cited of the Charter. It has horizontal application and no reference to any other charter right is needed. The case law concerning the interpretation of art. 47 CFREU shows that its impact differs depending not only on the areas of the law to which it is applied but also on the differences across Member States.[49] Its quantitative impact has been measured by the number of citations in CJEU judgments. A comprehensive quantitative analysis of its use by national courts is not yet available. Qualitative scholarly analysis shows that its impact on both substantive and procedural rules has been significant but uneven.

The impact of CJEU judgments on judicial powers at national level like *ex officio* and judicial review varies significantly across Member States but the

---

47 See K. Lenaerts, 'The Role of the Charter in the Member States', cit.

48 See D. Reichel and G. Toggenburg, 'References for a Preliminary Ruling and the Charter of Fundamental Rights , Experiences and Data from 2010 to 2018' in M. Bobek and J. Adam-Prassl (eds), *The EU Charter of Fundamental Rights in the Member States*, cit., p. 467 ff. European Union Agency for Fundamental Rights and Council of Europe, *FRA Handbook on European Law Relating to Access to Justice* (FRA, Vienna 2016).

49 See K. Gutman, 'Article 47: The Right to an Effective Remedy and to a Fair Trial' in M. Bobek and J. Adam-Prassl (eds), *The EU Charter of Fundamental Rights in the Member States*, cit., p. 371.

reasons for these variations remain unexplored.[50] Changes of interpretation of national procedural rules have not occurred with the same intensity across Member States and practices by the national judiciaries are not the same. In some legal systems the allocation of power between the parties and the judges has been revisited, in others it remained untouched.

In some legal systems judgments applying art. 47 have determined important procedural changes in the administrative and judicial proceedings, in others its application has been limited to specific areas without a significant general impact. The qualitative impact of CJEU art. 47 rulings on procedural laws provides some illustrations.

The relevance of the application of art. 47 in migration and asylum has varied among Member States.[51] Similarly differences have emerged in relation to the use of *ex officio* power in unfair contract terms.[52]

The principles spurring from CJEU jurisprudence related to States' duty to cooperate in asylum cases or the *ex officio* power in unfair contract terms may have very different impacts depending on the procedural rules of each Member State.

Whether the duty to cooperate between the State and the asylum seeker has been interpreted narrowly or has modified the legal features of the relationship between judges and parties is an empirical question that needs a comparative analysis of national judgments.[53]

An important dimension of the right to effective judicial protection concerns the right to be heard. How the content of the right to be heard has been defined depends on the interactions between national courts and the CJEU.

The scope and the remedies of the right to be heard in asylum and migration have been defined by a prolonged set of judicial interactions involving many national courts and the CJEU. The involvement of several national courts is often the expression of an implicit horizontal dialogue among them taking place through the interactions with the CJEU.[54] When the interpretation given by the CJEU is driven by specific conditions of one Member State, a court of a different Member State submits a preliminary reference seeking clarifica-

---

[50] See *FRA Handbook on European Law Relating to Access to Justice*, cit.

[51] See B. Zalar, 'Impact of Judicial Dialogue(s) on Development and Affirmation of the Right to Effective Legal Remedy from Articles 13 and 14 of the Return Directive' in M. Moraru, G. Cornelisse and P. De Bruycker (eds), *Law and Judicial Dialogue on the Return of Irregular Migrants from the European Union* (Hart, Oxford 2020), p. 369.

[52] See European Commission, Guidance on the interpretation and application of Council Directive 93/13/EEC of 5 April 1993 on unfair contract terms in consumer contracts, COM(2019) 5325 final.

[53] See M. Bobek, *Comparative Reasoning in European Supreme Courts* (OUP, Oxford 2013).

[54] See Chapter 18 by Moraru and Clement in this book.

tions on the basis of the different normative and social context it operates.[55] This is the process of decontextualization and recontextualization carried by national courts that can be supported by CJEU

The application of art. 47 has often translated into a process of judicial empowerment of national courts. The link between rights and remedies has driven the CJEU to change the powers of judges, creating new rights and new remedies to ensure effective protection. If those powers are not duly exercised by the judge, then private parties can use different tools, they can appeal the decision claiming that there has been an *error in procedendo*, they can seek compensation if the failure to exercise the power by the Court violates a duty to exercise *ex officio* power that entails state responsibility under *Kobler* jurisprudence.[56]

In some judicial training programmes *ex post* impact evaluation has been carried, highlighting the different impact of a single judgment in various legal systems.[57] The casebooks in those projects have tried to define the impact of single judgments and those of clusters of judgments that reflect the dialogue between national courts and the CJEU. As it is often the case the dialogue over the same issue does not end in a single round but includes several rounds often played by different courts within a national legal system as occurred in Spain about unfair contract terms or between national systems as exemplified by the *Google* or the *Facebook* cases[58] in the field of data protection and in the field of asylum and migration.[59]

It is often the case that the referring judge includes questions on principles and questions on rules to which 47 must applied. References are made both to

---

55 On the right to be heard see the Irish High Court in *M.M.* (ECLI:EU:C:2012:744) versus the French Tribunals of Pau and Melun in Case C-166/13 *Mukarubega* (ECLI: EU:C:2014:2336) and Case C-249/13 *Boudjlida* (ECLI:EU:C:2014:2431), the right to be heard shaped in the first case in the context of a specific Irish dual international protection adjudication system, versus the right to be heard of returnees within the French specific combined return procedure (rejection of asylum was served together with the return order).

56 See the application of *Kobler* principles in Case C-168/15 *Tomášová*, ECLI:EU: C:2016:602.

57 See ACTIONES Handbook on the Techniques of Judicial Interactions in the Application of the EU Charter , 2017, accessed 3 November 2021 at https://cjc.eui.eu/projects/actiones/actiones-platform/ and ReJUS casebooks, 2018, accessed 3 November 2021 at https://www.rejus.eu/content/materials.

58 See Case C-507/17 *Google*, ECLI:EU:C:2019:772: and Case C-645/19 *Facebook Ireland and Others*, ECLI:EU:C:2021:483.

59 The right to be heard is of general application to both administrative and judicial proceedings. In relation to the former it is part of the right to good administration, in relation to the latter it is part of the right to a fair trial covered by art. 47 CFR and by art. 6 ECHR. See Chapter 18 by Moraru and Clement in this book.

specific provisions of secondary legislation and to general principles that can be associated with the interpretation of the specific rule.[60]

JD has involved not only the scope of the right and the correlation between administrative and judicial proceedings but also the remedies. National courts have, for example, asked for guidance on the consequences of violations of the right to be heard within administrative proceedings. The CJEU in collaboration with national courts has crafted remedies that would allow quashing the administrative decision to grant the asylum seeker the necessary protection. Similarly in the field of data protection it broadened the scope of existing remedies and expanded the protection by recognizing extraterritorial effects to injunctions.[61]

The relationship between administrative and judicial remedies has been addressed by the CJEU in relation to art. 47.[62] Whereas the *Puškár* judgment concerns data protection the principle stated by the Court is meant to have general application. The framing of the *Puškár* ruling permits Member States to sequence remedies and make access to the Court conditional upon the exhaustion of administrative remedies if three conditions occur: it is regulated by legislation, it does not excessively delay the access, it is proportionate.[63] The quantitative impact of *Puškár* has been limited but its qualitative impact is potentially very significant. An *ex post* impact evaluation of the judgment could provide national courts in other areas like competition, consumer, environmental to define the relationship between administrative and judicial remedies.

Art. 47 includes also the relationship between alternative dispute resolution and judicial proceedings.

In *Menini Rampanelli*, the questions of the national court addressed the scope of Directive 2013/11 concerning compulsory mediation (question n. 1) and the use of mediation as a precondition for the admissibility of legal proceedings by the consumer (question n. 2).[64] The answer given by the Court did not elaborate on the limits of compulsory mediation and its compatibility with the right to a judicial remedy under art. 47 CFR. The framing of the answer provided by the CJEU was clearly narrow and avoided engaging in a general

---

[60] For an analysis of Case C-73/16 *Puškár*, ECLI:EU:C:2017:725 see Chapter 22 by Casarosa and Sabato in this book.

[61] See, for example, Case C-18/18 *Eva Glawischnig-Piesczek*, ECLI:EU:C:2019:821, paras 49–50.

[62] See Case C-73/16 *Puškár*, ECLI:EU:C:2017:725.

[63] See Case C-73/16 *Puškár*, cit. On the reference to art. 47 see K. Gutman, 'Article 47: The Right to an Effective Remedy and to a Fair Trial', cit., pp. 379–81.

[64] See Case C-75/16 *Menini and Rampanelli*, ECLI:EU:C:2017:457.

analysis of the relationship between the directive on mediation and the right to effective judicial protection.

The impact of *Menini Rampanelli* has been limited. Had the Court been willing to elaborate on the relationship with the principles of effectiveness and the right to effective judicial protection the impact would have likely been much wider. The possibility and the type of opt-out mechanisms available for those who have to engage in compulsory mediation remains an open issue at EU level and the solutions adopted at the national level by national courts differ.

Within the institutional impact attention must be paid to the scope of judicial review.[65] Making use of art. 47 CFR the CJEU has expanded the scope and intensity of judicial review especially in those legal systems where procedural hurdles prevented national courts from imposing public administrations to comply with their judgments.[66] By expanding the scope of judicial review the CJEU has changed the relationship between judiciaries and national administrations.

The example of *Toruharov* in asylum is illustrative of the expansion but similar cases have been decided in tax and other areas.[67] National courts have been given, through art. 47, the power to change decisions of the administrations when these decisions did not comply with previous judgments.[68] In *Torubarov* the national court was given the power to grant international protection to a refugee after the administration had wrongly denied it without complying with a previous judgment.[69]

The impact of the case law concerning art. 47 needs to be further explored through a rigorous and comparative analysis. However, on the basis of the material collected in the judicial training projects it is clear that there has been an impact on judicial power and on the reallocation of power between judiciary and public administration. The scope and intensity of judicial review as an expression of the right to effective judicial protection shows that national courts have been given deeper and broader powers to scrutinize the activities of both public administrations and independent administrative authorities. Clearly the differences on impact are related to the national differences con-

---

65 See Chapter 22 by Casarosa and Sabato in this book.

66 See Case C-682/15 *Berlioz*, ECLI:EU:C:2017:373.

67 See Case C-556/17 *Torubarov*, ECLI:EU:C:2019:626.

68 For a very rich comparative analysis see Association of the Councils of State and Supreme Administrative Jurisdictions of the European Union, *General Report*, accessed 3 November 2021 at https://www.aca-europe.eu/seminars/2021_Fiesole/2021_Fiesole_General_Report_en.pdf.

69 See Case C-556/17 *Torubarov*, cit.

cerning the scope and intensity of judicial review.[70] But a more radical change is taking place. In areas where fundamental rights are at stake national courts have been given by article 47 the power to correct administrative failures and shortcomings often replacing with their own judgments administrative acts violating those rights. These changes, driven by the necessity to increase legal protection and to ensure the respect of fundamental rights are likely to change the allocation of powers within Member States and to redefine the separation of powers as the national constitutions implicitly or explicitly have designed it.

As clearly demonstrated by Moraru and Clement and in Chapter 18 the right to be heard featured at the same time a vertical judicial interaction between the Irish High Court, the Irish Supreme Court, and the CJEU and a horizontal dialogue between the Irish Court and the Dutch Council of State in relation to the scope of the right to an oral hearing in administrative and judicial proceedings related to asylum and migration.[71]

Both the *M.M.* and the subsequent *M.* judgments demonstrate the iterative structure of judicial interaction and the necessity to evaluate the impact of the CJEU not just based on a single judgment but on the series of interactions that include reactions not only by the referring national court but also by the administration and, sometimes, by the legislator.[72] The right to be heard in asylum is another example of institutional dialogue driven by JD but involving multiple institutional actors.

The analysis has shown that impact of CJEU judgments in Member States may depend on the features and geometry of JD. The intensity of the impact depends on the existence of mutual trust among national courts and between them and the CJEU which feeds the preliminary reference mechanism. The geometry of dialogue affects the intensity of the impact. The interdependence of vertical and horizontal dialogue is an institutional factor that deeply influences the quality of the impact of the CJEU. Hence the causal relationship between dialogue and impact is bilateral. Effective dialogue based on mutual trust increases the impact. Distrust impairs the dialogue and reduces the impact of the CJEU.

---

[70] See ACA, *General Report*, cit.

[71] See Chapter 18 by Moraru and Clement in this book.

[72] See Case C-277/11 *M.M.*, ECLI:EU:C:2012:744; Case C-560/14 *M.*, ECLI:EU:C:2017:101.

Index